A DOCUMENTARY HISTORY OF EDUCATION IN THE SOUTH BEFORE 1860

A
Documentary History
of
Education in the South
Before 1860

Edited by

EDGAR W. KNIGHT

IN FIVE VOLUMES

Volume I

EUROPEAN INHERITANCES

Chapel Hill

THE UNIVERSITY OF NORTH CAROLINA PRESS

PJ

NC
370,995
D
V.I

CONSULTANTS

Charles F. Arrowood
Stuart G. Noble
Dorothy Orr
Nita K. Pyburn
James B. Sellers

PREFACE

The first difficulties met in the preparation of this volume and the volumes that are to follow were in locating the documents wherever these could be found and then in getting at them for reproduction. Location was greatly facilitated by suggestions and advice of interested people too numerous to mention here, but to whom the editor, consultants, research-fellows, and the University of North Carolina Press are most grateful. Then came the task of reproduction, by microcopying, photocopying and typing. But for the compiler and editor the most difficult task of all, made so by the abundance of documents located and reproduced and verified with as great care as possible, was the matter of selecting the documents to be included. Although he had competent advice, the compiler and editor had to make, and he alone must be held responsible for, the final selection of the documents. Selection by another compiler and editor might well have resulted in a different work.

The region for the documents selected for the volumes in this study comprised the Confederate States. After careful consideration these states were chosen because they seemed to furnish a unity which another group, organized, for example, to include all slaveholding states, could not so well provide. The period of the study extends from colonial beginnings to 1860. After that date source materials in education in the South are more abundant and are more easily accessible.

Acquaintance with original sources has long been properly recognized as the foundation of all sound historical knowledge. Nowadays good practice in teaching history, whether educational and social, political, economic, or of other aspects, requires that students of the subject have access to and acquaintance with the original sources. But one difficulty in providing for such acquaintance is generally the inaccessibility of such materials. In an effort partially to remove this difficulty, the present work has been undertaken.

When George H. Martin in 1894 published his *The Evolution of the Massachusetts Public School System* he said in the preface that a complete history of education in that state could not be prepared until the source materials, very abundant but widely scattered, were made available and properly used. This complaint, made more than fifty years ago of Massachusetts, always careful to preserve its records, has often been heard in and of the Southern States, which too long have been careless with theirs. The need for doing what has here been undertaken has been felt by teachers and students of the educational and social history of the Southern States, and it is hoped that such need may be partially met by this study and that it also will stimulate similar studies in educational and social history here and elsewhere in the United States.

The first volume covers the period from the early part of the seventeenth century through most of the third quarter of the eighteenth century and, we hope, includes most of the major documents of educational importance during that time, though some of them necessarily extend beyond the colonial period. While only a few of the documents here presented are new or even rare, many of them have not until now been made generally accessible to students and teachers of American educational history of the colonial period. The documents have been drawn from many, and some of them from unexpected, places. Not all of those located and reproduced could be included. But it is believed that those here used are sufficient to explain the educational theories and practices inherited by the South from Europe during the colonial period.

The second volume deals with efforts to gain educational and cultural independence; the third volume is devoted primarily to higher education, the rise of state universities and of denominational colleges, especially after the Dartmouth College Decision; the fourth with the rise and growth of academies including those of the manual labor and military type; and the fifth and concluding volume will contain documents on arguments and proposals for and legislation on state school systems, support and supervision, the education of teachers, materials and methods of teaching, textbooks, and closely related subjects.

The compiler and editor is especially indebted to the consultants whose names appear on the copyright page. In addition he is indebted to many other people: Professors R. D. W. Connor, Fletcher M. Green, J. G. deR. Hamilton, and Hugh T. Lefler of the University of North Carolina; Librarian-emeritus Earl G. Swem, John M. Jennings, formerly in charge of manuscripts of the Library of the College of William and Mary, now Librarian of the Virginia Historical Society; Robert H. Land, Librarian of the College of William and

Mary; William J. Van Schreeven and Dr. Wilmer L. Hall and other members of the staff of the Virginia State Library; Dr. Ed McCuistion of the State Department of Education in Arkansas; Dr. A. F. Kuhlman, of the Joint University Libraries, Nashville; Professor-emeritus I. L. Kandel, of Columbia University; Professor S. J. Folmsbee, of the University of Tennessee; Professor R. L. Meriwether and members of the staff of the South Caroliniana Library, University of South Carolina; A. S. Salley, State Historian of South Carolina; Professor J. H. Easterby, South Carolina Historical Society; Mary A. Sparkman, Secretary of the Historical Commission of Charleston; H. O. Strohecker, principal of the Charleston High School, South Carolina; Mrs. J. E. Hays, State Historian, and members of the staff of the Department of Archives and History of Georgia; Clarence S. Brigham, Director of the American Antiquarian Society; Dr. St. George L. Sioussat and members of the staff of the Division of Manuscripts, the Library of Congress; and many others.

The compiler and editor has been most fortunate also in the research-fellows: George A. Beebe; Selby Coffman; Carolyn A. Daniel; Ellen Diggs Bodman; Clifton L. Hall; Robert S. Lambert; Margaret E. Lerche, and Roberta McKenzie Hamilton. In addition, graduate students who have been most helpful include J. C. Colley, George W. Patrick, Thomas L. Patrick, William R. Risher, C. M. Clarke, Katherine McGeachy, Olena S. Bunn, H. B. Story, R. H. Hamilton, John Littleton, William F. Burton, Jr., and Isaac Copeland, to all of whom I am most grateful. Thanks are due also to Mrs. Mabel T. Hill and Mrs. Dorothy Lyon for assistance with the classification and arrangement of the documents and with most competent help in typing and editing.

Special thanks go to the General Education Board, whose grants-in-aid helped to make this study possible and to Mr. C. T. Council of Durham, North Carolina, for generously providing some research fellowships.

Edgar W. Knight

The University of North Carolina
December, 1948

CONTENTS

VOLUME I

EUROPEAN INHERITANCES

I

HENRICO COLLEGE AND EAST INDIA SCHOOL

I. PREVIEW AND COMMENTS

THE FIRST STEPS toward educational efforts in English North America were taken for the colony of Virginia under the auspices of the Virginia Company of London in plans for Henrico College and East India School. The original charter of Virginia in 1606 referred to the need for "propagating of Christian religion to such people, as yet live in darkness and miserable ignorance of the true knowledge and worship of God, and may in time bring the infidels and savages...to human civility and quiet government" and the second charter of 1609 made reference to the same need. Eight years later King James the First requested the archbishops to instruct the bishops to "give orders to the ministers and other zealous men of their Dioceses" to move the people to contribute as liberally as possible "to so good a Worke." From these early efforts to provide education in Virginia, and at least until the Indian massacre in 1622, there were many evidences of interest in these undertakings. The early and romantic efforts at education in Virginia have been many times referred to, but the best secondary statement and summary of available information on the subject has been given by R. H. Land.[1]

Sir Thomas Dale went to Virginia under instructions from the Virginia Company of London to establish and "to inhabit" an English settlement near the Falls of the James River. This settlement,

1. "Henrico and Its College," *William and Mary College Quarterly Historical Magazine*, Second Series, vol. 18, No. 4 (October, 1938). This excellent study was made after extensive research by Land to meet the need "for a restatement and summary of information on Henrico and its college." Land used many sources, including the excellent work of Susan Myra Kingsbury (editor), *The Records of the Virginia Company of London* which was published in four volumes by the Library of Congress between 1906 and 1935. Most of the documents in the pages that follow in this section have been drawn from Kingsbury with her permission and that of the Library of Congress.

In the preface to Vol. I of Kingsbury the late Professor Herbert L. Osgood, wrote: "The records, especially the Court Book, of the Virginia Company of London, have long been regarded as among the most precious treasures which have found lodgment in the United States." In the present work the spelling in the documents as edited by Kingsbury has been preserved with no attempt to modernize the text of the extracts drawn from that source.

named "Henrico" [2] in honor of Henry, Prince of Wales, seems not to have flourished and apparently was practically abandoned in 1618. Nevertheless, Henrico had become fairly well known in England because of the college and school proposed to be located there and the project enlisted the interests and activities especially of those English people who had concern for missionary work in America.

Land says (p. 483) that the proposed East India School at Charles City ·(now City Point) was planned as a free public "collegiate school with dependence on Henrico College" and the idea of this institution "resulted from gifts solicited by the Reverend Patrick Copland to build a school or church in Virginia." One statement which was used to justify building East India School instead of a church was that the planters of Virginia through the lack of schools had been "hitherto constrained to their great costs to send their Children from thence hither [to England] to be taught." [3] Land notes also (pp. 496-97): "Possibly a greater blow to Henrico College than the massacre was the revocation of the charter of the Virginia Company on June 16, 1624.. The company had attempted to revive Henrico College after the massacre; but when the colony became a royal province, nothing more was done for it. However, the commissioners appointed by the crown to administer affairs in Virginia did try to establish the East India School. A year after the dissolution of the company, the council in Virginia wrote to those commissioners that they would be ready to assist with their utmost endeavours 'that pious work of the East India Free School.' " And as late as 1629-30 the "Plantation of the College" was represented in the House of Burgesses of the General Assembly of Virginia.

Academia Virginiensis et Oxoniensis.

Two years after the Indian insurrection Good Friday, March 22, 1622, the idea of a university in the colony of Virginia was revived through the will of Edward Palmer. On July 3, 1622, "16 shares of lands in Virginia" had been passed over by the Virginia Company of London to "Edward Palmer of the Middle Temple London esquire

2. Land notes: "Of late years, writers have found it convenient to refer to this settlement as Henricopolis, thus avoiding confusion with Henrico County which took its name from this settlement when counties were formed in Virginia in 1634. Since the town was never contemporarily known as Henricopolis, it has been thought best to use the original form of the name which was Henrico or Henricus."— *Op. cit.*, 453, note.

3. John S. Flory, "The University of Henrico," *Southern History Association Publications*, VII (January, 1904), 43. Quoted by Land, *op. cit.*, p. 487.

with allowance of the Auditors and Approbacon of this Court; and said Shares being parcell of the later 40 Shares assigned vnto him from the Right Hono^ble the Lady D'Lawarre." [4] Under his will of November 22, 1624, Palmer left all lands and tenements in Virginia and New England for "the foundinge or maintenance of a Universitie, and such schooles in Virginia, as shall be there erected and shall be called *Academia Virginiensis et Oxoniensis* and shall bee divided into several streets or alleyes of Twentye foot broade. Provided always that all such as can prove their lawful descent from John Palmer, Esq., of Lemington aforesaid, my grandfather deceased, and my late grand-mother his wife, being sonnes, shall be there freelye admitted and shall be brought upp in such schooles as shall be fitt for their age and learnings, and shall be removed from time to time as they shall profitt in knowledge and understandinge.

"And further, my will is, that the schollers of said Universitye for avoydinge of Idleness at their houres of recreation shall have two paynters, the one for oyle cullors, and the other for water cullors wch shall be admitted fellowes in the same College to the end and intent that the said scollers shall or may learne the arts of paynting, and further, my will and mind is, that two grinders, the one for oyle collours, & the other for water collours, and also coullers, oyle, and gumme waters shal be provided from tyme to tyme at the charges of the said College, beseeching God to add a blessing to all these intents." [5]

Although plans for Henrico College and a university called *Academia Virginiensis et Oxoniensis* failed, the latter perhaps because of the death of its chief advocate, Edward Palmer, the idea of a university for Virginia did not die. In 1660 the General Assembly of Virginia voted "that for the advance of learning, education of youth, supply of the ministry, and promotion of piety, there be land taken upon purchases for a Colledge and free schoole, and that there be, with as much speede as may be convenient, houseing erected thereon for entertainment of students and schollers." [6]

The General Assembly also voted in 1660 that the commissioners of the county courts on court days should take subscriptions for the benefit of the proposed college and that they should send instructions

---

4. Kingsbury, *op. cit.*, II, 77, 217, 218.
5. Will of Edward Palmer, November 22, 1624. Edward D. Neill, *Virginia Vetusta*, pp. 183-84. See also Herbert B. Adams, *The College of William and Mary*. Circulars of Information of the United States Bureau of Education. No. 1, 1887, pp. 11-12.
6. Hening, *Statutes at Large*, II, 25.

throughout their counties to the vestrymen of the parishes to raise money from those people who "have not already subscribed." But three decades were to pass before a higher educational institution was provided for Virginia. In 1693 the charter of The College of William and Mary was granted by the crown,[7] the first college to be established in the South and next to Harvard (1636) the oldest in English North America. But this ancient ecclesiastical institution failed to become a state university, notwithstanding the efforts of Thomas Jefferson to transform his alma mater into such an institution when, as Governor of the State, he became a member of the Board of Visitors in 1779. This effort failed as did also the effort in the early 1820's to move The College of William and Mary to Richmond. In 1819 the University of Virginia was chartered, to be opened in 1825.

Documents on Henrico College and East India School follow: [8]

II. DOCUMENTS

1. EXTRACT FROM THE CHARTER OF VIRGINIA, 1606

... We greatly commending, and graciously accepting of, their [members of the Virginia Company of London] desires for the furtherance of so noble a work, which may, by the providence of Almighty God, hereafter tend to the glory of his divine Majesty, in propagating

7. This charter (In Latin and in English) is given below beginning on p. 397.

8. Dès 1619, c'est-à-dire une douzaine d'années avant que le *Mayflower* aborde sur la côte de Massachusets, l'idée de l'*Université* est vivante en Virginie. Le Président de la *Virginia Company*, sir Edwin Sandys, signe en Angleterre la concession de 10,000 acres (un peu plus de 40,000 hectares), attribués à la construction d'un "Seminary of Learning" à Henrico. De cette munificence une part spéciale était réservée aux Indiens (1,000 acres); aux Indiens aussi fut attribuée une donation de 1,500 livres, faite par l'épiscopat anglais, sous l'influence du roi.

Cette union de l'Eglise et de l'Etat dans une même pensée produisit quelques bons résultats immédiats. Les colons virginiens prélevèrent sur leurs maigres ressources les éléments d'une souscription de 150 livres, des *settlers* prirent possession des terres *universitaires*, un surintendant, sir George Thorpe, *of His Majesty's Privy Chamber*, vint tout exprès de Londres; mais les Indiens, surexcités par les vexations des nouveaux venus, peu touchés par les promesses de ceux qui confisquaient leurs forêts de chasse, se soulevèrent en 1622, et tout fut massacré, surintendant et planteurs.

Les promoteurs de la cause de l'éducation ne se laissent point décourager: *uno avulso non deficit alter*. Dès 1624, M. Edward Palmer obtint du gouvernement anglais une île dans la Susquehanna, tout près de l'emplacement actuel du Havre-de-Grâce, où, loin des atteintes des Indiens, serait bâtie l'Université, dont le nom annonçait les prétentions, *Academia Virginiensis et Oxoniensis*. Ainsi, jadis, au milieu des barbares northumbriens, le monastère de Lindisfarne s'était élevé, protégé par les eaux contre ses peu hospitaliers voisins. Mais l'*Académie d'Oxford* ne devait pas s'établir: la mort du principal promoteur de l'entreprise, M. Palmer, arrêta ces projets, avant même un commencement d'exécution.—Charles Barneaud, *Origines et progrès de l'éducation en Amérique* (Paris, 1898), p. 41.

of Christian religion to such people, as yet live in darkness and miserable ignorance of the true knowledge and worship of God, and may in time bring the infidels and savages, living in those parts, to human civility and to settled and quiet government; Do by these our letters pattents, graciously accept of, and agree to, their humble and well intended desires; . . .—Extract from "Letters Patent to Sir Thomas Gates, Sir George Somers and others," April 10, 1606. In Alexander Brown, *The Genesis of the United States*, I, 53-54.

2. EXTRACT FROM THE CHARTER OF VIRGINIA, 1609

And lastly, because of the principal effect, which we can desire or expect of this action, is the conversion and reduction of the people in those parts unto the true worship of God and Christian religion, in which respect we should be loath, that any person should be permitted to pass, that we suspected to effect the superstitions of the church of Rome . . .—Extract from the second charter of Virginia, May 23, 1609. In *ibid.*, p. 236.

3. KING JAMES THE FIRST TO HIS ARCHBISHOPS, 1617

You haue heard ere this time of ye attempt of diuerse Worthie men, our Subjects to plant in Virginia (under ye warrant of our L'res patents) People of this Kingdom, as well as for ye enlarging of our Dominions, as for propagation of ye Gospell amongst Infidells: wherein there is good progresse made, and hope of further increase; so as the undertakers of that Plantation are now in hand wth the erecting of some Churches and Schooles for ye education of ye children of those Barbarians w'ch cannot but be to them a very great charge, . . . In wch wee doubt not but that you and all others who wish well to the encrease of Christian Religion will be willing to give all assistance and furtherance you may, and therein to make experience of the zeal of deuotion of our well minded Subjects, especially those of ye Clergie. Where fore Wee doe require you and hereby authorize you to write yor Letters to ye severall Bishops of ye Diocese in yor Province, that they doe giue order to the Ministers and other zealous men of their Dioceses, both by their owne example in contribution, and by exhortation to others, to move our people within their seuerall charges to contribute to so good a Worke in as liberall a manner as they may for the better aduancing whereof our pleasure is that those Collections be made in the particular parishes four seuerall tymes within these two years next coming: and that the seuerall accounts of each parish together wth the moneys collected, be retourned from time to time to ye Bishop of ye Dioceses and by them be transmitted half yearly to you: and so to be deliuered to the Treasurer of that Plantation to be employed for the Godly purposes intended and no other.—King James the First to his Archbishops, 1617. In Edward D. Neill, *Virginia Vetusta*, 167-68.

4. INSTRUCTIONS TO GOVERNOR-ELECT GEORGE YEARDLEY, 1618

And Whereas by a special Grant and licence from his Majesty a general Contribution over this Realm hath been made for the building and planting of a college for the training up of the Children of those Infidels in true Religion moral virtue and Civility and for other godly uses We do therefore according to a former Grant and order hereby ratifie confirm and ordain that a convenient place be chosen and set out for the planting of a University at the said Henrico in time to come and that in the mean time preparation be there made for the building of the said College for the Children of the Infidels according to such Instructions as we shall deliver And we will and ordain that ten thousand acres partly of the Lands they impaled and partly of other Land within the territory of the said Henrico be alotted and set out for the endowing of the said University and College with convenient possessions.—Instructions to Governor-elect George Yeardley. Kingsbury (ed.), *The Records of the Virginia Company of London*, III, 102 (November 18, 1618).

5. A GIFT TO THE COLLEGE, 1619

Giuen to the vse of the College, certaine good Bookes of Diuinitie, by an vnknowne person.—*Ibid.*, p. 241 (January, 1619).

6. REPORT OF THE TREASURER ON FUNDS FOR THE COLLEGE, 1619

It was also by m^r Trer propounded to the Co^{rt} as a thing most worthy to be taken into consideracon both for the glory of God, and hono^r of the Company, that forasmuch as the King in his most gracious fauo^r hath graunted his Lres to the seuerall Bishops of this Kingdome for the collecting of monies to erect and build a Colledge in Virginia for the trayning and bringing vp of Infidells children to the true knowledge of God & vnderstanding of righteousnes. And considering what publique notice may be taken in foreslowing to sett forward the accon, especially of all those W^{ch} hath contributed to the same, that therefore to begin that pious worke, there is allready towards it—1500li,—or thereabouts, whereof remayning in cash 800li, the rest is to be answered out of the Stock of the Generall Company for so much Wch they borrowed, besides the likelihood of more to come in; ffor mr Treasuror hauing some conference Wth the Bishop of Lichfield, he hath not heard of any Colleccon that hath beene for that busines in his Diocese; but promiseth when he hath a warrt therevnto he will Wthall dilligence further the enterprize; Wherevpon he conceaued it the fittest; that as yet they should not build the Colledge, but rather forebeare a while; and begin first with the meanes they haue to provide and settle an Annuall revennue, and out of that to begin the ereccon of the said Colledge: And for the performance hereof also moued, that a certaine peece of Land be Laid out at Henrico being the place formerly resolued of Wch should be called the Colledge Land, and for the planting of the same send presently ffifty good persons to be seated thereon and to occupy the same according to order, and to haue halfe the benefitt of their Labor and the other halfe to goe in setting forward the worke, and for mayntenance of the Tutors & Schollers.—*Ibid.*, I, 220 (May 26, 1619).

7. COMMITTEE ON THE COLLEGE IS APPOINTED, 1619

It was moued by mr. Threr that the Court would take into consideracon to appoint a Comittie of choice Gentlemen, and others of his Mats Counsell for Virginia concerning the Colledge; being a waighty busines, and so greate, that an Account of their proceedings therein must be giuen to the State. Vpon Wch the Cort vpon deliberate consideracon haue recomended the care thereof vnto the Right Wor Sr Dudley Diggs, Sr Iohn Dauers, Sr Nath: Rich, Sr Io: Wolstenholme, mr Deputy fferrar, mr Anthony, and mr Dr Gulson to meete at such time as mr Treasuror shall giue order therevnto.—*Ibid.*, p. 231 (June 14, 1619).

8. WORKMEN TO BE SENT FOR ERECTING THE COLLEGE, 1619

The fifte Petition is to beseeche the Treasurer, Counsell and Company that, towards the erecting of the University and Colledge, they will sende, when they shall thinke it most convenient, workmen of all sortes, fitt for that purpose.—*Ibid.*, III, 161 (July 31, 1619).

9. CONCERNING THE FUNDS FOR THE COLLEGE, 1619

Mr Trer desired the allowance of this Court of one thing agreed of by the Auditors and Comittees of the Colledge, Wch was that 1400li

—od mony in all being receaued of the Colleccon monyes by Sr Tho: Smith, of Wch vpon seuerall occasions, therewas vented by way of Loane for the vse of the Company Eight hundreth poundes, the Remainder being 500li odd money was paid vnto mr. Treasuror; Therefore that the said 800li—might be reimbursed out of the Comon Cash in to the Colledge mony, Wch was ratified and allowed of by the Court.—*Ibid.*, I, 263 (November 15, 1619).

10. CONCERNING GIFT OF 500 POUNDS FOR EDUCATION, 1619

Whereas the last Court a speciall Committee was appoynted for ye mannaginge of the 500li given by an vnknowne pson for educatinge the Infidles Children Mr Threr: signified that they have mett, and taken into consideracon the proposicon of Sr Iohn Wolstenholme, that Iohn Peirce and his Associates might have the trayninge and bringing vpp of some of those Children butt the said Comittee for divers reasons think itt inconvenyent, first because they intend not to goe this 2 or :3: monneths and then after there arryvall wilbe longe in settlinge themselves, as allso that the Indians are not acquainted wth them, and so they may stay 4 or 5 years before they have account that any good is donne.

And for to putt itt into the hands of pryvate men to bringe them vpp att xli a Childe as was by some proposed they hould itt not soe fitt by reason of the Causuality vnto wch itt is subiect.—*Ibid.*, pp. 310-11 (February 16, 1619).

11. UNKNOWN PERSON PROMISES 500 POUNDS, 1620

A Lre from an vnknowne person was read dyrected to mr Treasuror pmisinge five hundred pounds for the educatinge and bringinge vpp Infidell Children in Christianytie wch Mr Treasuror not willing to meddle therwith alone desyred the Court to apoynt a select Comittee for the mannadginge and imployinge of itt to the best to wch purpose they have made choyse of the

Lord Pagett.	mr Tho: Gibbes.
Sr Tho Wroth.	Dr Winstone.
mr Io: Wroth.	mr Bamforde &
mr Deputie.	mr Keightley.

The Copy of wch Letter ensueth.

Sr yor Charitable endeavors for Virginia hath made you a ffather wee a favourer of those good works wch although heretofore hath com neer to their birth yett for want of strength could never be delivered, (envy & division dashinge these younglings even in the wombe) vntill yor helpfull hand wth other honorable psonages gave them both birth and beinge, for the better cherishinge of wch good and pious worke seeinge many castinge guift into the Treasury, I ame encourraged to tender my poore mite and although I cannott wth the Princes of Issaker bringe gould and silver Coveringe yett offer here what I cann, some Goat hayre necessary stuffe for the Lords Tabernacle, protestinge heer in my sinceritie wth out papisticall merritt or pharasaicall applause wishing from my part as much ynitie in yor honorable vndertakinge as theris sinceritie in my designes, to the furtherance of wch good worke, the Convertinge of Infidles to the fayth of Christe I pmised by my good frends 500^li for the mayntnenance of a Conveyent nomber of younge Indians taken att the age of Seaven years or younger & instructed in the readinge and vnderstandinge the principalls of Xian Religion vnto the Age of 12 years and then as occasion serveth to be trayned and brought vpp in some lawfull Trade wth all humanitie and gentleness vntill the Age of one and Twenty years, and then to enioye like liberties and pryveledges wth our native English in that place and for the better pformance thereof yo^u shall receave 50^li more to be delivered into the hands to two religious psons wth securitie of payment who shall onve every Quarter examine and certifie to the Treasuror herein England the due execucon of these premises together wth the names of these Children thus taken, their ffoster ffathers and ouerseers not doubtinge butt yo^u are all assured that guiftes devoted to Gods service cannott be diverted to pryvate and secular advantages without sacriledge, if yor graver iudgments can devise a more charitable course for such younge Children, I beseech yo^u informe my frend wth yor securitie for true pformance and my benevolence shalbe allwaies redy to be delivered accordingly, the greatest Courtesie I expect or crave is to conceale my frends name least importunytie vrge him to betray that trust of secresie wch hee hath faythfully promised, hee that moved my harte to this good worke, dyrect yor Charitable endeavours herein, whylest I rest as I ame

Dust and Ashes

Directed to Sr Edwin Sandys ye faithfull Treasuror for Virginia.
—*Ibid.*, pp. 307-8 (February 2, 1620).

12. Bequest of 300 Pounds, 1620

Intelligence was given yt mr Nicholas fferrar thelder beinge translated from this life vnto a better, had by his will bequeathed 300li
towards the convertinge of Infidles Children in Virginia to be paid
vnto Sr Edwin Sandys and mr Io: Ferrar att such time as vppon Certificate from thence ten of the said Infidles Children shalbe placed in
the Colledge to be then disposed by the said Sr Edwin Sandys and Io:
Ferrar according to the true intent of his said will, and that in the
meane, till that were pformed hee hath tyed his executors to pay 8
p Cent for ye same vnto 3 seuerall honest men in Virginia (such as the
said Sr Edwin Sandys and Iohn Ferrar shall approve of) of good life
and fame that will vndertake each of them to bringe vpp one of the
said Children in the grounds of Christian religion that is to say 8li
yearely apeece.
An vnknowne pson hath allso given 10li for some good vses in
Virginia.—*Ibid.*, p. 335 (April 8, 1620).

13. The Letter of "Dust and Ashes" Presented, 1621

The Letter subscribed D and A was brought to the former Court
by an vnknowne Messenger was nowe againe presented to be read
the Content whereof are as followeth.[1]

Ianuary 28th 1621

Most worthie Companie
Whereas I sent the Treasuror and yor selues a letter subscribed
Dust and Ashes wch promised 550li to such vses therein expressed,
and did soone afterward, accordinge to my promise send the said
money to Sr Edwin Sandys to be deliuered to the Companie, In
wch letter I did not strictly order the bestowinge of the said money
but shewed my intent for the conversion of Infidell Children, as it
will appeare by that letter wch I desire may be read in open Court
wherein I chiefely comended the orderinge thereof to the wisdome
of you the Honoble Companie, And whereas the gentlement of the
Southampton Hundred haue vndertaken the disposinge of the said
550li I haue longe attended to see the erectinge of some Schoole or
other waye whereby some of the Children of the Virginians might
haue bin taught and brought vp in Christian religion and good
manners wch not beinge donne accordinge to my intent but the

---

1. This Document was copied into the manuscript at a later date. (Kingsbury's
note.)

money deteyned by a priuate hundred all this while contrary to my minde, though I iudje verie charitably of that honoble Society, And as already you haue receaued a great and the most painefully gained part of my estate toward the layinge of the foundacon of Christian religion and helpinge forward of this pious worke in that Heathen nowe Christian land, So nowe I require of the whole Body of yor Honoble and worthie Companie (whome I entrusted with the dispose of the said moneyes,) to see the same speedily and faithfully converted to the worke intended: And I do further propound to you the honoble Companie that if you will procure that some of the male Children of ye Virginians (though but a fewe) be brought ouer into England here to be educated and taught, and to weare a habbit as the Children of Christ Hospitall do, and that you wilbe pleased to see the said 550li converted to this vse then I do faithfully promise that when eight or ten of the Virginians Children are brought ouer, and placed in London either in Christ Hospitall or el in the Virginian Schoole or Hospitall (as it may be called and by the will and guift of good men may be yearely augmented) where the Companie may haue an ey ouer them and be (as it were) nursinge ffathers vnto them then I say I faithfully promise to add 450li more to make the Sume 1000li wch if God permitt I will cheerfully send you only I desire to nominate the first Tutor or Gouernor who shall take charge to nurse and instruct them: But if you in yor Wisedomes like not of this mocon then my humble Suite vnto ye whole body of yor Honoble Companie is that my former guift of 50li be wholly imployed & bestowed vpon a free Schoole to be erected in Southampton Hundred (so it be presently imployed) or such other place as I or my freind shall well like of wherein both English and Virginians may be taught together and that the said Schoole be endowed with such priuiledges as you in yor wisdomes shall thinke fitt: The Mr of wch Schoole I humbly craue may not be allowed to goe ouer except he first bringe in to the Companie sound testimony of his sufficiency in learning and sincerity of life The Lord giue you wise and vnderstandinge hart that his worke herein be not negligently performed.

D and A

Directed
   To the right Honoble and wortt the Treasuror Counsell and Company of Virginia.

This letter beinge referred to the consideracon of this Court for somuch as it did require an Account of the Companie howe they haue expended the saide money vizt the 550li in gold for the bringinge vp of the Infidell Children in true religion and christianity, Sr Edwin Sandys declared that the said money cominge vnto him enclosed in a box in the time of his beinge Treasuror, not longe after a letter subscribed Dust and Ashes had bin directed vnto him in the quality of Treasuror, and Deliuered in the Court and there openly read he brought the money also vnto the next Court in the Box vnopened: Wherevpon the Court after a large and serious deliveracon howe the said money might be best imployed to the vse intended, at length resolued that it was fittest to be entertayned by the Societies of Southampton Hundred and Martins Hundred and each to vndertake for a certaine number of Infidell Children to be brought vp by them, and amongst them in Christian Religion and some good Trade to lyue by accordinge to the Donors religious desire; But Martins Hundred desired to be excused by reason their Plantacon was sorely weakened and as then in much confusion: Wherevpon it being pressed that Southampton Hundred should vndertake the whole they also consideringe together with the waight the difficulty also and hazard of the buissines were likewise verie vnwillinge to vndertake the mana+ginge thereof and offered an addicon of 100li more vnto the former some of 550li that it might not be put vpon them. But beinge earnestly pressed therevnto by the Court and findinge no other means howe to sett forward that great worke yealded in fine to accept thereof: Wherevpon soone after at an Assembly of that Society the Adventurers entred into carefull a consideracon howe this great and waightie buissines might with most speed and great aduantag be effected: Wherevpon it was agreed and resolued by them to imploy the said money together with an Addicon (out of the Societies purse) of a farr greater Some toward the furnishinge out of Captaine Bluett and his Companie beinge 80 verie able and sufficient workmen wth all manner of prouisions for the settinge vp of an Iron worke in Virginia, whereof the proffitt accruinge were intended and ordered in a ratable proporcon to be faithfully imployed for the educatinge of 30 of the Infidell Children in Christian Religion and otherwise as the Donor had required: To wch end they writt verie effectuall letters vnto Sr Geo: Yeardley then Gouernor of Virginia and Capt: also of Southampton Plantation: not onely recomendinge the excellencie of that worke, but also furnishinge him at large with aduise & direccon howe to proceed therein with a most earnest adiuracon (and that often it-terated in all their succeedinge Letters) so to imploy his best care and industrie therein, as a worke whereon the eyes of God, Angell, and men were fixed: The Coppie of wᶜʰ letter and Direccon through some omission of their Officer was not entred in their booke, but a course should be taken to haue it recouered.—*Ibid.*, pp. 585-88 (January 30, 1621).

14. COMMITTEE TO CONFER WITH MR. COPLAND ON DISPOSITION OF FUNDS, 1621

The said Comittee meetinge this Afternoone to treat with mʳ Cop-land touchinge the dispose of the money giuen by some of the East Indy Companie that came with him in the Royall Iames to be be-stowed vpon some good worke for the benefitt of the Plantacon in Virginia, the said mʳ Copland beinge nowe present did deliuer in a note of the names of those that had freely and willingly contributed their moneyes herevnto, Wᶜʰ money mʳ Copland said they desired might be imployed towardes the buildinge either of a Church or Schoole in Virginia (Wᶜʰ the Companie should thinke fitt). And that although this Some of money was but a smale proporcon to pforme so great a worke, yet mʳ Copland said he doubted not, but to pswade the East Indy Companie (whome he meant to solicite), to make some Addicon therevnto, besides he said that he had very ef-fectually writt (the Coppie of Wᶜʰ letter he shewed and was read) to diuers ffactories in the East Indies to stirr them vp to the like Con-tribucon towardes the pformance of this pious worke as they had already donne for the buildinge of a Church at Wappinge where by his Report they haue giuen about 400ˡⁱ.

It beinge therefore nowe taken into consideracon whither a Church or a Schoole was most necessarie and might nearest agree to the in-tencons of the Donors: It was conceaued that for somuch as each pticuler Plantacon aswell as the generall either had or ought to haue a Church appropriated vnto them, there was therefore a greater want of a Schoole then of Churches: As also for that it was impossible with so smale a proporcon to compasse so great a charge as the buildinge of a Church would require, they therefore conceaued it most fitt to re-solue for the erectinge of a publique free schoole Wᶜʰ beinge for the educacon of Children and groundinge of them in the principles of religion Ciuility of life and humane learninge serued to carry with it the greatest waight and highest consequence vnto the Plantacons as that whereof both Church and comonwealth take their originall foundacon and happie estate, this beinge also like to proue a worke most acceptable vnto the Planters, through want whereof they haue bin hitherto constrained to their great costes to send their Children from thence hither to be taught.

Secondly it was thought fitt that this schoole should be placed in one of the fower Citties and they conceaued that Charles Citty, of the fower did affoord the most convenient place for that purpose as well in respect it matcheth with the best in holesomnes of Aire, as also for the comodious scituacon thereof, beinge not farr distant from Henrico and other perticuler Plantacons.

It was also thought fitt that in honor of the East Indy Benefactors, the same should be called the East Indy Schoole who shall haue precedence before any other to preferr their Children thither to be brought vp in the rudimentes of learninge; It was also thought fitt that this as a Collegiate or free schoole should haue dependance vpon the Colledge in Virginia Wch should be made capable to receaue Schollers from the Shoole into such Scollershipps and fellowshipps as the said Colledge shalbe endowed withall for the aduancement of schollers as they arise by degres and deserts in learninge.

That for the better mayntenance of the Scholemr and Vsher intended there to be placed it was thought fitt that it should be moued at the next Quarter Cort that 1000 acres of land should be allotted vnto the said Scolle, and that 5 psons besides an ouerseer of them should be forthwith sent vpon this charg in the condicon of Apprentices to manure and cultiuate the said land, and that ouer and aboue this allowance of land and Tenantes vnto the Schoolemr, such as sent their Children to this Schoole should giue some benevolence vnto the scoolemr for the better encrease of his mayntenance.

That it should be speacially recommended to the Gouernor to take care that the Planters there be stirred vp to put their helpinge handes towardes the speedy buildinge of the said Schoole in respect their Children are like to receaue the greatest benefitt thereby in their educacon: And to let them knowe that those that exceed others in their bounty and Assistance herevnto shalbe priuiledged with the preferment of their Children to the said Schoole before others that shalbe found lesse worthie.

It is likewise thought fitt that a good Schoolemr be poruided forthwith to be sent vnto this Scoole.

It was also informed by a gentleman of this Comittee that he knewe one that desired not to be named that would bestowe 30li to be added to the former Some of 70li to make it vp 100li towardes the buildinge of the said schoole: This report beinge read was well approued of and thought fitt to be referred for confirmacon to the next Quartr Court.—*Ibid.*, pp. 538-41 (October 31, 1621).

15. COMMITTEE RESOLVES TO USE FUNDS FOR SCHOOL, 1621

Whereas the Comittee appointed to treat with mr Copland about the buildinge of the East India Church or Schoole, in Virginia towards wch a Contribucon of 70li was freely giuen by some of the East Indy Company that came home in the Royall Iames did nowe make report what speciall reasons moued them to resolue for the bestowinge that money towardes the erectinge of a Schoole rather then a Church Wch report is at large sett downe at a Court held the last of October: And further that they had allotted 1000 acres of land and fiue Apprentices besides an Ouerseer to manure it, besides that beneuolence that is hoped wilbe giuen by each man that sendes his Children thither to be taught for the Schoolemr mayntenance in his first begininge: Wch allowance of land and Tenantes beinge put to the question was well aproued of and referred for confirmacon to the Quarter Court Prouided that in the establishment hereof the Companie reserue vnto themselues power to make lawes and orders for the better gouerment of the said Schoole and the Revenues and profittes that shall therevnto belong.—*Ibid.*, p. 550. (November 19, 1621).

Whereas there was a contribucon of 70li freely giuen by certaine gentlemen and Marriners of the East India Companie yt came home in the Royall Iames wch they desired might be imployed towardes the buildinge either of an East Indy Church or Schoole in Virginia at the Choise of the Virginia Companie: Wherevpon it beinge referred to a Comittee and by them taken into consideracon they did nowe certifie that many important reasons had moved them to agree in opinion yt the said moneyes were fitt to be imployed for the buildinge of a free schoole in Virginia wch they likewise thought fitt should be called the East Indy Schoole in honor of the said Benefactors they also signified further that an vnknowne person out of a zealous affeccon to aduance so pious a worke had giuen 30li more, both wch Somes were nowe brought into the Court and laid vpon the Table It was also further declared in the report of the said Comittee beinge entred at large in the Court held the last of october that they thought fitt for the mayntenance of the said Schoolemr and his Vsher to be placed in the said Schoole to allowe no lesse than 1000 acres of land and fiue persons besid and Ouerseer of them wᶜʰ they thought fitt should be forthwith sent vpon this former charge (in condicon of Apprentices) to manure and culture the said lands, wᶜʰ allowance of land and Servante beinge intended for this as a Collegiate Schoole, the Court conceaued to be verie reasonable and therevpon beinge put to the question were accordingly confirmed.—*Ibid.*, pp. 550, 558-59 (November 19 and 21, 1621).

16. PASSENGERS AND CREW ON ROYAL JAMES MAKE CONTRIBUTION TO FREE SCHOOL IN VIRGINIA, 1621

There is one thinge likewise that hath lately hapned vnto us, not great in itself but of great good hope; the gentlemen and Mariners of the Royall James belongeing to the East India Company, being mett at Cap Bona Speranza by some English Shipps outward bound, and certified of the prosperitie of Virginia, did there (vppon the exhortation of Mr Copland theire Minister) bestowe the sume of 70ˡⁱ towardes the buildinge of a free schoole in Virginia: wᶜʰ pious guift hath lately received an addiccon of 30ˡⁱ by an vnknowne person. The maner of employeinge the mony wᶜʰ the Company hath resolued vppon, we send yoᵘ here inclosed, desiringe that yoᵘ would likewise take it into yoʳ considerations.—*Ibid.*, III, 531 (December 5, 1621).

17. THANKS RETURNED TO JOHN BRINSLEY, "A PAINEFULL" SCHOOLMASTER, FOR COPY OF HIS *A Consolation for our Grammar Schooles*, 1621

Mr Bamfeild signified vnto the Court of a booke [1] compiled by a painefull Schoolmr one mr Iohn Brinsly: Wherevpon the Court gaue

---

1. *A Consolation for our Grammar Schooles*, by John Brinsley, was printed in London in 1622 and was dedicated "To the Right Honourable his Majesties Lord Deputy of Ireland, and to the Right Honourable the Lord President and Lord Lieutenant of Wales, and the Principalities thereof, the Gouernours of the Iles of Gernsey and Iernsey; and to the right Honourable and right Worshipfull, the Treasurer, Councel and Company for Virginia, and of the Sommer Ilands; and to all other Gouernours within his Majesties dominions, to whom the charge and care of Schooles; namely, those of the inferiour sort, are assigned; with all true fauourers of good Learning, who vnfainedly wish the perpetuall flourishing of the Church of God, and of their natiue Country, all grace and happinesse in Christ eternally."

The full title of Brinsley's book was: "A Consolation for our Grammar Schooles: or a faithful and most comfortable incouragement for laying a sure foundation of all good learning in our Schooles, and for prosperous building thereon. More especially for all those of the inferiour sort, and all ruder countries and places, namely for Ireland, Wales, Virginia with the Summer Islands, and for their most speedie attaining of our English tongue by the same labour, that all may speak one and the same language. And withall, for the helping of all such as are desirous speedily to recover order that the Companies thanke should be giuen vnto him, & appointed a select Comittee to pvse the said Booke vizt

Sr Iohn Dauers.	mr Bamfeild.
mr Deputy.	mr Copland.
mr Gibbs.	mr Ayres.
mr Wrote.	mr Nicho: ffarrar.
mr Binge.	

who are entreated to meete when mr Deputy shall appoint and after to make report of their opinions touchinge the same at the next Court. —*Ibid.*, I, 574 (December 19, 1621).

18. COMMITTEE TOO BUSY TO PERUSE THE BOOK; COPLAND ASKED TO DO SO, 1622

The Comittee appointed to pvse the bookes Wch mr Io: Brinsly Schoolmr presented at the last Court touchinge the educacon of the younger sort of Schollers, for somuch as they had yet no time to pvse the same by reason of many buissinesses that did occurr they desired of the Court some longer respite Wch was graunted vnto them mr Copland being present was entreated to pvse it in the meane time and deliuer his opinion thereof vnto the said Comittees at their meetinge about it.—*Ibid.* (January 16, 1622).

19. UNKNOWN DONOR SENDS BOOKS FOR THE COLLEGE, 1622

In the middest of this narracon a stranger stept in presentinge 4 books fairely bound sent from a pson refusinge to be named who had bestowed them vpon the Colledge in Virginia being from the same man that gaue heretofore fower other great book the names of these he nowe sent were these vizt a large Church Bible, the Comon

---

that which they had formerly got in the Grammar Schooles, and to proceed aright therein, for the perpetual benefit of these our Nations and of the Churches of Christ."

In his *Epistle Dedicatore* Brinsley said of the aims of education: "... The first and chiefe whereof (as I conceiue) is this, That his pure religion, honour, and true worship, may be set vp, and aduanced in them; the next, that the wealth and sauing of all his poore people in those places, both of their soules and bodies, may be by you procured, so farre as in your power shall lie. And these things to be effected principally, by a learned, holie, and faithfull Ministerie, protected and assisted by a godlie Magistracie, and of propagating and spreading all good learning and knowledge amongst them. To this purpose God hauing ordained Schooles or learning to be a principal meanes ... for the breeding and nourishing of such a holy Ministerie, with a wise and godlie Magistracie, and people to be perpetuallie preserued; your care, as I take it, in the next place (that I may speak with all reuerence and submission) ought to be for prouision of meete Schooles and Seminaries for them, according to the natures and conditions of the places, and as God shall raise vp meanes thereto ..."

prayer booke, Vrsinus[1] Catichisme and a smale Bible richly im-
broydered: The Court desired the Messeng[r] to returne the gent. that
gaue them their generall acknowledgm[t] of much respect and thank
due vnto him.—*Ibid.*, I, 589 (January 30, 1622).

20. Mr. Copland recommends master for the school, 1622

M[r] Copland moued that whereas it was ordered by the last Quarter
Court that an Vsher should be sent to Virginia with the first conveniency to instruct the Children in the free schoole there intended
to be erected, that for somuch as there was nowe a verie good
Scholler whome he well knewe and had good testimony for his
sufficiency in learninge and good carriage who offered himselfe to
goe for the prformance of this seruice he therefore thought good to
acquaint the Court therewith and so leaue it to their better iudgement
& consideracon wherevpon the Court appointed a Comittee to treat
with the said Party. vizt

m[r] Gibbs.	m[r] Copland.
m[r] Wroth.	m[r] Balmford.
m[r] Wrote.	m[r] Robert.

who are to ioyne herein the rest of the Comittee and to meet about it
vpon Monday next in the morninge about eight at m[r] Deputies and
thereof to make report.—*Ibid.*, pp. 600-1 (February 13, 1622).

21. The young man seems unwilling to go to Virginia, 1622

The Comittees report touchinge the allowance graunted vnto the
Vssher of the ffree Schoole intended in Virginia beinge read m[r]
Copland signified that the said Vsher havinge lately imparted his
minde vnto him seemed vnwillinge to goe as Vsher or with any less
title then m[r] of the said Schoole and to be also assured of that allowance that is intended to be appropriated to the m[r] for his propper
mayntenance, but it was aunsweared they might not swarue from

---

1. Zacharias Ursinus (1536-1583), German reformed theologian and writer. The
"Heidelberg Catechism" is said to have been "the most attractive of all the catechisms of the Reformation." It was drawn up on instructions of Frederick III, elector
of the Palatinate, by Ursinus and Caspar Olevianus (1536-1587), published in 1563,
officially recognized by the Synod of Dort in 1619, was widely used in France, England, and America and is said to share with *The Imitation of Christ* by Thomas à
Kempis (1380-1471), *Pilgrim's Progress* by John Bunyan (1628-1688) "the honour of
coming next to the Bible in the number of tongues into which it has been translated."
This catechism was generally accepted by Calvinists as a faithful and authoritative
exposition of the reformed churches and was used as a manual of Christian doctrine
and public profession of faith. See *Catholic Encyclopedia*, V, 763; *The Encyclopaedia
Britannica*, Fourteenth Edition, II, 387.

the order of the Quarter Court wch did appoint the Vsher to be first
established for the better aduancemt of wch Accon diuers had vnder-
written to a Roll for that purpose Drawne wch did already arise to
a good Some of money, and was like Daylie to encrease by reason
of mens affeccons to forward so good a worke: In wch respect many
sufficient Schollers did now offer themselues to goe vpon the same
condicons as had bin proposed to this Party, yet in fauor of him for
somuch as he was speacially recomended by mr Copland whome the
Companie do much respect the Court is pleased to giue him some
time to consider of it between this and the next Court desiringe then
to know his direct aunsweare whither he will accept of the place of
Vsher as had bin offered vnto him And if he shall accept thereof
then the Court haue entreated.

> mr Balmefore.
> mr Copeland.
> mr Caswell.
> mr Mellinge.

to conferr with him about the methode of teachinge and the bookes
he intends to instruct Children by.—*Ibid.*, pp. 606-7 (February 27,
1622).

22. CONCERNING MR. DIKE, PROPOSED AS USHER FOR THE SCHOOL, 1622

The Court takinge into their consideracon certaine proposicons
presented vnto them by mr Copland in the behalfe of mr Dike
formerly comended for the Vshers place in the free Schoole intended
at Charles Citty in Virginia they haue agreed in effect vnto his seuerall
requestes namely that vpon certificate from the Gouernor of Virginia of his sufficiency and Diligence in framinge vp of youth comitted
to his charge he shalbe confirmed in the place of Mr of the said
Schoole, Secondly that if he can procure an expert writer to goe
ouer with him that can withall teach the groundes of Arithmaticke
whereby to instruct the Children in matters of Account, the Companie
are contented to giue such a one his passage whose paines they doubt
not, but wilbe well rewarded by those whose Children shalbe taught
by him, and for the allowance of 100 acres of land he desireth for his
owne propper inheritance, it is agreed that after he hath serued out
his time wch is to be fiue yeares at least and longer duringe his owne
pleasure he givinge a yeares warning vpon his remoue whereby another may be prouided in his roome the Companie are pleased to
graunt him 100 acres as before. It is also agreed he shalbe furnished

with bookes fitt for the Schoole for wᶜʰ he is to be accountable, and for yᵉ Children the Companie haue likewise vndertaken to prouide good store of bookes fittinge for their Vse for wᶜʰ their Parentes are to be aunsweareable, lastly it is ordered that the agreemᵗ between him and the Companie shall accordinge to his owne request be sett downe in writinge by waye of Articles indented.—*Ibid.*, pp. 616-17 (March 13, 1622).

23. MR. DIKE PREFERS TO REMAIN IN ENGLAND, 1622

Whereas mʳ Dike was entertayned to be vssher in the free scoole intended in Virginia it was nowe signified that he hauinge since shewed a willingnes to resigne that place by reason of some other hopes he had to preferr himself here in England the Comittee thought fitt in reguard of his longe waitinge and Dependance vpon that imployment to bestowe vpon him 3ˡⁱ to discharge him wᶜʰ agreement and allowance this Court did well approue of.—*Ibid.*, p. 629 (April 10, 1622).

24. LIST OF GIFTS FOR THE FREE SCHOOL IN VIRGINIA, 1622

	l.	s.	d.
The Gentlemen and Mariners that came in the *Royall Iames* from the *East Indies* (being at *Cape Bona Speranza* homeward bound) gaue towards the building of a Free Schoole in *Virginia*, to be called the *East India Schoole*, the summe of	70.	8.	6.
Towards the furtherance of the said *East India* Schoole, an vnknowne person hath added the sum of	30.	00.	00.
A person refusing to be made known, hath giuen the sum of 40.s. a yere for euer, for a Sermon, before the *Virginia* Comp.	30.	00.	00.
At a Quarter Court held the 30. of *Ianuary* 1621. by a person not willing as yet to be knowne, was sent in gold to helpe forward the *East India* Schoole	25.	00.	00.
At the same Quarter Court, a small Bible, with a couer richly wrought; a great Church Bible; Bookes of Common Prayer; and other Bookes were presented to be sent to *Virginia*, in the name of a person who had the yeere before sent, for the vse of the Colledge at *Henrico*, diuers Bookes, and an exact Map of *America*; the Giuer is not knowne, but the Bookes are valued at	10.	00.	00.

Giuen also by M. *Thomas Bargraue*, Preacher in ⎤
Virginia deceased, for the vse of the Colledge, a Library ⎬ 100. Marks
valued at   ⎦

—*Ibid.*, III, 642-43 (end of May, 1622).

25. THE COLONY SHOULD BE GIVEN CHOICE OF SCHOOLMASTER OR USHER, 1622

There comes also along one Leonard Hudson a Carpenter wth his
wife and fiue of or Apprentices for the erecting of the East India
Schoole, the monies would not reach vnto the sending of an Vsher
as was first intended; and besides vppon a second consideration, it
was thought good to giue the Collony the choise of the Schoolemr;
or Vssher, if so be there be any there fitt for the place, if not, we
desire to vndr stand what proportion of manteinance they will alowe
and accordingly, wee will do or best, to procure from hence an
honest, and sufficient man for such a charge. The building of a
Schoole and setting out the land at Charles Cittie is not so absolutely
required, but that if an other place shalbe iudged more convenient
by the Colonie, it is lefte to yor choise; but there be such a proportion
of land some where laid out, and that those people now sent be kept
together for cultivating the land and buildinge of a howse; may not
vppon any reason whatsoever be altred: wherefore wee pray you
to lett the buissines proceed in that course, where in the notice of a
good begininge, we are assured will stirr vpp the mindes of diurs
good people to add liberaly to this foundation: There is very much
in this buissines that wee must leaue to yor cares and wisdomes; and
the help and assistance of good people, of wch we doubt not.—*Ibid.*,
p. 650 (June 10, 1622).

26. CONCERNING PLACING AND ENTERTAINING MR. COPLAND IN THE COLLEGE, 1622

The placeinge and entertainement of mr Copland in Virginia being
referred by the former Court to the consideracon of a Comittee they
hauinge accordingly aduised about it did nowe make report of what
they had donne therein as followeth (vizt).

1 ffirst they thought fitt that he be made Rector of the intended
Colledge in Virginia for the conversion of the Infidelles and to haue
the pastorall charge of the Colledge Tenantes about him.

2 In reguard of his Rectorshippe to haue the Tenth part of the proffittes due to the Colledge out of their landes and arisinge from the labors of their Tenantes...

The report of the Comittee touchinge mr Coplandes placinge and entertainement in Virginia was nowe read, they hauinge thought fitt he be made Rector of the intended Colledge there for the conuersion of the Infidelles and to haue the Pastorall charge of the Colledge Tenantes about him and in reguard of his Rectorshippe to haue the Tenth part of the proffittes due to the Colledge out of their landes and arising from the labor of their Tenantes, and in respect of his Pastorall charge to haue a Parsonage there erected accordinge to the generall order for personages Wch this Court hath well approued of and haue likewise admitted him to be one of the Counsell of State in Virginia.—*Ibid.*, II, 75-76, 91 (July 3, 1622).

27. "OF NO LESSE WAIGHT DO WE ESTEEME THE COLLEDGE AFFAIRES," 1622

Of no lesse waight do we esteeme the Colledge affaires, wch wee pray you to take into yor considerations not only as a publique, but a sacred bussines; and in pticuler we very earnestly request the care, and paines of mr George Sandys for the settling and ordering of the Tennts; who beinge now by long experience growne skilfull in all maners of the Cuntrie, we are informed it will not be lesse advantageable vnto vs, and of farr more content to themselues, to be left to theire owne disposinge and goverment, and to reduce the vncertaintie of halfes to the certaintie of a Rent; wch we haue therefore agreed, shallbe for eury prson 20 bushelles of Corne; 60t waight of good leafe tobacco, and one pound of Silke, to be yearely paid, together wth six dayes labor in publique workes, and over and aboue that they be bound to buildinge of convenient howses, plantinge of orchardes, gardins &, on the Colledg Land and not elswhere: they that will accept of these Condicons, you shall leaue to themselues, but so, as for better conveniencie of living, fowr, or at least three of them, sorte themselues to work, and liue together, and be bound each for other for the true prformance of theire Covenantes: those other that shall not be willing or worthie of such agreementes, we leaue to you to take the best order in disposinge of them; as for those that shalbe Artificers and of Manuall trades and occupacons, we conceiue that they may likewise prforme this bargaine although they follow theire trades, wch rather then that they should not do, wee leaue it to you to contract otherwise wth them, as you shall thinke best, allwaies reservinge that theire living be vppon ye Colledge Landes. As for the Brick-makers, we desire they may be held to theire Contract made wth mr Thorpe, to the intent that when opportunitie shalbe for the erecting of the fabricke of the Colledge, the materialles be not wanting...

Wee send you a Copie of or Letters by the Furtherance wch wee doubt not but is safely long ere this arived wth you the suplies therein sent of Shipwrightes, and East India Schoole, wee cannot but againe most effectually and earnestly recomend vnto yor care and favors, wch prhapps by the chaing of thinges wth you they will the more need. The improving of the Companies revenues, and recoverie of theire Debtes is, of those thinges wthout wch neither wee nor you can subsist. Many other matters we haue to write if time would giue leaue for want whereof, we must reserue them till the departure of the Abigaile: And now comitting you and all yor affaires, to the good guidance and proteccon of the Almightie. we bid you hartily fare-well.—*Ibid.*, III, 671, 673 (August 1, 1622).

28. CONCERNING ANOTHER BEQUEST OF 100 POUNDS, 1622

Mr Deputy further acquainted the Company that mr George Ruggle lately fellowe of Clare hall in Cambridge beinge a Brother of the Company and newly deceased (wch he said he could not without great greife mencon) had by his will bequeathed 100li for the educacon of Infidell Children wch he had caused to be put into the Table: wch the Court well approued of; but seemed (at least the most part) to be vtterly ignorant of the person or qualities of the man: Wherevpon desiringe to be informed of both; mr Deputy told them that he was a man second to none in knowledge in all manner of humanity, learninge, and was so generally reputed in the Vniuersity of singuler honestie and integritie of life, sincere and zealous in Religion, and of verie great wisdome and vnderstandinge: All wch good part he had for these last three yeares, wholly almost spent and exercised in Virginia buissinesses, hauinge (besid continually assistinge his Brothers and himselfe with Counsell and all manner of helpe in their places) written sundrie treatises, for the benefitt of the Planta-tion and in pticuler that worke so highly comended by Sr Edwin Sandys, concerninge the Gouermt of Virginia but such was his modestie that he would by no meanes suffer it to be knowne duringe his life: But nowe beinge dead, mr Deputy said he could not with a

good conscience, depriue him of that Honor wch he so duely de-
serued.—*Ibid.*, II, 136 (November 20, 1622).

29. ANOTHER LIST OF GIFTS, 1619, 1620, 1621

	l.	s.	d.
A person vnknowne gaue for the vse of the Colledge, a Communion-cup with a Couer, and a Plate for the bread, a Siluer guilt: a crimson veluet Carpet with gold lace and fringe, and a linnen damaske Tablecloath: all valued at	30.	0.	0.
A person vnknowne sent a Letter, the Copy whereof is registred; directed thus, *To Sir Edwin Sandys, the faithfull Treasurer of* VIRGINIA: and subscribed, *Dust and Ashes:* And afterwards by an vnknowne person sent a box to the house of Sir *Edwin Sandys* with the same direction: which being opened in Court, therein was found in gold 550. pounds, to be disposed of for the education of children of the Infidels, in Christian religion and ciuility.	550.	0.	0.
Master *Nicholas Farrar* of London, deceased, hath by his Will giuen, 300 li. to the Colledge in VIRGINIA, to bee paid when there shall be ten of the Infidels children placed in it; and in meane time 24. pounds by the yeare to bee disbursed vnto three discreete and godly men in the Colonie, which shall honestly bring three of the Infidels children in Christian Religion, and some good course to liue by.	300.	0.	0.
A person refusing to be named, hath giuen to the benefit of the Plantation	10.	0.	0.
The Gentlemen and Mariners that came in the *Royall-Iames* from the *East Indies*, being at *Cape Bona-Speranza*, homeward bound, gaue towards the building of a Free Schoole in VIRGINIA, to be called the *East Indie Schoole*,	70.	8.	6.
Towards the furtherance of the *East Indie Schoole*, an vnknowne person hath added the summe of	30.	0.	0.
A person refusing to be named, hath giuen the summe of 40. shillings *per annum* for euer, for a Sermon, to be preached before the VIRGINIA Company.	40s. *per an.*		

At the Quarter Court held the 30. of *Ianuary* 1621. by a person not willing as yet to be knowne, was sent in gold 25 li. to helpe forward the *East Indie Schoole.* — 25. 0. 0.

At the same Quarter Court a small Bible with a Couer richly wrought, a great Church-Bible, the Booke of Common Prayer, and other bookes were presented to be sent to *Virginia*, in the name of a person who had the yeare before sent for the vse of the Colledge at *Henrico; S. Augustine De ciuitate Dei,* Master *Perkins* his workes, and an exact Map of *America:* the giuer is not known, but the books are valued at — 10. 0. 0.

Giuen by Master *Thomas Bargraue,* a Minister in VIRGINIA deceased, for the vse of the Colledge, a Library valued at — 100. *marks*

There is a Contribution made by the Inhabitants in VIRGINIA for the building of a house of entertainment for new commers, at *Iames-Citie:* amounting to the value of — 1500. 0. 0.

The Gentlemen and Mariners that came lately home from the *East Indies,* in the two Ships called the *Hart* and *Roe-Bucke,* being at the Cape of *Bona Speranza,* homeward bound, gaue towards the building of the aforesiad Free-Schoole in VIRGINIA the summe of — 66. 13. 4.

—*Ibid.,* III, 575 (1619, 1620, 1621).

30. Report of the Indian Massacre, March 22, 1622

The country being in this estate, an occasion was ministered of sending to *Opachankano* the King of these Sauages, about the middle of *March* last, what time the Messenger returned backe with these words from him, That he held the peace concluded so firme, as the Skie should sooner fall then it dissolue: yea, such was the treacherous dissimulation of that people who then had contriued our destruction, that euen two dayes before the Massacre, some of our men were guided thorow the woods by them in safety: and one *Browne*, who then to learne the language liued among the *Warrascoyacks* (a Prouince of that King) was in friendly manner sent backe by them to Captaine *Hamor* his Master, and many the like passages, rather increasing our former confidence, then any wise in the world ministring the least suspition of the breach of the peace, or of what instantly ensued; yea, they borrowed our owne Boates to conuey themselues crosse the Riuer (on the bankes of both sides whereof all our Plantations were) to consult of the diuellish murder that ensued, and of our vtter extirpation, which God of his mercy (by the meanes of some of themselues conuerted to Christianitie) preuented; and as well on the Friday morning (the fatal day) the 22 of *March*, as also in the euening, as in other dayes before, they came vnarmed into our houses, without Bowes or arrowes, or other weapons, with Deere, Turkies, Fish, Furres, and other prouisions, to sell, and trucke with vs, for glasse, beades, and other trifles: yea in some places, sate downe at Breakfast with our people at their tables, whom immediately with their owne tooles and weapons, eyther laid downe, or standing in their houses, they basely and barbarously murthered, not sparing eyther age or sexe, man, woman or childe; so sodaine in their cruell execution, that few or none discerned the weapon or blow that brought them to destruction. In which manner they also slew many of our people then at their seuerall workes and husbandries in the fields, and without their houses, some in planting Corne and Tobacco, some in gardening, some in making Bricke, building, sawing, and other kindes of husbandry, they well knowing in what places and quarters each of our men were, in regard of their daily familiarity, and resort to vs for trading and other negotiations, which the more willingly was by vs continued and cherished for the desire we had of effecting that great master-peece of workes, their conuersion. And by this means that fatall Friday morning, there fell vnder the bloudy and barbarous hands of that perfidious and inhumane people, contrary to all lawes of God and men, of Nature & Nations, three hundred forty seuen men, women, and children, most by their owne weapons; and not being content with taking away life alone, they fell after againe vpon the dead, making as well as they could, a fresh murder, defacing, dragging, and mangling the dead carkasses into many pieces, and carrying some parts away in derision, with base and brutish triumph...

Here following is set downe a true list of the names of all those that were massacred by the treachery of the Sauages in VIRGINIA, the 22 *March* last, To the end that their lawfull heyres may take speedy order for the inheriting of their lands and estates there: For which the Honourable *Company of Virginia* are ready to doe them all right and fauour...

Slaine of the Colledge People, about two miles from Henrico-Citie.

Samuel Stringer.
George Soldan.
William Basset.
Iohn Perry.
Edward Ember.
Iarrat Moore.
Thomas Xerles.
Thomas Freeman.
Iohn Allen.
Thomas Cooke.
Iohn Clements.
Iames Faulkoner.
Christopher Henley.
William Iordan.
Robert Dauis.
Thomas Hobson.
William Baily.

—*Ibid.*, pp. 550-51; 564-65; 566 (1622).

31. REPORT OF THE MONEY COLLECTED ON THE ROYAL JAMES, 1622

A Declaration how the monies (viz. *seuenty pound eight shillings sixe pence*) *were disposed, which* was gathered (by *M. Patrick Copland,* Preacher in the *Royall Iames*) at the Cape of good hope, (towards the *building of a free Schoole in* Virginia) *of the Gentlemen and Marriners in the said Ship: A list of whose names are under specified, for Gods glory, their comfort, and the incouragement of others to the furthering of the same, or the like pious worke.*

		li.	s.	d.
Captaine Martin Prines		6	13	4
Patrick Copland, Preacher		5	0	0
George Baal	Merchants	5	0	0
Adam Denton	Merchants	5	0	0
Thomas Iohns	Merchants	5	0	0
Ieremy Shuker	Merchants	1	0	0
Iohn Leman, Master		2	0	0
Thomas Adison	Masters mates	1	0	0
Iames Slade	Masters mates	1	0	0
Rich. Wedmore	Masters mates	1	0	0
Iames Dauice	Masters mates	1	0	0
Iames Burgesse	Masters mates	0	10	0
Thom. Hartnell	Masters mates	0	13	4
Samuel Butta	Masters mates	0	10	0
Will. Massam	Masters mates	0	10	0
Edward Hewet	Masters mates	0	10	0
Henry Ienings		0	3	0
Ioseph Bowry		0	10	0
Robert Blanchard		0	10	0

	li.	s.	d.
Iohn Butler	0	5	0
Anthony Fensham	0	5	0
Francis Browne	0	5	0
Henry Bennet	0	5	0
Iohn Daniel	0	2	0
Thomas Hall	0	3	0
George Gresham	0	2	6
Richard Hayward	0	2	0
Iohn Elliot	0	5	0
Thomas Read	0	5	0
Marke Robinson	0	10	0
Charles Nuttal	0	10	0
Edward Turner	0	2	0
Henry Smith, Purser	1	5	0
Arthur Suffield, Pursers mate	0	5	0
Tobias Parice, Steward	0	7	0
Steuen Goad, Boatswaine	1	0	0
Philip Worgan, Carpenter	0	10	0

	li.	s.	d.		li.	s.	d.
Andrew Dawson	0	5	0	Frances Terry	0	5	0
Thomas Burch	0	5	0	Iohn Siluer	0	5	0
Thomas Badger	0	5	0	Robert Thacker	0	5	0
Iohn King	0	2	0	Luke Browne	0	10	0
Iohn Feny	0	15	0	Iohn Mason	0	4	0
Rober Smith	0	5	0	Robert Moore	0	3	0
Iohn Austed	0	5	6	Iohn Hilles	0	4	0
Richard Fewater	0	5	0	Iames Newcomb	0	5	0
Richard Langford	0	2	0	William Coulston	0	10	0
Rowland Shepherd	0	2	0	William Stoke	0	1	0
Iames Searles	0	2	0	Thomas Samson	0	2	0
Thomas Croome	0	5	0	William Mousley	0	2	6
Iohn Dring	0	1	0	Nicholas Medland	0	2	6
Iohn Sarier	0	3	4	Christopher Isop	0	2	0
Philip Wood	0	10	0	Nicholas Smith	0	2	0
Iohn Stauely	0	5	0	Humfrey Stanfield	0	1	0
William Burrouse	0	5	0	William Constable	0	2	0
Robert Eldred	0	2	6	Robert Geyton	0	5	0
Thomas Griffin	0	2	0	George Blades	0	2	0
Thomas Iohnes	0	3	0	Iohn Pauy	0	5	0
Iohn Seabrooke	0	3	0	Christopher Read	0	5	0
Thomas Alredge	0	7	0	Nicholas Cage	0	5	0
Iohn Tachus	0	3	0	Thomas Woolman	0	3	0
William Bishop	0	10	0	Austen Bernard	0	2	6
Thomas Haget	0	5	0	Samuel Basse	0	10	0
Thomas Hughes	0	10	0	William Yeomans	0	3	0
Thomas Russell	0	5	0	Robert Owen	0	10	0
Henry Blake	0	5	0	Thomas Vrine	0	2	6
William Baly	0	5	0	George Browne	0	5	0
Iohn Grant	0	2	0	Fabian Hopkins	0	5	0
Iohn Winter	0	2	0	Iohn Pindleton	0	5	0
Arthur Dauice	0	2	0	Rouse Waller	0	5	0
Richard Elrye	1	0	0	Henry Rothermaker	0	5	0
Henry Hanfield	0	5	0	Iohn Roe	0	5	0
Ioseph Kiduile	0	18	0	Iohn Carman	0	2	0
Giles Whitehead	0	5	0	William Ashley	0	5	0
Dauid Hailes	1	0	0	Iohn Pearson	0	2	0
William Tod	0	5	0	Iohn May	0	2	0
William Chandler	0	10	0	Iohn Doule	0	2	0
Iohn Coker	0	5	0	Alexander Cunningham	0	2	6
George Paulet	0	5	0	Roger Falwood	0	5	0
Iohn Fletcher	0	5	0	Ieremy Lampin	0	5	0

	li.	s.	d.		li.	s.	d.
Iames Mitten	0	3	0	Thomas Wood	0	5	0
Michael Hazard	0	5	0	Thomas Hutchins	0	3	0
Iohn Garrets	0	6	0	Ieremy Eliard	0	10	0
Christopher Tiffen	0	2	0	Hugh Roberts	0	2	0
Iohn Walter	0	1	0	Iohn Went	0	2	0
William Walker	0	5	0	Thomas Wylicocke	0	10	0
William Wilie ⎫ Surgeons	1	0	0	Hans Martin	0	3	0
John Long ⎬	0	10	0	George Read	0	5	0
Thomas White ⎭	0	3	0	William Chambers	0	3	0
Iohn Wilcocke	0	5	0	Richard Thomas	0	5	0
Nathaniel Grosse	0	2	6	An vnknowne person	30	0	0

which 70. pound 8. shillings 6. pence, together with 30. pound added thereunto by an vnknowne person, for the furtherance of the said free Schoole, was paid vnto the Right honourable Henry Earle of Southhampton, for the honourable Company of *Virginia*, at their great and generall Quarter Court, held the 21. of Nouem. 1621. And the said Court, for the better maintenance of the said Schoole, Schoolemaster, and Vsher intended there to be placed, granted 1000. acres of land to the said free Schoole, to bee at *Charles* Cittie, as the most commodious place for health, security, profit, and conueniency: And appointed that with the said 100. pound 8. shillings 6. pence, there should be sent ouer presently an Vsher, for the instructing of the children there, in the principles of Religion, ciuility of life, and humane learning: as also the fiue persons (besides an ouerseer of them) should be foorthwith sent in the condition of Apprentices, to manure and cultiuate some part of the said land, for the vse and benefit of the said Vsher, till God stirred vp the hearts of others to be further helpefull to the said Schoole.

Likewise the said honourable *Virginia* Court, thought fit in honour of the said *East-India* Benefactors, the said free Schoole should bee built, and the said 1000 acres set out in *Charles* Citie, to be called *The East-India Schoole:* And that the *East-India* Companies seruants, should haue precedence before any other, to preferre their children thither, to be brought vp in the rudiments of learning.

They thought fit also, that this (as a Collegiat or free Schoole) should haue dependance on *Henrico* Colledge in *Virginia*, which should be made capable to receiue Schollers from the Schoole, into such Schollerships and Fellowships as the said Colledge shall be endowed withall, for the aduancement of Schollers, as they shall rise by degrees and desert in learning.

There was since by a person refusing to be named, sent in to the great and generall Quarter Court held for *Virginia*, the 30. of Ianuary 1621. 25 pound toward the furtherance of this godly worke: So that now there is in all 125. pound 8. shillings 6. pence.

They that be wise shall shine as the brightnesse of the firmanent; and they that turne many to righteousnesse, shall shine as the Stars for euer and euer, Dan. 12. 3. For publike actions of vertue, besides that they are presently comfortable to the doers, are also exemplary to others; and as they are more beneficiall to others, so are they crowned in vs: our principall care should bee, that while our soules liue in glory in heauen, our good actions may liue vpon earth, and that they may be put into the banke and multiply, while our bodies lie in the graue and putrifie. *Whosoeuer shall receiue such a little child in my name, receiueth me.* Mat. 18. 5.—*Ibid.*, pp. 537-40 (1622).

32. CONCERNING MONEY ISSUED OUT OF THE STOCK OF THE COMPANY, 1623

The Court beinge made acquainted by m^r Deputie that for sattis-fiinge the monney issued out of the Stocke given for buildinge of the East India Schoole intended in Virginia and employed vppo the publique business of the Company, the Committee vppo a Treaty wth m^r Copeland thought fitt an allowance be made either in Cattle or by turninge ouer some of the Companies Tenants for the vse of the saide Schoole; Did therevppon agree that accordinglie sattisfaccon should be made by the Company to the full for the monney soe borrowed and employed.—*Ibid.*, II, 496-97 (November 19, 1623).

33. THE COMPANY READY TO ASSIST THE EAST INDIA SCHOOL, 1625

We should be redie wth our vtmost endevors to asiste y^t pious worke of ye East India freescoole, but we must not dissemble, that besides theire vnseasonable arivall, we doupt y^t the age of m^r Careleff will over ballance all his other sufficyency, though exceedinge good, and the number soe few, as little wilbe expected from them, They were not liable to subsist of them selves vppon certen Cleered grounde wch they might have had in Martins hundred, and cam in so late as they could hardlie haue howsed themselves, But what Accomodations they could possiblely give them, was offered by m^r Horwood and m^r Emersone, but m^r Careleff vtterly refused to seate there, though we advised him to it, he pretending y^t many of you disliked of that place, and y^t the charge of disposinge ye men lay vppon him, The accoumpt of ye people and goodes formerly sent for the Easte India scoole, we heerwith send you, We desire y^t theire zeale who haue traduced us in that busines may heerafter be ioyned wth some better knowledge, and y casuall faylings by mortalitie and otherwise, may not be charged uppon us.—*Ibid.*, IV, 565-66 (June 15, 1625).

II

FOR POOR, ORPHAN, AND ILLEGITIMATE CHILDREN

I. PREVIEW AND COMMENTS

APPRENTICESHIP PRACTICES were common in the Southern as in all the American colonies and represented a significant practice of "class education." So important was this system that Marcus W. Jernegan gave to one of the chapters of his useful treatment of the subject [1] the title of "Compulsory and Free Education for Poor Children and Apprentices." This book dealt, however, chiefly with Massachusetts and Virginia, although it could have dealt with the subject in other colonies perhaps as well.

While the importance of this system in American colonial history has almost been forgotten, apprenticeship played a significant role in education during the colonial period through the churchwardens, justices of the peace, or other authorities. This change from the one to the other form of control may be seen by examination of the laws on the care of the poor, orphan, and illegitimate children; and legislation on these subjects, whether in one or another section of colonial America, reflected concern for this kind of "class education." [2]

In the earliest development of this country, so-called compulsory education seems to have included and emphasized not, as nowadays, "secular book education," but rather instruction in a trade, in morals and religion, and later in the elements of the language arts and the arts of calculation, reading, writing, and arithmetic to the "rule of

1. *Laboring and Dependent Classes in Colonial America, 1607-1783* (University of Chicago Press, 1931).
2. For the change in control of this economic or social "problem" in one colony, see "The Evolution of Public Education in Virginia," *Sewanee Review*, January, 1916, by Edgar W. Knight. See also "Public Education of Dependents: The Apprenticeship System," in his *Public Education in the South*, (Boston: Ginn and Company, 1922). Additional light was thrown on this interesting subject by Jernegan in his "Compulsory Education in the American Colonies," "The Educational Development of the Southern Colonies," and "Compulsory Education in the Southern Colonies," *School Review*, XXVII (January, May and June, 1919). For an excellent treatment of "bound labor" see Richard B. Morris, *Government and Labor in Early America*, Chapters VII, VIII, IX. (New York: Columbia University Press, 1946.) See also A. E. Smith, *Colonists in Bondage: White Servitude and Convict Labor in America*. Chapel Hill: The University of North Carolina Press, 1947.

three." [3] Practices in the American colonies on the notion or principles of "compulsory education" had their roots in the English Statute of Artificers (1562) and in "An Act for the Relief of the Poor" (1601). The former of these pieces of legislation seems less important, however, when viewed historically, in the development of the theory and practice of education in the American colonies. While that act is omitted here, it seemed to express the hope that skilled labor would tend to "banishe Idlenes, advance Husbandrye and yeelde unto the hired person bothe in tyme of sacrsitee and in the tyme of plentye a convenient proporcon of Wages."

The act of 1601 is included here as the statutory foundation of the theories and practices of apprenticeship which early appeared in the American colonies as direct inheritances from England and were continued by law and practice in the United States, in some cases late into the nineteenth century. Parts of the language of the act of 1601 appeared in the statutory legislation on the subject of apprentices in the American colonies and were continued in such legislation after the colonies became States; moreover, there are traces of practices of apprenticeship before the enactment of colonial legislation on the subject. Apprenticeship legislation and practices reflected the genesis of the conscience and concern of the public for the welfare and at least the rudimentary education of underprivileged youth in the community.

The documents that follow seem to reveal that the theories and practices of the apprenticeship system were economic, humanitarian, and religious in purposes. The laws on the subject generally recognized first the economic or industrial or vocational purpose because of the need for skilled artisans or workers, but the humanitarian, religious, or philanthropic purposes also appear. The system applied to poor children, orphans, illegitimate children and sometimes to Negro and mulatto children although the indentures did not always make it obligatory on the master to teach Negro or mulatto apprentices to read and write. After the Nat Turner Insurrection in Virginia August 21, 1831, which "started a wave of contagious fear in other Southern states," legal prohibitions against teaching Negroes became very extensive throughout the slave-holding states. Prior to that insurrection, however, there were cases of the apprenticing of free

3. Proportion. Single rule of three, simple, and double rule of three, compound, proportion.

Negro children under indentures which promised the benefits of the usual educational features of the system.

It appears that legislation and practices in Virginia were copied or imitated somewhat in detail in the other Southern colonies. This seems especially true of North Carolina which was in close contact with Virginia; but the system was in operation in North Carolina before legislation on the subject was enacted in that colony.

Legislation on apprenticeship in Georgia was not unlike that of the older states. In the main that legislation required the appropriate officer to bind out children in this manner:

Where it shall appear to the said court that the annual profits of the estate of any orphan is not sufficient for the education and maintenance of such orphan, it shall be the duty of such court forthwith to bind out the said orphan for the whole or such part of the time of such orphan's minority as to them shall seem best; and the person to whom such orphan shall be bound, shall undertake to clothe and maintain such apprentice to be taught to read and write the English language, and the usual rules of arithmetic.

A later enactment in Georgia provided:

It shall be the duty of the master to teach the apprentice the business of husbandry, house service, or some other useful trade or occupation, which shall be specified in the instrument of apprenticeship, shall furnish him with protection, wholesome food, suitable clothing, and necessary medicine and medical attendance; shall teach him habits of industry, honesty, and morality; and shall cause him to be taught to read English; and shall govern him with humanity, using only the same degree of force to compel his obedience as a father may use with his minor child.

The first legislation enacted in what became Tennessee was practically the same as the law of 1762 of the parent state of North Carolina.[4] The law required the master or mistress of every apprentice to provide for him or her diet, clothes, lodging, and accommodations fit and necessary and to teach or cause him or her to be taught "to read and write and cipher as far as the rule of three." A later enactment required the master or mistress, at the expiration of apprenticeship, to pay the apprentice the sum of $20 and to furnish him with a good suit of clothes.

Similarly, legislation in Louisiana required the master to instruct

4. See pp. 51-52.

the apprentice in his art, trade, or profession and to teach him or cause him to be taught to read, write and cipher. In addition, legislation in that State required that:

> In every case where any person shall be bound in any place, where there shall be a school established, either an apprentice or servant, who shall be under the age of twenty-one years, there shall be a clause in the indentures binding the master or mistress to teach or cause to be taught the said apprentice or servant to read and write, as also to instruct him in the fundamental principles of arithmetic.

As early as 1807 a law in what became the state of Mississippi required the overseers of the poor twice a year to make to the county courts returns of all poor orphans in their districts and of such other children "whose parents they shall judge incapable of supporting them, and bringing them up in honest ways." Such children were later to be bound apprentices whose master or mistress was required by covenant entered in the indenture

> to provide the apprentice with a sufficiency of good and wholesome provisions, necessary clothing, washing, and lodging; to teach the said apprentice the business or occupation which he pursues for a livelihood, and also, to read, write, and cipher as far as the rule of three; and at the expiration of said apprenticeship, to furnish the said apprentice with one complete new suit of clothing, and two shirts; if a female, one complete new suit of clothes and two shifts.

By early legislation in Alabama the justices of the county courts were to appoint overseers of the poor whose duties, among others, were to make returns of poor orphans and other underprivileged children who were to be bound apprentices, and

> the person to whom such apprentice shall be bound, shall engage by a covenant entered in the indenture to provide the apprentice with a sufficiency of good and wholesome provisions, necessary clothing, washing, lodging; to teach the said apprentice the business or occupation which he pursues for a livelihood; and also to read, write, and cipher, as far as the rule of three; and at the expiration of said apprenticeship to furnish the said apprentice with one complete new suit of clothes and two shirts; if a female one complete new suit of clothes and two shifts.

Legislation on apprenticing poor children in Arkansas was also similar to that in the older states. The earliest enactment in 1840 remained essentially unchanged throughout the nineteenth century.[5] So also was the law in Florida. Near the close of the nineteenth century the law in that state provided that the master or mistress must

teach the apprentice some art, trade, business or occupation to be particularized [in the indenture], and also the elements of reading, writing, and arithmetic, and to give said apprentice a new suit of cloths, shoes and blanket upon the lawful expiration of the term of apprenticeship.

Legislation in Texas applied to males until they were twenty-one and to females until they were eighteen years of age, and the master was required by indenture to furnish the apprentice sufficient food and clothing, to treat him humanely, to furnish him medicine and medical attention when necessary, and to teach or cause him to be taught to read and write. Under the law the master was also required "if practicable, to send said minor to school at least three months in each year during the continuance of such apprenticeship, after said minor has arrived at the age of ten years..."

Although hundreds of indentures have been located and reproduced, far more than can be used here, the full extent of the practice in the South is most difficult accurately to ascertain. This difficulty has been increased by the loss of local records through fire, negligence of local officers, or other causes. But it is believed that the material here presented on this system is sufficient to illustrate in theory and practice social concern for underprivileged children in the days before orphanages, juvenile courts, children's home societies, boards of charities, and public-welfare agencies were established.

It has not seemed desirable to try to observe a strict chronological limitation on the subject of this section and to include only documents of the period prior to the American Revolution. Inasmuch as the theory and practice of apprenticeship extended far into the nineteenth century[6] it has seemed well to include or refer to documents from the newer Southern States. Students of the subject will find it of

---

5. By an act of 1889 North Carolina required the master to provide his apprentice Diet, clothes, lodging and accommodations fit and necessary; that the apprentice be taught to read and write and the rules of arithmetic to the double rule of three; six dollars in cash, a new suit of clothes and a new Bible at the end of the apprenticeship; and such other education as may be agreed upon and inserted in the indenture by the clerk.

6. For legislation on apprenticeship in Alabama, Arkansas, Louisiana, and Mississippi see editorial comments above and consult session acts. For legislation in Florida, see *Acts of Florida*, 1822, p. 11; in Texas, see Gammel (compiler), *Laws of Texas*, II, 640-41, and III, 297.

interest during the past century, not only in the South but in other parts of the country as well, and especially those movements for "public welfare" legislation and practices that displaced the practice of "binding out" children.

II. DOCUMENTS

1. ENGLISH ACT FOR THE RELIEF OF THE POOR, 1601 [1]

Be it enacted by the authority of this present parliament, That the church-wardens of every parish, and four, three or two substantial householders there, as shall be thought meet, having respect to the proportion and greatness of the same parish and parishes, to be nominated yearly in *Easter* week, or within one month after *Easter*, under the hand and seal of two or more justices of the peace in the same county, whereof one to be of the *quorum*, dwelling in or near the same parish or division where the same parish doth lie, shall be called overseers of the poor of the same parish: and they, or the greater part of them, shall take order from time to time, by and with the consent of two or more such justices of peace as is aforesaid, for setting to work the children of all such whose parents shall not by the said church-wardens and overseers, or the greater part of them, be thought able to keep and maintain their children; and also for setting to work all such persons, married or unmarried, having no means to maintain them, and use no ordinary and daily trade of life to get their living by; and also to raise weekly or otherwise (by taxation of every inhabitant, parson, vicar and other, and of every occupier of lands, houses, tithes impropriate, propriations of tithes, coal-miners, of saleable underwoods in the said parish, in such competent sum and sums of money as they shall think fit) a convenient stock of flax, hemp, wool, thread, iron and other necessary ware and stuff, to set the poor on work: and also competent sums of money for and towards the necessary relief of the lame, impotent, old, blind, and such other among them, being poor and not able to work, and also for the putting out of such children to be apprentices, to be gathered out of the same parish, according to the ability of the same parish, and to do and execute all other things, as well for the disposing of the said stock as otherwise concerning the premises, as to them shall seem convenient:

II. Which said church-wardens and overseers so to be nominated, or such of them as shall not be left by sickness or other just excuse,

---

1. The statutory basis of the theories and practices of apprenticeship in America.

to be allowed by two such justices of peace or more as is aforesaid, shall meet together at the least once every month in the church of the said parish, upon the *Sunday* in the afternoon after divine service, there to consider of some good course to be taken, and of some meet order to be set down in the premisses; (2) and shall within four days after the end of their year, and after other overseers nominated as aforesaid, make and yield up to such two justices of peace as is aforesaid, a true and perfect account of all sums of money by them received, or rated and sessed and not received, and also of such stock as shall be in their hands, or in the hands of any of the poor to work, and of all other things concerning their said office; (3) and such sum or sums of money as shall be in their hands, shall pay and deliver over to the said church-wardens and overseers newly nominated and appointed as aforesaid; (4) upon pain that every one of them absenting themselves without lawful cause as aforesaid, from such monthly meeting for the purpose aforesaid, or being negligent in their office, or in the execution of the orders aforesaid, being made by and with the assent of the said justices of peace, or any two of them before-mentioned, to forfeit for every such default of absence or negligence twenty shillings.

III. And be it also enacted, That if the said justices of peace do perceive, that the inhabitants of any parish are not able to levy among themselves sufficient sums of money for the purposes aforesaid; That then the said two justices shall and may tax, rate and assess as aforesaid, any other of other parishes, or out of any parish, within the hundred where the said parish is, to pay such sum and sums of money to the church-wardens and overseers of the said poor parish for the said purposes, as the said justices shall think fit, according to the intent of this law; (2) and if the said hundred shall not be thought to the said justices able and fit to relieve the said several parishes not able to provide for themselves as aforesaid; Then the justices of peace at their general quarter-sessions, or the greater number of them, shall rate and assess as aforesaid, any other of other parishes, or out of any parish, within the said county for the purposes aforesaid, as in their discretion shall seem fit.

IV. And that it shall be lawful, as well for the present as subsequent church-wardens and overseers, or any of them, by warrant from any two such justices of peace, as is aforesaid, to levy as well the said sums of money, and all arrearages, of every one that shall refuse to contribute according as they shall be assessed, by distress and sale of the offender's goods, as the sums of money or stock which shall be behind upon any account to be made as aforesaid, rendring to the parties the overplus; (2) and in defect of such distress, it shall be lawful for any such two justices of the peace to commit him or them to the common goal of the county, there to remain without bail or mainprize until payment of the said sum, arrearages and stock: (3) and the said justices of peace, or any one of them, to send to the house of correction or common gaol, such as shall not employ themselves to work, being appointed thereunto, as aforesaid: (4) and also any such two justices of peace to commit to the said prison every one of the said church-wardens and overseers which shall refuse to account, there to remain without bail or mainprize until he have made a true account, and satisfied and paid so much as upon the said account shall be remaining in his hands.

V. And be it further enacted, That it shall be lawful for the said church-wardens and overseers, or the greater part of them, by the assent of any two justices of the peace aforesaid, to bind any such children, as aforesaid, to be apprentices, where they shall see convenient, till such man-child shall come to the age of four and twenty years, and such woman-child to the age of one and twenty years, or the time of her marriage; the same to be as effectual to all purposes, as if such child were of full age, and by indenture of covenant bound him or her self. (2) And to the intent that necessary places of habitation may more conveniently be provided for such poor impotent people; (3) be it enacted by the authority aforesaid, That it shall and may be lawful for the said church-wardens and overseers, or the greater part of them, by the leave of the lord or lords of the manor, whereof any waste or common within their parish is or shall be parcel, and upon agreement before with him or them made in writing, under the hands and seals of the said lord or lords, or otherwise, according to any order to be set down by the justices of peace of the said county at their general quarter-sessions, or the greater part of them, by like leave and agreement of the said lord or lords in writing under his or their hands and seals, to erect, build, and set up in fit and convenient places of habitation in such waste or common, at the general charges of the parish, or otherwise of the hundred or county, as aforesaid, to be taxed, rated and gathered in manner before expressed, convenient houses of dwelling for the said impotent poor; (4) and also to place inmates, or more families than one in one cottage or house; one act made in the one and thirtieth year of her majesty's reign, intituled, *An act against the erecting and maintaining of cottages,* or any thing therein contained to the contrary notwithstanding: (5) which cottages and places for inmates shall not at any time after be used or employed to or for any other habitation, but only for impotent and poor of the same parish, that shall be there placed from time to time by the church-wardens and overseers of the poor of the same parish, or the most part of them, upon the pains and forfeitures contained in the said former act made in the said one and thirtieth year of her Majesty's reign.

VI. Provided always, That if any person or persons shall find themselves grieved with any sess or tax, or other act done by the said church-wardens, and other persons, or by the said justices of peace; that then it shall be lawful for the justices of peace, at their general quarter-sessions, or the greater number of them, to take such order therein, as to them shall be thought convenient; and the same to conclude and bind all the said parties.

VII. And be it further enacted, That the father and grandfather, and the mother and grandmother, and the children of every poor, old, blind, lame and impotent person, or other poor person not able to work, being of a sufficient ability, shall, at their own charges, relieve and maintain every such poor person in that manner, and according to that rate, as by the justices of peace of that county where such sufficient persons dwell, or the greater number of them, at their general quarter-sessions shall be assessed; (2) upon pain that every one of them shall forfeit twenty shillings for every month which they shall fail therein.

VIII. And be it further hereby enacted, That the mayors, bailiffs, or other head officers of every town and place corporate and city within this realm, being justice or justices of peace, shall have the same authority by virtue of this act, within the limits and precincts of their jurisdictions, as well out of sessions, as at their session, if they hold any, as is herein limited, prescribed and appointed to justices of the peace of the county, or any two or more of them, or to the justices of peace in their quarter-sessions, to do and execute for all the uses and purposes in this act prescribed, and no other justice or justices of peace to enter or meddle there: (2) and that every alderman of the city of *London* within his ward, shall and may do and execute in every respect so much as is appointed and allowed by this act to be done and executed by one or two justices of peace of any county within this realm.

IX. And be it also enacted, That if it shall happen any parish to extend it self into more counties than one, or part to lie within the liberties of any city, town or place corporate, and part without, That then as well the justices of peace of every county, as also the head officers of such city, town or place corporate shall deal and inter-meddle only in so much of the said parish as lieth within their liberties, and not any further: (2) and every of them respectively within their several limits, wards and jurisdictions, to execute the ordinances before-mentioned concerning the nomination of overseers, the consent to binding apprentices, the giving warrant to levy taxations unpaid, the taking account of church-wardens and overseers, and the committing to prison such as refuse to account, or deny to pay the arrearages due upon their accounts; (3) and yet nevertheless, the said church-wardens and overseers, or the most part of them, of the said parishes that do extend into such several limits and jurisdictions, shall, without dividing themselves, duly execute their office in all places within the said parish, in all things to them belonging, and shall duly exhibit and make one account before the said head officer of the town or place corporate, and one other before the said justices of peace, or any such two of them, as is aforesaid.

X. And further be it enacted by the authority aforesaid, That if in any place within this realm there happen to be hereafter no such nomination of overseers yearly, as is before appointed, That then every justice of peace of the county, dwelling within the division where such default of nomination shall happen, and every mayor, alderman and head officer of city, town or place corporate where such default shall happen, shall lose and forfeit for every such default five pounds, to be employed towards the relief of the poor of the said parish or place corporate, and to be levied, as aforesaid, of their goods, by warrant from the general sessions of the peace of the said county, or of the same city, town or place corporate, if they keep sessions.

XI. And be it also enacted by the authority aforesaid, That all penalties and forfeitures before-mentioned in this act to be forfeited by any person or persons, shall go and be employed to the use of the poor of the same parish, and towards a stock and habitation for them, and other necessary uses and relief, as before in this act are mentioned and expressed; (2) and shall be levied by the said church-wardens and overseers, or one of them, by warrant from any two such justices of peace, or mayor, alderman, or head officer of city, town or place corporate respectively within their several limits, by distress and sale thereof, as aforesaid; (3) or in defect thereof, it shall be lawful for any two such justices of peace, and the said aldermen and head officers within their several limits, to commit the offender to the said prison, there to remain without bail or mainprize till the said forfeitures shall be satisfied and paid.

XII. And be it further enacted by the authority aforesaid, That the justices of peace of every county or place corporate, or the more part of them, in their general sessions to be holden next after the feast of *Easter* next, and so yearly as often as they shall think meet, shall rate every parish to such a weekly sum of money as they shall think convenient; (2) so as no parish be rated above the sum of sixpence, nor under the sum of a half-peny, weekly to be paid, and so as the total sum of such taxation of the parishes in every county amount not above the rate of two-pence for every parish within the said county: (3) which sums so taxed shall be yearly assessed by the agreement of the parishioners within themselves, or in default thereof, by the churchwardens and petty constables of the same parish, or the more part of them; or in default of their agreement, by the order of such justice or justices of peace as shall dwell in the same parish, or (if none be there dwelling) in the parts next adjoining.

XIII. And if any person shall refuse or neglect to pay any such portion of money so taxed, it shall be lawful for the said churchwardens and constables, or any of them, or in their default, for any justice of peace of the said limit, to levy the same by distress and sale of the goods of the party so refusing or neglecting, rendering to the party the overplus: (2) and in default of such distress, it shall be lawful to any justice of that limit to commit such person to the said prison, there to abide without bail or mainprize till he have paid the same.

XIV. And be it also enacted, That the said justices of peace at their general quarter-sessions to be holden at the time of such taxation, shall set down what competent sums of money shall be sent quarterly out of every county or place corporate, for the relief of the poor prisoners of the King's bench and marshalsea, and also of such hospitals and alms-houses as shall be in the said county, and what sums of money shall be sent to every one of the said hospitals, and alms-houses, so as there be sent out of every county yearly twenty shillings at the least, to each of the said prisons of the King's bench and marshalsea; (2) which sums ratably to be assessed upon every parish, the churchwardens of every parish shall truly collect and pay over to the high constables in whole division such parish shall be situate, from time to time, quarterly, ten days before the end of every quarter; (3) and every such constable at every such quarter-sessions in such county, shall pay over the same to two such treasurers, or to one of them, as shall by the more part of the justices of peace of the county be elected to be the said treasurers, to be chosen by the justices of peace of the said county, city or town, or place corporate, or of others which were sessed and taxed at five pounds lands, or ten pounds goods at the least, at the tax of subsidy next before the time of the said election to be made; (4) and the said treasurers so elected to continue for the space of one whole year in their office, and then to give up their charge, with a due account of their receipts and disbursements, at the quarter-sessions to be holden next after the feast of *Easter* in every year, to such others as shall from year to year, in form aforesaid, successively be elected treasurers for the said county, city, town or place corporate; (5) which said treasurers, or one of them, shall pay over the same to the lord chief justice of *England*, and knight marshal for the time being, equally to be divided to the use aforesaid, taking their acquittance for the same, or in default of the said chief justice, to the next antientest, justice of the King's bench, as aforesaid: (6) and if any church-warden or high constable, or his executors or administrators, shall fail to make payment in form above specified, then every church-warden, his executors or administrators, so offending, shall forfeit for every time the sum of ten shillings; (7) and every high constable, his executors or administrators, shall forfeit for every time the sum of twenty shillings; (8) the same forfeitures, together with the sums behind, to be levied by the said treasurer and treasurers by way of distress and sale of the goods as aforesaid, in form aforesaid, and by them to be employed towards the charitable uses comprised in this act.

XV. And be it further enacted, That all the surplusage of money which shall be remaining in the said stock of any county, shall by discretion of the more part of the justices of peace in their quarter-sessions, be ordered, distributed and bestowed for the relief of the poor hospitals of that county, and of those that shall sustain losses by fire, water, the sea or other casualties, and to such other charitable purposes, for the relief of the poor, as to the more part of the said justices of peace shall seem convenient.

XVI. And be it further enacted, That if any treasurer elected shall wilfully refuse to take upon him the said office of treasurship, or refuse to distribute and give relief, or to account, according to such form as shall be appointed by the more part of the said justices of peace; that then it shall be lawful for the justices of peace in their quarter-sessions, or in their default, for the justices of assize at their assizes to be holden in the same county, to fine the same treasurer by their discretion; (2) the same fine not to be under three pounds, and to be levied by sale of his goods, and to be prosecuted by any two of the said justices of peace whom they shall authorize. (3) Provided always, That this act shall not take effect until the feast of *Easter* next.

XVII. And be it enacted, That the statute made in the nine and thirtieth year of her Majesty's reign, intituled, *An Act for the relief of the poor*, shall continue and stand in force until the feast of *Easter* next; (2) and that all taxations heretofore imposed and not paid, nor that shall be paid before the said feast of *Easter* next, and that all taxes hereafter before the said feast to be taxed by virtue of the said former act, which shall not be paid before the said feast of *Easter*, shall and may after the said feast of *Easter* be levied by the overseers and other persons in this act respectively appointed to levy taxations, by distress, and by such warrant in every respect, as if they had been taxed and imposed by virtue of this act, and were not paid.

XVIII. Provided always, That whereas the island of *Fowlness* in the county of *Essex*, being environed with the sea, and having a chapel of case for the inhabitants thereof, and yet the said island is no parish, but the lands in the same are situated within divers parishes far distant from the said island; (2) be it therefore enacted by the authority aforesaid, That the said justices of peace shall nominate and appoint inhabitants within the said island, to be overseers for the poor people dwelling within the said island, and that both they the said justices and the said overseers shall have the same power and authority to all intents, considerations and purposes for the execution of the parts and articles of this act, and shall be subject to the same pains and forfeitures, and likewise that the inhabitants and occupiers of lands there shall be liable and chargeable to the same payments, charges, expences and orders, in such manner and form as if the same island were a parish; (3) in consideration whereof, neither of the said inhabitants or occupiers of land within the said island, shall not be compelled to contribute towards the relief of the poor of those parishes wherein their houses or lands which they occupy within the said island are situated, for or by reason of their said habitations or occupyings, other than for the relief of the poor people within the said island, neither yet shall the other inhabitants of the parishes wherein such houses or lands are situated be compelled, by reason of their resiancy or dwelling, to contribute to the relief of the poor inhabitants within the said island.

XIX. And be it further enacted, That if any action of trespass or other suit shall happen to be attempted and brought against any person or persons, for taking of any distress, making of any sale, or any other thing doing, by authority of this present act, the defendant or defendants in any such action or suit shall and may either plead not guilty, or otherwise make avowry, cognisance or justification for the taking of the said distresses, making of sale, or other thing done by virtue of this act, alledging in such avowry, cognisance or justification, That the said distress, sale, trespass or other thing whereof the plaintiff or plaintiffs complained, was done by authority of this act, and according to the tenor, purport and effect of this act, without any expressing or rehearsal of any other matter or circumstance contained in this present act: (2) to which avowry, cognisance or justification, the plaintiff shall be admitted to reply, That the defendant did take the said distress, made the said sale, or did any other act or trespass supposed in his declaration, of his own wrong, without any such cause alledged by the said defendant; (3) whereupon the issue on every such action shall be joined, to be tried by verdict of twelve men, and not otherwise, as is accustomed in other personal actions: (4) and upon the trial of that issue, the whole matter to be given on both parties in evidence, according to the very truth of the same; (5) and after such issue tried for the defendant, or nonsuit of the plaintiff after appearance, the same defendant to recover treble damages, by reason of his wrongful vexation in that behalf, with his costs also in that part sustained, and that to be assessed by the same jury, or writ to enquire of the damages, as the same shall require.

XX. Provided always, That this act shall endure no longer than to the end of the next session of parliament.—*The Statutes at Large, from the Thirty-Ninth Year of Q. Elizabeth, to the Twelfth Year of K. Charles II, inclusive. To which is prefixed, A Table containing the Titles of all the Statutes during that Period. By Danby Pickering, of Gray's Inn, Esq; Reader of the Law Lecture to that Honourable Society, VII, 30-37.*

2. LEGISLATION ON APPRENTICESHIP IN VIRGINIA

1642

WHEREAS sundry laws and statutes by act of parliament established, have with great wisdome ordained, for the better educateing of youth in honest and profitable trades and manufactures, as also to avoyd sloath and idlenesse wherewith such young children are easily corrupted, as also for releife of such parents whose poverty extends not to give them breeding. That the justices of the peace should at their discretion, bind out children to tradesmen or husbandmen to be brought vp in some good and lawfull calling, And whereas God Almighty, among many his other blessings, hath vouchsafed increase of children to this collony, who now are multiplied to a considerable number, who if instructed in good and lawfull trades may much improve the honor and reputation of the country, and noe lesse their owne good and theire parents comfort: But forasmuch as for the most part the parents, either through fond indulgence or perverse obstinacy, are most averse and unwilling to parte with theire children, *Be it therefore inacted by authoritie of this Grand Assembly*, according to the aforesayd laudable custom in the kingdom of England, That the comissioners of the severall countyes respectively do, at theire discretion, make choice of two children in each county of the age of eight or seaven years at the least, either male or female, which are to be sent vp to James Citty between this and June next to be imployed in the public flax houses vnder such master and mistresse as shall be there appointed, In carding, knitting and spinning, &c. And that the said children be furnished from the said county with six barrells of corne, two coverletts, or one rugg and one blankett: One bed, one wooden bowle or tray, two pewter spoones, a sow shote of six months old, two laying hens, with convenient apparell both linen and woollen, with hose and shooes, And for the better provision of howseing for the said children, *It is inacted*, That there be two houses built by the first of April next of forty foot long a peece with good and substantial timber, The houses to be twenty foot broad apeece, eight foot high in the pitche and a stack of brick chimneys standing in the midst of each house, and that they be lofted with sawne boardes and made with convenient partitions, And it is further thought fitt that the commissioners have caution not to take vp any children but from such parents who by reason of their poverty are disabled to maintaine and educate them, *Be it likewise agreed*, That the Governour hath agreed with the Assembly for the sume of 10000 lb. of tob'o. to be paid him the next crop, to build and finish the said howses in manner and form before expressed.—Hening, *Statutes at Large*, I, 336-37 (1642).

1705

And be it further enacted, That every county court shall take good security of all guardians, for the estates of the orphans committed to their charge, and that they shall yearly inquire into such securities; and if any of them become defective or insufficient, shall cause new security to be given: And if it shall appear that the said estates are likely to be imbezzelled, or that the orphans are not taken care of, and educated according to their estates; then the said court shall have power to remove the said orphans (not being of age to choose their guardians) and their estates, and to place them under the care of such other persons, as to them shall seem most proper; always taking good security for the said orphans estates, that when the same shall become paiable to the said orphans, they shall be paid without making any abatement or allowance (other than of the profits of the said estates) for diet, cloathing, or any other matter whatsoever: And if the estate of any orphan be of so small a value, that no person will maintain him for the profits thereof, then such orphan shall, by direction of the court, be bound apprentice to some handicraft trade, or mariner, until he shall attain to the age of one and twenty years. And the master of every such orphan shall be obliged to teach him to read and write: And, at the expiration of his servitude, to pay and allow him in like manner as is appointed for servants, by indenture or custom. And if it shall appear, that any such apprentice be ill used by his master, or that he fails to teach him his trade, the court shall have power to remove him, and to bind him to such other person as to them shall seem most proper.—*Ibid.*, III, 375-76 (1705).

1769

WHEREAS the laws now in force are not sufficient to provide for the security and indemnifying the parishes from the great charges frequently arising from children begotten and born out of lawful matrimony: For remedy whereof, *Be it enacted, by the Governor, Council, and Burgesses, of this present General Assembly, and it is hereby enacted, by the authority of the same*, That, from and after the passing this act, if any single woman, not being a servant or slave, shall be delivered of a bastard child which shall be chargeable, or likely to become chargeable, to any parish, and shall, upon examination to be taken in writing, upon oath, before any justice of the peace of the county wherein such parish shall lie, charge any person, not being a servant, with being the father of such bastard child, it shall and may be lawful for any justice of the peace of the county wherein the person so charged shall be a resident or inhabitant, upon application made to him by the church-wardens of the parish wherein such child shall be born, or by any one of them, to issue his warrant for the immediate apprehending the persons so charged as aforesaid, and for bringing him before such justice, or before any other justice of the peace of the county wherein he is a resident or inhabitant; and the justice before whom such person shall be brought is hereby authorized and required to commit the person so charged as aforesaid to the common gaol of his county, unless he shall enter into a recognizance, with sufficient security, in the sum of ten pounds, upon condition to appear at the next court to be held for such county, and to abide by and perform such order or orders as shall be made by the said court; and if, upon the circumstances of the case, such court shall adjudge the person so charged to be the father of such bastard child, and that such child is likely to become chargeable to the parish, they shall, and may, by their discretion, take order for keeping such bastard child, by charging the father with the payment of money or tobacco for the maintenance of such child, in such manner, and in such proportions, as they shall think meet and convenient, and for such time as such child is likely to become chargeable to the parish, and no longer. And the father of such child shall enter into a recognizance, with sufficient securities, before the said court, in such sum as the said court, in their discretion, shall think fit, payable to his majesty, his heirs and successors, to observe and perform such order or orders of the court as aforesaid. And if the father, charged with the maintenance of such bastard child as aforesaid, shall make default, and not pay the money or tobacco so as aforesaid charged upon him by order of the said court, to the churchwardens of the parish, for the maintenance of such child, the court before whom such recognizance was entered into, shall, from time to time, upon the motion of the churchwardens of the said parish, or any one of them, enter up judgment and award execution for the money or tobacco in such order or orders mentioned, as the same shall become due, against the said father and his securities, their executors or administrators; provided ten days notice be given to the parties against whom such motion is made, before the making thereof. And if the father of such child shall refuse to enter into recognizance as aforesaid, such father shall be committed by the said court to the common gaol of the county, there to remain, without bail or mainprize, until he shall enter into such recognizance as aforesaid, or until he shall discharge himself by taking the oath of an insolvent debtor, and delivering in a schedule of his estate in manner directed, by the laws now in force, for debtors in execution (and which estate shall, by order of the court, be applied towards indemnifying the parish as aforesaid) or until the churchwardens of the parish concerned shall otherwise consent to his discharge.

II. *Provided always,* That it shall not be lawful for any justice, or justices of the peace, to send for any woman whatsoever, before she shall be delivered, in order to her being examined concerning her pregnancy, or compel her to answer any questions relating thereto, before her delivery.

III. *And be it further enacted, by the authority aforesaid,* That if any single woman, not being a servant, shall be delivered of a bastard child, she shall be liable to pay the sum of twenty shillings, current money of Virginia, to the churchwardens of the parish wherein she shall be delivered; to be recovered, with costs, before a justice of peace, and on such judgment execution may issue as in other cases: But the person so convicted shall not be liable to be whipped for failing to make payments, or to give security for such fine, any law to the contrary notwithstanding; which fine, recovered as aforesaid, shall be applied by the churchwardens to the use of the poor of the parish.

IV. *And be it further enacted, by the authority aforesaid,* That every such bastard child shall be bound apprentice by the churchwardens of the parish, for the time being, wherein such child shall be born, every male until he shall attain the age of twenty-one years, and every female until she shall attain the age of eighteen years, and no longer; and the master or mistress of every such apprentice shall find and provide for him or her diet, cloaths, lodging, and accommodations fit and necessary, and shall teach, or cause him or her to be taught to read and write, and at the expiration of his or her apprenticeship, shall pay every such apprentice the like allowance as is by law appointed for servants, by indenture or custom, and on refusal, shall be compellable thereto in like manner. And if, upon complaint made to the county court, it shall appear that any such apprentice is ill used, or not taught the trade or profession to which he or she may be bound, it shall be lawful for such court to remove and bind him or her to such other person or persons as they shall think fit.

V. And whereas by an act of assembly made in the twenty-seventh year of the reign of King George the second, intituled An act for the better government of servants and slaves, it is amongst other things enacted, if any woman servant shall be delivered of a bastard child, within the time of her service, that, in recompense for the loss and trouble occasioned her master or mistress thereby, she shall, for every such offence, serve her said master or owner one whole year, after her time, by indenture, custom, or former order of courts, shall be expired, or pay her master or owner one thousand pounds of tobacco; and the reputed father, if free, shall give security to the churchwardens of the parish to maintain the child, and keep the parish indemnified, or be compelled thereto, by order of the county court, upon the complaint of the churchwardens. And whereas it frequently happens that convict servants are delivered of such bastard children, who, being disabled to give testimony, cannot be examined, nor for that reason can the reputed father of such bastard child be discovered, and the parish indemnified from the charge of its maintainance: For remedy whereof,

VI. *Be it enacted,* That where any convict servant woman shall be delivered of a bastard child, during the time of her service, the master or owner of such servant shall be obliged to maintain such child, or be compelled thereto by the county court, on complaint of the churchwardens, and, in consideration of such maintainance, shall be intitled to the service of such child, if a male until he shall arrive to the age of twenty-one years, if a female until she shall arrive to the age of eighteen years.

VII. *Provided always,* That such master or owner shall find and provide for such child, the like accommodations, education, and freedom dues, and shall be compelled to answer his or her complaint, made to the county court, for default therein, or for ill usage, in like manner; as is before directed in the case of other apprentices.[1]—*Ibid.,* VIII, 374-77 (1769).

3. Legislation on Apprenticeship in South Carolina, 1687

And it is further enacted, by the authority aforesaid, that the age or ages of the severall servants that may arrive without indentures or contracts, to bee by theire said masters brought before the Grand Coun-

---

1. For additional legislation on this subject in Virginia see Hening, *op. cit.,* II, 298 (1672); IV, 212 (1727), 482 (1736); VI, 32 (1748), 368-69 (1753).

sell, within six months after the arrivall of such servant or servants as aforesaid, whose severall ages shall bee adjudged by the Grand Counsell, or any other by them appoynted. And all and every such servant or servants arriving without indentures or contracts as aforesaid, and serving according to the limitation of this Act, shall and may have and receive from the master or masters of such servant or servants, att and upon the expiration of theire terme of service, lymitted as aforesaid, one suite of Apparell, one barrel of Indian Corne, one Axe and one Hoe.—Cooper, *Statutes at Large of South Carolina*, II, 30-31 (1687).

4. Legislation on apprenticeship in North Carolina, 1715

IV. And Be It Further Enacted by the Authority afors'd that all Orphans shall be Educated & provided for according to their Rank & degree out of the Income or Interest of their Estate & Stock if the same will be sufficient Otherwise such Orphan shall be bound Apprentice to some Handycraft Trade (the Master or Mistress of such Orphan not being of the Profession of the People called Quakers) till they shall come of Age unless some of kin to such Orphan will undertake to maintain & Educate him or them for the interest or income of his or her Estate without Diminution of the Principal whether the same be great or small shall be always delivered to the Orphan when at Age. (1715)—Walter Clark (ed.), *The State Records of North Carolina*, XXIII, 70.

5. Legislation on apprenticeship in Tennessee, 1762

When the estate of any orphan shall be of so small value that no person will educate and maintain him or her, for the profits thereof, such orphan shall, by direction of the court, be bound apprentice; every male to some tradesman, merchant, mariner, or other person, approved by the court, until he shall attain to the age of twenty-one years; and every female, to some suitable employment, until her age of eighteen years; and also, such court may, in like manner, bind apprentice all free, base-born children; and every such female child, being a mulatto or mustee, until she shall attain the age of twenty-one years; and the master or mistress of any such apprentice, shall find and provide for him or her, diet, clothes, lodging and accommodations, fit and necessary, and shall teach, or cause him or her to be taught, to read and write; and, at the expiration of his or her apprenticeship, shall pay every such apprentice the like allowance as is by law appointed for servants, by indenture or custom, and on refusal, shall be compelled thereto, in like manner; and if upon complaint made to the county court, it shall appear that any such apprentice is ill-used, or not taught the trade, profession or employment, to which he or she was bound, it shall be lawful for such court to remove and bind him or her to such other person or persons as they shall think fit.

SEC. 20. The binding of such apprentice by order of the court, as aforesaid, shall be by indenture, made in the name of the *chairman* of the court, and his successors, of the one part, and of the master or mistress, to whom he or she shall be bound, of the other; which indenture shall be acknowledged or proved, before such court, and recorded, and a counterpart thereof shall remain and be kept in the clerk's office, for the benefit of such apprentice, and any person or persons injured, may and shall, at his or her costs and charges, prosecute a suit thereon, in the name of such chairman, or his successors, and recover all damages which he or she may have sustained by reason of the breach of the covenants therein contained; and if any verdict or judgment shall pass for such master or mistress, he or she shall receive costs.—Caruthers and Nicholson, *A Compilation of the Statutes of Tennessee*, p. 98 (1762).

6. LEGISLATION ON APPRENTICESHIP IN GEORGIA, 1786

Art. VII. *And be it enacted by the authority aforesaid,* That the senior justice in each county shall issue his warrant, annually, to not less than seven of the justices of their respective counties, to meet at the place appointed by law for building the court house and gaol, within thirty days after the adjournment of the March circuit court; and the justices so summoned, or not less than five of them, being met, shall have full power and authority to enquire into the number and circumstances of the poor of the county, bind out orphans, and other children that have not a comfortable subsistence, or ability to procure an English education, to some mechanic trade, or other lawful occupation, and appoint fit and discreet persons as overseers of the poor; and the aforesaid justices shall have power to levy a tax, not exceeding six-pence on every hundred pounds value of all taxable property belonging to the residents, in their respective counties, which shall be collected by the sheriff of the county, in such manner and way as the said board of justices shall direct; and, in case any person or persons shall neglect or refuse to pay the aforesaid tax when thereunto required, it shall and may be lawful, and the sheriffs of the different counties are hereby required to distrain for the same, in like manner as they would do in collecting the general tax, and shall have the like commissions therefor: And the monies arising from the aforesaid tax shall be paid into the hands of the senior justice in each county, to be applied, at the discretion of the board of justices, for the relief of the poor of the county, who are not otherwise provided for by the legislature; and, in case a surplusage should remain in the hands of the senior justices after provision made for the poor, the same shall be laid out by the aforesaid board of justices in building and keeping in repair the court houses, gaols, pillories, and stocks, in their respective counties, and such buildings and repairs shall at all times be let to the lowest bidder.

—Robert and George Watkins, *A Digest of the Laws of the State of Georgia*, p. 339.

7. PRACTICES AS SHOWN BY INDENTURES [1]

YORK COURT, 20 Oct., 1646.—It is ordered, with the consent of Mr. Edmund Chisman, father-in-law to John Lilly, orphant; William Barber, father-in-law to the orphans of John Dennett, vizt.: Thomas Dennett, Margaret Dennett, and Sarah Dennett; & Daniel ffoxe, father-in-law to the orphants of Clark & Munday, that the estates belonging to the s^d sev^rall orphants, wch this day they have filed on accot of to this co^{rt}, shall henceforward with all there increase freely come & belong unto the said orphants wth out any charges for the future subsistance or education of the s^d orphants, or for there care, paines, or charge in p^rserving & looking to ye s^d sev^rall orphants estates, as long as they or any of them shall remaine under the tuition of ye above s^d Edmund Chisman, William Barber, & Daniel ffoxe, &c.

YORK COUNTY.—Orphants Co^{rt} held August 24th, 1648.

Present: Capt Nicholas Martin, Capt John Chisman, Mr Hugh Gwyn, M^r ffrancis Willis, M^r ffrancis Morgan.

Whereas John foster, orphant to John foster, late of Hampton pish, deceased, whoe is left without any mentaynance or estate whatsoever, and Stephen Gill, godfather to ye s^d foster, haveing made humble suite to this court that the s^d John foster, whoe hath by him beene already provided for and kept about a yeare, that he may have the tuition and bringing upp of ye s^d John foster, and that he may be put wth him for some certayne tyme by this co^{rt}. It is therefore ordered

1. Indentures and other evidences of the actual practice of the apprenticeship system are presented for Virginia, North and South Carolina and Georgia.

that the sd John foster shall live & remaine under tuition & bringing upp of ye sd Stephen Gill, for ye space of nine yeares from ye date hereof. Dureing which tyme ye sd Gill is hereby injoined to p'vide sufficiently for ye sd foster, & to take care that he bee brought upp in ye feare of God and taught to Reade.

LANCASTER COUNTY, Jan'y 6, 1655.—The court hath ordered Jno, ye base child of Thomas Mannan, borne of Eliza: Tomlin, shall, according to ye will of ye mother, bee kept by Roger Harris & his wife until he arrive at ye Age of 18 years, he, ye sd Harris providing yt ye sd child be taught to write & reade. And yt ye sd Harris have all of ye tobacco due from Jno Robinson pd him at ye crop on ye 10th of November next, the same being 600 & caske.

SURRY COUNTY, June 15, 1681.—Wm. Rogers bound apprentice to Thomas Bage to serve till 21—his master to teach him his trade of blacksmith, and to read & wright, &c.

April 15, 1701. Sarah, the daughter of John Allen, deced, is bound to Thomas Bentley until she shall arrive at the age of eighteen years —the said Bentley obligeing himselfe to instruct her in the rudiments of the Christian Religion, to learne or cause her to be learnt to reade perfectly, and at the expiration of the said tearm to provide and give her a decent suit of Apparell, and ordered that Indentures be drawne accordingly.

Similar order in reference to her brother John.

May 4, 1697. Ordered that unless Jno Clements do put John High to school to learne to reade & write, he do appeare at the next court, and bring ye said John with him, that the court may then do therein as shall be found fitt.

ELIZABETH CITY COUNTY, July 18, 1698.—Ann Chandler, orphan of Daniel Chandler, bound apprentice to Phyllemon Miller till 18 or day of marriage, to be taught to read a chapter in the Bible, ye Lord's prayer, and ten commandments, and sempstress work.

ISLE OF WIGHT COUNTY.—At an Orphan's Court held on the 1st May, Anno 1694.

Prsent: Col. Arthur Smith, Capt. Henry Applewhait, Mr. Hen. Baker, Mr. Thos. Giles, Mr. Antho. Holladay, justices.

Charles Edwards having exhibited a peticon to this Court for Grace Griswood, an Orphan Girl, that she might live with him, ye sd Charles, till eighteen years old or marryed. It is thereupon ordered yt the sd Orphan doe live & abide with the sd Edwards till age or marryage as aforesaid, & ye sd Charles doth hereby oblige himselfe to mainteyn her decently & see yt she be taught to read, sew, spinn & knitt, & at the expiration of the tyme to have sufficient cloathing as shall be thought well by the court.

YORK COURT, May ye 26th 1690.—Whereas Thomas Thorpe and Ellinor his wife sued Robt Green to this court, and in their peticon declare that they did binde Richard Gilbert there son An Apprentice to ye Defent for the space of nine yeares by one Indenture under hand and seale to bee Instructed and taught in ye Arts and Mistery of a taylor and to teach or cause him to be taught to reade & to write a Leagable hand, and not to Imploye him to Labour in the Grownd, Excepting in helping to make corne for the Defendts ffamely, but ye Defendt without regard to ye said Indenture Dayley keeps the said Apprentice to Labour in the Ground from year to year and omitts giveing him Learning or teach him his trade which is to ye said Apprentice utter Rewing and undoing. Therefore itt is ordered that ye said Robt Green doe at ye next court Enter into a Bond of 4000 lb tobacco & cash, with good and sufficient security for the true pformance of ye said Indenture and to fulfill every clause and Artickle therein expressed, according to ye true Interest and meaning ye same. —*William and Mary College Quarterly Historical Magazine*, V, 221-23.

Upon a petition exhibited by Jabell Alford praying to have liberty to chuse a Guardian. Ordered that the said Jabell Alford be bound to Mrs Susanna Hartley Widow untill he be one and twenty years of age & that ye said Mrs Hartley be bound and enter into bond to learne him the trade of a Carpenter or Joyner wthin ye said time.—William L. Saunders (ed.), *The Colonial Records of North Carolina*, I, 398 (August 7, 1694).

Upon ye Peticōn of Honell Thomas Harvey esqr Ordered yt Wm ye son of Timothy Pead late of the County of Albemarle Decd being left destitute be bound unto ye sd Thomas Harvey esqr and Sarah his wife untill he be at ye age of twenty one years and the said Thomas Harvey to teach him to read.—*Ibid.*, p. 448. County of Albemarle, February, 1694/95.

Elisabeth Gardner ye Rellock William Gardner desesed prsented hir selfe before ye Court to bind hir Son William Gardner to ye Honbl Govener Thomas Harvi or his Heires thay Ingagen to Learn him to Reed Which In or to Was doon till he comes to ye Age of

Twenty on yeares he being five years ould now a fortnite before Crismas—*Ibid.*, p. 495. Perquimans Precinct, October, 1698.

North Carolina }
Wake County } ss

December Term 1771

This Indenture made the third Day of December in the Year of our Lord one thousand and Seven Hundred and Seventy One; Between Theophilus Hunter Esq. Chairman of our Inferior Court of the said County, and John Fox of the one part and Jacob Uttley of the other part, Witnesseth, That the said Theophilus Hunter on Behalf of the said Court hath put the said John Fox, Apprentice to the aforesaid Jacob Uttley, and to be taught in Reading and Writing Agreeable to Law and to serve Eight Years from the Day of the Date of these presents, until He attains to the age of Twenty One being now Thirteen years old, and to serve Eight Years; During which time He shall behave himself as an honest and faithfull Apprentice ought to do: and the sd Jacob Uttley shall teach or cause to be taught his said Apprentice in the Art and Mistery of a Planter. And procure and provide for him sufficient, Meat, Drink, Washing and Lodging and apparal, fitting for such an Apprentice, during the said Term.

And further do and perform all other things mentioned in an Act of General Assembly of this Province. In Witness whereof, We have hereunto set our Hands and Seals, the Day and Year first above written.—*Record Book, 1771-1782*, Wake County Clerk of the Superior Court, pp. 9-10.

At a court of Pleas and Quarterly Sessions begun and held at the Court House in Raleigh on the 3rd Monday of February, 1822 being the forty-sixth year of American Independence (and the 18th day of February).

Ordered that A. Johnson,[1] an orphan boy and son of Jacob Johnson, deceased, 14 years of age, be bound to Jas. J. Selby till he arrive at lawful age to learn the trade of a Tailor.

TEN DOLLARS REWARD

Ran away from the Subscriber, on the night of the 15th instant, two apprentice boys, legally bound, named William and Andrew Johnson. The former is of a dark complexion, black hair, eyes, and

1. Johnson became the seventeenth president of the United States.

habit. They are much of a height, about 5 feet 4 or 5 inches. The latter is very fleshy, freckled face, light hair, and fair complexion. They went off with two other apprentices, advertised by Messrs. Wm. & Chas. Fowler. When they went away, they were well clad—blue cloth coats, light colored homespun coats, and new hats, the maker's name in the crown of the hats, is Theodore Clark. I will pay the above Reward to any person who will deliver said apprentices to me in Raleigh, or I will give the above Reward for Andrew Johnson alone.

All persons are cautioned against harboring or employing said apprentices on pain of being prosecuted.

James J. Selby, *Tailor*.

Raleigh, N. C. June 24, 1824.

—*The Raleigh Gazette*, June 24, 1824.

Order'd that Charles Purdy be bound to Mrs Levis Planter until he is of the age of 21 years and that the Parish pay her ten pounds in Consideration of her giving him a years Schooling. (1733)—A. S. Salley (ed.), *Minutes of the Vestry of St. Helena's Parish, South Carolina*, 1726-1812, p. 21.

You may judge of my Hurry, when I tell you I am, (and have been these 4 Months) the sole Inhabitant of my Printing office, (excepting a Negro boy, whom I'm teaching to serve me at the Press). I discharged my villainous Apprentice; gave him two years time, quitted all Claims on him for Monies received and gamed away, for loss of Time, and Charges for taking up etc. etc. etc. A Lad very capable of the Business, and might have been of vast Service to me but for 3 years has always pulled the contrary way; owing to an unhappy affection for Drink, Play, and Scandalous Company.—Letter by Peter Timothy, June 14, 1754. In *The South Carolina Historical and Genealogical Magazine*, XXXV (1934), 125.

This Indenture Witnesseth that John Alston [1] the sonne of William Alston of Hamersmith in the County of Midlelsex gent doth put himselfe apprentice to James Jones of the County of Carolina merchant to Learne and follow his Art with him after the manner of an apprentice & to serve him his s^d master the full end & terme of Seaven yeares from the day of the date hereof dureing wch s^d Terme he the Afores^d James Jones doth hereby covenant to finde unto his said

---

1. John Alston (the name was later spelled Allston) was the founder of a family distinguished in the history of South Carolina.

Apprentice meate, drinke, apparell Lodgeing and all other necessaryes which shall be needfull and convenient for him provided neverthelesse and it is hereby further Agreed by and between the said James Jones and the Aforesd William Alston ffather of the said John that if the sd William Alston shall at any tyme or tymes hereafter cause to require or call home to him his sd sone within the aforesd Terme of seaven yeares and before that time be compleated he the sd James Jones doth hereby covenant and Oblige himselfe to returne him Carefully (if alive) The said William defraying the money due for his passage into England and returne In Wittness whereof the pties above named to these prsent Indentures have put their hands and seales Interchangeably this sixteenth day of May Anno Dni 1682.—Miscellaneous Records of the Governor of South Carolina, 1672-1692, p. 123. In *The South Carolina Historical and Genealogical Magazine,* VI (1905), 114.

.Know all men by these presents that I Charles Smith am held and firmly bound unto the Court of Ordinary for said County and their successors in office in the sum of five hundred dollars for which payment well and truly to be made I bind myself my heirs executors etc. sealed and dated this 16th day of July 1833.

The conditions of the above obligation is such that whereas Ezkiel Miller has this day bound unto the said Charles Smith his son Gilford Miller until he becomes to the age of twenty-one: even if the said Charles Smith shall use his best endeavours to teach the said Gilford, the occupation of farming, and provide for him sufficient meat, drink, apparel and lodging & during the said time and the said Master is to give the said apprentice schooling sufficient to do the common business of the country & further the said Charles Smith can obligate himself provided the said Gilford do faithfully serve the said term, one horse with sixty dollars saddle & bridle and a suit of clothes extra to common ward.—Records of the Ordinary, Baldwin County, Georgia, 1833.

At an Orphan's Court held for the Isle of Wight County on the first of May, 1694. Prsent, Col. Arthur Smith, Capt. Henry Applewhaite, Mr. Hen. Baker, Mr. Tho. Giles, Mr. Anthony Holladay, Justices. Charles Edwards having exhibited petition to this court for Grace Griswood, an Orphan Girle, that she might live with him ye sd. Charles, till eighteen years old or married. It is thereupn ordered yt the sd. Orphan doe live and abide with the sd. Edwards till ye age or marryage as aforesaid, and yᵉ sd. Charles doth hereby oblige him selfe to mainteyn her decently and see yᵗ she be taught to read, sow, spin, and knitt and at the expiration of the tyme to have sufficient cloathing as shall be thought well by the Court.

It is ordered by the court yᵗ Jno. Moore doe forthwith returne to his apprenticeship with his master Jno. Davis shoemaker, and faithfully serve out his tyme appointed him by indenture, and if the Prentice be any ways abused, then complaint thereof to be sett forth to this courte yᵗ yᵉ same may be duly regulated, the sd. Davis being now admonished by the court not to abuse the boy.—*William and Mary College Quarterly Historical Magazine*, VII, 257-58.

David Alexander and Thomas Cooke Church wardens of Pettsoe [Petsworth] Parrish in yᵉ County of Gloucestʳ Doe in yᵉ name and behalfe of yᵉ Vestrey Therof by this Indenture Bind unto Nathaniell Mills an orphant Boy named John Lewis untill He comes to yᵉ Age of one and twenty years In all Such Service as the Said Mills will imploy him about he yᵉ Said Mills obligeing himself by this Indenture to give unto yᵉ Sd orphant John Lewis two years scooleing and yᵗ to be given at nine years of Age and not before he comes to yᵉ afore Said Age as Also for to find and alow yᵉ Said Lewis Suffitient aparrell Meat Drink washing and Lodging Dureing yᵉ afore Said term of time as Also to Pay unto yᵉ above Bound John Lewis all Such Necrssary Alowanchess as to him Due according to the Custome of this Countrey, In wittness whereof yᵉ Partiess above mentioned have interchangably Sett their Hands and Seales yᵉ Day and year above written [1700]. —C. G. Changerlayne (ed.), *The Vestry Book of Petsworth Parish, Gloucester County, Virginia, 1677-1793*, p. 66. Scores of indentures are given in this work. If the other parishes were as energetic as Petsworth in this activity, there were countless cases of "binding out" children in Virginia.

This Indenture made the eighth day of Novembʳ 1701. & the fourteenth year of our soveraigne Lord William of Great Brittain ffrance & Ireland King Witnesseth That Wee Thomas Cooke & Davis Alexander Church Wardens of Petsoe parish In yᵉ County of Gloster Doe firmly in the name & behalfe of yᵉ Vestry of yᵉ sd parish bind unto Mr Jnᵒ Day of yᵉ forsd parish one Orphan boye called James Luis of yᵉ age of seven yeares (who was formerly bound unto James Hayes now deceast & now takne from his widow for want of maintinance) unto the sd Day his heires exors &c: untill he arrive att the full age as the law directs to serve him & them in all maner of service & imploy that he or they shall sett him about And ye sd Jno Day does oblidge himselfe his heires exors &c: to Give him ye sd Orphan three yeares shooling & to carefully instruct learn & educate the sd Orphan in all such wayes that he may able after his indented tyme expyre to gett his own living & to allow him sufficient meat Drink lodging & apparele untill the expyration of ye sd tyme, & after the finishing of the same To pay unto the sd James Luis Double apparell wt all other such allowances necessary as the law Directs in such cases As also to keep the afosd parish During the aforsd intented tyme from all manner of charges or being any wayes burdensome to the sd parish & the abovenamd Church Wardens Doe oblidge themselves in quality aforsd to have allowed to the sd Day five hundred lb: tob, att the nixt levie In consideration of his three yeares schooling In witness whereof both ye sd parties have heerunto sett their hands & seals Day & year first above written.—*Ibid.*, pp. 70-71.

This Indenture made ye: Thirtieth day of octobr: in ye Yeare of our Lord God one Thousand Seven Hundred & Sixteen & in ye Second yeare of our Sovereign Lord George of Great Brittain France & Ireland Defender of ye faith &c Wittnesseth that I Thos May Cleark of Petso Parish In Gloster County do firmly in ye name and behalf of ye Vestry of ye Parish above Sd: Bind unto Ralph Bevis of ye Sd Parish & County a Molatto Boy Named George Petsworth of ye age of two yeares old ye Sixth day of March Next Insuing ye Date of these prsents untill he arives att ye Age as ye Law Directs to Serve him ye Sd Ralph Bevis his heirs &c: in all maner of Lawfull Services & Imployments yt he Shall Sett him about and ye Sd Ralph Bevis doth Bind and Oblidge himself his heirs &c: to give ye Sd Molatto Boy Three years Schooleing & to Carefully Instruct him afterwards that he May read well in any part of ye Bible also to Instruct & Leare him ye Sd Molatto Boy Such Lawfull way or ways that he may be able after his Indented time Expiared to gitt his own Liveing & to alow him Sufficient Meat Drink washing & Apparrill untill ye: Expiration of ye Sd time & after ye finishing of ye Sd time to pay ye Sd George Petsworth all such alowances as ye Law Directs in Such Cases as also to keep ye aforeSd Parish Dureing ye aforesd: Indented time from all manner of Charges or being any way Burdensome to ye Sd Parish in Witness Whareof I have hereunto Sett my hand & Seale ye. Day & yeare above written.—*Ibid.*, pp. 135-36.

At a Court held for Caroline County on Friday the 14th day of March, 1734/35. It is ordered and considered by the Court that Edmund Pendleton [1] son of Henry Pendleton decd., be bound and is hereby bound unto Benj. Robinson, Clerck of this Court, to serve him the full end and term of six years and six months as an apprentice to be brought up in the said office, which time the said apprentice his said master faithfully shall serve according to the usage and custome of apprentices. In consideration whereof, the said Benjamin Robinson doth agree that he will use the said the utmost of his endeavours to instruct his sᵈ apprentice in all things belonging to a Clerk's office and that he will provide for him sufficient meet, drink, apparell & fitting for an apprentice during yᵉ sᵈ time.—*William and Mary College Quarterly Historical Magazine*, XXVII (1918), 139.

1. Edmund Pendleton (1721-1803), eminent jurist and revolutionary patriot of Virginia.

III

THE SOCIETY FOR THE PROPAGATION OF THE GOSPEL IN FOREIGN PARTS

I. PREVIEW AND COMMENTS

THE SOCIETY FOR THE Propagation of the Gospel in Foreign Parts was chartered in England in 1701 "for the purpose of providing the ministrations of religion for our countrymen in the Colonies, and of bringing the surrounding heathen to the Knowledge of the truth." It had been preceded (1699) by the Society for Promoting Christian Knowledge which also engaged in missionary and educational work. The Established Church through these societies undertook to get a firmer grip on the colonists, but the SPG was the more active in such effort. The Reverend James Blair became the Bishop of London's Commissary for Virginia and The Reverend Thomas Bray for Maryland. The activities of the SPG were discontinued in America with the Revolution; but prior to that event much of the money expended by the organization had been used for work in the American colonies, with Negroes and Indians being special objects of its solicitude.[1]

At the initial meeting of the Society June 27, 1701, the first matter of importance considered was "the state of religion in the American Colonies" and at a meeting September 19 of that year an account of the state of religion in the British plantations in North America was presented by Colonel Dudley, Governor of New England. He pointed out that South Carolina contained 7000 souls and would admit and support 3 ministers; North Carolina 5000 souls and would admit and support 3 ministers; and that both colonies stood in need of schools. Virginia with 40,000 souls was "divided into about 40 parishes, with an established maintenance by act of Assembly, but is not fully supplied, and the maintenance hurt by disuse; but will be always encouraged by Colonel Nicholson, the present Governor." At that same meeting a letter was read by Reverend George Keith,

---

1. Useful secondary accounts of the work of the SPG include C. F. Pascoe, *Two Hundred Years of the S.P.G., 1701-1900*, London, "Published at the Society's Office," 1901; Ernest Hawkins, *Historical Notices of the Missions to the Church of England in the North American Colonies, Previous to the Independence of the United States*, London, 1845; and James S. M. Anderson, *History of the Church of England in the Colonies and Foreign Dependencies of the British Empire*, London, 1845.

the first missionary maintained by the Society, who had quit the Church of Scotland where he was born, had joined the Quakers, gone to Pennsylvania where he created some disturbances, got into trouble and was tried for the publication of his doctrines. His fine was later remitted and he joined the Church of England. In the letter referred to he wrote at length about "the state of Quakerism" in North America—and thought it "a good expedient" that ministers be sent to America by the Church of England through the SPG; they should not reside constantly in one place but preach at several places; and he recommended "that a considerable number of little books, such as the Pastoral Letter, and those against swearing, drunkardness, and sabbath-breaking" should be spread in the colonies, "and if a little book were printed by some able man, to shew the sin of schism, to persuade to the communion of the Church of England, and sent among them, it would be of great service."

If it should appear that the SPG was relatively inactive in Virginia, this condition may be due to the better organization and control by the Established Church of religious and educational activities there than in the other Southern colonies. Another condition which may have caused this relative inactivity appears to have developed from the "incendiary" personality of James Blair who seems to have resented Thomas Bray from the outset. This could have amounted to an insurmountable obstacle in the way of progress of the SPG in Virginia. Commissary Blair had large control over many things in Virginia from the latter part of the seventeenth century until his death in 1743, "and was certainly not a man to be trifled with." [2]

The missionaries sent by the SPG to South Carolina often complained about conditions including the dangers of malaria, dysentery, other problems of health, the high rate of mortality, and troubles caused by dissenters. As for North Carolina, Stephen B. Weeks [3] wrote that the educational backwardness of that colony was due "to the pernicious activities" of the SPG missionaries, some of whom were probably not very exemplary. From the appearance of the first of these in North Carolina in the early part of the eighteenth century to the beginning of the administration of Governor Tryon

2. Letter from John M. Jennings, in charge of manuscripts and rare books, the Library of The College of William and Mary, to Edgar W. Knight, February 19, 1947.

3. *Church and State in North Carolina*, p. 22. See also David D. Oliver, "The Society for the Propagation of the Gospel in the Province of North Carolina," *James Sprunt Historical Publications*, Vol. IX, No. 1.

in 1765 the Society seems to have accomplished very little in that province. When Tryon became Governor he pledged his efforts to secure good clergymen for the colony and urged the SPG not to send to North Carolina "the sweepings of the Universities but some clergy of character." [4] Opposition of the Quakers and other dissenters seems to have been one of the causes of the failure of the SPG in North Carolina. Other conditions under which the Society undertook to conduct its work there were not favorable. The activities of the Society in Georgia were less extensive than elsewhere in the South.

Frank J. Klingberg [5] says that 353 missionaries were sent to the American colonies and served as important "religious reporters." These representatives of the SPG were instructed to give on a questionnaire twice a year exact information concerning many subjects, including the Indians and Negroes. "Moreover, they were encouraged to relate, independently of enquiry, any and all observations of their own on colonial society ... these records from the colonial world won the financial support for the vast undertaking of the Society. It was supported not by taxes but primarily by the wells of private charity... The missionary, however, with his necessary data of adversity and achievement, covered the colonial scene as a whole better than any other observer."

II. DOCUMENTS

General

1. Charter of the Society for the Propagation of the Gospel in Foreign Parts, June 16, 1701

William the Third, By the Grace of God, of England, Scotland, France, and Ireland, King, Defender of the Faith. To all Christian People, to whom these Presents shall come, Greeting

Whereas Wee are credibly informed that in many of our Plantacons, Colonies, and Factories beyond the Seas, belonging to Our Kingdome of England, the Provision for Ministers is very mean. And many others of Our said Plantacons, Colonies, and Factories are wholy destitute, and unprovided of a Mainteynance for Ministers,

---

4. *Colonial Records of North Carolina*, VII, 103-6.

5. *Carolina Chronicle: The Papers of Commissary Gideon Johnston, 1707-1716* (Berkeley: University of California Press, 1946), p. 3. Pascoe, *op. cit.*, p. 847, reports 309 missionaries to the "older Colonies, now the United States, 1702-1785."

and the Publick Worshipp of God; and for Lack of Support and Mainteynance for such, many of our Loveing Subjects doe want the Administration of God's Word and Sacraments, and seem to be abandoned to Atheism and Infidelity and alsoe for Want of Learned and Orthodox Ministers to instruct Our said Loveing Subjects in the Principles of true Religion, divers Romish Preists and Jesuits are the more encouraged to pervert and draw over Our said Loving Subjects to Popish Superstition and Idolatry

And whereas Wee think it Our Duty as much as in Us lyes, to promote the Glory of God, by the Instruccon of Our People in the Christian Religion And that it will be highly conducive for accomplishing those Ends, that a sufficient Mainteynance be provided for an Orthodox Clergy to live amongst them, and that such other Provision be made, as may be necessary for the Propagation of the Gospell in those Parts:

And whereas Wee have been well assured, That if Wee would be gratiously pleased to erect and settle a Corporacon for the receiving, manageing, and disposeing of the Charity of Our Loveing Subjects, divers Persons would be induced to extend their Charity to the Uses and Purposes aforesaid

Know yee therefore, That Wee have, for the Consideracons aforesaid, and for the better and more orderly carrying on the said Charitable Purposes, of our speciall Grace, certain Knowledge, and meer Mocon, Willed, Ordained, Constituted, and Appointed, and by these Presents, for Us, Our Heires, and Successors, doe Will, Ordaine, Constitute, Declare, and Grant, That the most Reverend Fathers in God, Thomas Lord Archbishopp of Canterbury, and John Lord Archbishopp of Yorke, The Right Reverend Fathers in God, Henry Lord Bishop of London, William Lord Bishop of Worcester Our Lord Almoner, Simon Lord Bishop of Ely, Thomas Lord Bishop of Rochester Deane of Westminster; *and the Lords Archbishops of Canterbury and Yorke, the Bishops of London and Ely, the Lord Almoner and Deane of Westminster for the Time being:* Edward Lord Bishop of Gloucester, John Lord Bishop of Chichester, Nicholas Lord Bishop of Chester, Richard Lord Bishop of Bath and Wells, Humphry Lord Bishop of Bangor, John Mountague Doctor of Divinity Clerke of Our Closett, William Sherlock Doctor of Divinity Deane of St. Paules, William Stanley Doctor of Divinity Arch Deacon of London and the Clerke of the Clossett, of Us, Our Heires and Successors, *the Dean of St. Paul's and Arch Deacon of London for the Time being; The two Regius and two Margaret Professors of Divinity of both Our Universities for the Time being;*—Earle of Thannet, Thomas Lord Viscount Weymouth, Francis Lord Guildford, William Lord Digby, Sir Thomas Cookes of Bentley, Sir Richard Bulkley, Sir John Phillipps and Sir Arthur Owen, Baronetts: Sir Humphrey Mackworth, Sir William Prichard, Sir William Russell, Sir Edmund Turner, Sir William Hustler, Sir John Chardin, and Sir Richard Blackmore, Knights: John Hook, Esquire Serjeant at Law, George Hooper Doctor of Divinity Deane of Canterbury, George Booth Doctor of Divinity Archdeacon of Durham, Sir George Wheeler Prebendary of Durham, William Beveridge Doctor of Divinity Arch Deacon of Colchester, Sir William Dawes Baronett, Thomas Maningham, Edward Gee, Thomas Lynford, Nathaniel Resbury, Offspring Blackhall, George Stanhope, William Heyley, and Richard Willis, Doctors of Divinty and Our Chaplaines in Ordinary; John Mapletoft, Zacheus Isham, John Davies, William Lancaster, Humphrey Hody, Richard Lucas, John Evans, Thomas Bray, John Gascorth, White Kennett, Lilly Butler, Josiah Woodward, Doctors in Divinity; Gideon Harvey and Frederick Slare, Doctors of Phisick, Rowand Cotton, Thomas Jervois, Maynard Colchester, James Vernon Junr. Joseph Neale, Grey Nevill, Thomas Clerk, Peter King, —— Rock, John Comins, William Melmoth, Thomas Bromfeild, John Raynolds, Dutton Seaman, Whitlock Bulstrode, Samuel Brewster, John Chamberlaine, Richard King, and Daniel Nicoll, Esquires; Benjamin Lawdell, John Trimmer, Charles Toriano, and John Hodges, Merchants; William Fleetwood, William Whitfeild, and Samuel Bradford, Masters of Art, and Our Chaplains in Ordinary; Thomas Little, Batchelor in Divinity; Thomas Staino, Henry Altham, William Loyd, Henry Shute, Thomas Frank, and William Meeken, Clerks, and their Successors to be elected in Manner as hereafter directed, Be, and shall for ever hereafter be, and by Vertue of these Presents shall be one Body Politick and Corporate, in Deed and in Name, by the Name of, The Society for the Propogation of the Gospell in Forreigne Parts: And them and their Successors, by the same Name, Wee doe by these Presents, for Us, Our Heires, and Successors, really and fully Make, Ordaine, Constitute, and Declare One Body Politick and Corporate, in Deed and in Name.

And that by the same Name, they and their Successors shall and may have perpetuall Succession.

And that they and their Successors by that Name shall and may, for ever hereafter, be Persons Able and Capable in the Law to Purchase, Have, Take, Receive, and Enjoy to them and their Successors, Mannors, Messuages, Lands, Tenements, Rents, Advowsons, Liberties, Priviledges, Jurisdictions, Franchises, and other Hereditaments whatsoever, of whatsoever Nature Kind and Quality they be, in Fee and in Perpetuity, not exceeding the Yearly Value of Two Thousand Pounds beyond Reprizalls and alsoe Estates for Lives and for Yeares and all other Manner of Goods, Chattells, and Things whatsoever, of what Name Nature Quality or Value soever they be, for the better Support and Maintenance of an Orthodox Clergy in Forreigne Parts, and other the Uses aforesaid: And to Give, Grant, Let, and Demise, the said Mannors, Messuages, Lands, Tenements, Hereditamts, Goods, Chattells, and Things whatsoever aforesaid, by Lease or Leases, for Terme of Yeares in Possession at the Time of Granting thereof, and not in Reversion, not exceeding the Terme of One and Thirty Yeares from the time of Granting thereof: on which, in Case noe Fine be taken, shall be Reserved the Full Value; and in Case a Fine be taken, shall be Reserved at least a Moyety of the full Value that the same shall reasonably and *Bona Fide* be worth at the Time of such Demise.

And that by the Name aforesaid they shall and may be able to Plead and be Impleaded, Answer and be Answered unto, Defend and be Defended, in all Courts and Places whatsoever, and before whatsoever Judges Justices or other Officers of Us, Our Heires and Successors, in all and singular Actions Plaints Pleas Matters and Demands, of what Kind, Nature or Quality soever they be: And to act and doe all other Matters and Things, in as ample Manner and Forme as any other Our Liege Subjects of this Our Realme of England being Persons able and capable in the Law, or any other Body Corporate or Politique within this Our Realme of England, can or may have, purchase, receive, possesse, take, enjoy, grant, sett, let, demise, plead and be impleaded, answer and be answered unto, defend and be defended, doe permitt and execute.

And that the said Society for ever hereafter shall and may have a Common Seale to serve for the Causes and Businesse of them and their Successors: And that it shall and may be lawfull for them and their Successors to change, breake, alter, and make New the said Seale from Time to Time, and at their Pleasure, as they shall think best

And for the better Execucon of the purposes aforesaid, We doe give and grant to the said Society for the Propagation of the Gospell in Forreigne Parts, and their Successors, That they, and their Successors for ever, shall, upon the Third Friday in February Yearely, meet at some convenient Place to be appointed by the said Society, or the major Part of them, who shall be present at any Generall Meeting, betweene the Houres of Eight and Twelve in the Morning; and that they, or the major Part of such of them that shall then be present, shall choose one President, one or more Vice-president or Vice-presidents, one or more Treasurer or Treasurers, two or more Auditors, one Secretary, and such other Officers, Ministers, and Servants, as shall be thought convenient to serve in the said Offices for the Yeare ensueing. And that the said President and Vice-presidents, and all Officers then elected, shall, before they act in their respective Offices, take an Oath to be to them administered by the President, or in his Absence by one of the Vice-presidents of the Yeare preceding, who are hereby authorized to administer the same, for the faithfull and due Execucon of their respective Offices and Places dureing the said yeare

And Our further Will and Pleasure is, That the first President of the said Society shall be Thomas, by Divine Providence, Lord Arch Bishop of Canterbury, Primate and Metropolitan of all England: And that the said President shall, within Thirty Dayes after the passing of this Charter, cause Summons to be issued to the severall Members of the said Society herein particularly menconed, to meet at such Time and Place as he shall appoint: And that they, or the major Part of such of them as shall then be present, shall proceed to the Eleccon of one or more Vice-president or Vice-presidents, one or more Treasurer or Treasurers, two or more Auditors, one Secretary, and such other Officers, Ministers, and Servants, as to them shall seem meet; which said Officers, from the Time of Their Eleccon into their respective Offices, shall continue therein untill the Third Friday in February, which shall be in the Yeare of Our Lord One Thousand Seaven Hundred and One, and from thence forwards untill others shall be chosen into their Places, in Manner aforesaid

And that if it shall happen, that any of the Persons at any Time chosen into any of the said Offices shall dye, or on any Account be removed from such Office at any Time between the said yearly Dayes of Election, that in such Case it shall be lawfull for the surviving and continueing President, or any one of the Vice-presidents, to issue summons to the several Members of the Body Corporate, to meet at the usuall Place of the Annuall Meeting of the said Society, at such Time as shall be specified in the said Summons; and that such Members of the said Body Corporate, who shall meet upon such Summons, or the major Part of them, shall and may choose an Officer or Officers into the Roome or Place of such Person or Persons soe dead or removed as to them shall seem meet

And Wee doe further Grant unto the said Society for the Propagation of the Gospell in Forreigne Parts, and their Successors, That they and their Successors shall and may, on the third Friday in every Month yearely for ever hereafter, and oftner if Occasion require, meet at some convenient Place to be appointed for that Purpose to transact the Businesse of the said Society, and shall and may at any Meeting on such Third Friday in the Month Elect such Persons to be Members of the said Corporation, as they or the major Part of them then present shall think Beneficiall to the Charitable Designes of the said Corporation

And Our Will and Pleasure is That noe Act done in any Assembly of the said Society shall be effectuall and valid, unlesse the President or some one of the Vice-presidents and Seaven other Members of the said Company at the least be present, and the major Part of them consenting thereunto

And Wee further Will, and by these Presents for Us, Our Heires and Successors doe Ordaine and Grant unto the said Society for the Propagation of the Gospell in Forreigne Parts, and their Successors, That they, and their Successors, or the major Part of them who shall be present at the first and second Meeting of the said Society, or at any Meeting on the Third Friday in the Months of November, February, May, and August, yearely for ever, and at noe other Meetings of the said Society, shall and may Consult, Determine, Constitute, Ordaine, and Make any Constitutions, Lawes, Ordinances and Statutes whatsoever; as alsoe to execute Leases for Yeares, as aforesaid, which to them, or the major Part of them then present shall seem reasonable, profitable, or requisite, for, touching or concerning the Good Estate, Rule, Order and Government of the said Corporation, and the more effectuall promoteing the said Charitable Designes: All which Lawes, Ordinances, and Constitucons, soe to be made ordained and established, as aforesaid, Wee Will, Command, and Ordaine, by these Presents, for Us, Our Heires, and Successors, to be from Time to Time and at all Times hereafter kept and performed in all Things as the same ought to be, on the Penalties and

Amercements in the same to be imposed and limited, soe as the same Lawes, Constitucons, Ordinances, Penalties, and Amercements, be reasonable, and not repugnant or contrary to the Laws and Statutes of this Our Realme of England

And Wee doe likewise Grant unto the said Society for Propagation of the Gospell in Forreigne Parts and their Successors, that they and their Successors, or the major Part of such of them as shall be present at any Meeting of the said Society, shall have Power from Time to Time, and at all Times hereafter, to depute such Persons as they shall think fitt to take Subscriptions, and to gather and collect such Moneys as shall be by any Person or Persons contributed for the Purpose aforesaid

And shall and may remove and displace such Deputyes as often as they shall see Cause soe to doe, and to cause publick Notification to be made of this Charter, and the Powers hereby granted, in such Manner as they shall think most conduceable to the Furtherance of the said Charity

And Our further Will and Pleasure is, That the said Society shall Yearely and every Yeare give an account in Writing to Our Lord Chancellor, or Lord Keeper of the Great Seale of England for the Time being, the Lord Cheife Justice of the King's Bench, and the Lord Cheife Justice of the Common Pleas, or any two of them, of the severall Summe or Summes of Money by them received and laid out by vertue of these Presents or any Authority hereby given, and of the Management and Disposicon of the Revenues and Charityes aforesaid

And lastly Our Pleasure is, That these Our Letters Patents, or the Inrollment thereof, shall be good, firme, valid, and effectuall in the Law, according to Our Royall Intentions herein before declared In Witnes whereof, Wee have caused these Our Letters to be made Patents Witnes Ourselfe at Westminster the Sixteenth Day of June, in the Thirteenth Yeare of our Reigne.

Per Breve de Privato Sigillo,

Cocks

—Pascoe, *op. cit.*, II, 932-35. The charter may also be found in Hawkins, *op. cit.*, 415-21.

2. INSTRUCTIONS FOR THE CLERGY EMPLOYED BY THE SOCIETY, 1706

Upon their Admission by the Society.

I. That, from the Time of their Admission, they lodge not in any Publick House; but at some Bookseller's, or in other private and reputable Families, till they shall be otherwise accommodated by the Society.

II. That till they can have a convenient Passage, they employ their Time usefully; in Reading Prayers, and Preaching, as they have Opportunity; in hearing others Read and Preach; or in such Studies as may tend to fit them for their Employment.

III. That they constantly attend the Standing Committee of this Society, at the Secretary's, and observe their Directions.

IV. That before their Departure they wait upon his Grace the Lord Archbishop of *Canterbury*, their Metropolitan, and upon the Lord Bishop of *London*, their Diocesan, to receive their Paternal Benediction and Instructions.

Upon their going on Board the Ship designed for their Passage.

I. That they demean themselves not only inoffensively and prudently, but so as to become remarkable Examples of Piety and Virtue to the Ship's Company.

II. That whether they be Chaplains in the Ship's, or only Passengers, they endeavor to prevail with the Captain or Commander, to have Morning and Evening Prayer said daily; as also Preaching and Catechizing every Lord's Day.

III. That throughout their Passage they Instruct, Exhort, Admonish, and Reprove, as they have occasion and opportunity, with such Seriousness and Prudence, as may gain them Reputation and Authority.

Upon their Arrival in the Country whither they shall be sent.
First, *With Respect to themselves.*

I. That they always keep in their View the great Design of their Undertaking, *viz.* To promote the Glory of Almighty God, and the Salvation of Men, by Propagating the Gospel of our Lord and Saviour.

II. That they often consider the Qualifications requisite for those who would effectually promote this Design, *viz.* A sound Knowledge and hearty Belief of the Christian Religion; an Apostolical Zeal, tempered with Prudence, Humility, Meekness and Patience; a fervent Charity towards the Souls of Men; and finally, that Temperance, Fortitude, and Constancy, which become good Soldiers of Jesus Christ.

III. That in order to the obtaining and preserving the said Qualifications, they do very frequently in their Retirements offer up fervent Prayers to Almighty God for his Direction and Assistance; converse much with the Holy Scriptures; seriously reflect upon their Ordination Vows; and consider the Account which they are to render to the Great Shepherd and Bishop of our Souls at the last Day.

IV. That they acquaint themselves thoroughly with the Doctrine of the Church of *England*, as contained in the Articles and Homilies; its Worship and Discipline, and Rules for Behaviour of the Clergy, as contained in the Liturgy and Canons; and that they approve themselves accordingly, as genuine Missionaries from this Church.

V. That they endeavour to make themselves Masters in those Controversies which are necessary to be understood, in order to the Preserving their Flock from the Attempts of such Gainsayers as are mixed among them.

VI. That in their outward Behaviour they be circumspect and unblameable, giving no Offence either in Word or Deed; that their ordinary Discourse be grave and edifying; their Apparel decent, and proper for Clergymen; and that in their whole Conversation they be Instances and Patterns of the Christian Life.

VII. That they do not board in, or frequent Publick-houses, or lodge in Families of evil Fame; that they wholly abstain from Gaming, and all such Pastimes; and converse not familiarly with lewd or prophane Persons, otherwise than to order to reprove, admonish, and reclaim them.

VIII. That in whatsoever Family they shall lodge, they persuade them to join with them in daily Prayer Morning and Evening.

IX. That they be not nice about Meats and Drinks, nor immoderately careful about their Entertainment in the Places where they shall sojourn; but contented with what Health requires, and the Place easily affords.

X. That as they be frugal, in Opposition to Luxury, so they avoid all Appearance of Covetousness, and recommend themselves, according to their Abilities, by the prudent Exercise of Liberality and Charity.

XI. That they take special Care to give no Offence to the Civil

Government, by intermeddling in Affairs not relating to their own Calling and Function.

XII. That, avoiding all Names of Distinction, they endeavour to preserve a Christian Agreement and Union one with another, as a Body of Brethren of one and the same Church, united under the Superior Episcopal Order, and all engaged in the same great Design of Propagating the Gospel; and to this End, keeping up a Brotherly Correspondence, by meeting together at certain Times, as shall be most convenient, for mutual Advice and Assistance.

Secondly, *With respect to their Parochial Cure.*

I. That they conscientiously observe the Rules of our Liturgy, in the Performance of all the Offices of their Ministry.

II. That, besides the stated Service appointed for Sundays and Holidays, they do, as far as they shall find it practicable, publickly read the daily Morning and Evening Service, and decline no fair Opportunity of Preaching to such as may be occasionally met together from remote and distant Parts.

III. That they perform every Part of Divine Service with that Seriousness and Decency, that may recommend their Ministrations to their Flock, and excite a Spirt of Devotion in them.

IV. That the chief Subjects of their Sermons be the great Fundamental Principles of Christianity, and the Duties of a sober, righteous, and godly Life, as resultng from those Principles.

V. That they particularly preach against those Vices which they shall observe to be most predominant in the Places of their Residence.

VI. That they carefully instruct the People concerning the Nature and Use of the Sacraments of Baptism and the Lord's Supper, as the peculiar Institutions of Christ, Pledges of Communion with Him, and Means of deriving Grace from Him.

VII. That they duly consider the Qualifications of those adult Persons to whom they administer Baptism; and of those likewise whom they admit to the Lord's Supper; according to the Directions of the Rubricks in our Liturgy.

VIII. That they take special Care to lay a good Foundation for all their other Ministrations, by Catechizing those under their Care, whether Children, or other ignorant Persons, explaining the Catechism to them in the most easy and familiar Manner.

IX. That in their instructing *Heathens* and *Infidels*, they begin with the Principles of Natural Religion, appealing to their Reason and

Conscience; and thence proceed to shew them the Necessity of Revelation, and the Certainty of that contained in the Holy Scriptures, by the plainest and most obvious Arguments.

X. That they frequently visit their respective Parishioners; those of our own Communion, to keep them steady in the Profession and Practice of Religion, as taught in the Church of *England*; those that oppose us, or dissent from us, to convince and reclaim them with a Spirit of Meekness and Gentleness.

XI. That those, whose Parishes shall be of large Extent, shall, as they have Opportunity and Convenience, officiate in the several Parts thereof, so that all the Inhabitants may by Turns partake of their Ministrations; and that such as shall be appointed to officiate in several Places shall reside sometimes at one, sometimes at another of those Places, as the Necessities of the People shall require.

XII. That they shall, to the best of their Judgments, distribute those small Tracts given by the Society for that Purpose, amongst such of their Parishioners as shall want them most, and appear likely to make the best Use of them; and that such useful Books, of which they have not a sufficient Number to give, they be ready to lend to those who will be most careful in reading and restoring them.

XIII. That they encourage the setting up of Schools for the teaching of Children; and particularly by the Widows of such Clergymen as shall die in those Countries, if they be found capable of that Employment.

XIV. That each of them keep a Register of his Parishioners' Names, Profession of Religion, Baptism, &c. according to the Scheme annexed, No. I. for his own Satisfaction, and the Benefit of the People.

Thirdly, *With respect to the Society*.

I. That each of them keep a constant and regular Correspondence with the Society, by their Secretary.

II. That they send every six Months an Account of the State of their respective Parishes, according to the Scheme annexed, No. II.

III. That they communicate what shall be done at the Meetings of the Clergy, when settled, and whatsoever else may concern the Society.

Notitia Parochialis; to be made by each Minister soon after his Acquaintance with his People, and kept by him for his own Ease and Comfort, as well as the Benefit of his Parishioners.

I. Names of Parish- ioners	II. Profession of Religion	III. Which of them baptized	IV. When baptized	V. Which of them Com- municants	VI. When they first com- municated	VII. What Obstructions they meet with in their Ministration

N⁰ II.

Notitia Parochialis; or an Account to be sent Home every six Months to the Society by each Minister, concerning the spiritual State of their respective Parishes.

I. *Number of Inhabitants.*

II. *No. of the Baptized.*

III. *No. of Adult Persons baptized this Half-year.*

IV. *No. of actual Communicants of the* Church of England.

V. *No. of those who profess themselves of the* Church of England.

VI. *No. of Dissenters of all Sorts, particularly Papists.*

VII. *No. of Heathens and Infidels.*

VIII. *No. of Converts from a prophane, disorderly and un-christian Course, to a Life of Christian Purity, Meekness, and Charity.*

—Pascoe, *op. cit.,* II, 837-40.

3. INSTRUCTIONS FOR SCHOOLMASTERS EMPLOYED BY THE SOCIETY, 1706

I. That they well consider the End for which they are employed by the Society, *viz.* The instructing and disposing Children to believe and live as Christians.

II. In order to this End, that they teach them to read truly and distinctly, that they may be capable of reading the Holy Scriptures, and other pious and useful Books, for informing their Understandings, and regulating their Manners.

III. That they instruct them thoroughly in the Church-Catechism; teach them first to read it distinctly and exactly, then to learn it perfectly by Heart; endeavouring to make them understand the Sense and Meaning of it, by the help of such Expositions as the Society shall send over.

IV. That they teach them to write a plain and legible Hand, in order to the fitting them for useful Employment; with as much Arithmetick as shall be necessary to the same Purpose.

V. That they be industrious, and give constant Attendance at proper School-Hours.

VI. That they daily use, Morning and Evening, the Prayers composed for their Use in this Collection, with their Scholars in the School, and teach them the Prayers and Graces composed for their Use at Home.

VII. That they oblige their Scholars to be constant at Church on the Lord's Day, Morning and Afternoon, and at all other Times of Publick Worship; that they cause them to carry their Bibles and Prayer Books with them, instructing them how to use them there, and how to demean themselves in the several Parts of Worship; that they be there present with them, taking Care of their reverent and decent Behaviour, and examine them afterwards, as to what they have heard and learned.

VIII. That when any of their Scholars are fit for it, they recommend them to the Minister of the Parish, to be publickly Catechized in the Church.

IX. That they take especial Care of their Manners, both in their Schools and out of them; warning them seriously of those Vices to which Children are most liable; teaching them to abhor Lying and Falsehood, and to avoid all sorts of Evil-speaking; to love Truth and Honesty; to be modest, gentle, well-behaved, just and affable, and courteous to all their Companions; respectful to their Superiors, particularly towards all that minister in holy Things, and especially to the Minister of their Parish; and all this from a Sense and Fear of Almighty God; endeavouring to bring them in their tender Years to that Sense of Religion, which may render it the constant Principle of their Lives and Actions.

X. That they use all kind and gentle Methods in the Government of their Scholars, that they may be loved as well as feared by them; and that when Correction is necessary, they make the Children to understand, that it is given them out of kindness, for their Good, bringing them to a Sense of their Fault, as well as of their Punishment.

XI. That they frequently consult with the Minister of the Parish, in which they dwell, about the Methods of managing their Schools, and be ready to be advised by him.

XII. That they do in their whole Conversation shew themselves Examples of Piety and Virtue to their Scholars, and to all with whom they shall converse.

XIII. That they be ready, as they have Opportunity, to teach and instruct the *Indians* and *Negroes* and their Children.

XIV. That they send to the Secretary of the Society, once in every six Months, an Account of the State of their respective Schools, the Number of their Scholars, with the Methods and Success of their Teaching.

[The following form appears in the "Standing Orders" of the later edition]:

Notitia Scholastica; *or an Account to be sent every Six Months to the* Society *by each* Schoolmaster, *concerning the State of their respective Schools.*

1. Attendance daily given.	
2. Number of Children taught in the School.	
3. Number of Children baptized in the Church of *England*.	
4. Number of *Indian* and Negroe Children.	
5. Number of Children born of Dissenting Parents.	
6. Other Schools in or near the Place.	
7. Of what Denomination.	
8. Other Employments of the Scholmaster.	

—Ibid., pp. 844-45.

4. QUALIFICATIONS OF THE SOCIETY'S SCHOOLMASTERS, 1711/12

8th Febry 1711/12

The Secretary reported from the Com^ee that they had, according to order, Consider'd of Rules & orders for the qualification & Conduct of Schoolmasters, and having Inspected the Society's Collection of Papers, had adapted these following for that purpose, wch they agreed to lay before the Society vizt.

1 That no person be admitted as Schoolmaster till he bring Certificates of the following particulars

    1 his age
    2 his condition of life whether Single or mary'd
    3 his temper
    4 his prudence
    5 his Learning
    6 his Sober & pious Conversation
    7 his Zeal for the Xtian Religion & diligence in his calling
    8 his affection to the present government
    9 his conformity to the doctrine & discipline of the Church of England

2 That no person Shall be employ'd as a Schoolmaster by the Society till he has been tryed and approved by three members appointed by the Society or Committee who Shall testify by word or writing his ability to teach reading, writing and the Catechism of the Church of England and Such exposition thereof as the Society Shall order.

3 That they obServe the Instructions given to the School masters by the Society, Set down page 33.34.35. of the Said *Collection of papers.*

4 That no Testimonyal Shall be allowed of, but Such as are Signed by the respective minister of the parish; and where that is not practicable, by Some other persons of Credit and note, three at least of the Communion of the Church of England, whereof one Shall be a Clergyman, and Such as Shall be well known to some of the members of the Society.

5 That all Schoolmasters, in matters which they desire Shou'd be Laid before ye Society do Correspond only with the Secretary of this Society.

6 That if any Schoolmaster, in the Service of the Society, Shall return from the Plantations, without leave first had from the Society,

Such School master Shall receive no farther allowance from the time he Shall leave his Service there.

7 That all School masters sent over to the plantations by the Society, being Marryed men, be obliged to take their wives with them, unless they can offer such reasons as Shall induce ye Society to dispense there with.

8 That the Salary of every Schoolmaster who is not dismis'd the Service for Some misdemeanour Shall continue one year, and no longer, after the Society have resolved at their bord to dismiss Such Persons from their Service.

The above Report of the Committee being Read and consider'd was Agreed to be laid before the Society anniversary meeting in order to be confirm'd at that time if it Shall be thou't fit.

15 Febry 1711/12.

The Report of the Comee for Rules and Orders for the qualifications and conduct of Schoolmasters being consider'd, ye Same was read and approv'd wth these Alterations vizt in the second Rule That no Schoolmaster be Sent instead of Employ'd—In the 4th to ye word (Parish) be added the words Where he last liv'd. In the 5th before the Word Secretary be inserted (President or)

Order'd that there be added to ye said Orders, That no Schoolmaster be sent in ye Societys Service till he be espiscopally Ordain'd Deacon, and that he have a Sallary not under Thirty pounds p ann..

Agreed that the Rules, and Orders aforemention'd relating to Schoolmaster be made Standing Orders and that ye Title of the Instructions be Instructions for Schoolmasters Sent by ye Society &c. —Gertrude Foster (comp.), Documentary History of Education in South Carolina (Typescript doctoral dissertation, University of South Carolina, 1932), VI, 16-19.

Activities of the Society in North Carolina

5. GOVERNOR HARVEY NOTIFIED OF APPOINTMENT OF THOMAS BRAY, DECEMBER 20, 1699

Gentlemen

The Reverend Doctor Bray a learned pious & Charitable man, coming into America Suffragan & Comissary to ye Bishop of London yor Diocesan & designing to give you a vist Wee thought fit to let you know it & desire you to treat him with all kindness & respect &

place ye charge to ye publique acco Among other good offices he will be able to mediate, in any difference that may be betweene Virginia & us concerning wch & your other affayrs you are like suddenly to heare from us at large

We are

Gentlemen

Your very affectionate

friends

BATHE Palatine

CRAVEN

BATHE for LORD CARTERET

M ASHLEY.

Wm THORBURGH for Sr

JOHN COLLETON

THO AMY

Wm THORNBURGH

To Tho: Harvey Esqr

Deputy Governour &

to our Deputys & Coun-

cell of North Carolina.

—William L. Saunders (ed.), *The Colonial Records of North Carolina*. I, 520.

6. HENDERSON WALKER WRITES TO THE BISHOP OF LONDON, OCTOBER 21, 1703

North Carolina, 21st *October*, 1703.

MAY IT PLEASE YOUR LORDSHIP:—

The great and pious designs of your lordship towards these American parts, for the propagation of the Christian Church, of which you are so pious and good a pillar, emboldens me to lay before your lordship the present state of North Carolina, as to their Christian well-being; and I was the more encouraged to do it by reason that our lords proprietors were pleased to write to us concerning Mr. Bray, your lordship's commissary, coming to visit us.

My lord, we have been settled near this fifty years in this place, and I may justly say most part of twenty-one years, on my own knowledge, without priest or altar, and before that time, according to all that appears to me, much worse. George Fox, some years ago, came into these parts, and, by strange infatuations, did infuse the Quakers' principles into some small number of the people; which did and hath continued to grow ever since very numerous, by reason of their yearly sending in men to encourage and exhort them to their wicked principles; and here was none to dispute nor to oppose them in carrying on their pernicious principles for many years, till God, of his infinite goodness, was pleased to inspire the Rev. Dr. Bray, some time about four years ago, to send in some books of his own particular pious gift, of the explanation of the Church catechism, with some other small books, to be disposed of and lent as we thought fit, did, in some measure, put a stop to their growth; and about a year after, did send to us a library of books for the benefit of this place, given by the honorable the Corporation for the Establishing the Christian Religion, by one Mr. Daniel Brett, a minister appointed for this place. He for about half a year behaved himself in a modest manner, but after that, in a most horrid manner, broke out in such an extravagant course that I am ashamed to express his carriage, it being in so high a nature. It hath been a great trouble and grief to us who have a great veneration for the Church, that the first minister who was sent to us should prove so ill as to give the dissenters so much occasion to charge us with him. My lord, I humbly beg you to believe that we do not think that the Rev. Dr. Bray knew anything of the life and conversation of the man. We did, about this time two years, with a great deal of care and management, get an Assembly, and we passed an act for building of churches and establishing a maintenance for a minister amongst us; and in pursuance thereto we have built one church, and there are two more a going forward; and his excellency, Francis Nicholson, Esq., governor of Virginia, was pleased, of his pious goodness, to give us £10 to each church, and we sent copies of that act of Assembly to our lords proprietors to get the same ratified, and likewise a copy to Dr. Bray, to entreat his favor with them to obtain a ratification, which we are in hopes to obtain this shipping; but they not being come, we are in a great loss. My lord, I humbly beg leave to inform you, that we have an Assembly to sit the 3d November next, and there is above one half of the burgesses that are chosen are Quakers, and have declared their designs of making void the act for establishing the Church; if your lordship, out of your good and pious care for us, doth not put a stop to their growth, we shall the most part, especially the children born here, become heathens. I humbly entreat your lordship to send some worthy, good man amongst us to regain the flock, and so perfect us in our duty to God, and establish us by his doctrine, life, and conversation in the fundamentals of our

Christian profession, that we in our time, and those as come hereafter, may bless God that he has raised up so noble a pillar as your lordship to regain those who are going astray, and put a stop to the pernicious, growing principles of the Quakers.

Your lordship may see the copy of our act by Dr. Bray, and I humbly beg your lordship's pardon for giving you this trouble, and take leave to subscribe myself, my lord,

Your most humble and obedient servant,

HENDERSON WALKER.

—Ibid., 571-73.

7. JAMES ADAMS COMPLAINS ABOUT THE BEHAVIOR OF MR. GRIFFIN, SCHOOLMASTER, OCTOBER 4, 1709

Sir:-- . . .

. . . I wrote to you formerly of one Mr. Griffin, who had behaved himself very remarkably in the office of a reader and schoolmaster: he has fallen into the sin of fornication, and joined with the Quakers' interest, which has proved great stumbling-block to many of our persuasion.*—Ibid.*, p. 721.

8. WILLIAM GORDON REPORTS ON RELIGIOUS AND EDUCATIONAL IN-TERESTS IN PASQUOTANK AND CRAVEN PRECINCTS, MAY 13, 1709

. . . This precinct was one of the two I attended, and being very large, and divided by the Great Sound and several rivers and branches, was very troublesome; however, I was in all the parts of it, baptized almost a hundred children, distributed those small tracts which were sent over, settled a schoolmaster, and gave some books for the use of scholars, which the church-wardens were to see left for that use, in case the master should remove . . .

. . . The next precinct is Pasquetank, where as yet there is no church built; the Quakers are here very numerous; the roads are, I think, the worst in the country; but it is closer seated than the others, and better peopled in proportion to its bigness. In their way of living they have much the advantage of the rest, being more industrious, careful and cleanly; but above all I was surprised to see with what order, decency, and seriousness they performed the public worship, considering how ignorant people are in the other parishes. This they owe to the care of one Mr. Griffin, who came here from some part of the West Indies, and has for three years past lived amongst them, being appointed reader by their vestry, whose diligent and devout example has im-

proved them so far beyond their neighbors and by his discreet behavior has gained such a good character and esteem, that the Quakers
themselves send their children to his school, though he had prayers
twice a day at least, and obliged them to their responses, and all the
decencies of behavior as well as others. After Mr. Adams was settled
here I found it improper for Mr. Griffin to stay, and therefore, notwithstanding the large offers they made him if he would continue, he
consented to fix in Chowan, where I left him, having procured for
him a small allowance from the vestry; but I am afraid the hardship
he will meet with in that part of the country will discourage him, if
not force him from thence, though he promised me to hold out as
long as he could. . . . —*Ibid.*, pp. 712, 714.

9. GILES RAINSFORD WRITES ABOUT INDIANS' SCHOOLING AND MASH-
BURN'S SCHOOL AT SARUM, JULY 25, 1712

. . . I had several conferences with one Thomas Hoyle King of
the Chowan Indians who seem very inclinable to embrace Christianity and proposes to send his son to school in Sarum to have him taught
to read and write by way of foundation in order to a further proficiency for the reception of Christianity I readily offered my service to
instruct him myself and having the opportunity of sending him to Mr
Garratts where I lodge being but three miles distance from his Town.
But he modestly declined it for the present till a general peace was
concluded between the Indians and Christians I found he had some
notions of Noahs flood which he came to the knowledge of and
exprest himselfe after this manner—My father told me I tell my Son
But I hope in a little time to give the Society a better account of him
as well as of those peaceable Indians under his Command Theres one
Mr Mashburn who keeps a school at Sarum on the frontiers of Virginia between the two Governments and neighbouring upon 2 Indian
Towns who I find by him highly deserve encouragement and could
heartily wish the Society would take it into consideration and be
pleased to allow him a Salary for the good services he has done and
may do for the future. What children he has under his care can both
write and read very distinctly and gave before me such an account of
the grounds and principles of the Christian religion that strangely surprised me to hear it. The man upon a small income would teach the
Indian Children gratis (whose parents are willing to send them could
they but pay for their schooling) as he would those of our English
families had he but a fixed dependency for so doing and what ad-

vantage would this be to private families in particular and whole Colony in general is easy to determine . . . —*Ibid.*, p. 859.

10. MISSIONARY URMSTONE COMPLAINS ABOUT CONDITIONS,
OCTOBER 22, 1712

I acquainted the Honorable Society with the death of my fellow Labourer the Revd Mr Adams late Missionary in this province per the first opportunity after the same and withall that being disappointed of that Library brought in by Mr Gordon, and for which I stand bound, I demanded that which belonged to Mr Adams, which upon inquiry I found safe and entire but was refused it. The precinct where the deceased last dwelt, pretending the Books belonged to them and would not part with them except I would live with them. I am told Mr Rainsford had the like answer. Thus Society is abused and their Missionaries in this as well as other cases ill treated by an ungrateful worthless people. I hope you will either cancel my obligation or send me other books instead of those lost by Mr Gordon I aver and testify that those . . . . Mr Adams were brought in were at the time of his death safe and entire as above and therefore see no reason his heirs should suffer but what is since become of them perhaps neither you nor I shall ever know. I've more than once complained of the injust usage I have met with in reference to a very valuable collection of choice books detained at Bath, nowe the seat of war many of which are spoilt and the rest will infallibly, be destroyed by the Heathen, at least the Ministry will never be much better for them for whose use they were chiefly intended. That place will never be the seat of Government nor supplied by an Incumbent a remote obscure dangerous place of it felt incapable of subsisting a Minister and inconsistent with any other part of the Colony. I have not been favoured with a line since I arrived here from the Society. I hope I shall be so happy within a short time and that my requests per Col. Quarry will be granted, otherwise you must expect to hear I am Bankrupt & forced to run for it, since Col^l Hides death the Quakers and their adherents threaten to act over again the late Tragedy in Order to settle and establish themselves overthrowe the Church & in the end finish the ruin of this poor country if the Indians do it not for them but these Meeting with little or no opposition cannot fail of destroying us all; We are in expectation of succour from Ashley River but that is very uncertain. Our cowardice and Quaking principles render us the scorn & contempt of all our neighbours. We are to have an assembly on the 4th of next month I hear few but quakers and their party are chosen Burgesses so that we may expect but little good, they give out already they'l have new Lords and new Laws or rather no Laws that will best please the generality of our Gentry —*Ibid.*, pp. 884-85.

11. GILES RAINSFORD REPORTS ON CATECHISING CHILDREN AND BAP-
    TISING SIX NEGROES, FEBRUARY 17, 1712/13

... On the account of my late indisposition I have been able only to Catechise children and baptize six Negroes with the advantage of what Good I might do thro' God's blessing by preaching and conference ... I have nothing more to add but that I am with all truly Christian gratitude for favors already done me—*Ibid.*, II, 18.

12. URMSTONE WRITES TO GENERAL NICHOLSON, 1714

As soon as possible after I was favoured with one from the Society inclosed in your honor's I sent to the several Vestries within this wretched Government in number seven and exhorted them to lay hold of this opportunity of obtaining Missionaries and School masters which are much wanted—I know not how quick they may be in complying with your commands if know them I am not apt to believe they'l not be over forward, such slow bellys to all that concerns souls health: most here had rather be without them. I am sure they are not worthy of any and were their usage of me known I am persuaded none would be so mad as ever to come among them they'l neither pay Minister nor Schoolmaster nay they had need to be hired to go to church or send their children to school I and all my predecessors have been laden with calumnies reproach and scandalous falsehoods instead of wealth nay having had the hard fortune of staying against my will longer with them than any of my function ever did— I find them more prone to take from us by fraud and extortion what we bring with us and seem unwilling we should live though at our cost by them— ...

I cannot see how it will ever be possible to settle a Ministry here the people live so scattered and remote the Parishes so large that they cannot be supplied without much labour and charge—I have been open exposed to great danger and a great expense and at last bought a couple of Negroes and a canoe in order to serve my cure and forced to hire a white hand to teach them as well as make them work, weary of that charge I resolved to buy me an English Servant was cheated with one by Thomas Jones who out of pure kindness spared me one whom his brother had tried for 8 months and not being able to manage him let me have him for £14 Sterling he could not have found such another villain in all America he first robbed me and at 3 weeks end ran away—I sent after him but cannot hear of him—This is the 4th white servant I've lost since I left England I was most abominably cheated with a Negro who died within ten days after I bought him—I've been very unfortunate in cows and horses my Salary spent in Bills the worst way of improving it; My attorney abuses me has suffered two Bills to come back protested and I fear will serve other two which I since drew upon him in like manner, so that I shall be very miserable, nothing coming in from the Country nor credit— ...

I acquainted your honor in a former if I mistake not that the Library my Predecessor Mr Gordon should have brought in was left with Mr Wallace of Virginia he is dead and I fear the Books will be lost—I have desired an order more than once from the Society or Mr Gordon to demand them but have no answer from that or a thousand other things very material relating to my Mission; surely paper and ink must be dear in England The Vestry of Coratuck where Mr Adams late Missionary died detain his Books on pretence they were at some charge in fetching them out of Virginia and will appropriate them to that Parish where no Minister will scarce ever reside. The famous Library sent in by Dr. Brays directions is in a great measure destroyed I am told the books are all unbound and have served for some time for waste paper ... —*Ibid.*, 125-28.

13. CHARLES EDEN WRITES TO THE SOCIETY, MAY 10, 1716

...I take the liberty to enclose with this an Abstract of an Act of Assembly made here the last Winter which I beg Sir you will lay before the Society. It may serve to give those Gentlemen a specimen of the inclinations of these poor people Tennts to my Masters the Lords proprietors wch are not so black as they have been painted, but on the Contrary are as willing as any of his Majesty's Subjects on the Continent to contribute to the utmost to the subsisting of Ministers that are Gentlemen of good lives and affable behaviour & conversation. Though hitherto it has been their misfortune to be in a manner void of such necessary instructors, I dare not presume to ask any favor of the Gentlemen of the Society. They being the only Judges how, for they can extend their nursing care to a poor uninstructed people. But if we cannot be so happy as to procure ministers for each four parishes would they but please to send us schoolmasters qualified, as mentioned in their most excellent rules.. I verily believe the Inhabitants would willingly pay them the greatest part of their Salaries established by the Act for reading the Service and Catechising the Children reserving the overplus to any of your Missionaries who should visit them twice or thrice in the year.

In most of the parishes they have already established two or three readers who are the most capable persons we can get here. To some of which they allow pr. Ann thirty pounds. To others twenty pounds and to none less than Ten pounds . . . —*Ibid.*, pp. 227-29.

14. GILES RAINSFORD ON NEED FOR MISSIONARIES AND SCHOOLMASTERS IN NORTH CAROLINA, AUGUST 17, 1716

. . . That poor Colony will soon be overrun with Quakerism and infidelity if not timely prevented by your sending over able and sober Missionaries as well as Schoolmasters to reside among them.. These two years past every third Sunday I constantly preached in Albemarle County in North Carolina and have engaged others from going to Quakerism as can be attested by the Inhabitants: While I was in the Society's employ I served 'em faithfully and to the uttermost of my power . . . —*Ibid.*, p. 245.

15. MR. TAYLOR TO THE SOCIETY ON TEACHING THE CATECHISM TO SLAVES, APRIL 23, 1719

. . . In this year I caused a pretty many of the children to learn our catechism, and catechis'd them, in public, in this year I Baptized one Adult White Young Woman, and Thirty White Children, and one Adult Negro Young Woman, and one Mustee Young Woman and three Mustee Young Children, in all 36. I hope I took a method with the Negro Young Man, and with the Mustee Young Woman, whom I baptized, which will please the Society, which was this, I made them get our Church Catechism perfectly without Book, and then I took some pains with them to make them understand it, and especially the Baptismal Covenant, and to persuade them, faithfully and constantly to perform the great things they were to promise at their Baptism, and ever after to perform to God: and then I caused them to say the catechise, one Lords Day, and the other another Lord's Day before a large congregation, without Book which they did both distinctly, and so perfectly, that all that heard them admired their saying it so well, and with great satisfaction to myself, I baptized these two persons.........................,I had for some time great hopes of being the Minister that should convert and Baptize the rest of the Esq.r Duckenfield Slaves, which I was very desirous and ambitious to be, and I would have begrudged no pains, but would most freely and with the greatest pleasure have done all I could to promote and accomplish this so great, and so good work. And in order thereunto I was preparing 4 more of them for Baptism, and had taught one of those 4 their Catechism very perfectly, and the other 3 a good part of it, and now as I was about this good work, the enemies to the conversion and baptism of slaves, industriously and very busily buzzed into the Peoples Ears, that all slaves that were baptized were to be set free, and this silly Buckbear so greatly scared Esqu.r Duckenfield that he told me plainly I should Baptize no more of his slaves 'till the Society had got a Law made in England that no Baptized Slave, should be set free because he is Baptized and send it here, and many more are of the same mind, and so this good work was knocked in the head which is a great trouble to me, because so many slaves are so very desirous to become Christians without any expectation of being set free when they are Baptized—I fear this good work will not be revived and prosper here till such a Law is enacted by the Parliament of Great Britain and this people are acquainted with it, for I perceive nothing else will satisfy them; This and some other rubs I met with, and the great need of a Church of England Minister, which the interest of the Church of England stood in here, where there are many Quakers, who make it their business to gain as many of our Friends over to them as they can; wherein they have been too successful and leavened some of our people with their Principles and practices too much and especially with anti-Baptism, and many of their children and of themselves too are unbaptized, and used commonly to go to the Quakers Meeting because there was no Public Place of Worship for them to go. These things were the chief Reasons of my leaving the Southwest Shore of Chowan and coming here where I hope I shall increase the Interest of the Church of England and cause the Interest of the Quakers to decrease and then I persuade myself that the most excellent Society will not be offended at my removing here—*Ibid.*, pp. 331-33.

16. MISSIONARY URMSTONE COMPLAINS ABOUT BEING "BURIED ALIVE IN THIS HELL OF A HOLE," FEBRUARY 5, 1720/21

Since my last of Xber 22nd nothing of any moment occurs save that I am still detained here against my will in this wretched country in hopes of getting my money but greatly suspect I shall be disappointed I was to have had f120 the first of last month and got but f54 and the f122 due six years ago is not yet raised notwithstanding an act of Assembly which I obtained with great struggling last August for the payment of it on or before 25th Novr last nor do I believe I shall ever have it. I will wait till May and if there be no more likelihood than I see at present I think to come home—I did hope to have something to come home to but am forced to draw Bills for everything I want I was not very happy in my late wife's days upon divers accounts but I am now quite weary of my life and worse put to it than ever to subsist what I've received from the parish is all gone towards paying for a Negro within ten days after I bought him and a white man who ran a way with in the like time If I had not received the money I verily believe I never should have received a penny from the parish. I endured 4 or 5 arrests to make me give Bills of Exchange but being restive my creditors were obliged to take parish pay with the advance of f150 per Ct in lieu of Stg money.

I desired in my last as I now do that if any one came to the Society or Treasurer that called himself my Son that no notice should be taken of him I have been forced to turn him adrift for his undutifulness in combining with my Servants to ruin me he got a servant wench with child who had 2 years to serve rendered her not only useless but even a burden to me yet am forced to keep her not knowing where to get a better being in great want of provisions I sent a Bill of Exchange for f20 to Coll. Heathcoat at New York but after divers since the date thereof which was July 15th 1719 I cannot hear from him I pray you or the Treasurer to acquaint him whether it was ever tendered or paid I hear he is poor which makes me fear my money is lost we are informed our late good for nothing proprietors have sold their interests in these parts to 3 Quakers if so the Church is like to flourish others say we are under the Crown—I can not hear from England I am buried alive in this hell of a hole....—*Ibid.*, pp. 416-17.

17. CLEMENT HALL TO THE SOCIETY, DECEMBER 27, 1749

In Septr & Octr past I journied thro' the north part of my Mission, rode about 200 miles—preached 14 sermons, Bapd 265 white & 20 Black children & 4 Black adults The congregations were very numerous & behaved exceedingly well; tho' the continued travel & duty went very hard with me by reason of my Indisposition having had bad health of long time.

The state of our church is as before, but Mr. Corben Earl Granville's agent, says that he will do his true endeavours to have it finished and there is another chapel now Building in the Parish, which will make 4 places of Publick Worship in the compass of 60 or 70 miles, I have baptized 3945 white & 139 Black children; 45 white & 92 Black adults: in all 4221 persons.—*Ibid.*, p. 925.

18. DANIEL EARL WRITES ABOUT LACK OF SCHOOLS, 1760

Since my letter to you of April 25. I have received the Box sent me by the Society, containing my instructions and the Books &c to be distributed among the Parishioners which shall be faithfully done; and am steadfastly resolved with the assistance of Gods grace to ev'ry article of my instructions . . .

. . . I shall beg leave to mention to you, the want of schools in this province, and as the depressed and mean circumstances of the inhabitants render them incapable of educating their children, & as the good education of the youth of the country would be a great means of impressing upon their minds the principles of Religion & virtue which the Revd & Honble Society earnestly endeavours to promote in these his Majestys colonys: I hope therefore that this poor & illiterate Province will feel the effect of their benign & pious institution in this, as it has, in many other instances; as I believe there is no other part of this continent, that calls louder for it than this government. If the society would be pleased to grant any assistance for this purpose, I should with the greatest alacrity, exert myself to establish a School in this Parish and should always (as far as my Parochial duties would permit me) superintend the same & inspect into the conduct of the teacher . . . —*Ibid.*, VI, 240-41.

19. ALEXANDER STEWART REPORTS ON BAPTIZING NEGROES AND TEACHING THEM TO READ, 1763

As soon as my health would permit, I set out for the benefit of the sea air, to a part of Hyde County called Atamuskeet (this Place I formerly informed the society) is separated by an impassable morass from the other parts of that county and is only to be come at by water and upwards of 70 miles from Bath, while I was there I preached twice at the Chapel and baptized 64 white children one Adult white, 11 black adults and 11 do. infants, and at the other chapels in Hyde County 42 white infants and 5 black do. the remains of the Attamuskeet, Roanoke and Hatteras Indians, live mostly along that coast, mixed with the white inhabitants, many of these attended at the Places of Public Worship, while I was there & behaved with decency seemed desirous of instruction & offered themselves & their children to me for baptism. & after examining some of the adults I accordingly baptized, 6 adult Indians, 6 Boys, 4 Girls & 5 Infants & for their further instruction (at the expence of a society called Dr. Bray's associates, who have done me the Honor of making me Superintendant of their schools in this Province, have fixed a school mistress among them, to teach 4 Indian & 2 negro boys & 4 Indian girls to read & to work & have supplied them with Books for that purpose & hope that God will open the eyes of the whites everywhere that they may no longer keep the ignorant in distress but assist the charitable design of this Pious society & do their best endeavours to increase the kingdom of our Lord Jesus Christ.—The baptisms in this Parish have been since I wrote last 63 white infants & 2 adult whites., 17 Black infants & 1 adult, number of communicants, inhabitants &c. as much as usual, so that the number baptized by me in all is 236.—I have nothing to add to the society but that I am now living in the 1st Glebe House ever finished in this Province, & tho' I have much impaired my health, by fatigues & duty in so large a district, yet that I go thro' with it cheerfully, as I hope for a more lasting inheritance for myself hereafter & if it please God to spare me, but a little to put everything in order in this Parish that my successor may find a comfortable subsistance —*Ibid.*, pp. 995-96.

20. JAMES REED ON SCHOOLHOUSE AT NEWBERN, JULY 10, 1765

The Schoolhouse is now in building and I am sorry to say that the work goes on but very slowly, as indeed all Public Buildings generally do in Infant Colonies. Men Money and Material are wanting but Money chiefly—For I was obliged to take the subscriptions in Notes of hand payable six months after date and tho' most of the money has been due these six months past yet it comes in very slowly and rigorous methods in such cases would be very imprudent——However I have no reason to despond and will spare no pains to complete the undertaking——Mr Tomlinson continues a useful member of Society amongst us, and attends his school with very great diligence—He is still unprovided with an assistant but expects one daily though a little dubious whether the advantages arising from keeping an — — — — Assistant will be proportionable to the trouble and expense unless he should be so happy as to meet with a person better qualified for such a place than he can reasonably expect according to his Proposal. He has thirty scholars at Twenty shillings proc: by the quarter which acording to the present exchange amounts to sixty pounds sterling per annum, and reaps no other advantages as perquisite whatsoever that I know of—For the people in general are poor and he may think himself extremely happy in being regularly paid according to contract—In this respect he says he has no reason to complain which I am glad to hear for he is the first person I verily believe that ever taught school in Newbern for any considerable time without complaining of bad pay and very loudly, such complaints I have seen nailed up at the Church Door.

I must beg leave further to observe that all sorts of wares and merchandize are excessive dear much dearer I believe in this province, than in any other on this continent which may in some measure be owing to our bad navigation but principally to the want of a proper staple commodity—Board is likewise very high not less than Twenty five pounds sterling per annum in any regular decent family and indeed hardly any such families to be found that will take in Boarders on any terms whatever—Mr. Tomlinson is obliged to lodge in a public house which he says is very disagreeable but as the children belonging to the family are under his Tuition—he meets with some indulgence in his expenses and therefore submits to the inconvenience on account of his Interest—A house of his own in the honourable state of matrimony I presume would be agreeable would his circumstances permit and I know of no other method of living that can be attended with the least satisfaction to a regular and virtuous man in this place.—*Ibid.*, VII, 98-99.

21. Governor Tryon writes to the Society, July 31, 1765

As no British colony on this continent stands in more, or so much need of regular moral clergymen, as this does, I hope the Society will give all possible assistance to contribute to the happy effects of the present orthodox bill; should I be so happy to meet with a favourable regard to my recommendations, I shall on a proper opportunity communicate to the Society the future state and progress of religion in this colony. Chapels are established in every county which is served by a Reader where no clergy can be procured, they have two, three, or four more or less, in each county according to the number of the inhabitants, or extent of the county. If the Society would send for my distribution or the Governor's for the time being as many well-bound bibles and prayer-books for the ministers desks as there are parishes, it would have a better effect than a ship load of small books recommending the duty of a christian. The ignorant would hear their duty delivered out of the former, when they could not instruct themselves in the latter, This incapacity prevails from a want of schools in the province which consideration brings me lastly to solicit the Society's bounty, and encouragement to Mr. Tomlinson, at present seated at Newbern. His memorial I enclose at his request certified by many gentlemen some of whom I am acquainted with, I had a long conversation with Mr Tomlinson and from the sense and decency of his behaviour, and the general good character he maintains, obliges me warmly to solicit the society in his behalf, He is the only person of repute of that profession in the country; He was invited to America by a brother who has a plantation near Newbern. I really think him deserving the favourable attention of the Society and as such I recommend him. I cannot conclude this letter without acquainting the Society the Rev^d Mr Whitefield preached a sermon at Wilmington in March last which would have done him honour had he delivered it at St James's allowing some little alteration of circumstances between a discourse adapted for the Royal Chapel and the Court House at Wilmington. As considerable sums of money have been raised by subscription for furnishing the churches of Wilmington and Brunswick I expect they will both be completed in less than twelve months—*Ibid.*, pp. 103-4.

22. Governor William Tryon to the Society on Mr. Tomlinson, April 30, 1767

. . . Mr Tomlinson entertains a grateful sense of the Society's generosity in granting him an additional salary: He now presides at the head of the only school established in this country by legislative authority, in virtue of an Act passed the last Session of Assembly held at Newbern.—*Ibid.*, p. 458.

23. The Society offers to aid fund to provide schoolmaster for German settlers in Rowan County, July 19, 1771

Copy of the pious countenance of the Honourable Society for the propagation of the gospel in foreign parts.

At a General Meeting of the Society for Propagation of the Gospel in Foreign Parts held in Dean's Yard Westminster on Friday July

19th 1771, A Petition with a Testimonial thereunto annexed by his Excellency Governor Tryon From the German Settlers on Second Creek in Rowan County North Carolina having been laid before the Board

The Society did approve the pious & useful design therein contained, and declared that in case the proposed Subscription shall meet with success and such a sum shall be raised as shall afford a reasonable prospect of establishing a fund adequate to the permanent support of a Minister and Schoolmaster in the said settlement. They will contribute to such fund and give such encouragement thereto as corresponds with their ability and the Nature of their Institution.— *Ibid.*, VIII, 631.

24. JAMES REED ON THE SCHOOL AT NEWBERN, JULY 2, 1771

I am sorry to inform you that our little Academy is not in the most flourishing condition. The scarcity of money and the dearness of Board very much disappointed Mr Tomlinson's expectations, and obliged him to dismiss a very able assistant. He never wants sufficient employment for himself, and has generally upwards of Thirty Scholars, children of the Inhabitants of the Town, But several that live remote, and are desirous of sending their children, cannot get money to defray the expense of Board and Tuition, so that the benefit of the school at present is too local, and confined in a great measure to the Town of Newbern. However, I hope the Legislature will very shortly find out some expedient to remove this obstacle and that the School will become more generally useful.—*Ibid.*, IX, 6.

25. CHARLES E. TAYLOR WRITES FROM ST. GEORGE'S PARISH, NORTHAMPTON COUNTY, ABOUT THE NEED FOR BOOKS, AUGUST 20, 1771

... There is a great want of Books in this parish as there were never any distributed here The Vestry have desired me to write home for three prayer Books and Bibles for three of the churches, one being provided. I told them I would write and enquire if the Society were willing to send them, and if they are not must beg the favor of you to give my respects to Mr Rivington and desire him to send them, as I shall direct, and should desire he were paid for them out of my Salary the Society allow. Respecting the balance of last years Salary I have judged it most expedient to defer drawing for it till this present years Salary becomes due, I shall take the liberty to preadvise you thereof.—*Ibid.*, p. 23.

26. James Reed on the school at Newbern, February 15, 1772

My last was on the 2d of July 1771, since which, there has been great Contention about our little Academy. I should have sent you a more early account of it, cou'd I have done it with any satisfaction; but I found it difficult to find out the whole truth & the real causes of Discontent. The most material Intelligence I have been able to receive, even after the most diligent search, has been only from Mr. Tomlinson himself, Mr. Parrot, Mr. Tomlinson's late assistant, & one dissenting Trustee. The rest of the Trustees whether from a Consciousness of having acted wrong, or some worse motive entirely declined all conversation with me about it.

When Mr. Tomlinson opened his School, he was apprized of the excessive Indulgence of American Parents, and the great difficulty of keeping up a proper discipline; more especially as his school consisted of numbers of both Sexes. He was therefore very cautious, and used every little artifice to avoid severity as much as possible. But when the children grew excessive headstrong, stubborn and unruly, & likely to endanger the welfare of his School, he used to correct and turn them out of School, & make some little difficulties about their Readmission. Unfortunately for Mr. Tomlinson, this piece of policy gave very great umbrage to two of the trustees, who ever since their children were corrected and turned out of School, have been his most implacable Enemies. One of them has acquired a very considerable fortune by trade, & has four or five of the trustees entirely at his Devotion. The Circumstances & Influence of the others are inconsiderable.

You may see by the Act of Assembly for establishing the School, which I sent you the 23rd of January 1767, that one penny per Gallon, for a limited time, is laid upon all spiritous Liquors imported into Neuse River, for the Benefit of the School; out of which Twenty pounds per ann: is to be paid to the Schoolmaster, to enable him to keep an assistant & the rest is to be applied to the education of poor children, not exceeding Ten. Mr. Tomlinson presuming that this duty upon Spiritous Liquors wou'd be honestly applied by the Encouragement of the trustees, wrote to his correspondent in London, who procured him an assistant, Mr. Parrot, properly qualified in every respect, & entered into bond with him for a term of years in behalf of Mr. Tomlinson. About twelve months after the arrival of Mr. Parrot, great umbrage was given to the potent trustee, by Mr.

Tomlinson correcting and turning one of his children out of school for very disobedient & stubborn Behaviour; and a dissenting Minister, about the same time opened a School at Wilmington, which is near one hundred miles distant, when Six Boys, which Mr. Tomlinson had under his Care from that place, were taken away, for the Conveniency of being nearer home, which reduced his scholars to about forty four. The trustees had never sent more than five poor children to School, And as Mr. Tomlinson found his School reduced, he petitioned the trustees to send him five more, the better to enable him to continue Mr. Parrot. But behold the consequence! a meeting of the trustees was appointed (not a general one, for I had no notice of it, but such as could be depended upon to answer particular purposes) & an order made, the original inclosed, that he should dismiss the five poor Children which were then at school, under a pretext of want of money to repair the Schoolhouse. I call it a Pretext, because their own Accounts will shew, that they had money enough then due & in their treasurer's hands, not only to have made all necessary repairs, & continued the five poor children, but likewise to have educated five more according to Mr. Tomlinson's Request. And tho' some repairs were really wanting, yet they have not laid out a single shilling in any Repairs from that day to this. And the dissenting trustee, who was at that Meeting, lately informed me, that the five poor children were taken away, not for want of Money, but with a design to distress Mr. Tomlinson.

When Mr. Tomlinson found his School still more reduced by the dismission of the five poor children, he represented to Mr. Parrot the hardship of continuing him as assistant, who generously consented to cancel the Bonds & provide for himself. The greatest difficulty seemed then to be removed. Mr. Tomlinson had sufficient Employment for himself in the School, & Mr. Parrot who is a good Mathematician & Penman supported himself by Hackney writing.

But tho' Mr. Tomlinson was now perfectly easy, yet resentment could not sleep. The Correcting and turning the children of two of the trustees out of the School, was, like the Sin against the Holy Ghost, never to be forgiven. Mr. Tomlinson's Destruction was determined upon, but how to accomplish it was the difficulty. Mr. Parrot was therefore tampered with to open a School in opposition to him. But Mr. Parrot saw thro' their design to making a tool of him; and tho' he detested their proposal yet he gave soft answers, implying, that if the School should be at any time vacant, he would accept it, provided he had no better employment. Mr. Tomlinson was therefore to be turned out to make room for him; but Governor Tryon was in the way, who had been an Eye Witness of Mr. Tomlinson's conduct, and had a particular value and esteem for him. But at length Governor Tryon was removed to New York, and a new Governor succeeded him, who was a Stranger to Mr. Tomlinson, and then was the time to strike the fatal Blow. Accordingly on the 14th of last September, there was a meeting of the trustees (not a general one, for tho' a Trustee, I had no notice of it, not being a proper person for such business as they were then about) when they did their utmost to turn Mr. Tomlinson out of the School. A copy of their proceedings on that day, you have enclosed, & upon which I would beg leave to remark; That when they took the poor children away, there was no Complaint of neglect, but only of want of money. But now Mr. Tomlinson is accused of neglecting his School by the Trustees, & what is very surprising by no body else. They were the only accusers & the only Judges.

Mr. Tomlinson has taught School here upwards of Eight years, and I never heard him accused of neglecting his School till after the 14th of September 1771, & since that time, only by one Person, who is greatly in his Debt, besides the trustees that endeavoured to displace him. And I verily believe, they might with as much Justice have accused him of Robbery or Wilful Murder.

Two or three days after, Mr. Tomlinson informed me, how the trustees had used him, & was very desirous of a public hearing before the Governor. And tho' I was at that time very sick, yet I waited upon the Governor along with him, who received us very graciously. But his Excellency being a Stranger, & not knowing how far he was legally authorized to interfere, prudently declined granting him a public Hearing, till he had the Attorney General's opinion, a copy of which I have sent you inclosed, & by which you will perceive, that he could not legally interfere at all. Mr. Tomlinson's Case therefore seemed to be desperate, & nothing was to be done but turn out immediately.

The full number of Trustees is Eleven. At that time there were two vacancies, & I had no notice of their meeting. Eight met, and one dissented; therefore Mr. Tomlinson was dismissed by the voice of Seven. But to give this Dismission the appearance of a more general voice, they proceeded immediately to fill up the vacancies, & elected two new Trustees, sent for them & swore them in, & then signed a nomination for Mr. Parrot. I have sent you coppies both of the Dismission & Nomination, which you will find of the same date, & the nomination signed by Ten, to induce the Governor to believe that Mr. Tomlinson was dismissed by the voice of Ten, tho' he was dismissed by the voice of Seven only, for they got the two new elected Trustees, as well as the trustee that dissented to sign the nomination for Mr. Parrot.

But here the Trustees met with a difficulty, they were not aware of. They knew Mr. Parrot's distressed circumstances, & never doubted but he would readily accept the School. But when the time of trial came, he let them see, that he had too much sense to be made a Tool of, and too much honor to supplant a worthy honest man.

In short, he refused to accept the School when offered in such a base and dishonourable manner; which redounded so much to his Credit, that he has lately got into decent Employment in the Secretary's office; which I hope will give him a comfortable subsistance at present, & be a step towards his future advancement. And now for the last Effort of disappointed Resentment.

After the trustees had sent for Mr. Tomlinson with an Intention to dismiss him (tho' he had not the least notice or suspicion of it, having never heard of any Accusation) they settled accounts with him, & gave him an order upon their treasurer for his money, & then the president, in the name of the Society, in a very abrupt manner, dismissed him. But a few days after, finding Mr. Tomlinson not very willing to turn out, & Mr. Parrot unwilling to accept the School, the potent trustee went to the Treasurer & by his own authority, forbade the payment of Mr. Tomlinson's order. The treasurer accordingly refused payment & Mr. Tomlinson is obliged to sue for his money, tho' the Treasurer has due and in his hands about two hundred pounds.

I never despaired of bringing about a Reconciliation, till this last affair happened. It showed such a depravity of mind, that I thought it dangerous to continue any longer a Member of the incorporated Society, & I therefore resigned. And I believe the venerable Society, will never blame me for resigning in such a Situation. I saw I cou'd do no Good, and therefore wou'd not suffer my Name to give a Sanction to others to do mischief. Besides I was obliged to resign for my own preservation, & to keep out of the way of Strife and Contention.

The majority of the Trustees are wealthy men, but I cannot learn that any of them ever passed thro' a reputable School, or have the least knowledge of any of the Learned Languages, or liberal Sciences, or of the difficulty of governing a School. And I shall leave you to judge of the honor & Integrity of some of them, by the list of Debts inclosed, which Mr. Tomlinson gave me last Christmas. The want of such considerable sums must greatly distress any man in his station. He therefore grew urgent in his Demands, which united his Debtors more firmly in their opposition, and caused them to speak very disrespectfully of him before their Children. For such as will not pay their honest debts, seldom fail to abuse their injured Creditors.

You see it was not either for want of inclination or power, that they did not turn Mr. Tomlinson out of the School, but only for want of a proper Person to succeed him. He is therefore determined to resign the School next April, & follow some other employment.

I have been the more particular in the above Relation, from the duty I owe to the venerable Society & the great regard I have for Mr. Tomlinson, who, I believe, is a sincere Xtian, and has been very basely treated. He is certainly one of the most peaceable & inoffensive men living, enters into No Parties, meddles with nobodys business, but his own, & is not addicted to any one visible vice. And if the Trustees did really think him guilty, either of too much severity, or negligence, or any other Indiscretion or Misdemeanor, why did not they admonish or reprimand him? But that wou'd neither have paid their Debts, nor sufficiently gratified their Malice & Resentment.

I sincerely wish the Act for establishing the School was repealed. I am sure it will never answer any good intention, while such an unlimited power is intrusted in the hands of the Trustees. They shou'd be obliged to lay their accounts annually before the Commander in Chief for his inspection, who should have a Check upon them both in the admission & dismission of the Master. Tis true, the Governor has a power of licensing the Master, which I thought would have been a sufficient restraint, but you may see by the Honorable Marmaduke Jones's opinion inclosed, which is fuller than the Attorney General's, the Governors License is a mere trifling, if any restraint at all. And if the Bishop of London would point out the Defects of the present Act & get it repealed, I believe it would not be difficult to get a much better passed at the next Session of the Assembly. Or if that cou'd not be done, the Schoolhouse had better revert to the Subscribers in general than remain the property of a few, who so shamefully abuse their trust.

After having said so much relative to the School, tis time to say some thing with regard to myself, and tho' I cannot complain of ill usage, yet I never had so much reason to lament the want of Health. About the last of August I was seized with the bilious fever, which baffled every human effort for Relief, & the effects of which I feel too sensibly to this day. Sometimes I was confined to my Bed, at other times I could walk about a little or ride a little, but never enjoyed one Days health till after Christmas, when indulgent providence gradually relieved me by the variation of the Seasons. In this lingering sickly condition I was obliged to attend remote chapels; and in the month of November was so weak, that I cou'd not travel on Horseback, but was obliged to get a Chair; and when I had not strength to go thro' the whole Duty, I got the Clerk or Reader to do such parts of it, as I thought most proper. With great difficulty & bodily pain, I attended all the Chapels as usual, except one, the road to which is hardly passable for a wheel carriage.

After being clogged & surfeited with medicine & finding no Relief, I wrote to an eminent Physician who had lately removed from Newbern, for his advice; which I have sent you enclosed, & which, tho' probably very salutary, is not agreeable either to my circumstances or inclination. Removing is very expensive, & a new parish must be attended with a new Sett of acquaintances, which I wou'd avoid, if possible in the Decline of life. Besides I do not know of any parish in this province, in which a Clergyman cou'd be exempted either from long Journies or indifferent Lodgings. I am therefore determined to continue where I am, I wait the Effects of the returning Spring, which are generally very salutary. But if I should meet with a Return of my old Disorder, I humbly beg, the venerable Society will give me Leave, either to remove according to the Doctor's Advice, or to go to some of the Northern Colonies for a few months, or to return home for the Recovery of my Health.—*Ibid.*, pp. 238-44.

27. GOVERNOR MARTIN PROTESTS TO THE BISHOP OF LONDON ABOUT DISMISSAL OF TOMLINSON, JUNE 20, 1772

As I am well acquainted with your Lordship's good disposition to promote all useful knowledge, and above all that of the Christian Religion, it becomes my duty to inform your Lordship that an Act of the General Assembly for establishing a public School in this Town was passed here in the year 1766 in consequence of which Mr. Thomas Tomlinson a man of unexceptionable good character and qualifications was invited here from England by the Reverend Mr. Reed a most worthy Clergyman and one of the Society's missionaries, to take the conduct of it, and that under his auspices and the encouraging countenance of that venerable Society it promised to become an Institution of the greatest utility until the Trustees of the School actuated by most unjust resentment and taking advantage of a most extraordinary and unreasonable power given to them by the Act of Assembly dismissed him from his charge without notice, and without complaint or reprehension; colouring since, their arbitrary proceeding, with general suggestions of neglect which they cannot in one instance prove although repeatedly called upon to do so by the injured Mr. Tomlinson, it hath grieved me extremely to find it out of my power to redress this worthy man, but the Act of Assembly vests the Governor with a power perfectly nugatory, making his Licence necessary to the appointment of a master while the absolute power of dismission and removal of Masters is reserved to the Trustees, and requires not his consent or participation, thus, My Lord, the Kings Governor is rendered the mere Instrument of the Trustees power, which they have most capriciously exercised in the present instance, and who being ignorant and uneducated men, are as little capable of judging of the merits of a pedagogue, as inclinable to do justice.

Matters of this nature falling particularly under your Lordships notice as a patron of religion and letters, and a coadjutor in the laudable and pious designs of the Society for the propagation of the Gospel whose countenance and encouragement hath been heretofore extended to this Institution I humbly beg leave to urge to your Lordships consideration, as a member of His Majesty's most honorable privy council the expediency of recommending the aforementioned Act of the General Assembly of this Province for His Majestys Royal disallowance, as depriving the Governor of power with which he ought to be invested, to oppose the injurious and arbitrary proceedings of the Trustees, who left to the free exercise of their caprice must ruin an Institution that might under proper regulations become of the utmost advantage to society, by promoting useful knowledge. I have lately written to the Earl of Hillsborough on this subject, and I have every reason to believe that your Lordship will find that virtuous nobleman and able Minister disposed to concur with your Lordship, in all such proper measures as may be taken on the occasion . . . —*Ibid.*, pp.305-7.

28. Thomas Tomlinson asks for his salary, July, 1772

I hope my last letter accompanied by those of the Reverend Mr Reed, have reached you before this time. I have now to acquaint you that I quitted the School on the 13th of April and surrendered my Licence to his Excellency.

What a hardship that this affair in which both my interest and character have been *so* deeply concerned, should be smothered up without a fair and public hearing!

The suit which I brought against the incorporated Society, so called, as mentioned in former Letters would have been brought to trial last May Superior Court, but the Treasurer a few days before the Sitting of Said Court, paid me down the money (though without any previous public Meeting of the Socity) ordered the suit to be dismissed and paid the Costs thereof amounting to about £4 16s. 0d.

Whether this sum is to be paid out of the fund, or out of the Treasurer's own pocket, or of any other individual, is what I cannot pretend to say. Perhaps this may be Kept a Secret as they are not liable to be called to account for any of their proceedings.

I have taken the liberty of drawing on the Society for my Salary for the Quarter which I attended the School in the present year. But to prevent any dispute about paying it, as being only a single quarter, I have directed the Possessor of the Bill to wait upon you for your opinion in the matter, before it be presented to the Treasurer.—*Ibid.,* pp. 317-18.

Activities of the Society in South Carolina

29. An act for securing the provincial library at Charleston, South Carolina, 1700

WHEREAS, at the promotion of the Reverend Dr. Thomas Bray, and the encouragement and bounty of the Right Honourable the true and absolute Lords and Proprietors of this Province, and the aforesaid Dr. Bray, and the inhabitants of this Province, a library hath been sent over to Charlestown, for the use of this Province, and it is justly feared that the books belonging to the same will quickly be embezzeled, damaged or lost, excepting a law be passed for the effectual preservation of the same—

I. *Be it therefore enacted,* by his Excellency John Earl of Bath, Palatine, and the rest of the true and absolute Lords and Proprietors of this Province, by and with the advice and consent of the rest of the members of the General Assembly, now met at Charlestown, for the South-west part of this Province, and by the authority of the same, That the Provincial Library of Carolina shall be, continue and remain in the hands, custody and possession and safe-keeping of the incumbent or minister of the Church of England, in Charlestown, in this Province, for the time being; which said incumbent is and shall be hereby bound and obliged to keep and preserve the several and respective books therein, from waste, damage, embezzlement, and all other destruction, (fire and all other unavoidable accidents only excepted,) and is and shall be hereby accountable for the same, and every book thereof, to the commissioners hereafter nominated: And to that end and purpose, the incumbent of Charlestown, and his successors, shall pass two receipts for the books belonging to the library aforesaid, one to the commissioners hereafter named, and the other to the church-wardens of Charlestown for the time being, in which receipts the titles of each book shall be inserted; and in case all or any of the books is or shall be found to be wasted, endamaged or embezzeled, or any otherwise destroyed, except as before excepted, the respective incumbent, his executors or administrators, are and shall be hereby bound and obliged to answer double the value of the same; and the said commissioners are hereby impowered to sue for the same, in any court of record in this Province, by bill, plaint or information, or other action wherein no essoign, protection, injunction or wages of law shall be allowed; and what thereby shall be recovered, reasonable charge and expences deducted, to employ and dispose towards the compleating and perfecting the aforesaid library, so wasted, endamaged, embezzled or otherwise destroyed, within the space of twelve months after such recovery.

II. *And be it further enacted* by the authority aforesaid, That in case of the death or removal of the incumbent of Charlestown, in this Province, that then the respective church-wardens of Charlestown shall immediately take into their respective hands, custody, possession and safe-keeping, all the books belonging to the said library, and shall be answerable for the same to the commissioners hereafter nominated.

III. *And be it further enacted* by the authority aforesaid, That the church-wardens of Charlestown, upon their receiving of the books belonging to the said provincial library, into their custody, shall compare the same with the catalogue and receipt for the same, in their custody, and if any of the books are wanting or damaged, they shall give an account thereof in twenty days time at farthest, to the commissioners hereafter mentioned, who are hereby impowered to sue the said incumbent, or, in case of his death, his executors or administrators, for the same, as aforesaid: And in case the said church-wardens refuse to give such account, then they, their executors and administrators, are hereby made accountable to the commissioners hereafter named, for all the books belonging to the said library, and contained in the catalogue thereof.

IV. *And be it further enacted* by the authority aforesaid, That the inhabitants of this Province shall have liberty to borrow any book out of the said provincial library, giving a receipt for the same to the incumbent of Charlestown, for the time being, with a promise to return the said book or books; if a folio, in four months time; if a quarto, in two months time; if an octabo, or under, in one month, upon penalty of paying three times the full value of the said book or books so borrowed, in case of failure of returning or damnifying the same: And the said incumbent is hereby obliged to enter such receipt in a book, to be fairly kept for that purpose, and upon the same being returned, shall note it returned, on the other side or column of the said book, and not cross or blot the same: And in case the persons that borrowed any book or books out of the said library, doth refuse to return the same, or doth damnifie the said book, upon complaint thereof given by the said incumbent, his executors or administrators, to two or more of the commissioners, and by them, or any five of them, to the chief justice of this Province for the time being, or any two justices of the peace, it shall be lawful, and the said chief justice, or any two justices of the peace, are hereby impowered and required, by warrant of distress, directed to any of the constables of this Province, to levy three times the value of such book or books, on the goods and chattels of the person so refusing to deliver, or damnifying the same; and for want of such distress, to commit the person to prison, till satisfaction be made to the incumbent.

V. *And be it further enacted* by the authority aforesaid, That the commissioners hereafter named shall make, or cause to be made, seven catalogues of all and singular the books in the said library, and the same being fairly written, one of which shall be sent to England to the Right Honourable the Lords Proprietors of this Province; one to the Right Reverend Father in God the Lord Bishop of London; one to the aforesaid Reverend Dr. Bray; one to be entered on record in the Secretary's office of this Province; one to be in the custody and for the use of the commissioners hereafter named, under which the incumbent shall sign a receipt for the respective books; one to be in the custody of the church-wardens of Charlestown, for the time being, under which the incumbent shall also sign a receipt for the respective books; and one to be fairly entered in a book for that purpose to be kept by the incumbent in the said library, that so any person may know what books are contained in the said library.

VI. *And be it further enacted* by the authority aforesaid, That the commissioners hereafter named, after making an exact catalogue of all and singular the respective books in the said library, shall, and are hereby impowered to, appraise and rate each book, at a price certain, in the current money of this Province; which appraisment shall be an established rule to judge and determine the value of the said books, in case any suit is brought by the said commissioners against any person that shall detain or damnify any of the said books, or against the incumbent of Charlestown, or his executors or administrators.

VII. *And be it further enacted* by the authority aforesaid, That the commissioners hereafter named, or any five of them, shall, every year, on the fifth day of November, resort to the house built for the incumbent of Charlestown, where the said library shall be kept, and there examine the books thereof by the catalogue, and see that there be the full number, and that they are not damnified nor spoiled: And therefor, the incumbent is hereby required, in lending of any of the several books out of the said library, notwithstanding the time usually allowed by this Act, to oblige the said persons to return all such books as they borrow, to the said incumbent, ten days before the said fifth day of November, that so all and singular the books belonging to the library aforesaid, may be exposed to the view of the said commissioners, the better to enable them to judge if they are any way damnified or spoiled, and to give their order accordingly.

VIII. *And be it further enacted* by the authority aforesaid, That James Moore, Esq., now Governor of Carolina, Joseph Morton, Nicholas Trott, Ralph Izard, Esqrs., Capt. Job Howes, Capt. Thomas Smith, Mr. Robert Stevens, Mr. Joseph Croskeys, and Mr. Robert Fenwicke, or any five of them, be, and they are hereby nominated to be, commissioners and trustees, for the due inspection and preservation of the library aforesaid, and all and singular the respective books to the same belonging: And they, or any five of them, shall have power to commence or bring any suit or action given by this Act: And in case, by death or absence, there be not five of the said commissioners in this Province, that the Governor for the time being shall nominate such person or persons as shall make the number of the commissioners five, which shall have all the power given the said commissioners in this Act, and shall so continue till the next meeting of the General Assembly of this Province, who shall then chose so many persons as shall make up the full number of nine; which persons so chosen by an ordinance of a General Assembly, shall, and are hereby declared, to be the commissioners and trustees required by this Act; and they, or any five of them, to have and execute all and singular the powers given the commissioners above named by this Act.

IX. *And be it further enacted* by the authority aforesaid, That the commissioners above named, after having examined the respective books belonging to the library aforesaid, if they find any books wanting, shall summon such persons as have the said books in their custody, to deliver the same in twenty days after such notice in writing left with the persons, or their places of abode; and in case any persons shall fail or refuse to deliver the said respective books to the said commissioners, or any five of them, that upon complaint being made by the said commissioners, or any five of them, to the chief justice of this Province, for the time being, or any two justices of the peace, against such persons refusing to deliver the said books, that the said chief justice, or any two justices of the peace, are hereby authorized, impowered and required, by warrant of distress, directed to any of the constables of this Province, to levy to the treble value of such respective book or books, on the goods and chattels of the person or persons so refusing the same, and to make sale of the same, rendering the overplus to the owner; and for want of such distress, to commit the persons to prison till satisfaction be made.

X. *And be it further enacted* by the authority aforesaid, That all persons that have borrowed or have in their custody any of the books belonging to the provincial library aforesaid, shall, on or before the first day of January next, return the same to the present incumbent of Charlestown, upon the penalty of the forfeiture of treble the value of each book not returned as aforesaid, the better to enable the commissioners before named to make a perfect catalogue of the books belonging to the library aforesaid.

Read three times, and ratified in open Assembly, November 16, 1700.—Cooper, *The Statutes at Large of South Carolina,* VII, 13-16.

30. Francis Le Jau writes to the Society, February 1, 1709/10

...Mr Wood is not well used in his parish and thinks of taking a Schoolmasters employment in or near the Town...

...I shou'd say something of Propagating the Xtian Knowledge; We want a Schoolmaster in parish for our White peoples Children but as for the Negroes or Indians with all submission I wou'd desire that such a thing shou'd be taken into Consideration as the importance of the matter and the Consequences wch may follow do deserve. The best Scholar of all the Negroes in my Parish and a very sober and honest liver, thro' his Learning was like to Create some Confusion among all the Negroes in this Country; he had a Book wherein he read some description of the several judgmts that Chastise Men because of their Sins in these latter days, that description made an Impression upon his Spirit, and he told his Masters abruptly there wou'd be a dismal time and the Moon wou'd be turned into Blood, and there wou'd be dearth of darkness and went away: When I heard of that I sent for the Negroe who ingeniously told me he had read so in a Book; I advised him and Charged him not to put his own Constructions upon his reading after that manner, and to be Cautious not to speak so, which he promised to me but yet wou'd never shew me the Book; but when he spoke those few Words to his Master, some Negroe overheard a part, and it was publickly blazed abroad that an Angel came and spake to the man, he had seen a hand that gave him a Book, he had heard Voices, seen fires &c As I had opportunities I took care to undeceive those who asked me about it; now it is over. I fear that those Men have not judgment enough to make a good use of their Learning; and I have thought most convenient not to urge too far that Indians and Negroes shou'd be indifferently admitted to learn to read, but I leave it to the discretion of their Masters whom I exhort to examine well their Inclinations.. I have often observed and lately hear that it had been better if persons of a Melancholy Constitution or those that run into the Search after Curious matter had never seen a Book: ...—Foster, *op. cit.*, II, 73-74.

31. Francis Le Jau thanks the Society for "such an able School Master," September 17, 1711

The Inhabitants of this Parish have charged me with the care of returning to your Lordship their most humble Thanks for sending to us such an able School Master as Mr Dennys, I acquit my self of that obligation with the most Profound Respect and Beseech your Goodness to accept our humble Acknowledgment of your Paternal care and Permit us to beg the Continuation of your Lordships favour and Protection with your holy Blessing for ourselves and our familyes.

We shall endeavour to settle Mr Denys and his family as advantageously as our Circumstances can afford.—*Ibid.*, pp. 120-21.

32. COMMISSARY GIDEON JOHNSTON WRITES TO THE SOCIETY, JULY 5, 1710, MARCH 25, 1712, MAY 28, 1712, JUNE 17, 1712, JANUARY 27, 1715

...God has been pleased to bless my endeavrs with our late Govr and the Assembly towards the laying the ffoundation of a good School[1] here. But to give this Project the greater life and dispatch, it will be in my opinion, necessary for the Venble Society to put the Govr and Assembly here, for the time being, in mind of it, and to press them to perfect that, which they have so commendably begun: Nor ought the Lords Proprietors to be forgotten on this occasion; who, by the Venble Society's application to them may be prevail'd upon to Contribute somthing towards this design...

We are extremely in want here of Common Prayer Books for our own use; and wish the Venble Society wou'd send us 100. of them: with the New Version of Psalms in them: I believe most of these may be bought, and the People will be glad to get them at any reasonable price; provided the Books be a good Print and well bound. I have continual complaints made to me on this occasion for want of Prayer Books: and I will undertake the Venble Society, shall be reimburs'd for all these Books, unless it be for a few that may be given gratis to the poorer sort. Bp Beveridges Book concerning the necessity and advantage of publick prayer & frequent Communion, wou'd be greatly acceptable to my Parishioners, so likewise wou'd the Christians way to heaven; an Essay toward making the knowledge of Religion easy to the meanest capacity; an answer to all the excuses and pretences, which men ordinarily make for their not coming to Holy Communion; plain Instructions for the Young and ignorant comprised in a short and Easy Exposition of the Church Catechism; in which it were

1. The reference is to "An Act for the Founding and Erecting a Free School for the use of the Inhabitants of South Carolina," passed April 8, 1710.

to be wished, that all the Texts or places of Scripture refer'd to in it, were printed at full length, for the greater ease & advantage of those, who may read that small Treatise: Some short and plain directions for spending one day well: the Sick Christian's Companion, a few of which I formerly had; as also a perswasive to a serious preparation for death & Judgment; and a familiar Guide to the right and profitable receiving of the Lord's Supper; a number of those little Tracts wou'd be of singular use, & highly acceptable to most of my parishionrs and I am perswaded, they wou'd be soon bought up, a few only excepted which shou'd be given to those who are not well able to buy them; the reason which induces me to suppose they may be bought is, because I was Offer'd money for many of those little Books, which the Society upon my coming hither, gave me to distribute among the People: but as I freely reced them, so I freely gave them away.

The Provincial Library in this place is greatly imbezl'd between Mr Marston and Mr Marsden, a third part of the books being wanting. And shou'd the Venble Society be pleased to favour me with some Books for my own use, as their own Missionary, it wou'd be of great advantage to me. I have taken all the pains I can in endeavouring to recover the Library Books, having charged the Clergy to give their parishionrs publick Notice to return such as they have in their hands, and to make the narrowest enquiry they can in their respective P (ar) ishes about them; but the success hitherto has not answer'd my expectation, altho' this attempt has not proved altogether fruitless. The plain truth is, the Act concerning the Provincial Library here, is altogether wrong; nor have I ceased upon proper occasions to express my dislike of it: ffor it makes it a Lending Library to every Inhabitant of this province; whereas it is evident by the Catalogue of Books, and by the very Original design and foundation of this Library, that it was purposely intended for the use of the Missionaries that shou'd be sent hither, who had not Books of their own, to enable them to prosecute their necessary Studies and to qualify them thoroughly for the business of their function; and what farther confirms me in this opinion is; that there is a Lending Library here for Laymen, which is much more imbezel'd than the other. Mr Marston is greatly to blame for this, who obstinately refuses to give in a list of such Books as he in his time gave out, as well as Mr Marsden, my immediate predecessors in this Place ....

I reced the two Boxes of Spanish New Testaments &c., which you sent me, and have made a distribution of them, as there was Occasion. The Spanish Testaments are of little use at present and most of them lie on hand Your Missionaries, for so I call the whole Clergy of this Province, not knowing how to dispose of them . . . —Frank J. Klingberg (ed.), *Carolina Chronicle: The Papers of Commissary Gideon Johnston, 1707-1716* (Berkeley: University of California Press, 1946), pp. 39, 43-44, 55.

June 17th 1712

Hond Sr

. . . The Assembly have settled a Schoolmaster in this Town one Mr Douglass newly come from Philadelphia and an Usher as a beginning or Essay towds greater Matters. The one at 6of and the other at 3of of this Country mony and they have Likewise by Act adjusted the Schoolmastrs Wages at 3f P Ann for Every Boy that he Instructs either in Latin or Greek. They have Given Mrs. Marston likewise 7of to sett up a Small Shop with to maintain her family and they have given a Poor Widow I also recommended to them 4of and a Brief. Something also is done with Relation to Parochiall affairs, but the Clerk of the Lower House who has the Acts being Sick, I cant Exactly tell what they are as yet. As soon as my Son is gone off, I intend to goe into the Country for the Benefit of the Air and to relax and unbend my mind a little in hopes this may be of some advantage to me; & my kind Bretheren have promised to change some turns with me for that Purpose. In the mean time let me be in wt state or Condition of Life God is best pleased with whether Rich or Poor in Sickness & in Health I shall never cease to pray for the prosperity and Success of the most Illustrious Society and shall to the utmost of my Power Endeavour to convince them with how great Respect & Gratitude I am to them & you Honoured Sr

A most humble & most Obedient Servant
Gideon Johnston

—*Ibid.*, pp. 114-15.

Jan 27 1715 (1715/16)

Sir.

. . . It wou'd be Some Satisfaction to me, to have the three last years Sermons and abstracts, as likewise that of this Current year; not doubting but that it will be published, before you can well return an answer to this Letter. And I do once more humbly recommend it to the Society, that they wou'd order Such Books as are given to the Missionaries of Each Parish, to be lodg'd in the Publick Library here, in case they shoud die, or go off, or be displaced; because, the lodging them in the Churchwardens hands, is of ill consequence, in regard Many of them are, and still may be in Such cases lost and Embezeled, and those that are left, miserably spoild and Mangled.

Mr. Whitehead is chosen Master of the free School here, which is 100 L P an Salary of this Country money, perquisites; and I hope he will be made very Easy by this means . . .—*Ibid.*, p. 159.

33. THOMAS MORRITT OUTLINES HIS TEACHING PROGRAM AT THE
    CHARLESTON FREE SCHOOL, JUNE 11, 1723

The Latin tongue is the Intent of my Mission and for that Method I shall observe no other than what is usually practis'd in other Gramer Schools in Engld. I shall chiefly use Lilly for the rudimental part & then I shall proceed to Sententia puerites, Corderii Colloquies, Latin Test., Erasmus, Ovid's Metamorphoses, Virgil, Horace, Lucius, Justine, Tacitus Suetonius or Valerius Maximus & Claudian and as for the Greek Authors I shall teach such parts of Isocrates & Lucian's Dialog: as are usually published for the use of Schools, the Minor Poets with Hesiod's Greek Test. Homer & Euripides & in order to give the Boys a tast of Class Geography I shall cause to be read Dionysious Periegetis and Cluver Geographia and these I shall be somewt particular upon to Compare them wth the modern Geography . . . Justin & others I shall cause to be frequently read & perused to give the boys a Tast of Cronology . . . Kennet's Goodwin and Potter's Antiquity shall be also read in order to be acquainted with the rights Customs & Ceremonies of the Antients these at Spare times or at home I shall endeavor to oblige the boys to read over together with the History of the Heathen Gods, Pantheon &c. but as for those boys wch I shall have constantly in the House wth me & such as are boarders I do intend besides these Books already menconed to make them read 3 times a week at least if not every night Classick History especialy such historians as we have Translated into our Language. those books I will cause to be read an hour at nights between 8 & 9 & I shall not omit at that time to instruct them in Cronology & Geography & teach them the use of the Globes.—"Papers relateing to Mr. Merrit and School at Charles Town," in S.P.G. MSS. (L.C. Trans.), B 4, Pt. 2, pp. 569-70. In Helen E. Livingston, "Thomas

Morritt, Schoolmaster at the Charleston Free School, 1723-1728,"
Historical Magazine of the Protestant Episcopal Church, XIV,
158-59.

34. Thomas Morritt complains to the Society about "intruders" as schoolmasters, December 11, 1723

I cou'd heartily wish they were Suppress'd for instead of being
a furtherance to Learng they're a great hindrance. It Is Customary
here for a Newcomer to set up for a Schoolmr and in a little time
either grow weary or meet with some other employ. In the meantime
these Intruders amuse the people and baulk the Publick School so
much that I wish the honble Society wou'd be pleased to interest themselves & represent this grievance to the Govnt.—*Ibid.*, p. 162.

35. Thomas Morritt tells how his boys progress in the school at Charleston, October 27, 1725

... Some of 'em who cou'd scarce read wn they came to me are
now capable of rendering a whole Chapt of the English Testamt into
Latin, in one morning, according to Castalio's Version, & withall get
a Lesson by 'emselves out of Erasmus or Ovid, & many can read Besa
Gramaticaly into English ... My method is to keep my boys in
Corderii Coloq: & Bezas Test: so long till the same become familiar
on openg to any part of before I put any other Books into their hands
by wch means I find they are easily brot to be Capable of understanding Erasmus or Lucius. I have 10 Boys sent me out of the Country
beside one that came from Philada & another that came from the
Bahaman Islands which are Boarders & 10 Charity Boys recommended by the Comrs two of wch are Mulatos in all 52 of wch I daily
expect an Augmentation rather than a decrease.—*Ibid.*, pp. 163-64.

36. Thomas Morritt has some complaints about his work, July 8, 1726

When I arrived I found neither a House nor a Salary setled nor
any Steps taken towards sounding the mind of the People to know
wether they wou'd give any encouragemt to a Lecturer, so that finding myself thus bubbled & seeing I cou'd not immediately return to
England because my Wife was wth child, I writ to the Honble
Society to get me appointed to a parish but discovering my overtures,
I had that disingenuous piece of Service done me to have it represent'd that I was hankering after a Parish, and therefore application

was made to some Members to attend all Committees & get my
address set aside, this I was not made acquainted with till I had
begun the School, but in reality the ground of this war, least my
return or non acceptance of the School should reflect upon Some
Gent. that Subscribed to the Letter to invite me over for Mr. Moore
speaker of the Assembly told me their House knew nothing of my
coming, & wch I urged to him that they had Sign'd a Petition for that
intent, answer'd, it was forgot, & they thought no more of it, wn I
brought things to bear, wch I had never done if I had not happily
preach'd at Goose Creek, another attempt underhand was contrived
to be offer'd to comprise the Lecturer in the Augmentation of the
Salary, no sooner was I inform'd of it, but I instantly applied myself
to Coll. Moore Speaker, who advised me to Petition that the School
might be consider'd apart wch accordingly I did & his Excellency
has the Petition to produce if not I have a Copy by me. Such are the
difficultys I have met & Strugl'd with, yet I thank God I have brought
the School to something even beyond expectation, but yet wou'd
be much better was I in a Convenient House both Convenient for
Boarders & more convenient for the Town Children. But this I live
in is so Crazy that some make a Scruple of sending their Children by
day least it fall down, it is a Brick house 2 story & a half high &
supported by 16 Shoars, wch is a hindrance to the increase of my
Boarders, & as for new House as it will not be ready agt the Hurrican
Season, so I must be oblig'd to have one at my own Expence for the
Security of my Goods & Books, in wch I suffered no small damage
abt two years ago, so much that I was obliged to write for new Furniture wch are now I hope in God safe at Sea, wth £35 Sterl. School
Books, & part of my Library I left behind me. I have drawn over a
Considerable Interest into this Country so much that I cannot be able
to remove out of it this two years, at least, without a considerable
loss, & I have likewise 1000 £ this Currency owing me wch is not
readily called in, as it is known I am fetter'd so I am insulted and used
the worse for it, wch is very hard. I must thus be disturbed of my
quiet & as it were ferreted out of my Settlemt. . . . .—*Ibid.*, pp. 165-66.

37. Accounts for the building of a Negro schoolhouse in
Charleston, South Carolina, 1743

NEGRO SCHOOL-HOUSE AT *CHARLES-TOWN* ACCOMPT.

1743 DEBTOR.		1743 CREDITOR.	
To cash paid Mr. *John Cart*, for Timber, Boards, &c., as per *his* Accompt and Receipt.	£109: 3:6	By Benefaction received from the Honourable *Charles Pickney*, Esq;	£10: 0
To ditto paid Mr. *Jacob Fiddling*, for framing and finishing the Carpenter's Work of the said Negro School, as per Agreement and Receipt.	90: 0:0	By ditto from the Hon *Jos: Wragg*, Esq;	20: 0
		By ditto from the Hon *Edmond Atkin*, Esq;	10: 0
		By ditto from the Rev. Mr. *William McGilchrist*	10: 0
To ditto paid Mr. *John Cart*, for Shingles, &c. as per Accompt and Receipt.	11:10:0	By ditto from a Person that desires to be unknown	10: 0
		By ditto from Mr. *Robert Pringle*	10: 0
To ditto paid Mr. *Jacob Motte*, for Nails and Iron Work, as per his Accompt and Receipt.	17:10:0	By ditto from Mr. *Charles Theodore Patchabel*	4: 0
		By ditto from Mrs. *Mary Hext*	10: 0
To ditto paid Mr. *Jacob Fiddling*, for making Benches, Brestwork, and Desk for the said Negro School House, as per his Accompt and Receipt.	32: 0:0	By ditto from Mr. *Jacob Motte*	10: 0
		By ditto from Colonel *Othmiel Beale*	10: 0
		By ditto from Mr. *William Stone*	10: 0
		By ditto from Mr. *Andrew Dupuy*	5: 0
To ditto paid Mr. *Edmond Atkins*, for 4 M. plaistering Laths, as per Accompt and Receipt.	8: 0:0	By ditto from Mr. *John Watsone*, sen	10: 0
		By ditto from Mr. *Peter Benoist*	10: 0

1743 DEBTOR.		1743 CREDITOR.	
To ditto paid Mr. Hugh Cartwright, for 30 Bushels of Lime, as per his Accompt and Receipt.	3:15:0	By ditto from Mr. James Osmond	10: 0
		By ditto from Mr. William Hopier	5: 0
Indebted to Mrs. Sarah Trott, for Brick work and plaistering, about	12: 0:0	By ditto from Mr. Benjamin Smith	10: 0
		By ditto from Mrs. Sarah Trott	10: 0
Borrowed from the publick Magazine near the Work house, 3M. 5 C. Bricks at £.7 per M.	24:10:0	By cash received for 200 Feet of overplus Boards sold Mr. Dupuy.	2:10
		By ditto from another Person who desires to be unknown	50: 0
	£308: 8:6		£.226:10

Charles-Town, Nov. 26, 1743.
Errors excepted.

ALEXANDER GARDEN.

December 12, 1743. This Day the above Accompt was audited and examined by the proper Vouchers, and approved by the Vestry of the Parish of St. Philip, Charles-Town. William Smith, Clerk.	The above Accompt was sworn to, by the Reverend Mr. Garden, before me this 12th Day of December, 1743. JAMES WRIGHT, F.P.

—*The Magazine of History*, I (January–June), 64.

38. Richard St. John says the Presbyterian schoolmaster will conform to the rites of the Established Church, August 2, 1747

...We have the Other Day got a Presbyterian Schoolmaster Mackenzie by Name, Who after some Cavils and Objections, has promised in every thing to conform exactly to the Rites of the Establish'd Church, and has ever Since been very Urgent wᵗʰ me about the salary, which the Honourable Society are pleased to Appoint the Cathechist and Schoolmaster of these Islands. I assured him it did not depend on Me, tho possibly it might on his own Behaviour; Which he might depend on my laying faithfully before the Society.—Foster, *op. cit.*, V, 752.

Activities of the Society in Georgia

39. THE TRUSTEES OF GEORGIA MEMORIALIZE THE S.P.G., JANUARY 17, 1732

That in pursuance of powers granted to them by His Majesty they have sent out a number of families of His Majestie's subjects to settle in Georgia, and that to provide for the establishing a regular Ministry according to the Church of England they have already directed the laying out a site for the Church, and have allotted three hundred acres of land for glebe for the Minister but in regard it will be some years before the glebe can produce a sufficient maintenance for the said Minister, they humbly hope that the Society will deem it to be within ye intent of their Charter to make the like allowance to the Rev. Mr. Samuel Quincy [1] the Minister chosen to be settled among them as they do for the Missionaries establisht in the other Colonies till such time as the glebe shall be sufficiently improved for his maintenance as likewise that they will favour the Trustees with a benefaction of such books or furniture as they have usually given upon the first foundation of Churches. That they have received some benefactions for religious purposes which they have already set apart for erecting a Church for the town of Savannah clearing the glebe land and building the Minister's house.—Pascoe, *Two Hundred Years of the S.P.G.* (London, Published at the Society's Office, 1901), I, 26.

40. THE REQUEST OF THE TRUSTEES IS GRANTED, JANUARY 16, 1736

A memorial of the trustees for establishing the Colony of Georgia in America was read, setting forth that the Rev. Mr. Samuel Quincy, to whom the Society had been pleased, upon their recommendation, to allow a salary of fifty pounds per annum, has by letter certified to the said trustees, that he is desirous of leaving the said Colony of Georgia, and returning home to England in the month of March next to which they have agreed; and the said trustees recommend the Rev. Mr. John Wesley to the Society, that they would allow to him the said fifty pounds p. annum from the time Mr. Quincy shall leave the said Colony, in the same manner Mr. Quincy had it. Agreed that the Society do approve of Mr. Wesley as a proper person to be a Missionary at Georgia, and that fifty pounds per annum be allowed to

1. Quincy was the first S.P.G. missionary to Georgia. He was stationed at Savannah 1733-1736.

Mr. Wesley from the time Mr. Quincy's salary shall cease.—*Ibid.*, pp. 26-27.

41. HARMAN VERELST, ACCOUNTANT TO THE TRUSTEES, TO JAMES OGLETHORPE, JUNE 17, 1736

The Trustees have received from the Society for Promoting Christian Knowledge the Sum of £50 they desire you will pay to M[r] Bolzius for his M[r] Gronau [1] and the Schoolmaster's Salarys for half a year ending the 1st of November next and take his Receipt for the same; they will send you the Value in Georgia Bills.

And as the Trustees have received Money from several Benefactors for the Maintenance of the Missionaries who went with you to Convert to Christianity the Native Indians in Georgia They desire you will pay M[r] Charles Wesley and M[r] Ingham [2] 50 £ a piece and take Receipts for the same. And as the Incorporated Society for propagating the Gospel in Foreign Parts have agreed to Continue to M[r] John Wesley from Lady Day last the £50 a year they gave M[r] Quincy & which they will Pay to him to that time. The Trustees think it right that M[r] John Wesley should have a year's Salary advanced him and they will receive it from the Incorporated Society in Repayment And they will send you the said £150 Value in Georgia Bills...—Allen D. Candler (compiler), *The Colonial Records of Georgia*, XXIX, 274. These records have been published through Vol. XXVI with the exception of Vol. XX. Vols. XXVII through XXXIX, secured by Candler from England in typescript, are in the Georgia Department of Archives and History, Atlanta, and materials drawn from these unpublished records are here used with the permission of Mrs. J. E. Hays, Director of that Department.

42. MEMORIAL OF THE TRUSTEES TO THE SOCIETY, JULY 11, 1739

That the Settlements in Georgia being greatly extended and requiring two Missionarys one for Savannah and the other for Frederica besides an Itinerant Missionary, and a Missionary for instructing and converting to Christianity the Native Indians in Georgia.

---

1. John Martin Bolzius and Israel Gronau, with Henry Lemke and Christian Rabenhorst, were leaders of the Salzburgers in Georgia.

2. Rev. Benjamin Ingham, missionary and teacher to the Indians, seems to have taught at Irene for two years, learned the Indian language, and undertook to write a Creek grammar. See E. Merton Coulter, *Georgia: A Short History* (Chapel Hill: University of North Carolina Press, 1947), p. 70.

That the Trustees not finding themselves in a Condition to provide for their Support are necessitated to apply for the Assistance of this Society and therefore hope for an Allowance of fifty Pounds a Year to be paid to the Reverend Mr William Norris[1] appointed Missionary at Frederica who is well known to some of this Venerable Society until they shall be enabled to raise a sufficient maintenance for him out of the Lands now Cultivating in Georgia for the Religious uses of the colony.—*Ibid.*, XXXIII, 56.

43. THE TRUSTEES OF GEORGIA PETITION THE SOCIETY, JUNE 10, 1743

That Whereas the Society were pleased upon the application of the Trustees dated July 11th 1739 to grant an Allowance of Fifty Pounds p Annum for three years to be paid to a Missionary in Georgia Which was accordingly paid to the Revd Mr William Norris for the time he Officiated there which was a year and a half of the said Term of three Years And as the Payment of the same ceased when he returned to England in the year 1741 And the Trustees did themselves from that time pay the Salary to the Revd Mr Christopher Orton till the time of his Death which happened a little before Michaelmas last, and whereas the Revd Mr Thomas Bosomworth lately ordained by the Right Reverend the Lord Bishop of London is going over to the Colony in Order to succeed the late Mr Orton But the Trustees are unable to give him any Allowance out of the Supply (granted in the last Session of Parliament for the further Settling and Improving the Colony) it being Appropriated for other Uses They find themselves under a Necessity of Applying to this Society and therefore desire an Allowance of fifty Pounds p Annum to enable them to pay the said Mr Thomas Bosomworth.

The Trustees have Ordered That three hundred Acres of good Land shall be appropriated for the Use of a residing and officiating Minister, and have Appropriated out of the money a sufficient Sum for Allowing to the Minister two Servants with their Maintenance for the Cultivation of the same which is all they have Ability at present to do but it must be a great while before the Lands can be in a condition to yield a proper Support.

There has always been a Place convenient for Public Worship and a Parsonage House has been built by the Trustees for the Minister and they have sent Orders in the most pressing Terms to expedite

---

1. According to Pascoe, *op. cit.*, II, 851, Norris served as missionary at Frederica 1739-40.

the Building of the Church for which they have appropriated a sufficient Sum of Money.—*Ibid.*, 226.

44. THE TRUSTEES APPOINT THOMAS BOSOMWORTH AS CLERGYMAN
IN GEORGIA, JULY 4, 1743

Whereas by the Death of the late Reverend Mr Christopher Orton at Savannah in the Colony of Georgia in America, and the Return of the Reverend Mr William Norris from Frederica in the said Colony, there is no appointed clergyman in Georgia to perform Religious and Ecclesiastical Offices there. And whereas the Reverend Mr Thomas Bosomworth has lately received full Orders from the Right Reverend the Lord Bishop of London to qualify himself to go over a Missionary to Georgia, and has agreed to perform all Religious & Ecclesiastical Offices on his being allowed after the Rate of fifty pounds a Year from Midsummer last from the Incorporated Society for propagating the Gospel in Foreign Parts; And for the Maintenance and Cloathing of two Men Servants Twelve pounds three shillings and four pence a Year for each Servant from the Trustees for establishing the said Colony, to be employed in the Cultivation of three hundred Acres of Land appropriated for a Residing Minister in Georgia We the Trustees for establishing the Colony of Georgia in America have authorized and empowered and by these Presents do authorize & empower the said Reverend Mr Thomas Bosomworth to do and perform all Religious and Ecclesiastical Offices that shall be necessary for the better establishing and promoting the Christian Religion in the said Colony and all other the good Ends and Purposes thereby intended agreeable to the Laws of England and the Tenour of our Charter In Witness whereof the said Trustees have to these Presents affixed their Common Seal the fourth day of July in the Seventeenth year of the Reign of our Sovereign Lord George the Second by the Grace of God of Great Britain France and Ireland King Defender of the Faith and so forth And in the Year of our Lord One thousand seven hundred and forty three.—*Ibid.*, pp. 258, 259.

45. MEMORIAL OF THE TRUSTEES TO THE S.P.G. ON THE APPOINTMENT OF BARTHOLOMEW ZOUBERBUHLER, NOVEMBER 11, 1745

Whereas the Incorporated Society upon a Memorial from the Trustees dated the 10th of June 1743 appointed the Reverend Mr Thomas Bosomworth their Missionary at Savannah in Georgia with a Salary of Fifty pounds a Year from Midsummer 1743; And Whereas the said Mʳ Bosomworth hath left Georgia, and returned without Leave to England, Application having been made to the Trustees by the Reverend Mʳ Bartholomew Zouberbuhler, lately admitted into the Holy Orders of the Church of England by the Lord Bishop of London, that he might be permitted to exercise his Holy Function in the Province of Georgia, the Colony being then destitute of a Minister of the Church of England, and a Ship being instantly about to sail for Georgia, the Trustees embraced the Opportunity of sending the said Mʳ Zouberbuhler to Georgia therein.

The Trustees therefore recommend the said Reverend Mʳ Bartholomew Zouberbuhler to the Society, to succeed the said Mʳ Bosomworth in the Mission of Savannah in Georgia, with the usual Salary for such time as the Society shall think proper; The Trustees on their Part having provided for the Maintenance of two Servants to be employed in the Cultivation of Three Hundred Acres of Land for the Use of a Residing and Officiating Minister there, the Produce of which three hundred Acres of Land, they hope after some Years, will be as ample Provision for a Missionary at Savannah.—*Ibid.*, pp. 320, 321.

46. THE TRUSTEES APPOINT BARTHOLOMEW ZOUBERBUHLER MISSIONARY IN SAVANNAH, NOVEMBER 11, 1745

That the Society having been pleased to grant an Allowance of Fifty pounds a Year for a Missionary at Savannah in the Province of Georgia; And the Reverend Mʳ Thomas Bosomworth who was the Missionary at the said Place, having returned to England, and quitted his Office there, the Trustees have appointed the Reverend Mʳ Batholomew Zouberbuhler the Missionary at Savannah in his Room.

They therefore desire the Society will transfer the Allowance of Fifty pounds a Year from the Reverend Mʳ Thomas Bosomworth to the said Reverend Mʳ Batholomew Zouberbuhler. . .

The Trustees have given it in Charge to the said Mʳ Zouberbuhler, as well as to their President and Assistants, to forward the Cultivation of the Lands appropriated for the Use of the Residing and Officiating Minister at Savannah, by his Servants they maintain for that Purpose.—*Ibid.*, pp. 315, 316.

47. The Trustees agree to additional pay for Bartholomew Zouberbuhler, March 1749

The Parliament in the last Session having granted the Sum of £5304..3..4 for the further settling and improving the Colony for the Year 1749. The Trustees embraced an Opportunity then offered, of sending 63 Foreign Protestants as Servants to the Saltzburghers at Ebenezer, being 39 men, 12 Women, 4 Boys and 8 girls under Contract that every married Couple should serve together, and no girl under 10 Years of Age, or Boy under 12, to be separated from their Parents; And that in Case any of them should within three Months from their Arrival in Georgia pay £6. the charge of their Passage for the Use of the Trust in Georgia, such Servants were to be free, and each Man of 21 Years of Age was to have as much Land as he could cultivate, not exceeding 50 Acres. Which Servants arrived in Georgia the 2d of October last.

The Reverend Mr Zouberbuhler, the Missionary in Georgia, coming to England, with the Leave and Recommendation of the Inhabitants, to represent to the Trustees his Inability of discharging the great Duty required from him, for the Stipend allowed him by the Incorporated Society, and the Offer that was made him of a Living in Carolina. The Trustees thereupon agreed to allow him Fifty pounds a Year in addition to the fifty pounds a Year the Incorporated Society gave him, and also the Maintenance of two Servants to cultivate the Lands allotted him; And Mr Zouberbuhler returned to his Duty on board the Ship with the said Foreign Protestants. By which Ship the late Dr. Crow's Library (the Disposal whereof was left to Dr Hales and Mr Smith, and they agreeing to give it for Georgia) was also sent over, under the Care of the Minister, To be kept for the Use of the Colony, and to be divided in Georgia as the Trustees may see Occasion.—*Ibid.*, pp. 411, 412.

48. The Trustees request the S.P.G. to send a missionary to Augusta, August 8, 1750

That in the Month of June 1749 the Society were pleased to continue the Reverend Mr Bartholomew Zouberbuhler a Missionary at Savannah in the Province of Georgia, with a Salary of £50 a Year, to which he had been appointed above three Years before.

That the said Mr Zouberbuhler is the only missionary in the said Province.

That the Settlements round Savanah are grown so numerous, that the said Missionary's Time must be wholly engross'd in performing his Duty at Savanah, and in his Attendance on the said Settlements.

That the Town of Augusta in the said Province is large, and contains a great Number of Inhabitants, and at so great a Distance from Savanah and (being at least 140 miles) that Mr Zouberbuhler's Duty at Savanah and the adjoining Settlements will not suffer him to perform any Duty there.

That the Inhabitants of the said Town of Augusta have at their own Expence erected an handsome and convenient Church, and have transmitted a Petition to the Trustees, to procure from this Venerable Society a Minister to be appointed for the said Town, a Copy of which Petition is herewith enclos'd, with a Plan of the Church.

That the Smallness of the Parliament's Grant for the Trustees, and the short Time during which They can hope for any (as their Power of governing the said Province will expire within three Years) make it impossible for the Trustees to engage such a Missionary, or settle any Stipend upon him; But They intend to grant to the Petitioners, the Ground for the Church and Church Yard, and 300 Acres of Land to be cultivated for the Support of the Minister there, and the Pulpit Cloth, and other Things which they desire.—*Ibid.*, pp. 469, 470, 471.

49. THE INHABITANTS OF AUGUSTA MEMORALIZE THE TRUSTEES OF GEORGIA, APRIL 12, 1750

The principal Inhabitants at a General Meeting here, having taken into Consideration the Numbers of Settlers, and the daily Increase of them, together with the many Traders and Servants by them employed in the Indian Countries round us (who twice a year reside two Months each Time in this Place) The Necessity of a Place of Divine worship was too evident not to be taken Notice of by them, more especially, as those People for many years had quite been Strangers to the Church Service, till lately at the Fort.

For this therefore, and other Reasons, your humble Servants the Subscribers were appointed by all at the said Meeting, to act in the Nature of a Committee, in collecting Subscriptions, agreeing with proper Workmen, & superintending the building of a Church.

Pursuant to the said Resolution, we have collected several Sums of Money, and erected a Church, a Plan of which is herewith sent to your Honours; And we believe we may venture to say, there is no Church so far advanced in the Indian Country as this, and so soon finished; But as Indian Friendship is sometimes precarious, we have built it opposite one of the Curtains of the Fort, that the Guns of the Bastions may secure it, and that it may be a Place of Retreat for the Inhabitants of the Place in sudden Alarms.

What we have therefore to beg of your Honours is that you'll be pleas'd to procure for us a Clergyman of the Church of England from the Society for Propagation of the Gospel, and as a well quali-fied one is not only necessary for the Instruction and Edification of the lower Sett of the Inhabitants, but may also in Time assist the Religious Work for which that Society was first established, we hope He will be put upon a good footing; And We assure your Honours, that our little Mites, and those of several other Subscribers shall not be wanting to make this Place agreable to such a One.

We beg also that your Honours will be pleased to grant to the Inhabitants of this Town the Ground on which the Church; the Church yard, and avenue leading to it, independent of the Com-manding Officer of the Fort, excepting in Time of Danger, or in such manner as your Honours shall think most expedient.

We have already in some Measure experienced the good Effects of Divine Service being celebrated in the Officers Room in the Fort by a Layman, as Numbers of the Inhabitants have regularly and decently attended every Sunday.

We have nothing more to ask, unless your Honours are inclined to add some little Decoration vizt Some Glass for the Windows, Pulpit Cloth, Sacramental Ornaments &c. which will be thankfully accepted, and always gratefully acknowledged by your Honours.—The originals of this document and of the next eight that follow are the property of the S.P.G., 15 Tufton Street, Westminister, London, S.W. 1. Photocopies are in the Library of Congress and microcopies of these photocopies now are in the Library of the University of North Carolina. These materials are here used with the permission of Mrs. M. W. Landers, B.A., Archivist of the Society.

50. BARTHOLOMEW ZOUBERBUHLER TO THE S.P.G., DECEMBER 20, 1750

Since my last I have visited as many neighbouring Towns and Villages as my Constitution & the Cure of my Parish would admit; & in discharge of my duty, as well as from an affecting View of the deplorable circumstances of the Inhabitants in regard to their Spiritual Affairs, I have instructed them in the saving Truths of the Gospel & endeavoured to bring them to a Sense of true Religion; & I hope my labours have not been in vain. They receiv'd me kindly, & seemed very desirous of having more frequent Opportunities of attending divine worship, and hearing the glad Tidings of the Gospel.—I receiv'd many other Invitations especially from Augusta, a Town about 170 miles from Savannah, where the Inhabitants (who are pretty numerous) have built a large Chappel at their own Expences, & would willingly contribute to the Support & Comfort of a Minister in the holy Order of our Church, if the Society would be pleased to send them One. It gives me no little uneasiness to see so many in this Colony destitute of divine worship, & I cannot, but with very great concern think of going to Officiate at such a Distance and neglect those whom divine Providence hath more immediately comitted to my care. The Harvest would certainly be great, if there was more labourers.

I therefore desire you would not impute my delay of writing to any neglect in me, but to the want of sending you a true account of the State of my Parish, which is as follows.

No of Inhabitants 800
    of the baptized Since last Christmas . . 25
    of Adult persons baptized since Do . . 1 Negroe Woman
    of Communicants of the Church of Engd 65
    of Negroe Infidels . . . . . abt 200
    of converts 1

The 7th of last July was Spent in dedicating our New Church to God's solemn worship & the Offices of Religion, in praising & adoring the most High God for two other memorable blessings accidentally met together, viz. Our being on that Day initiated into the happy Priviledges of British Subjects; & Our great & wonderful deliverance out of the bloody hands of the Spaniards, when above 4000 of them had in a manner actually taken possession of this Colony, but were happily repelled to the everlasting honour of that brave Comander General Oglethorpe. The building is large, beautiful & Comodious. My parishioners are constant in their Attendance & I have the pleasure to see many Negroes decently join our Service. And as there is now among us an Encrease of religion, So in the Trade of our harbour, many Vessells have taken in their lading this year, & we have great reason to hope that this will yet be a flourishing Province & soon answer the care & diligence which the Trustees have hitherto employ'd for it's Prosperity. But as the general good of a Country depends upon a Christian & careful Education of Children, I hope due care will also be used in this Matter, at least nothing in my power shall be wanting to promote it. Our School in Savannah at present consists of 41 children, & might encrease to many more, if Masters of Slaves would shew a greater concern to have their young Negroes instructed & brought up in the Knowledge & fear of God. It would be very Acceptable if the Society would be pleased to send us a few Bibles, Testaments, Psalters with the comon prayers, Primars, Lord Bishop of Man's Essay towards an Instruction of Indians & some other useful & pious Tracts, as the venerable Society shall think proper of all which there is great want for the Instruction of white as well as Negroe Children. May God bless the Society & all their pious & laudable designs, is the hearty desire of him, who begs the Continuance of their favour.

P.S. If the Society thinks proper to send me the desired books, please to recomend it to the care of Mr Harman Verelst Accomt to the Trustees, in Queen Square. Westminster. I should be glad to have the annual Accounts of the Societys proceedings & if not too troublesome every year left wth sd Mr Verelst. You will likewise much oblige me by sending me such Acts of Parliament as are ordered to be publickly read in Churches.

51. Dr. Richard Barford and Rev. William Chambers write
    Testimonial for Rev. Samuel Murthwaite May 15, 1762

The Revnd Mr Samll Murthwaite A:M: of St John's College in Cambridge Curate to the Revnd Mr Chambers Rector of Achurch & Master of the grammar school at Oundle in the County of Northampton, understanding from the Revnd Doctr Smith [1] Provost of the College of Philadelphia that there is now a vacancy in the Mission for the Province of Georgia hath applied to us, whose names are underwritten for letters Testimonial of his good behaviour & Abilities; in compliance wth wch request we humbly beg leave to recommend to your notice & choice the said Samll Murthwaite as a Person, that has been well known to us for the space of six years last past, that he is of great Probity of life, Integrity of Morals, & proficiency

1. For a useful account of Smith's life and work, see A. F. Gegenheimer, *William Smith: Educator and Churchman, 1727-1803*. Philadelphia: University of Pennsylvania Press, 1943.

in sacred & profane Learning, well skilled in the arts, particularly Mechanics & Mathematics, & in all respects qualified for the office we here recommend him to supply, & wch he is willing & desirous to undertake, provided the emoluments & stipend thereof be found to be such as to be a sufficient encouragement to leave his present engagements & connections here.

In witness whereof we have hereunto set our hands this 15th day of May 1762.

> Richd Barford D.D. Rector of
> Tichmarsh North-tonshire.
> Wm Chambers A.M. Rector of Achurch
> Northtonshire

52. CHURCHWARDENS OF ST. PAUL'S IN AUGUSTA TO THE S.P.G., MARCH 24, 1763

We are favour'd with your obliging Letter of the 22d May 1762. for which we beg your acceptance of our best thanks.—

we shall always retain a grateful sence of the venerable and honourable societies readiness to send us a Clergyman, with the additionall favour of contributing towards his support amongst us; give begg leave to assure their Lordships of honours, that we will faithfully comply with what we proposed in our Letter of the 8th feby 1762.. so far as it depends upon us, or is in our power to do, & which for clearness & perspicuity's sake we will beg leave to repeat here.—

The sallery of Twenty five pounds sterling pr ann: setled by an act of the General Assembly of this province, is indisputable, & as there is a perpetual fund Establish'd for that purpose it will be always certain and not in the least precarious.—The fifteen or Twenty pounds sterling that we proposed to raise by a private subscription amg the principal inhabitants of this parish shall be, always from time to time, or year to year paid punctually, & this shall be obligatory upon us so to do, for which reason we send a Duplicate. that the Gentleman with whom the society may be pleased to honour us, may if he thinks proper accept of it—The seventeen pounds sterling, formerly allow'd by s. Carolina, for a sermon once a month at New windsor, do's not depend upon us, therefore to that article we can only say, that we have not the least doubt but that province will allow it, as heretofore, & be glad of the opportunity of doing so.— and we hereby promise, that if there should be the least Occassion for it to use our best Interest, & that of our friends in s. Carolina to get it allow'd as before—the perquisites for marrying, we again assert will rather exceed, than fail of what we formerly mention'd viz. £15 or £20 P ann:—The advantage of the school in this parish we shall most certainly give the preference off to the Gentleman, that may be sent us if he shall think proper to accept it—As Mr Copp is no more, we would beg leave to say as little as possible in answer to what he was pleas'd to assert in his letter of 9th feb. of 1756 to the society. some of us who were generally concerned in collecting the subscriptions rais'd for him, very well know & do hereby assert that Mr Copp never had less but much more from those subscriptions every year than what was Originally intended & promised him viz. £20 P ann & even the first year of his residence here, he had more than double that sum when Mr Copp first arrived here, some of his friends who was very warm in his interest had promoted that sub-scription to £50.. which they signified to him would be paid An-nually & which was done the first year, but afterwards many of the subscribers refused to pay their subs alledging that they never engaged to Continue it but for one year & this we believe was what led Mr Copp to complain that the promises made for his support were not comply'd with but tho that Gentn never rece'd £50 P ann; after the first year he never fell short of it £15 every year after, during his stay here—

Our new Church has been for some time past retarded by some unavoidable accidents but we have now a pleasing prospect of its going on with spirit & in order to promote divine worship among us we have just purchased a Genteel Organ for the Church & have a proper hand to perform on it—our prospect of Quietness with re-gard to the Indians is every day more confirmed & our possession of the Neighbouring Countries of Mobille and saint Augustine will not admit of the most distant apprehensions of any future Trouble from them—we are with Esteem ...

53. SAMUEL FRINK, MISSIONARY AT SAVANNAH, TO THE S.P.G.
JANUARY 7, 1768

I have received your Letter of the 20th of April with a Postscript of the 16th of May last, by the Hand of the Revd Mr Ellington,[1] who arrived the latter End of August in Charles Town So. Carolina, from thence after a stay of a Fortnight he came to Savannah, where he continued about 5 weeks waiting for a proper Conveyance to

1. Ellington was stationed at Augusta 1767-1770.

Augusta, & where I hope he will prove serviceable, as he seems to be an honest well-disposed Christian, as far as the heat of an Enthusiastical Imagination will permit—

I return my *thanks* to the Society, not only for their providing so soon for Augusta; but for their kind Approbation, & Indulgence, in my Removal from my former Mission to Savannah, where I have enjoyed my Health the Year past to a greater Degree, than since my first coming into the Province, notwithstanding the Parochial Labors are 3 times greater than in my former Mission—

In One Year I have Baptized 80—Baned 120. Preach twice every Sunday, & upon the principle Holy-Days always once— Besides affording all the assistance in my Power, to this & the Neighbouring Province of So. Carolina— Communicants last Christmas 55— I should be sorry to hear that the venerable Society have diminished the Sallary allowed my Predecessor—

It is true the Revd Mr Zouberbuhler, as I have been informed had an allowance from the Crown, & there is Provision made in this Province of 50 £ Sterling. That of the Province is certain, but that of the Crown uncertain, as far as I can learn, I have not received any thing of the Crown as yet, whether I shall or no, I am not able to determine till trial is made,— Now if I should be deprived of that allowance of my Predecessor, & a diminution of Sallary by the Society, my Situation must be uneasy, & Consequently shall be under a necessity of leaving Savannah.—

I am not avaritious—I want no more than a comfortable Support— I am obliged to assert, & that justly too, that what I was allowed, whilst in my former Mission, I mean the last year of it, was preferable to what I shall have here, even Upon the Supposition, that both the Crown, & Society should yet continue their Bounty & Generosity.—

The Situation of the two Places makes a vast difference, I find— To be in the principal Place of the Province, where most strangers resort, & to have nothing to entertain a Friend & Acquaintance must be disagreeable to any Clergyman. However, I shall submit this matter to the better Wisdom of that venerable Body, whom I desire to serve in promoting the Redeemer's Kingdom, & whose Instruction, & great design, it will be the height of my ambition to obey & promote, at all Times, & doubt not but the divine assistance will accompany the same—

I have drawn a Bill of 25 £ Sterling on the Treasurer, from the 25th of last June, to the 25th of December past, & hope it will be accepted. If the Society can depend upon my Representations from time to time—every thing shall be related in the most unreserved & honest manner that humane Nature is capable of— When I can have the least prospect, of easing the Society, in order to extend their Bounty to other Places, I shall immediately make it known to them.—

And I make no doubt, but that in three or four years at the most, some Method will be adopted in this Province, to support the Clergy, themselves— I have been moving this thing to Members of the Assembly of the Province, which I hope will be considered in their approaching Sessions— But this Province is yet in its Infancy, & Poor withal. I know of no part of America, that deserves the Society's Notice more than this Province of Georgia—a little Bestowed in the Beginning, will soon raise it above want of Assistance in this Respect— The Religious Necessities of all Parts of the Province are deplorable; whole Families there are who have not even a Form of Godliness, much less the Power; many are worse than the aboriginal Natives themselves— Now how is this to be Remedied, but by Instructing the rising Generation in the Principles of Religion, & how can they be Instructed without Teachers, & how shall Teachers live amongst them unless they have a proper support— Besides, all Societies arise from Families, & where Instruction is wanting, & a deficiency in the educating, & training up Children in the way that they ought to go, all Societies of Men—Governments Civil & Ecclesiastical, must at last fall— But I am too tedious—

I must refer you to another Letter for the Result of a private Enquiry into Mr Alexander's Character, with some other Things, which I chuse should be seen by no one but yourself.

54. SAMUEL FRINK FROM SAVANNAH TO DR. BURTON, JUNE 29, 1769

My last Letter dated the 4th January last I have reason to believe got safe to hand, in which I gave you an account, of my Labors, & the success which has attended, since my Change from Augusta to Savannah— I have been chiefly Active in the Circle of my own Parish, & particularly in the Town, where I am so much Confined to the Duties of my Function, that I can scarce make an Excursion for a Day— It is therefore out of my power, to render those frequent good Offices to the poor People in the Parishes around me according to inclination. These People/ without using any bold Rhetorical Figures/ in General seem to have but very little more Knowledge of a Saviour than the Aboriginal Natives— Many Hundreds of—poor

People, both Parents, & Children, in the Interior, & extreme Parts of the Province, have no Opportunity of being instructed in the Principles of Christianity, or even in the Being of a God, any farther than Nature dictates. This is Shocking indeed! This argues the want of a—Number of Churches to be Erected & sober Ministers Employed to open their Minds, & Instruct them in divine Truths, by the divine Aid, & especially those that concern their Everlasting Welfare hereafter— I have often tho't upon these poor unhappy Mortals with Grief, But how to remedy it is past my Skill, unless I was to move in a Sphere somewhat different—Or at least be Seconded and Supported in some proposals for Remedying that—Remissness of those in whose power it is to do better— We have good & wholesome Laws in this Province— But what does this Signify, if they are never put in Execution?— The Church of England is Established by Law, and that Law is Confirmed by the King— But all this is of no avail, unless some Person is invested with more Power, than a Poor Missionary commonly has in order to inspect these things more narrowly, to see that the Church is not neglected amidst the Bustle & Noisey Politicks—and that the Clergy are not imposed upon by those who delight in destroying all Order both in—Church, & State— The Province is divided into a Number of Parishes. And there are Commissioners appointed by a Law, to provide Glebe-Lands, & to see that Churches are Built in every Parish— In short they are impowered to take out Grants for such Lands, & that without any Expense to themselves— But they had rather have Lands, & Houses called by their own Names. The Commissioners before mentioned have a power to fix even the Spot for to Build a Church upon, where any Dispute may arise upon that Head— So far from Acting agreeable to the Intention of the Church Act, that they have never troubled their Heads about it— There is not a Grant for a Glebe Land in the Province, which my worthy Friend the Bearer of this will inform you of— There are but two Churches in the Province and those 150 Miles distant from each other— There is a fine Field open here not only for enlarging the Redeemer's Kingdom, but of Episcopacy too, which is built upon the Foundation of the Apostles, Jesus Christ being the Corner-Stone, if those to whom these things are committed would exert themselves— I have often endeavoured to stir up their—Minds by way of Remembrance, but it has answered no purpose at all— I could wish that my Lord of London would take particular Notice of such Neglect, but investing some person with a power to call them to an

Account for such an abuse of that which has been entrusted with them— In these Licentious Times the Notion of Order both in Church, & State seems to be forgotten; Headings, or anything that bears the least Impression or Character of an Establishment upon Order and decency, & good Government, meets with too cold a Reception. There is such a Consonancy between the present Government & the Established Church, that it is impossible that the One should suffer without the other. But we hope for better things than the Dissolution of either— I hope the happy Time is not far distant when we shall be favored with a Bishop [1] in some part of America, tho' we have so many Enemies amongst our Dissenting Brethren both in England, and America, respecting this Matter.. But it always seemed strange to me that the Church of England should not be entitled to as great Privileges in America as the Dissenters are; which is really the Case in the Northern Provinces— Why those who possess themselves of the Established Church should be at such an Expense, & even such risks of Life, to obtain Orders in that Church in which they would always wish to Live & die in the Communion of, when those of a Different Persuasion enjoy every Privilege whatsoever with regard to their way— Why should these Schismaticks frighten a whole Nation with their Blustering? Surely they cannot deny no liberty of Conscience. which they are so fond of— Are not Churchmen entitled to as many Privileges as Dissenters in America? I hope to more—tho' they have not as yet Experienced it— Why all this Clamour, & Noise with regard to sending a Bishop to America? Nothing surely less than consummate Impudence, & a desire to be in the Saddle that they may Ride over us, as they have always endeavoured to do both in Church, & State— God preserve us from such Masters!— Certainly we should have more Order amongst us, if we could have proper Governors in the Church— The Clergy would be kept under proper Government. We should have perhaps more deserving Clergymen than have sometimes been in these parts, who have served for the purpose of bringing the Ministry into disgrace, & for the Triumph of Dissenters— I dare say could this of sending a Bishop to America, once be accomplished, a man of Calmness & deliberation, not vigorous, but easy of access, & of an exemplary deportment, many hundreds that now vociferate in

1. According to Pascoe (*op. cit.*, 849-51), the Diocese of Virginia was founded in 1790; that of South Carolina in 1795; that of North Carolina in 1823; that of Georgia in 1841. For the history of the Anglican Church in Virginia, see George M. Brydon, *Virginia's Mother Church*. Richmond, Va.: Virginia Historical Society, 1947.

Conventicles, would be turned from their Errors, & see their Vileness in renting the seemless Garment of their Saviour— The Future Generation Educated in their Colleges would conform to Order, by observing its harmony— The hindrance of many now in our Colleges in America from entering into holy Orders, is the danger of the Voyage,[2] & the Expense only.—If the thing that I have been mentioning could once be accomplished, we should in a great measure be freed from the gross Impositions of every pragmatical Genius. We should then be freed from, & keep at a distance, Coblers and Thinkers, Butchers, & Bakers, watchmakers, & Cattle russlers Thieves, & Robbers, & every Vagrant, in such a manner so not to dare to assume the sacred Character of the—Priesthood— They would be then kept from leading astray the Ignorant, & Unwary, from the Truth, & from endeavouring to overthrow that little Order, that now scarcely subsisted amongst us—

I can't but observe with Regret, that consistent with my own Knowledge, that all Sectaries are always Encouraged more in our Colonies, than the strict adherents to the Established Church— Whether there is anything peculiar in the Air since Mr. Whitf—ld's Enthusiastick fumes have Evaporated, I do not pretend to determine— But this I know that something has had a great Effect amongst us— Dissenters have had such Encouragement, that they have had the Impudence to demand, & absolutely take a small Surplus Fee established by Law, to belong to the Minister of the Established Church— But however all their Impudence will not do— I do not speak this without Book— I am sorry to find those that profess themselves of the Church of England so remiss, when it is in their own power to keep these Disturbers at a Distance— But alas the Laodicean Temper is too prevalent—

Reverend Sir, I have said too much already, but I hope your Candour will excuse me, as there are so few of us to fight the Battle, we certainly must be—more sensible when we ought to be supported, in rewarding of those continual Strokes that are aimed at us. My zeal/ which I trust is according to godliness/ is for supporting the Establishment of Church, & State, and I pray God that I may never be Instrumental of hurting either. I could say many things more, & with greater plainness; but I must forbear— My worthy good Friend —Henry Gouge Esqr Surveyor-General of Georgia, & Brother to

2. See below B. Franklin's lively letter to "Messrs. Weems and Gant, Citizens of the United States in London," July 18, 1784.

the Bishop of Norwich, will throw Light upon any Thing you may think Mysterious in this Letter, and will readily answer you to any Question you may be pleased to ask him in private, relating to the Religious State of the province of Georgia. He is a Man worthy of Notice, & Regard—of strict veracity, good sense, & Honesty— In short a good Christian—I could wish that you might have a few hours Conversation with him Relating to some matters that I have mentioned—

This same Gentleman will present a Subscription for assistance to Build a New Church in Savannah which is greatly wanted, as the present one is much decayed—he is authorized so to do from the vestry—which I hope will meet with Encouragement—

I have drawn a Bill upon the Treasurer of the Society for 25 £ Sterling, my last half years Salary— How far I may be deserving, it would be presumption in me to say— The Society by Enquiry no doubt are Judges—I heartily thank them for past Favours—I hope the Bill will meet with a kind Reception, if I can find out the Name of the Treasurer, if not I must Crave your Assistance in the Matter— It would give me great pleasure to peruse an Abstract of the Society's proceedings for the last 3 Years, & shall esteem myself under the greatest obligations to that Venerable Body for a few cheap Bibles & Common prayer Books to distribute among the poor People who are not able to buy— My Parochial List since the Last stands thus— Baptized 30—at the Communion   Easter 65—Whitsunday 40. . .

55. BENJAMIN FRANKLIN TO "MESSRS. WEEMS AND GANT, CITIZENS OF THE UNITED STATES IN LONDON," JULY 18, 1784

On receipt of your letter, acquainting me that the Archbishop of Canterbury would not permit you to be ordained, unless you took the oath of allegiance, I applied to a clergyman of my acquaintance for information on the subject of your obtaining ordination here. His opinion was, that it could not be done; and that, if it were done, you would be required to vow obedience to the Archbishop of Paris. I next inquired of the Pope's Nuncio, whether you might not be ordained by their Bishop in America, powers being sent him for that purpose, if he has them not already. The answer was, "The thing is impossible, unless the gentlemen become Catholics."

This is an affair of which I know very little, and therefore I may ask questions and propose means that are improper or impracticable. But what is the necessity of your being connected with the Church of England? Would it not be as well, if you were of the Church of Ireland? The religion is the same, though there is a different set of bishops and archbishops. Perhaps if you were to apply to the Bishop of Derry, who is a man of liberal sentiments, he might give you orders as of that Church. If both Britain and Ireland refuse you, (and I am not sure that the Bishops of Denmark or Sweden would ordain you, unless you become Lutherans,) what is then to be done? Next to becoming Presbyterians, the Episcopalian clergy of America, in my humble opinion, cannot do better than to follow the example of the first clergy of Scotland, soon after the conversion of that country to Christianity. When their King had built the Cathedral of St. Andrew's, and requested the King of Northumberland to lend his bishops to ordain one for them, that their clergy might not as heretofore be obliged to go to Northumberland for orders, and their request was refused; they assembled in the Cathedral; and, the mitre, crosier, and robes of a bishop being laid upon the altar, they, after earnest prayers for direction in their choice, elected one of their own number; when the King said to him, "*Arise, go to the altar, and receive your office at the hand of God.*" His brethren led him to the altar, robed him, put the crosier in his hand, and the mitre on his head, and he became the first Bishop of Scotland.

If the British Islands were sunk in the sea (and the surface of this globe has suffered greater changes), you would probably take some such method as this; and, if they persist in denying you ordination, it is the same thing. A hundred years hence, when people are more enlightened, it will be wondered at, that men in America, qualified by their learning and piety to pray for and instruct their neighbours, should not be permitted to do it till they had made a voyage of six thousand miles out and home, to ask leave of a cross old gentleman at Canterbury; who seems, by your account, to have as little regard for the souls of the people of Maryland, as King William's Attorney-General, Seymour, had for those of Virginia. The Reverend Commissary Blair, who projected the College of that Province, and was in England to solicit benefactions and a charter, relates, that, the Queen, in the King's absence, having ordered Seymour to draw up the charter, which was to be given, with two thousand pounds in money, he opposed the grant; saying that the nation was engaged in an expensive war, that the money was wanted for better purposes, and he did not see the least occasion for a college in Virginia. Blair represented to him, that its intention was to educate and qualify young men to be ministers of the Gospel, much wanted there; and begged Mr. Attorney would consider, that the people of Virginia had souls to be saved, as well as the people of England. *"Souls!"* said he, *"damn your souls. Make tobacco."* I have the honor to be, Gentlemen, &c.—Jared Sparks (ed.), *The Works of Benjamin Franklin*, X, 109-11.

56. SAMUEL FRINK FROM SAVANNAH TO DR. BURTON, JULY 6, 1770

I have the pleasure of addressing you again On a Subject most pleasing because long wished for & desired, & consequently must give the highest Satisfaction. I have at last gained my point, with respect to the general Commissioners for erecting of Churches, & settling Glebe-Lands, that is, in assisting those in applying for a few hundreds of Acres to be granted for the use of every Minister of the Church of England, which the Governor would always readily do when applyed for; This Law of appointing Commissioners to provide for these Things is of long standing but they never applied for one Glebe Land till I/ tho' I sound my own Trumpet/ in some measure roused them from their Lethargy— They have agreeable to the Request of the people of St. George's Parish, assisted them, with regard to a Glebe which has been my aim & their Endeavours for these 9 Years past— There is nothing now wanting with regard to the Gospel's being preached among them, but for that Venerable Society for the propagation of the Gospel, to reach forth their well known beneficent hand, to promote the present as well as future happiness of the risen & Rising Generation in said Parish, which I think I can say they never refused to the Necessitous; I will not refuse to a Province more Necessitous in this respect, I dare aver, than any on the Continent.—

There is now a happy Door opened in St. George's Parish,/ which has been long shut thro' the Negligence of the Commissioners before mentioned/ for the propagation of the Gospel among a great number of People, who have been so long without the Gospel preached,/ as I have in former Letters observed/ that the greatest part have no Religion at all, & Consequently, their children have never been taught by them, to make any difference with respect to days, except that of merrymaking & diversions after their mode, on the Sabbath— which indeed is too much the Case with those where the Gospel is regularly preached—

The Bearer of this Letter is Mr Alexander Findlay, a Young Gentleman who has resided in Savannah for these three Years past the People of St. George's Parish have made choice of to be their minister when he shall receive holy Orders, well knowing him to be a Sober and discreet person, ever since his residence in Georgia— At his first arrival he often visited me, & as soon we we were a little acquainted he made known his design of taking Orders, & settling in Georgia from his good Behaviour, & very intimate acquaintance with him, I encouraged him in his good Intentions, & from time to time have given him the best advice I was capable of, with regard to the necessary steps to be taken before his entry upon such an important work as that of the Ministry— And for that end have put into his hands such Books, & advised him to such as I tho't would answer the End proposed.

Soon after his arrival in Georgia He with Mr Seymour a Relation of his, engaged in keeping the Publick School in Savannah, & have the happiness both of them of being universaly esteemed, for their Method of Instruction, modest deportment, & Gospel Conversation, as well as Learning—

Mr Findlay was born at Aberdeen in Scotland and educated at the University in the same place, where he made good proficiency, in the Languages Philosophy, & Mathamaticks, & other branches of Learning, as well as divinity—

I must therefore from a personal knowledge & acquaintance, recommend him as a person not only as to Age, but in all other respects fit for holy Orders, and deserves the Society's particular notice; I must beg the Society in behalf of him (Mr. Findlay) & the people, among Whom he proposes to reside, to assist him & them as far in them lies with regard to allowing him part of a maintenance as neither the parish, nor province are able to raise a Man in that respect above Contempt, thro' want & poverty— His Mission will be very laborious the Parish is about 50 Miles in length, & so in breadth, & Consequently there must be two Chappels—

The Society I doubt not after mature deliberation on the matter before mentioned, at the same time sensible of the Necessity of having more missionaries in this province than now are, as I myself am left alone will in their great wisdom & Generosity, will grant the thing prayed for.

57. GOVERNOR JAMES WRIGHT FROM SAVANNAH TO DR. BURTON, MAY 8, 1771

Your letter of the 19th of October last I Recd by Mr. Findlay the Second instant and am very glad to hear that the Recommendation I gave him was so well confirmed & approved &c.

Joseph Brookes Schoolmaster at Augusta I never saw, but Mr Ellington, and some gentln of Veracity who Live at Augusta have mentioned him to me as an useful wellbehaved & deserving Man.[1]

58. JAMES SEYMOUR FROM AUGUSTA TO DR. HIND, SECRETARY OF THE SPG FEBRUARY 24, 1774

Your kind favour of date May 22nd 1773 I have received, tho' the Books mentioned therein have never as yet been heard of—

Since my last, a Methodist Minister of the Name of Piercy (sent out some time ago by the Countess of Huntingdon) came to Augusta; I did not chuse to admit him into my Pulpit, as he always had, on his first arrival, introduced himself to the dissenting Congregations, and not to the Ministers of the established Church.—

Lady Huntingdon has likewise sent out to the Orphan House Academy in this Province, four young Men, itinerant Lay Preachers, who ride about in the different Parishes, endeavouring by their Preaching to insinuate themselves into the good Opinion of the Country People, for the Purpose of obtaining Letters recommendatory to my Lord of London—One of them, in particular of the Name of Cook, has already obtained some instruments of writing to that Purpose, from an Ignorant frontier Settlement, not yet established into a Parish, and I am told that he intends to go to England in a few Weeks...

My Cure has been very much alarmed lately, by the Nation of Creek Indians, who threaten a War, and have already murdered about 20 white People on the Frontiers of our Parish; I brought my family down a few days ago to Savannah & I should set out again for Augusta tomorrow or next day.—

1. James Wright is described as "able, successful as an executive, and a patriotic Britisher. He arrived in 1760, and befittingly enough, this same year George III succeeded to the throne of England, ... Of the three colonial governors, Wright was the most successful despite the fact that he had the most difficult position to fill, and he was the best liked, even though he was finally driven out in the Revolution."— E. Merton Coulter, *Georgia: A Short History* (Chapel Hill: The University of North Carolina Press, 1947), pp. 88, 89.

Since my last, I have baptised 16 white Children and 3 Mulattoes, married 13 Couple, buried 3 Corpses, Communicants the same as before—I have drawn on the Treasurer of the Society for half a years Salary, and I hope the Bills will be favoured as formerly.[1]

Activities of The Society in Florida

59. REQUEST CONCERNING SCHOOLMASTERS FOR EAST AND WEST FLORIDA, JULY 20, 1764

I request the favour of you to acquaint the Lords Commissioners for Trade and Plantations, that the Society for propagating the Gospel not having yet been able, in pursuance of their Lordships desire, to procure proper Schoolmasters for the New Settlements of East and West Florida, humbly recommend to their Lordships, that the Ministers, who are appointed to those Settlements, may for the present be directed to execute the office of Schoolmasters also, who are willing to undertake that Trust, with the allowance of the Salary alone designed for Schoolmasters, the Lands alloted for them being reserved, 'till such time as Schoolmasters can be provided, wch the Society will use their best endeavours to procure as soon as may be.— *Transcription of the British Colonial Office Records*, copied from the Library of Congress Collections for the Files of Florida Writers' Project, I, 51.

60. REQUEST FOR SCHOOLMASTER FOR EAST FLORIDA, MARCH 25, 1765

Sir

Mr William Knox hath desired me to procure the recommendation of the Society for propagating the Gospel, in favour of Mr Jones Read, that He may be appointed Schoolmaster at St Marks in East Florida. the society will have no meeting till the 19th of April, & if Mr Read waits for a recommendation in Form. He will loose an opportunity of a most convenient passage.

I desire the favour of You to assure the Lords Commissioners of Trade & Plantations, that the Society have no person immediately in view for that department, & that I believe It will be most perfectly agreable [sic] to Them, if their Lordships will be pleased to give Mr Read, in case They think him properly qualifyed, that appointment.—*Ibid.*, p. 69.

1. Seymour was stationed at Augusta 1771-1779, was a refugee at Savannah 1780-1782 and in Florida in 1783 and died en route to the Bahamas 1784.

IV

DR. BRAY'S ASSOCIATES

I. PREVIEW AND COMMENTS

CLOSELY CONNECTED WITH the Society for the Propagation of the Gospel in Foreign Parts was the organization known as "Dr. Bray's Associates" which was confirmed by a decree in chancery in 1731 and among whose purposes were provision for parochial libraries and the conversion of Negroes in the British plantations. With regard to this latter purpose:

The Case stands as followeth.– Dr. Bray had, by the many known Instances of his Zeal for the Propagation of Christianity recommended himself to the Esteem of Mr D'*Alone*, private Secretary to King *William*. This pious gentleman bequeathed a certain proportion of his Estate to Doctor Bray and his associates, towards erecting a Capital Fund or Stock for Converting the Negroes in the *British* Plantations. This Bequest amounted to the neat Sum of Nine Hundred pounds, and was immediately vested in the South Sea Annuities. By a Feoffment made by Dr. *Bray* before his Death, as well as the Tenor of his Last Will, this Trust was devolved on the Associates: and their Authority was farther confirmed by a Decree in Chancery, 1731.

Out of the Interest of this Fund an annual Stipend was paid for several Years towards the Support of a Catechist to teach the Negroes in *Georgia:* But the strong Prejudices which adult Negroes retain in favour of their own Superstition, the lively Resentment they felt for the Loss of their Liberty and native Country, and the continual Labours they are forced to undergo, together with their intire Ignorance of our Language, proved almost insuperable Obstacles to their Instruction; hereupon the Associates finding their Endeavours in this Way ineffectual, thought it advisable to turn their Attention to the Instruction of the *Negroe* Children, who being born and educated in our Colonies, and understanding our Language, may as easily be taught the great Truths of our holy Religion as *white* Children of the same Age; and where it might be reasonably hoped that the good Seed sown will take deep Root, and in due Time, with God's Blessing, bring forth a plentiful Harvest. With this View Schools for Negroe Children have been opened in different Provinces of *America*, under the Care and Inspection of worthy Persons, who have charitably engaged to see that the Children be properly instructed in the Principles of true Religion; and that the great and necessary Duties of Obedience and Fidelity to their Masters, Humility and Contentedness with their Condition, be duly impressed on their Minds.[1]

The original MSS. of the Associates are in London, "preserved in the building of the Society for the Propagation of the Gospel in Foreign Parts in the custody of the Association, by whose permission they may be inspected." Photofilm copies are in the Library of Congress and microcopies of those are in the Library of the University of North Carolina and in the Library of the College of William and Mary. The introduction to Pascoe's *Two Hundred Years of the Society for the Propagation of the Gospel in Foreign Parts* (London, 1901) states that this work is based, in part at least, on the minutes of the meetings of the Associates. W. W. Kemp's *The Support of Schools in Colonial New York by the Society for the Propagation of the Gospel in Foreign Parts* (New York: Teachers College, Columbia University, 1913) refers to the minutes of the Associates of January 2, 1760, and contains a lengthy quotation from the Minutes of January 17 of that year. In "Thomas Bray's Associates and Their Work Among the Negroes," in *Proceedings of the American Antiquarian Society* (Worcester, Mass., 1939) are citations to photofilm reproductions (largely resumés), in the Library of Congress, of the minutes of the Associates, and to references to, quotations from, or descriptions of the letters from Bartholomew Zouberbuhler, Alexander Stewart, John Barnett, and others, and of some of the minutes of the Associates that follow below.[2]

II. DOCUMENTS

1. SOME MINUTES OF DR. BRAY'S ASSOCIATES

January 2, 1760: At the Angel Ave Mary Lane
Present: Peter Le Keux Esq
        Mr John Spiller
        Mr Jos. Waring
        Revd Mr. Waring
        Revd Mr. Skinner

1. *An Account of the Designs of the Associates of the Late Dr. Bray; with an Abstract of Their Proceedings.* London: Printed in the year MDCCLXVI, pp. 7-8.
2. The editor does not know whether all the materials that follow have ever before been published. After diligent inquiry of those scholars who should but turned out not to know, he is inclined to believe that some of these documents are now being published for the first time. Here it may be noted that Benjamin Franklin became a member of Dr. Bray's Associates January 2, 1760, for a time served as chairman of the organization, and took intelligent interest in its work.

Revd Mr. Berriman
Mr. Nixon
Revd Mr. Dixon

John Waring recommended Benjamin Franklin Esq of Philadelphia in Pennsylvania as a proper person to be an Associate & also Rich Morhall Esq of St Andrews Holbourn,

Benjamin Franklin Esq & Richard Morhall Esq were unanimously elected by Ballot

Agreed that three Schools for negro Children be opened with all Convenient Speed in some part of the British Plantations, & that J. Waring be desired to inform the worthy person who offered ten Guineas a year for five years for that purpose, of this resolution of the Associates.

Agreed that the Thanks of the Associates be returned to the aforesaid worthy person.

Agreed that J Waring be desired to inform Mr Franklin of the above Resolution & to request the favour of his Assistance in settling these Schools.

Agreed that for the future the Associates do meet on the first Thursday in each month at 11 oclock in the forenoon & at all other times by adjournmt

17th January: 1760 At the Angel Ave Mary Lane
Present: Peter Le Keux Esq in the chair
Benjamin Franklin Esq
Mr John Spiller
Mr Joseph Waring
Revd Mr Waring

Mr. Franklin declared that in his opinion New York, Williamsburgh in Virginia, & Newport in Rhode Island are the most proper places in the British Plantations for Schools for the Instruction of negro Children.

Mr. Franklin recommended Sr S: Johnson President of the College, the Revd Mr Barclay Minr of Trinity Church, & the Revd Mr Auchmuty at New York

William Hunter Esq, Postmaster The Revd Dr Dawson President of William & Mary College & Minr of the Church at Williamsburgh & also

The Revd Mr Pollen Minr of Newport Rhode Island as very proper persons to be requested to take upon them the Care & Management of the several schools in the places aforesd

Agreed that one school for the Instruction of thirty negro Children be opened with all convenient speed at each of the aforesd places viz

New York, Williamsburgh Virginia & Newport Rhode Island & that the Salary of the Master or Mistress do not exceed twenty pounds Sterling a year

Agreed that Mr Franklin be desired to write to the aforesd gentlemen & request the favour of their kind Assistance in establishing these Schools, that they would occasionally & as often as they may judge consistent visit & inspect them, & from time to time transmit to the Associates an account of their proceedings and the Progress the children make & the reception the design meets with from the Inhabitants in general

Agreed that three parcels of Books for the use of the above Schools be immediately prepared & that J Waring be desired to procure from the Society for promoting Christian Knowledge such as may be necessary & are not in the Associates store

Adjourned

Thursday Febr 7: 1760 Ave Mary Lane
  Peter Le Keux the Chair
  Benjn Franklin Esq
  Richard Morhall Esq
  Mr Spiller
  Mr Nixon
  Revd Mr Merriman
  Revd Mr Skinner
  Revd Mr Waring
  Dr Burton
  Revd Mr Dixon

Agreed that Dr Burton & Mr Skinner be requested to draw up an account of the Last Years Proceedings of the Associates & that 500 copies thereof be printed.

Adjourned to the first Thursday in March

March. 6: 1760 Avemarylane
Present
  Revd Mr Berriman
  Revd Mr Skinner
  Mr Spiller

Mr Jos. Waring
Benjn Franklin Esq
Richard Morhall Esq
Mr Nixon
Mr Jams Waring
Revd Mr Waring

J Waring reported that he had received 2: 2: 0 of Benjn Franklin Esq & 1: 1: 0 of Richard Morhall their Benefactions at admission.

[Agreed that copies of certain books be sent to the libraries at Philadelphia, Williamsburg, New York City, and Newport Rhode Island]

J. Waring reported that he had sent three boxes of Books for the negro Schools in America as directed on the 17. Jany Last

Ave Mary Lane   At a meeting of the Associates Novr 6: 1760
    Present Dr Franklin in the chair
        Revd Mr Skinner
        Revd Mr Waring

Dr Franklin reported that he had received a letter from Mr Hunter of Williamsburg Virginia dated June———— acquainting him that he had received a packet of Books for the use of the negroes that he was much pleased with the commission he had received to open a negro School & that he and Dr Dawson would use their best endeavours to open a School with all convenient speed.

J. Waring reported that in consequence of the Resolution of the association at their last meeting to open two more Negroe Schools. He had consulted with Mr Bacon on that Subject, who upon Mature Deliberation thought it most advisable to open one School at Eden Town North Carolina, & the other in Maryland at Such place as his Br. shoud most approve of & further that He had wrote upon this Subject to the Revd Mr. Bacon in Maryland & also to Thos Child Esq. & Mr Hazlewood Mercht at Eden Town North Carolina—and also that proper packets of books had been sent to each province for the use of the Schools, the freight of which Mr. Bacon very kindly paid.

Read a Letter from Mr Hunter of Williamsburgh Virginia dated Feb: 16: 1761 who says a School was opened there Michaelmas last for 24 Negroes (which he thinks are as many as one woman can take care of) that he & Dr Dawson were of opinion 20 a year was not a sufficient salary & therefore they agreed to give 10 more for rent which Mr Dawson undertook to raise by subscription, but he dying soon after nothing was done, that Mr Hunter judged it more for the Credit of the associates to pay the whole Salary than to be aided by a trifling contribution that he thinks 30 £ Sterling as little as it can be done for. He saith the Design of the associates was generally well received. That the progress & improvement of the Children in so short a time has greatly exceeded his Expectations & he has reason to hope that the good Intentions of the Associates will be fully answered by the Care & good conduct of the mistress. . .

Agreed that J. Waring do write to Mr Hunter & acquaint him that the associates are much obliged to him for his kind Letter, and are sensible persons on the Spot are best judges what Salary may be sufficient for a Mistress, & therefore they certainly acquiesce with his Opinion, & will increase the appointment for Williamsburgh to thirty pounds a year. That the Ass. return him Thanks for his generous assistance & will order a Letter to be sent of Robt Carter Nicholas to request the Favour of his kind concurrence.

Agreed that in the Opinion of the Associates present it is very proper & Expedient that at their Several Meetings for the Dispatch of Business they shou'd jointly offer up their prayers to Almighty God to implore his Assistance & Blessing upon their several undertakings, and that the Clergy present be desired to prepare suitable forms of Prayer to be used before & after the Business of each meeting.

Agreed that the Revd Dr Owen & Revd Mr Waring be desired to draw up an account of the proceedings of the Associates for the last year & 250 copies thereof be immediately printed.

Agreed that a meeting be held here on Wednesday next to consider whether it may not greatly contribute to promote the charitable Designs of the Associates, if they were to dine together at their own Expense and to consider of the proper Time & place for that purpose.

Adjourned to Wednesday next 13th

Associates Office Octobr 1. 1761
Present   Dr Franklin in the Chair
           Revd Mr Berriman
           Mr Waring
           Thos Linquist Esq
Read a Letter from the Revd Mr Marge Junr of St Thomas's Parish Orange County Rapalanoch River Virginia who says that he succeeded the Late Mr Marshall in his Living to Whom the Associates

had sent a parcel of Books which arrived safe, that his parishioners had promised, on the arrival [word not clear] Parcel to build a House entirely for a Library... He hath many negroes in his Parish who bring their Children to be baptised, & Many of the adults are desirous of Baptism. He desired the Associates to send him some more Books. . .

Dr Franklin & Mr Waring reported that they had not yet come to any resolution where to put any more negro schools for want of better information

> Novr 5: 1761 Associates Office
> Richd Morhall Esq
> Thomas Toiquist Esq
> Revd Mr Waring
> Mr Joseph Waring

Richd Morhall in the Chair in the absence of Dr Franklin.

Benefactions reported a collection of Books valued at 4:4:0 for the Lending Library . . . from Revd Mr Waring.

Agreed that Mr Waring be desired to acquaint Mr Marge in answer to his letter read at the last meeting that the Associates wou'd very readily send him the Books he requests, if their Fund wou'd allow of it; but that at present, in the Choice of Books for parochial Libraries, they must confine themselves to such as are most immediately useful to the Clergy in the discharge of their pastoral Function; that their view in presenting Books to Mr Marge & the late Mr Marshall toward Parochial Libraries was to encourage them to promote the Instruction of the negroes in the Christian Religion to which Books further additions will be made as soon as Mr Marge shall favor the Associates with a particular account of the progress he hath made in converting & instructing the Negroes

Agreed that eighteen Indians Instructed & some Tracts against swearing & gaming be sent to Mr Marge for the use of the Negroes in his parish

> Associates Office Jan. 1762
> Dr Franklin—Chairman

Mr Waring reported that he had received the following letter relating to the designs of the Associates, viz:

> Williamsburgh Virg. [date not clear].

Sir

Yours of June the 1st directed Mr Hunter with a letter to Mr Yates and another for Mr Nicholas came to our Hands about ten days ago.

Mr Hunter being dead, Mr Yates and Mr Nicholas will accept of the Trust and will write to you: and to them we have delivered your Letters & Papers relating to the Negro school & have directed the Mistress (Mrs Wager) to apply to them for Instructions and her pay for the future. Mr Hunter by his will appointed Mr James Tarpley (now in London) & ourselves his Executors. We have duly proved the will here, and finding by Mr Hunter's Books that £ 10 is due to his Estate for two Quarters salary paid the Mistress, exclusive of the first Quarter which he drew on you to Mr Tarpley, we have this Day drawn an Order on you to Mr Tarpley for the sum which we desire you will be pleased to pay him for the use of Mr Hunter's Estate, We are

Sr Yor & C
Ben Waller
Thos Everett

Sr   Williamsburgh 17 Sept 1762

 I have lately had the pleasure of receiving your Favour of the first of June under Mr Hunters cover who died a few days before it came to Hand. You Judged very right of my sentiments in not allowing yourself to doubt of my ready compliance with the Associates request, as I should always be ready most cheerfully to concur in any measure tending to promote Christianity. I took the earliest opportunity in waiting on the Revd Mr Yates to converse with him on the subject of your Letter, and found him, as I knew he would be, heartily disposed to cooperate with me, in supporting the school to the utmost of his power. I have also seen the school Mistress and understand from her matters stand pretty much as they did when Mr Hunter wrote you his last letter. From what I have already discovered, for I have not had time yet to enquire minutely, I find there are several regulations necessary to be made; and tho I have no very sanguine expectations of the schools insuring the Intentions of the pious Founders you may assure the Society that no endeavours of Mine shall be wanting to procure the wishes for success. The Exectors of Mr Hunter inform me that they have paid for the 3d Quarters salary, & I suppose we shall have permission to draw for the fourth as I understand the year is nearly expired. I am, Sir, with good regards

Yours &c
Rob C. Nicholas

Agreed that the Thanks of the Associates be returned to Mr Nicholas for his kind letter, that he be informed that His & Mr Yates's Resolution charitably to superintend the Negroe School gave most sincere Pleasure to the Associates who entirely leave it to Mr Nicholas & Revd Yates to make such Regulations for the future good [word not clear] of the School as they shall Judge expedient, & hope Mr Yates will in a little Time find the good effects of the School exceed his expectations..

Copy of Letter from Revd Mr Dan Earl
N. Carolina Edentown 3 Oct-61
Sir
Mr. Hazlewood a merchant in this Town Showed me a Letter from you, wherein you signifyed to him that a Society called Dr Brays Associates were desirous that a School may be opened here for the Education of Negroe Children under the Care of him Mr Child and myself. But as Mr Child, some time ago moved from hence into Virginia, neither Mr Hazlewood nor myself cou'd learn the Societys Plan till very lately when I waited on him myself for that Purpose. Since which Time I have used my utmost Endeavours to recommend this beneficient and charitable Design to the Inhabitants of this Town, & to represent it in the Light it ought to appear in to all who profess our holy Religion: But am sorry to acquaint you, that my Exhortations and Remonstrances have not as yet had the desired effect, but hope they will consider better of it and not suffer so fair an opportunity of having their young slaves instructed in the Principles of Religion fall to the ground.

They all allow of the great Expediency of the Design but say, that as their Circumstances are low and distressed (which is generally the Case) They cannot spare their Negroes from Service at the age that they are susceptible of Condition, and those that are in affluent Circumstances are so very few that the number of Children sent by them wou'd be so inconsiderable as not to be worth any persons acceptance, as the Teaching of Negroes precludes the taking of White Children, the Parents not allowing their Children to be educated among such. If it shou'd be proposed by your worthy Society to allow any Salary for the Education of white Children, it wd be readily embraced, & wou'd be productive of great Utility to the poor and ignorant Colony as the great part of them are brought up in profound

Ignorance of every kind of Literature, occasioned chiefly by the Poverty and Indigence of the Inhabitants.

I sometime ago signifyed to the Incorporated Society for propagating the gospel in foreign Parts the Want of Education in this Province, as I have the Honour of being in their Service, but have not as yet received any answer.—The Society may rest assured that as I have hitherto, so I shall hereafter incessantly endeavour that their munificent and laudable & charitable Design may answer all the good purposes thereby intended

I am etc

Agreed that the Thanks of the Associates be returned to Mr Earl for his kind Letter & that he be requested to continue his good Endeavours that the Design of the Associates may be carryed into Execution.

Agreed that the Part of Mr Earls Letter relating to the utility of a School for white Children at Edenton be communicated to the Society for propagating the Gospel in foreign parts.

> Associates Office Feb:4:1762
> Present Revd Mr Waring
> Peter Le Kean Esq
> Revd Dr Owen
> Revd Mr Berriman. . . .

Agreed, upon Reconsidering the Revd Mr Marge's Letter from Orange County Virginia, that four small collection of Books on practical Religion be sent to Mr Marge to be placed at his 4 places of publick Worship as Lending Libraries for the Use of the respective Congregation:

> Associates Offices March 4: 1762
> Present Revd Mr Egerton
> Mr Spiller
> Revd Mr Waring
> Mr Nixon
> Peter Le Kean Esq
> Mr Joseph Waring Junr
> Revd Mr Berriman
> Revd Dr Owen

Mr Egerton in the Chair in the absence of Dr Franklin.

Mr Waring reported that he had received a Benefaction of one guinea from Mrs Goditha Martin Daughter of the Late Dr Bray.

Agreed that Thanks be returned to Mrs Martin

Agreed that the Revd Mr Egerton, Mr Nixon & M^r Le Kean be appointed a Committee to audit the Accounts.

The Committee reported that the Ballance of Account in Mr Warings hands due to the Associates is ninety six pounds eighteen shillings & sixpence.

Mr. Waring recommended the Revd Mr Arch deacon Yardley of Highgate as a proper person to be an Associate.

Agreed that Mr Arch deacon Yardley be immediately balloted for.

The Chairman reported that Mr Arch deacon Yardley was unanimously chosen.

Agreed that Proposals for opening negroe schools for 30 children each, be sent to the following Places, with a Salary not exceeding 20 £ p anon

Annapolis Maryland

Chester on Chester River

York on York River ⎫
Norfolk ⎬ Virginia

Bath Town North Carolina

St James's Goose Creek Parish South Carolina. . .

Associates Office May 13: 1762

Present Mr Joseph Waring jun

Revd Mr Archdeacon Yardley

Revd Mr Waring

Revd Mr Berriman

Revd Mr Skinner

Peter Le Kean Esq

Mr Berriman in the Chair in the Absence of Dr Owen. . .

Mr. Waring reported that in pursuance of the Direction of the Associates at their Meeting March 4th He had sent proposals for opening a School for 30 negroe Children at Chester on Chester River Maryland

York on York River Virginia

Norfolk Virginia

Bath Town North Carolina . . .

He has been informed that in the Parish of St James Goose Creek South Carolina the Inhabitants Lived at such a distance from each other that a Sufficient Number of Children for a School were scarce to be met with in one place.

Associates Office Ap. 1: 1762
Present Dr Franklin in the Chair
    Revd Mr Waring
    Revd Mr Archdeacon Yardley
    Revd Mr Berriman. .

Mr Waring reported that the Revd Mr Jonathan Boucher Mins of Hannover Parish in King George County Virginia had assured him that on his Return to Virginia he wou'd use his best Endeavours to instruct the Negroes in his Parish in the Principles of Religion, & requested the Associates to favour him with a few Books to found a Parochial Library in his Parish.

Agreed that Mr Waring do acquaint Mr Boucher that in Consideration of his offer to instruct the Negroes in his Parish The Associates will allot a Parcel of Books towards a Parochial Library in Hannover Parish for the Use of him & successors. . .

Associates Office October 7: 1762
Present Revd Mr Berriman
    Revd Mr Waring
    Revd Mr Skinner. . .
Extract of a Letter from Rob. Carter Nicholas
           Williamsburgh in Virginia 23d June 1762

I have had the number of Children augmented Thirty as You desired. The Mistress is very diligent, and I am in hopes we shall be able to give you soon an agreable account of the Progress They Make under her care & Tuition. I must own to you that I am afraid the School will not answer the Sanguine Expectations its pious Founders may have formed but we will endeavour to give it a fair Trial. . .

Associates Office Jany 6th 1763
Present Revd Mr Waring
    Revd Mr Egerton
    Mr Jos: Waring Junr
Read a Letter from the Revd Mr Alexander Stewart dated Bath North Carolina Aug. 12. 1762 wherein he says "he made known the Associates Intention of supporting a Negroe School, & found the People at Bath & in his Several Chapelries approved of it & many of them promised to be encouragers of so good a Design But He says

there are Difficulties almost peculiar to that Province, The Towns are Small, Bath particularly has the fewest Inhabitants of any, so that the Number of Negroes Sufficient for a School cou'd not be had in any one Town, that the Towns which abound with Negroes are situated on Rivers which are generally impassable, however, he Saith, he hath advertised for a Mistress, & will make an Essay on the Associates Plan.

The most probable Method of making the Associates Scheme take footing in that Province till it is better peopled he thinks wou'd be to divide their Salary among three or four Schoolmasters in different Towns, & that He will take upon him to visit the Several Schools twice in the Quarter, & catechise the remote Children on the Evenings of those Days he preaches at the Chapels & every Easter. & Christmas Day will oblige the Masters to have their Negroe Scholars brought to the Church to be publickly & all together catechised & y[t] he will take care to keep a publick Register of the Ages, Baptisms, & Times of Admission on the different Children.

The Schoolmasters he woud recommend he says are such as already keep publick Schools for white Children to whom it wou'd be great Encouragement to have this small Bounty from the Associates.

He Saith he wrote to Governour Dobbs, who, he doubts not, will be an Encourager of the Design, but lives at too great a Distance to have any immediate Influence on a School in that or any of the neighbouring Parishes.

Agreed that M[r] Waring do return the Thanks of the Associates to M[r] Steward for his kind Letter & acquaint him that they refer it to him to make choice of the Method of promoting the Instruction of the Negroes, which to him may seem most likely to be attended with success, only they desire he will not exceed twenty pounds Sterling for teaching thirty Children & so in proportion for a greater or Less Number:

Associates Office March 3[d] 1763
Present M[r] Joseph Waring Jun[r]
  Rev[d] Archdeacon Yardley
  Rev[d] D[r] Owen
   M[r] Spiller
  Rev[d] M[r] Waring
  Rev[d] M[r] Skinner
  Rev[d] D[r] Burton

Revd Mr Berriman

Mr A. Yardley in the Chair in the absence of the Chairman

Read a Letter dated at Williamsburgh Virginia 30th Sept. 1762 from the Revd Mr Yates & Robt Nicholas Esq: wherein They say They have sent a List of the Black Children at present in the School, but can give no Satisfactory Account of those who have left the School the Mistress having kept no regular account. That at a late Visitation of the School they were pretty much pleased with the Scholars performances as they rather exceeded their Expectations, that They believe all the Children have been baptized & that it is general Practice in the Province for Negroe Parents to have their Children baptized that the many Difficulties They have to Struggle with in the Prosecution of the good Work made them Apprehensive that the Success might not answer the Expectation of the Associates but they shall think themselves very Fortunate if any Endeavours of theirs can contribute to the Spiritual Welfare & Happiness of the poor Negroes. They hope, notwithstanding the several obstacles to the Instruction & Reformation of the Negroes (which they enumerate) that this Scheme of Negro Schools properly conducted may have a good Effect. They say the People of that City were very willing to send their Young Negroes to School, & believe that double the present Number of Scholars might easily be procured, wou'd the Fund admit of it; but are fearful Many People do not send them upon right Motives, because They do not suffer them to continue at School long enough to be properly instructed, but keep them at Home as soon as they can be of the least Service in the Family. They add, that the Planters urge it a sin & politick to enlarge the understanding of their Slaves, which will render them more impatient of Slavery. They are apprehensive that the good Impressions made on the Childrens Mind whilst at School will afterwards be too easily effaced by the bad Examples of other Slaves, especially of their Parents: howevery They are resolved not to be discouraged, but hope by the Blessing of God the undertaking will prosper—They think that Designs of this Nature cannot properly be conducted without certain Uniform Regulations, by which all parties concerned may know how to conduct themselves, & have therefore drawn up a Set of Rules for this Purpose a Copy of which They sent to be submitted to the Judgement of the Associates. They shall soon have Occasion for a few Testaments, Psalters Spelling Books for the use of the School &

a Number of Baccu's Sermons to be dispersed among the Planters & conclude with wishing Success to the Associates in all their Designs.

Agreed that the Sincere & hearty Thanks of the Associates be returned to the Revd Mr Yates & Mr Nicholas for their full and very Satisfactory Account of the present State of the Negroe School, & for their generous assurances that notwithstanding the manifold Difficulties & Discouragements they have to contend with, They are resolved to persevere in the Prosecution of this pious & charitable Undertaking.

Agreed that hearty Thanks be returned also for their Care in drawing up Rules & Regulations for the Better Government of the School & that They be made acquainted that the Associates do entirely approve thereof as Judiciously calculated to answer the good End proposed

Agreed that 25 Spelling Books 25 Psalters 20 Testaments & 25 Baccus Sermons be sent for the Use of the Negroe School at Williamsburgh.

Associates Office April 7: 1763
Present Richard Morhall, Esq.
   Revd Mr Waring
   Revd Mr Archdeacon Yardley
   Revd Dr Burton
   Revd Mr Egorton
   Revd Mr Berriman
  Revd Mr Archdeacon Yardley in the Chair.

Read a Letter from Revd Mr Charles Smith dated Portsmouth Parish Virginia Sep.. 22: 1762, in answer to a proposal sent last Year for opening a Negroe School at Norfolk, wherein he Says he received the Box but the letter of advice not coming for some time after, he had disposed of some of the Books to poor whites & blacks, that his Parish was lately divided into three & he had retired into the Country where there are few Negroes that he communicated the Proposal to Mr Rhonnald his Successor, who desired him to impart the Scheme to his Vestry & Parishoners before he begins the School.

Read a Letter from Mr Rhonnald dated Norfolk Virginia, Sep. 27: 1762 who assigns several Reasons why he cou'd not proceed in setting on foot a Negro School at Norfolk but especially the smallness of the Salary allowed by the Associates.

Agreed that the Design of having a Negroe School at Norfolk be laid aside for the present.

Read a Letter from the Revᵈ Mʳ Boucher dated King George County Rappahanock River Virginia Decʳ 21, 1762 where in he says that many Difficulties prevent his opening a Negroe School in his parish at present, but that he uses his best Endeavours to promote their spiritual Improvement, that since his Arrival he had baptized upwards of 108 Negroe Children & between 30 & 40 adults, desires to continue his Correspondence in hopes that in some part of his life he might be enabled to lend a helping Hand to this desirable Work...

Associates Office Oct.. 6: 1763
Present Revᵈ Mʳ Waring
      Revᵈ Mʳ Berriman
      Revᵈ Dʳ Mayo
      Mʳ John Spiller...

Read a Letter from Dʳ Franklin dated New York June 27, 1763, who says He had been at Williamsburgh & gives a good account of the School there, Says he intends to visit the School at New York, Newport Rhode Island, & on his Return to Philadelphia will very minutely enquire into the State of the School There. He Inclosed a List of the Black Children at Present in the School...

ASSOCIATES OFFICE FEBY: 2: 1764

Read a Letter from the Revᵈ Mʳ Marge dated Orange County Rapahanock River Virginia Octobʳ 24: 1763 Wherein he says (referring to a former Letter) he finds it impracticable to set on foot a Negroe School in his Parish on Account of the dispersed Situation of the Inhabitants & the various Employments They have for the Young Negroes as soon as They are well able to go about. to remedy which he recommends the Distribution of proper Books to the Planters, who in general are destitute of such Aids were they ever so well disposed to instruct their Negroes. He says there is a Town on the River (the name of which he doth Not mention) a Place of great Trade populous and abounding with Negroes where a School, he Thinks, might be placed with great advantage. He refer to his former Letter for the Books he requested of the Associates but does not take any Notice of the Books which were sent to him last so that tis to be feared he never received Them & concludes with assuring the Associates he will cheerfully execute any orders They will be pleased to send him. ...

ASSOCIATES OFFICE SEPT^R 6TH 1764

Read a Letter from the Revd Mr Boucher, dated Hanover Parish King George County Rappach^k River Virginia Ap. 28: 1764. Wherein He says that to remedy the Want of a School for Negroes as much as He cou'd He has employed a very sensible well disposed Negro belonging to a Gentleman who lives about a Mile from Him, to endeavour at instructing his poor fellow Slaves in reading and some of the first Principles of Religion, with which, He hath taken Care that He shou'd not be totally unacquainted. Saturdays and Sundays afternoons He employs to this Purpose and He has as Mr Boucher believes between twenty and Thirty who constantly attend him and that he may be the better qualified for his Office Mr Boucher obliges him to visit him two or three times every week when either himself or some young gentlemen who live with him give his lessons, and once at least a month he brings his Scholars to be examined by Mr Boucher who Thinks the Progress they have made not inconsiderable. He finds them in Books and endeavours to encourage the industrious by alloting some small Reward for extraordinary Diligence as well as to their Master. Mr Boucher hopes, that tho he hath deviated from the plan of the Associates, they will not think the few Books sent improperly bestow'd. He wou'd be glad of a further supply to the value of 30s or 40s which he wou'd willingly purchase, but that he shall in a little Time remove to St Marys, about 20 miles higher up the River. He is fearful his little Seminary may upon his Departure dwindle away for want of some person to encourage its President Aaron. He will endeavour to introduce such a scheme into St Marys Parish & hopes to meet with the Approbation and Assistance of the Associates.

The Revd Mr Stewart in a Let^r dated Bath N. Carolina May 1: 1764 says that upon Shewing the Secretarys Letters to some of the Inhabitants He was fed with Hopes of erecting three Schools in that and the Neighbouring Counties in a short Time, but after He had distributed part of the Books among the Schoolmasters and encouraged them all He cou'd, He found at Length that it was but Labour & Sorrow owing to the mean low Prejudices of the People. He made one short lived Effort to erect a school (not altogether on the Plan of the Associates) for the Instruction of Ten Indians and Negro

Children at Attamusket in Hyde County. He says the Master James Francis instructed Six Indian Boys whom Mr Steward baptized in Octor 1763. A List of their names & ages with the Masters Receipt for a Quarters Salary amounting to 1L:13s:9p were inclosed. He is uncertain whether the School is continued it being above 10 miles by water from Bath. He says He shall always be ready upon the least Dawn of Success to renew his Endeavours.

Associates Office April 4: 1765

Mr Waring reported that He had received of the Revd Mr Broughton the Sum of One Hundred Pounds. Being a Benefaction of Mr Thomas Wycliffe, Merchant of Liverpool, towards promoting the Instruction of the Negroes in the British Plantations in the Christian Religion.

Agreed that Thanks be returned to Mr Wycliffe for his very generous Benefaction and that he be requested to grant Permission to be elected an Associate.

Read a Letter from Robt C. Nicholas Esq of Williamsburgh Virginia dated 21 Decr 1764. wherein he says The Rules for the Negro School formerly transmitted by Him were rather what He wished to have complied with than what He expected wou'd be given into at once, however He will endeavour to enforce them by Degrees, however strange it may appear He assures it is a very difficult Business He is engaged in and finds it necessary to manage with great Delicacy. The School is in much the same State as when he wrote last except in the Change of a few Scholars. The Mistress is very diligent. He is sorry for the death of the Revd Mr Yates, by which He is left alone in this Business, He is succeeded as President of the College & Minr of the Parish by the Revd Mr James Horrocks, who, He doubts not wou'd cheerfully give his assistance if it were asked, and recommends that He be wrote to on the subject.

Agreed that Mr Waring be desired to write to the Revd Mr Horrocks to request him to join with Mr Nicholas in conducting the Negro School at Williamsburg.

Read a Letter from the Revd Mr James Marge Minr of Orange County Virginia dated Sept. 25. 1764 wherein He says that He had been at Fredericksburgh lately, on a Visit to his Father who is Minr of the Parish and made Inquiry what number of young Negroes might be sent Shou'd a school be opened there, & cou'd not learn it wou'd be possible to get above four or five of thereabout, and They not to go constantly but only at Spare times as it suits their Owners. The number of adult Negroes in his Parish He thinks may be about one Thousand and the same number of young ones. The numbers attending divine service on Sundays differs at different Churches, in general there are about 30 or 40 on some Sundays He has seen 60 or more. The number of Negroe Communicants is very small not exceeding half a dozen or thereabout. All that understand English and are tolerably convenient for the Church bring their Children to be baptized.

ASSOCIATES OFFICE OCT. 3D: 1765

The Revd Mr Boucher Rector of St Marys Carolina County Virginia saith in a Let. dated Jany 22.-65 The Associates have his hearty Thanks for their attention to his opinion and Endeavours that had it been in his Power to have established a Negroe School agreable to their Expectations He wou'd cheerfully have attempted it but he still thinks it impracticable, yet many important services may be done among the poor Negroes. He hope he hath been instrumental in doing some good among them. He knows no way so likely as that happily taken by the Associates. Prayer Books distributed among them and proper Inquiries after their Improvement seems to be all that is in the power of the Best of Us to do, in parishes like his. A great deal this is of itself, he saith I might surprise you were I to relate some of the Conversation I have had with the Negroes to whom I had given Books, and adds it must be a Satisfaction to the Ass. to have the Prayers and Blessings of many of these unfortunate People which he hath often heard expressed with Tears of Gratitude.

He laments that the Box of Books sent last year was not yet come to Hand and concludes with assuring that he shall always cheerfully concur in any Schemes for the Spiritual welfare of any part, how inconsiderable, of the human Race.

Mr Lewis De Rossett of Wilmington N. Carolina in a Lett dated Ap 22: 1765 saith the Secys Lettr & Box of Books came to his Hands last Year. that he thought it wou'd be best to defer writing until he had tryed all Methods to carry into Execution the laudable Designs of the Associates, but is sorry to say that all his Endeavours for that purpose have proved ineffectual as he can find no person properly qualified to instruct the black Children in the Manner proposed. & that if such Person cou'd be found yet in that Country Twenty pounds is by far too little to support them and is much afraid that nothing more can be got there, for that he spoke to several gentlemen who He thought might send Black Child^n to School & proposed that they should give something to encourage the undertaking, but did not find any of them willing to do it, he thought the same person might teach white Children as....

ASSOCIATES OFFICE DEC^R 5. 1765

Mr Nicholas of Williamsburgh Virginia in a Lett^r dated Sept. 13: 1765 says he intended this Fall to have sent a circumstantial Account of the State of the Negroe School there, but that a long Indisposition hath interrupted his attention to Business of every kind. The number of Scholars is much the same, about thirty: the Mistress is pretty much advanced in years & he fears the Labours of the School will be Shortly too much for her, if this is the Case He will endeavour to procure another, but is apprehensive of great Difficulties in fixing on a proper person, He has tried to enforce some of the Rules approved by the Associates, but finds they are not well relished however he will persevere. He finds it extremely difficult to procure a proper House for the Mistress & her Scholars, Rents being so high There: He will make his Business very soon to visit his Charge, & will send a more particular Account by some future opportunity.

Fielding Lewis Esq of Fredericksburgh in Virginia in a Letter dated Sept 14.-65 saith that he had received a Box of Books with the Secretarys Lett^r & will with pleasure do every Thing he can to promote the pious Design of the Associates. He had some Difficulty in procuring a proper person to undertake the School for the Education of Negroe Children the allowance being so small that the greatest part of it will be paid for House Rent and Fireing, Mr Nicholas has furnished him with the Rules established in the School at Williamsburgh, which are so well calculated for the good government that he Hath established the same at Fredericksburgh. The School was opened in April last and there are now he says Sixteen Children who constantly attend and who have improved beyond his Expectation. The Revd Mr James Marge Minister of the parish hath given him all the Assistance He cou'd, & hath promised to call frequently and examine the Children, as they begin already to read prettily there will be occasion for a few Testaments & common prayer Books, for the purpose to introduce them to Church as soon as they are capable of joining in the Service, in his next he promises to send a Copy of the School Register with the ages of the Children.

Agreed that Parochial Libraries of about the same size and value with those formed last year be sent to the above places with all convenient speed & that Mr Howell be designed to superintend the Establishment of them.

ASSOCIATES OFFICE APRIL 3D 1766

Mr Robt Carter Nicholas of Williamsburgh Virginia in a Letter dated Decr 27. 1765 sent a List of thirty four negroe Children then at School in that City; Tis, impossible for him to fix their ages: but he supposes them to be from about four to ten years. The Time standing in the School, from the Mistress's Account which is not scrupulously exact, from about Six Months to two yrs & half. The Rules which He formerly drew up for the better government of the School, and which were approved of by the Associates, He wou'd gladly have observed, but soon found that the Masters & Mistress's were so averse to every Thing that looked like Compulsion that He Thought it adviseable to relax a little in hopes that Things might be put upon a more agreable Footing. The present Number exceeds what the Mistress stipulated to teach, for as it is not in her power to oblige them to attend constantly She is willing to instruct all Such as offer themselves. The Owners, as soon as the Children are able to do little offices about the House, either take them away from School entirely, or keep them from it at Times so that they attend only when there is no employment for Them at Home. The term He proposed for the Children to continue at School was three Years at Least, but few are allowed to stay so long; those who do generally learn to read pretty well, to say their prayers & the Catechism. He had lately visited the School and examined the Children who seemed to have made a reasonable Progress. The Mistress is far advanced in years, & He is afraid the Business will soon be too laborious for Her: & how to Supply the School better He at present doth not know, for He is satisfied She take a deal of pains with the Children. He will not fail to encourage her and do every thing he can to promote the Success of so pious an Institution.

Robt C. Nicholas Esq. of Williamsburgh, says in a Lettr dated Decm 27. 1766 that the School there goes on as well as usual, in this Lett was inclosed a State of Accounts relating to the School There.

ASSOCIATES OFFICE APRIL 2D 1767

Filling Lewis Esq. of Fredericksburgh, Virginia, says in a Letr dated Decr 12th 1766 that He had received a Second Box of Books for the Negroe School, that the Children when admitted into the School were very young, which wou'd be no disadvantage to them, provided they cou'd be kept at School a Sufficient Time, which he fears the proprietors will not consent to & therefore He is apprehensive this undertaking will not succeed so well as He at first hoped. He will admit none hereafter, unless the Masters will engage to continue them at School at least five Years, which Form he thinks necessary for their attaining a proper Degree of Instruction, for unless there is some Regulation of this kind, few will be kept longer than two or three years which, considering how Young they are admitted, is too short a time for them to make any great progress, & therefore He recommends it to the Associates to discontinue the School after this Year unless the proprietors will agree for the time proposed otherwise he thinks the money will be expended & no good purpose obtained. He desires the direction of the Associates in his Letter was inclosed a list of Seventeen Children then in the School with their respective Ages at Admission, by which it appears they were from five to Eight years old.

Agreed that Thanks be returned to Mr Lewis for his charitable Inspection of the Negroe School, & that He be requested to continue the School on the best terms He can, & endeavour that the Number may be compleated as soon as may be & that He be acquainted that the Associates are desirous of keeping the School on foot Some time longer, in hopes that much good may result from it.

The Revd Mr Boucher Rector of St Marys, Carolina County Virginia, in a Letter dated March 9. 1767 saith—The Box of Books at length came safe, and that he had distributed many of them among the poor Slaves in his Parish, as it is impracticable to establish a School by reason of the dispersed Situation of the Negroes. He endeavours to find out an old Negroe or Conscientious Overseer who can read, to whom He gives Books, with an Injunction to them to instruct such & such Slaves in their respective Neighbourhoods, and afterwards to report to him the Success of their Endeavours. This He thinks is the most practicable Method of accomplishing the good End in View, the Instruction of the poor Slaves.

Last Summer He baptized in one Day Three Hundred & fifteen

Adults, and delivered a Lecture of an Hour, after reading prayers to about Three thousand. It was the Hardest Days Service, saith He, I ever had in my Life, yet I know not that I ever before felt such a pleasing Exultation of Heart, as I then did; for I cou'd not but think my Employment truly primitive & Apostolical: It was in Whitsun Monday which is a general Holiday for Slaves throughout the Colony; and as I had given Notice that I wou'd on that Day preach to them in particular, They eagerly flocked to me from all Quarters, in greater Numbers than my Church Yard cou'd contain.—In his own Parish He believes there are upwards of a Thousand Negroes, Many of them attend Church duly, and behave decently: In Summer They are frequently so numerous as not to be able to find Room. There are five or Six who have prayer Books, and make the Responses with great Regularity & Propriety, and on Christmas Day last He believes there were fifteen of Them Communicants, and he is perswaded very worthy Ones. Some of his Brethren in the remoter Parishes have interceded with him for some Books which he supplied them with, & he doth not doubt but They will heartily & vigorously concur in promoting this good work in their respective parishes.

The Revd Mr Boucher Rector of St Marys Carolina County Virginia in a Let.. received in August without a Date, says He thinks no considerable Services can be done amidst the Slaves any where in America & get some little Instructions it is in the power of the Clergy to give them: & in them to receive & that little, doubtless every conscientious Minister will think it his Duty to do, & gratefully acknowledge the Assistances received from the Associates. The Negroes in his Parish are too numerous for his Church to contain, were they all constantly to attend divine Services. He believes, however, he hath more than any other man at least. Their numbers are complained of by the white people, during the hot weather Months, when They realy are very offensive. They are regularly & universally baptized in St Mary's & the Number of Communicants amongst Them constantly increases. No longer ago than Yesterday saith He, I am pretty certain I distributed upwards of two Dozen Books. so that at this Time the Stock you sent me, tho' pretty considerable is almost entirely out. The gentleman who succeeded him in Hanover is so very inform that he is by no means able to discharge his other parochial Duties with charging himself with the additional Burthen of the Negroes. He is told the Negroe School at Fredericksburgh about seven miles from his doth much Service.

ASSOCIATES OFFICE MARCH 3D: 1768

Read a Letter from Mr Nicholas of Williamsburgh Virginia dated 1st Decr 1767 acquainting that the Mistress is diligent as usual & the Children are managed in the manner he formerly mentioned that He has drawn for Thirty pounds Sterl. which will not quite defray the Expenses of the last year & yt the Balance will be brought to an After Account.

Agreed that Mr Nicholas be acquainted that no other Negroe School Supported by the Associates stands them in more than twenty pounds Sterl. P Ann, & hoped that the School at Williamsburgh when first opened wou'd not have cost them more than twenty five pounds Sterl P An. & that if be needful to find a School Room for the Mistress, they don't doubt but the worthy Inhabitants of Williamsburgh will Chearfully contribute towards payment of the Rend as was proposed by some of them at the first Opening of the School, & that no more than 25 £ P An be paid after Mid summer next.

ASSOCIATES OFFICE APRIL 6TH 1769

Read a Letter from Mr Lewis of Fredericksburgh Virginia dated Oct. 21: 1768 wherein he expresseth his Concern that the Negroe School there did not answer the good Intention of the Associates, there being only Nine young Negroes who constantly attend the School, that in the Summer there were only four and he has reason to fear the present Number will soon be greatly reduced. He Observes that several of them have left the School as soon as they cou'd read tolerably. He hopes however the little Time These have remained there may be of Service, as great Care is taken by the Mistress to impress on their Minds the Duties of our holy Religion, & He will call at the School so long as the Associates think proper to continue it to see that the Mistress doth her Duty.

Agreed that Thanks be returned to Mr Lewis for his kind attention to the Negroe School & that he be requested to acquaint the Proprietors of Slaves that unless the number of Scholars be increased to Twenty before the Expiration of the present Year. the School will be discontinued...

Read a Letter from Mr Nicholas of Williamsburgh Virginia dated Jan 1: 1770 wherein he acquaints the Associates that if the Expenses of the Negro School there exceeds 25 £ Sterling the Surplus shall be made up by the People there.

ASSOCIATES OFFICE MAY 3: 1770

The Revd Mr Tho.. Baker of Hengston Glebe in Gloster Counter Virginia in a Letter dated Apl 23. 1770 says many masters are not only averse to learning their Slaves to read, but did not the Law oblige them, wou'd not have them baptized. However many attend both his Churches every Sunday, both Infant & adult Negroes. He hath baptized some upwards of Sixty Years old, who have with tears running down their Cheeks repeated the Lords Prayer & Creed & behaved in such a manner as wou'd have pleased every good Christian.—He hath disposed of some of the Books given by the Associates to the best advantage he cou'd, & hopes when he hath a Parish of his own to promote this good work with greater Success than he can at present.

The Revd Mr Barnett of Northampton North Carolina in a Letter dated June 9: 1770 says about Sixty adult Negroes joyfully accepted the offer of Instruction.

ASSOCIATES OFFICE APRIL 4TH 1771

Mr Nicholas in a Letr dated Jany 22. 1771 says There have no material Alterations happen'd in the School since his last on account he hath nothing new to offer.

ASSOCIATES OFFICE MAY 7: 1772

Mr Nicholas of Williamsburgh Virginia in a Letr Dated Decr 17: 1771 says the Affairs of the Negroe School go on much as formerly, that the Mistress has been sick for some time past, & he himself very much indisposed, otherwise he wou'd have sent a List of the Scholars with proper remarks on their Progress, which he promises at some future opportunity.

Mr Lewis of Fredericksburgh in a Letter dated Feb. 1st 1772 says that pursuant to the Request of the Associates He had endeavoured to the utmost of his power to procure a competent number of Negroe Children to be instructed but without Effect, that the Mins The Revd Mr Marge gave an excellent discourse in the Church on the Occasion, but the good purpose was not answered. He therefore at the End of the Year discontinued the School which had subsisted five years at the Expense of one hundred pounds Sterling which leaves a Bal due to him of thirty pounds. He laments that so much money shoud have been expended to so little purpose.

Read a Letter from Mr Nicholas dated 1st Decr 1771 wherein he saith that he intended to have sent a list of the Negroe Children at School, but was prevented by the Indisposition of the Mistress, & a variety of publick Business, however he will venture to say that Matters are conducted much as formerly, the number of scholars is fluctuating, & some few of the Inhabitants do join with him in contributing towards support of the School, tho' there is far from a general disposition to promote its success.—He desire that the Associates will request the Revd Mr Josiah Min^r of the Parish to concur with him in countenancing & promoting this charitable design.

Agreed that the Sec^y do write to Mr Johnson to request his kind & charitable Concurrence.

Read a Letter from Mr Nicholas dated 5th Jany 1774 wherein he says the Situation of the School is much as it was when he wrote last, the number of scholars is between 20 & 30 & he believes the Mistress gives them proper Attention, he says The Revd Mr Johnson to whom the Sec^y wrote last year is dead, & wishes the Associates wou'd request the Patronage of the Revd Mr John Bracken his Successor who is a worthy Man & may be of Service to the School.

Agreed that the Revd Mr Bracken's Assistance in inspecting the School be requested.—Original MSS are the property of the SPG. Photocopies are in the Library of Congress and microcopies of those are in the Library of the University of North Carolina and in the Library of the College of William and Mary.

2. LETTER FROM JOHN THOMPSON, ORANGE, VIRGINIA, AUGUST 25, 1743

Revd Sir,

I receiv'd your kind letter of ye 2^d of February 1741, with a Present of books from ye venerable Society for promoting Christian Knowledge, as also a Benefaction from ye Associates of ye late Dr Bray; for which, I desire ye favour of you, Sir, to return them my hearty & unfeigned thanks, hoping y^t I shall make such a good use of their repeated favours, as to answer, in some measure, their pious & laudable Designs. My Parish was so extensive, as to admit of a Division, & a new one erected; but notwithstanding, my labour & diligence is nothing abated, having, still three Places of Worship to preach at; & give ye Sacrament at each place three times in ye year; where I have a considerable number of Communicants, & to my great comfort, perceive, their number yearly increasing. The people seem better disposed, & to have more of ye christian temper, than when I first settled amongst them. I baptiz'd, this last year, 290 white children, 43 negroes & a mulatto, & hope in a short time to have several Negroes, so far instructed, as to be fit to come to ye Lord's table. I have taken all possible care for ye Encouragement of Schools in my Parish of which, now, we have a good number, & have distributed amongst them Lewis's Catechism, & Lessons for children &c—which I received from ye Society. Practical pieces of Divinity wou'd be of great use here; but as I have already receiv'd many Favours from my good friends, shall not intrude any further upon their good nature; but whenever they think proper, to present me with a few Books, they shall be receiv'd with all thankfulness, & converted to a proper Use. Sir, I have nothing of moment to acquaint you with, but gratefully acknowledge ye obligations I am under to you, & remain wth ye profoundest veneration & respect, Reverend Sir,

Your most obliged

Humbl Servt . . . . . Jno Thompson

P.S. Pray give my very humble Service to my good friend Mr Henry Newman: I thank him for his kind Letter, & readiness to serve me—Present my Respects to your good Lady. Commissary Blair is dead, & left a fine Character behind him.

3. EXTRACT OF LETTER BY BENJAMIN FRANKLIN FROM LONDON TO HIS DAUGHTER, JUNE 27, 1760

London, June 27, 1760

My dear child, . . .

The Paragraph of your Letter inserted in the Papers, related to the Negro School. I gave it to the Gentlemen concern'd, as it was a Testimony in favor of their pious Design. But I did not expect they would have printed it with your Name. They have since chosen (me) one of the Society, and I am at present Chairman for the current year. I enclose you an Account of the Proceedings.—Albert H. Smyth, *The Writings of Benjamin Franklin*, IV, 23.

4. LETTER FROM WILLIAM HUNTER, WILLIAMSBURG, VIRGINIA, FEBRUARY 16, 1761

Sir.

I received some Time ago a letter from Mr Franklin, informing me that I had been nominated as one of the Mannagers of a School to be erected here, for the Education of Negroes in the Christian Faith,

&c—Mr Dawson, Commissary and Minister of this Parish, received at the same Time your Letter on the same Subject. We consulted together and agreed with Mrs Anne Wager for the opening a School at Michaelmas last: which was accordingly done.—We judged that the allowance of £ 20 Sterling was not Sufficient, we gave the Mistress therefore the whole Sum as a Salary, and Mr Dawson undertook to raise Ten Pounds Sterling by Subscription for the Payment of House Rent. But he dying soon after, nothing has been done to that purpose, neither do I believe did he ever answer your Letter.—I should have done it sooner myself, but I could not, 'til lately, procure your Letter of his Executor.

As I did not approve of raising the additional Money, by a petty Subscription, I have not attempted it, but am myself liable for the present Year.—I judged it more to the Credit of the Associates to pay the whole Expense necessary, than to be aided by a trifling Contribution.—I would therefore recommend it to them to increase the allowance to £ 30 Sterling if they would maintain the School in any tolerable Credit.—And this I think is as little as it can be done for.

I have the Pleasure of informing the Associates that their Design has been generally well received..

The School was opened with 24 Scholars, (as many I think as one Woman can well manage). Their Progress and Improvement in so short a Time, has greatly exceeded my Expectation, and I have Reason to hope that the good Intentions of the Associates will be fully answered by the Care and good Conduct of the Mistress.

At present I stand single in this Undertaking but Mr Yates being last Week elected minister of the Parish in the Room of Mr Dawson, I shall communicate to him your Letter, and doubt not his Concurrence.—As it was the Intention of the Associates to nominate three Trustees, not knowing that Mr Dawson was a Minister of The Parish, I would recommend a Letter to be written to Robt Carter Nicholas Esqr to whom I have never mention'd it, imagining that a Letter from the Associates would best secure his Compliance.

The Mistress was paid one Quarter's Salary at Christmas, for which I have given Mr Tarpley an order on you, but may probably for the future draw but once a Year, to prevent the Trouble of small Bills.

Be pleas'd to assure the Associates of my hearty Endeavours to further their good Designs, by making this Establishment, at present in its Infancy, as generally beneficial as possible.

5. LETTER FROM DANIEL EARL, EDENTON, NORTH CAROLINA,
OCTOBER 3, 1761

No Carolina Edenton 3 October 1761

Sir

Mr Hazelwood Merchant in this Town Shewed me a Letter from you, wherein you signified to him, that a Society called Dr Brays Associates were desirous that a School may be opened here for the Education of Negroe Children: under the Care of him, Mr Child, and myself; but as Mr Child, some time ago, moved from here into Virga, neither Mr Hazelwood or myself could Learn the Societys Plan 'till very lately, when I waited upon him myself for that Purpose: Since which Time, I have used my utmost Endeavour to recommend their beneficient and charitable Design to the Inhabitants of this Town; and to Represent it in that Light that it ought to Appear to all who Profess our Holy Religion: But am sorry to Acquaint you, that my Exhortations and Remonstrances have not as yet had the desired Effect; but hope they will consider better of it, and not suffer so fair an Opportunity of having their young Slaves instructed in the Principles of Christianity fall to the ground. They all Allow of the great Expediency of the Design, but say, that as their Circumstances are low and Depressed, (which is generally the Case) they can't spare their Negroes from their Service at the Age that they are susceptible of Education: And those that are in Affluent Circumstances are so very few, that the Number of Children sent by them would be so inconsiderable, as not be worth any Person's Acceptance; and as the teaching of Negroes precludes the taking of white Children, the Parents not Allowing their Children to be Educated among such.

If it should be proposed by your worthy Society to Allow any Sallary for the Education of white Children, it would be readily Embraced, and would be productive of great Utility to this poor and ignorant Colony, as the greatest part of them is brought up in profound Ignorance of every Kind of Literature, occasioned chiefly by the Poverty and Indigence of the Inhabitants.

I sometime ago signified to the Incorporated Society for Propagating the Gospel in foreign Parts, the want of Education in this Province as I have the Honour of being in their Service; but have not as yet received any Answer.

The Society may rest assured that as I have hitherto, so I shall hereafter incessantly Endeavour that their Munificent, laudable, and charitable Design may Answer all the good Purposes thereby intended.

6. LETTER FROM ALEXANDER STEWART, BATH, NORTH CAROLINA, AUGUST 12, 1762

Revd Sir

Your favour of ye 20th of April, came safe to hand a few days ago, and I shou'd be unworthy of the Honour the Associates have done me in appointing me Superintendent of this Seminary here, Did I not to ye utmost of my Capacity & Station endeavour to promote this their truly pious & Christian design. To this purpose I have already made known ye Associates Intentions at ye Church In Bath & ye Several Chappels within my Parish, & with pleasure found most People approved & many ye promised to be encouragers of this publick utility. But, there are many Difficulties wch we Labour under in this Province, wch other Provinces are Exempt from. For the towns of N. Carolina are all of them very Small, & Bath particularly has ye fewest Inhabitants of any of them, so that ye number of Scholars to fill up a School cou'd by no means be had in any of ye towns of this Province. Our towns likewise on ye Seaboard, (where negroes are most to be had,) are all of them built on very wide Rivers, often Impracticable to Cross, this Cutts off one half of ye Country Children & added to the Expence of boarding Negroe Children, ye Loss of their time, & ye Prejudices of the Ignorant, are ye Difficulties wch at present Stand in ye way. However I have advertised for a mistress according to the Directions of ye Associates, & if a well recommended one can be had will make an Essay on their plan & open ye School starting by sending two boyes & two girls out of my own family, one of wch boys has already been at school, & will send ye rest of my young negroes as they grow up & can be spared.

The most probable method to make ye Associates Scheme take footing in this County till we are somewhat better peopled wou'd be to divide their Bounty among three or four Schoolmasters, one in this town & ye others in ye Country, & as some of these school masters that I wou'd recommend have Wives who wou'd be capable of teaching ye girls to work, these Masters might have charge of the girls & ye single men of ye Boys. The Parishes here . . . In my attendancd of my Parish I will take upon me to Visit ye Several Schools at least twice in ye Quarter & Catechize ye remote Children on ye Evenings of those days when I preach at ye Chappel & Every Easter & Christmas day will oblige ye masters to have their Negro Schollars brought to ye Church to be publickly & all together Catechized, & will take care to have a publick Register of ye ages, Baptisms, & times of Admission of ye Different Children.

As this Societies Charity, (I presume) is not bound; I make bold to propose to them this method of making it an extensive & beneficial as ye Nature of this thin Settled Country will admit of & will be always ready with my best endeavours to forward their Laudable, publick Spirited & truly Christian Intentions.

I have wrote to Governour Dobbs (who is a member of ye Incorporated Society, to whom likewise I am a missionary;) & inclosed to him a Coppy of your Letter & ye Abstracts of ye Associates, & make no doubt but he will be an Encourager of your Design, but he lives at too great a Distance to have any Influence on a School in this many of ye neighbouring Parishes.

Mr Palmer was gone for England before your letters & Books arrived; & as he is now in London & knows well the Situation of this Country I shall refer you to him for further Information & am Rev^d S^r with my best wishes for ye Society your most obedient & humble Servt.

P.S. The School Masters that I wou'd recommend are such as already keep publick schools in this Parish for White Children, to whom it wou'd be great encouragement to have this Small Bounty from your Society.

7. LETTER FROM CHARLES SMITH, PORTSMOUTH, VIRGINIA, SEPTEMBER 22, 1762

Your very courteous letter of Ap^l 8 relative to the design of Doctor Bray's Associates I received Septr 1st—& the package of books in July; but as they came without a letter, I concluded they had been sent, by the old Sociaty, & distributed some of them to poor white Children, & likeways to Negroes of whom I had a good opinion, to learn & practice Christian dutys: But what remains of the books shall be kept for the purpose you imparted—By the printed Memoirs of the Associates, & their correspondents, it appears, they intend to erect their Schools for young Negroes in the principal Towns of North America, and of which, Norfolk in Orng^e promises to become one & whereof I was Minister almost twenty years; But the Town & Country About it, being too large for one Parish, It was divided abt 10 months ago into three, And I am now retired into one of them in the Country,

After being pretty well worn out, with fatigues of Mind & body, that I can not be of any great Service to the pious design of the Associates, there being but few Negroes in my Neibourhood, whom I will do my utmost, (as I always did) to instruct, & make them in love with Christianity—whose rewards, they of all others, have most reason to aspire after, as finding little or none in their present State—I communicated your letter to the Revd Mr Rhonald, My Successor in the Town of Norfolk, whom I satisfyed, that your letter would have certainly been addressed to, had you known that he was the Incumbent there. He expressed (as he could not otherways do) a great esteem for the Associates, but begs some time till he imparts the Scheme to his Vestry, & parishioners before he begins the School, & upon your writing to him it is not to be doubted, but he will undertake its superintendency to the Satisfaction of the Associates which is the Sincere prayer of Reverend Sir,

Portsmouth Parish
in Virginia, Septr 22
1762

P.S. Colo Ludwells favorable opinion of me, you may be sure was pleasing, which proceeded from his own candour & good nature, & which all Virginians are remarkable for, towards their Clergy, that it must be our own faults, if we are not, on a good footing here.

8. Letter from Alexander Rhonnald, Norfolk, Virginia, September 27, 1762

Revd Sir

On the 21st of this current the Revd Mr Charles Smith my Predecessor waited on me at my School, where he produced a Letter from you, intending a School for Negroes in Norfolk. I was agreeably surprized at it, but when I had read your letter, I was likewise heartily sorry that in the Method & manner proposed it will not answer here for many reasons, as—

1st I find that a School Mistress is rather desired than a Master, for which reason it is obvious, that more girls are to be benefited than Boys, as they are to be educated in Affairs more proper for that Sex. —which thing will answer exactly the Ladies of this place who have many such to send, & will hinder others, so that this Charity must consequently be wrong applied.

2dly If a mistress must be had, qualified with such accomplishments, but especially with the Fear of GOD the only Principle Qualification, such a One may be found Super valuable, who might instruct in some measure about five or Six, but there is not that Woman in this County young or old who could manage Thirty negro Children at one & the same time, however worthy or wicked she may be, which I can attest by Experience, who have had but a few under my Care, within these last Twenty Years of my Life.

3dly Supposing that such a Mistress could be found in this or any other Govermt with all due Accomplishments, the Salary of £ 20 is not much above half the Trouble, or what is paid here for Whites, which is little more respected Employmt as there are 24 Sterl paid for each, & proportionably more according as girls are taught in the Branches of Work, or Boys at Arithmetic, &c, so that the Salary must be equal, at least, with what is given for White Children, otherwise, no woman, however gracious, would undertake the Charge. I myself would be will to add £ 5 of this Currency to the £ 20 Sterl which will make it exactly £ 30 a Year, but I can perceive none willing under £ 50 & a House found for that purpose which will be about Ten pounds. So that this must be a great Bar in this pious proposal.

4. If these Difficulties could be happily Surmounted, There is one Obstacle which I can plainly foresee, would attend it, and that would be, That the gentlemen & their Ladies would fill up the number with their Negroes first, in spite of all Opposition here, otherwise endeavour by Insinuations either to ruin a School in the place, or by Misrepresentations to inform the honourable Society of the Minister of the parish [not clear] who would be only for promoting all he could the pious & worthy Dr Bray's intentions, & that there was no need for such a School here. To that at last, finding nothing in his favour, it would drop of course, which would exactly be the Case with me, so that there is a necessity of adding more Trustees to that School, & in my humble Opinion, appointing Mr Commissary the chief Trustee, to whom the Minr of this parish is to answer & account from limited Time to Time, concerning the number of Scholars, whose they are, & what progress they make, that he may place or remove any as he sees most convenient, but not to depend on the Minr of the parish as chief Visitor, only, as it would occasion him the Unwill of most of his parish, if he insisted on a charity School for poor Negroes, & not for the great & powerful of this place.

5thly There are many poor Free Negroes & Mulattoes in this Borough & Parish, who could not be the better of this School, by reason of the Gentlemen insisting that their small Negroe Boys, whom they perhaps design for Domesticks or Livery Men, shall be preferred before them, & so of the girls who are to be brought up in Needlework or Knitting, fitting them for the House, when at the same time, I can plainly discern, That these girls will be more instructed for the latter Employment, than in that which may conduce to the Saving of the Souls, if well applied, & for that reason I am not a proper Person to be chief Manager of that School here, because

6thly If I could not without offence, I would go through the Borough Parish among such free Negroes, or poor people who cannot afford to teach them themselves & if I could find any Young hopeful Lad or gentleman of that Colour, who after good Education at a School, would [word not clear] a Visit Such a School I would not only place but promote them all that lay in my power by boarding some of them, or giving them what I thought might the more encourage them, altho' I am poor & just entering on the World in an Age when many are above Want, having a large family of children & servants in my house, & other Necessities abounding which I would never mention, had I not thought that the society might conceive that I trifled with them & truckled to Interest here, I have no ends of my own to Serve, being above all things willing to serve my master in whose work I am now more particularly engaged, but still it is my Endeavour to follow peace with all men, & to cut off Occasion from them who Seek Occasion.

I observed in the end of Mr Smith's Letter, a Small List of Books sent for that purpose, which he says, he hath distributed almost to such whites as he pleased, but that he has a few remaining on his hands that he has not yet given away. He might have sent them to my house not being above 30 yards from his house, when he had them, as he does not design to bring the People about his Ears, but he was careful enough not to mention any thing of that kind till he moved out of his place about 6 Weeks ago from his dwelling House to his Glebe in Portsmouth parish.

I also assure the honourable Society That if the great ones here have the sole property & privilege of the Schools, no Master nor Mistress will undertake it for Negro Children in general are very dull & stupid, & they will always be for telling Tales to the prejudice of the Teacher, to which, I have all along experienced that Masters or Mistresses will most greedily listen, & then Such Persons are ruin'd for ever from that time, if they stay any longer there, so that in Seven Years space, there possibly may be a Change of a Dozen of

Teachers unless some barefaced convict, an old undaunted Soldier, or an impudent Sailor, who are all void of Shame or Fear, should happen to have the Charge. Three sorts of people I should always be careful not to encourage, those I dare to affirm, none could match the People better, but GOD forbid that I should be the Witness of either, as I want youth instructed only by the good & praise worthy where they may be found. And now if I may be allowed to add my own sentiment to the end of this long Epistle, I would not undertake such a Charge tho' I had nothing else to support my Consideration of money, neither as I have before said, should I be willing to be the chief Trustee of the School, lest I might find it worse than it was when I had a Charity School in a neighbouring County where the gentlemens children were many years Educated, & the objects of Charity disdained till I was oblig'd to leave the School & lodge a Complaint in the Assembly, which has presented the grandees to-reign longer, but from that time they use one with the most invidious Terms of ill or abuse for my pains, & because I baptize more Negroes than other Brethren here & instruct them from the Pulpit, out of the common road, & encourage the good among them to come to the Communion after a due sense of the matter, I am criticised & branded by such as a Negro Parson, for which reason & many more might be offered, I do not chuse to throw myself out of the respect of my Parish altogether for unholding a Thing where I have none to stand by me, but shall most readily do it, if supported by the honorable Society & the Worthy Revᵈ Mr Commissary Robinson.

All I have now to add is That considering my Years, & the sorry circumstance of my family, the honourable Society will be pleased to pity my case, who mean nothing but the good & spiritual Advantage of those poor unhappy illiterate Creatures, and if the honourable Society will insist on me to be an Inspector, to regulate the School, they would be good enough to find out a proper Expedient to strengthen my hands that with the Strength of GOD, I may be Instrumental in their eternal Happiness, which is the earnest prayer & hearty desire of . . .

9. LETTER FROM DANIEL EARL, EDENTON, NORTH CAROLINA,
MARCH 1, 1763

Sir,

Your favour of June 1ˢᵗ I some time ago Received, to which I should have Wrote an Answer before now, only waited to See if my

Persuasions seconded by your very eloquent and Affecting Letter could Remove the Objections the Inhabitants of this Town made to your Society's pious and laudable Institutions, to all which, I am sorry to Acquaint you, they give a deaf Ear so that I have no Expectation of having it established here.

I have repeatedly Wrote to the Society for propagating the Gospel concerning a School for the Education of white Children, but never was favoured with their Sentiments upon it, which I impute to my Letters being miscarried thro the Casualties of war. I have not as yet Received the Books sent to Mr Child, but when they come to hand shall Take Care of them, untill I am favoured with your Orders concerning the Disposal of them.

To Mr John Waring

10. ACCOUNT FOR THE SCHOOLING OF SIX INDIAN CHILDREN IN NORTH CAROLINA, FEBRUARY 20, 1764

Aramaskeet Feby ye 20th 1764

Doct^r Alexander Stewart, to James Francis,
To the Schooling Six Indian Children
Three Months, as Pr Agreement at   £   s:
7/6 Each, Pr Quarter   2:   5: —
A List of the above Six Indians.
1763 With Their Entrance &c
Novr 7th Then Entered for the Schooling, Two Indian Boys,
    Vizt Solomon Russel, about 17 Years of Age
    and John Squires abt———16 Ditto
The Same Day Entered, Two Indian Girls,
    Vist. Bet Squires about 13 Years of Age
    and Poll: Mackey abt 13   Ditto ———
Novr 18 Then Entered Two Indian Boys
    Vist Joshua Squires abt 9 Years of Age
    and Bob; Mackey at 7   Ditto
    All Which made out their Quarter
                            Jam^s Francis,
Sir/ Please to pay Capt John Goddard the above Sum of Two P^{ds} five shillings, and his Receipt shall be a Discharge in full for the same from

Feby 20th 1764   Sir, Y^r very hum, Serv,
                            Jam^s Francis
The Revd Doct^r Alex^{dr} Stewart.

11. LETTER FROM ALEXANDER STEWART, BATH, NORTH CAROLINA, MAY 1, 1764

Revd Srs

I recd your favr of ye 7th of April 1763 wch I shou'd have answered much sooner, had I not waited to return a more Satisfactory one, than that I am at present obliged for to give.

Upon Shewing your Letters, to some of ye Inhabitants I was fed up with hopes of erecting these Schools in this & ye neighbouring Counties in a Short time; but after I had distributed part of your Books among ye Schoolmasters & encourag'd them all I could, I found at length that it was but Labour & Sorrow owing to ye mean, low prejudices of ye People of North America. I made a Short lived Effort, you may see by ye Inclosed to erect a School (not altogether on ye Societies plans) for ye Instruction of ten Indians & negroe Children at Attamuskeet in Hyde County; The Master in ye Letter signed Jas Francis shews you ye objections of ye people, & ye Expectations we are to have. He instructed six Indian Boys & Girls whom I baptized in October 1763, their ages & names you may see by ye Inclos'd rect for his Quarters Sallary wch I have paid, but whither He continues or not, I am uncertain of having not since heard from him, it being above 70 miles by Water from this place.

The other Letter from Anthony Kinnin who lives about 30 miles to ye Westward of this town, I likewise inclose to you, that your Society may see that I have not been regardless of their good & pious Design, and tho' it has not been in my power hitherto to carry it on to any Purpose, yet that my best wishes attend it & yt I shall always be ready upon ye least dawn of Success again to renew my endeavours.

The 1st Box of Books directed to Mr Palmer I have never had in possession but remains in his Stores unopened, the 2d Box I almost distributed and am Sorry to no better purpose. The remainder may be ordered to any place where they will be made useful but they can be carried to no place where they are more wanted among poor & Ignorant Whites.

It wou'd give me great pleasure to correspond with ye Society, & to know whether an Indian School in ye manner I have begun comes within their Scheme.

12. LETTER FROM JOHN BARNETT, BRUNSWICK, NORTH CAROLINA,
AUGUST 17, 1767

Dear Sir

About a month since I receiv'd your letter, dated 25th March last in Answer to one I wrote you Novr 24th 1765.

My letter I intended only for your own perusal, that, on making yourself acquainted with the Man, you might be able to form an opinion of him, and represent him accordingly to Dr Burton: therefore it was I did not write the Dr to whom I know all letters on business *immediately relative* to the Society shou'd be address'd. The Bishop last year wrote to our Govr and therein mention'd his having seen my letter, to you and was satisfy'd with the contents.

I find his Lordship had refus'd Mr Stevens Orders before he saw that letter; and if I remember right you shew'd it him on the very day of Ordination, (Trinity Sunday).

I fear I shall be no more successful in my endeavors for the establishment of a Negroe School than Mr Lewis [not clear].

Allow me to say no one is more earnestly desirous such an institution than myself, nor has any struggled with more difficulty, solely arising from the unhappy prejudices of the People. I had agreed with a widow woman here of good character, some months since, and had propos'd opening School with so small a number as fifteen but I cannot make up more than 8 or 9, therefore must for a time drop the design.

I had agreed with the Mistress to teach the girls to Sew, knit and Mark, thinking that wou'd excite people to send young negroe girls, but I find they wou'd rather their Slaves shou'd remain Ignorant as brutes.

In the course of the year I ride near fourteen hundred miles to visit the out parts of my Parish. In our place thirty miles from Town where I officiate nine times in the year a great number of Negroes always attend with great seeming devotion, of them I have baptised twelve Adults and eighteen of their Children. Several among them can read and having promised me to take pains to instruct such of their fellow slaves as are desirous to learn I have given them many of the Associates books.

I write to the society to beg leave of Absence from my Mission for six months from Easter next on some business of real importance.

I am too bashful publickly to own the business but to you will confess. I want to follow the example you have set me, and take unto myself a Wife.

Let me beg you to contribute your aid on the Affair; which you can facilitate by speaking to the Bishop of London or good Dr Burton.

I have had a long and dangerous illness; and my health yet is in so poor a State, that I am assur'd by every body I cannot perfectly recover till I have taken a Voyage at Sea to England or the Northern Colonies or Bermudas.

The latter place my Physicians advise me to sail to immediately, but I am determined to run the hazard of a stay here this summer; in hopes of the Society's Indulgence on leave for me to visit London next Spring. By my errand to England then (if please God I live) I shall avoid the heats of the next summer, get my health perfectly re-established and get a good Wife to return with me. Let Mr Lawrence (one of your Lecturers) know that I have found the right Magnolia or Laurel Tree. If he will immediately write me how to propagate it I will bring it over with me, no one here can give me any instruction My Father the Corner of little Queen Street High Holborn will take care of and forward any letters for me.

If you will favor me with a letter (which I very much desire) pray write immediately.

But pray use your interest for my leave of absence.

I am glad to hear Mr Skinner and family are well—beg my complements to them, and Mr Hopkins & family.

V
EARLY EDUCATIONAL INTERESTS AND ACTIVITIES IN GEORGIA

I. PREVIEW AND COMMENTS

GEORGIA, THE LAST OF THE English colonies to be established in America, was formed as a barrier against the rivalry of the colonizing powers of the Spanish and the French—as protection against foreign attacks and a safeguard of the interests of England in America. To this purpose was added a philanthropic motive. Georgia was to be a refuge for the king's "poor subjects" and an asylum for those unfortunate people in England who in America might "not only gain a comfortable subsistence for themselves and families, but also strengthen our colonies and increase the trade, navigation, and wealth of England." Both of these motives were set out in the charter granted in 1732 to "the Trustees for establishing the colony of Georgia in America." [1] Moreover, both of these purposes were exemplified in James Edward Oglethorpe, the founder of the colony and its first governor, who as a member of the House of Commons for many years exhibited intelligent and wide public interest and a deep humanitarian concern for honest debtors and for reform of England's penal system. Parliament granted ten thousand pounds to promote the establishment of Georgia.

The provisions of the charter and the legislation and rules of the trustees for regulating and directing the new colony reveal "clearly the benevolent paternalism of the founders." The trustees had authority to bring to Georgia people willing to become subjects of the king; religious liberty was promised everybody except "papists"; slavery and the importation of rum were prohibited (in 1749 the importation of slaves was permitted under certain conditions); and efforts were made to promote the moral welfare of the colonists as well as to protect them against their own thriftlessness. The first settlement was made at Savannah in 1733. The early colonists of Georgia con-

---

1. The original charter of Georgia may readily be found in B. P. Poore, *The Federal and State Constitutions, Colonial Charters, and Other Organic Laws of the United States*, Part I, pp. 369-77. Washington: Government Printing Office, 1877. In the same work may be found the charters of Virginia and the Carolinas. For a good general history of Georgia, see E. M. Coulter, *Georgia: A Short History*. Chapel Hill: The University of North Carolina Press, 1947.

sisted of English, Lutherans (Salzburgers), Swiss, Scottish High-landers, some Portuguese, and some Jews; and after 1752 when the colony became a royal province, with a governor and council on recommendation of the lords commissioners for trade and plantations, there was much immigration from Virginia and the Carolinas. It appears that the work of the founders of the colony appealed to charitably disposed people in England who made contributions from time to time for the benefit of the colonists. Apparently very accurate records were kept of such contributions and accounts.[2] In the documents that follow are set out some evidences of the educational interests and activities of the trustees of this colony.

II. DOCUMENTS

1. Gifts of money and books to the Trustees for educational and religious purposes, 1732-1749

Receiv'd by Mr Hales from an Unknown Hand for the Use of the Colony of Georgia, 40 Bibles Minion, 60 Testaments Long Primer, 100 Common Prayer Minion, 50 Duty of Man Small 120. 50 Christian Monitor and Companion, 50 Christian Monitor and Answer to Excuses, 72 Psalters, 50 Bishop Gibson's Family Devotion, 100 Horn Books. 100 Primmers. 72 Spelling Books. 100 Lewis's Catechism. 100 A B C with the Church Catechism (November the 1st 1732)

Receiv'd by Mr Hales from an Unknown Hand the further Addition of Books for the use of the People going to Georgia in their Passage, Six Bibles, twelve Guides to Christian Families, Nine Duty of Man, One Do larger, twelve Christian Monitors, twelve Do with Answer to Excuses, One Quarto Common Prayer, twelve Lewis's Catechism, twelve Common Prayer, Six Testaments, Six Bishop Gibson's Family Devotion, three Nelson's Practise of Free Devotion. (November the 8th 1732)

That a Memorial be drawn up to be presented to the Incorporated Society for propagating the Gospel in Foreign Parts, setting forth, that the Trustees have sent forth a Number of his Majesty's subjects to be settled in Georgia, and appointed a Site for the Church, and a sufficient Glebe for the Minister, and desiring the Society to make the usual Allowance for the Minister in Georgia, as is given to their Missionaries in the other Colonies, till such time as the Glebe shall be

2. See Allen D. Candler (compiler), *The Colonial Records of the State of Georgia*, III.

sufficiently improved for a Minister; and Desiring the usual Benefaction of Books and Furniture. (November 23d 1732)

Receiv'd by the hands of Captain Coram from an Unknown Benefactor One hundred Books of the great Importance of a Religious Life consider'd, for the use of the second Imbarkation. (December the 7th 1732)

Receiv'd One thousand Spelling Books the Benefaction of Mr James Leake pursuant to his Letter (Janry 31st 1732)

3

Receiv'd of Mr Hales an Account of the following Books. Vizt One Bible, two Bibles of a less Value, three Common Prayer Books, One hundred Catechisms, fifty Young Christians Instructed; Part of the Benefaction from an Unknown Person, Which were sent by Mr Oglethorpe, but not enter'd with the rest November the 1st 1732. (Febry the 14th 1732)

3

Receiv'd by Mr Hales the following Books forty Eight Faith and Practise of a Church of England Man, in Sheets, Eight Christian Monitors, Nine Lewis's Catechism. the Benefaction of the Revd Mr Stanley Rector of Hadham Hertfordshire for the Use of the Colony. (Febry the 28th 1732)

3

Receiv'd by the Hands of Mr Hales from an Unknown Person for the Use of the Colony of Georgia the following Books. Vizt two Hundred of Dr Thomas Gouch's shewing how to walk with God. two Hundred Help and Guide to Christian Families by William Burkitt. two Hundred Gibson's Family Devotion. two Hundred Common Prayer Books. Minion 12me two Hundred Horn-Books. two Hundred Primmers. One Hundred Testaments. One hundred Psalters. two Hundred A. B. C with the Church Catechism. One hundred Lewis's Catechism. One hundred of the The Young Man Instructed. two Hundred Friendly Admonition to the Drinkers of Brandy. the Whole to the Value of fifty four Pounds ten Shillings. (May 30th 1733)

Mr Christopher Ortman attended and proposed to go over to Georgia as School Master and Parish Clerk to the Saltzburghers. (October 17th 1733)

Receiv'd by the hands of Dr Hales the following Books being the Benefaction of a Person Who desires to be unknown for the use of the new Settlement which is going to be made at the Southward Part of Georgia Viz^t One Bible Quarto. One Common Prayer Book Q^to twenty Bibles Minion 12mo twenty five Testaments long Primer 8vo. fifty Common Prayer Books minion 12mo twenty five Bishop of Man on the Lords Supper. fifty Christian Monitor and Companion to the Altar, fifty Christian Monitor and Answer to Excuses. One hundred Horn Books. One hundred Primmers. One hundred A B C with the Church Catechism. two hundred friendly Admonitions to the Drinkers of Brandy. (July 16th 1735)

Receiv'd ten German Grammars the Benefaction of Mr Thomas Lediard for the Use of the Colony. (October 10th 1735)

Receiv'd fifty four Books for the Library in Georgia the Benefaction of the Earl of Egmont, for Which the Board return'd their thanks to his Lordship. (June 2 1736)

Receiv'd a Receipt from the Bank for fifty Pounds paid in June 4 1736 by William Tillard Esqr for the Honble Society for promoting Christian Knowledge, to be Applied for the payment of Salaries for half a Year from the said Society to the Missionaries, and School Master for the Saltzburghers in Georgia ending November the 1st next. (June 9th 1736)

Receiv'd by the hands of the Revd Dr Hales Eighteen Pounds Eighteen Shillings the Benefactions of the following Persons to be applied towards the Support of the Missionaries and Schools for instructing and converting the Native Indians in Georgia. Viz^t

£

A Gentleman Who desires to be Unknown............	1.	1.	0
A Gentlewoman Who desires to be Unknown.........	1.	1.	0
A Gentlewoman Who desires to be Unknown..........	3.	3.	0
A Gentle Woman Who desires to be Unknown........	2.	2.	0
A Gentle Woman Who desires to be Unknown........	10.	10.	0
The Revd Dr Metcalfe of Sunbury in Middlesex........	1.	1.	0
	£ 18.	18.	0

(Feb^ry 9 1736/7)

Receiv'd by the hands of Dr Hales One hundred Pounds the Benefaction of a Gentlewoman Who desires to be Unknown to be applied towards the Support of the Missionaries and Schools for instructing and converting to Christianity the Native Indians in Georgia. (March 17th 1736/7)

Receiv'd by the hands of Dr Hales the sum of ten Pounds ten Shillings the Benefaction of a Gentle Woman Unknown to be applied towards defraying the Expences of the Revd Mr George Whitefield and the School Master Who go's to Frederica for the Service of the Mission.

Receiv'd by the hands of the Revd Dr Hales four Pounds four Shillings the Benefaction of the Revd Mr Vallois Rector of East Tisted near Alton Hampshire to be applied towards defraying the Expences of the aforesaid Revd Mr Whitefield and School Master. (June 29th 1737)

Receiv'd a Receipt from the Bank for ten Pounds ten Shillings paid in by the Revd Dr Hales being the Benefaction of a Gentlewoman Unknown to be applied towards defraying the Expences of the Revd Mr George Whitefield and the School Master Who go's to Frederica for the Service of the Mission. (July 6. 1737)

Receiv'd the 6th Instant of Mr Edmund Parker twenty five London New Method and Art of teaching Children to spell and read, to be sent to Georgia for the use of the Children there, being the Benefaction of a Person Who desires to be unknown. (August 8th 1739).

Read a Letter from Mr Henry Newman Secretary to the Society for promoting Christian Knowledge with an Inclos'd Extract of a Letter from the Revd Mr Martin Bolzius at Ebenezer in Georgia dated March 15th 1742. Requesting the Assistance of the Trustees and their Other Benefactors in Europe to build a small House for Divine Service at What they call the Plantations; And also to support a School Master for instructing the Children (July 12th 1742).

Read a Letter from Mr Orton dated March 4th 1741 acquainting the Trustees with the Progress in his Ministry at Savanah And that he had taken upon him the Management of the School for want of a Person fitly Qualified to undertake the Duty. (July 26th 1742.) Resolved

That it be recommended to the Consideration of the Common Council as the Opinion of the Trustees to add ten Pounds pr Ann to the Allowance to the School Master at Savanah on Condition that he shall not take any Gratuity from the Scholars for instructing them. March 12. 1742

3

The Trustees being acquainted that the Revd Dr Hales and the Revd Mr Smith, to whom the Revd Dr Crow left his Library to dispose of for Parochial Libraries in England, or for the Use of the

Colony of Georgia, had agreed, that the said Library should be given for the use of the Colony.
Resolved
That the Thanks of the Trustees be given to Dr Hales and Mr Smith for the same.
Resolved
That two Catalogues of the said Library be made, and that the Library be sent to Georgia under the care of the Revd Mr Zouberbuhler the present Minister, and be kept in his Custody for the use of the Trust; That Mr Zouberbuhler do sign both the Catalogues One to be sent to Georgia with him, and the Other to be left with the Trustees. That it be in the Trustees Power to divide the said Library hereafter as they may see Occasion; And that the President and Assistants do Once in a Year visit the same, and see that it is carefully preserv'd.
Resolved
That One hundred Horn Books, two hundred Spelling Books, One hundred Primmers, fifty Psalters And fifty Testaments, Part of those in the Custody of the Trustees, be sent to Georgia under the Care of Mr Zouberbuhler. (July 4th 1749)
Read a Paragraph in a Letter from the President and Assistants Dated   that Mr Holt the School Master behaved for some time pretty well, and had a thriving School, but of late his Behaviour has been so bad, that he has but few Scholars; And that it was very probable that They should be obliged to send him to England, When They should have an Opportunity of sending him directly from Savanah
Resolved
That it be recommended to the Common Council that if Mr Holt the School Master is desirous of returning to England, rather than continue, and settle as a Planter in Georgia, the Freight of his and his Wife's Passage should be paid by the Trust. (March 7 1752)— *Journal of the Trustees for Establishing the Colony of Georgia, in* Allen D. Candler (compiler), *The Colonial Records of the State of Georgia*, Vol. I, pp. 83, 84, 87, 89, 98, 100, 102, 121, 142, 222, 234, 254, 270, 275, 290, 291, 356, 399, 403, 413, 534, 575.

That Mr Vernon and Dr Bundy be desired to propose to the Society for promoting Christian Knowledge, that on paying over three thousand Pounds to the Trustees, they will engage under their Seal to pay three several Salaries of fifty, thirty, and ten Pounds pr

Ann to the Minister, Catechist and School Master of the Saltzburghers in Georgia. (November 14th 1733.)

Resolved

That the Benefactions to be collected by Mr Whitefield under the Commission he desires shall when Collected be particularly applied for erecting an Orphan House in Georgia, and building a Place of Worship for the Saltzburghers at Ebenezer. (December 20th 1738.)

That six Pounds be paid to the Revd Mr Whitefield as desired to buy Necessaries for Mr Habersham the School Master for the Year ensuing. (December 20th 1738.)

That fifteen Pounds be paid to the Revd Mr Whitefield Which he furnish'd Mr De la Motte with who was late School Master at Savanah on his Return to England. (December 20th 1738.)

Read a Letter from the Revd Mr George Whitefield acquainting the Board that he had collected upwards of five hundred Pounds for the Orphan House in Georgia, and praying a Grant of five hundred Acres of Land in trust for the use of the said Orphan House, with the privilege of naming Who shall succeed him in it. (May 2. 1739.)

The Revd Mr George Whitefield attended and acquainted the Board that he declin'd the Acceptance of any Salary as a Minister at Savanah, or for the management of the Orphan House in Georgia. (May 9th 1739)

The Revd Mr George Whitefield having acquainted the Board that Mr Robert Hows of Savanah in Georgia is willing to alienate his fifty Acre Lot to the said Mr Whitefield for building an Orphan House. (May 30th 1739.)

Resolved

That Robert Hows have liberty to alienate his said Lot to the Revd Mr George Whitefield, and that a License be made out for his Alienation of the said Lot.

Read a Draught of a Grant for four hundred and fifty Acres to the Revd Mr George Whitefield in Trust for the Orphan House subject to a Quit Rent of three Pounds pr Ann.

Order'd

That the said Draught be engross'd, And that the Seal of the Corporation be affix'd thereto, and to the aforesaid License in the presence of any three of the Trustees.

Order'd

That the Secretary do countersign the same when seal'd, and a

Memorial of the same in order to be register'd with the Auditor of the Plantations. (May 30th 1739.)

Do to the School Master at Savanah in lieu of Food........10.   ____

Salary to the School Master of the Saltzburghers a Gratuity.. 5.   ____

(May 30th 1739)

Read a Letter from the Revd Mr Whitefield to the Accomptant dated Janry 16th 1739 relating to the Orphan House, and desiring an Alteration in the Grant of Land to Him in Trust for the Orphan House, to be made to him and his Successors forever, And that it may be free from Quit Rents &c. and signifying his Intentions to resign his Ministry both at Savanah and Frederica, and to apply himself only to the care of the Orphan House.

Read Another Letter from Mr Whitefield to the Accomptant dated Janry 28th 1739 relating to the Orphan House, and desiring that the Money for building of the Church may be put into his hands.

Read Another Letter from Mr Whitefield to the Trustees dated March 10th 1739 acquainting them that he had been in the Southward $\overline{40}$ Part of the Province to fetch all the Orphans he could meet with; And that he brought with him four from the Darien (and inclosing a Letter from General Oglethorpe to Mr Mackintosh Moore, and Mr Macleod with their Answer) and desiring to know whether Orphans, tho' fourteen or fifteen Years old, are not to reap the Benefit of the Orphan House, and desiring again that the Money to be expended in building of the Church may be paid into his Hands. (May 7th 1740.)

Read a Petition of John Dobell setting forth that he was employ'd almost three Years in teaching the Children of the Free School at Savanah to read and cast Accounts And that from December 1739 to January 1740 he was intrusted with the sole Charge and Direction of the said School, and praying to be appointed School Master there. (December 5th 1741.)

That as Several Persons have not Ability to pay for the Education of their Children at Savanah, Ten Pounds pr Ann be added to the Allowance of the Schoolmaster on Condition that he shall not take any Gratuity from his Scholars or their Friends. (Aprill 18th 1743)

To a Schoolmaster at Savanah......10. o. o. (Aprill 18th 1743.)

To the Schoolmaster at Ebenezer... 5. o. o (Aprill 18th 1743.)

Resolved

That Mr John Ulrick Driezler be appointed School Master at Frederica with a Salary of ten Pounds pr Ann. And that the Revd Mr Burton be desired to appoint the said Mr Driezler to Officiate for him as shaplain to Genl Oglethorpe's Regiment. (May 23 1745)

That the President and Assistants at Savanah be directed to order the Surveyor to lay out two Acres being part of the vacant Land between Vernonburgh and Acton, in order to erect a Tabernacle for Divine Worship, Which may serve likewise for a School. (February 16 1746)

$$\frac{}{7}$$

Order'd

That the Secretary write to Mr Stephens, and acquaint him, that the Trustees entirely disapprove of and disallow the Settlement of twelve pounds a Year made on Mr Christopher Ortman, for acting as School Master at Vernonburgh and Acton, by the President and Assistants. That the Trustees are surpris'd at the Resolution, Which the President and Assistants came to, Vizt "That the said Mr Ortman had been misrepresented to the Society for promoting Christian Knowledge" without their hearing Any Body on that Subject but Mr Ortman himself. And that the Trustees cannot but take notice of, and condemn the Inference drawn by them, that the Placing Mr Ortman at Vernonburgh and Acton, is a Saving to the Trust, as if they were oblig'd to maintain Every Body Who for Misbehaviour may have been discharg'd. (February 16 1746.)

$$\frac{}{7}$$

Resolved

That the Freight of Mr Holt the Schoolmaster at Savanah, and his Wife's Passage from Georgia to England be paid by the Trustees, in case They desire the same and return during the Existence of the Trust. (March 21st 1752.)—*Minutes of the Common Council of the Trustees for Establishing the Colony of Georgia in America*, in Allen D. Candler, *op. cit.*, Vol. II, pp. 46, 260, 272, 273, 274, 275, 323, 376, 408, 417, 418, 460, 478, 479, 520.

A Benefactor whose Name is desired to be concealed, by the hands of the Reverend Mr Burton, being the first Annual Payment for the Endowment of a Catechist in Georgia, which the Benefactor agrees shall be annually paid for five Years certain, and afterwards (if living) for the term of his life   £10

(February 26, 1733)
A Benefactor whose Name is desired to be concealed, by the same hands, being the second Annual
Payment to be continued for the Term of the Benefactor's Life; but given for Five Years certain, for
the Endowment of a Catechist in Georgia........   £ 10

(February 21, 1734)
The Honourable Society for promoting Christian
Knowledge by the Hands of William Tillard Esq;
to be applied for the Payment of half a Years Salaries for the said Society to the Missionaries and
Schoolmaster for the Saltzburghers in Georgia to
the 1st of November 1736 ....   £ 50

(June 4, 1736)
A Benefactor whose Name is desired to be con-
ceal'd, by the same Hands, being the third Annual
Payment, to be continued for the Term of the
Benefactor's Life, but given for Five Years certain,
for the Endowment of a Catechist in Georgia.....   £ 10

(May 18, 1736)
The Honourable Society for promoting Christian
Knowledge, by the Hands of William Tillard Esq;
for twelve Months Provisions supplied the Saltz-
burghers, who went to Ebenezer in Georgia with
Mr: John Vat their Conductor, over and above the
the Three Months Provisions they carried with
them, £ 287:-: And for the Freight of Copper
Halfpence, Books, and other things sent by the said
Society, to the Saltzburghers in Georgia by the Ship
Two Brothers in June last £ 1: 17: 6—making to-
gether ....   £ 288   s17   d7

(February 1, 1736)
The use of the Missionaries and Schools for in-
structing and converting to Christianity the Native
Indians ....   £ 239   s8

(June 9, 1737)
A Benefactor whose Name is desired to be concealed by the Hands of the Reverend Mr: Burton
being the fifth annual Payment to be continued for

the Term of the Benefactors Life for the Endowment of a Catechist in Georgia................ £10
 (June 1, 1738)
A Benefactor whose Name is desired to be concealed, by the Hands of the Reverend Mr Burton,
being the seventh annual Payment, to be continued
for the Term of the Benefactor's Life, for the Endowment of a Catechist in Georgia............. £10
 (June 5, 1740)
A Benefactor whose Name is desired to be concealed, by the Hands of the Reverend Mr Burton,
being the eighth Annual Payment, to be continued
for the Term of the Benefactor's Life, for the Endowment of a Catechist in Georgia............. £10
 (June 9, 1741)
Paid the Catechist sent to Savannah in Georgia,
as an Encouragement to him on his going over to
Instruct in Christianity the Negroes there, on the
Annual Stipends allowed him by the Association of
the Late Dr Bray, and the Incorporated Society for
propagating the Gospel in Foreign Parts.......... £30

       —*Ibid.*, Vol. III, *passim.*

	£	s	d
1736			
10 Febry Mrs Dionisia Long by the hands of the Rev- end Dr Hales	100	—	
A Gentleman who desires to be unknown by the same Hands	1	1	—
A Gentlewoman who desires to be unknown, by the same Hands	1	1	—
A Gentlewoman who desires to be unknown, by the same Hands	3	3	—
A Gentlewoman who desires to be unknown, by the same Hands	2	2	—
A Gentlewoman who desires to be unknown, by the same Hands	10	10	—
The Reverend Dr Metcalf of Sunbury in Middlesex, by the same Hands............	1	1	—
5 Mar. The Reverend Mr Williams of Devonshire, by the same hands	10	—	—

10 Ditto A Gentlewoman whose Name is desired to be
      concealed, by the same Hands............   10 10   —
22 Ditto A Lady who desires to be unknown, by the
      same Hands   100   —   —
                                        £239   8   —
                                    —*Ibid.*, p. 140.

2. REVEREND BENJAMIN INGHAM WRITES TO SIR JOHN PHILLIPS ABOUT INDIAN SCHOOL, 1736

Notwithstanding all the Opposition of Men & Devils, I Trust there is A Door now Opening for the Conversion of the Indians. There is already A School almost built amongst them. The House 60 Foot long & 15 Wide. it will be divided into 3 Rooms, One at Each End, consisting of 15 Foot Square, & the School Room in the Middle as large as both the Other. Under one of the End Rooms they have dug A Cellar. The Foreside of the House faces the rising Sun, And the two Ends are due North & South. It Stands on A little Hill which we call Irene, by a Brook Side, about half a Quarter of A Mile above Tomo-chachees Town, where the River Savannah divides it Self into 3 Streams. This Hill has been made Some Hundred Years ago, for what Reason I can't tell; Perhaps to perpetuate the Memory of Some Illustrious Hero or famous Action. In digging the Cellar, they found Abundance of Oister Shells, and some Bones and Buck Horns. When I fixed upon this Place, the Indians ask'd me if I was not afraid to live upon A Hill, I Answer'd no. They said, the Indians were, because they believed that Fairies haunted Hills. The Moravian Brethren out of their Zeal for the Work, Undertook the Building at a low Price; As soon as it's finish'd, which will be within A few Dayes, One of them with his Wife is to live there with me. I believe in A little Time we Shall have a good Number of Scollars. The Indians, tho' at first they would hardly be persuaded to let one child learn, yet now they are very willing to have them taught, and even Some of the Men Seem to have a desire to learn. . .

Tomochachee is lately recovered from A dangerous Sickness, wherein their own Doctors gave him up, but it pleas'd God to restore him by the Care of Mr Oglethorpe, thro' the Prayers of several Christians for him, I hope he will live to hear the Glad Tidings of the Glorious Gospel, he has been very earnest to promote the School. I don't despair of acquireing their Language, I begin to understand a little of it, And I hope thro' the Prayers of my good Friends in

England, I shall be enabled to make a daily Progress in it. I have three Boys that I think will be able to read their Language as Soon as I shall be able to Speak it.

If Mr Oglethorpe, was in England, he would Undertake to Collect Charities towards founding and maintaining Schools amongst the Indians; he saies, he will subscribe £200 himself, but as his Affairs Here will not permit him to return immediately, that Work must be deferr'd, Unless it would please Almighty God to Stir up the Hearts of Some Zealous Christians to set forward so Good A Work in his Stead. What I wish for at present is One or more of my dear Oxford Friends to come over and help me. Cannot indeed Say that I am alone because the Moravian Brethren join heartily with me, and from Such Helpers One may expect Good Success, As your Worthy Society has Sent over two Transports of Saltsburghers, I heartily wish they would Contribute towards bringing over Some more of the Moravian Brethren from Hernhuth, for they are not only the most useful People in the Colony, But also they are certainly the holiest Society of Men in the whole World. They would be very willing to come hither because they are persecuted at home, not only by the Papists, but also and that very likely, by the Lutherans. . . .—*Ibid.*, XXI, 221-23.

3. Expenses for instructing and converting the Indians to Christianity, April, 1736—April, 1737

Expended for the Missionaries and Schools to instruct & convert to Christianity the Indians in Georgia.

	£	s	d
Paid the said Missionaries, & for Necessaries for the Indian School	154	1	2¼
Expended for the Missionaries and Schoolmaster for the Saltzburghers. viz.			
For half a Year's Salarys to the said Missionaries and School-master to the 1st of Novr 1736	50	-	-

—Ibid., III, 147.

4. Reverend William Norris writes to the Trustees, 1738

Savannah Decr the 12th 1738

On my Enquiry into the State of the Church here. I have been surprized to find, that she had retained but little more than the Titles of her most excellent Institutions & Ordinances pure from many

Romish & German Corruptions; & that she has lost that true, equal, & unpassionate Frame of Spirit, which is so agreeable to the Genius & Temperature of the Gospel, & to the Bases on which all her Duties are settled...

One day in every Fortnight I visit the People of Highgate & Hamstead, & read the full Service of the Church & a sermon to them. At my first going among them, they were so utterly unacquainted with our Form of Worship, that they knew not where to join with the Minister, nor the Decency observed in the several Parts of it. This I have been the more surprized at, because Mr Doble the School-master there reads Prayers to them every Night. I have therefore recommended to him strictly to observe the prescribed Form & Liturgy of the Church, that they may become uniform Members of the same. These People have been upwds of two Years without re-ceiving the Sacrament, & tho' they profess the Faith & Articles of our Church, have ever been excluded by Mr Wesley from communicat-ing in it. They have erected a Tabernacle here, which serves also for the School; the Number of Children which are instructed here rarely exceeds twelve, & but seldom makes up that. The publick School of Savannah consits now of forty Boys, those I catechise twice every Week in School, & every Sunday Even in Church. I have in-troduced Lewis's Explanation of the Church Catechism, which has been received with general Approbation; & nothing is wanting to recommend & make it as generally useful, but the Scarcity of them. I must with these beg some Supplies of Bibles & Common-Prayer-Books, & such other Books as you will judge proper for the School &c...–*Ibid.*, XXII, Pt. I, 351-56.

5. JOHN MARTIN BOLZIUS REPORTS COMPLAINTS ABOUT SCHOOLMASTER
ORTMAN AND HIS WIFE, 1739

Ebenezer in Georgia July 19th 1739.
...His Excellency General Oglethorpe was much troubled by a great many Groundless Complaints of our School Master Ortman & his Wife, which he took the Trouble almost half a Day to inquire into. His Wife was allways exceeding troublesome by her scandalous Behaviour to my Congregation, & since Necessity for stoping Wickedness in the Bud, obliged me to forbid her the holy Table till she would make satisfaction by leading a better life, it occasioned the School Master to grieve me & my Fellowlabourer very much by Oppositions, slanderings & false Imputations before the Magistrates

at Savannah as well as before General Oglethorpe, but to their own shame & Confusion. Since the man is grown by his Wifes wicked Contrivances, & Insinuations obstinat & disobedient, he is a great Burthen to us, & not at all useful to our School, which my Duty obliges me to acquaint your Honour with. He could not be used in any measure to instruct our Children in the English Tongue, which was heretofore a great Disappointment to us. Notwithstanding he pretended strongly to be a English School Master, but his wrong Pronunciation & great many Mistakes in spelling, reading & writing occasioned General Oglethorpe to order me not to give him leave to teach any Child English. I dare not trouble you any longer by my Writing in your Weighty Affairs, . . .—*Ibid.*, pp. 182-83.

6. JAMES OGLETHORPE WRITES ON THE NEED FOR SCHOOLMASTERS, 1741

We want here some men fit for Schoolmasters, one at Frederica and one at the Darien, also a sedate and sober minister, one of some experience in the world and whose first heat of youth is over. These are things I should chiefly think necessary.—James Oglethorpe to "Honble the Trustees." April 28, 1741. *Collections of Georgia Historical Society*, III, 113.

7. SCHOOLMASTER JOHN DOBELL WRITES TO THE TRUSTEES, 1743

Savannah the 14th of May 1743.
Two Days ago Coll Stephens sent for me to Breakfast with him, and told me that by his last packet to your Honours sent about a Week or Two since he had mention'd my uneasiness in that I am not able to Discharge the Duty of the Office of Register of the Grants of Lands for want of Instructions; that he had mentioned me in the most favourable manner; & was pleas'd to tell me he was my Sincere and Cordial Friend and as an Instance thereof made me an offer of the Place of Secretary to the Indian Trade & Affairs willing me to accept thereof telling me that the Revenue of it would amount to about £8 or 10 pr Year, and that the business of this Place would not interfere with my other business or be any Cause of taking the Office of Register from me, but rather be a means of recovering for me such Instructions from your Honours as would enable me to discharge the Duty of it. Therefore with much Thankfulness I accepted of this place of Secretary and the rather, because I find the 20£ pr. Year as Register and the £10 Schoolmaster full little to maintain me with my utmost Care. Five pounds pr Yr was Added to the £20

for Register which together with y^t of the School would amount to £35 pr Y^r my L^d of Egmont was pleas'd to tell me: But I have rec^d no more than £20 pr. Y^r as Register, & 10£ as Schoolmaster. And indeed all I have received for the performing that Office hath hitherto been above my Desert, I not having been able to perform any thing Material therein, as yet, for want of Instructions which I have continually appli'd to Col^l Stephens &c for; But to this Day have had none from Col Stephens....—Candler, *op. cit.*, XXIV, 28-31.

8. John Martin Bolzius astonished at the behavior of
Schoolmaster Ortman, 1743.

Ebenezer June 20th 1743

It grieved me very much, that Mr Thomas Stephens endeavours still as much as he can, to blacken my Character & to misrepresent the present state of our Settlement, by publishing several Falsehoods & Calumnies. Please to remember, that I acquainted you in a Letter of the 24th of May 1742 with the poor Errand of the said Stephens at our Place, of which I send you now a Copy n.1. supposing, it would make the shameful Contrivances of his a little clear to you. The Schoolmaster Ortman says, that Mr Stephens had penned that Writing, to which he, Kieser & Pichler have set their names, & which Stephens has concealed for me like a great Secret. Lyes & Calumnies, of which Stephens's Writing is full, are Darkness, which shuns the Light, I desired Mr Wm Ewen at Savannah to let me see the Pamphlet of Stephens, but he excused himself much, & I believe, he was ashamed of it. I thank you therefore that you took the trouble to send me a copy of that, which concerns chiefly myself & my Congregation. I am astonished, that the Schoolmaster by Instigation of his Wife could subscribe & sign such a Paper, of which his Conscience convinced him, that it contained nothing else but lyes & Calumnies, yea that he proceeded so far in his Wickedness to be a Agent of Stephens, to induce other people under Pretence of an innocent & harmless Writing in Stephens's seditious Ways & Contrivances. What Ortman alledges for his defence, you'll see here inclosed n.2.

But Sir, since the great Crime of exercising over the people here an arbitrary power, is laid to my Charge by Stephens & Ortman, besides many more false Accusations in the said Writing, I must beg of you. & His Excellency the General to instruct me, what means I must use to clear my Innocency from such heinous Imputations. John Spielbiegler once Inhabitant of Ebenezer declared on Oath before Mr Beale in Charles-Town the same, tho' I am sure, there is not one Person at Ebenezer, who takes me to be such a one as is set forth in the Deposition & Attestation, except (perhaps) Ortman & his Wife, tho' I have given them no Offence, but aime only at the promoting of their true Welfare. You know yourself, how often I have laid before you & the Magistrates matters of Weight, which I thought myself not to be able to devide with Mr Gronau & other Friends. As for Spielbiegler's Behaviour here, it was very bad, & he could not be brought to any good Order, giving by Obstinacy, Wilfulness, Quarrels, & strives with his own Mother & other people, Drunckeness & other Vices, many scandels. He hired himself out by the Month for gaining so much Money as would be required for his Passage back to Europe, where he hoped to find the old Steps of a free dissolute life. As long as he was at Ebenezer he hardly could be admitted any time to the Lord's table by reason of his bad behaviour. . . .—*Ibid.*, pp. 38-43.

9. JOHN MARTIN BOLZIUS AGAIN COMPLAINS TO THE TRUSTEES ABOUT ORTMAN, 1743

Ebenezer June 30th 1743.

I must beg leave to trouble you for the present with a dismal Account of the bad Behaviour of our Schoolmaster Ortman. As he has been from the beginning of our Settlement by his Wife's Instigation an Enemy to me & our Congregation (which he has testify'd frequently by his own Letters to England) so he has proved the same, when Mr Thomas Stephens in October. 1741 came to our Place, & lodged in his House in order to get our people into his snares for a subscription against the Welfare of our Settlement, Ortman & his Wife have been then his Interpreters & Agents to some of our people, persuading them with all their might & subtility to the said Subscription by giving them many groundless Promises. The 2 men, Thomas Bichler & John Michael Keiser, whose Names are underwritten in Mr Stephens's Paper, are quite innocent, which will appear from their Attestations sent home by Mr Thomas Jones, but as for Ortman, who understood the Contents of Mr Stephens's Writing, & was his Interpreter & Agent to some of our people, he is not able to speak any true thing for his Defence, nither can he prove the least Article of his Attestation, penned by Mr Stephens & himself. Our inhabitants in general were astonished at the palpable Calumnies & falsehoods of the said Ortman, & have declared by a new Attestation penned &

signed amongst themselves, that they abhorr the Contents of Mr Stephens's paper as a Libel, signed by Ortman, which new Attestation I send now to you so, as it was written in the German Language, which easely an Interpreter in London will translate in the English Tongue for the Information of the Honble Trustees & Society for promoting Christian Knowledge. I beg of the Honble Trustees to free our Place from such a Schoolmaster, who gives Children & grown people such heinous scandals, as his & Mr Stephens's poor groundless Attestation contains. Tho' his Wife is the chief Cause of his signing such a Libel, as also of many bad Contrivances, yet it must be laid to his Charge, what he has attested against his Conscience & the Experience of all Inhabitants of Ebenezer. . .—*Ibid.*, pp. 53-56.

10. CHRISTOPHER ORTMAN APPOINTED SCHOOLMASTER AT
VERNONBURGH, 1744

At a Meeting of the President and Assistants for the Colony of Georgia on Friday the fourteenth Day of December in the Year of our Lord 1744.

Present {William Stephens   President
Henry Parker ⎫
William Spencer ⎬ Assistants
Samuel Marcer ⎭

A Petition of Christopher Ortman being read, wherein He greatly complains of hard Dealings being used which has occasioned his being discharged by the Society from his Office of Schoolmaster at Ebenezer: The Board taking the same into Consideration are of Opinion, that the said Christopher Ortman has been misrepresented to the said Society, And by that means he is reduced to great Poverty, both He and his Wife being uncapable by Reason of their old Age and Infirmities for any Labour; and They never hearing any otherwise of Him than that He was an honest, sober and inoffensive Man Do therefore in Charity appoint him Schoolmaster for the Village of Vernonburgh and Acton (the Inhabitants there having often complained for Want of Such) And for the Subsistance of Himself and Wife, the Board doth allow him at the Rate of twenty Shillings per Month, till the Trustees Pleasure is therein known: And they also think 'twill be a Saving to the Trust for his being so placed, rather than to be oblidged to maintain him otherwise for doing of Nothing: And whereas five Pounds a Year has been by the Trustees Order paid to the said Christopher Ortman as Schoolmaster at Ebenezer We think it reasonable that the said five Pounds be paid towards defraying the said Expenses—*Ibid.*, VI, 121-22.

11. John Martin Bolzius writes about the need for instruction in English, 1746

Ebenezer in Georgia Feby 22th
1745/6.

...As for the Instruction of our young people in the English Tongue, I wish, I had it in my power to do it myself, knowing very well how much it contributes in many Respects to the German Inhabitants's Good to be acquainted with the Language of the English Dominions: but Ortman was not able, & one Hamilton, a Perwig-Maker, who was sent over some years ago by Mr Verelst, was neither willing nor able to teach the children & others the English Tongue, tho' I endeavoured to incourage this most necessary & useful thing to the utmost of my Ability. If the Lord would send me some supply of Money, I would readily lay it out for a Salary of an English School Master, then I believe, that either the Revd Mr Whitefield or an other Minister, who is a Friend to our Congregation, would recommend me a well qualifyed Man to keep an English School for the young people in Town & upon the Plantations, so as we have two German School Masters for the Use of our Children. . .—*Ibid.*, XXV, 3-4, 6.

12. John Dobell delivers keys to school and quits as schoolmaster, 1746

At a Meeting of the President and Assistants for the Colony of Georgia on Monday the twenty first Day of July in the Year of our Lord 1746.

Present
{
William Stephens   President
Henry Parker
William Spencer   Assistants.
Samuel Marcer
Patrick Graham
}

...Mr John Dobell attended the President some Days agoe, and offered to deliver him the Key of the School, which he refused to receive in that manner but ordered him to attend when the Board next met; whereupon he now did so, and delivered up the Key of the

School together with a List of the Scholars, declaring that he was leaving the Colony and the Trustees Service: He was thereupon asked what Books, Papers, &c he had of the Trustees in his Custody; The Board acquainting him that it was proper as he was quitting the Colony to deliver all Things relating to the Trust to the Presidents Order: And being farther asked what Progress he had made relating to his Office of Register, He frankly confessed that he had made no Entry of any Kind in any Book, but had sent to the Trustees an Account of all he had done, except a List of Grants which he now delivered contained in several Sheets of Paper, which had been lately put into his Hands by Order from the Trustees for him to make perfect, and when so perfected by Him, the Seal of the Province was directed by their Honours to be affixed to it. Mr Dobell's leaving the Colony so abruptly lais Us under some Difficulties in providing a Master sufficiently qualified for the School to take upon him the present Charge and to be recommended to the Trust; Which would require a few Days Deliberation.—*Ibid.*, VI, 59-60.

13. RELIEF IS PROVIDED FOR SCHOOLMASTER ORTMAN, 1747

At a Meeting of the President and Assistants for the Colony of Georgia on Monday the twenty first Day of December in the Year of our Lord 1747.

Present
{
William Stephens   President
Henry Parker   ⎫
William Spencer   ⎪ Assistants
Samuel Marcer   ⎬
Patrick Graham   ⎭
}

. . . Christopher Ortman having several Times petitioned this Board Setting forth his unhappy Circumstances and the miserable Condition He is reduced to, being entirely uncapable of Labour owing to his great Age and decrepid State, and that He and his Wife must inevitably perish if not immediately relieved by this Board having no where else to apply: We knowing the Truth of it to be such and being in a Straight how to relieve him under his present Necessity, as he is unhappily under the Trustees Displeasure, but being well assured of their Honours humane Dispositions, that They will not suffer any Person to perish for Want under their Protection, Do presume thus farr as to allow forty Shillings to be given him from Time to Time as this Board shall think proper; Having set forth his unhappy

Case in our Letter to Mr Secretary Martyn of the second of October last, hoping We might soon have Directions relating to him.—*Ibid.*, VI, 202-3.

14. Peter Joubert is discharged as schoolmaster, 1749

At a Meeting of the President and Assistants in Council assembled for the Colony of Georgia on Wednesday the 20th Day of December 1749.

Present
{
William Stephens President
William Spencer
Samuel Marcer
Patrick Graham
James Habersham
}
Assistants

... The Revd Mr Zouberbuhler and the Inhabitants of this Town having made repeated Complaints to this Board, that Mr Peter Joubert Schoolmaster had for some Time past neglected to give proper Attendance to his Scholars, and likewise that He has been of late so much addicted to Drinking, that He gives great offence to the Inhabitants, and what is more pernicious sets a bad Example to their Children.— The Board being too sensible of this Complaint, and with concern finding that, their repeated Admonitions have not been duly regarded They are now obliged to discharge him.—*Ibid.*, VI, 302-3.

15. Proposal to build a Schoolhouse, 1750

His Excellency also proposed to the Board that a public School should be erected, on the old burying Ground, forty Feet in Length, Twenty Feet in Breadth, Two Stories, each Story to be ten Feet in heighth: And that as the Burying Ground included two Lots, his Excellency proposed that one of the Lots should be sold at public Vendue And the Moneys arising thereby to be made Use of towards defraying the Expence of such Building All which the Board unanimously approved.—*Ibid.*, VIII, 136.

16. Complaint about ill conduct of schoolmaster Holt who is suspended, 1750

At a Meeting of the President and Assistants in Council assembled for the Colony of Georgia on Wednesday the 17th Day of October 1750

Present
{
Henry Parker   President

William Spencer
Patrick Graham   } Assistants
James Habersham
}

The Reverend Mr Zouberbuhler and most of the Inhabitants of this Town, having frequently complain'd of the ill Conduct of Mr Holt the Schoolmaster, towards many of the Children under his Instruction— The Board could no longer hear these repeated Complaints without examining into the same; therefore He was sent for (Mr Zouberbuhler by Request being present) who returned for answer, that He would come when He had Time; the Messenger was again sent to acquaint Him, that his Attendance was required immediately, the answer was, when He dismissed the School, He wou'd attend, and that He was the properest Judge of the Time; this insolent Behaviour occasioned the Board to order their Messenger to fetch Him as an Officer—When He was brought, his Behaviour to the Board, as well as to Mr Zouberbuhler was so intollerably abusive; that it was thought proper, in order to reduce him to a sense of his Duty, to order him into Confinement; but before, He reached the Place, Mr Zouberbuhler at the request of the Board, overtook him, and endeavoured to convince Him of his Error, which kind Service, Mr Zouberbuhler said, He returned with the utmost Scorn and Contempt, and added that He could not in Conscience ask any Favours for Him; 'till He was convinced of his Folly, which He thought could only be done by shewing a proper Resentment, as He had often declared, that He was not under the Controul of any authority here.

Mr John Milledge petitioned for four Hundred Acres of Land on the South side of little Ogechee River at the back of Lands granted to William Wilson and his Son John, setting forth, that He some Years ago made considerable Improvements on a Tract of Land on the Great Ogechee, while He commanded the Garrison on the said River, but the same having never been confirm'd to him, and the Provincial Troops being broke, made it inconvenient for him to desire to be fixed there; and that He has since been industriously employ'd in cutting Lumber &c. but now conceives it to be high Time to make a Settlement for his future Welfare— The Board having for some Time past observed, that this good natur'd Young Man has been employing his Strength and Industry rather for the Service of others, than for himself, could not but approve of his Design of making a Settlement, therefore granted his Request; and they cannot omit observing, that He has at all Times appeared peculiarly Active to serve the Colony, whenever required, especially in all Disturbances with the Indians, being a good Horseman and well acquainted with the Woods.

Thursday the 18th Day of October 1750

The Board thought proper before they separated to desire Mr Habersham, one of their Members, to get Mr Zouberbuhler to go with Him to have a further Discourse with Mr Holt concerning his late Behaviour, which Mr Zouberbuhler for some Time refus'd, saying He look'd upon him to be in his present Temper incorrigible, and that he ought to be humbled by Confinement but was at length prevail'd on to go, who soon return'd together, reporting that his Behaviour was the same or rather worse; but the Board having Compassion on the Infirmities of his decrepit Body, thought rather to Suspend him from acting as a Schoolmaster under the Trustees (at least 'till he came to a sense of his Duty) than to keep him longer confin'd, accordingly he was sent for and acquainted of the same, but that He might keep a private School for such Children whose Parents should think proper to send to Him.—*Ibid.*, VI, 343-45.

17. SCHOOLMASTER HOLT IS RESTORED, 1750

Saturday the 10th Day of November 1750

The Revd Mr Zouberbuhler acquainted the Board, that Mr Edward Holt had been with him several Times, and acknowledg'd, that He had been induced by the Reports of idle People to act in the Manner he had done, unbecoming his Station; but that if He might be restor'd to his Office, He would take Care to give no Offence for the future—The Board were pleas'd to hear, that their Suspension had wrought so good an Effect, and brought him to a Sense of his Duty, which was what they intended; therefore they readily sent for him, and upon his repeated promise, that He wou'd conduct himself agreeable to his Station, they restor'd him.

At a Meeting of the President and Assistants in Council assembled for the Colony of Georgia on Wednesday the 14th Day of November 1750

Present
{
Henry Parker — Vice President
William Spencer
Patrick Graham
James Habersham
Noble Jones
} Assistants

Last Monday Mr Edward Holt open'd his School, and his Behaviour is so much alter'd for the better that He seems to give general
Content—*Ibid.*, p. 354.

18. Thomas Eastham receives license to teach school, 1754.

By his Excellency John Reynolds Esquire Captain General
Governor and commander in chief in and over his majestys Province
of Georgia, and ordinary of the same.

To Thomas Eastham
out of the assourance of the Sobriety, ability and loyalty of you the
said Thomas Eastham I do hereby licence you to keep a Scholl for
the instruction of youth within this province (You having first before
me taken the state oaths and subscribed the test required by law)
and for so doing this shall be your Sufficient License which is to continue my pleasure—

Given under my hand and Seal at Savannah the twenty fifth day
of november in the year of our Lord one thousand seven hundred and
fifty four and in the twenty eighth year of his majestys reign—Will
Book AA, Georgia Department of Archives and History, p. 2.

19. Petition of German Protestants for land for schoolmaster, 1760

Read a Petition of the German Protestants inhabiting the District
of Goshen setting forth that by Subscription they had purchased
from Matthias West fifty Acres of Land for the Use and Benefit of
a School Master, but unadvertently had let the Time expire by Law
limited for claiming and taking out his Majestys Grant for the same
That the Petitioners were in low Circumstances and the Expence
falling on a few of them by Reason of some Subscribers being removed without paying their Subscriptions Therefore they humbly
pray that as the Land was for a Charitable Purpose a Grant for the
same might be ordered to pass unto John Sheraus and Michael Bore-
man In Trust for the Use aforesaid and that the Fees of taking out
the same might be remitted.

RESOLVED That the Prayer of the said Petition is granted so
far as the Board may grant the same; his Excellency the Governour
particularly remits his Fees.—Candler, *op. cit.*, VIII, 364-65.

VI

PHILANTHROPY AND EDUCATION:
THE SYMS-EATON SCHOOL

I. PREVIEW AND COMMENTS

SO FAR AS IS now known, the first endowment for an educational institution in English North America was provided in Virginia under
the will of Benjamin Syms February 12, 1634, which was confirmed
by the House of Burgesses in 1642.[1] Twenty-five years later Thomas
Eaton also of Elizabeth City County left by his will property which
was later combined with the gifts of Syms and became the foundation
on which the Syms-Eaton School was established and had a long and
rather continuous history. The school established by Syms and that
provided by Eaton were incorporated as one, by an act of the General Assembly December 12, 1805, under the name and style of the
"Trustees of Sym's and Eaton's Free School." A quarter century
later the inhabitants of Elizabeth City County engaged in controversy
over a proposal to divide the funds and provide for two schools. The
petition and the counter-petition to the General Assembly, and the
interrogation of the head of the school on the subject, are included
here as parts of the documentary history of this interesting educational effort. Between 1829 and 1840 feeling in the county was so
sharply divided as to take on the "proportions of a feud" between
the supporters of George Cooper and C. J. D. Pryor as candidates for
the principalship of the school, a dispute that finally resulted in the
murder of Cooper by Thomas Allen, a strong supporter of Pryor for
the post.[2] During the Civil War the town of Hampton was burned
and the house of the Syms-Eaton School destroyed. The mortgage
bonds in which the funds had been invested were taken by the
family of Col. J. C. Phillips along with their own papers when early
in the war they became refugees to Richmond. A new school house
was built after the war and in 1902 the school became known as the
Syms-Eaton Academy.

In 1940 the General Assembly of Virginia enacted a bill to restore

1. There are many references to this school, but perhaps the best account of it is by
Mrs. F. M. Armstrong, *The Syms-Eaton Free School*. This was published for the
Daughters of the American Revolution and the Association for the Preservation of
Virginia Antiquities, but no date or place of publication is given.
2. See Armstrong, *op. cit.*, pp. 21-25.

the school, perhaps as a sort of "museum piece," but the governor disapproved the measure, in the nature of a "pocket veto," without giving any reasons. At that time the endowment of the Syms-Eaton fund amounted to $10,000, which is now invested in United States Government Bonds. The Will Book for Elizabeth City County in which the will of Benjamin Syms should be recorded is lacking, but the Virginia State Library [3] has a certified copy of it.

II. DOCUMENTS

1. THE WILL OF BENJAMIN SYMS, 1634

In the name of God Amen this Twelfth day of Febry Anno Domini one thousand Six hundred and thirty four I Benjamin Syms being of perfect health, & memory praised be God make & ordain this my last Will and testament, in manner & forme following Viz

I commend my soul into the hands of God my Creator and Redeemer and my body to the Earth from whence it came to have Christian burial whereas there is due to me two hundred acres of land lying in the old Poquoson River and Eight Milch cows—I bequeath it as followth Viz The use of the said land with the milk and Increase Male of the said cattle to be for the mantayance of an honest & learned man to keep upon the said Ground a free School to Educate & teach the Children of the adjoining Parishes of Elizb City & Poquoton from Mary's Mount downwards to the Poquoson River.

Item My Will and desire is that the Worshipful the Commander and ye rest of the Commissioners of this liberty with the ministers and Church Wardens of the said Parish where the said School is founded to see it from time to time justly & truly performed.

Item My Will and Desire is that when it please God there is sufficient Increase of the said cattle yt some part of them be saved for the erecting a very sufficient School house and the Rest of the Increase that are left to be disposed of before nominated and in Repairing the said School.

Item My Will is that the Increase of the said Cattle after the said School Master is sufficiently stocked for his maintaynance shall be spent according to the directions of the said Commander &

3. Letter from W. J. Van Schreeven, Head Archivist, Virginia State Library, to Edgar W. Knight, May 21, 1947. A typescript copy of the will is in the Library of the University of North Carolina.

Commitions with the rest of them to manteyne poor children, or decayed or maimed persons of the said parish.

Item I give and bequeath unto George Thompson the Soun of Roger Thompson, late of Barstable in the County of Duenshire decd one thousand, pos weight of Tobacco in leafe.

Item Whereas there is due unto me one bond of one hundred pounds from Thomas Worth in the County of Cornewall, which said bond is now in the hands of Wassell Webbing of Baching in the County of Essen I Doe also give & bequeath to the said George Thompson.

Item My Will and desire is that if the said George Thompson or Angell Thompson should decease that then whatever I have bequeath In this my Will & testament to Remaine to the surviver.

Item I Doe further will and desire that if should please God to take away both the Said George & Angell Thompson that then whatever I have bequeath them in this my will to Return to the use and benifit of the said School for want of Heirs of Either of their bodys lawfully begotten.

Item I give and bequeath unto Angell Thompson son of the said Roger Thompson decd three thousand pounds of Tobacco in leaf with twelve young Cattle with all the Increase of those cattle which belongs unto me unto this my Will be with all such goods, hoggs Poultry and household stuffe as are or shall be found belonging unto me with twelve barrels of corn.

Item I give and bequeath unto the said Angle Thompson two hundred and fifty acres of land which is due unto me for transportations, of five Servants in the Peter & John of London in the year our Lord one thousand Six hundred twenty Six Capt. John being the commander of the said ship.

Item I give and bequeath five hundr Pounds of Toba to be imployed to the use of the Church of the old Poquoson.

Item I give and bequeath to the minister of the said Parish which shall beat the time when this my will shall be two hundd pounds of Tobacco.

Item I request my well beloved friends Mr. Thomas Oldis and John Snode to be Overseers to see those legacies Performed according, to the full Intent and meaning of my last will and Testament. To whom I give as a rememberance of my love three hundd Pounds of Toba and one Ewe goate being at the house of John Branch at Back River.

In witness whereof I have hereunto set my hand and seal the day and year first above written

his mark

Benjamin Syms

—Copy of this will is in the Virginia State Library. Photocopy of that copy is in the University of North Carolina Library.

2. THE LEGISLATURE CONFIRMS THE WILL, 1642

Be it also enacted and confirmed upon consideration had of the godly disposition and good intent of Benjamin Symms, dec. in founding by his last will and testament a freeschool in Elizabeth county, for the incouragement of all others in the like pious performances, that the said will and testament with all donations therein contained concerning the freeschool and the scituation thereof in the said county and the land appurteining to the same, shall be confirmed according to the true meaning and godly intent of the said testator without any alienation or conversion thereof to any place or county. —March, 1642-3: 18th Charles 1st. Hening, *Statutes at Large*, I, 252.

3. THE WILL OF THOMAS EATON, 1659

To all Christian people to whom these presents shall come, I, Thos. Eaton of Black River, in the County of Elizabeth City (hereby) send Greeting in our Lord God everlasting. Know ye that I the said Thomas Eaton, being at present weake in body but whole & (perfect) in memory, praised be God, out of my own free will (and the love) that I beare towards the Inhabitants of the County of Elizabeth City, I have for the maintenance of an able school master (to) educate and teach the children borne within said County of Elizabeth City—

Given, granted, assigned, set over and confirmed and doo by these presents give, grant, assign, set over and confirm after the time of my decease for the use aforesaid, Five hundred acres of land whereon the (sd) Free school shall bee kept being a part of a dividend of six hundred and (f———) acres graunted unto me by pattent bearing date the fifth day of June Anno 1638, Beginning from the beaver damm———westerly towards the head of the Back River & Southerly ———Woods, with all houses, edifices, orchards and Rights to——— belonging to it. Two negroes called by the names of———Twelve Cows and two bulls, twenty hogs, young and old, one bedstead, a table, a cheese press, twelve milk trays, an Iron kettle, contayning about twelve gallons, pot rack and pot hooks, Milk Pailes, water tubs and powdering tubbs, to have and to hould the said land with all other the premises before mentioned for the use afores'd, with all ye male increase thereof, for ye maintenance of said schoolmaster such one as by the Commissioners, Mynister & churchwardens whom I doo nominate and appoint as trustees in trust for the ordering and settling thereof from time to time shall be thought fit, and I, the said Thomas Eaton do further order & appoint that no free education bee allowed but to such children as shalbe borne within the said county. And that when there shall be found to bee sufficient maintenance for the sd. schoolmaster that ye overplus thereof shalbe imployed for the maintenance of poor impotent persons Widowes and Orphans, inhabitants in the said county as by my said Trustees shalbe thought fit. All wch the premises before mentioned to be enjoyed for the use aforesaid, without anie manner of claime or demand, disturbance, incumbrance or hindrance of anie person or persons, clayming by from or under mee forever by these presents, and further know ye, that I, ye said Thomas Eaton have delivered at the time of the ensealing and delivery hereof, part of the sd. land in name of all the rest of the premises before mentioned.

In witness whereof I have hereunto set my hand & seal this nineteenth day of September, Anno Dni. 1659.

THO. EATON Seale

—Records in Clerk's Office, Elizabeth City County.
In Armstrong, op. cit., pp. 8, 9.

4. ITEMS FROM THE RECORDS OF ELIZABETH CITY COUNTY, 1692-1728

19 Xber, 1692.—Whereas Mr Ebenezer Taylor, late schoolmaster of Eaton's ffree-school, his time being expired & having had ye Benefitt & pquisetts thereof, It is thought reasonable yt a negroe woman belonging to ye sd schoole should be cloathed at ye charges of ye sd schoolemaster, she being almost naked. It is therefore ordered y sd Taylor doe wthin fourteen dayes next pvide and deliver unto Mr Henry Royall. one of ye ffeoffees, one new cotton wastecoate and pettycoate, 3 yards of good new canvis for a shift, one pare of new shoes & stockins & alsoe 3 barrels of sound Indian Corn for ye said negroes use wth costs als exon.

Nov. 20, 1693.—It is ordered yt Robert Crook Schoolmaster at Symmes School be allowed and paid for his charges in repairing ye schoole House two old cowes in lieu thereof.

May 20, 1695.—It is ordered yt a negroe Joan belonging to Eaton's free school by reason of age for ye future be free from paying Levyes and what crop she makes of Corne, Tobacco or Pulse y^t shee keepe ye same to her owne use for her maintainance.

18 Nov. 1697.—Mr. George Eland with consent of this court is elected Schoolemaster, of Eaton's free school & he to continue in place as he shall be approved of from year to year Teaching all such children in English and gramer learninge as shall be sent to him y^t are belonging to this county, and he shall have all such pquissets & pfitts as is belonging to ye s^d schoole.

19 June 1699.—Upon ye peticon of William Williams wee doe hereby give, grant, possess, and confirm unto the said Williams & his heirs &c all that plantation or tract of land whereon John Tams lately lived, belonging to Eaton's free-school land, being part thereof, beginning from Tony Kings along ye Dam side & extending in breadth Eastward as far as the next swamp or branch of ye s^d dams and soe into ye woods as far as ye head Lyne (the term is stated to be 21 years and the consideration that Williams should build or cause to be built one substantial thirty-foot dwelling house, and plant one hundred apple trees at usual distances, and keep the same well trimmed and fenced, and pay yearly 200 lbs. of tobacco "unto such pson as the same in right shall belong or apptayn, and ye expiracon of ye s^d time Deed the said Williams should deliver up the said plantation and houses tenantable.")

Aug. 17, 1720—Upon complt made by Henry Irvin gent ag^t Jno Curle about Eaton's free schoole land of waste being made of the timbers, it is orderd that the Clk. brings s^d Eaton's will and Deed to next court concerning the premises and a copy of the vestry ord^r whereby Curle hath the land granted to him.

Nov. 17, 1725.—Upon the motion of William Tucker setting forth that he is willing to take the school land and provide a schoolmaster, it is ordered that the said Tucker have possession of the said land with this proviso and condition, that he constantly keep ·and provide a schoolmaster to teach children in said land.

Dec. 18, 1728.—Ordered that the quit rents due for the school land according to the rent rolls thereof be paid out of the money arising from the sale of wood from the said land to Henry Cary.—Record Book of Elizabeth City County. Armstrong, *op. cit.*, pp. 10, 11.

5. The minister of Elizabeth City Parish comments on two endowed schools, 1724

There are two schools endowed, though very meanly, whereof John Mason and Abram Paris are teachers. There is also a very good private school where, besides reading, arithmetic and writing, Latin and Greek are very well taught, whereof William Fyfe, a man of good life and conversation is master.—Minister of Elizabeth City Parish. W. S. Perry, *Historical Collections Relating to the American Colonial Church*, I, 294.

6. Advertisement for tutor in the Syms' School, 1752

NOTICE is hereby given, That *Symes*'s Free School, in *Elizabeth-City* County, will be vacant on the 25th of *March* Inst. a Tutor of a good Character, and properly qualified, may meet with good Encouragement, by applying to the Trustees of the said School.

N. B. The Land Rent of the said School is 31 *l. per Ann.* besides Perquisites.—*The Virginia Gazette* (Williamsburg, William Hunter), March 5, 1752, p. [3]; also March 12, 1752, p. [3]

7. Legislation concerning the Syms' School, 1753

Whereas Benjamin Sym, late of the county of Elizabeth-City, deceased, was in his life-time seised in fee-simple, of a tract or parcel of land, containing two hundred acres or thereabouts, with a marsh contiguous thereto; situate, lying, and being, in the county of Elizabeth-City, and being so seised, by his last will and testament bearing date the twelfth day of February, in the year of our lord, one thousand six hundred and thirty four, devised the use of the said land, (by the description of two hundred acres of land being in the Poquoson river) with the milk, and increase of eight milch cows, for the maintenance of a learned honest man, to keep upon the said ground a free school for the education and instruction of the children of the adjoining parishes of Elizabeth-City and Kiquotan, *viz.* from Mary's mount downwards, to the Poquoson river, and declared his will and desire to be, that the justices of the peace of the said county, (by the name and title of the worshipful the commanders, and the rest of the commissioners of this liberty) with the minister and church-wardens of the said parish of Elizabeth-City, should see his said will, from time to time justly and truly performed, and further declared his will and desire to be, that when there should be a sufficient increase of the said cattle, part of them should be sold, and the money raised by such sale, laid out in building a school-house; and that the residue of the said increase, after the school-master should have a sufficient stock, should be applied towards repairing the school-house, and maintaining poor children, or decayed or maimed persons, according to the direction of the said justices, minister, and church-wardens.

II. And whereas the charitable intention of the said Benjamin Sym, the donor, hath not been effectually fulfilled. To the end that the said charity may be more beneficial for the future,

III. *Be it enacted by the Lieutenant-Governor, Council, and Burgesses of this present General Assembly, and it is hereby enacted by the authority of the same,* That the present justices of the peace of the said county of Elizabeth-City, and such as after them shall succeed to be justices of the peace for the said county, during the time they shall so continue justices; the present minister of the said parish of Elizabeth-City, and such as after him shall succeed to be minister thereof, during the time they shall so continue or be in the same office, and the present church-wardens of the said parish of Elizabeth-City, and such as after them shall succeed to be church-wardens thereof, during the time they shall so continue in the same office; shall and may be trustees and governors of the said free school, and of the said tract or parcel of land and marsh, with the appurtenances at all times hereafter for ever: And that the said trustees and directors shall for ever hereafter stand and be incorporated, established and founded, in name and deed, a body politic and corporate, to have continuance forever, by the name of the trustees and governors of Sym's free school in the county of Elizabeth-City, and that they the said trustees and governors may have perpetual succession, and that by that name they and their successors may forever hereafter have, hold, and enjoy the abovementioned tract or parcel of land, containing by estimation two hundred acres, according to the known and reputed bounds thereof, and the marsh aforesaid, with the appurtenances; and that the said trustees and governors, and their successors, or the greater part of them, by the same name shall and may have power, ability and capacity, to demise, lease, and grant the said tract or parcel of land and marsh, with the appurtenances, and the present stock of cattle being thereon, and belonging thereto, for any term of years not exceeding twenty one years, or for any term of years determinable upon one, two, or three lives, or for one, two or three lives, reserving the best and most improved rent that can be got for the same; and

to take, acquire, and purchase, and to sue, and be sued, and to do perform, and execute all other lawful acts and things, good and necessary, and profitable, for the said corporation, in as full and ample a
manner and form, to all intents constructions and purposes, as any
other incorporation, or body politic or corporate, fully, and perfectly
founded and incorporated may do. And that the said trustees and
governors, and their successors for the time being, may have and use
a common seal for the making such their demises, leases, and grants,
and for the doing all and every other thing and things, touching or
in anywise concerning the said incorporation; and that the said
trustees and governors, and their successors for the time being, or
the greater part of them, shall and may have full power and authority,
by writing under their common seal, to nominate and appoint when,
and as often as they shall think good, the said free school; which
said master, before he be received or admitted to keep school, shall
undergo an examination before the minister of the said parish, for the
time being, and produce a certificate of his capacity, and also a
licence from the governor or commander in chief of this dominion,
for the time being, agreeable to his majesty's instructions. And the
said trustees and Governors, and their successors for the time being,
shall and may have full power and authority to visit the said free
school, and to order, reform, and redress all disorders and abuses in
and touching the government and disposing of the same, and to remove the said master, as to them, or the greater part of them shall
seem just, fit, and convenient, And that the said trustees and governors, and their successors, or the greater part of them for the time
being, shall apply the rents to be paid for the said tract or parcel of
land, with the appurtenances, and stock or cattle, aforesaid, to the
maintenance of the said school-master, and erecting and keeping in
repair, a sufficient school-house for his dwelling, and teaching the
children of the adjoining parishes of Elizabeth-City and Kiquotan,
viz. from Mary's Mount downwards, to the Poquoson river; and the
surplus, in case there shall be any, to the maintenance of such poor
children, or decayed or maimed persons, as the said trustees and
governors, and their successors, or the major part of them shall think
fit.

III. *And be it further enacted by the authority aforesaid,* That
the said trustees and governors, and their successors, or the greater
part of them for the time being, shall have full power, ability and
capacity, by the name aforesaid, to sue for, and recover all rents,

and arrears of rent, and all and every sum and sums of money, due
for this occupation of the said tract or parcel of land, by virtue of any
agreement or contract, heretofore made with the present justices of
the peace of the said county, and minister and church-wardens of
the said parish, or their predecessors or the greater part of them
against the person and persons from whom the same are due, his
and their executors and administrators; and also all damages sustained
by occasion of not repairing the houses on the said tract of land, or by
the occasion of the breach of any other part of such contract or
agreement, any law, or custom to the contrary, notwithstanding.

IV. Saving to the king's most excellent majesty, his heirs and successors, and to all and every other person and persons, bodies politic
and corporate, their heirs and successors, other than the person and
persons claiming as heir or heirs of the said Benjamin Sym, all such
estate, right, title, claim and demand, which they, or any of them
should or might have, of, in, to, or out of the premises or any of them,
or any part thereof.—Hening, *op. cit.,* VI, 389-92 (November, 1753).

8. LEGISLATION CONCERNING THE EATON SCHOOL, 1759

Whereas notwithstanding the act of general assembly, made in the
third and fourth years of the reign of his present majesty, intituled,
An Act to enable the justices of the peace of the county of Elizabeth-
City, and the minister and churchwardens of the parish of Elizabeth-City, in the said county, for the time being, to take and hold
certain lands, given by Thomas Eaton, and to let leases thereof, part
of the said lands hath been unprofitable, the trustees having neglected
to let the same; and it is doubted whether the said trustees have
power to recover damages for any waste committed on the said land
by the tenants, or for breach of contract in not building and planting
thereon according to the terms of the leases, or for any arrearages of
rent, the said trustees not being incorporated by the said act, and
some of the said leases being either lost or in the custody of the
tenants who will not produce them: *Be it therefore enacted, by the
Lieutenant-Governor, Council, and Burgesses, of this present General
Assembly, and it is hereby enacted, by the authority of the same,*
That the present justices of the peace of the said county of Elizabeth-
City, and minister and churchwardens of the said parish of Elizabeth-City, and their successors, during the time they shall so continue in their respective offices, shall and may be trustees and gov-

ernors of the charity-school on the said land, with the appurtenances, and shall for ever hereafter stand and be incorporated, established and founded, in name and deed, a body politic and corporate, to have continuance for ever by the name of Trustees and Governors of Eaton's Charity-School, in the county of Elizabeth-City, and shall and may have perpetual succession, and by that name forever hereafter have, hold and enjoy the said land with the appurtenances; and that the said trustees and governors, and their successors, or the greater part of them, by the same name, shall and may have power, ability and capacity to demise, lease and grant any part of the said tract of land, with the appurtenances, not already letten, for any term of years not exceeding twenty-one, or for any term of years determinable upon one, two or three lives, reserving the best and most improved rent that can be got for the same; and to take, acquire and purchase, sue and be sued, and to do, perform and execute all other acts and things good, necessary and profitable for the said incorporation, in as full and ample manner and form, to all intents, constructions and purposes, as any other incorporation or body politic or corporate may do: And may have and use a common seal for making such their demises, leases and grants, and for doing all and every other thing and things touching or concerning the said incorporation. And that the said trustees and governors, and their successors, for the time being, or the greater part of them, shall and may have full power and authority, by writing, under their common seal, to nominate and appoint, when, and as often as they shall think good, such person as they shall approve of to be master of the said charity-school, such master having been first examined by the minister of the said parish for the time being, and producing from him a certificate of his capacity, and a license from the governor or commander in chief of this dominion, for the time being, agreeable to his majesty's instructions: And the said trustees and governors, and their successors, for the time being, shall and may have full power and authority to visit the said charity-school, and to order and reform the government thereof, and to remove the said master as to them, or the greater part of them, shall seem just and convenient: And that the said trustees and governors, and their successors, or the greater part of them, for the time being, shall apply the rents of the said land, with the appurtenances, to the maintenance of the said master and erecting and keeping in repair sufficient houses for his dwelling and teaching the children entitled to the said charity, and the surplus, in case there shall be any, to the other purposes mentioned in the will of the said Thomas Eaton, recited in the said act.

II. *And be it further enacted, by the authority aforesaid,* That the said trustees and governors, and their successors, or the greater part of them, for the time being, shall have full power, ability and capacity, by the name aforesaid, to sue for and recover damages for any waste or trespass committed on the said land, and for not building, planting on and improving the same according to the terms of any leases heretofore made, and all rents and arrears of rent against the person and persons from whom the same are due, his and their executors and administrators: And in case any person or persons, holding any part of the said land by virtue of any lease or leases, will not produce such lease or leases, or accept of a new lease or leases, and cause the same to be recorded in the court of the said county of Elizabeth-City, within six months after the passing of this act, such lease or leases shall be void, and the said trustees and governors, and their successors, or the greater part of them, shall and may demise and let such tenements in the same manner as if such lease or leases had never been made.

III. And whereas it will be for the benefit of the said charity if part of the timber and woods on the said land are sold: *Be it therefore enacted,* That the said trustees and governors, and their successors, shall have full power to sell the said timber and woods off the said land, reserving as much as will be sufficient for building on, repairing and fencing the same, in such manner as shall appear to them to be most beneficial for the said charity, and shall apply the interest thereof, and of the money to be recovered for the damages, rents and arrearages aforesaid, to the purposes herein before mentioned.

IV. And whereas the said foundation hath been abused, by admitting a great number of children into the said school, whose parents are well able to pay for their education: For remedy whereof, *Be it enacted, by the authority aforesaid,* That no person shall enjoy the benefit of the said charity-school without consent of the master, for the time being, except such poor children as the said trustees and governors, and their successors, or the greater part of them, shall from time to time declare to be the proper objects of the pious founder's charity.

V. Saving to the king's most excellent majesty, his heirs and successors, and to all and every other person and person, bodies politic and corporate, their heirs and successors, other than the person and persons claiming as heir or heirs of the said Thomas Eaton, all such estate, right, title, claim and demand which they, or any of them, should or might have of, in, to, or out of the premisses, or any of them, or any part thereof.

VI. *Provided always*, That no lease hereafter be made of the said land, or any part thereof, to the said trustees, or their successors, or to any other person or persons to their use or benefit.—*Ibid.*, VII, 317-20 (February, 1759).

9. The benefits of the Eaton School restricted to poor children, 1759

IV. And whereas the said foundation has been abused, by admitting a great number of children into the said school, whose parents are well able to pay for their education: For remedy whereof *Be it enacted by the authority aforesaid*, That no person shall enjoy the benefit of the said charity-school without consent of the master, for the time being, except such poor children as the said trustees and governors and their successors, or the greater part of them, shall from time to time declare to be the proper objects for the pious founder's charity.—*Ibid.*, p. 319 (February, 1759).

10. Indenture between the trustees of Syms' School and George Wythe, 1760

This Indenture, made the fifteenth day of July, in the year of our Lord, one thousand seven hundred and sixty, between John Tabb, Robert Armistead, Cary Selden, Charles Jennings, John Tabb the younger, Starkey Robinson, George Wray, James Wallace, David Wilson Curle, and Thomas Warringten, Trustees and Governors of Sym's Free School in the County of Elizabeth City, of the one part, and George Wythe of the other part. Witnesseth:—that the said Trustees and Governors, for and in consideration of the rent herein after reserved to be paid, and of the covenants hereinafter contained to be performed by the said George Wythe, have demised and granted and by these presents do demise and grant unto the said George Wythe and to his assigns all that tract or parcel of land called and known by the name of the Sym's Free School land; now in the tenure of the said George Wythe scit. in the Parish and County of Elizabeth City (excepting and reserving one acre at the south-west corner thereof unto the said Trustees and Governors; and their successors,) with all houses orchards, way and waters, water-courses, woods, trees, marshes low grounds, profits and commodities to the said tract or parcel of land appertaining, together with eleven head of black cattle belonging to the said lands; to have and to hold, the said tract or parcel of land and premises, with the appurtenances unto the said George Wythe and to his assigns from the date of these presents for and during the natural life of the said George Wythe; he the said George Wythe and his assigns yielding and paying therefor Thirty one pounds and five shillings current money of Virginia, unto the said trustees and Governors and their successors on the fifth day of February in every year during the said term. Provided that if the said yearly rent of Thirty-one pounds and five shillings or any part thereof, being first lawfully demanded, shall be behind and unpaid by the space of sixty days next after any day on which the same ought to be paid, it shall and may be lawful for the said trustees and Governors and their successors or any of them in the name of the whole to re-enter into the said tract or parcel of land with the appurtenances, and to have and repossess the same. And the said George Wythe for himself his executors and administrators, doth by these presents, covenant with the said Trustees and Governors and their successors that he the said George Wythe or his assigns will deliver or cause to be delivered to and for the use of the Master of the above mentioned Free School, for the time being, four good milch cows in the month of April in every year during the said term; to be returned to their calves in good order in the November following, unless the said Master shuld chuse to keep them during the winter in which case he may retain them instead of others and return them in November afterwards. And that the said George Wythe or his assigns within twelve months after the date thereof will plant an orchard, consisting of one hundred apple trees on the said land and at the expiration or determination of this lease, leave the same complete as to the number of good bearing trees, and keep and leave the houses to be built on the said land (except the houses on the acre of land before excepted and reserved unto the said trustees and governors and except in cases of tempests and accidents by fires) in good repair, and leave three thousand fence rales and eleven head of black cattle on the said land, and pay his Masjestie's quit rents of the said land annually during the said ease. And the said Trustees and Governors for themselves and their successors do covenant with the said George Wythe and his assigns, that the said George Wythe and his assigns, paying the said yearly rent of Thirty one pounds and five shillings, and performing all the covenants herein before contained, which on his or her parts ought to be performed, may at all times during the said lease peaceably and quietly enter into and have and possess the premises hereby demised, with the appurtenances, without any denial or interruption of the said Trustees and Governors or their successors or any person or persons claiming under them.

In witness whereof, the parties to these presents have hereunto interchangeably sett their hands and affixed their seals the day and year first above written.

	John Tabb	(Seal)
Sealed and delivered	George Wray,	(Seal)
in the presence of	David Wilson Curle	(Seal)
	John Tabb Junr.	(Seal)
W. Wager,	James Wallace,	(Seal)
William Armistead,	Thomas Warrington	(Seal)
John Hay,	George Wythe,	(Seal)

—Records in Clerk's Office, Elizabeth City County. In Armstrong, *op. cit.*, pp. 13-16.

11. A MASTER IS WANTED FOR THE SYMS' SCHOOL, 1766

A MASTER is wanted for *SYME'S* CHARITY SCHOOL, in *Elizabeth City* county. Any person inclined to undertake that office, may apply to the Governours and Visitors of the school.—*The Virginia Gazette* (Williamsburg, Alex. Purdie, and John Dixon), July 11, 1766, p. [2]; also July 18, 1766, p. [3]; July 25, 1766, p. [4]

12. THE LEGISLATURE COMBINES THE SYMS' AND THE EATON FUNDS, 1805

Whereas application is made by the inhabitants of Elizabeth City, to appoint and incorporate trustees of two free schools directed by the will of a certain Benjamin Symms, and the deed of a certain Thomas Eaton, to be maintained and kept on two separate tracts of land lying in the said county, and given by them for that purpose; and also to authorize a sale of the said lands by those trustees, if in their opinion such a measure will be beneficial and expedient; representing that for a number of years past, the schools thereon established, have been most shamefully neglected, the buildings suffered to tumble into ruins, and the land dismembered of nearly all its most valuable timber, and used for purposes not designed by the donors: That the magistrates of the said county, who heretofore have considered themselves as answering the description of "commissioners," and "commissioners of the liberty," designated and declared in the said deed and will, trustees to carry into effect the benevolent intentions of the aforesaid donors, are unwilling to exercise any authority over the said property and schools, because there are now no persons in the said county under the denomination of church wardens, with whom they can associate, and who are required by the said charters of conveyance to be co-trustees with those commissioners described therein; in consequence whereof, one school is totally discontinued, and the other under no control, but in the most wretched and deplorable situation:

1. *Be it therefore enacted by the general assembly*, That the freeholders and housekeepers residing in said county shall assemble on the first day of March in the present year at the courthouse of the said county, and vote for eleven able and discreet men, being residents of the said county, who shall act as trustees of the aforesaid lands and schools; and that polls shall be kept of the names of the voters and persons voted for, by some person or persons called upon and sworn for that purpose, who shall sign the same in the presence of two or more credible witnesses, and return them to the next court to be holden for the said county, which court shall declare such eleven persons duly elected to be trustees, and enter the same of record.

2. The trustees so elected, shall be a body corporate, by the name and style of the "Trustees of Symm's and Eaton's free schools," and shall have perpetual succession. By that name they may sue or be sued, plead and be impleaded, in all courts of law and equity, and shall be capable to take, purchase and receive lands and tenements, goods and chattels; shall, in short, be clothed with every legal power necessary to constitute a body corporate, and particularly shall hold the lands herein before denominated for the purposes hereinafter declared.

3. The said trustees, or a majority of them, shall appoint a president, treasurer and a tutor or tutors, properly qualified to teach the most useful and important branches of science, and may make such bye-laws, rules and regulations, for the well ordering the affairs, and for the good government of the said schools, as to them may seem proper; provided they do not contravene the constitution and laws of this land.

4. Before the treasurer shall undertake the duties of his office, he

shall execute a bond with so many good and sufficient securities as shall be approved of by the said trustees, or a majority of them, payable to the said trustees and their successors, in such penalty as they may require, with a condition to collect and account for all monies due and belonging, or which may be due, or belong hereafter to the said institutions; and upon failure to pay and account for all monies by him received in the capacity of treasurer as aforesaid, he and his securities, his and their executors and administrators, shall be subject to judgment on said bond, by motion at the instance of the said trustees, or a majority of them, in the court of said county; provided he or they have ten days previous notice of such intended motion. And the said treasurer shall, on the first day of January annually, or oftener, if in the opinion of such trustees, or a majority of them, it should be necessary, render a true and just account to the said trustees of all his actings and doings in his official capacity.

5. At the end of every three years, a like election of trustees shall be held, who shall have all the powers herein granted to their predecessors; and in case of the death, resignation or removal of any of the trustees, his or their place or places shall be supplied by the remaining trustees, and those thus elected shall act until the period of a new election.

6. If an election of trustees should not be held at the time prescribed by this act, it shall be lawful for the same to be held at any time thereafter; provided public notice be given of the time when such election is to take place, by the sheriff of the said county, under the direction of the court thereof. After the first appointment, and forever thereafter, until an election shall be held according to the provision in this act, the trustees in office shall continue to act.

7. The said trustees shall have power, and they are hereby authorized, at any time hereafter, when in the opinion of a majority of them, it will be most conducive to the end contemplated by the donors thereof, to make sale of the aforesaid lands, together with all the property of every description belonging, or in any wise appertaining thereto, upon such terms as they may deem most advantageous, and invest the money in such way, as that the same shall constitute a fund for the purpose of establishing an academy or seminary of learning in that part of the said county, which to them, or a majority of them, shall seem most convenient and eligible; the same to be called by such a suitable and appropriate name as may be adopted by them.

8. And in case such sale should take place as is herein authorized, the trustees of Symm's and Eaton's free school lands, to be appointed according to the first and fifth sections of this act, shall be and are hereby appointed trustees of the academy, or seminary of learning, which shall be established; shall be elected in like manner, and shall have the same powers and privileges herein before vested in them as the trustees of the said free school lands.

9. And whereas, it appears from the aforesaid will of Benjamin Symms, that the parish of Poquoson, adjoining that of Elizabeth City, is equally entitled with the latter to all the benefits which might result from the establishment of a school on the particular tract of land therein devised for that purpose.

10. Be it further enacted, That the said parish of Poquoson, expressed in the last mentioned will, shall be, and is hereby authorized to send six poor and indigent children to be educated at the said academy, should the sale herein authorized ever be accomplished; who, together with the poor and indigent children residing in the county of Elizabeth City, shall be instructed in those branches of knowledge which may be taught at the aforesaid academy, without fee or reward. All children other than the poor and indigent herein spoken of, shall receive the benefit of tuition at the said academy, paying therefor an adequate and reasonable compensation. And the money arising from this source, shall be vested in the funds of the said institution, for the use of the same, to be appropriated in such way as may seem most beneficial, by the said trustees, or a majority of them.

11. This act shall commence and be in force from and after the first day of February next. (December 12, 1805).—Samuel Shepherd (compiler), *The Statutes at Large of Virginia, from October Session, 1792, to December Session 1806, Inclusive,* III, 164-66.

13. Some Inhabitants of Elizabeth City County petition for division of funds, 1830

To the General Assembly of Virginia

The Petition of the Freeholders and House-Keepers of the County of Elizabeth-City.[1]

1. The originals of this petition, the counter-petition, and of the interrogation of Christopher Pryor, teacher in Hampton Academy, by the legislative committee on schools and colleges in 1830, on the question of dividing the funds of the academy, are in the Virginia State Library. Photocopies are in the library of the University of North Carolina.

Your Petitioners belong to the great body of the people; a body in whom, they are proud to acknowledge, the sovereign power is vested, and which no authority can take from them, but by their free and voluntary consent. They address themselves to the representatives of the people, who are their agents and servants, bound by a connection so close and intimate, that their grievances are only to be stated, but to be promptly heard, and redressed. With these feelings and impressions, your petitioners beg leave most respectfully to introduce a subject of vital interest to themselves, and one which it is believed, you will regard as being not entirely indifferent to yourselves; because it is connected with the great subject of public education, on which you have justly spent, so much time and money, thereby evincing its importance and magnitude.

This subject is the rise, progress, and present condition of the Hampton Academy; a brief history of which they take occasion to give, in order that it may be seen, whether your petitioners are right in the conclusions to which they have arrived.

It seems that as long ago as the 19th Sept. 1659, one Thomas Eaton, a pious and patriotic citizen, granted 500 acres of land and some little personal estate, in the county of Elizabeth City, near the head of Back River, for the support of an able schoolmaster, to educate and teach the children born within the county, on which land a free school was to be kept, with the express injunction that no free education should be allowed but to such children as shall be born within the said county, and that when there should be a sufficient sum raised for the teacher, the overplus should be employed for the maintenance of poor impotent persons, widows and orphans, inhabiting the said county.

Afterwards to wit, on the 15th June, 1715, Benjamin Syms, another kind and benevolent man, devised 200 acres of land, in the said county, near Poquoson River, for the maintenance of an honest learned man, to keep upon the said ground, a free school to educate and teach the children of the adjoining parishes of the said county, with a direction to apply the surplus to the maintenance of poor children, or decayed, or maimed persons of the parishes.

These donations were used though in a very limited degree, as far as your petitioners can ascertain, in advancing the objects of the donors; but in 1805, a law was passed, on the petition of a number of the people of the county, directing a sale of the said lands, and the establishment of the Hampton Academy, under the management of trustees elected by the people triennially, and the Academy so established has continued to the present time, and is now in operation at Hampton, in the said county.

The sales of the lands devised by Syms and Eaton compose almost the entire fund of the institution; perhaps there may have been a small accession from the personal estate, attached to the glebe, but of this, your petitioners are by no means certain. It is represented, that the annual income of the academy, is between 6 and 7 hundred dollars, which is now paid to the principal of the academy, who is entitled to receive stated fees from those attending the academy, who are able to pay.

Your petitioners have endeavored to give a brief history of the facts, connected with the academy, without exageration or disguise. They certainly do not intend to misrepresent.

They now assert, that this academy is so located and conducted, as to defeat the objects of the donors, and these are some of the prominent reasons for this assertion.

The donors in terms, established schools at different points, in the county, the better to distribute their benefits: for they do expressly direct that the schools are to be kept on the lands devised. But at Hampton, those who were the immediate objects of the donors' bounty, are excluded: for they are too distant to attend a school in Hampton, and by establishing the school in Hampton, a class of people enjoy the benefit of the fund, who if they were in the donors' mind, certainly were not the first objects of their bounty, unless it is supposed that they had a greater regard for those at a distance, than for their immediate neighbors and friends; an opinion which it is believed will not be hazarded by any one, however zealous he may be in the cause of the academy.

The people of Hampton now enjoy almost the entire benefit of the fund. With a population equal to about one third of the whole population of the county, the Hampton people are enjoying a fund which was designed to be general to the county, and thus the other two thirds are entirely excluded, and these two thirds in all probability, the favorites of the donors. This is the effect of the present location of the school. It may be said that the school is equally open for the country as well as the Hampton people, and that this obviates the objection: but can all the country people move to Hampton? unless they live there, they cannot send to school there. This is obvious. Besides, the country people have a right to locate the schools where the donors intended, or where the objects of their bounty may get the benefit of them. And if this right be perfect, (which it is believed it is), then it is manifest, that it was not only wrong, but unjust to establish the academy at Hampton, having the controul of the whole fund.

The donors' first object was the promotion of education. The second was the care of the poor. This is proved by reference to the spirit and terms of the different donations. In the grant by Thomas Eaton, he says he gives to educate and teach *the children born within the county*. Again, he says, a *Free School* shall be kept on the land. And in the devise by Benjamin Syms, he expressly states that he makes the devise, for the maintenance of an honest learned man, to keep upon the ground, a *free school*, to educate and teach the children of the county. Then it is manifest from both donations, that the schools were to be free, and for children generally, and not for poor children exclusively. The Hampton academy, is not conducted on this principle. Free instruction is not given, except to the poor, all others must pay, and thus the object of the donors, is again defeated.

Your petitioners stated that the second object of the donors was the care of the poor. A reference to the same means, will prove the statement. By the grant from Thomas Eaton, he directs that when the school master shall be sufficiently provided, the overplus shall be employed in the maintenance of poor impotent persons widows and orphans of the county. And by the will of Benj. Syms he says, that after the schoolmaster is sufficiently stocked for his maintenance, the residue is to be applied to maintain poor children, or decayed, or maimed persons of the county.

It is manifest then, that both donors intended to establish a free school, for educating the youth of the county, generally; and when that object was attained the *surplus* was devoted to the poor. But the trustees of the Hampton academy, do not recognize this principle, for they exclude from the school, those who are able to pay, unless they will pay tuition fees, equal to the ordinary price of education, and thus, again the object of the donors is frustrated.

There can be no doubt, but that both donors intended to confine the benefits of their donations, to children born in the county—Benjamin Syms does not say so, in terms, though he does in effect; but Thomas Eaton, does expressly say, that none but children, born in the county, shall be educated without fee. The trustees do not adhere to, or recognize this feature of the donation. Any poor person, wheresoever born, may go to this school, free of charge. And hence, the town of Hampton, is thronged with poor children, who come over to live in Hampton, in order that they may attend the Academy free of charge. This is very kind in the Trustees, and no doubt, is a very popular regulation. But have they the power, thus to use the funds? Do they not by this course, again conflict, with the express injunctions of the donors?

Your petitioners are, in this view, presenting the subject, according to strict right, and in pursuance with the manifest intention of the donors. They do not wish, to be understood, as conveying the idea, that they object to the use of this fund, exclusively for the poor. On the contrary, they here freely express their decided approbation, to the appropriation of the fund to that object. But then, all the poor of the county, have equal claims on the fund, not the poor of Hampton, who now enjoy almost the exclusive use of it. If the fund is to be applied in aid of education generally, let all the youth of the county enjoy its benefits. If for the poor only, let all the poor participate. This is common Justice.

Your petitioners may be told, that the act establishing the academy, was enacted on the petition of the people of the county, and that therefore the General Assembly ought not further to interfere. It is admitted that there was such a petition, and that it was signed by a number of respectable persons. But it is confidently believed, that many of those who signed that petition, did not for a moment reflect on what they were doing; few of them, knew of the terms of the donations; others, were flattered with the prospect of having a great school in the county, which all should enjoy, whilst to others, was held out the idea, that schools should be located in different parts of the county, and supported by the profits of the funds. In this way, a great number of friends were gained over to the project, the lands were sold, and the academy established in Hampton, to the great joy of the Hampton people, who were the prime movers of the plan.

It is evident that the academy, and its funds, belong to the people of the county. The trustees say, they have no power to change the location of the academy, or to divide its funds; then, if the General Assembly cannot give relief, it follows, that the people own a fund which they cannot control, and which must forever take a direction against their express will; a conclusion too absurd for this enlightened age. But, it is believed, that the General Assembly does possess power to give relief on this subject; not to take the funds from the county, or to destroy the school altogether, but to assist the people, in giving the funds a direction which shall be accordant with their wishes.

The General Assembly cannot call a Convention, but yet a Law has been passed to assist the people in that object, by giving them an opportunity to collect the voice of the State. It is upon this principle, that the General Assembly may act, with perfect propriety, by passing a law to assist the people of the county to give the funds such a direction as they wish.

Your petitioners are by no means unfriendly to the academy, or to the Hampton people. But they feel themselves bound to speak, and to speak plainly. They feel, that they have been injured, and, they think, that the Hampton people, if called upon, are bound to acknowledge it. They seek and ask redress for this injury, in a spirit of moderation and forbearance, which they would be sorry to find assailed even for one unkind expression. Let the academy then continue at Hampton, give it its proper share of the income of the fund, that being the portion which the population of Hampton would command, and let the ballance go to establish schools in other parts of the county, and thus the objects of the donors will be completely attained. There will then be three or more schools, instead of one; and these properly located, will place education within the reach of every person in the county; an object so desirable, that every man must assent to its justice.

To conclude, your petitioners pray that a Law may pass, dividing the said funds and locating two or more schools in other parts of the county, as the people may determine, to be kept up under the management of the present and all future trustees of the academy; or that the said trustees may be authorized and empowered to locate two or more schools in other parts of the county, under their management and control, and to be supported out of the said funds.

And your petitioners, as in duty bound, will ever pray, &c.

14. Other inhabitants present counter petition, 1830

At a meeting of the citizens of the county of Elizabeth City, held at the courthouse, on the 29 day of December 1830, to take into consideration the means best calculated to defeat the memorial, presented to the General Assembly of Virginia, by divers citizens of the county; praying that a law may pass, dividing the Funds of the Hampton Academy and locating two or more schools in other parts of the county; Capt. Robert Lively was called to the chair, and John

C. Pryor appointed secretary; Whereupon the following resolutions were unanimously adopted.

Whereas, from the dificulty of obtaining a copy of the memorial, and the inclemency of the weather, since a copy was procured, together with the urgent necessity, of forwarding this counter memorial, it became impracticable to obtain the signatures of but a small number of these, opposed to the division of the Funds of the Academy; Be it therefore Resolved, that the following Memorial be adopted, and transmitted, together with these proceedings, to our Representative in the General Assembly of Virginia.

Resolved that the Chairman and secretary be requested to sign these proceedings.

Robt Lively Chairman
Jno C. Pryor Sect.

To the General Assembly of Virginia

The subscribers, citizens of the State of Virginia and residents of the county of Elizabeth City, respectfully shew;

That a memorial has been presented, to your body, by divers citizens of the same county, praying, that a Law may pass, for dividing the funds of the Hampton Academy, and locating two or more schools in other parts of the county.

That memorial was sedulously withheld from those, who did not agree to sign it, and though repeated applications were made, by persons opposed to its objects, no copy, or even a view of it could be obtained, until after the original had been placed in the Post-Office, to be transmitted to Richmond. This is stated in no querulous spirit, but to account for the tardiness of this counter memorial.

The Hampton Academy, the destruction of which is sought; and will be certainly effected, by the success of that memorial, owes its existence to an act of the Legislature, passed on the 18th Jany 1805, to which your Petitioners beg leave to invite your special attention. That Act was passed at the application of the citizens of Elizabeth City county, refers to, and recites the substance of their memorial, and confirms, by legislative sanction, the statements there made, as inducements for the passage of the Law. It enacted, among other things, that Trustees, to be biannually elected by the freeholders and housekeepers of Elizabeth City county, should be encorporated with power to sell certain lands, which had been conferred by Benjm Syms and Thos Eaton, and to apply the proceeds as a fund for establishing an Academy, or seminary of learning, in that part of the county which, to them, or a majority of them, should seem most convenient and eligible; The same to be called by such suitable and appropriate name, as they might adopt. Pursuant to that law, these agents, elected for that very purpose sold the land and established an academy at Hampton, as the most convenient and eligible part of the county, and conferred upon it, the name of the Hampton Academy.

The funds, of this Institution, were afterwards, augmented by the proceeds of the Glebe property, and now amount to about $10,000, producing an annual income of between six and seven hundred dollars. The success of the academy, has surpassed the expectation, even of its founders; nor do the memorialists themselves either impeach its prosperity, or the order, discipline, and propriety, with which this administered. The plan of education, pursued at this Academy, embraces, besides the ordinary branches of English education, Rhetoric, Mathematics, Metaphysics, Moral Philosophy, the elementary principles of Chemistry and Natural Philosophy, and the Latin language. These subjects are divided into four classes. The tuition fees of the first class, are $2.50 of the second $3.50, of the third, $6.50, and of the fourth $8.50 per quarter. The Academy is conducted by a principal teacher—and an assistant, and the average number of pupils may be estimated at 60 pay scholars, and 25 who are instructed gratuitously. The number attending the school, at present, exceeds even this computation.

These facts are submitted, that your honourable body may judge, whether in a country, in which the means of education are so limited, and too often so wastefully applied, an Institution, embracing within its benevolent operation, both the needy and the competent; affording the means of education, to so large a number of both, at so small an expense, ought, upon light grounds, to be arrested in its course of usefulness. The memorial professes to give a history of the rise, progress, and present condition, of the Hampton Academy. The argument chiefly relied on, to sustain their application is, that the Academy is so located and conducted, as to defeat the intention of the donors, Syms and Eaton. The remedy proposed, to obviate that evil, is to divide the funds, and locate two or more schools, in other parts of the county.

That the history of the Academy, given by the Memorialists, is incomplete, must be obvious from its suppresion of every circumstance, most material to the enquiry; (to wit) The plan of education, its success, and the number of scholars. That it is not altogether authentic, in what it states, is also certain. Whether the argument be more orthodox than the history, remains to be considered.

To sustain the position, that the location of the Academy defeats the intention of the donors, the Memorialists refer to the donations, made by Syms on the 10th of Feb 1734, (incorrectly stated to be on the 15th June 1715,) made by Eaton, on the 16th of Sept. 1659. A copy of the will and deed of Syms & Eaton will accompany this petition, to enable your body to ascertain their intention, as expressed by themselves.

It will be seen that in the very first of these donations, the education of the children of Poquoson Parish, was provided for, as well as those of Elizabeth City parish. Though these were adjoining parishes, the former was not within the county of Elizabeth City. The act of 1805, however much it has been reproached by the Memorialists, did not pretermit the claims of the poor children of Poquoson parish, but expressly provided for them; and they are protected by, and embraced within, the operation of the Hampton Academy.

The Memorialists, however, at the very moment they express a sort of religious honor, at the supposed profanation of the intention of the donors, by the act of 1805, and profess a holy zeal to bring back the fund to the objects contemplated by them, with most remarkable consistency prey, that the funds may be divided, and two or more schools located in the same county, as the people of Elizabeth City may determine; to the entire exclusion of the people of Poquoson, whose children were equally, with those of Elizabeth City, the object of Sym's bounty It will be found, on an inspection of Syms and Eaton's donations, that the funds provided by them were of a very miscellaneous character, comprehending not only lands, but slaves, cattle, hogs, poultry, and various articles of household and kitchen furnature; and that at the time the donations were made, there were buildings upon the lands for the accommodation of the master and the pupils. It was manifestly the interest and expectation of the Testators, that the school master, residing on the land, should have the use and profits of the houses, as the means of enabling him to maintain his school.

It should excite not surprise, that after the lapse of nearly two centuries, the houses, personally, and every thing save the soil, were wasted and had become extinct. But when, to this, is added, the circumstance, that the worshipful, the commander, and the rest of the commissioners of the liberty, with the ministers and church wardens, who were the Trustees, had all become extinct, both in fact and in law,—it must be manifest, that the literal and exact execution of the intention of the donors, had become impossible prior to 1805. It is therefore, certain, as the Memorialists themselves have stated, that these donations were never used, but, in a very limited degree, in advancing the intention of the donors. But in 1805, and for many years before, schools had entirely gone down.

By their own admissions, then, the benevolent designs of the founders had been entirely frustrated, prior to 1805.

The Act of that year, whatever may be its other offences, cannot be charged with the sin of violating the design of Syms and Eaton. That act was the effect, and not the cause, of the total frustration of their scheme. And it cannot but excite surprise, that with his actual experience, attested by the Memorialists themselves, of the insufficiency, in their separate and divided state, to fulfill the benevolent designs of the donors, and the total failure of the plan of separate schools; and effort should now be made to renew the same experiment, and to bring about the same mischief, at the very moment when the advantages of their union are illustrated and confirmed, by the prosperous condition of the Hampton Academy.

It is not for your petitioners to judge, if the rights, vested by law, in the corporation, can be divested by the legislature. If the power exists, to do so, it is one of two delicate and dangerous a character,— to be wantonly and lightly exerted; and nothing short of a gross abuse of the powers—conferred on the corporation, or the experience of some great mischief from its operation, would justify its exercise. No abuse of trust is imputed, or can be imputed. The only complaint is, that the people of Hampton now enjoy almost the exclusive benefit of the funds. If that change means, that either by the arrangement of the Institution, or by its practical administration, any favoritism, preference, or priority whatever, is bestowed, on the people of Hampton, your petitioners deny it, in the most explicit terms, and require that, that matter—may be investigated, and proved if true. On the contrary, they assert, that no preference whatever has been conferred on them; that the benefits of the Academy are indiscriminately, and equally open to all the people, and that pupils attend the Institution from all parts of the county, and even from other counties. If the charge means, however, nothing more than that the Academy does not equally accommodate every part of the county, your Petitioners need only say, that, in the nature of things, that equality is unattainable. Every Institution of the sort must be more convenient to those residing near its site, than to those more distant. It is not, in the power of man, to bestow ubiquity, or annihilate space. Should your Memorialists succeed in their object, that imaginary equality, at which they profess to aim, could not be realized. The children, nearest the sites of the new schools, proposed to be established, by the destruction of the Academy, would still be more accommodated than those more distant.

All that is practically attainable, or ought to be aimed at in the location, is, to produce the greatest amount of convenience for education. That was settled by the people of Elizabeth City in 1805, has been recognized by general acquiscence since, and confirmed by the actual condition of the Institution.

The memorial assails the Act of 1805, and the motions and intelligence of the people of the county, on whose application it was enacted. Your Petitioners deem it unnecessary to indicate either. Their own memorial shows the utter annihilation of the schools before that act, the present condition of the Academy proves the wisdom and benevolence of the measures then adopted, to reanimate those endowments. There is certainly no proof, that those who applied to the Legislature, in 1805, did not reflect on what they were doing, or were ignorant of the terms of the donation, or were flattered with prospects which have not been realized, or were cajoled and deceived by false ideas held out to them. Your Petitioners persuade themselves that this is only a picture of imagination; but if it be a portrait of actual life, they are confident, that the original is not to be found in the Petitions of 1805, but in some more recent applicants to the Legislature.

The Memorialists represent that they belong to the great body of the people, and very plainly intimate, that their prayer must be granted, that their grievances are only to be stated, to be redressed. Did not the Petitioners of 1805, do not your present petitioners, also, belong to the great body of the people, or is it intended to disenfranchise all that do not concur in the scheme, of destroying the best school, of its grade, in lower Virginia. If not, what meaning is to be attributed to that unnecessary reference to first principles, which are not more dear to those, who aim at destroying the Academy, than to those who wish to sustain it. Your Petitioners know, that the best, if not the only preservation of free institutions, is the intelligence and morality of the people, and that Education is the prolific parent of both. With this conviction deeply impressed on their minds, and the actual experience of the benefits, diffused by the Hampton Academy, they are unwilling to revive the experiment, which failed before 1805.

They therefore pray, that the prayer of the said Memorial may not be granted.

15. CHRISTOPHER PRYOR TESTIFIES ON THE CONTROVERSY, 1830

Interrogatories proposed in the Committee of Schools and Colleges to Christopher D Pryor, teacher of the Hampton Academy, a witness examined, under authority of a resolution of the House of Delegates, touching the petition and counter petition of sundry citizens of Elizabeth City county: with the answers thereto, upon oath. Question by

Mr. Maxwell—What is the present number of pupils in the Hampton Academy?

Ans—I think there are 64 pay scholars, and about 20 poor children who pay nothing.

Question by

the same—What is the present annual income of the Academy; and what proportion of it is paid to the teacher?

Ans—The annual income is between $600 and $700, as stated in the counter memorial; of which the teacher received $400. The rest is applied to repairs and contigent expenses.

Question by

the same—What are the present rates of tuition?

Ans—They are as set forth in the counter memorial.

Question by

the same—Whence do the pupils principally come?

Ans—At present, chiefly from Hampton and its vicinity. Some however are sent from other parts of the County. There are 2 from Fox-hill, and more are expected from other parts of Elizabeth City.

Question by

the same—Could the Academy be kept up in its present condition, in your judgment, if the funds were divided?

Ans—I think it could not.

Question by
the same—Are the poor of the county, or any other persons of the
county excluded from the benefits of that institution, because of
the admission of poor persons, or any other persons, from any
other county?

Ans—I think they are not.

Question by
Mr. Goode—Has any poor scholar ever been excluded, within your
knowledge, from the benefits of the institution?

Ans—None ever has, within the last three years; during which
time I have been the teacher.

Question by
Mr. Jones—During the last three years, has not a Mr. Cooper kept an
opposition school in the town of Hampton?

Ans—He kept such a school until about July last.

Question by
the same—Can you inform the Committee what number of scholars
Mr. Cooper had?

Ans—I cannot. But for some short time he had a greater number
of pay scholars than were at the Academy. His school however
declined, and the Academy increased as that declined, until Mr.
Cooper left Hampton. Other opposition schools afterwards
established also declined, and at present there is no opposition
to the Academy within the town.

Question by
the same—Was not your assistant teacher, at the time of his appointment, a teacher of the school kept at Harris's Creek Meeting
house, at Fox-hill?

Ans—My present assistant was a teacher at Fox-hill, at the time
of his appointment.

Question by
Mr. Booker—By a division of the funds, in conformity to the prayer
of the petitioners, do you suppose as many persons could receive
the benefits of education from those funds: and from your
knowledge of the county and its inhabitants, do you believe that
any permanent benefit may reasonably be anticipated from such
division of the funds?

Ans—Perhaps the number of scholars might be increased; but I am
satisfied they could not be as well instructed as they are at
present.

Question by

Mr. Leland—Have the Trustees purchased a building for the school? and if they have what is its value?

Ans—They have purchased one, but I do not know its value. It is a large frame building in good repair.

Question by

Mr. McDowell—Is there any apparatus or library belonging to the Academy?

Ans—There is none belonging to the Academy. The teacher has a small apparatus which is used by the pupils; and a private library which some of the larger scholars occasionally use.

Question by

Mr. Semple—Are not the great body of the people, whose names are signed to the petition from Elizabeth City, residents of that district of the County called Fox-hill:—and are the former sites of the schools farther from Fox-hill than the present site?

Ans—A large majority of the petitioners reside in Fox-hill; and are more distant from the former sites of the schools, than from the Academy. A considerable number of them are emigrants from the Eastern Shore.

Question by

the same—Is there a school in Fox-hill district at this time, and did one exist there in 1830?

Ans—I believe there is one, and one existed in 1830.

Question by

the same—Is the proportion of the Literary Fund belonging to the county of Elizabeth City regularly expended in that county?

Ans—It is not.

Question by

the same—Were the trustees of the Hampton Academy at the last election chosen chiefly by the residents of Fox-hill; and what was their purpose in the election?

Ans—They were chosen chiefly by the people of Fox-hill, and for the very purpose of dividing the funds of the Academy.

Question by

the same—Was it generally understood that all the trustees elected were favourable to a division of the funds?

Ans—It was generally so understood; and those only were elected who were supposed to be favourable to such division.

Question by
the same—Were you present when the poll appended to the petition
was taken?
Ans—I was frequently present during the day.
Question by
the same—Did you hear the petition publicly read; or have you heard
any one say they heard it read or explained?
Ans—I did not hear it read myself; nor did I hear any one say that
they heard it read or explained.
Question by
the same—Do you know or believe that the trustees of the Academy
have, in their corporate character, authorised an application for
a division of the funds?
Ans—I am satisfied that they never have.

16. HAMPTON SCHOOL BOARD TAKES ACTION ON THE SYMS-EATON
FUND, 1944

Mr. Lindsay reported that the City of Hampton School Board had
concurred in the judgment of the Elizabeth City County School
Board that the $1200 repaid to the Syms-Eaton Fund should be in-
vested in Government Bonds. He reported that Frank H. Roberts,
County Treasurer, had requested that the school board adopt a resolution authorizing him to invest this money in bonds. The following
resolution was proposed by Dr. Burbank, seconded by Mr. Saunders,
and unanimously adopted:
WHEREAS a mortgage in the amount of $1200.00 has been repaid
the Syms-Eaton Fund by Stephen C. Clark, and
WHEREAS the City of Hampton School Board has concurred in
the recommendation of the Elizabeth City County School Board
that this $1200.00 be invested in United States Government Bonds,
NOW, THEREFORE, BE IT RESOLVED by the Elizabeth City
County School Board that the Treasurer of Elizabeth City County
be hereby directed to invest said $1200.00 in United States Gov-
ernment Bonds in the name of the Elizabeth City County School
Board.
The board authorized the investment of $600, now held by the
County Treasurer for the Syms-Eaton Fund, in Government Bonds.
Mr. Lindsay reported that the American Legion had repaid its loan
from the Syms-Eaton Fund in the amount of $400.00, whereupon the
board unanimously adopted the following resolution:

WHEREAS, the American Legion has repaid its loan from the Syms-Eaton Fund in the amount of $400.00, and same has been deposited to said fund by the County Treasurer,

NOW, THEREFORE, BE IT RESOLVED that the County Treasurer be authorized and instructed to invest the $400.00 now standing in the Syms-Eaton Fund in United States Government Bonds.—Letter from Superintendent C. Alton Lindsay to Edgar W. Knight, July 5, 1947.

VII

PHILANTHROPY AND EDUCATION: BETHESDA ORPHAN HOUSE

I. PREVIEW AND COMMENTS

AMONG THE EARLY educational efforts in Georgia were those of a school at Irene for the religious instruction of Indians, and the work of Bethesda Orphan House. The school at Irene seems to have been conducted for only a short time by the Moravians before they left for Pennsylvania.[1]

The idea of Bethesda Orphan House was suggested to Reverend George Whitefield by Reverend John Wesley[2] and with the aid of his friend, James Habersham, the distinguished evangelist established the institution a few years later somewhat on the pattern of the remarkable educational and charitable institution which had been founded at Halle in 1695 by August Hermann Francke (1663-1727), the German Lutheran religious leader and educational reformer. A grant of land had been given by the Trustees of Georgia and Whitefield raised in the colonies funds for the enterprise into which he put so much of his immense zeal and energy.[3] The orphan house was built near Savannah on land granted by the Trustees of the colony and one of the earliest collections for the institution was taken at a church in Charleston where Whitefield was invited to speak on the

---

1. "In 1735 a Moravian settlement was begun, but the unwillingness of these people to perform military service made them unpopular and they soon found a more congenial home in Pennsylvania." E. B. Greene, *Provincial America*, 259.

2. John and Charles Wesley went to Georgia in 1735. John was sent over by the Society for the Propagation of the Gospel in Foreign Parts as missionary among the Indians, but the mission seems not to have been practicable. John Wesley, described as "a stiff High Churchman," was not widely and warmly popular and left after a period of less than two years. Charles became secretary to James Oglethorpe but ill health took him back to England.

3. Whitefield must have been a very persuasive and compelling platform performer. Benjamin Franklin, in his *Autobiography*, tells how this thrifty gentleman emptied his pockets for Bethesda Orphan House after or while hearing Whitefield speak so persuasively in Philadelphia. David Garrick, the English actor, poet, and dramatist, who often enjoyed hearing Whitefield in London, is reported to have said that the Evangelist's voice was so marvelously modulated that "he could make men either laugh or cry by pronouncing that blessed word Mesopotamia." (In his report for 1924-25, p. 37, President Nicholas Murray Butler, commenting on Garrick's admiration for Whitefield's preaching, said that the "word research has come to be something like the blessed word Mesopotamia. It is used to reduce everyone to silence, acquiesence, and appropriation.")

orphans of Georgia. Shortly after Whitefield's death in Massachusetts in 1770 Bethesda Orphan House, "the most prominent institution of learning in the colony prior to the Revolution," was destroyed by fire. It was later partially rebuilt, only to suffer "a second demolition by hurricane and fire" and the institution soon ceased to have active existence. By legislative act in 1808, the trustees of the institution were directed to sell the property and, after the payments of its debts, to distribute the remainder of the proceeds to charitable institutions in Savannah. As the documents below indicate, Whitefield tried to have Bethesda Orphan House converted into "a seminary of literature and academical learning" on the plan of the College of New Jersey (Princeton), but his petition to the crown for a charter was refused. Whitefield left his property to the Countess Dowager of Huntingdon, a legacy which apparently did not fully please the people of Georgia.

II. DOCUMENTS

1. EXTRACTS FROM THE JOURNALS OF GEORGE WHITEFIELD, 1737; 1739

Sunday, May 7, (1737). Arrived at *Savannah* Town about seven this Evening...

Monday, May 8. Begun to read publick Prayers, and expound the second Lesson at five in the Morning to seventeen Adults and twenty five Children.... I was received with great Civility, and our chief Conversation ran upon the Place of my Settlement; at last it was resolved that I should have a House and Tabernacle built at *Frederica*, and serve at *Savannah*, when, and as long as I pleased. ...

June 11—Opened a school to Day for the Girls of *Savannah*.— George Whitefield, *A Continuation of the Reverend Mr. Whitefield's Journal from his Arrival at Savannah to his Return to London.* Second Edition. London, 1739. Pp. 1-2. A copy of this book is in the Duke University Library. Microcopy is in the University of North Carolina Library.

SAVANNAH.

FRIDAY, *January* 11. 1739/40. Went this Morning with some Friends to view a Tract of Land, consisting of 500 Acres, which Mr. H———— whom I left School-Master of *Savannah*, was directed, I hope by Providence, to make Choice of for the *Orphan-House*. It is situated on the Northern Part of the Colony, about 10 Miles off

Savannah, and has various Kinds of Soil in it; a Part of it very good. —Some Acres, through the Diligence of my Friend, are cleared. He also stock'd it with Cattle and Poultry. He has begun the Fence, and built a Hut; all which will greatly forward the Work. I choose to have it so far off the Town, because the Children will then be more free from bad Examples, and can more conveniently go upon their Lands to work. For it is my Design to have each of the Children taught to labour, so as to be qualified to get their own Living.— *LORD, do thou teach and excite them to labour also for that Meat which endureth to everlasting Life.*

. . . .

Tuesday, January 29. Took in three *German* Orphans, the most pitiful Objects, I think, that I ever yet saw.—No new Negroes could possibly look more despicable, or require more Pains to instruct them. —They have been used to exceeding hard Labour, and tho' supplied with Provisions from the Trustees, yet treated in a Manner unbecoming even Heathens.—Was all the Money I have collected, to be spent in freeing these three Children from Slavery, it would be well laid out.—I have also in my House near twenty more, who, in all Probability, if not taken in, would be as ignorant of GOD and CHRIST, comparatively speaking, as the *Indians*. Blessed be God, they begin to live in order. . . .

Tuesday, January 29. This Day I began the Cotton Manufacture, and agreed with a Woman to teach the little ones to spin and card.— I find annual Cotton grows indifferently well in *Georgia*: And to encourage the People, I this Day bought three hundred Pounds weight, and have agreed to take all the Cotton, Hemp, and Flax that shall be produced the following Year through the whole Province. —I see more and more the Excellency of the Charity in which I am engaged. I trust it will make *Savannah* lift up her drooping Head. Tho' there are fewer Inhabitants, yet I think they are in a better Situation than when I was here last.—They now live independent on a Public Store, Provisions, (Flour especially) are much cheaper, Cattle more plentiful; and by the Divine Blessing, if any Manufacture can be raised amongst themselves, to prevent their exporting so much Money, they may yet do well.—I bless GOD my Congregations are as large as usual. . . .

Wednesday, January 30. Went this Day with the Carpenter and Surveyor, and laid out the Ground whereon the Orphan-House is to be built. It is to be sixty Feet long, and forty wide. A Yard and

Garden before and behind.... There are near thirty working at the Plantation already, and I would employ as many more, if they were to be had.—George Whitefield, *A Continuation of the Reverend Mr. Whitefield's Journal After his Arrival at Georgia, to a few Days after his second Return thither from Philadelphia*. First Edition. London, 1741. Pp. 2-5. A copy of this book is in the Duke University Library. Microcopy is in the University of North Carolina Library.

2. BENJAMIN FRANKLIN COMMENTS ON GEORGE WHITEFIELD AND BETHESDA ORPHAN HOUSE, C. 1739

In 1739 arrived among us from Ireland the Reverend Mr. Whitefield, who had made himself remarkable there as an itinerant preacher. He was at first permitted to preach in some of our churches; but the clergy, taking a dislike to him, soon refus'd him their pulpits, and he was oblig'd to preach in the fields. The multitudes of all sects and denominations that attended his sermons were enormous, and it was matter of speculation to me, who was one of the number, to observe the extraordinary influence of his oratory on his hearers and how much they admir'd and respected him, notwithstanding his common abuse of them by assuring them they were naturally *half beasts and half devils*. It was wonderful to see the change soon made in the manners of our inhabitants. From being thoughtless or indifferent about religion, it seem'd as if all the world were growing religious, so that one could not walk thro' the town in an evening without hearing psalms sung in different families of every street.

And it being found inconvenient to assemble in the open air, subject to its inclemencies, the building of a house to meet in was no sooner propos'd, and persons appointed to receive contributions, but sufficient sums were soon receiv'd to procure the ground and erect the building, which was one hundred feet long and seventy broad, about the size of Westminster Hall; and the work was carried on with such spirit as to be finished in a much shorter time than could have been expected. Both house and ground were vested in trustees expressly for the use of any preacher of any religious persuasion who might desire to say something to the people at Philadelphia; the design in building not being to accommodate any particular sect, but the inhabitants in general; so that even if the Mufti of Constantinople were to send a missionary to preach Mohammedanism to us, he would find a pulpit at his service.

Mr. Whitefield in leaving us, went preaching all the way thro' the colonies, to Georgia. The settlement of that province had lately been begun but, instead of being made with hardy, industrious husbandmen, accustomed to labor, the only people fit for such an enterprise, it was with families of broken shop-keepers and other insolvent debtors, many of indolent and idle habits, taken out of the jails, who, being set down in the woods, unqualified for clearing land, and unable to endure the hardships of a new settlement, perished in numbers leaving many helpless children unprovided for. The sight of their miserable situation inspir'd the benevolent heart of Mr. Whitefield with the idea of building an Orphan House there, in which they might be supported and educated. Returning northward, he preach'd up this charity and made large collections, for his eloquence had a wonderful power over the hearts and purses of his hearers of which I myself was an instance.

I did not disapprove of the design, but as Georgia was then destitute of materials and workmen and it was proposed to send them from Philadelphia at a great expense, I thought it would have been better to have built the house here and brought the children to it. This I advis'd; but he was resolute in his first project, rejected my counsel and I therefore refus'd to contribute. I happened soon after to attend one of his sermons in the course of which I perceived he intended to finish with a collection, and I silently resolved he should get nothing from me. I had in my pocket a handful of copper money, three or four silver dollars, and five pistoles in gold. As he proceeded I began to soften and concluded to give the coppers. Another stroke of his oratory made me asham'd of that and determin'd me to give the silver; and he finish'd so admirably that I empty'd my pocket wholly into the collector's dish, gold and all. At this sermon there was also one of our club who, being of my sentiments respecting the building in Georgia and suspecting a collection might be intended, had, by precaution, emptied his pockets before he came from home. Towards the conclusion of the discourse however, he felt a strong desire to give and apply'd to a neighbour who stood near him to borrow some money for the purpose. The application was unfortunately (made) to perhaps the only man in the company who had the firmness not to be affected by the preacher. His answer was: *"At any other time, Friend Hopkinson, I would lend to thee freely; but not now, for thee seems to be out of thy right senses."*

Some of Mr. Whitefield's enemies affected to suppose that he would apply these collections to his own private emoluments; but

I, who was intimately acquainted with him (being employed in printing his Sermons and Journals, etc.), never had the least suspicion of his integrity but am to this day decidedly of opinion that he was in all his conduct a perfectly *honest man;* and methinks my testimony in his favor ought to have the more weight as we had no religious connection. He us'd, indeed, sometimes to pray for my conversion but never had the satisfaction of believing that his prayers were heard. Ours was a mere civil friendship, sincere on both sides, and lasted to his death.

The following instance will show something of the terms on which we stood. Upon one of his arrivals from England at Boston, he wrote to me that he should come soon to Philadelphia but knew not where he could lodge when there as he understood his old friend and host, Mr. Benezet, was removed to Germantown. My answer was: "You know my house; if you can make shift with its scanty accommodations, you will be most heartily welcome." He reply'd, that if I made that kind offer for Christ's sake, I should not miss of a reward. And I returned: *"Don't let me be mistaken; it was not for Christ's sake, but for your sake."* One of our common acquaintance jocosely remark'd that, knowing it to be the custom of the saints when they received any favour, to shift the burden of the obligation from off their own shoulders and place it in heaven, I had contriv'd to fix it on earth.

The last time I saw Mr. Whitefield was in London, when he consulted me about his Orphan House concern and his purpose of appropriating it to the establishment of a college.

He had a loud and clear voice, and articulated his words so perfectly, that he might be heard and understood at a great distance, especially as his auditories, however numerous, observ'd the most exact silence. He preach'd one evening from the top of the Courthouse steps, which are in the middle of Market-street, and on the west side of Second-street, which crosses it at right angles. Both streets were fill'd with his hearers to a considerable distance. Being among the hindmost in Market-street, I had the curiosity to learn how far he could be heard, by retiring backwards down the street towards the river; and I found his voice distinct till I came near Front-street, when some noise in the street obscur'd it. Imagining then a semicircle, of which my distance should be the radius, and that it were fill'd with auditors, to each of whom I allowed two square feet, I computed that he might well be heard by more than thirty thousand. This reconciled me to the newspaper accounts of his having preach'd to twenty-five thousand people in the fields, and to the antient histories of generals haranguing whole armies, of which I had sometimes doubted.[1]

November 29th, 1739—On Friday last, Mr. Whitefield arrived here with his friends from New York, where he preached eight times. He has preached twice every day to great crowds, except Tuesday, when he preached at Germantown, from a balcony, to about five thousand people in the streets. And last night the crowd was so great to hear his farewell sermon, that the church could not contain one half, whereupon they withdrew to Society Hill, where he preached from a balcony to a multitude, computed at not less than ten thousand people. He left this city to-day.

December 5th.—On Thursday last, the Reverend Mr. Whitefield left this city, and was accompanied to Chester by about one hundred and fifty horse, and preached there to about seven thousand people, On Friday he preached twice at Willing's Town to about five thousand; on Saturday at Newcastle to about two thousand five hundred; and the same evening at Christiana Bridge to about three thousand; on Sunday at White Clay Creek he preached twice, resting about half an hour between the sermons, to about eight thousand, of whom three thousand it is computed came on horseback. It rained most of the time, and yet they stood in the open air.

May 15th, 1740.—This evening the Reverend Mr. Whitefield went on board his sloop at Newcastle to sail for Georgia. On Sunday he preached twice at Philadelphia. The last was his farewell sermon, at which was a vast audience. On Monday he preached at Derby and Chester; on Tuesday at Wilmington and White Clay Creek; on Wednesday at Nottingham; on Thursday at Fog's Manor. The congregations were, at every place, much more numerous than when he was here last. We hear that he has collected in these parts, in goods and money, between four and five hundred pounds sterling for his Orphan House in Georgia.

1. In the early part of his life, Mr. Whitefield was preaching in an open field, when a drummer happened to be present, who was determined to interrupt his pious business, and rudely beat his drum in a violent manner, in order to drown the preacher's voice. Mr. Whitefield spoke very loud, but was not as powerful as the instrument. He therefore called out to the drummer in these words, "Friend, you and I serve the two greatest masters existing, but in different callings; you beat up for volunteers for King George, I for the Lord Jesus. In God's name, then, let us not interrupt each other; the world is wide enough for both; and we may get recruits in abundance." This speech had such an effect on the drummer, that he went away in great good-humor, and left the preacher in full possession of the field.

May 22d, 1740.—Monday next will be delivered to the subscribers two volumes of the Reverend Mr. Whitefield's works; viz. one of Sermons and one of Journals. The other volumes being nearly finished, will be ready in a short time. The whole number of names subscribed far exceeds the number of books printed. Those subscribers, who have paid, or who bring the money in their hands, will have the preference.—Jared Sparks (ed.), *The Works of Benjamin Franklin*, I, 136-40.

3. COMPLAINTS ABOUT THE TREATMENT OF A BOY AT BETHESDA ORPHAN HOUSE, 1741

Tuesday. Complaint being made to Bailiff *Parker*, that one of the Orphan Boys, under the Care of Mr. *Whitfield*, had been treated with unwarrantable Correction, by Mr. *Barber* the Presbyterian Minister there, he was summoned to appear at *Savannah*, by Warrant to the Constable, under the Hands of Mess. *Parker, Fallowfield*, and *Pye* the Recorder: To which he appeared; and the Matter was examined into by them, at Mr. *Fallowfield's* House, Mr. *Jones* declining to act in it, partly (it may be presumed) from his particular Attachment to that House, where he was unwilling to believe they could do any Thing amiss; and at this time more especially he was not willing to join any Thing with those who had dealt so ill with him lately. (*Vide* 9th and 11th instant.) As I never interpose in the Magistrates Execution of their Office, unless when they desired me to be present; which sometimes they have done in particular Cases; and not being made privy to this, I cannot say what passed, otherwise than from the best Information I could get; which I apprehended I had from an impartial Hand, to this Effect. The Boy who had suffered (it seems) had run away to Mr. *Parker* for Protection, at his Plantation in the *Isle of Hope;* where *Parker* being not well at that Time, had delay'd coming to Town for near a Fortnight, to have it enquir'd into; by which Means the Stripes he had seen fresh upon the Boy, did not now appear so terrible as at first: However, the Boy being now present, and stripp'd, it is yet too visible from Scars and Wounds not yet healed, that great Cruelty had been used: It was not denied, that the Boy was made naked to the Waist, after the Manner of common Malefactors, and lashed with five strong Twigs tied together, as long as they would hold, whereby his whole Back, Shoulders, Loins, Flank and Belly, were in a dreadful Condition. The

Cause of this Severity, as alledged by the Boy, was that he had wrote a Letter some Time before, to Mr. *Parker*, therein then complaining of severe Usage; which Mr. *Parker* now owned he received, but did not take great Notice of it, thinking it the common Case of many School-Boys under the Chastisement of a Rod; but now it was made appear, that the Boy's writing that Letter, was come to their Knowledge, and was the Occasion of his being thus dealt with and threatened to have his Punishment renewed, unless he would write to Mr. *Parker* again, and contradict all he had said before; which the Anguish he was under forced him to promise; but he made his Escape as aforesaid. During this Proceeding, it is said Mr. *Barber* found courteous Treatment; but upon offering nothing in his own Vindication, only that he thought himself the proper Judge, without Controul, in what Manner to govern the Boys that he had the Care of, and questioning the Powers by which they acted; they told him, they should convince him farther of that very soon, when they intended, by Virtue of that Power, to visit the Orphan-House, and make farther Enquiry into whatever they found amiss, and appeared to them contrary to the Design of the Trustees, by their Grant: And thereupon taking the Boy away, with Intent to dispose of him by Apprenticeship, as they saw proper, they parted. Whether or not Mr. *Jones* took part either Way in this Affair, came not to my Knowledge; but by the great Regard he had shewn always, beyond most others, to the Family of *Bethesda*, and their spending most Part of this Day with him at his House, some were apt to think he took Counsel with them there how to obviate, if not defeat, whatever the other Magistrates attempted to enquire into, where they had the Direction of every Thing under Mr. *Whitfield* (with Heads too green in my poor Opinion.)—*Journal of Colonel William Stephens.* In Allen D. Candler (compiler), *The Colonial Records of the State of Georgia.* Supplement to Vol. IV, 166-68.

4. SAMUEL FRINK, MISSIONARY AT AUGUSTA AND AT SAVANNAH, TO THE S.P.G. ABOUT WHITEFIELD'S PLAN FOR A COLLEGE, AUGUST 4, 1760

... it gives me great pleasure, & Satisfaction to hear that his Grace, the worthy, the venerable, and the Good Archbishop of Canterbury, in his great wisdom, thinks it not proper to Encourage Mr Whitefield's College, in Georgia, with its intended broad bottom.

I must beg leave to detain you a while in making an Observation or two on the Letters which he wrote to his Grace: with regards to his broad bottomed plan of a College.[1]

Mr Whitefield seems to intimate, that the Governor, Council & Commons House of Assembly in Georgia favoured his Broad-bottomed Scheme: far from any thing of the Kind—They favored the erecting a College it is true, but never supposed that it would ever be established upon any other Foundation than that of the Established Church of England: all the well-wishers to the Church very well foresaw that if ever such a Plan as Mr Whitfield has since proposed, (which was never hinted to the Legislature of this province that I can learn) would over set the present Establishment in Georgia, which is that of the Church of England. As to his saying that People here are waiting with Impatience for his broad bottomed College: this is News to me, all that I am acquainted with—I know of none, unless his Brother broad bottom, One Mr H-b-rsh-m formerly a School-M-st-r, but now Pr-s-d-nt of the C--nc-l in Georgia; and by Courtesy of the Province consequently styled H-n-r-bl-. perhaps there may be some of his puritanick Friends in New England, the Seat of Contention, & place for broad bottoms, that may wish that such a Plan may be carried into Execution. But Georgia has nothing to do with New England in this matter, as they are upon a much better footing, as to Religion—I can assure his Grace, from my own certain Knowledge, there are but very few in Georgia, except the Person before Mentioned, & my Successor at A-g-sta, that ever desire to see a College in Georgia, established in Confusion, (if I may be allowed the Expression) or which is all one, according to Dr. broad bottoms Plan; (excuse the Expression)—

As to the two Thousand Acres of Land granted to him by the Governor & Council near the River Alatamaha, as I am informed it was granted for no broad bottomed purpose; and I can say, that none except his Friend, & brother before mentioned ever dreamed of such a Church and even this his best Friend has been heard to say, that a College could never be erected upon any other Plan, than that of the Church of England however secretly both might wish, & hope to the Contrary—And I have not the least doubt but what both have endeavored to have such a College, for neither of them are friends to any Establishment, but that of a broad bottom—As to the 1000 Acres of Land he mentions, left by the late Revd Mr Zouberbuhler:

---

1. Whitefield hoped to convert the orphanage into Bethesda College, but the British government insisted on conditions he would not meet.

The Will determines this matter. The Will says "That nine Acres of Land is given to the Orphan House, if ever erected into the College, provided it is upon the Foundation of the Church of England: Mr Zouberbuhler, it seems, by this proviso, was afraid of this broad bottom, which Mr Whitefield mentions in his Letters—

It is needless for me to Expose the many Errors which Mr Whitefield labors hard to maintain, in order to accomplish his Broad bottomed Scheme, as it would exceed any present design—

It is enough to say that we know the Man and his Communication. This Gentleman has sat upon a broad bottom too long—And done more Mischief, not only in England, & America, more particularly in Georgia, than he himself could undo; if we suppose him as zealous in promoting Enthusiasm, Disorder, & Confusion, as he has been for Encouraging them. It is more, I say, than he could undo, in three Centuries. He has been a Destroyer of Order, & Peace, and of the Church of England where ever he came. An Encourager of every Sectary; a publick condemner of the Church of England Clergy, persuading the People in every Preachment that 9/10 of the Clergy of the Church of England are absolutely perjured &c. &c. &c. And this is now said from the Pulpit by one of his Stamp, in my former Mission. However I pity the Man, whilst I condemn his rashness and censorious humour.

It is my prayer to God, and the utmost of my wishes, that this lying Spirit that is gone forth into the world; may cease from Troubling. And I heartily wish that all the Friends to Government, & the Established Religion, which is the main prop, would give no Encouragement to such Destroyers of peace, & Harmony, & fomentors of feuds, Discontents, & Rebellions in the State.

I must say that I never desire to see Whitfield in Georgia in the capacity of a Clergyman any more. how to behave with regard to admitting him into the Pulpit here in Savannah when he arrives I am utterly at a Loss; some I shall please, & others displease; I could wish I had your advice on this Head, & upon many others—Broad bottoms are best at a distance—.

His Orphan House has always been a Nest for the Enemies of the Church. Ignorance & Enthusiasm its concomitant, is the Characterisitck of all those that have received any Instruction there. If my zeal for the present Establishment in Church and State, carried me to too great Lengths in this Epistle, I shall be willing to be convinced & ask pardon for it, if it is a zeal not according to knowledge. However I shall always look upon the disturbers of our tranquility, to be the Vermin and Rats of any State.

Believe me to be a Lover of all, excepting those that oppose the Progress of Christ's Kingdom down upon Earth—Enthusiasm opposes the regular Progress of our Religion, & brings every thing into Confusion, & gives Satan an Advantage, & therefore cannot be pleasing to the Deity—Original in the offices of the S.P.G.; photocopy in the Library of Congress; microcopy of that copy in the Library of the University of North Carolina.

5. WHITEFIELD PETITIONS THE COUNCIL FOR LAND TO ENDOW COLLEGE, DECEMBER 18, 1764

Read a Memorial of the Reverend George Whitefield Clerk setting forth that about twenty five Years ago, the Memorialist assisted by the voluntary Contributions of charitable and well disposed Persons, at a very great Expense and under many Disadvantages. Did erect a commodious House with necessary out-Buildings suitable for the reception of Orphans and other poor and deserted Children and that with repair of the Buildings, Purchase of Negroes, and supporting a large Orphan Family for so many Years, he had expended upwards of Twelve thousand Pounds Sterling, as appeared by the Accounts which from Time had been audited by the Magistrates of Savannah. That since the Commencement of this Institution he had the Satisfaction of finding that by the Money expended thereon, not only many poor Families were assisted, and thereby kept from leaving the Colony in its infant State but also that a considerable Number of poor helpless Children had been trained up who had been and were then useful Settlers in this and the other neighbouring Provinces That in order to render the Institution aforesaid more extensively useful the Memorialist as he perceived the Colony gradually rising for some Years past, designed within himself to improve the original Plan by making further Provisions for the Education of Persons of superior Rank who thereby might be qualified to serve their King, their Country and their God either in Church or State That he did with inexpressible Pleasure see the present very flourishing State of the Province but with concern perceived that several Gentlemen had been obliged to send their Sons to the Northern Provinces who had much rather have had them educated nearer Home, and thereby prevented Affection being alienated from their native Country and also considerable Sums of Money from being carried out of this into other Provinces. The Memorialist further observed that there was no Seminary for Academical Studies as yet founded Southward of Virginia, and consequently if a College could be established here (especially as the late Addition of the two Floridas rendered Georgia more centrical for the Southern District) it would not only be highly serviceable to the rising Generation of this Colony, but would probably occasion many Youths to be sent from the british West India Islands and other Parts The many Advantages accruing thereby must be obvious to all. From these Considerations the Memorialist was induced to believe that the Time was now approaching, when his long projected Design for further serving this his beloved Colony, should be carried into Execution That a considerable Sum of Money was intended to be laid out in purchasing a large Number of Negroes for the further Cultivation of the present Orphan House and other additional Lands, and for the future Support of a Worthyable, President, Professors and Tutors and other good Purposes intended— Therefore praying for in Trust for the Purposes aforesaid Two thousand Acres of Land on the North Fork of Turtle River called the lesser Swamp if vacant, or where Lands might be found vacant South of the River Alatamaha—

Resolved That on Condition only that a Grant or Grants be taken out for the said Land within seven Months from this Date and that the same be registered in the Register's Office of the said Province within Six Months from the Date thereof that his Majesty may not be defrauded of his Quit Rents the Prayer of the said Petition is granted—Candler, *op. cit.*, IX, 259-61.

6. The General Assembly and the government approve
Whitefield's petition, December 19, 1764

It appearing to this House that the Reverend Mr Whitefield has applied to his Excellency the Governor in Council for lands for the Endowment of a Colledge in this Province.

RESOLVED That an Address be presented to his Excellency the Governor requesting his Recommendation and Encouragement of so laudable an Undertaking and that he may be pleased to transmit Home the Wishes of this House for the Completion thereof.

ORDERED That a Message be sent to the Commons House by the Master in Chancery acquainting them with the said Resolution and desiring their Concurrence therein and that they will appoint a

Committee of their House to join a Committee of this House to prepare an Address accordingly.

A Message was brought from the Commons House by Mr Crooke in the following Words vizt

Commons House of Assembly 19th December 1764.

Honourable Gentlemen,

In Answer to your Message of yesterday desiring the Concurrence of this House and that a Committee might be appointed to join a Committee of your House in preparing an Address to his Excellency the Governor requesting his Recommendation and Encouragement of so laudable an Undertaking as the Endowment of a College in this Province by the Revd Mr Whitefield, And that his Excellency may be pleased to transmit Home our Wishes for the Completion thereof This House doth agree thereto and hath appointed a Committee accordingly.

Committee Messrs Jones, Braddock, Ewen, Sir Patrick
    Houstoun and Mr Milledge

The House adjourned during Pleasure and the Committee of this House joined the Committee of the Commons House to prepare the aforesaid Address, And after some Time the Committee being returned the House was resumed, And Mr Elliott reported that the Committee of both Houses had prepared an Address to his Excellency on the aforegoing Subject Matter which he was directed to report when the honourable House will please to receive the same.

ORDERED That the Report be now received.

And Mr Elliott accordingly read the same in his Place and afterwards delivered the Address in at the Table where it was read and agreed to by the House.

A Message was brought from the Commons House by Sir Patrick Houstoun Bart in the following Words vizt

Commons House Assembly 19th Decr 1764.

Honourable Gentlemen

This House having taken into Consideration the Report of the Committee appointed to join a Committee of your House to prepare an Address to his Excellency the Governor requesting his Recommendation and Encouragement of so laudable an Undertaking as the Endowment of a College in this Province by the Revd Mr Whitefield; and that he may be pleased to transmit home the Wishes of both Houses for the Completion thereof; This House doth agree to the Address so prepared.

A Message was sent to the Commons House by the Master in Chancery in the following Words Viz^t

Upper House of Assembly 19th Decr 1764.

Mr Speaker

Upon report from the Committee of this House appointed to join a Committee of your House to prepare an Address to his Excellency the Governor requesting his Recommendation and Encouragement of so laudable an Undertaking as the Endowment of a College in this Province by the Revd Mr Whitefield; and that he may be pleased to transmit home the Wishes of both Houses for the Completion thereof: This House doth agree to the Address so prepared.

ORDERED That the Address be ingrossed.

The Address of both Houses of Assembly

May it please your Excellency

We his Majesty's most dutiful and loyal Subjects the Council and Commons House of Assembly of Georgia in general Assembly met beg leave to acquaint your Excellency that with the highest Satisfaction we learn the Reverend Mr George Whitefield has applied for Land in order to the Endowment of a College in this Province.

The many and singular obligations Georgia has continually lain under to that Reverend Gentleman from it's very Infant State would in gratitude induce us by every Means in our power to promote any Measure he might recommend but in the present Instance where the Interest of the Province, the Advancement of Religion and the pleasing Prospect of obtaining proper Education for our Youth so clearly coincide with his Views, We cannot in Justice but request your Excellency to use your utmost Endeavours to promote so desireable an Event: And to transmit Home our sincere and very fervent Wishes for the Accomplishment of so useful so beneficent and so laudable an Undertaking.

ORDERED That Mr President do sign the Address.

ORDERED That Mr Powell do with a Member of the Commons House wait on his Excellency the Governor to know when he will please to receive the two Houses with their Address.

Mr Powell reported that his Excellency the Governor having been waited on pursuant to Order to know when the two Houses should attend him with their Address had been pleased to answer that he was then ready to receive them.

Accordingly the House adjourned during Pleasure and with the Commons House attended his Excellency the Governor with their

Address; And being returned the House was resumed, and Mr President reported that his House with the Commons House had attended his Excellency with their Address, which he (Mr President) had delivered And his Excellency was pleased to give his Answer thereto in the following Words vizt

Gentlemen

I am so perfectly sensible of the very great Advantages which will result to the Province in general from the Establishment of a Seminary for Learning here that it gives me the greatest Pleasure to find so laudable an Undertaking proposed by the Reverend Mr Whitefield The friendly and zealous Disposition of that Gentleman to promote the Prosperity of this Province has been often experienced and you may rest assured that I shall transmit your Address home with my best Endeavours for the Success of the great Point in View.—*Ibid.*, XVII, 140-46.

7. JAMES HABERSHAM WRITES TO GEORGE WHITEFIELD, JANUARY 27, 1766

I had the pleasure of writing you [1] a long letter of the 17th August last, and intend now to give you all the News here, which however insignificant to almost all mankind, cannot be so to you, who are so much interested in our Welfare; but we are in so much Confusion here about the Stamp Act that every Friend of Government and Good Order, I may say of the Province, gives his whole attention to prevent, if possible, the most fatal Consequences—My very Flesh trembles while I am writing to you, at, I must say, the Madness of People here, we mean to be as good patriots, as they have shewn themselves—Surely the violent measures that have been persued must rather retard than forward a repeal of the Act, which I must be free to say, I think was passed with too much Precipitation—You know my Principle especially as a public officer, is to obey all orders and Acts of Government, for no longer, than I can do so, no longer will I act in a Public Character, persuaded that the Crown have as good a right to faithfull servants, as you and I have to those we pay wages to. On this account I have had an incendiary letter written to me, have been threatened to be mobbed at Night, and have my House pulled down, and while I am writing this, a friend has whispered to me to be in

1. Habersham came from England to Georgia in 1737, worked closely with Whitefield in promoting the orphanage, was a merchant, and served as acting governor of the colony.

some Place out of, Town 2 or 3 days hence, least I should meet with some severe Insult which advice I shall follow, as we are well informed two or three Hundred People are gathering together in the Country, and intend to encamp near the Town; in order I suppose to intimidate the Governor and public officers to comply with their Demands—What they may be, I can only guess, but probably one will be to put a totall stop to issuing Stamp Papers, for you must understand that we have so far prevailed on the Sons of Liberty as they call themselves in this Town that the Stamp Papers be issued to clear out Vessells, otherwise I should not have had an opportunity of sending you this—We have now I believe, Sixty Sea Vessels in this Harbor, but I am afraid that commerce will be again interrupted and all public officers, as well as Law Proceedings continue, as they have been since the 1st Nov last, to be stopt. Dreadfull it is to find one's Person and Property at the Disposal of a giddy multitude for surely we are no longer Freeman, than the Laws of our Country can freely operate to protect them—I must insist on your not making a public use of this scrawl as I have not only wrote in a great hurry, but with unreservedness—God bless you—I can say no more—My Heart bleeds—I shall only add that you have enclosed, a Bill of Lading for a quarter Cask Maidera Wine, which I think extremely good—It has lain by two or three months, and may have leaked, and want two or three quarts to fill it, but I do not chuse to mix any other wine with it I know you will accept it as a small token of my unfeigned regard—Young Capt Ball has promised to take it in his Cabin and deliver it safe and in good order to you—I would have paid him the Freight, but he says that all Freights are paid in London—As the wine, I know, is extraordinary, I hope no adulteration will be attempted on board.

P. S. The People at Bethesda are all well. Our honest Governor has on this Critical occasion behaved like himself, I mean like a man of honor and a faithful Servant of the Crown.—"Letters of Hon. James Habersham, 1756-1775," in *Collections of the Georgia Historical Society*, Vol. VI (Savannah, 1904), 54-55.

8. THE GOVERNOR AND ASSEMBLY ATTEND SERVICES AT BETHESDA ORPHAN HOUSE, 1770

Last Sunday, his excellency, the governor, council assembly, having been invited by Rev. Mr. Whitefield, attended divine services in the chapel of the orphan Academy. The company were very politely entertained with a handsome and plentiful dinner, and were greatly pleased to see the useful improvements in the house, the two additional wings for apartments for students, one hundred and fifty feet in length, other lesser buildings.—*Savannah Gazette*, January 31, 1770.

9. THE COUNCIL EXTENDS THANKS TO REVEREND GEORGE WHITEFIELD
FOR HIS SERMON, FEBRUARY, 1770

This House having at the Invitation of the Revd Mr George Whitefield, attended divine Service at the Orphan House Academy on the twenty Eighth Day of January last and heard a Sermon preached by him from Zachariah 4th Chap^r 8th 9th & part of 10th Verses.

RESOLVED That the Thanks of this House be given to the said Mr Whitefield for his said Sermon; And that the Clerk do acquaint him therewith by Letter.—Allen D. Candler (compiler), *The Colonial Records of Georgia*, XVII, 520.

10. EDWARD ELLINGTON TO THE REV. DR. BURTON, SECRETARY TO THE
S.P.G., FEBRUARY 10, 1770

I think it my duty to take the most early opportunity of acquainting the worthy Society that I have been applied to by the Rev^d Mr. Whitefield to take upon me ¹ the present care of management of his intended college, now known by the name of the Orphan House Academy, & tho' I am truly sensible of my insufficiency for such an undertaking, yet as it is Mr. Whitefield's intention to have stated Worship of that Seminary agreeable to the Liturgy of the Church of England, & he finds it difficult to procure a Clergyman of the established church to take the charge in its present infant state, I hope the Society will not be displeased at my having accepted his offer, & accordingly I propose removing there at Midsummer.—I thank God I have reason to hope that my ministerial services in my Parish have been attended in some degree with a divine blessing, & the kind behaviour of my parishioners to me ever since I have resided among them gives me no less reason to believe that my poor labors have been generally acceptable to them.—I have no prospect by my intended removal of improving my mortal circumstances, tho' I hope I shall not thereby be less useful to the Church.—The Orphan House Academy is but 12 miles from this place, therefore I shall have it in my power occasionally to assist the Rev^d Mr. Frink & also to officiate in places contiguous which are destitute of any public worship

1. Ellington was missionary at Augusta, 1767-1770.

& at the same time the Society will have an opportunity of supplying the province with another Clergyman without expense.

I have drawn upon the Society's Treasurer for twenty Pound sterling, payable to Mr Joseph Clay on order, due at Christmas last.—In my last letter I acquainted the Society of the death of Mr Theobald Maighereaux the late Schoolmaster at Augusta, who is succeeded by Mr Joseph Brooks, a sober young man, & from some months experience, I think he is properly qualified, & appears to be worthy of the Society's countenance.—

I propose leaving this town in a day or two, & on my getting to Augusta, I shall inform the Vestry of my intention to leave them next Midsummer, & I hope the Society will continue their kind assistance to the Parish—Since my last, I have christened 89, married 13 couples, buried 4 & have 13 added to my communicants. . .—Original in the offices of the S.P.G.; photocopy in the Library of Congress; microcopy of that copy in the Library of the University of North Carolina.

11. The Churchwardens of Augusta to Dr. Burton, February 27, 1770

We are sorry that we are again under a necessity of applying unto the Society for their further assistance regarding a Missionary for this Parish, The Revd Mr Ellington, our present Minister, having acquainted us within these few days, that through the Solicitations of The Reverend M. Whitefield, he had Consented to take upon him the Care of his intended College, Known by the name of the Orphan house Academy, and that he is to remove from this Parish, about midsummer next.

We therefore take the earliest opportunity of informing the Society with our present Situation, hoping they will be pleased to Continue their kind indulgence toward us; by providing us with a proper Pastor, in the room of Mr Ellington: a Gentleman we have hitherto been much Oblig'd to for his exemplery life, and Care in Preaching & propagating the Gospel among us.

We beg leave to Observe, that this Parish increases dayly, and the Contiguousness of South Carolina, where a number of people are settled on the Banks of this river, for many miles above & below this town, will make us the more regret the want of a good Clergyman.

We are hard press'd with parish expenses, but are Still willing to allow the same Salary, unto the Gentleman the Society Shall be pleased to Send us: as we have done to our former & present Ministers. Should a Gentleman with a family offer, we would wish to prefer such a one, as it may tend to fix him more permanently among us.

We beg leave to assure you that we are with the greatest esteem and respect—Original in the offices of the S.P.G.; photocopy in the Library of Congress; microcopy of that copy in the Library of the University of North Carolina.

12. SAMUEL FRINK FROM SAVANNAH TO DR. BURTON, JULY 6, 1770

It is not from want of Inclination that I have not wrote since Christmas last to the Society: but for want of health, accompanied with that weight of parochial Dutys which have pressed so hard upon me as to be scarcely able to perform them all; But God be thanked I am so far recovered as to be able, /tho' not without Pain & Fatigue/ to perform the several Duties of my Function— Tho' I have had a great show of those Disorders peculiar to the Climate, Yet since my Mission here in Georgia I have omitted preaching only 2 Sundays, & one Ashwednesday— I hope God will prosper the pious intentions of the Society, so as to make my Labors in their Service efficacious, for promoting the true, & real Interest of Religion, & the propagation of the Gospel according to the Church of England, Jesus Christ himself being the Chief Corner Stone.

When I have entered upon this Topic, I think I am in duty Bound, not to pass over in Silence one thing, which my late indisposition prevented my writing upon before—

Mr Ellington's leaving the Mission at Augusta—/tho' I am told that few tears were lost on the occasion/ The people there have always treated him with the greatest kindness, have ever been punctual with regard to paying the Money annually which they engaged to do. In short to my certain Knowledge; they have ever endeavoured to make everything agreeable, particularly so, and a great prospect before him of some Lands being sold which in Town Common, for the Purchase of 5 or 6 Slaves for the use of the missionary for the time being— Notwithstanding all the Circumstances before mentioned, with others which I think not worth naming, Yet he has left the poor people destitute, who always go beyond their abilities with regard to the support of a Minister. He is now come to a part of the Province, where he is likely to do as little service to Religion as the Man in the Moon. It is said he is to be Mr Whitefield's Chaplain professor of Oratory, or rather a kind of Superintendant at the Orphan House;

I doubt not he has informed the Society of these things, & made some plausible excuse for such unprecedented Conduct— I have heard from some of his late parishioners, that he informed the Society in a Letter not long since that he was occasionally to assist me in Savannah, what he intends by the word occasionally, I am at a loss to know, unless it is occasionally to make a disturbance in my Parish, which he attempted two or three times whilst at Augusta, when occasionally at Savannah but without Success, however the Society must judge for themselves in these matters. But I could wish that Venerable Body could once be satisfied that Men of Temper & turn in Religion will never Answer their pious Intentions, or ever be of any real service to promote godliness in any part of the world, especially when instead of uniting Christians in one mode & form of worship they take the direct Contrary way as for Instance in continually endeavouring to overturn that best of Churches, viz the Church of England which they have engaged to support,— And also in speaking with so much disrespect against the present worthy & wise Guides of the Church—I have said too much already—

I shall only pray & beseech that venerable Body, the Society, in behalf of the new destitute people of Augusta, to assist them once more in sending them a Gentleman of a different turn from the late Gentleman, endowed with a little more good Nature & Charity— The people are really in want of a steady serious Man of sound Church of England Principles, they are not so fond of the modern puffs of Methodistick Insanity— They were once my Parishioners, & I make it a particular point to interest myself in their behalf & render them any service in my power—

I shall now give an account of my Stewardship to that worthy & Venerable Body, whom I have the honor to serve in promoting the Interest of the Redeemer— Since my last I have Baptized 50 Whites and two adult Negroes, Buried 70, married 20, on Easter, & Whitsunday 60 Communicants— I have drawn a Bill of Exchange from Christmas Last to the 25th of June, on the Treasurer for £25 Sterling, being the last half Years Sallary, which I doubt not will meet with the usual kind reception—

I have much more to say, but I must refer you to a Letter sent by Mr Alexander Findlay who is going for holy Orders, for St. George's Parish in this Province—who will inform you of many little anecdotes, & the little Battles I am obliged to fight, to preserve the Established Churchs being overturned here by its Enemies, & lately by some

Cold attacks made by the late Commons House of Assembly, so far intoxicated with Liberty Principles /rather Libertine/ as to endeavour to put Jews & Dissenters of all Denominations upon a footing with the Church here established—the Bills had actually passed the Lower House, so far as to make them all one Body Politic Incorporate which were thrown out by the Upper House. . .—Original in the offices of the S.P.G.; microcopy in the Library of Congress; microcopy of that copy in the Library of the University of North Carolina.

13. THE WILL OF GEORGE WHITEFIELD, 1770

In the name of the Father son and Holy Ghost three persons But One God I George Whitefield clerk at present residing at the Orphan House Academy in the Province of Georgia in North America being through infinite mercy in more than Ordinarily bodily health & a perfectly sound Disposing mind knowing the certainty of Death and yet the uncertainty of the time I shall be called by it to my long wish'd for home do make this my last will & Testament in manner & form following Viz. . . In respect to my outward American concerns which I have engaged in simply & solely for his great name sake I leave [several words here not clear] Province of Georgia together with all the other Buildings lately erected thereon & likewise all other building land's Negroes Books furniture and every other Thing whatsoever which I now stand possessed of in the province of Georgia aforesaid to that Elect Lady that mother in Israel that mirrow of truth undefiled religion the right Honorable Salina Countess Dowager of Huntington desiring that as soon as may be after my Decease that plan of the intended orphan House Bethesda college may be prosecuted or if not practicable or eligeble to pursue the present plan of the Orphan House Academy on its Old Foundation & usual channel But if Her Ladyship should be called to enter into her glorious rest before my Decease I bequeath all the Building Land Negroes & every thing before mentioned which I now stand possessed of in the province of Georgia aforesaid to my Dear first Fellow Traveller & Faithful invariable Friend the Honorable James Habersham Esqr President of his Majesty's Honorable Council and should He Survive Her Ladyship I earnestly recommend Him as the most proper person to succeed Her Ladyship or to act for her during Her Ladyship's life time in the affairs of the Orphan House Academy with regard to my Outward Affairs in England whereas there is a Building commonly called the Tabernacle set apart many years ago for Divine Worship I give & bequeath the said Tabernacle with the Adjacent House in which I usually reside when in London with the Stable & Coach House in the Yard adjoining together with all Books Furniture & everything else what soever that shall be found in the House and Premises aforesaid and also the Building commonly called Tottenham Course Chapel together with all the other Buildings Houses Stable Coach House and every thing else whatsoever which I stand possessed of in that part of the Town to my worthy trusty Friend David West Esqr...

[Other bequests in Whitefield's will included "my late wifes gold watch," to Habersham; fifty pounds to each of Whitefield's brothers, Richard and Thomas, a brother-in-law and a niece; "one hundred pounds sterling" to his favorite Countess and he begged "Her Lady-ship's acceptance of so small a mite"; forty pounds to "John Grave-now a faithful stewart at the Orphan House Academy"; and to "my Humbler Faithful Servent & Friend W. Ambros Wright if in my service and employ at the time of my Decease" the sum of five hun-dred pounds.

[The crowning educational ambition of Whitefield, to establish "Bethesda College in the Province of Georgia," apparently on a plan similar to that of the College of New Jersey, was never realized. For this ambition he expressed willingness to give up all the Bethesda property. While his petition for a charter for the proposed college was not granted and he was disappointed, he did not allow himself to become discouraged but rather seemed determined to develop at Bethesda an academy similar to that which Benjamin Franklin had established in the 1750's in Philadelphia and on which the University of Pennsylvania was later developed.

[Whitefield died in Newburyport, Massachusetts, September 30, 1770, while on a trip to the Northern States, without seeing the col-lege established. Under his will, made six months earlier and given in part above, the estate of the Orphan House was vested in the Countess of Huntingdon, who he doubtless believed could build a college in Georgia by enlarging Bethesda. But her efforts were un-successful, and shortly after Whitefield's death Bethesda Orphan House was destroyed by fire, was later partially rebuilt but only to suffer a second destruction by hurricane and fire. The institution ceased to exist and by Legislative Act of December 22, 1808, the estate was ordered sold and the proceeds used for institutions in

Savannah,– The Savannah Poor House and Hospital Society, The Union Society, the Chatham Academy.–Will Book AA, Georgia Department of Archives and History, 354 ff. By "N.B." to this will Whitefield left "a mourning ring to my Honrd and Dr. Friends and Disinterested Fellow Labours the Revd Messs John and Charles Wesley in token of my indissoluble union with them in heart and Xtian affection notwithstanding our Difference in judgment about some particular points of Doctrine Grace be with all them of whatever denomination that love our lord Jesus our common Lord in sincerity."]

14. JAMES HABERSHAM TO THE COUNTESS DOWAGER OF HUNTINGDON ON THE DEATH OF WHITEFIELD, DECEMBER 10, 1770

I make no doubt but that your Ladyship heard of the truly lamented Death of that dear and much Honoured Servant of Jesus Christ,–the Revd George Whitefield at Newburyport in New England, about the same time as we did here, which was the beginning of last Month, and as your Ladyship must know the Character and Usefullness of the Worthy deceased, in the Church, it will be needless for me to say any thing on that subject. I have however lost in him The oldest and Dearest Friend I had upon Earth. My first acquaintance with him was 34 years ago soon after he left Oxford and on his first visit to London, before he was known as a popular preacher and from the first hour we saw each other, to the hour of Death, our affectionate and real Friendship never abated; indeed it was so deeply founded, that we knew not how to part, and when he first set off for this, then Infant Colony in December 1737, I left my Business, Contrary to the Sentiments of all my Friends, and embarked with him, without having any particular design in View, otherwise than to accompany him, and since my Arrival here near 33 years ago, I have not once seen my native Country, and perhaps never may. Some of the first years of my being here, I was wholly engaged with, and for him, in erecting the Orphan House and conducting his Affairs there. He has long appeared to be particularly designed by divine Providence to be singularly usefull in promoting the Interests of real Religion in this new and very extensive World, and I believe his death has been very truly and very Generally Lamented, wherever he has had an opportunity of being known throughout this Continent, and the Inhabitants of this province have in him, lost a Friend indeed, which they appear to be sensible of, and so does the Legislature now convened: who have publickly and genteely expressed their Gratitude, which I have endeavoured to Acknowledge in the enclosed Gazette, and at the same time mentioned some Incidents, well known to a few, yet alive of our first Settlers in memory of my Valuable Old Friend under the signature of *An old and real Friend to the deceased and to Georgia*—among the papers inclosed with this: your Ladyship will find an Authenticated Copy of his Will under the Great Seal of this Province, which I have sent, the better to enable your Ladyship and the London Executor to Act—The Original is wholly in his own Hand writing which he made a Short Time before he last embarked from hence, and left it in the care of Honest Mr Ambrose Wright, his faithful Friend and Servants who delivered it to me, on hearing of the Certainty of his Death, by which your Ladyship will find, he has left all his Affairs in this province absolutely to your Ladyship: a circumstance I am happy to find, but could have wished to have had the perusal of it, and particularly an other Friend (I mean our Worthy Governor) as we should have doubtless pointed out the necessity of adding a few Words more fully to extend the power of his devises, agreable I am persuaded to his *Intention*, and what he *really thought* he had done, having told me so in one of our last Conversations—I must own, it's appearing rather defective, has given me no small pain, as it is well known there are many, too many who would gladly improve every pretence to put the Worst Constructions on the Conduct of the deceased, who I need not say to your Ladyship acted in every respect, with a *disinterested and pure View*, to promote the Honour of the Great God, but in order that I may be better understood I shall take the Liberty of Tresspassing on your Ladyship's patience, while I make a few remarks. It is conceived as I before remarked, that the Will is not so clear and express as it might have been in regard to the Trust invested in your Ladyship and the London Executors, for tho' there is strong Implication of a *Trust* to your Ladyship, (and to myself in Case of your Ladyships demise) as to the Georgia Affairs, there is not a Word to that purpose to Mr West and Mr Keen in respect to the Tabernacle and Tottinham Court Chappel and unless the Leases of the Lands, on which these buildings are Erected, declare their Uses, I am afraid the deceased's Heir will (unless he will release—or the Executors or one of them should Survive 'till the Expiration of the respective Leases), have an Absolute Right to them for, the term, if any may remain unexpired— Your Ladyship will please to observe by the Copys of the Grants enclosed of the lands here, that there are seven, three of which are *in trust for the Use and Benefit of the Orphan House*, three in Trust for the Endowment of a College, which is a happy Circumstance, and there is one for 500 Acres Called Huntingdon granted generally and without any Trust expressed, which after your Ladyships Decease will undoubtedly come to the deceaseds Heir, if he does not before that period release This Tract, I many years ago took up unknown to my late Friend and after he knew it, he gave its' Name out of respect to your Ladyships: and, if my memory does not fail me, I believe I advised him to have the Grant in his own Name only, that he might add it with his many other Donations to the Orphan House, as his own Gift and property which I am sure he did not advert to on making his Will, otherwise it would have been 'specially devised to your Ladyship, for the use of the Orphan House, having *repeatedly* heard him say that none of his Relations should possess a Foot of property, he had dedicated to the Service of God. This Land as yet unimproved adjoins to the plantation called Ephata, is valuable and will be extremely convenient for the future Improvement and Support of the Institution; and if the Heir is not prevented from Claiming it in future, it would much grieve me, as I had it in my power to have had the Grant in my own Name, and to give it for the Use I very truly intended, when I took it up,—I need not observe to your Ladyship, that neither the lands in England, or Here, are by the Will devised in *Fee*, and, from what I have understood, my late Friends Heir, and any that may Succeed, is by no means fit to have the Trust, (and he can have no more, unless, if not prevented, Huntingdon) of the deceased's landed Affairs here, which however was the most distant from the Testators Intention—The Negroes, and all the personal Estate, the Heir at Law cannot interfere with, and, if I am not mistaken in my observations, I should think it might be expedient to have some Instrument drawn up, declaring the Uses of all the Lands, Negroes &c, agreable to what your Ladyship and the Executors know was the deceased's Intention, and in the deeds (for, if any are thought necessary, there must be two, one from your Ladyship in respect to the Georgia Affairs, and another from Mr West and Mr Keen for the London Affairs) to insert a Clause by which the Heir at Law Releases all Claims &c to the Lands (if any he has) and join in the Declaration of uses or Trusts &c, but, if it's thought the Heir will make any difficulty, then it may perhaps be better to say nothing to him about it but of this your Ladyship and the Executors will be better able to Judge, after taking advice on the Will—And, as I cannot doubt, but your Ladyship will condescend to accept of the Trust—I take the Liberty to recommend to your Ladyship to send me a particular power of Attorney, and as I am in years, and Life is Uncertain, I also recommend to your Ladyship to join the following persons with me—The Honourable Francis Harris Esqr John Smith Esqr Mr Joseph Clay, Mr Ambrose Wright and Mr James Habersham Junior, that if your Ladyship thinks proper, they may apply here to endeavour to obtain a Law to establish the College, as the deceased intended to have done, had he lived, or to act in such other Manner as your Ladyship may judge most proper for perfecting the desirable, Object of the Testator—I hope your Ladyship will excuse my presuming to give my Opinion, and attribute it to my hearty Inclination to serve an Institution, I have devoted so much Time, and have been at great Pains to Support and render Usefull, agreable to the pious purposes of the Founder; and I am extremely concerned, that your Ladyship should have any trouble, that might have been spared, had the good man known as much about Law, as he did of the Gospel. I purpose sending this, with the several Inclosures, by Mr Cornelius Winter, who it's expected will embark to morrow, or at farthest the day following for London, to endeavour to obtain Ordination, as a Missionary to, the poor Negroes, and whatever Objections our Revd Fathers may have to a Methodist preacher, being instrumental in Converting Christians, I should add Nominal ones, I hope they will have none against Converting Negroes who are almost totally in a perfect State of Heathenism, he carries with him perhaps better Credentials, than most do who go from America for Holy Orders, and if your Ladyship has time to peruse them, I believe they will appear reputable, and cannot fail of being attended to, unless his pious and Exemplary Behaviour, and (should it be known, as it probably may) his connection with my deceased Friend, should operate against him. I suppose your Ladyship may have seen him having been one of Mr Whitefields family in London, and he has been esteemed so here, and consequently is in some measure able to answer, any enquiry's, your Ladyship may chuse to make in regard to the Orphan House. My acquaintance with him has only been for about a year past, and I am greatly mistaken, if he does not engage with a Single Eye in the Work he has undertaken if permitted. Your Ladyship will please to observe that the Will was not proved, 'till this day, as I thought it Necessary that it should be on its's Way to your

Ladyship, before the contents were known here, as well on Account of the respect due to your Ladyship as that a Malicious and near relation of the deceased in this Town, might not have it in his power to circumvent any measures your Ladyship might think proper to take with the Heir at Law in England, who I suppose is well known to Mr Keen—I have found among, my late Friends Papers, a Sketch of a Law to establish a College, and I shall immediately employ a Lawer to put it in Town, and send your Ladyship a copy by the next Conveyance for your Ladyships Approbation, in which I may perhaps be indulged with our very Sensible and kind Governors advice, who is esteemed an exceedingly Good Lawer, having formerly been in great practice in South Carolina, where he was many Years Attorney General. He proposes going to England with his Family next May, when this Government will probably devolve upon me, and being sensible of my own Inability for such an Undertaking, I truly Tremble at the Thought— He has very Great property here, which I shall have the principal Charge of: he goes to England as Governor of Georgia, having the King's Leave to return to his Government, if he chuses, which is a favour not granted to every Governor, and I am sure, he will very readily assist and advise your Ladyship in promoting the Testators Intentions of which he is acquainted, having had many conversations with him, on that Subject, when last here— Among the Inclosures, your Ladyship will find a Schedule of the lands and Negroes of the deceased, also a copy on an account enclosed with his Will of his Money Matters, he left with Mr. Keen, which I suppose is all his *great Worthy Estate*, so much talked of by his Enemies, and I think when his Legacy's are paid there will be but very little left for the Orphan House, the Accounts of which were all settled and Audited last February, and It's debt paid to that time, and what has been necessarily contracted since, I am told will not be very Considerable, which I shall take care to discharge, and duly render your Ladyship an account—I shall likewise have an Inventory taken of the deceased's real and personal Estate, as soon as possible, which I am obliged to have done within 3 months, agreable to Law, and my Oath on Qualifying as Executor—I have informed your Ladyship, that I only qualifyed to day and could not 'till that was done, legally act, tho I have not been Idle in my Friends Affair since I heard of his Death—I do, not precisely know the Number of poor Children at the Orphan House, but I believe there are not many, of which and every other particular, I shall inform myself, and consequently your Ladyship. I have had several Applications since my Friend last left this province, and some lately, to take in poor Children, but I have determined not to enlarge the Family or make any other alteration in it, untill I hear from your Ladyship—The Institution will want further Support, and I know it's Founder intended, as his ability permitted, to add 15 to 20 Negroes more, which if he had lived to do, I think it would have been Sufficient to Support the president-Tutors, and Servants, and as many Orphan Children, as could conveniently be taken in. The Students when a College is superadded must pay all their Expenses of Board &c, and some settled sum towards Supporting the president and other Offices: The additional Buildings for the Accomodation of Students are in great forwardness, and will soon be finished, but they will be of no Service without a person properly qualified to preside, without which nothing can be—done to purpose as a College. I would beg leave to recommend to your Ladyship the obtaining such a person as a *principal Object*, and as such, I can make no doubt of your Ladyships considering it; he must necessarily be well acquainted with Classical Learning, and should have a tolerable Knowledge of the Sciences; He should be a Clergyman of the Church of England, of sound principles, and no Stranger to Experimental Divinity and I may add he should not only be a Gentleman by profession, but in practice capable of Governing with Dignity, tho' with Tenderness— Such an one my Lady would, I had almost said, be the Greatest Benefaction that could be given to the Institution and to the province in General. The Chappell is very neat, and nearly completed, and the two Wings for Students, and other Buildings are in great forwardness, and all together they are very convenient and make a handsome appearance; and Mr. Wright assures me, he will see them all finished, and will Execute any further Business your Ladyship may require of him. It has been extremely chagrining, and a disagreable State of Suspence to Mr. Whitefields Friends here, not to have even heard till within a few days past from Richard Smith, the Servant who waited upon him on his last Journey, and was with him at the time of his death. In his Letter, I am informed he acquaints Mr. Wright that he intended to embark from Boston for London by the advice of a Friend there, tho' his own Judgement, and the knowledge he had of, his Master's affairs here should I—think have directed him to return with all speed to Georgia, with what Effects and Money his good Master had with him— It appears by Will, which he could not be acquainted with,—

that he is intitled to all the Wearing Apparel his Master had with him, but not to several little things, Mr. Wright informs me, the deceased's carryed for his convenience, belonging to the Orphan House, and especially a Gold Watch my dear Friend left me, of which I am in no want, otherwise than I should preserve, and Esteem it as a token of his Love and Regard. Mr Smith has also a Legacy left him of 50 £ and I suppose when Mr Keen settles *that* with him, he will take care, that he Accounts for what money he found in the possession of his kind Master at the time of his Death. He has a Son at the Orphan House, and I must think this part of his Conduct is by no means pleasing— I shall endeavour to write to Mr West and Mr Keen by this Opportunity much to the same purpose I have done to your Ladyship, and I am sorry I have been obliged to be so prolix and intruding upon your Ladyships patience but I thought it my Duty, to be as particular as in power at present and beg your Ladyship will believe me to be

Your Ladyship's Obedient & very humble Servt

P. S. I shall endeavour to inform your Ladyship from Time to Time as Circumstantially as possible of the Affairs of your Trust— I forgot to mention that I have enclosed Copys of 3 papers I found of my late Friends Writing, intitled Subjects for Annual prizes, College Rules and a List of Wardens for the intended College, which I shall send for your Ladyships amusement— I have just seen Mr Wright, who says that Mr Smith wrote him, that the money he found of his late Masters, was between £24. and £25. I understand that Mr Thomas Adams, Mr Howell Davies, and Mr Stirk, late of this province dyed before the Testator, and if so as the Legacys are only to the Legatees and not their Heirs, they will I presume remain as part of the Testators Estate.—"Letters of Hon James Habersham, 1756-1775," in *Collections of the Georgia Historical Society*, VI (1904), 102-9.

15. JAMES HABERSHAM TO COUNTESS DOWAGER OF HUNTINGDON, DECEMBER 31, 1770

I had the Honour of writing your Ladyship a long Letter the 10th of this Month, which was forwarded by Mr Cornelius Winter, who came over with my late deceaseded Friend, the Revd George Whitefield, and went to England in the Ship Georgia Packet, with intention to obtain holy Orders as a Missionary to the poor Negroes to which I must beg leave to refer your Ladyship, hoping Mr Winter will arrive safe, and there by render it unnecessary to trouble your Lady-ship with Duplicates I then enclosed an authenticated Copy of the deceased's Will, and sundry other Papers, by which your Ladyship will find yourself solely invested with his whole property in this Province: and at the same time I mentioned, that I should send your Ladyship a draught of a Bill for establishing a College, which has been considered agreed upon by our worthy Governor and my late Friend, and has intended to be laid before the Legislature now to be convened to be passed in to a Law, with a Clause to suspend its taking Effect till it has obtained his Majestys royal Allowance and Approbation upon perusing the Sketches of this intended Law, found among my Friends papers, they are so imperfect, that in some In-stances I am at a Loss to understand their Meaning— I am however in hopes that your Lordship, is before this Time possessed of the real Copy, as I find my Friend carryed it with him, whence he last went from hence— Lewis Johnson Esqr one of his Majesty's Council of this province embarked with him for Philadelphia for the recovery of his Health, and being lately returned, informs me that he had the Perusal of the draught of this intended Law, and had also several Conversations with Mr Whitefield on the subject Matter in Phila-delphia, that, I must suppose, his Servant Richard Smith who was with him, and who I have before acquainted your Ladyship em-barked for London from Boston, instead of first returning here, has doubtless delivered it, with what ever Papers and Effects he found in the Possession of his Master at the Time of his Death to your Lady-ship— I must therefore beg leave to request your Ladyship to send me a Copy of it, with the Names of the Wardens or Trustees, that, if your Ladyship approves of it. I may endeavour to have it passed into a Law— I must observe that my deceased Friend intended pre-vious to the passing this Law to have made over his real and Personal Estate in this province to some Persons in Trust for the Purposes reposed by the Law, as a Ground to obtain his Majesty's royal Ap-probation, which I have not the least doubt, would have been granted, especially as it would have been countenanced and recommended by the Governor as well as the whole Legislature; and I presume such a Power or deed of Trust may be necessary for your Ladyship to effect the intention of the deceased— In two or three days I shall have an Inventory taken by sworn Appraisers of all the Goods and Chattels of my late Friend in this Province, and by a good opportunity I shall send your Ladyship a Copy thereof with the Accounts of the Orphan House settled to this day.

My deceased Friend before he last left us, engaged a young Clergyman of the Church of England, the Revd Edgard Ellington, to reside at Bethesda *for-the present*, for which he agreed to give him £50. pr Annum and his Board &c expecting he might be further supported by becoming an Assistant to the rector of the Parish— He has accordingly officiated in our Church for about six months past, once and sometimes twice every Sabbath day, and with almost Universal Approbation, tho, he has yet had no other reward than the satisfaction of doing his duty. Several of the Inhabitants want him to remain here, and would make some provision for his Support but the rector differs with him in religious Sentiments, and it's believed does not want, and will therefore probably not agree to give him the free use of his Pulpit once every Sunday, and occasionally on other Days, he does not seem inclined, (and neither indeed can I advise him,) to remain here on disagreable Terms with the rector, and at best to move in a contracted Sphere, especially as he has been offered one of the best Parishes of South Carolina, where he will probably be as usefull as he can be here. I think him to be a serious young Gentleman, and of promising Abilities, which, however he has not had the best opportunity of improving, and although I am persuaded, he will acquit himself as a Parish Minister, usefully and with reputation, he does not I believe think himself sufficiently qualifyed to instruct Youth in Classical and other usefull Learning, and *such a Person*, I must recommend to your Ladyship to procure to preside at Bethesda College, without which no Law, nor all the Countenance that can be given it, will effectually answer the good Purposes of the Founder, and your Ladyship—*Ibid.*, pp. 109-11.

16. JAMES HABERSHAM TO THE EARL OF DARTMOUTH, JANUARY 9, 1771

Was I not well informed of the Amiable and condescending Disposition of your Lordship, I could not presume to take the Liberty of this Address, especially as I have not the Honour of being personally known to your Lordship, tho' I suppose your Lordship may not be unacquainted with my Name, by means of my Worthy deceased Friend—the Revd Mr Geo. Whitefield,—who, I have understood was Honoured with your Lordships Friendship and Esteem. Our first acquaintance and Friendship commenced soon after he left

Oxford upwards of 34 years agoe, and continued unabated till the Hour of his Death— I came over with him, when he first embarked for this Province, and have had a principal Charge in conducting under many and unknown Difficulties, his Disinterested and generous concerns Here, and in him, I have lost the dearest and oldest Friend I have upon Earth. Before he last embarked for the Northern Provinces on this Continent, he made his Will, and left the whole of his affairs here to good Lady Huntingdon, and in case of her Death, to me desiring, that as soon as may be, his intended plan here may be effectually prosecuted, God's Thought's are not as our Thoughts, but to all Human Appearance it is to be wished he had lived to return here, as he had got the draught of a Bill prepared to Establish his intended College, which had been considered and agreed upon by our Worthy Governor and him, and was intended to be laid before the Legislature, now convened to be passed into a Law, with a Clause to suspend its operation, until it had obtained his Majesty's Royal allowance and Approbation, which I flatter myself would have been granted, as it would have been strongly recommended by the Governor and the whole Legislature. This Draught, my deceased Friend, took with him, but his Servant Richard Smith who attended him on his late journey, instead of first returning here, as I though he ought to have done, went from Boston to England, and doubtless carried the Copy of this Bill, and what papers and Effects he found in his Masters possession at the time of his Death, with him, which I must Suppose he has delivered to Lady Huntingdon, who I have requested to furnish me with a Copy, that I may endeavour to have his intention carryed into Execution, as far as may be in my power— I have sent her Ladyship an Authenticated Copy of his Will, and also of every paper I could find relative to his Affairs in this Province, and likewise sent an Authenticated Copy of the same to his Executors in London— (Mr West and Mr Keen) for their Information and Guidance with respect to Tottenham Court Chappell, and the Tabernacle. I must however wish he had communicated the Contents of his Will to a friend here (the Governor) and myself, as he would have probably been advised to express his Intentions better and more agreable, to what I am persuaded he meant, of which I have written to her Ladyship, as well as Mr West and Mr Keen very fully and circumstantially by Mr Cornelius Winter who lived some years with my Deceased Friend in London, and came with him from England. I think him to be a very serious humble and pious young man. He embarked about three weeks ago for London, and goes well recommended for holy Orders, as a Missionary to the poor Negroes agreable to the Will of our late Rector the Revd Mr Bartholmew Zuberbuhler, who had thereby made a handsome Provision for that Purpose, and I am persuaded he engaged in this laudable design with an Honest and single Eye to promote the real Good of these truly benighted People. I very heartily hope he will succeed. I have to day seen one of the South Carolina Gazettes of the 31st Ult. in which is the following Paragraph taken from a London paper of the 8th November last "Yesterday on receiving the Account of the Death of the Revd Mr George Whitefield, a Caveat was entered at Doctors Commons by a principal Creditor, to whom a considerable sum of money is said to be owing." This Intelligence early as he died the 30th September preceding, and as I well know my Lord that every aspersion that can be invented by the Enemies of the Son of God, will be thrown out to hurt his Memory. I can scarcely give creditt, that any such Caveat Exists, and if it does it must be without any real Foundation. I am sure my Friend was Incapable of deceiving, and am not afraid of staking my reputation, which I esteem dearer than any other Consideration, on his Veracity, in the minutest Instance. I found enclosed and sealed up with his Will a State of his Money Matters, which is all in the Hands of his trusty Friend Mr Robt Keen in London, and after his Legacy's, which are principally to his Servt who more than deserved all he had in his power to do for them, and some inconsiderable Sums to his relations, and particular Friends, are paid, I believe there will be very little of anything left for the Support of his Institution here. I am well informed that the only Debt he owed in England—which was to a kind Friend, who lent him the Use of a Sum of Money without Interest, he has taken care to make provision to discharge, as will appear, if please God, Mr Winter arrives Safe to deliver my letters to his London Executors,. His Accounts and every demand on him here, were settled paid and audited last February, and what has been unavoidably contracted since, I shall discharge, tho' I have not a farthing of his Money, not doubting but I shall be reimbursed; and this my Lord, I am persuaded is a true Account of his Great Worldly Estate, which his Enemies have charged him with secretly amassing for his private purposes— The time is now come my Lord, to evince to the whole world, the uprightness of his Intentions, and that his Views were Solely and disinterestedly terminated in promoting the Glory of God, and the

Good of Mankind. The Additional Buildings necessary for the College he intended to superadd to the Orphan House, are going on, and will soon be finished, and they will be not only Extremely Usefull and convenient, but make a handsome and ornamental Appearance, and must Effect a lasting Honour on the founders Memory. My deceased Friend has appeared to be particularly designed by Divine Providence to be singularly usefull in promoting the Interest of religion in the new and Extensive World, and his Death has been Universally lamented throughout this Continent. The Inhabitants of this province seem very sensible of *their* Loss in particular, and the Legislature here have very genteely expressed their Gratitude to their departed Friend, which I have endeavoured to acknowledge in the enclosed Gazette, under the Signature of *"an Old and Real Friend to the deceased and to Georgia"* I have likewise taken the Liberty to enclose your Lordship two Funeral Sermons, one published here, and the other in So. Carolina, and the latter is the production of a good old Gentleman, who is far advanced in Years, and is Labouring under the Natural Infirmities of Age. For several years past he has appeared very little in the pulpit, but I suppose could not be satisfied without leaving this last Testimony for the deceased. in which the Warmth of a truly Friendly and good Heart is Visible. He has been a very sensible usefull writer, and is the Mr Smith mentioned by Mr Newton in his Life, which I have lately read with great pleasure. The real Affection that has subsisted between me and my old Friend, and the regard your Lordship had expressed for him, I flatter myself will plead my excuse for this intruding on your Lordship, and if your Lordship will not be displeased with my requesting your Lordships Friendship to a worthy Gentleman I shall think myself highly honoured. This Gentleman is Lewis Johnson Esqr a Usefull and sensible Member of his Majesty's Council in this Province, who embarked with my late Friend when he last left us, to Philadelphia for the recovery of his Health, having been long affected with sickness, and thereby deprived of attending his profession as a physician. His journey to the Northward has answered his purpose, and he is returned in as good a State of Health, as he has enjoyed for some years past, and his Judgement is esteemed equal, if not Superior to any of the Practitioners in the Medical Way here, his late absence, and his frequent and tedious sickness before, and, I am sorry to say, his steady and faithfull Conduct to Support Government during our late disturbances, on Account of the Stamp and American duty Acts, has not a little contributed to throw the Greatest part of his Business into other Hands. He is my Lord, the Father of a reputable and Large Family, a carefull and prudent Wife and thirteen young Children, who depend upon him for Support. He has had a Liberal Education, and has been regularly brought up in his profession, and I believe this Attention to his Business especially in the Latter part of the Summer, which is our Sickly Season, has hurt his Constitution, and as the Same Cause will probably have the same Effect he is desirous of getting some Employment that may secure a certain and decent support for himself and large Family during his Life. The Collector of his Majesty's Custom here is very old and according to the Course of Nature cannot be expected to live long, and if Mr Johnson could succeed him, I am persuaded he would Execute the office Faithfully, and with reputation. Our Governor and his Friends here very heartily wish it and I know the former has a real respect for him, and will recommend him to the Commissioners of the Customs at Boston./I find our present Collector's Appointment is from the Commissioners of the Customs in London, but it was before any board of Commissioners was Established in America, and as it is a revenue Office, perhaps it may lay with the lord of the Treasury in the first Instance, and if your Lordship can Serve this Worthy Man by Insuring the reversion to him, I am sure he will not dishonour your Lordship's Countenance for him: as I express the Sentiments of my deceased Friend, who, I have not the least doubt, would have done every thing in his power to serve him had he lived to return to this Province. Our Worthy Governor's Leave of Absence, proposes going with his Family next May, when this Government will probably devolve on me, during his absence.—*Ibid.*, pp. 112-16.

17. JAMES HABERSHAM TO SAMUEL LLOYD ON THE DEATH OF WHITEFIELD, FEBRUARY 6, 1771

You have doubtless heard of the Death of my late dear Friend, the Revd Mr Geo. Whitefield in New England, an Account that too sensibly affects me to wish to dwell too much upon. He has left the Trust of his Affairs here, to good Lady Huntingdon, and in case of her Demise to me, who am also his only Executor here, by which a very weighty concern devolves on me. There have been many Publications throughout this extensive Continent, on his much lamented Death and I beg leave to enclose our Gazette, in which is a short one of mine, under the signature of "an Old and real Friend to the deceased and to Georgia." I am the only one left in America of his first Friends, and must soon follow him. I have no doubt of his laudable and disinterested Institution Succeeding, tho' at present the Means of its visible Support are indeed very small, and by no Means adequate to the Undertaking.—*Ibid.*, pp. 119-20.

18. JAMES HABERSHAM TO ROBERT KEAN ON BETHESDA ORPHAN HOUSE, MARCH 28, 1771

Our Friends the Messieurs Wright and Mr Crane, have by this Conveyance sent a special Power of Attorney from each of them to my Friend Mr John Clark in Billiter Sqr, with whom my second Son lives, to enable him to receive, and fully to acquit you, and our late dear Reverend Friends other Executors in London for the Legacy's he kindly left them, when it may be convenient for you to pay them. I have had the best advice on the will *in respect to this Matter*, and was advised to this Mode of doing it, as the most proper. Our friend Ambrose has lately married, I think a prudent and discreet Woman, and as he proposes to remain at the Orphan House, while he may be thought usefull, and I trust that will be during his Life, she will be a good Helpmate to him. He has also bought a House and Lott in this Town for £250. which I have advanced him for the residence of his ingenious, and industrious Brothers, who have more Employment, and that from the best People, that they can possibly undertake, Mr Reynolds the Bricklayer, who came over with them, has more than full employ. Mr Crane will probably marry, and end his Days among us, I mean at the Orphan House. That Institution is indeed bereaved, but God can, and I believe will supply our Loss. I must own I now and then, *in respect to it*, feel a Damp on by Spirits, and seem to be encompassed with Clouds and Darkness, but in general, blessed be God, I experience a chearful and undoubting Dependence on him, that he will raise us Means and Friends in his own Way, for he must have the Honour, to support and enable us to go on, and bring forth the Head Stone with shoutings, crying Grace, Grace unto it. I have already advanced to Mr Ambrose Wright £200.—to pay Expenses to the 1st January last, which I hope good Lady Huntingdon, who is our Friend's residuary Legatee, will be enabled to reimburse me. I hope in all next Month, I shall hear from her Ladyship, and you and our other good Friends, because 'till I do, I am scarcely at Liberty to act, or rather am acting without her Ladyship's Direction and approbation in every Instance Last Monday, (Lady Day) was our Anniversary at the Orphan House Academy, when our new, very decent and plainly elegant little Chappell was opened, where a numerous and very polite Company attended. Perhaps when I tell you, that you will see very few such genteel Auditory's in London, you will smile, but, nothwithstanding, it may be, and I believe is a Fact, if I know anything of London. Last January I Employed Mr Langworthy, and began an Academy with 4 little Boys, sons of the first Gentlemen here, and they are now doubled and I have no doubt will encrease, and now and then, we add an Orphan Child to those there, but we must go on softly. On the Anniversary, Peter Edwards, son of our late Friends Brother the Captain deceased, introduced the Solemnity with a Speech, which he delivered with great Propriety and Modesty, Much, very much to my Satisfaction, and the whole Audience. When I tell you, he did me Justice you will suppose I penned it, This Speech with Mr Langworthy's on the conclusion, and a short account of the Proceedings on that Day, you will find in the enclosed Gazettes, of which you will furnish Mr Hardy, Mr West, and your other Friends with a Copy. These Transactions are published on the Spott, and cannot be contradicted. There were four young Gentlemen who spoke on a Stage erected for the Purpose, *they were indeed young,* but acquitted themselves with applause, but one of them, not seven years of age, amazed the whole Company, and if you will not think me *too proud,* he was my own Nephews Son. The Governor gave Peter Edwards £5. and some other People gave him near as much more, which if added to his deceased Benefactors Legacy, may, if properly disposed of be of future Advantage to him. I have great Hopes, he will turn out a usefull Man. Mr Ambrose, Mr Robert and Jacob Wright are all now with me, as is Mr Crane, and I believe they live in Love and cordial Friendship, Mr Ellington has left the Copy of his Sermons preached on opening the Chappell, with me to publish if I chuse to do it, but I know not what I shall determine for although I like the Matter, the Method, that is the Management of the Discourse, may admit of objections, and if I would, I have neither Time nor Leisure to put it in an unexceptionable Dress, and therefore I shall probably let it sleep in Silence. I have a short account of our Friends Money Affairs in your Hands in your own writing, which I shall send by our Governor, who will probably sail for England in about two Months, and as I expect he will go in a Man of War, he will probably go safe, if there should be a rupture with Spain. If you will please to pay Mr Clark Ten Pounds left me and take his Receipt, in Discharge of it, you may depend I will return it with full interest, to my beloved Bethesda here. I hope you have got from Richard Smith the Gold Watch left me, and pray send me a ring of the size of the Pattern enclosed. These are Memorials I should be sorry to want, and hope they will remain with my latest Posterity. Their Value otherwise would be of very small Consideration with me.

Mr. Benjamin Stirk to whom a small Legacy is left by our late Friend dyed last July and was buryed at the Orphan House, so that Legacy will elapse. We are here very poor, and I hope you and the other Executors will continue your Friendly assistance to us. Please to assure them of my cordial Respects. How happy should I be to manifest it in Person, but I now begin to dispair of ever being favoured with making a Visit to my native Country, as Business seems to multiply on my Hands, with growing Years, consequently with growing Infirmities, . . .—*Ibid.*, pp. 123-25.

19. JAMES HABERSHAM TO JAMES WRIGHT, MAY 30, 1772

I thank you for undertaking the Cause of the Orphan House, now truly an Orphan, which I find by your Letters, as also another from Lord and Lady Huntingdon, lately received— It was sometime ago industriously rumoured here, that it was to go to Mr Whitefield's Heirs, and indeed by a Letter I received from Her Ladyship, about the same time she wrote to me almost in the same Terms, and in a Strain, I did not relish and understand, and have not answered it, but Her Ladyship's last Letter is kind and affectionate, and therefore I shall as kindly reply— I am between 2 and £300 in Advance for that House— When this report first prevailed, there were about 16 Boarders, and every thing appeared to go on agreeably, but on Mr Lowten's proposing to keep a School, and it being propagated, that the Scheme of a College or School wou'd come to nothing, the Children were by Degrees withdrawn, untill reduced to Mr Graham's and Clay's Sons, and Mr Langworthy concluding, that he could not at present be of use, came to Town, and has now opened a School with Mr Holmes, in which I believe they meet with success, and the Parson has also another in his Library— As it at present appears to me, I think Lady Huntingdon wou'd promote its Interest best, by giving it up to be the Public, as the best means of its meeting with Support, and rendering it usefull— In this I only give my Opinion, and by no means wish or intend to dictate. Mr Lowten gains the Affections of his Parishioners more and more— He is confessedly clever in the Pulpit, and has perhaps not many Equals— His private Conduct is, I believe, unexceptionable, both as a Gentleman and a Christian, and the Tongues of his Opposers seem to be stoped— In his Public Exhibitions, he does not touch, on matters of Government, and in private, if he mentions his Opinion, it has been as far as I have seen, in its Favour and Support, and at the request of a great Majority of the Vestry, and the general Sense of the best of his Parishioners, I have collated him, something in the Manner you did Mr Frink, and some weeks after at his own request, he subscribed what is prescribed by Law, which he did and declared before me in writing at my House, which I have in my Possession, and afterwards went to Church, and read the 39 Articles, and publickly declared his Assent and Consent to them, and then read the written Declaration made before me, which he signed, and my Certificate that he had so done— This latter Transaction was of a Sunday— At first I was at a loss to know the meaning of this, which he explained that N. W. J. and some few of his secret Friends had got Burns Eclesiastical Law, and given out, that his Living was ipso facto void, without he complyed with these requisites within a certain Time, so that you see, every thing is to be made a party Affair— I am now glad it is done, because it has put an End to all further Intrigues in this matter, and I have not the least doubt of Mr Lowtens giving Content, even to those, who first Opposed him—*Ibid.*, pp. 180-81.

20. James Habersham to "The Revd Mr ———— at Bethesda College," May 25, 1773

Although I feel myself constrained from the real Love I bear you to write this line, yet God knows how reluctant I do it, because I would not willingly, do or say anything to give my good Friend the least Pain; and from my Situation in Life, I feel a further difficulty, as it may not only be thought improper but presumptuous in me to offer my opinion in Matters out of my Sphere, but as I believe you, possess great goodness of heart, and an uncommon sweetness of temper, I am the less fearfull of offending you. You certainly chose a noble and most excellent subject to speak upon last Sunday Evening, and the general observations you made were serious and solemn truths, but they were so disjointed, that I think your auditory were disappointed, and not much benefitted by your Manner of handling the Text— A very dear friend, one of Lady Huntingdons Attorneys for the Orphan House, who has been absent from Savannah since your Arrival, and who you therefore are not acquainted with, was present, and when we came out of the House, observed, that he wished you would reduce your Thoughts into writing, before you delivered them in public— I perfectly agreed with him, and also very heartily wish you would do it— It would be a means of fixing the subject matter, you treat upon, better on your Memory, and enable you to divide the word of Truth with greater Precission and Clearness, and permit me to say, that there are Many sensible Men, who cannot speak their Sentiments extempore with gracefull Acceptance, who shine with great Lustre, when they deliver them in writing, or at least from short Notes well digested under proper Heads— This I know from my own Experience, and that when I have endeavoured to express myself, without previously reducing my Thoughts into writing at large, or the Substance in Notes, I have failed and indeed have not been able to speak My Sentiments to my own or the Hearers Satisfaction, or even to be sometimes clearly Understood— My Late dear Friend Mr Whitefield has more than once told me, that altho' he thought I could express by Thoughts tolerably in writing, I did not verbally, and I am sure his observation was right, and I have often found it so, in a public capacity, which has made me frequently more than blush—. . .—*Ibid.*, pp. 227-28.

VIII

PHILANTHROPY AND EDUCATION: WINYAW INDIGO SOCIETY

I. PREVIEW AND COMMENTS

A N INTERESTING EXAMPLE of philanthropy for education in colonial South Carolina was the Winyaw Indigo Society, which was founded about 1740 primarily for the purpose of improving the cultivation of indigo, one of the principal staples of that time and place. The society was formed largely as a convivial club by some planters who met in Georgetown on the first Friday in each month to discuss the latest London news, "to hold high discourse over the growth and prosperity of the indigo plant, and to refresh the inner man, and so to keep up to a proper standard the endearing ties of social life by imbibing freely of the inevitable bowl of punch." The manner by which the members became interested in education appears in the brief history of the Society given below. All of the documents here given on this Society have been drawn from the reference given at the end of this section.

The school founded by this Society had a very successful career from 1756 to 1861 and twenty-five or more children were annually educated in it. The trustees allowed the principal to receive a certain number of pay scholars in addition to the pupils for whom the school was originally designed, and for teaching these he was allowed a salary of $600 in addition to his annual salary of $1000. The Civil War practically destroyed the value of the Society's invested funds and the school building was occupied for more than a year by Federal troops, and the library was scattered. When the organization was allowed possession of the building again, funds were raised for a new endowment. The school continued its work from 1866 to 1886 when it was incorporated as one of the public graded schools of the State. During the past four or five decades the Society has engaged in no educational work but still retains its organization and library.

II. DOCUMENTS

1. THE CHARTER OF THE SOCIETY (1755) AND AMENDMENTS (1803, 1825, 1847)

Whereas, several inhabitants of the Parish of Prince George Win-yaw, and others, taking into consideration the great disadvantage the said inhabitants labored under from want of a School for the education of children, did, on or about the seventh day of March, one thousand seven hundred and fifty-five, enter into a voluntary Society for founding and erecting a Free School at Georgetown, in the Parish aforesaid, and have, at a considerable expense, employed masters of the said School, who already have a great number of children under their care and tuition; which undertaking they hope will in time, if duly encouraged and properly established, be of great advantage to the religious as well as the civil concerns of this Province, and are desirous of having the Society incorporated, thereby to put them upon a more solid and lasting foundation than they can be by their voluntary subscriptions only; for promoting, therefore, so good a work, we humbly pray his most sacred Majesty that it may be enacted.

I. *And be it enacted*, by His Excellency, William Henry Lyttleton, Esquire, Captain-General and Governor-in-Chief in and over the Province of South Carolina, by and with the advice and consent of His Majesty's Council, and the Common House of Assembly of the said Province, and by the authority of the same, That Thomas Lynch, Esquire, President; Mr. Joseph Poole, Senior Warden; Mr. Samuel Wragg, Junior Warden; Mr. Nathaniel Tregagle, Treasurer; Mr. Joseph Dubourdieu, Clerk; Mr. Charles Fysse and Mr. William Shackelford, Junior, Stewards, the present officers, and the rest of the present members of the said Winyaw Indigo Society, having been duly elected and being now members of the said Society, and all such other persons as shall be hereafter duly admitted or become members of the said Winyaw Indigo Society, according to the rules, orders, and Constitutions of the said Society, shall forever hereafter be, and they are hereby declared to be, one body corporate and politic, in deed and in name, by the name of the Winyaw Indigo Society; and by that name shall, from time to time, and at all times hereafter, have perpetual succession, and shall forever hereafter by that name be a body able and capable in law to purchase, have, hold, receive, take, retain, possess, and enjoy, to them and their successors forever, lands, tenements, rents, franchises, and hereditaments, in fee simple, not exceeding in the whole the clear yearly value of five hundred pounds, lawful money of Great Britain, and also goods and chattels, real or person effects and things whatsoever, of what nature, kind, or quality soever, by donation, subscription or otherwise howsoever; and also to give, grant, sell, alien, convey away, exchange, demise, or lease the same, or any part thereof, as they or their successors shall think proper and convenient, and for the benefit and advantage of the said Society, and according to the rules, laws, and others thereof; and by the same name, shall be forever hereafter a body able and capable to sue and be sued, plead and be impleaded, answer and be answered unto, defend and be defended, in all or in any Court or Courts, or other places, and before any Judges, Justices, and other persons whatsoever, in all manner of actions, suits, complaints, pleas, causes, and things whatsoever, and of what nature or kind soever, which shall to them in anywise belong, or appertain in, about, or concerning the premises.

II. *And be it also enacted*, by the authority aforesaid, That it shall and may be lawful for the said Winyaw Indigo Society, and their successors, from time to time, and at all times forever hereafter, to have one common seal for their use and benefit, with full power to change, alter, break, and make new the same, when and so often as they shall judge requisite.

III. *And be it also enacted*, by the authority aforesaid, That it shall and may be lawful for the said Society or Corporation hereby erected, and their successors, to assemble and meet together on the first Friday in November in every year, and at such other times as there shall be occasion, at such place in Georgetown, aforesaid, as they shall see fit, due and public notice being given at least ten days, by the Clerk of the said Society. in the public Gazette, or for want of such Gazette, by his affixing and posting at the most usual and notorious places in Georgetown aforesaid, before the times of such meetings, not only the day, hour and places of such meeting, but the cause thereof, and of the matters intended to be transacted at such meeting, and that they, the said Society or Corporation, and their successors, or any twenty-five of them, shall have full power and authority, from time to time, to make, constitute and establish such and so many by-laws, rules, and orders, as to the greatest part of them then present shall seem necessary and convenient for the better regulation, government, well ordering and directing the said Corporation or Society, and the officers, servants and persons by them employed, or to be employed, in or about the same, and for the better management, limiting and appointing of all and every the trusts and authority in them, and each of them reposed, and to be reposed, and for the admission of new members into the said Society, and for the doing, managing and transacting all things necessary for and concerning the government of the said Society or Corporation; and the same by-laws, rules and orders to put in use and execution accordingly, and the same again, at their will and pleasure, to alter, change or revoke; all which said by-laws, rules and orders so be made as aforesaid, shall be binding on every member of the Society or Corporation, and be, from time to time, by them, and each of them, punctually and inviolably observed, according to the tenor and effect thereof, under the several pains, penalties and disabilities therein appointed or declared; *Provided,* That the same shall be reasonable, and not contrary or repugnant to the laws and statutes of Great Britain or of this Province.

IV. *And be it also enacted* by the authority aforesaid, That it shall and may be lawful for the said Corporation or Society to found, erect, endow, maintain and support such school or schools, for the maintenance and education of such poor and helpless orphans or indigent children, and for binding them apprentices, as they shall judge proper objects of charity, and to appoint and choose, and at their pleasure displace, remove and supply such officers, school-masters, servants, and other persons to be employed for the use of the said school or schools, or other affairs of the Corporation, and to appoint such salaries, perquisites, or other rewards or their labor or service therein, as they shall from time to time approve of and think fit.

V. *And be it also enacted* by the authority aforesaid, That the better to enable the said Society or Corporation to support and carry into execution the good and laudable designs aforesaid, every person who now is or shall hereafter become a member of the Society or Corporation, his and their executors and administrators shall be, and they are hereby obliged to pay into the hands of the Treasurer of the said Society or Corporation for the time being, within twelve months after the same shall become due, all such sum and sums of money yearly, and at such days and times as by the rules, by-laws and Constitutions of the said Society or Corporation hereby erected and established, are or shall be appointed and directed. And for neglect or default in the payment thereof, or of any part thereof, shall be subject and liable to forfeit all right, title, benefit and interest in the said Corporation.

VI. *And be it also enacted* by the authority aforesaid, That this Act shall and may be given in evidence on the trial of any issue or cause in any Court of Law or Equity in this Province, without special pleading.

VII. *Provided always, and be it further enacted* by the authority aforesaid, That this Act, nor anything contained therein, shall not take effect or be of force until His Majesty's Royal approbation of the same shall be obtained and made known in this Province.

B. SMITH, *Speaker.*

In the Council Chamber, the 21st day of May, 1757.

Assented to. WILLIAM HENRY LYTTLETON.

AMENDMENTS.

XII. *And be it further enacted* by the authority aforesaid, That all the confiscated property to which this State is now entitled, in the election districts of Prince George Winyaw and All-Saints, and all such other property as hath heretofore accrued, or may hereafter accrue, to this State, in the said districts, under the operation of an Act entitled "An Act to appoint escheators and to regulate escheats," and all the vacant lots in the town of Georgetown, shall be, and are hereby, vested in the Winyaw Indigo Society. *Provided*, the aforesaid property shall not exceed five thousand pounds sterling. A.A. 1795.

I. *Be it enacted* by the Senate and House of Representatives of South Carolina, now met and sitting in General Assembly, and by the authority of the same, That so much of the charter incorporating the Winyaw Indigo Society, as fixes the annual meeting of the said Society on the first Friday of November, in each year, and requires ten days public notice of every other meeting and of the business to be transacted thereat, be, and the same is hereby repealed; and that the said Winyaw Indigo Society be and it is hereby empowered to fix, by its laws, the times of its annual and other meetings, and to transact at any meeting, all such business as shall be deemed by the Society necessary and proper.

II. *And be it further enacted* by the authority of the same, That so much of a charter amending the charter incorporating the aforesaid Winyaw Indigo Society, as authorizes nine members, at any other than an annual meeting, to transact business, but subjects their proceedings to revision at the next annual meeting, at which there shall be fifteen or more members, be and the same is hereby repealed, and that nine members be, and they are hereby empowered, to transact business at any other than an annual meeting, subject to revision at the first subsequent meeting, whether annual or not, at which there shall be fifteen or more members. AA. 1803.

XXII. *And be it further enacted,* That the Winyaw Indigo Society be, and they are hereby authorized and empowered to bind out to any trade or occupation, such pupil or pupils on the bounty of that institution, as they may deem expedient and proper. A.A. 1825.

XI. The hereafter seven members of the Winyaw Indigo Society shall constitute a quorum for the transaction of business of said Society. A.A. 1847.

2. A Brief History of the Society

All the records of the "Winyaw Indigo Society" were lost or destroyed at the close of the recent war, when Georgetown fell into the hands of the Federal forces. The Academy Building, with here and there a volume of what was once a very large and valuable library, is about all that is left of the property of which it was possessed as the capital upon which it did its noble deeds of charity. Few of its living members became such more than forty years ago, and its early history is, therefore, simply the tradition of the past.

As tradition hath it: the planters of Georgetown District, about the year 1740, formed a convivial Club, which met in the Town of Georgetown on the first Friday of each month, to talk over the latest news from London, which was never less than a month old, to hold high discourse over the growth and prosperity of the Indigo plant (then and for a long time after spelt, in the invoices to London, Indico,) and to refresh the innerman, and so keep up to a proper pitch the endearing ties of social life by imbibing freely of the inevitable bowl of punch. The Old Oak Tavern which stood on Bay street, not far from its intersection with Broad street, was the place of this monthly reunion. The first Friday in May of each year, was the anniversary meeting, and on these occasions anecdote and song (speech-making was not yet in vogue) added to the good cheer of the punch bowl, and many a staid and solid old planter became as blue as the residuum of the plant he cultivated. Indeed, tradition says, it always required great skill for these jolly old fellows to sit their prancing steeds, after one of these anniversary festivals, for a spur in the head always equals two in the heel, and master and horse became so mobile and agile that the ground and lofty tumbling was generally equal to a small sized circus.

There was an initiation fee and an annual contribution from each member, which went to defray the expenses of the meetings. These were always paid in Indigo. In those good old days, when there were no protective tariffs or license to sell poison under the euphonious names of Burbon and Summerdine, and no Maine Liquor Law to stop the trade in wholesome beverages; when there were no revenue inspectors prowling about under the guise of land speculators; when each man was permitted to sit under his own vine and fig tree and imbibe the best and purest Old Jamaica for fifty cents a gallon; the appetite did not grow upon what it fed on, and the brain did not reel under the maddening influence of narcotic poison; but our forefathers, with their peach and honey and genuine Old Rum, rose to the height simply of genial gentlemen and liberal benefactors. And so it came to pass that about the year 1753, the exchequer became plethoric of gold, and the hearts of our founders overflowed with the milk of human kindness. . .

And hence it became the question of the hour, to what good purpose shall we devote our surplus funds. As the tale runs, the discussion was brief, pertinent and solid. At the close of it the Presiding Officer called on the members to fill their glasses, he wished to close the debate by a definite proposition, if it met their approbation, each member would signify it by emptying his glass. He said: "There may be intellectual food which the present state of society is not fit to partake of; to lay such before it would be as absurd as to give a quadrant to an Indian; but knowledge is indeed as necessary as light, and ought to be as common as water and as free as air. It has been wisely ordained that light should have no color, water no taste, and air no ordor; so, indeed, knowledge should be equally pure and without admixture of creed or cant. I move, therefore, that the surplus funds in the Treasury be devoted to the establishment of an Independent Charity School for the Poor." The meeting rose to its feet. The glasses were each turned down without soiling the linen, and the Winyaw Indigo Society was established.

Such, in brief, was the origin of a Society whose School has been *the* School for all the country lying between Charleston and the North Carolina line for more than one hundred years. In its infancy it supplied the place of Primary School, High School, Grammar School and Collegiate Institute. The rich and poor alike drank from this fountain of knowledge, and the Farmer, the Planter, the Mechanic, the Artisan, the General of Armies, Lawyers, Doctors, Priests, Senators and Governors of State, have each looked back to the Winyaw Indigo Society as the grand source of their success or their distinction. To many it was the only source of education. Here they began, here they ended that disciplinary course which was their only preparation for the stern conflicts of life.

The Society received a royal charter from King George in the year 1755. Some other privileges have been since granted to it by the Legislature of the State. Its Constitution still contains the imprint of wisdom of its founders, few changes having been made to adapt it to the changed circumstances of the times. It lived through the rugged "times that tried men's souls," and came out of that contest with royalty, still clinging to its royal charter and cherishing with the recollection of a favored child the good old days and customs and practices of England, but yet not unmindful of its new duties in its new relations to Carolina, "the land of the free and the home of the brave." It has never suffered politics to enter its doors. In the wildest periods of political excitement it has kept its gaze undeviatingly fixed on its true—its only mission. Its cardinal rule was, never to close its door against any worthy, honorable citizen who desired to become a member, and never to dismiss from office any officer who was capable and willing to serve. The consequence was: its membership was of the best men of the county; its duties in every respect was discharged promptly and efficiently; it had grown rich, it had enlarged its operations, it had become the central object of the affection of all our people; and it was nobly doing its work in enlightening the minds, improving the morals, and imparting tone, dignity and practical wisdom to generation after generation of our children. It was the offspring of the rollicking liberality of the Cavalier and the inflexible spirit of the Huguenot, beautifully mingled and blended into harmonious action. It contained, as it had commenced, the foster mother of all that is good and commendable, personating the blindfolded Goddess in the distribution of her favors.

But the "civil war" came, and with it that disastrous result, which has swept away the accumulation of more than a century. And now when its charitable deeds are more needed than they were in 1753, and when the descendants of its founders are heavily taxed to support free schools, whose doors are virtually closed against their children, The Winyaw Indigo Society finds itself without funds, without school apparatus and without means to soothe its poverty-stricken children by the rich endowment of knowledge, the enduring heritage of learning. Is there no kind Maecenas who will consent to lift us out of the mire and place us once more on the plain of usefulness?

The Academy Building was occupied by the military as long as the Town of Georgetown was garrisoned, and the building and premises were very much abused by the soldiers. The best and most valuable works in the library were appropriated and carried off, including Audubon's great work on Ornithology, which cannot be replaced except at an enormous price. By dint of great efforts the members have raised among themselves money to repair the building and fences, and have during the past year once more employed a competent teacher and started their school, but have been compelled to charge a small sum for tuition to aid them in raising the salary of the preceptor. The school is entirely without apparatus of any kind, so useful and essential in teaching the sciences. In fact, the interior arrangement and appearance of the school with its rough benches and uncouth desks, resemble the traditional "old field" school that followed the first settlement of the State. The members are thoroughly alive to the importance of nurturing the school into something like its former brilliant success, but without aid from abroad, it must necessarily progress slowly, with probably many halts before it again reaches the summit of its great usefulness, and again scatters its steady gleam of light to dispel the shadows that are daily thickening over this once favored district, then the abode of princely wealth and courtly refinement. There are, however, no vain regrets, no gloomy brooding over the past. Trustful of the present, hopeful of the future, knowing that in the long run blood will tell, let us learn to "labor and to wait."

3. Rules and resolutions of the Society

RULE I.

Quorum.

THE WINYAW INDIGO SOCIETY shall consist of an unlimited number of members; nor cease to exist while there remain nine.

Seven shall constitute a quorum to transact business, subject, nevertheless, to revision at the first subsequent meeting, at which shall be present *fifteen* members or more.

RULE II.

Meetings.

This Society shall have two general meetings in the year, the one annual, on the first Friday in May—the other half-yearly, on the first Friday in November; and ordinary meetings on the first Friday in every month, (excepting when the Courts of Equity or Common Pleas may be in session in Georgetown,) in which case the meeting shall be adjourned to the succeeding Friday.

The Society shall always meet at ten o'clock in the morning; and the President may, at any time when he thinks the interest of the Society demands it, call an extra meeting; the members who shall have notice thereof, shall be liable to the same fines for non-attendance, as at ordinary meetings.

RULE III.

Election of Officers.

At every annual meeting, the members shall elect by ballot, a President, Senior and Junior Wardens, Treasurer, Secretary, Attorney, Escheator, and two Stewards, for the ensuing year.

Fines for not Serving.

Any member elected to either of the foregoing offices, and refusing to serve the full term of his election, shall forfeit and pay the sum of five dollars; and in case of the death, resignation, refusal to serve, or removal from office of any officer, within the year, another shall be chosen for the remainder of it.

RULE IV.

Fines for non-Attendance of Officers.

That every officer may be compelled to attend the meetings of the Society, the following fines shall be imposed upon absentees, viz:

The President, one dollar.

The Senior and Junior Wardens, each fifty cents.

The Secretary, two dollars.

The Treasurer, two dollars, whenever the peculiar duties of his office requires his attendance.

And the Stewards, five dollars each, for absence from their duty at the anniversary of the Society.

All fines imposed by the rules of the Society, may be remitted on satisfactory excuse being made.

RULE V.

Order of Business.

The Society shall not be considered as opened, until the Secretary has called the names of the members residing in Georgetown, or within six miles thereof, excepting the names of the members who may reside on Waccamaw Neck; and immediately thereafter, the minutes of the preceding meeting shall be read; nor shall the Society be deemed adjourned, until the Secretary shall have read the minutes of the meeting, and called the roll.

Fines on Absent Members.

Any member who shall be absent at either call of the roll, except such members as are sixty years of age, and who may not be officers thereof, or who shall leave the room during the sitting of the Society, without permission of the President, shall be fined twelve-and-a-half cents for each absence, unless he shall make such excuse as shall be deemed satisfactory.

These fines shall be collected by the Treasurer, and such members as shall incur fines for non-attendance upon the meetings of the Society, or for neglect of any duty imposed upon them by the Rules, shall be fined by default, at the meeting next after such fine shall have been incurred, unless they make a sufficient excuse, either personally, or by letter, or be absent from the State.

RULE VI.

Duty of the President.

The President, with the assent of the Society, shall issue orders on the Treasurer for money, shall declare elections, appoint Committees, and also appoint proxies to vote for Directors in the different Banks in which the Society may own shares; and shall preserve due order and decorum; and shall appoint a Quarterly Committee, though there should not be a quorum of members at such meeting.

Punishment for Disorderly Conduct.

Any member who persists in disorderly conduct, after being called to order by him, shall be subject to be fined by the Society, in any sum, not exceeding twelve dollars; and if any person, after he shall have been thus sentenced to be fined, continue to disturb the peace of the meeting, he shall be forthwith expelled the Society.

RULE VII.

Duty of Wardens.

The Senior Warden shall preside in the absence of the President—the Junior Warden, in case of the absence of both President and Senior Warden.

And should the President and both Wardens be absent, the members may proceed to ballot for a President *pro tempore*.

RULE VIII.

Term of Office.

A member having served in any office the time appointed by these Rules, shall not be compelled to serve in the same, or in any office, the succeeding year.

RULE IX.

Admission of Members.

Application to become members of this Society, shall be made by letter, enclosing fifteen dollars, being the amount of admission; and the votes of *two-thirds* of the members present, shall be required to entitle the applicant to membership; but no person, applying for admission, shall be balloted for, unless his letter contain the sum above required; and if a candidate be rejected, his letter, with its contents, shall be returned to him; and he shall not be again balloted for until a year after his rejection.

RULE X.

Secretary's Duties.

The Secretary shall, from time to time, and at the charge of the Society, provide books; and in one of them he shall keep a regular index; he shall enter all Rules that now are, or may hereafter be agreed upon as well as such resolutions as may hereafter be directed by the Society to be inserted therein.

In another book, he shall enter the names of the members and the times of their admission; the transactions of each meeting, with the names of members present.

He shall also keep files of letters written to, and copies of those written by the Society; it shall be his duty to give notice to members of extra meetings; to attend the Quarterly Committee whenever it meets, and other Committees when required; to furnish them with such extracts from the minutes and proceedings of the Society, as shall be necessary, and also to record their proceedings.

He shall notify the members of Committees of their appointments, and also the Chairman of the Quarterly Committee whenever he has any business to lay before them. He shall not mark as absent from any meeting of the Society any member who shall be notoriously absent from the State, or beyond the distance of six miles from Georgetown, at the time of meeting.

It shall be his duty, whenever the Rules are approved and printed by the Society, to furnish each member with a copy of them; and on the admission of any new member, to furnish him also with a copy; for the performance of the above prescribed duties, or any other that may hereafter be required of him, he shall receive a compensation to be determined by the Society. In case of the neglect of the Secretary to perform any of the duties required of him, he shall be fined at the discretion of the Society, in a sum not exceeding twelve dollars, or be deprived of his office.

RULE XI.

Treasurer's Duties.

The Treasurer shall take charge of the Cash, Plate, Bonds, Mortgages, and other securities; the Rules, Seal, papers and accounts, except the books and papers of the Secretary—all of which shall first be inspected by himself and the Quarterly Committee, and two exact schedules of the same shall be made out, one of which, signed by the President, shall be delivered to the Treasurer, and copied into the journals by the Secretary; the other, signed by the Treasurer, shall be kept by the President.

All bonds and other securities for money, shall be taken in the name of, and made payable to the Winyaw Indigo Society. The annual interest upon which he shall demand the payment of, and upon a refusal to pay the same, he shall proceed to collect the said interest in the most summary manner the law will permit.

No money shall be let out at interest but to such persons, and on such security, as shall be approved by the President, Senior and Junior Wardens, Treasurer and Secretary, or by a majority of them; and no money shall be loaned to private individuals unless by the special direction of the Society; nor shall any public or bank stock be purchased, except approved by the above mentioned officers, or a majority of them; and under their direction the Treasurer shall hire out or lease the Society's lands and houses. He shall receive the arrears and contribution of the members, and all other moneys payable to the Society. He shall pay no money without a written order from the President, or presiding officer, and shall render to the Secretary semi-annually, to be entered on the journals, an account of all disbursements.

He shall keep a set of books and enter therein an account of the stock, admission money, contributions, rents, interest money, arrearages, fines, forfeitures, donations and legacies, received or payable to, or belonging to the Society, and render a semi-annual statement thereof; and at every anniversary, a statement of the receipts and disbursements of the year preceding, together with a schedule of the funded stock, securities, and all other property belonging to the Society.

It shall be the duty of the Quarterly Committee, annually, to examine the books, accounts and vouchers of the Treasurer for the preceding year, and to make a special report thereon, in which shall be stated the sums received and disbursed; to whom paid, from what funds, and from whom received; with the balance to be carried to the next year's account.

The present and every future Treasurer shall, upon receiving the papers and property of the Society into his possession, give his bond for the value of the funds and other property so committed to his charge; also a joint and several bond, with one or more sureties, to be approved by the President and Wardens, in the sum of two thousand dollars, for the safe keeping of the funds of the Society: and, further, for the faithful discharge of every duty that now is, or may be prescribed for his government by any rule or resolution.

If at any time it shall appear to the President and Wardens that the Treasurer shall have become insufficient, then, and in that case, it shall be considered as their duty, and they are hereby enjoined to require of the Treasurer other and further security; and on a refusal to give the same, to report said refusal to the Society.

It shall be the duty of the President to keep the said bonds, having first recorded them in the Office of the Register of Mesne Conveyance, in Georgetown, and within eight days after their date. As a full compensation to the Treasurer for the performance of all the above duties, he shall be entitled to receive, and shall receive two and a half per cent. on all contributions, rents, and interest money received by him, and upon all sums lent or vested in the funds by him.

RULE XII.

Attorney's Duties.

The Attorney of the Society shall, at every anniversary meeting, and the meeting in January, in each year, render an exact account of the business entrusted to him; for neglect of which duty he shall be liable to a fine not exceeding fifty dollars.

RULE XIII.

Escheator.

In conformity with the Act of the Legislature, the Escheator of the District shall be required to give his bond to this Society for two thousand dollars, with four personal securities, in five hundred dollars each, to be approved of in like manner as the security of other officers of this Society.

RULE XIV.

Defaulting Members.

That whenever a member is sued for his arrears agreeable to the Rules of the Society, and two executions issued on the judgement obtained on such suit, and the return of *nulla bona* is made by the Sheriff, the said member shall no longer be considered one of the

Society; and the Attorney of the Society in such case, shall require the Sheriff to return the said executions on oath.

RULE XV.

Contributions and Arrears.

To increase the funds of the Society, each member shall pay the sum of two dollars at every general meeting; and at every annual meeting, the Secretary shall read the names of the members in arrears, together with the sums due by them; and it shall be the duty of the Treasurer to sue every member who shall neglect to pay his arrears on or before the next half yearly meeting.

RULE XVI.

Admission of Children.

Application for the admission of children upon the bounty of the Society, shall be made at a regular meeting by letter, to be signed by at least two members, to be considered at that, and determined at the next. The children of indigent members of the Society, shall be first entitled to its bounty; the poor orphan next; then the children of indigent widows or widowers; and, lastly, those of such poor parents, as the Society shall deem proper objects of their charity; but no child shall be admitted upon the bounty of the Society, who is not above six years of age, and who is not acquainted with the alphabet, unless the parents or guardian will state that he or she is unable to teach the child the same. The tuition of a scholar shall be discontinued, whenever the Society shall think proper; or whenever, without sufficient excuse, such scholar is irregular in attendance at school. The Society will also furnish the scholars upon their bounty, with books, clothing and boarding, or either, as may appear to them necessary or expedient. And it shall be the duty of the Society, to attend, at least once in every year, at their School, for the purpose of superintending the examination of the scholars on their bounty.

RULE XVII.

Funeral of Members.

It shall be the duty of the Society to attend the funerals of all members; and when a member dies, the Secretary shall summon the members who may be in Georgetown, to attend his funeral; and if any one leaves not funds sufficient to defray the charges of a decent interment, the President and Wardens shall provide for the same, at an expense, not exceeding thirty dollars, from the funds of the Society.

RULE XVIII.

Stewards.

The Stewards shall provide a dinner at every annual meeting for the numbers of members that may be directed by the Society; they shall be present at the dinner; and at 6 o'clock, P.M., they shall inform the members present that no expense incurred after that hour, will be defrayed from the funds of the Society.

Each member present at the annual meeting, as well as all others who reside in Georgetown, or within twenty-five miles thereof, shall pay the Treasurer two dollars and fifty cents to defray the expense of the dinner and liquors. Members may invite strangers to the dinner on paying two dollars and fifty cents for each one whom they introduce, and providing for him a ticket of admission signed by one of the Stewards.

RULE XIX.

Quarterly Committee.

The President shall from time to time appoint a Quarterly Committee, to consist of three members, who shall examine the scholars on the bounty of the Society semi-annually, and report their progress in education at the regular meeting following such examination, except in any case requiring early action. The said Committee shall examine all accounts against the Society which may be presented by the Secretary, and attend to any other business which may be referred to them.

RULE XX.

Chairman.

The person first named on all Committees shall be the Chairman, and it shall be his duty to summon the members of his Committee, to meet when business requires it, except for the examination of the Society's School.

RULE XXI.

Fines for Non-Attendance to Duty.

Every Chairman who shall neglect to summon his Committee, when business requires their meeting, with the exception contained in the 20th Rule, shall pay a fine of one dollar into the hands of the Treasurer, and each member of the Committee who shall neglect to meet at the time and place appointed by the Chairman, shall pay to the Treasurer a fine of fifty cents; and each member of the Quarterly Committee, who shall neglect to examine the scholars on the bounty of the Society, and to report separately thereon at each regular meeting, shall pay to the Treasurer a fine of fifty cents.

RULE XXII.

Sermon or Oration.

At every annual meeting, a Sermon, or an Oration, appropriate to the views of the Society, shall be delivered in one of the churches in this place, by any person who shall be appointed for that purpose, at a preceding meeting. And on that occasion, the Society shall assemble, and after transacting business, shall walk in procession, preceded by the officers of the Society, and accompanied by the scholars on their bounty, to the place where the Sermon, or Oration, is to be delivered.

RULE XXIII.

None of the foregoing Rules shall be repealed or amended, nor shall any new one be made, until the same has been proposed, read, and approved at three meetings, one of which must be annual or semi-annual. All questions in this Society shall be determined *viva voce*, by a majority of the members present, or by ballot if any two members require it.

RESOLUTIONS.

5th November, 1830. The Committee on Rules reported, which report was accepted.

Resolved, That the connexion between the Tutor elect and the members of the Society, continue so long as the same is mutually satisfactory, and when it becomes necessary to disolve the connexion, that three months' notice be given of it.

Resolved, That there be an annual public examination of the scholars on the bounty of the Society, on the 3d Friday in every December.

1st April, 1831, *Resolved,* That the Teacher of the Society's School be required to employ an assistant, approved by the Society, for the first fifteen scholars over and above those on our bounty, and another for every other twenty scholars under his care.

4th May, 1832. *Resolved,* That the arrears of any member exceeding twenty dollars, be put in suit by the Treasurer, unless paid before the next return day.

13th December, 1833. *Resolved,* That the Preceptor be required to report quarterly to the Society the names of the scholars, together with the studies they are pursuing; also to report monthly to the Quarerly Committee the number of vacancies in the School, and all absences of any of the pupils from School during that time.

Amended the 6th March.

6th February, 1835. *Resolved,* That in all future applications for admission to the School, the letter of application shall state the fact, that the parents or guardians have been informed of the existence of an Act of the Legislature authorizing the Society to bind out children on their bounty; and it shall be the duty of the members of this Society, who in future may recommend children, to notify parents or guardians of said resolution, and satisfy the Society of their acquiescence previously to such children being received.

6th April, 1838. *Resolved,* That it be the duty of the Secretary to notify the Preceptor, in writing, of the admission of scholars to the bounty of the Society, immediately upon their being admitted.

6th December, 1839. *Resolved,* That the 16th Rule be so understood, that no application for admission on the bounty of the Society shall be considered when no vacancy exists at the time of such application, but that said application be laid on the table.

Substance of a resolution passed 3d of May, 1844, and amended 7th March, 1845:

Resolved, That to secure to this Society a full knowledge of the causes of the absence of scholars, it be made the duty of the Principal, in case of the absence of any scholar, to obtain of the parent or guardian of such scholar a written excuse for such absence, and that he file the same, if deemed unsatisfactory, to be turned over to the

Secretary, and by him laid before the Society at the ensuing meeting. And that he duly note the same on his daily register.

1st May, 1846. *Resolved*, That the Rules of this Society be re-published in pamphlet form, with a corrected list of the members, and the Charter appended thereto, together with the various amendments to the same, and that the officers of the Society be charged with that duty.

7th January, 1848. *Resolved*, That the following recommendation of the Quarterly Committee be adopted and entered on the Minutes, viz: "We would recommend that the Society require the Teacher to keep a daily account (Register) of the absences of all the scholars, and present it to the Quarterly Committee, that the Society may know who attend school."

———

NOTE.—The Preceptor has been allowed for several years to suspend the exercises of the School during the month of September.

———

Bequests to this Society have been generously made by the late

Jonah Horry, Esq.,	$1,453	50
George T. Lathrop, Esq.,	500	00
Francis Withers, Esq.,	5,000	00

—*Rules of the Winyaw Indigo Society, with a Short History of the Society, and Lists of Living and Deceased Members.* Charleston, S. C.: Walker, Evans & Cogswell, 1874.

IX

PHILANTHROPY AND EDUCATION: EDUCATIONAL PROVISIONS IN WILLS

I. PREVIEW AND COMMENTS

WILLS AND INVENTORIES of the colonial period reflected a wider esteem for education than is perhaps generally recognized. Not only did men and often women provide in their wills for the education of their own children and other relatives, but people of humanitarian [1] and philanthropic interest made provisions also for the education of underprivileged children, through bequests and endowments, a practice of early origin. This form of philanthropic education was important, not only in making some provision for the rudimentary education of underprivileged children,—in reading, writing, spelling and arithmetic, and in training in morals and religion through the Bible and the catechism—but it may have helped also to pave the way for a feeling of the need for "common schools." Certainly the conception of the importance and value of education seems to have been enlarged somewhat by philanthropic interest.

Among the earliest provisions in wills for the education of children and relatives in the South was that made by John Waltham, of Accomack County, Virginia, who died in 1640 and left directions for his son's "instructions of good learning," beginning at the age of six, to a "good and godlye school master" who was to be selected with great care, from which it may be inferred "that school masters were sufficiently numerous on the Eastern Shore, or at least in Virginia, at this time, to allow a considerable latitude of choice." [2] Young Waltham was to remain under his teacher's guidance until he reached the age of eighteen, the expenses of his instruction to be provided from the income of the property inherited by the boy. Nicholas Granger, also of Accomack County, Virginia, provided for the education of his

1. "Almsgiving is as old as man," says *The Encyclopedia Britannica*, (Volume 17, Fourteenth Edition, 1929, p. 709) supporting the statement by quotation from the Egyptian *Book of the Dead* and invoking in proof the memorial ascription as old as the pyramids of the Nile that "He gave bread to the hungry, water to the thirsty, raiment to the naked; he gave a boat to the man who had none." This old idea of philanthropy, present among the Hebrews and other ancient peoples, was greatly strengthened under the Christian epic, and found its way from Europe to the American colonies.

2. Philip A. Bruce, *Institutional History of Virginia in the Seventeenth Century*, I, 296.

daughter in a similar manner. In some cases the testator set aside money for the education of relatives or others; sometimes the proceeds of the labor of slaves was stipulated as means of providing educational facilities; and often the property bequeathed included land, cattle, and tobacco or other produce.

For reasons which should be obvious, no attempt is made to include here all the wills that contained educational provisions; but it is believed that those which follow will serve to illustrate this interesting educational practice in the Southern colonies. Many other wills are in typescript in the library of the University of North Carolina.[3]

II. DOCUMENTS

1. WILL OF JOHN WALTHAM, VIRGINIA, 1640

Item. I give & bequeath unto my sonne John Waltham being of the age of one yeare or thereabouts one Black Cowe wth calfe, bee it so provided that I intend not my ould black Cowe, and one black heifer wth Calfe, and my desire and will according to this my bequest is, that the male increase of the said cattle hereby given to my sd sonne shall be freely allowed to and for the Keeping & well mainteyninge of my sd Child untill he shall as yt may please God atteyne to the age of six years compleate. As also that the ffemale increases of such cattell shall be & remayne & accrue to & for the sole & proper use Comfitt and behoofe of my said Child John Waltham until he shall accomplish the full age of six years as above said.

Item. My Will & desire is that after my sonne hath atteyned the age of six years he maye then be brought up & educated in the sole instruccons of good learning, and the better to effect the same that he may be grounded in the rudiments of schollershipp, and schoole learning. My Will & desire is that he maye then bee put to Schoole unto some good & Godlie Schoolmaster And that especial choice may be made of such schoolmaster wthin the Collonye of Virgenya for the better prefermt of my sd Child, ffor the comendable payment & defrayinge of wch charges of schoole learninge. In wch and abought wch learning my desire is he maye conteynue the space of ffive years & noe longer untill he shall accomplish the age of eleven years, after wch as aforesaid I will & bequeath that during those ffive yeares &

3. The will of Benjamin Syms of Virginia in 1634, apparently providing the earliest endowment for education in English North America, and that of Thomas Eaton a quarter century later, are included in the section of the Syms-Eaton School, above.

noe longer the whole increase boath male & female of such cattell as shall be livinge at his age of Six years, & untill he be att the age of Eleven yeares shall properlie & soelie bee remayne & redound & accrue to & for such expence & charges of such his schoolinge & the defraying thereof provided that att the expiration of the tyme of his age of eleven years the total some & quanity of such stock as he was possessed of at his age of six yeares be made good & not lessoned, abated, or decreased in the numbers of such cattell. And that afterwards & untill his age of eighteene yeares all the male increase of such his cattell shall redound & be allowed unto and for his maynteynnce educacon & keeping & all the female increase shall accrue & remayne unto & for his owne p'per use & behoofe. And that after his age of eighteene yeares the whole increase boath of male & ffemale shall soly be and remayne unto his p'per use wthout exception or limittacon.

Item I give & bequeath by this my last Will & testament unto my deare & wel beloved wife Grace Waltham, One cowe calfe, two steeres, and all and singular the rest of my goods, cattells, Chattells, & p'sonall estate wth all ymplemts of household as well moveables as unmoveables & all other things & things whatsoever I am nowe possessed of belonging unto my estate. Item, by virtue of this my last Will and testament I make & ordeyne my welbeloved wife Grace Waltham aforesaid my full and sole Executive of this my last Will and testament wthout anie restraynt or contradiction p'vided shee shall cearfullie & duly performe the execucon of this my sd Will. Item. by this my last Will & testament I ordeyne & apoint as also intreate & desire my well beloved brother Mr Stephen Challeton & my welbeloved ffrinde Capt William Rooper to be the supervisors of this my last Will & testamt and of the due p'formance & right execucon of the same in each particular earnestlie intreatinge as well my sd brother Mr Challeton as alsoe my beloved friende Capt Roper to have a tender care & respect unto my child John Waltham as well in his infancy as when he shall attayne his riper age and nowe especiallye in the p'ticular choyce of his education and breeding in the rudiments of good learninge not doubtinge in their care therein. (September 16, 1640).—Copy in the Virginia State Library; photocopy in the Library of the University of North Carolina.

2. WILL OF WILLIAM GORDON, VIRGINIA, 1684

I will I bequeath my Soull unto god my creatour and Redeimer who gave it and next my bodyto—buried in my own orchard acording to the decent maner of Christendome by my beloved wif

Secondly I give unto loveing wif Mary Gordon all my wholl estate both personall and reall as Land housing orchard and all things elles [else] upon said divident with househould goods of all Sorts now belonging to me with horse mears cattell of all sorts with hodges belonging to the plantation.   She fullfilling my will which is as follows that after debts is payit and Som Small Legacies is payit She mak Lawfull Seall of all and everie particullar aboresaid provyed She goe to hir own country and thar to Liv

but if the said Mary Gordon my Loving wif after my deceise Shall *conteiu* in Virginia and be maried to another man then I giv and bequeath unto christ church parish *on* hundreth acres of Land of that which I took up Lying upon the Lyne of Mr. Allex Smith the glyb and *cun*-Lyn and two *kows* for the proper use of a scoull for ever and that the court or vestrie shall within *on twell* month taik unto thar hands the said Land and cattell after the mariag of the above Said Mary Gordon in Virginia Wither my Loving wif shall goe to England or Stay in Virginia I desire that after my deceis thes small legacies be payt to Wm Trige *on* heaffer of two yeir ould to Wm Gibs *on* heaffer of two year ould to *dorbour* boodle my tables with dyce and men to Wm Batchelder *on* heaffer of three yeir ould as for the parish child we keip I leir hir only to the goodness of hir mistress only heirin is my will that if it pleas god to taik hir mistress before hir tyme of servitud is out the girll may be Set free and not to serve another and heir I make chois Mr Allexr Smith Mr Richard Willis my verie good freind to assist and give counsell to Loving wife—Mary Gordon and unto each of them I bequeth a ring of gould at the Vallue of twentie Shilling Starlling and to Mr. John (Batc) helder I bequeth a Ring at 20s for advyce to my wife and lykewayes [likewise] unto my Loving wif Mary Gordon—give and bequeth what goods or money is dew to me in England with a full power to Show for the same if neid be and heirby I confirme hir as my—aire and ymmediat executrix after my deceis She fulling everie part of the aboresaid Will And herein I Set my hand and Seall the *threttie* day of Feberwary 1684.—In the Virginia State Library. Typescript copy in the library of the University of North Carolina.

3. ACTION BY VESTRY OF CHRIST CHURCH PARISH, MIDDLESEX COUNTY, VIRGINIA, CONCERNING BEQUEST OF WILLIAM GORDON, 1685-1767

It is ordered by this prsent Vestrey that mr William Daniell psent Church warden for ye Middle precinq for this Ensueing years Doe Immediately take into his possession the hundred Acres of Land left by the Last Will and Testament of mr William Gordon Late Decd for ye use and bennifitt of a Free Schoole Together wth Two Cows and their Encrease, and that ye said mr Wm Daniell Ch. warden doe proceed according to the will of the Testator &c. (1685)

Ordered that the Church wardens doe Se and Enqr Into what Reparations is watning to the Gleab of this Prish, & Signifie the Same to the next Vestry, and also that they Enqr after Two Cows left forthe use of the Free School by mr William Gordon Decd and Delivered to mr Deuel Pead our late Minister, And also after Those Things Given by mr Pead for the use of the Gleab &c. (1671)

Order'd that the said Churchwardens let the freeschool Land at Such terms as they shall think best. (1745)

To the Churchwardens for the Rent of the Free school land to be employ'd towards schooling of poor children.   500* (1748)

To Do for the Rent of the Freeshool land to be Employ'd towards Schooling of poor Children   500 (1749)

To the rent of the free school Land	500
To the Quitrents of Ditto	110 (1755)
To the Rent of the Free School	500
To the Sherif for the Quitrents of Ditto	110 (1756)
To the Rent of the Free School Land	500
To the Sherif for the Quitrents of Ditto	110 (1757)
To the Rent of the free SchoolLand	500
To the Sherif for the Quitrents fo Ditto	110 (1757)
To the Rent of the free School Land	500
To the Sheriff for the Quitrents of Ditto	110 (1758)
To the Rent of the free School Land	500
To the Sherif for the Quitrents of Ditto	110 (1759)

* Pounds of tobacco.

| To the Rent of the free School Land | 500 | |
| To the Sheriff for the Quitrents of Ditto | 110 | (1760) |

| To the Rent of the Free School Land | 500 | |
| To the Sheriff for Quitrents of Ditto | 110 | (1761) |

| To the Rent of the Free school Land | 500 | |
| To the Sheriff for the Quitrents of Ditto | 110 | (1762) |

| To the Rent of the Free School Land | 500 | |
| To the Sheriff for the Quitrents of Ditto | 110 | (1763) |

| To the Rent of the Free School Land | 500 | |
| To the Sheriff for the Quitrents of Ditto | 110 | (1764) |

That the late Receiver pay the Rent of the Free School Land being 520 lb Tobo to the Church wardens. (1764)

Ordered That the former Receiver of the Parish Levy pay the Tobacco due for the Rent of the Free School Land for the years 1762 & 1763 and also the 1013½ pounds of Tobaco in his hands not accounted for to the present Church Wardens. (1765)

| To the Rent of the Free School Land | 500 | |
| To the Sheriff for the Quitrents of Ditto | 110 | (1765) |

| To the Rent of the Free School Land | 500 | |
| To the Sheriff for Quitrents of Ditto | 110 | (1766) |

| To the Rent of the free School Land | 500 | |
| To the Sherieff for Quitrents of ditto | 110 | (1767) |

Ordd That The Overplus of The Tobo Levied for the *free *School *Land Quitrents of the free School land be Accounted for at the Laying of the Next Parish Levey. (1767)—C. G. Chamberlayne (ed.), *The Vestry Book of Christ Church Parish, Middlesex County, Virginia, 1663-1767* (Richmond: Old Virginia Press, 1927), pp. 50, 70, 71, 265, 273, 275, 294, 296, 298, 301, 306, 311, 313, 317, 320, 325, 326, 328, 329, 331, 332, 334, 340, 342.

4. WILL OF PHILIP LEE, SOUTH CAROLINA, 1690

Item I confirm ye former gift I gave of ye Third of Eight Thousand pounds of Sugar towards ye yearly Schooleing of ye poor Children

---

* These words scratched through in original, but still legible.—C. G. C.

of St. John's Parish; withal willing that in Case there be not poor Children enough whose Schooleing at ye Rate of four hundred pounds of Sugar P head will amount to ye Sd Sum, Then that ye Receive thereof be Paid out For ye Clothing and other necesSaries for ye Sd poor Children.

Tenth day of February in ye first year of ye reign of their gracious Majesty William & Mary King & Queen of England &c a Anno Do 16 8/90—The original of this will is in Charleston. Copy is in the South Caroliniana Library, the University of South Carolina, and in the University of North Carolina Library.

5. THE WILL OF ISAAC REDFORD, SOUTH CAROLINA, 1696

Item My Will and Pleasure is that my Executrs hereafter do Sell & dispose of all my fore mentioned reall & Personal Estate for ye Education Bringing up of my said 2 daughters if they stay in this Province & if they shall by any means go in to England ye said Estate to be for both their uses as for their Passage & other necessary & what shall remain over & above ye Same to be sent home with them & to be equally divided between them.—The original of this will is in Charleston. Copy in the South Caroliniana Library in the University of South Carolina, and in the University of North Carolina Library.

6. THE WILL OF CHRISTOPHER SMYTH, SOUTH CAROLINA, 1706

Item I give & Bequeath unto my Said Grandson Christopher Smyth one Moiety or half Part of all Negroes Horses Mairs Cattle Plate Household Stuff & personall Estate Whatsoever of which I shall dye possessed to be Delivered unto my Said Grand Son wn he shall Arive to the Age of Twenty Years or before if my Said wife think it Convenient but in the Mean time & untill he my Said Grandson doe Attaine to the Age of Twenty Years as aforesaid my Will & pleasure is that my wife have the use of the said Land Slaves Cattle Hoggs & premisses for & in Consideration of my Said wifes finding my Said Grandson Meat Drink Washing Lodging & Apparell NeceSsary & Convenient & of her Educating of him at School & buying of his books & all things requisite for his Learning untill he be Twenty Years of Age.—The original of this will is in Charleston. A copy is in the South Caroliniana Library in the University of South Carolina, and in the University of North Carolina Library.

7. The Will of John Bennett, North Carolina, 1710

I Give & bequeith to my Son, Benjamin, half that Tract I bought of John Nicker joyning on ye line of ye afsd. Tract on ye South Side & on ye line of Edward Jones Senr. on ye North Side. I freely fully and Absolutely Give unto my sd. Son ye sd. half with ye appertenances & to ye heirs of his body lawfully begotten; & for want to Such Isue to revert decent & Come to my Son, Joseph, & ye heirs of his body lawfully begotten & for want of such Issue to revert, decend, & come to my Brother, Joseph Bennet, & to ye heirs of his body lawfully begotten; & for ye want of Such Isue to remaine & bee for ye use & bennefitt of poor Children To pay for their Schooling & to remaine unto ye worlds End.—J. Bryan Grimes (compiler), *North Carolina Wills and Inventories*, p. 39.

8. The Will of Richard Berresford, South Carolina, 1715

In the name of God Amen I Richard Berresford of Berkley County in the Province of South Carolina, Planter, being now in good and perfect health and of sound and disposing mind and memory Thanks be to Almighty God. But considering the uncertainty of this Transitory life and that all flesh must die. Doe make Publish and Declare these presents to be and contain my last Will and Testament Hereby revoking and making null and void all former and other Wills Testaments and Codicils by me heretofore made and published. And ffirst being heartily sorry and from my heart and penitent for my sins past I comitt my soul unto Almighty God my Creator hoping thro his infinite mercy and by the meritts of my Blessed Saviour Jesus Christ to have full and free Remission of all my sins. And as to my body I comitt it to the Earth to be decently interred according to the discretion of my Executor herein after named there to remain till the day of resurrection which I firmly believe expect and wait for.

In the next place I order will and appoint that all such debts and sumes of money which I owe at the time of my decease as also my funeral charges be paid by my executors in some short time after my decease. And for the settling the temporal Estate which it hath pleased God to bless me with far above my deserts I give and dispose of the same in manner following. Imprimis I give unto my Sister Mary Ford Wife of Nathaniel Ford Shipwright all my goods and household Stuff that shall be found in my house at the time of my decease and all the debts which shall be then due and owing to me from any person or persons whatsoever. Item I give Devise and bequeath unto my Nephew Charles King when he shall attain the age of one and twenty years and to his heirs and Assigns forever All those Six hundred Acres of Land with the appurtenances which I lately purchased of the Honble the Lords Proprietors Deputies Commissioners appointed for selling of Lands in this province situate on Cooper River in Berkley County and lying between the Lands of Thomas Burton and Richard Codner Upon condition nevertheless and under the Provisoes herein after menconed That is to say Provided always That he the said Charles King doe pay or secure to be paid unto his Sister Mary King when she shall arrive at her age of eighteen or marriage the sume of One hundred and Fifty pounds currt money of this province. But in case he shall refuse or neglect to pay or devise the said sume of One hundred and fifty pounds unto his said Sister at her age of Eighteen or marriage as aforesaid. Then I Will that the said Six hundred Acres of Land be sold by my Executor hereinafter named for the most money that can be got for the same and the moneys thereby arising to be divided between them the said Charles King and Mary King in manner following that is to say One hundred and Fifty pounds thereof to be paid to the said Mary King and the rest and residue thereof to be paid unto the said Charles King. Item It is my Will that in case the said Charles King shall happen to die before he attains his age of One and Twenty then I doe give devise and bequeath the said Six hundred acres of land unto the said Mary King her heirs and Assigns forever. Item I give devise and bequeath unto Colo Thomas Broughton my Executor hereinafter named One hundred pounds currt money to buy him a ring. Item I give unto Mr Andrew Allen of Charleston Merchant Fifty pounds to buy him a ring. Item I give unto my Brothers and Sisters in law Collo James Moore and Elizabeth his wife and to Nathanl Ford & his wife a gold ring each. Item I give and bequeath unto Robert Hunt son of Robert Hunt deceased the sume of Fifty pounds to be paid him within six months after he is free from his Apprenticeship. Item I give unto my negro man Mathias One suit of black cloath and alsoe forty Shillings pr anm during his life to be paid him over and above his common allowance as a slave. Item I give devise and bequeath unto my Son John Berresford his heirs Executors Admrors and assigns forever all and singular my goods and chattels Lands Tenements and Hereditaments whatsoever in the said Province of South Carolina or elsewhere except what is hereinbefore or hereinafter devised when he shall attain unto the age of One and twenty years. Item It is my Will that my said son John Berresford have all due and liberal education maintenance and subsistence out of the yearly profits and produce of all my real and personal Estate hereinbefore mentioned to be devised to him according to the discretion of my Executrs hereinafter named untill he shall attain the age of One and twenty years. Item I give devise and bequeath unto Colo Thomas Broughton hereinafter appointed my Executor the sume of Ten Pounds per centum per anm for every One hundred pounds he shall make of the clear yearly profits and produce of my said Real and personal Estate hereinbefore devised to my said Son for his care and trouble in the management thereof untill my said son shall arrive to his said age of one and twenty. Item I doe give devise and bequeath unto my said Executor the said Collo Thomas Broughton out of the yearly profits and produce of my said Real & personal Estate for the first year after my decease the sume of Three hundred pounds and yearly and every year next ensuing, the sume of Two hundred pound untill my said Son shall arrive to his age of One and Twenty upon the special trusts and confidence hereinafter mentioned that is to say upon trust that he the said Thomas Broughton doe pay and apply the said sume of Three hundred pounds for the first year after my decease and alsoe the said sume of two hundred pounds yearly until my said son shall arrive to his age of One and twenty for and towards buildings improvements repairs clothing of negroes and all other necessary charges and expenses incident or belonging to my said Real and personal Estate or whatever he shall think needful or convenient for the improving thereof. Item I give devise and bequeath unto the said Collo Thomas Broughton his Ex'ors & Admors all the rest and residue of the yearly profits and produce of my said Real and personal Estate not hereinbefore devised until my said son shall attain to his age of One and twenty years upon the further special trust and confidence and for the several uses intents and purposes hereinafter menconed, that is to say upon trust that he the said Thomas Broughton doe yearly and every year pay the same into the hands of the Vestry for the time being of the Parish of St. Thomas in Berkley County to be disposed of by the said Vestry or the Major part of them in manner following that is to say One third part thereof to the Schoolmaster or Schoolmasters of the said Parish for the time being and the other two thirds of the said residue of the said Profits and produce of my said Real and personal Estate until my said son shall come of age for and towards the support maintenance tuition and Education of the Children of the poor of the said Parish as shall be there sent to School during the time aforesaid there to be taught and instructed in reading writing and casting accounts learning of the several languages Mathematics or other liberal learning and Education as the said Vestry shall direct and in case there shall be no Schoolmaster or Schoolmasters residing and teaching in the said Parish of St. Thomas I will that the said Vestry doe employ the said profits of my said Estate soe paid into their hands towards the building of a school or schools in the said Parish until a Schoolmaster or School Masters can or may conveniently be had or put the same out at interest for any the purposes aforesaid as they shall think best and most convenient. Item It is my Will that the said Vestry of the said Parish for the time being shall have the nominacon and choice of all or any such Schoolmaster or Schoolmasters and at pleasure the same to remove and displace if they shall see occasion. Item It is my Will that the said Thomas Broughton shall have a vote or voice with the Vestry if present as well in the nominacon of the said Schoolmaster or Schoolmasters, as alsoe in the disposicon of the residue of the profits of my Real and personal Estate herein before given to and for the use of [half a line in the original obliterated] Item My Will is that if my said Son shall happen to die before he attains his age of One and twenty years without any issue of his body lawfully begotten, then I do give devise and bequeath all my goods and chattels lands tenements and hereditaments whatsoever (hereinbefore mentioned to be given and bequeathed unto my said Son John) unto the said Collo Thomas Broughton his Heirs Executrs Adm'ors and Assigns forever upon this special Trust and confidence nevertheless and for the several uses intents and purposes following that is to say upon trust that the said Thomas Broughton doe sell and dispose thereof for the most money that can or may be had or gotten for the same and the monies thereby arising doe pay into the hands of the said Vestry of the Parish of St. Thomas for the time being to the intent that the same may be placed out at interest on good security all which said interest shall be rece'd by the said Vestry and be applied & disposed of as followeth, that is to say One third part thereof to be yearly paid to the Schoolmaster or Schoolmasters of the said Parish of St. Thomas for the time being to be nominated & chosen by the Major part of the said Vestry of the said Parish of St. Thomas for the time being as aforesaid and the other two thirds to be yearly paid and applyed towards the support maintenance education and tuition of the children of the poor of the said Parish as shall be there sent to school there to be taught and instructed in manner as aforesd. And Lastly I doe hereby nominate constitute and appoint the said Collo Thomas Broughton sole Executr of this my last Will. In Witness Whereof I have to this my last Will contained in two sheets of paper set my hand to the first sheet and my hand and seal to the last sheet thereof the   day of May in the first year of the reign of our Sovereign Lord George by the grace of God of Great Britain ffrance and Ireland King and Defender of the faith.—The original of this will is in Charleston. A copy is in the South Caroliniana Library of the University of South Carolina and another copy is in the University of North Carolina Library.

9. THE WILL OF THOMAS GRIMBALL, SOUTH CAROLINA, 1721

All possible Endeavours be used to give each of my Children a competent measure of learning and education, at least that they may be taught to read perfect English, write a legible hand fitt for public business or office, and Arithmetick through the rule of Fellowship.— *The South Carolina Historical and Genealogical Magazine,* XXIII (1922), 7.

10. THE WILL OF JAMES CHILD, SOUTH CAROLINA, 1718

In the Name of God Amen the thirteenth day of September in the Year of Our Lord one thousand Seven Hundred and Eighteen, I James Child of Childsbery Town on the Western Branch of Cooper River in the Parrish of St. Johns in the County of Berkly Yeoman being in sound mind and good Health in Body and Perfect memory thanks be given to God, therefore calling into mind the mortality of the Body, and knowing that itt is appointed for all once to dye, do make and ordain this my Last Will and Testamt: in manner and form following that is to say first and Principally, I give my Soul into the hands of Almighty God who gave itt me, and for my Body I commend to the Earth to be buried in a Christian and Decent manner, in the burial place laid out by me, nothing doubting butt at the genl resurrection I shall receive the same again by the Mighty Power of God, and as touching such Worldly Estate, wherewth God hath been pleased to bless me wth in this Life, I give demise bequeath, all that square of Land upon Norwesternly of the Fferry Street containing five Chains Square wth two acres and a halfe of Land Butting on the River Bay, and also the Marsh, two Chains an

a halfe between the Bay & the River, as itt appears in the Town Platt
to my Trustees hereafter named, in trust to them and their Survivers,
forever to be sett out by them for a Colledge or University, when any
Pious and Charritable Parson, or People think itt fitting for that use
and putt to no other use one penalty of one hundred pounds of
Sterling English money to the Owners of Childsberry Town & my
son Isaac Child and his Heirs to enjoy and to have & to hold the
proffits of the aforesaid Gift untill itt be builded for the aforesaid use.
Item I give and bequeath to my son Isaac Child, two Lotts of Land
next to Ferry Street containing halfe an Acre, each Lott five Chains
Long, and one Chain apiece each lott over for the bredth which is one
Acre, butting on the River Bay together with the River Marsh, between the Bay and the River. Item. I give and Bequeath one acre and
a halfe of Land, for to build a Church or Chapple upon itt & for
a Buring Place, for the Inhabitants of Childsbery Town, and all wth
in the Western and Eastern Branch of Cooper River as itt is bounded
out wth Locas Trees and a Ceader fence butt the Timber Trees
growing or may hereafter grow in the Church Yard and also the
harbage & grass & pasture I give to my son Isaac Child and his Heirs
forever wth a proviso & uppon condition he keep the Church Yard
weeded & cleane & smooth from hoggs diggins upon penalty of Forfeiting all the Timber & Trees harbage & grass to my Trustees and
them to dispose of itt to whom they shall think fitting, Item I give &
bequeath nine Chains of Land a square in the middle of the Town as
itt appears in the Town Plat for a markett place Item I give and bequeath on lott of Land numbred wth the figure sixteen 16 to my
Trustees and the survivors of them forever to build a free School
uppon itt wth a house for the teacher schoolmaster, and my Trustees
to putt in a Learned Schoolmaster to keep a Gramer School to Teach
the Latin Tongue to Boys & Children, untill they are fitt for a
University wth Learning, & to teach English to Children & to Learn
them to Write and keep accts by Arithmetick the children of all the
Inhabitants of Western and eastern Branches of Cooper River, that
was contributers to the Ferry & causway, allways Provided the
Parents send fire Wood for their Children in Winter time, or else
pay two Shillings & Sixpence of Currte Carolina money a year to the
Schoolmaster, Item I give and bequeath unto my Trustees, One hun-
dred Pounds & all ye Rents of Luckins Plantation, wherein I now
Dwell for the term of three Year's commencing from the Twenty of
September last past the date above said to build a House upon the

School Lott and five hundred Pounds more wCH is secured for a sallary for the schoolmaster, the interest of itt to be paid every six months or half yearly, by my Trustees or them they shall appoint in Currte Carolina money. Item I give & bequeath to the Inhabitants of Childsberry Town the commoning or Pasture of Six Hundred Acres of Land situated and Bounding Northwesterly on the Strawberry Land, Northwesternly on the Halfe way Swamp Southeasternly on the Lands of Mr Anthony Boneaus Southwesternly on the Lands of Capn Elias Ball for the commoning of Two Cows, two to a Lott & no more wth Power to chuse & elect a Heyward, & this shall be their stint to them & their Heirs for ever, and if any one exceeds that number more them two cows to a Lott, the hayward shall have power by Vertue of this will to impound them & the owner or owners, shall pay five Shillings a head to the Heyward, and he shall have itt for their Perquesites, Item I give and bequeath that Hill by the Tan House and the River Bay containing one acre of Land to build & make upon itt in time of War for the defense & Security of the Town a strong fort or Cittadell upon itt, itt being halfe made naturally all these gifts and Bequests (that is to say) the Colledge Land the School Land & three Years Rent of Luckins Plantation the Church Yard, the Markett Place & forte together wth the moneys I give in trust to my Trustees & the survivers of them for forever to be imployed for the uses before mentioned in this Will, Item I give & bequeath to my grandson Robert Dixs, all that Plantations wch was part of the Strawberry now now called now called Luckins Farm, bounding Southeasternly on the Land of Elias Ball containing together wth the Ceader Swamp to five hundred Acres of Land and also the Tan House wth ye Land belonging to the & all that angle of Land between Blakwell Street & high middle Street called Craven Street sictuat between Porters Bay and the River as doth appear in the Town Platt wth all the appurtenances thereunto belonging, when he attain to the age of One & Twenty Years to him & his Heirs Lawfully begotten of his Body, and in case he dye before he comes to age or dyes wth out Issue male, also then I give & bequeath the aforesaid Plantation, Tan House & Lands with all the pEmises thereunto belonging to my grand son William Child son To Isaac Child to him & his Heirs Lawfully begotten of his Body forever, Item I give & bequeath to my grand son Robert Dixs the pine timber & Lightwood or Tar Wood of the six hundred acres of Land wch I have given for common of Pasture to the Town of Childsberry when he attains to the age of One

& Twenty Years to him & his Heirs Lawfully begotten of his body forever, nott exceeding for cutting & makeing of Tarr wood or pine fifty yearly and no more, upon penalty of One Hundred Pounds for future, to the next heir entail, or else this gift to be Void an of no effect & case he dyes before age, or wth out issue male then I give & bequeath to my grand son William Child all the aforesaid Premises to him & his Heirs Lawfully begotten of his Body for ever Item I give & bequeath to my grand Daughter Sara Child one One Hundred acres of Land in Cravin County situate & bounding Southeasternly one William Ball's Cowpen to she and her Heirs forever, Item I give & bequeath to my grand son Robert Dixs, the eldest of my Mare Colts & to my grand son William Child the next eldest of my mare Colts, Item, I give & bequeath to my grand son Isaac Child, one hundred acres of Land in Craven County situate and bounding northeasternly one Mr Normans southwesternly on Andrew Forguson Land to him and his Heirs forever, Item I give & bequeath to my grand son Isaac Child one Island in Craven County, containing one hundred Acres situate in Winyaw Bay against Mr Whitioms Plantation & to him and his Heirs forever and also all my mares & Colts wch I have in the Wood that can be found to him & his heirs for ever, Item I give & bequeath to my son Isaac Child six hundred and fourty Acres of Land, situated & bounding northwesternly thirty degree line marked wth old & new trees one mebkin northeasterly on Mr William Waties land & Mr Elias Balls Land Southwesternly on the Strawberry Land Southeasternly one the Comon Land & Halfeway Swampe, all the pine & Lightwood or Tarr Wood & all sorts of Wood for sixteen Years wth a provisor and a consideration of the sum of three Hundred Pounds, for the lightwood wch was due one Year agoe, and nott paid, whereas now if my son Isaac Child payes lawfull Interest for this three Hundred & Ten pounds commencing from the twenty-ninth of Septembr last past the date above said to his Father James Child dureing his life or sooner if he demands itt, and att his decease if nott paid, then payable to his Trustees for the use of the School & if then paid, I give & bequeath to my Grandson William Child to him & his Heirs Lawfully begotten of his Body forever, also in case the aforesaid Moneys, after my decease be not paid to my Trustees wth in three months, Item then I give & bequeath the aforesaid six hundred and forty Acres of Land to my Trustees & the survivers of them for ever in in trust to be employed for the use of the Schools and a Sallary forever, Item I give & bequeath to my son Isaac Child, forty five Lotts

Numbred from 51 to 95: as doth & may appear in the Town Platt to him and his Heirs forever wth a provisor & upon condition he pays to my grand Daughter Hana Dixs One hundred Pounds, when she attains the age of one & Twenty Years & if not then paid or she happen to dye under age, I give itt to my son Isaac, butt if she attains they age Twenty one Years, I give the aforesaid Lotts to the aforesaid Hana Dixs & her heirs for Ever, my Will and meaning is the Hundred to be made Sterling English money, Item I give & bequeath to Maj^r Andrew Foster five Pounds of Curr^{te} Carolina Money, towards building a store House upon the River Lott upon lease according to his Covenants and also my Will & meaning is that my Executors I give them power to Lett or lett by Lease the Land between Porter Bay & the River for storehouses nott to exceed Forty Foot wide by the River Fronting & Sixty foot in Length Backwards from the River and also Power to Lett or Sell all those Front Lotts of halfe Acres on the Bay that are to be sold or be forfeited or Demand for not building upon them, according to their covenant & also to Lett or set any back Lotts if my son Isaac doth nott except my gift of them, nor give security for payment of them that are nott sold & to make the buyers deeds and conveyances und^r their Hands & Seals according to the tenor & form of other Lotts granted und^r my hand & Seal & also to take an account of the forty five Lotts of Hana Dixs by themselves for her use and the other back Lotts for the use of her Brother Robert Dixs to render to them when they attain their ages of one & Twenty Years & also to take an acc^t of what Pitch and Tarr is made Yearly out of the Lease Land Lett to John Benoitt five Years yett to come before itt is expired or out, and also power to Lett, sell or to Farm let Luckins Plantation wherein I now Dwell excepting all sorts of Wood butt Pine yett granting Liberty to fell Oak at peeling time only uppon the Land which is fenced & Cleared of all the wood for two plant with corn for the use of Bark for Tanning to sell itt for money & account for itt & for what Rents the tan make of the farm or Plantation & whereas there is three Years yett to come When John Benoiet Lease is expired of the Tarrwood of the Common of Pasture of the six Hundred acres of Land, the tarrwood, given to my grand son Robert Dixs and to Render an account what pitch or tar is or shall be made upon dureing the three Years att fower shillings a Barr^l for Pitch & Two shillings a Barr^l for Tarr, and also to putt out my grandson Robert dixs after his three Years Schooling, to a Trade wch he shall like Best & my Execut^{rs} approve of itt, Item I give & Bequeath all my Books & survaying instruments to—of my son Isaac Childs sons to one of them wᶜʰ shall or can attain to be a Latin Scholar if no son of his doth nott attain to the Lattin Tongue, then I give & bequeath them to begin a Libreary in the School House, It: I give & bequeath to my Grand   my little Cabinett It: I give & bequeath to my grand son Robert Dixs all my Bedding wᵗʰ Curtains &   & all my waring apparel, Item I give & bequeath to my Daughter Sara Child all the Yearly Rent of my House & Lands in old England at Coleshill in the Parrish of   in the County of of Hertford wᶜʰ is due from the time & the date of the last accounts made upp by my son James Child the Twenteh day of March: 1712 untill the day of my Decease & also when my Grandson Robert Dixs comes to Twenty one Years of Age, to render & give an acct to my Trustees will be in Bank when Robert Dixs his on shaire deducted for is made off upon his one—Estate and Premises for what moneys then will be in Bank I give & bequeath one moyety to my Grandson Robert Dixs & the other moyety or halfe part to my Trustees for the use of the School. Item I make & ordain my Well beloved & Trusty Friends for the managᵐᵗ of the Colledge & School & of other & all the Premises wᵗʰ the moneys thereto belonging & if charritable Christians were wll wishers to Learning & would sett a helping to itt we might have our Youth Some of them fited for Church & Statesmen as well as other Countrys, itt would be an Honour to our Country & promote the Honˡ Coll: Thomˢ Broughton & Coll: George Chickens: Richard Berrisford Esqʳ Purcevall Pawley, Majʳ & Surveyer & Majʳ Andrew—Foster Merchant, Capᵗ John Harleston, Lieutᵗ Anthony Boneau also I do nominate & appoint my Loveing & Trust Friends Purceval Pawley, Andrew ffoster, and my son Isaac Child to be my Executors of this Last will and Testament and for their care and pains I give allow them ten Pounds apeace for each of them Currᵗ Carolina Money one year after my Decease, & Lastly I do by this my Last Will & Testament renounce frustrate & make Void, all Wills by me formerly made & do declare this to be my Will and Testament In Witness hereunto I have sett my hand seale the twenty ninth of October in the Year of Our Lord one Thousand and Seven Hundred & Eighteen and in the fift year of the Reigne of our Sovereign Lorg King George King of Great Britain, France & Ireland, Defender of the Faith, Etc Ano. Do: 1718.—The original of this will is in Charleston. Typescript copy is in the South Caroliniana Library of the University of South Carolina and photocopy of that copy is in the University of North Carolina Library.

11. THE WILL OF JOHN BAPTISTE ASHE, NORTH CAROLINA, 1731

Item. I will that my Slaves be kept to work on my lands, and that my Estate may be managed to the best advantage, so as my sons may have as liberal an Education as the profits thereof will afford; and in their Education I pray my Exers. to observe this method; Let them be taught to read and write, and be introduced into the practical part of Arithmetick, not too hastily hurrying them to Latin or Grammar, but after they are pretty well versed in these let them be taught Latin & Greek. I propose this may be done in Virginia; After which let them learn French, perhaps Some French man at Santee wile undertake this; when they are arrived to years of discretion Let them Study the Mathematicks. To my Sons when they arrive at age I recommend the pursuit & Study of Some profession or business (I could wish one to ye Law, the other to Merchandize), in which Let them follow their own inclinations.

Item. I will that my daughter be taught to write and read & some femanine accomplishments which may render her agreable; And that she be not kept ignorant as to what appertains to a good house wife in the management of household affairs.—Grimes, *op. cit.*, pp. 16-17.

12. THE WILL OF JOHN YEATES, VIRGINIA, 1731

Item.—I give and bequeath all my land or lands in Virginia, and all the rents and profits of the same to the following use and uses: The rents thereof, now by lease or otherwise, may be converted hereafter to the use of a free school or schools, in the lower parish of Nansemond, formerly so-called, being the parish I have so long lived in, among such friendly neighbors; and that there may be two schoolhouses continued in the same places already fixed, which I have built, so that one school-house will be very convenient for the children of the one side of Bennett's Creek, and the other on the other side thereof, which will complete that part of the parish, as formerly I have done; and by that means, with God's blessing, the most or all of the children in these parts will be educated from the Gleabe down to the extent of that part of the parish lying on the south side of Nansemond river, which formerly was called the Lower Parish of Nansemond.

Item.—It is my will and desire that none of the tenants lie in debt for rent; for that will be a means to ruin the tenants and the schoolmaster also; but that the yearly rent be yearly paid in something or other to the value, to and for the schoolmaster's use or order. . .

Item.—What books I have or shall give for the use of the school or schools may lie in the desk in the school-house, under lock and key, in each school-house as I have provided, that when children have read those books they may be there ready for other children also. —*Virginia School Reports, 1884-85*, Pt. III, pp. 230-31. Taken from that part of the volume entitled "School History of Nansemond County," by V. S. Kilby, Superintendent of Nansemond County Schools, 1885. It appears that Yeates had established two schools in Nansemond County prior to 1731 and had supplied them with books. Under his will in that year the property which he left and the schools for which he provided were placed in the hands of the vestrymen of the church to which he belonged; and in 1803 the General Assembly of Virginia passed legislation which created and incorporated a board of trustees of twelve free-holders to hold the property and manage the schools.

13. Act for erecting school at Childsbury, June 9, 1733

WHEREAS, nothing conduces more to the private advantage of every man, or the public benefit of a country in general, than a liberal education, and the same cannot be had without due encouragement to persons qualified to instruct youth; and Mr. James Child, late of this Province, deceased, desiring as far as lay in his power to promote the same, did in and by his last will and testament, give and bequeath the sum of five hundred pounds current money of Carolina, towards the encouragement of a grammar school and other learning at Childsbury in St. John's parish in Berkley county; and also did further give, devise and bequeath the sum of one hundred pounds like money, and a lot to build a convenient house for the said school, and left the same to certain trustees in his said will named, to manage the same according to the directions of his will; and the said sums being far too short for the said purposes, several gentlemen, well weighing the great want of necessary learning in this Province, and being desirous to encourage so good an undertaking, (according to their several abilities,) have by voluntary subscriptions raised the sum of two thousand two hundred pounds like current money, to be added to the legacy of the said James Child, and have also chosen trustees to be joined with those named in the said Mr. James Child's will, to manage the said sums for the use of the said school, and as visitors to order, direct and govern the said school; we therefore humbly pray your most sacred Majesty that it may be enacted,

I. *And be it enacted*, by his Excellency Robert Johnson, Esq. Governour, by and with the advice and consent of his Majesty's honourable Council and the Commons House of Assembly of this Province, and by the authority of the same, That the said several sums given and bequeathed in and by the last will and testament of the said James Child, for the use of the said school, and the several sums raised by subscription for the same use, be for the future united and declared to be one individual fund for the purpose aforesaid, and that the same shall not be applyed or diverted to any other use or uses whatsoever.

II. *And be it further enacted* by the authority aforesaid, That the honourable Thomas Broughton, Esq. Lieutenant Governour, the Reverend Mr. Thomas Hassell, Anthony Bonneau, John Harleston, Nathaniel Broughton, Thomas Cordes and Francis Lejau, Esquires, shall be trustees for the said school, and that they shall have full power and authority to manage the several legacys and subscriptions already given and made, and which shall from time to time hereafter be made, devised or given for the use of the said school, according to their discretion.

III. *And be it further enacted* by the authority aforesaid, That they, or the majority of them, shall have full power and authority to elect a master or masters, usher or ushers, and appropriate such a sum or sums for a salary or salarys out of the income of the said fund, as they shall think proper; and also the said master or masters, usher or ushers, to turn out, and others to elect; and to make such rules for the better ordering and governing the said school, as they or a majority of them shall in their discretion think necessary.

IV. *And be it further enacted* by the authority aforesaid, That the trustees are hereby impowered to receive from time to time, such sum or sums of money, houses, lands, tenements, or any other gifts or legacys, as any well disposed persons shall think fit to give or bequeath unto them for the use of the said school, and to build such house or houses as they shall think necessary and convenient.

V. *And be it further enacted* by the authority aforesaid, That no person shall be a trustee, except he hath subscribed an hundred pounds, and no person shall have a vote in electing trustees, except he hath subscribed fifty pounds for the use of the said school; and that after the death of any of the subscribers, their heirs or assigns by them appointed, shall have the same privileges as the subscribers themselves had, of right ought to have.

VI. *And be it further enacted* by the authority aforesaid, That upon the death or resignation of any of the trustees, the survivors of them shall give notice to the subscribers, or to the heirs or assigns of such of the subscribers as shall be dead, within three months to meet at Childsbury, at a certain day, to elect another trustee in the place of the person deceased.

VII. *And be it further enacted* by the authority aforesaid, That the trustees or the majority of them, be obliged to meet at Childsbury once in three months at least, to consider of all things for the benefit of the said school, and that if any of them omit meeting for the space of one whole year, without a reasonable excuse, to be approved of by the rest of the trustees or the majority of them, that then it shall be lawful for them to declare his place to be vacant; and in such case they shall give notice to the subscribers to meet and elect another trustee in his room, as in case of death or resignation; and if the trustees shall neglect or refuse to summon the subscribers to meet within the time aforesaid to elect a trustee or trustees, that then the subscribers may meet and elect a trustee or trustees of their own accord, and the said person or persons so elected, shall be deemed to be a trustee or trustees, and have the same power and authority to act jointly with the others as those named in this Act.

VIII. And whereas, Francis Williams, late of Berkley county, deceased, did in and by his last will and testament impower his executors to dispose of such sums as were remaining of his estate, to such charitable uses as they thought fit: his said executors have given the sum of two hundred pounds to the said school, *Be it enacted* by the authority aforesaid, That the interest of the said sum be appropriated to the teaching so many poor scholars as the trustees shall think proper.

IX. *And be it further enacted* by the authority aforesaid, That if any charitable person or persons, shall hereafter subscribe any sum or sums of money to the said school, or give the same by will, he or they so subscribing or giving (or their assigns by them appointed,) shall have the same privileges as those who have already subscribed, subject, nevertheless, to the exceptions in this Act mentioned.

X. *And be it further enacted* by the authority aforesaid, That the trustees above mentioned and their successors, are hereby impowered to lend the said moneys out at interest, and to take bonds or notes, or any other instruments of writing, and to purchase lands and let them out by the year or lease them for a term of years; and the said bonds, notes and other instruments of writing, shall be in the name of themselves and their successors, for the use of the said school; and they are hereby impowered to demand and sue for any rents, legacys, notes, bonds or any other moneys that are or shall hereafter become due unto them, and to take possession of any houses, lands or tenements which shall be given or bequeathed to them for the use of the said school.—Cooper, *The Statutes at Large of South Carolina*, III, 364-66.

14. ACT CONCERNING THE WILL OF RICHARD BERESFORD, 1736

WHEREAS, Richard Beresford, (late of the Province of South Carolina,) Esq. deceased, sometime in or about the month of May, in the year of our Lord one thousand seven hundred and fifteen, duly made and published his last will and testament in writing, and therein and thereby (amongst other things) did give, devise and bequeath unto his son John Beresford, his heirs, executors, administrators and assigns forever, all and singular his the said Richard Beresford's goods and chattels, lands, tenements and hereditaments whatsoever, in the said Province of South Carolina, or elsewhere (except what was therein before and thereinafter devised) when he the said John Beresford should attain unto the age of one-and-twenty years; and the said Richard Beresford therein and thereby declared, that his will was that his said son John Beresford, should have all due and liberal education, maintenance and subsistance out of the yearly profits and produce of all his real and personal estate therein before mentioned to be devised to his said son, according to the direction of his executor thereinafter named, until his said son should attain the age of one-and-twenty years; and the said testator did further give, devise and bequeath unto the honourable Colonel Thomas Broughton, thereinafter appointed his executor, the sum of ten pounds per centum per annum, for every one hundred pounds he should make of the clear yearly profits and produce of the real and personal estate devised to his said son, for the said Colonel Broughton's care and management thereof, until his the said testator's son should arrive to the age of one-and-twenty; and the said testator did, by his said will, further give, devise and bequeath unto the said Colonel Thomas Broughton, his executors and administrators, all the rest, residue and remainder of the yearly profits and produce of his said real and personal estate not therein before devised, until his said son should attain to his age of one-and-twenty years, upon special trust and confidence, and for the several uses, intents and purposes hereinafter mentioned, that is to say, upon trust that he the said Colonel Thomas Broughton, should yearly and every year, pay the same into the hands of the vestry, for the time being, of the parish of St. Thomas, in Berkley county, to be disposed of by the said vestry, or the major part of them, in manner following, that is to say, one third part thereof to the school master or school masters of the said parish, for the time being, and the other two thirds of the said residue of the said profits and produce of his said real and personal estate, until his said son should come of age, for and towards the support, maintenance, tuition and education of the children of the poor of the said parish, as shall be there sent to school during the time aforesaid, to be taught and instructed in reading, writing and casting accounts, learning of the several languages, mathematicks or other liberal learning and education, as the said vestry shall direct; and in case there should be no school master or school masters residing and teaching in the said parish of St. Thomas, the said Richard Beresford's will was, that the said vestry should employ the said profits of the said estate so to be paid into their hands, towards the building of a school or schools in the said parish, until a school master or school masters can or may conveniently be had, or put the same out at interest for any the purposes aforesaid, as they shall think best and most convenient; and his will further was, that the said vestry of the said parish, for the time being, should have the nomination or choice of all or any such school master or school masters, and at pleasure the same to remove and displace, if they shall see occasion. And whereas, Colonel Thomas Broughton, the executor in the said will named, proved the said will, and took upon himself the burthen of the execution thereof, together with the several trusts and confidences in him by the said will reposed, and hath paid all the testator's just debts, and also divers large sums of money which did arise from the profits and income of the testator's estate during the minority of the aforesaid John Beresford, the son, into the hands of several of the vestry of the said parish of St. Thomas, for the time being. And whereas, the said John Beresford, the son, is now arrived to his age of one-and twenty years, and the several trusts by the said will reposed in the said Colonel Thomas Broughton, are now ceased and determined. And whereas, it is highly reasonable and just that the charitable and pious intentions of the testator should be effectually put in execution, and that the moneys arising by the said legacy or donation, should be carefully continued and applyed to and for the several uses, intents and purposes in the aforesaid last will and testament directed and appointed, we therefore most humbly pray your most sacred majesty that it may be enacted,

I. *And be it enacted*, by his Honor Thomas Broughton, Esquire, your Majesty's Lieutenant Governor and Commander-in-chief, in and over your Majesty's Province of South Carolina, by and with the advice and consent of your Majesty's honourable Council and the Commons House of Assembly of the said Province, and by the authority of the same, That all and every the person and persons who shall be from and after the twentieth day of June, which shall be in the year of our Lord one thousand seven hundred and thirty-six, annually chosen and elected to serve as vestry men for the said parish for the time being, shall be, and they are hereby declared to be one body corporate and politick, in deed and in name, by the name of the vestry of the parish of St. Thomas, in Berkley county, and by the same name the said vestry so to be chosen and elected as aforesaid, shall from time to time and at all times hereafter, have perpetual succession, and a common seal, with full power and authority to change, alter, break and make new the same, when and as often as they shall see expedient; and that the said vestry, for the time being, so to be chosen as aforesaid, and their successors, the vestry of the said parish, for the time being, shall be and they are hereby declared, able and capable in law, to have, hold, receive, enjoy, possess and retain to them and their successors, the vestry of the said parish, for the time being, all such estate, real or personal, money, goods, chattels or effects, as by the said Richard Beresford were bequeathed or devised to and for the charitable uses and intents in the aforesaid will mentioned, or which have been purchased for the use or benefit of the said donation, and all securitys for the same; and by the same name shall sue and be sued, implead and be impleaded, answer and be answered, in any Court or Courts within this Province.

II. *And be it further enacted* by the authority aforesaid, That after an account shall be taken by the said vestry of the lands, moneys, and effects of and belonging to the said donation, the same shall be deemed and taken as the capital stock of the said vestry for the purposes aforesaid, and shall be kept or placed out at interest, and the future interest and produce thereof, shall hereafter be applyed towards building or repairing a school or schools, and paying a school

master or school masters, and for and towards the support, maintenance, tuition and education of the children of the poor of the said
parish of St. Thomas, as shall be thereafter sent to school, in such
manner and according to the rules of proportion mentioned and
directed in and by the said testator's last will.

III. And whereas, the said vestry will have paid into their hands a
very large sum of money, arising or to arise by virtue of the said
last will and testament of the said Richard Beresford, deceased, by
reason whereof the trust reposed in the faithfulness, integrity and
abilitys of the members of the said vestry, ought to have more than
ordinary security, *Be it therefore enacted* by the authority aforesaid,
That no person or persons whatsoever (the rector of the said parish
for the time being excepted) shall be elected, deemed or taken as a
member or members of the said vestry, or have a right to vote as such,
until he or they shall have taken and subscribed the following oath,
(any law, usage or custom to the contrary, in any wise notwithstanding) to wit, "I, AB, do solemnly and sincerely acknowledge
and swear, that I do not owe or am indebted to the vestry of the
parish of St. Thomas, in Berkley county, on account of the donation
of Richard Beresford, Esq. deceased, any sum or sums of money
whatsoever, and I do solemnly promise that I will not, during the
time of my being a vestry man, apply for, or take up at interest, any
sum or sums of money of or from the said vestry; and that I will
well and faithfully execute the office of a vestry man of the parish of
St. Thomas, and to the utmost of my power, observe and follow the
directions of the Act of the General Assembly, made for incorporating the said vestry and for other purposes in the said Act mentioned,
so help me God." Which oath shall be administered by some justice
assigned to keep the peace in and for Berkley county, and by him
certified to the said vestry.

IV. *And be it further enacted* by the authority aforesaid, That the
members of the said vestry being duly qualified, shall and may meet
and assemble together, in the vestry room of and belonging to the
said parish of St. Thomas, four times in every year, that is to say, on
the second Tuesday after Easter day, the first Tuesday in June, the
first Tuesday in September, and the first Tuesday in December, or
oftener if the affairs of the said vestry shall require, upon seven days
notice to be given and published in the parish church of the said
parish of St. Thomas; and that all and every the matters and things
that shall be moved, stirred, debated or done, in or by the said vestry,

shall be done, transacted, ordered and determined by the consent, advice and approbation of the greater part of the members of the said vestry that shall be present and together at the time of their assemblys or meetings; provided always, that nothing shall be done or transacted in relation to any matter or thing in this Act mentioned, at or upon any other day or time, than the days or times before limited for such assembly or meeting, and unless there shall be at least five members of the said vestry duly qualified, present and together at such assemblys or meetings; any thing in this Act contained, to the contrary thereof in any wise notwithstanding.

V. *And be it further enacted* by the authority aforesaid, That it shall not be lawful for the said vestry to purchase for the use of the said charity, any lands, servants or slaves, or to alien, sell or exchange any of the lands, tenements or hereditaments already belonging to, or purchased for the benefit of the said charity, any law, usage or custom, to the contrary thereof in any wise notwithstanding.

VI. *And be it further enacted* by the authority aforesaid, That the said vestry and their successors, shall not lend to any one person more than the sum of one thousand pounds currency of the money of or belonging to the said charity or donation, nor any sum of the said money whatsoever to any member or members of the said vestry for the time being, nor accept or take any mortgage or mortgages, bond or bonds or other securities, for any such moneys, unless the principal sum or sums so to be lent, together with the lawful interest thereof, be by the provisoes, conditions or defeazances of such mortgages, bonds or other securitys, made payable at or before the end of one year from the date thereof, upon pain of forfeiting for each offence treble the value of the money so lent, one half to the informer, and the other to the poor of the said parish of St. Thomas, to be recovered against the members assenting to such loan or loans, by action of debt, bill, plaint or information, in any of his Majesty's Courts of record within this Province, wherein no protection, wager of law, or more than one imparlance, shall be allowed.

VII. *And be it further enacted* by the authority aforesaid, That the said vestry or any five of them, shall and may, once in every year, to wit, on the second Tuesday after Easter day, elect and choose a Treasurer, and the said Treasurer to be chosen, shall continue in the said office for one year and no longer, unless rechosen, and shall keep and render to the said vestry, as often as he shall be thereto required, a true, just and exact account of all the receipts, payments, disbursements, and all other dealings and transactions of the said vestry, in and about the execution of the trust in them reposed, and shall at the end of every year, close, balance and settle the accounts of the said vestry, and shall yield up and deliver to the said vestry, all moneys, securitys and effects whatsoever, which he shall have received, taken or been in possession of, for the use of the said vestry, during his continuance in the said office; and upon the Treasurer's settling and balancing, fully discharging and paying off and delivering all such moneys, securitys and effects, as shall be due and owing to the said vestry, shall give the said Treasurer sufficient and legal discharges under their common seal.

VIII. *And be it further enacted* by the authority aforesaid, That duplicates of the said Treasurer's accounts, together with an authentick copy of the proceedings of the said vestry, shall once at least in every year, forever hereafter, be by the said vestry transmitted to or laid before the Court of Chancery, holden in this Province, which Court shall, and they are hereby authorised and impowered, forever hereafter, to visit the said vestry, and to inspect and inquire into their accounts, and of the gifts, limitations and appointments made in and by the will of the said Richard Beresford, and of the abuses, breaches of trusts, negligences, misemployments, not employing, concealing, defrauding, misconverting or misgovernment of any lands, tenements, rents, profits, hereditaments, goods, chattels, money or stocks of money, at any time heretofore given and belonging to the said charity, or which shall hereafter belong to the same, and to correct, reform and redress all such abuses aforesaid.

IX. *And be it further enacted* by the authority aforesaid, That all such estates, real and personal, rights of action or entry, and other rights, titles, trusts, powers and authorities, claims and demands whatsoever, devised or given to or vested in the aforesaid Colonel Thomas Broughton, or any other person or persons whatsoever, by virtue of the said last will and testament of the said Richard Beresford, to and for the charitable uses, intents and purposes in the said will mentioned, specified and declared; and also all the issues, produce and profits of the estate, real and personal, of the said Richard Beresford, which arose or accrued after the testator's decease and during the minority of the said John Beresford; and also all the estates, real or personal, goods, chattels or effects which have been purchased or bought by the produce of the said estate; and also all and every sum and sums of money, bonds, specialties, mortgages and other securities that have been entered into or taken for securing the payment of any sum or sums of money, in whose names soever they have been taken, or in whose hands soever the same are, do or shall remain; and all other rights of action or entry, estates, titles, trusts, claims and demands whatsoever, which have accrued since the death of the said Richard Beresford, by reason of the trusts aforesaid, are and shall be by virtue of this Act fully and absolutely vested and settled in the said Vestry forever, for such pious and charitable uses as are hereby and by the said last will and testament of the said Richard Beresford directed and appointed, subject always and liable, nevertheless, to all such just rights, claims and demands whatsoever, either in law or equity, which the aforesaid Colonel Thomas Broughton, or the aforesaid John Beresford, or either of them, or their or either of their heirs, executors or administrators, or any of them, now have or hereafter may have or claim of, in, or out of the proceeds or produce of the estate, real or personal, of the said Richard Beresford deceased, so vested as aforesaid by this Act in the said Vestry; excepting always, all such part of the profits and produce of the said testator's real and personal estate as have been expended in the discharge of the debts, legacies and funeral expenses of the testator, or in the defraying of the necessary charges and expenses laid out and expended in providing necessaries and managing and taking care of the testator's estate, real and personal; and all such sums of money as have been duly and necessarily laid out and expended in and about the execution and management of the trusts aforesaid; and subject nevertheless to the payment of all such debts, legacies and other sums of money, in such manner as by the aforesaid last will and testament they are given, bequeathed or appointed, in case it shall happen that any such debts, legacies or sums of money shall remain due, unpaid, and not satisfied.

X. *And be it further enacted* by the authority aforesaid, That the school master, usher and clerk, shall be elected, chosen and appointed, and removed, put out and displaced, by the said Vestry, or the major part of them.

XI. *And be it further enacted* by the authority aforesaid, That the said Vestry shall be and they are hereby declared able and capable in law to have, hold, receive, enjoy, possess and retain to them all such other estates, real and personal, money, goods, chattels and effects, as have already been devised or bequeathed, or hereafter shall be devised or bequeathed to charitable uses, within the said Parish of St.

Thomas, subject nevertheless to the will, directions or appointment of the donor or donors.

XII. *And be it further enacted* by the authority aforesaid, That this Act shall be deemed and taken as a public Act, and notice shall be taken thereof in all courts of justice and elsewhere in this Province, and shall be given in evidence on the trial of any issue or cause, without special pleading; saving to his Majesty, his heirs and successors, and to all persons, bodies politick and corporate, and their heirs, successors, executors or administrators, (except the executors and administrators of the aforesaid Richard Beresford, or such and such persons who have been vestrymen of the Parish of St. Thomas, as trustees or devisees under the aforesaid will,) all such right, title, estate, interest, power of redemption, claim or demand, in law or equity, as any of them have or shall have, of, in, to or out of the premises, as if this Act had never been made. (May 29, 1736.)—*Ibid.*, pp. 431-36.

15. The Will of Lewis Jones, South Carolina, 1743

Item I give and Bequeath the Sum of One hundred pounds Sterling for the Support of a School at Beaufort to be put out at interest for the said use, which Intrest shall be for the payment of a School master for Instructing and Teaching as many Poor Children as the intrest of the said Sum will allow of. Item I will also that when the Children to be taught by this Charity can read well in the Bible and are thoroughly instructed in the principles of the Christian Faith According to the Church of England and are taught to write a fair hand and Cast Accounts the Minister and Vestry & Church Wardens for the time being (whom I do hereby appoint as Trustees of this Legacey) shall from time to time Recommend Such Poor Children whose parents are not Capable to pay for their Schooling & above all others I will that such poor Children be preferred, who are Orphans, and are left poor and Destitute....—The original of this will is in Charleston. Copy is in the South Caroliniana Library of the University of South Carolina, and another copy is in the University of North Carolina Library.

16. The will of James Winright, North Carolina, 1744

Item, I Will and Appoint that the Yearly Rents & Profitts of all The Town land and Houses in Beaufort Town, Belonging unto me, with the other Land Adjoining thereto (Which I purchased of John Pindar), after the Decease of my wife Ann, to be Applyed to the

Uses hereinafter Mentioned for Ever, (to Wit) for the encouragement of a Sober, discreet, Quallifyed Man to teach a School at Least Reading, Writing, Vulgar & Decimal Arithmetick, in the aforesd. Town of Beaufort, wch. said Man Shall be Choosen and Appointed by the Chair Man (& the Next in Commission) of Carteret County Court, and one of the Church Wardens of St. John parish in the aforesd. County and Their Successors for Ever. Also, I Give and Bequeath the Summ of Fifty pounds Sterling (provided that my estate Shall be Worth so much after my Just Debts and other Legacys are paid and Discharged) to be Applyed for the Building and finishing of a Creditable House for a school & Dwelling house for the said Master to be Erected and Built on Some part of my Land Near the White house Which I bought of the aforesaid Pindar, and my True Intent and Meaning is, that all the Yearly profitts & advantages Arising by the aforesd. Town Lotts and Lands thereunto adjoining as aforesd., with the Use of the sd. Land for Making & Improving a plantation for the planting & Raising of Corn &c. (if the aforesd. Master or teacher of sd. School shall think proper to plant & Improve the Same) be entirely for the use & Benefitt of ye sd. Master and his Successors During his and their Good Behavior. Also, that the sd. Master shall not be obliged to teach or take under his Care any Scholar or Scholars Imposed on him by the Trustees herein Mentioned, or their Successors, or by any other person, But shall have free Liberty to teach & take under his Care, Such, and so many Scholars, as he shall think Convenient and to Receive his Reward for the Teaching of them as he and the persons tendering them Shall agree.—Grimes, *op. cit.*, pp. 456-57.

17. THE WILL OF EDWARD MOSELEY, NORTH CAROLINA, 1745

When it shall be necessary to give all or any of my sons Other Education than is to be had from the Common Masters in this Province; for I would have my Children well Educated, it is then my Will that Such expence be Defrayed Out of the profits of Such Childs Estate & not Otherwise.

Item, I Recommend it to my Dear & Loving Wife that one of my sons, as shall be Thought best Qualified for it, be bred to the Law, it being highly necessary in so Large a Family; and to him I give all my Law Books, being upwards of 200 Volumes, which are now or Shall be in My Closet at Brunswick, and are Exprest in a Catalogue of my Own hand Writing, in a Marble Cover Book in my Closet.

Item. I give to my Dear wife, Blomes History of the Bible in folio,

3 Volumes in folio of Arch Bishop Tillotsons Works, four volumes in Octavo of Dr. Stanhopes on the Epistles & Gospels, and all the Books of Physick.

Item, I give to my Daughter, Ann Humfries, 3 Volumes in folio on the Old & New Testament, and I will that my Exors. buy for her, the work of the Auther of the whole Duty of Man.. I give to the Eldest of my sons, that shall not Study the Law; Chambers Dictionary, two Volumes in folio; Locks Work, three Volumes in folio; Millers Dictionary; 2 Volms in folio, and LeBlond of Gardening in Quarto: And the rest of my Books, about 150 Volumes, to be Divided among my Other three Sons.—*Ibid.*, p. 317.

18. EXTRACT FROM THE WILL OF CHARLES PINCKNEY, SOUTH CAROLINA, 1752

To my son Charles Cotesworth Pinckney my gold watch (and after decease of his mother, the diamond mourning ring for my late wife), certain slaves with their increase, and my Library to be sold for his benefit. To my son Thomas Pinckney slaves with their increase. To my daughter Harriot slaves with their increase.. My son Charles to be virtuously, religiously, and liberally brought up and educated in the study and practice of the Laws of England, to serve his God and his country, to employ his abilities in support of private Right and Justice between Man and Man.—*The South Carolina Historical and Genealogical Magazine*, VIII (October, 1907), 217-18.

19. EXTRACT FROM THE WILL OF JAMES INNES, NORTH CAROLINA, 1754

I also give & bequeath, att the Death of my Loving Wife, Jean Innes, my plantation Called Point Pleasant, & the Opposite mash Land over the River, for which there is a Separate Patent, Two Negro young Women, One Negro young Man, and there Increase; all the Stock of Cattle and Hogs, halfe the Stock of Horses belonging att the time to that Plantation With all my Books, and one hundred Pounds Sterling, or the Equivalent thereunto in the currency of the Country, For the Use of a Free School for the Benefite of the Youth of North Carolina. And to see that this part of my Will be dewly Executed att the time, I appoint the Colonell of the New Hanover Regiment, the Parson of Willmington Church & the Vestrey for the time being, or the Majority, of them as they Shall from time to time be Choised or Appointed.—Grimes, *op. cit.*, pp.. 265-66.

20. Act concerning Peasley Free School, 1756

I. WHEREAS Henry Peasley, formerly of the county of Glocester, deceased, was in his life time, and at the time of his death, seized in fee-simple of a tract or parcel of land, containing six hundred acres, or thereabouts, lying and being in the parish of Abingdon, in the said county, and being so seized, by his last will and testament, in writing, bearing date the seventeenth day of March, in the year of our Lord, one thousand six hundred and seventy five, devised the same by the description of the land he then lived on, together with ten cows and one breeding mare, for the maintenance of a free school for ever, to be kept with a school-master for the education of the children of the parishes of Abingdon and Ware, for ever.

II. And whereas several slaves have been by different persons, since the above devise, given for the same purposes, but by reason of the inconvenient situation of the said land few children frequent the free-school kept there, so that the charitable intention of the said Henry Peasley, and the other donors is of little benefit to the said two parishes.

III. And whereas it is represented to this present General Assembly, by the ministers, churchwardens, and vestrymen of the said two parishes of Abingdon and Ware, that if proper persons were impowered to lease out the said land and slaves, the annual rents thereof would be sufficient to support and maintain a free-school in each of the said parishes for the education of the children residing there. *Be it therefore enacted, by the Lieutenant-Governor, Council, and Burgesses, of this present General Assembly, and it is hereby enacted by the authority of the same,* That the present ministers, churchwardens, and vestrymen of the said two parishes of Abingdon and Ware, and the ministers, churchwardens, and vestrymen of the same parishes, for the time being, shall and may be, and they are hereby nominated and appointed trustees and governors of the said lands, slaves, and other premisses for ever; and that the said trustees and governors shall for ever hereafter, stand and be incorporated, established, and founded, in name and deed, a body politic and corporate to have continuance for ever, by the name of the trustees and governors of Peasley's free-school; and that they the said trustees and governors may have perpetual succession, and that by that name they and their successors may for ever hereafter have, hold, and enjoy the above mentioned tract or parcel of land, slaves, and other premisses, with their increase and that the said trustees and governors and their successors, or the greater part of them, by the same name, shall and may have power, ability, and capacity to demise, lease, and grant the said tract or parcel of land, slaves, and other premises, for any term of years, not exceeding twenty-one years, or for any term of years determinable upon one, two, or three lives, or for one two, or three lives, reserving the best and most improved rents that can be got for the same, and to take, acquire, and purchase, and to sue and be sued, and to do, perform, and execute all other lawful acts and things, good, necessary, and profitable for the said incorporation, in as full and ample a manner and form, to all intents, constructions and purposes, as any other incorporation or body politic and corporate fully and perfectly founded and incorporated may do; and that the said trustees and governors, and their successors, for the time being, may have and use a common seal for making such their demises, leases and grants, and for the doing all and every other thing and things touching, or in any wise concerning the said incorporation.

IV. *And be it further enacted, by the authority aforesaid,* That they the said trustees and governors, and their successors, or the greater part of them shall and may, and they are hereby impowered and required, to erect and found a free-school in some convenient part of Abingdon and Ware, and by writing under their common seal, to nominate and appoint when, and as often as they shall think necessary, such person, or persons, as they shall approve of to be masters of the said free-schools, respectively, which master, before they be admitted to keep school, shall undergo an examination before the minister of the parish in which the school he shall be appointed master of shall be situated, and produce a certificate of his capacity, and also a licence from the governor or commander in chief of this dominion, for the time being, agreeable to his majesty's instructions; and the said trustees and governors shall issue and apply the rents of the said tract or parcel of land, slaves, and other premises for the erecting, maintaining, and supporting a free-school and schoolmaster, in each of the said parishes for ever, for the education of the children of the said parishes respectively, and the said trustees and governors, and their successors, for the time being, shall and may have full power and authority to visit the said free-schools, and to order, reform and redress all disorders and abuses in and touching the government and disposing of the same, and to remove the masters, as to them, or the greater part of them, shall seem just, fit, and convenient.

V. *And be it further enacted, by the authority aforesaid*, That the said trustees and governors, and their successors, or the greater part of them, for the time being, shall have full power, ability, and capacity, by the name aforesaid, to sue for and recover all rents and arrears of rent, and all and every sum and sums of money due for the use and occupation of the said tract or parcel of land, slaves, and other premises, by virtue of any agreement or contract heretofore made by any person or persons whatsoever.

VI.. Saving to the king's most excellent majesty, his heirs and successors, and to all and every other person and persons, bodies politic and corporate, their heirs and successors, other than the person or persons claiming as heir, or under the will of the said Henry Peasley, all such estate, right title, claim, and demand, which they, or any of them, should or might have, of, in, to, or out of the premises, or any of them, or any part thereof.[1]—Hening, *Statutes at Large*, VII, 41-43.

21. EDUCATIONAL PROVISIONS IN THE WILL OF BARTHOLOMEW ZOUBERBUHLER, GEORGIA, 1766

In the name of God Amen! I Bartholomew Zouberbuhler Rector of the Parish of Christ Church at Savannah in the Province of Georgia being at present under the afflicting hand of God but of Sound and Disposing mind and memory do make this my last Will and Testament in manner and Form following that is to say, First I recommend my Soul to God of whom through the merits and meditation of his Son Jesus Christ my Blessed Lord and Redeemer, I expect mercy pardon and Salvation... Item I give and bequeath to my Trustees hereinafter named and their Successors Trustees for ever my Tract of Land one Thousand Acres situate on the main branch of Turtle River in the Province of Georgia In Trust that they do assign the same to and for the use and support of the Intended College [2] on the Land belonging to the orphan House in the said province, whenever such foundation shall take place provided however that such foundation be upon the Principle of the Church of England as by law Established but if founded on any other or meant or intended as a College or Seminary for Dissenters or Separatists from the said church or the Government thereof Then I give and Devise this Tract of Land to

1. Peasley's will should have been probated in Gloucester County. The early records of that county are not extant and it is believed that the will is not in existence.
2. The idea of this proposed college, in which Whitefield was much interested, while never established seems to have been "warmly approved" by the colonists of Georgia.

the said Trustees and their successors Trustees In Trust to and for the several Uses and purposes hereinafter mentioned Item all the Rest Residue and Remainder of my Estate both Real and personal Including my three Tracts of Land containing together one thousand and two hundered and thirty seven acres situate in the Parish of Christ Church the said Province of Georgia on which is my Plantation called Belhas [?] and Forty three Negroes and the Use Rents Profits and Produce thereof And the future Increase of the said negroes I give and Bequeath unto the Honorable James Habersham Francis Harris Grey Elliott and James Read Esquires Joseph Clay John Smith and Noble Wimberly Jones Esquires and their Successors to be appointed as herein After is directed forever, In Trust and for the Uses Intents and purposes hereinafter mentioned and expressed, that is to say that the profits and produce of the said Plantation and Negroes or of any addition that may be hereunto made by the said Trustees applied in hiring and Employing a Person Properly Qualified for teaching and Instructing Negroes in the principle of the Christian Religion as held by the Church of England and that the person so hired be required to reside upon my said plantation and there to teach and Instruct the Negroes thereon and thereunto belonging and cause them to attend and Join in Morning and Evening Devotions and all other Christian Duties and Divine Services, and upon the Birth of any Negro Child upon or belonging to the same to give notice thereof to one or more of the Trustees who are hereby required to have such Negro Baptized and taught to read and be instructed in the saving Truths of the Gosple, and if any of the Male Children thus taught and brought up in the knowledge and fear of God should when grown up express an Inclination to convert other Negroes to the Christian Faith and the said Trustees be convinced of their Sincerity and abilities It is my Will that such Negroes may by the Said Trustees Manumitted and by them employed for that purpose an in case the yearly profits and produce of the said Plantation shall be Sufficient to repay the expence my Will is that the said Trustees do bestow a Competent Recompence to a sound catechist or Schoolmaster at Savannah who shall be obliged to teach and instruct all other Negroes or so many as the said Trustees or the Society for Propagating the Gospel in foreing [?] who I am confidint will aid and assist them in so good a Design Shall direct or be sent to him for that purpose An Whereas the erecting an Infirmary in or near the Town of Savannah for the reception of poor and Distress'd Sick persons and to provide for them in their calamitouse condition the Necessary means of Recovery is a work that will be attended with many beneficial Circumstances as well to the Publick as the Unhappy Objects that may be Relieved thereby It is my Will that the said Trustees after all other purposes and intentions of this my Will are performed do as far as the Profits of my said Plantation will enable them, help and Contribute to the support continuance and enlargement of so good and compassionate an Undertaking and my Will further is that the said Trustees do Yearly and every Year Lay an ccount of the receipts Isscus [issues?] and Profits of the said Plantation and an actual State thereof before the Governor and Council for the time being and I do authorize and Impower the said Trustees to sell and make title for the Tract of one Thousand acres of Land Situate on Turtle River in the province of Georgia and hereinbefore conditionally bequeathed towards the use and support of a college, In case the said College should by its foundation appear not to be entitled to said Bequest... In witness whereof the said Bartholomew Zouberbuhler have to this my last Will and Testament set my hand and seal the Twenty fifth day of November in the year of our Lord one thousand Seven hundred and sixty six and in the Seventh Year of His Majesty's Reign.—Will Book AA, Georgia Department of Archives and History, pp. 176ff. Typescript copy in the University of North Carolina Library.

22. An act "to quiet the heirs and representatives of the late Reverend Bartholomew Zuberbuhler," 1791

WHEREAS the aforesaid Bartholomew Zuberbuhler, in and by his last will and testament made certain dispositions of his estate for benevolent purposes, which were declared by the legislature of the State of Georgia to be impracticable, and could not be carried into execution, in and by an act entitled, "An act to establish an academy in the county of Chatham, and for vesting certain property in Selina countess dowager of Huntingdon," passed at Augusta the first day of February, one thousand seven hundred and eighty-eight: And it further appearing by the said act that the rights of any persons legally the heirs of the said Bartholomew Zuberbuhler should not be barred from their claims: *And whereas* the legislature by their act passed at Augusta on the third day of February, one thousand seven hundred and eighty-nine, did declare that Bartholomew and Jacob Waldburger, being then in possession of the said estate, should keep the same, subject to an action of ejectment or claim of the said trustees, that the right of the heirs and applicants to the same might be determined.

I. *Be it therefore enacted,* That the real estate of the said Bartholomew Zuberbuhler, and of which he died possessed of, or was entitled to in the then province now State of Georgia, shall go to and be vested in the said Bartholomew Waldburger as eldest son and heir of his father Jacob Waldburger, who was the nephew of the said Bartholomew Zuberbuhler, to hold to him the said Bartholomew Waldburger, his heirs and assigns for ever: And as to the personal estate of the said Bartholomew Zuberbuhler, it shall go to, and be equally divided amongst the said Bartholomew Waldburger, Jacob Waldburger, and Henrietta, the wife of Zachariah Hoskins, sons and daughter of the deceased Jacob Waldburger, being the grand nephews and neice of the said Bartholomew Zuberbuhler, and to their, and each of their heirs and assigns for ever, any law to the contrary notwithstanding; subject nevertheless to the payment of lawful and just debts, due and owing from the estate of the said Bartholomew Zuberbuhler; and such estate to be assets in the hands of the said Bartholomew and Jacob Waldburger; and subject also to an annuity of one hundred pounds for four years, payable to the trustees of the academy of the county of Chatham, to be applied for by them, and their successors in office, for the support of the said academy: On failure thereof the trustees aforesaid are empowered to sue for, and recover the same against the said Bartholomew and Jacob Waldburger in any of the courts of law within this State.

II. *And be it further enacted,* That all claims of the said trustees of Chatham county, in and to the said estate of the said Bartholomew Zuberbuhler (except as to the annuity herein directed to be paid) shall be and is hereby barred.—Robert and George Watkins, *A Digest of the Laws of the State of Georgia,* pp. 430-31.

23. THE WILL OF ALEXANDER DOWNER, SOUTH CAROLINA, 1818

Item. I give and bequeath to such of my blood relations as can prove themselves so, One hundred Cents each, if called for in due time—Having been myself an orphan, and having received a partial education at the Orphan house [1] in Georgia, by which I have learnt how to estimate the value of an education, and by which I have been able to obtain a Sufficiency to support myself, my wife and seven orphan Children which I have raised, I do now feel an inclination

1. Betheseda Orphan House. See above.

and am willing to dispose of the ballance of my Estate, for the benefit of the Orphans of Edgefield District—*In the first place*. I will and
desire that the land whereon I now live containing three hundred
acres (more or less) shall be leased every year, or for a term of
years not exceeding five with the rent payable to my Executore
(whom I shall hereafter appoint) and that they build a School house
with said money on the land (if I do not build one before my decease)
and employ a school master to teach Orphan Children in the School
House aforesaid— The rent of the Land to be appropriated yearly
to the same purpose.— As the amount of funds will have to regulate
the number of Scholars I wish it so arranged for one fourth the
number to be taken from Richmond County in the State of Georgia
and the ballance from Edgefield district— It is my wish for no child
to remain after he attains the age of Fourteen years. The Negroes I
now own (to wit,) old Charles, Old Rose, Cuff, Jinney, Lucy, Sam,
Jack, Sue, Robert Miley, young Rose, young Charles, Ned, Harry.
and all I may be possessed of at my decease (except old Charles and
old Rose, those two negroes I do not wish sold but comfortably
provided for in food clothes and house during their natural lives
and that the funds necessary for that purpose be taken from any
monies that my executors may have, after the first year, but for that
year I wish a Sufficiancy reserved for them, from what I may leave
on the plantation, and before the Sale of the Personal property.— The
ballance of the Negroes I will and desire may be Sold by my Executors, within Six or twelve months after my decease as may appear
best to them, in the following way— Each negro shall have a ticket
from one or more of my Executors to make a choice of a Master or
Mistriss and such person shall have the liberty to purchase such Negro
at a fair and true Valuation—and my Executors or any two of them
are at liberty if they think proper to give a credit of One or two
years by taking a Mortgage on such negro or negroes with Bond
and Security for the Amount of Sale and Interest from the date that
all my personal property of every discription except the Negroes
(and a support for Charles and Rose as before mentioned) be sold by
my Executors as soon after my decease as they may think proper—
that the Money arising from such sales as well as that arising from the
sale of the Negroes as aforesaid, and all the Money I have by me or
entitled to with all debts due, I will and desire my Executors rest in
Bank Stock in the "Bank of the State of South Carolina" or in the
"Bank of the State of Georgia" and the profits and dividends or

Interest arising on such shares, I will and desire they appropriate (together with the money arising from the rent of the land as aforesaid) to the Boarding, Clothing and Schooling of orphan Children as aforesaid— Should the number of Scholars and their expenses together with the Salary of the teacher, not be sufficient to consume the sum appropriated, then and in that case, I wish the overplus appropriated to the Schooling of Orphan Children at the Academy at Edgefield Court House— In no case whatever are my Executors to deminish the Principal Sum in Bank, which I wish to remain Forever as my Bounty for the good of the Orphan, but the Interest or profits arising on that sum to be annually appropriated as before mentioned.—I do now request and desire the Judges of the Court *of Equity* to act and do and I empower them or either of them for the time being in the event of the decease of my Executors, their removal, incapacity or refusal to act, to act and do every thing that may appear equitable and Just and necessary to carry my intentions into full effect. And I request the Gentlemen of the Bar who may feel interested in the object I have in view, or any of them to make such observations (when necessary) as will secure to the orphan the benefit of my intentions.—And Lastly —I do hereby nominate and appoint Thomas L. Mills of the State and district first aforesaid, and Wilson Navey and William Rogers of the State of Georgia and County of Burk my Sole Executors, to this my last Will and testament, with full confidence in their integrity and friendly exertions to carry as far as they or any of them may be able my intentions into effect.—Original in Volume I, Book C, of Wills in Edgefield, South Carolina. Copy in the South Caroliniana Library of the University of South Carolina, and another copy in the University of North Carolina Library.

X

PHILANTHROPIC AND BENEVOLENT SOCIETIES IN SOUTH CAROLINA

I. PREVIEW AND COMMENTS

IN ADDITION TO THE Syms-Eaton School in Virginia, Bethesda Orphan House in Georgia, and the Winyaw Indigo Society in South Carolina, philanthropic and benevolent interests were expressed in the organization of charitable societies especially in South Carolina and in the latter part of the eighteenth century for the education of orphans and indigent children. The charters of five such societies and the rules of one are given below.

Meriwether says that the South Carolina Society (chartered in 1751) which was founded for the free education of indigent children of both sexes, "had funds to the amount of $137,000 by the opening of the following century." [1] In addition to the work of these societies, apparently more numerous in South Carolina than elsewhere in the South, interest in providing through wills of charitably inclined persons for the education of underprivileged children was very extensive in the South.[2]

II. DOCUMENTS

1. CHARTER OF THE SOUTH CAROLINA SOCIETY, 1751

WHEREAS, Robert Raper, John M'Call, and Benjamin Addison, in behalf of themselves and sundry other persons, inhabitants of this Province, who have associated themselves together for certain pious and charitable purposes, and have subsisted these thirteen years last past, under the name of "The South Carolina Society," have preferred a petition to the General Assembly, therein setting forth, that by small contributions from time to time, made and improved to the best advantage, the said society hath now collected a considerable sum of money, which they are desirous to apply in part towards those good and charitable uses which first called them together, and, in particular, towards erecting, endowing and supporting proper schools and alms-houses, for the maintenance and education of poor and

---

1. C. Meriwether, *History of Higher Education in South Carolina*, p. 19.
2. See the section above on educational provisions in wills.

helpless orphans; and therefore pray to be incorporated as a body politic, and to be invested with such powers and authorities as may be most conducive to answer and further the good intentions of the said association. We therefore pray his most sacred majesty that it may be enacted:

I. *And be it enacted*, by his Excellency, James Glen, Esq., Governor-in-Chief and Captain-General in and over his Majesty's said Province of South Carolina, by and with the advice and consent of his Majesty's Honorable Council and the Assembly of the said Province, and by the authority of the same, That Robert Raper, the present steward, John M'Call and Benjamin Addison, the present wardens, and the several persons who now are, or shall hereafter be, members of the society in this Province commonly called the South Carolina Society, and their successors, in the manner hereinafter directed, to be elected officers or members of the same, shall be, and they are hereby declared to be, one body corporate and politic, in deed and in name, by the name and style of "The South Carolina Society," and by the same name shall have perpetual succession of officers and members, and a common seal, with power to change, alter and break, and make new the same, as often as they shall judge expedient. And they and their successors shall be able and capable in law to have, hold, receive, enjoy, possess and retain, to them and their successors, all the monies or other personal estate, and all the securities for the same, which have arisen from the contributions aforesaid, and the interest or proceeds thereof, and which are now in the hands of or vested in any of the said officers or members, in trust for the said society; and also, at their discretion, to call in and replace at interest the said monies, or any part thereof. And they and their successors, by the said corporate name of the South Carolina Society, shall be capable in law, out of the said monies and the produce thereof, to purchase, receive, have, hold, enjoy, possess and retain, to them and their successors, in perpetuity or for any term of years, any estate or estates, real or personal, messuages, lands, tenements or hereditaments, of what kind or nature soever, not exceeding, in the whole, five hundred pounds sterling per annum, above reprises, and to sell, alien, exchange, demise, or lease the same, or any part thereof, as they shall think convenient; and by the same name to sue and be sued, implead and be impleaded, answer and be answered unto, in any court of record; and to make such rules and by-laws for the benefit and advantage of the said corporation, as shall be, from time to time, agreed to by the majority of the members of the said society.

II. *And be it further enacted* by the authority aforesaid, That it shall and may be lawful for the said corporation hereby erected, to take and hold, to them and their successors, forever, any charitable donations or devises of lands, not exceeding, in the whole, five hundred pounds sterling per annum; and also to take and hold moneys or chattels, real and personal; and therewith, and out of their common stock, to erect, endow and support proper schools; *provided*, that the masters of the said schools be members of the Church of England; and alms-houses for the relief of such indigent persons, and especially for the maintenance and education of such poor and helpless orphans or indigent children, and for binding them apprentices, as they shall judge proper objects of the charity hereby intended; and to appoint and choose, and at their pleasure displace, remove and supply, such officers, school-masters, servants, and other persons to be employed for the purposes herein mentioned or intended, or other affairs of the corporation, and to appoint such salaries, perquisites or other rewards, for their labor or service therein, as they shall, from time to time, approve and think fit.

III. *And be it further enacted* by the authority aforesaid, That this Act shall and may be given in evidence on the tryal of any issue or cause, in any court of law or equity, without special pleading.

IV. *And be it enacted* by the authority aforesaid, That this Act, nor any thing therein contained, shall not be of force until his Majesty's royal approbation thereof shall be obtained and signified to the Governor or Commander-in-Chief in this Province.—Cooper, *The Statutes at Large of South Carolina*, VIII, 106-7.

2. CHARTER OF SALEM SOCIETY, 1768

WHEREAS, sundry inhabitants of the district of Ninety-six, have formed themselves into a society by the name of the "Salem Society," for the express purpose of endowing and supporting a school and seminary of learning, and have fixed upon a spot between Catawba and Savannah rivers, near Little River Meeting House, as being the best situated to answer the designs of the society, and have made humble application to the General Assembly of this State to be incorporated and invested with such powers and privileges as may most effectually advance the views of the society:

I. *Be it therefore enacted*, by his Excellency Rawlins Lowndes, Esquire, President and Commander-in-Chief in and over the State of

South Carolina, by the honourable the Legislative Council and General Assembly of the said State, and by the authority of the same, That the Reverend James Creswell, present President of the said society, and John Williams, (son of Daniel) and James Griffin, the present wardens, and the several persons who now are, or shall hereafter be, members of that society in this State commonly called the Salem Society, and their successors, officers and members of the same, shall be, and they are hereby declared to be, one body corporate and politic, in deed and in name, by the name and title of the "Salem Society," and by the same name shall have perpetual succession of officers and members, and a common seal, with power to change, alter, break, and make new the same, as often as they shall judge expedient; and they and their successors, shall be able and capable in law, to purchase, have, hold, receive, enjoy, possess, and retain, to them and their successors, in perpetuity, or for any term of years, any estate or estates, real or personal, messauges, lands, tenements or hereditaments of what kind or nature soever, not exceeding ten thousand dollars per annum, and to sell, alien, exchange, demise, or lease the same, or any part thereof, as they shall think proper, and by the same name, to sue and be sued, implead and be impleaded, answer and be answered unto, in any court of law or equity in this State, and to make such rules and by-laws (not repugnant and contrary to the law of the land,) for the benefit and advantage of the said corporation, and for the order, rules and good government and management of the said school, and for the masters, teachers and scholars thereof, as shall be from time to time agreed to by the majority of the members of said society.

II. *And be it further enacted* by the authority aforesaid, That it shall and may be lawful for the corporation hereby erected, to take and hold to them and their successors forever, any charitable donations or devises of lands and personal estate, not exceeding in the whole the above mentioned sum of ten thousand dollars per annum, and to appropriate the same to the endowing and supporting the said school, and to the maintenance and education of such poor and helpless orphans and indigent children as they shall judge proper objects of the charity hereby intended; and to appoint and choose, and at their pleasure to displace, remove and supply such officers, school-masters, teachers and servants, and other persons to be employed for the above purposes, or other offices of the said society, and to appoint such salaries, perquisites, or other rewards for their labour or service therein, as the said society shall from time to time approve of and think fit.

III. *And be it further enacted* by the authority aforesaid, That this Act shall and may be given in evidence on the trial of any issue or cause in any court of law or equity, without special pleading.—*Ibid.,* 117-18.

3. CHARTER OF MOUNT SION SOCIETY, 1777

Whereas, several of the Inhabitants of this State have associated themselves together, under the Name of the *Mount Sion Society*, for the Purpose of founding, endowing, and supporting a Public School in the district of Camden, for the Education and Instruction of youth, and have made humble Application to the General Assembly of this State, to be incorporated as a Body Politic, and to be invested with such Power and Authorities as may be most conductive to answer and further the good Intentions of the said Association:

Be it Enacted by his Excellency *John Rutledge*, Esquire, President and Commander in Chief in and over the State of South-Carolina, by the Honourable the Legislative Council and General Assembly of the said State, and by the authority of the same, that *John Wynn*, Esquire, the President of the said Society, and, *Robert Ellison* and *William Strother*, Esquires, the Present Wardens, and the several Persons who now are, or shall hereafter be, Members of that Society, in this State commonly called the *Mount Sion Society*, and by that Name shall have perpetual Succession of Officers and Members, and a Common Seal, with Power to change, alter, break, and make new the same, as often as they shall judge expedient, and they and their Successors shall be able and capable in Law, to purchase, have, hold, receive, enjoy, possess, and retain to them and their Successors, in Perpetuity, or for any Term of Years, any Estate or Estates, real and personal, Messuages, Lands, Tenements, or Hereditaments, of what Kind or Nature soever, not exceeding in the whole *Three Thousand Dollars Per Annum*, and to sell, alien, exchange, demise, or lease the same, or any part thereof, as they shall think proper, and by the same Name to sue and be sued, implead and be impleaded, answer and be answered unto, in any Court of Law or Equity in this State: and to make such Rules and Bye-Laws, not repugnant and contrary to the Laws of the Land, for the Benefit and Advantage of said Corporation, and for the Order, Rule and good Government and Management of the said School, and for the Masters, Teachers, and Scholars thereof, as shall be from Time to Time agreed to by the Majority of the Members of the said Society.

And Be it Further Enacted by the Authority Aforesaid, That it shall and may be lawful for the Corporation hereby erected, to take and hold to them and their Successors for ever, any charitable Donations or Devises of Lands and Personal Estate, not exceeding in the whole the above mentioned Sum of *Three Thousand Dollars per Annum*, and to appropriate the same to the endowing and supporting the said *School*, and to the Maintenance and Education of such poor and helpless Orphans and indigent Children as they shall judge proper Objects of the Charity hereby intended; And to appoint and choose, and at their Pleasure to displace, remove, and supply such Officers, School-Masters, Teachers, and Servants, and other Persons to be employed for the above purposes, or other Affairs of the said Society, and to appoint such Salaries, Perquisites, or other Rewards for their Labour or Service therein, as the said Society shall from Time to Time approve of and think fit.

And Be it Further Enacted by the Authority aforesaid, That this Act shall and may be given in Evidence on the Trial of any Issue or Cause, in any Court of Law or Equity without special Pleading. —McCord's *Statutes at Large of South Carolina*, VIII, 114-15. (February 13, 1777).

4. RULES OF MOUNT SION SOCIETY

PREAMBLE

ISAIAH, Chap. LX, ver. 1, and Chap. LXI, ver. 3 *Arise, shine, for thy Light is come, and the Glory of the Lord is risen upon thee,—to appoint unto them that mourn in Sion, to give unto them Beauty for Ashes; the Oil of Joy for Mourning; the Garment of Praise for the Spirit of Heaviness; that they might be called the Trees of Righteousness, the Planting of the Lord, that he might be glorified!*

When we cast our eyes around, and behold a rising generation, the greatest part thereof must live in ignorance, on account of there being no place of instruction near them, where they can be properly educated: Also, when we behold the orphan left forlorn, and the children of indigent parents, growing up more like a race of savages than Christians, becoming thereby useless to their country, to society, and themselves; we cannot help being sensible of those tender feelings which the Divine Being hath impressed on our natures, as a spur to prompt us to lend a helping hand to succor and assist the destitute.

If men will look into their own bosoms, and consider the generous seeds which are there planted, that might, if rightly cultivated, ennoble their lives, and make their virtue venerable to futurity, surely they cannot, without tears, reflect on the many fine geniuses, in the remote parts of this State, who are entirely buried in oblivion, through lack of education.

Our country calls, nay the voice of reason cries aloud to us to promote knowledge as the firmest cement of a state; and conscience insists that it is our indispensible duty to instruct the ignorant in the Principles of Christianity: The more efficaciously to do which,—

> WE, whose names are annexed hereunto, have chearfully entered into a Society, at Charlestown, in South-Carolina, the Ninth Day of January, Anno Domini One Thousand Seven Hundred and Seventy-Seven, and have agreed to the following Rules and Regulations for the good government of the same:

RULES OF THE MOUNT SION SOCIETY

ARTICLE I. This Society shall be known by the Name of THE MOUNT SION SOCIETY, and shall consist of an unlimited number of Members, not cease to be while there remain five.

II. This Society shall have four General Meetings in the year, to wit, on the last Friday in every February, which shall be the Society's Anniversary; and on the last Friday in May, August and November, which shall be termed Quarterly Meetings: There shall be also Weekly Meetings, on every Friday throughout the year; which shall be held from the last Friday in February, to the last Friday in August, from Seven o'clock in the Evening till Ten: and from the last Friday in August to the last Friday in February, from Six o'clock in the Evening till Nine.

III. At every Anniversary Meeting the Members met, shall, by a majority of votes, elect by ballot, a President, Senior and Junior Wardens, Treasurer, and Secretary, for the ensuing year: Whoever shall be so elected, and refuses to act, he or they so refusing, or not serving the full term of one year, shall forfeit the sum of *Fourteen shillings* sterling, each. And in case of the death, resignation, refusal to serve, or removal from the State, of any officer within the year, another person shall be chosen for the remaining part of the year, who shall be liable to the same forfeiture, on not serving, or refusing to serve the full term for which he was elected.

IV. At the Anniversary and Quarterly Meetings, two Stewards

shall be chosen, who shall attend every Meeting of the Society, and whose business shall be to order a certain quantity of liquor for each respective Meeting; and to do any other business relating to the Society, which may be required of them by the President, for the time being. Their time in office shall be only three months, and fine for not serving, *six shillings* sterling.

V. That every officer may attend duly to the duties of the Society, the following fines shall be paid by absentees, viz. The President, *two dollars*, the Senior Warden, *seven shillings* sterling, the Junior Warden, *six shillings* sterling, the Treasurer, *one dollar*, Secretary, *three shillings and six pence* sterling, the Stewards, *three shillings* sterling each; unless the absentee makes such excuse at the next Meeting, as shall be satisfactory to a majority of the Members then present.

VI. The Society shall not be considered as opened, until the minutes of the preceding meeting are read—Nor closed till after the reading of the minutes of the then present evening.

VII. The President, assisted by the Wardens, shall preserve due order and decorum; and at the request of the other Governors, and with the assent of the Society, shall issue orders on the Treasurer for monies; shall declare elections, appoint committees' and cause a peaceable and inoffensive behaviour to be observed by all the Members at their respective Meetings; and when he gives the signal for attention, every Member must observe it, and take his seat, under the penalty of *three shillings* sterling.—He shall quash all disputes respecting State matters or Religion: Any person who persists in a debate of that kind, or behaves indecently, after being admonished by him, shall be subject to any fine the Society shall inflict, not exceeding *fourteen pounds* sterling: if any person after he shall be thus sentenced to be fined, continues to disturb the peace and harmony of the Meeting, on that or any other account, the President shall command him to quit the Room, and on his refusing to comply therewith, and not making a proper concession for his offensive behaviour, at the next succeeding Meeting, he shall be expelled the Society.

The President shall also, at the request of a majority of the Members present, at any regular Meeting, sue for any monies that shall be due the Society: and execute all other matters and things which shall be thought by the Society to appertain to his office.

VIII. The Senior Warden shall officiate in the President's absence, and the Junior Warden in the absence of the President and Senior Warden. But in case the President and both the Wardens should be absent, the Members present may proceed to ballot for temporary officers, who as soon as elected, shall have power to transact business for that night, provided thirteen Members are present; without which number no meeting shall be considered perfect, or capable of doing business.

IX. Any person elected into the office of President, Senior or Junior Warden, Treasurer, or Secretary, and having punctually, regularly and faithfully served the time appointed by these rules and regulations, shall not be liable (unless with his own consent) to serve in the same or any inferior office the succeeding year.

X. Once in three years, there shall be also chosen, by ballot, by a majority of Members present, at an Anniversary Meeting, Thirteen Governors or Directors, from the Society at large; Seven of whom shall reside in the country, and the other six shall be inhabitants of Charlestown; who shall have the entire direction and management of the buildings, the appointment of House-keepers and other necessary attendants; together with the power of fixing their respective salaries, and drawing on the Treasurer for monies, with the consent of the Society.

They shall likewise have authority to agree with the parents or guardians of children, who shall be sent to the school as boarders or scholars, and not on the charity. All monies resulting therefrom must be paid by them into the hands of the Treasurer, for the use of the General Fund.

Any person chosen a Governor or Director, who shall refuse to serve, shall forfeit *three pounds* sterling.—The appointment shall be for three years.

XI. Any person desirous of becoming a member of this Society, must apply by letter, directed to the President, Warden and Members, which application the Secretary shall enter on the minutes, and it shall lie over until the next meeting (unless from a person residing in the country, who may be balloted for immediately) and if two-thirds of the Members present are for the candidate, he shall be admitted, on paying into the hands of the Treasurer *one pound seventeen shillings and four pence* sterling; but if rejected, he shall not be eligible to be balloted for again, until the full end and term of one year.

XII. The Secretary shall from time to time provide books at the Society's charge; in one of which he shall enter all the rules, that now or hereafter may be agreed upon, together with the names of the members, and the times of their admission. He shall likewise keep regular minutes of the transactions of each Meeting, with the names of the Members present; as also, a fair and regular account of entrance money, fines, forfeitures, donations, receipts and disbursements of every kind whatsoever; likewise, a file of all letters and copies of letters.—Every other article and expence (besides books) which the Society shall think useful or necessary, shall be paid out of the General Fund.

XIII. The Treasurer shall also provide a proper book, in which he shall enter all monies received or disbursed; and keep a true state of the fund of the Society. He likewise, as soon as elected, shall give bond with security to the Society, for double the sum or value of the monies, bonds, and other securities then delivered into his hands; with condition to be accountable for, and deliver the same, together with all other monies or effects belonging to the Society, that may come into his hands during his Treasurership (fire and other inevitable accidents excepted) to the next succeeding Treasurer, or to the order of the Governors and the Society, when required by a majority of the Members at a regular Meeting; which bond shall be kept by the President, after being recorded in the Secretary's office.

All bonds and other securities for money shall be taken in the name of, and made payable to, the MOUNT SION SOCIETY. No monies belonging to this Society shall be let out at interest by the Treasurer, but with the consent of the President, Senior and Junior Wardens and Secretary: And no member of this Society shall be permitted to borrow any money belonging to the Society, or be security for any other borrower of the same.

XIV. Every Member who shall be appointed on any committee, and neglects to attend at the time and place appointed for the meeting thereof, and at the time and place to which the said committee may be adjourned, such Member or Members, so neglecting to attend, shall pay a fine of *two dollars*, unless he or they shall make a satisfactory excuse to the Society.

XV. In order to increase the fund of this Society, every Member shall pay the sum of *five shillings* sterling on every Anniversary and Quarterly Meeting—Any person neglecting to contribute such annual and quarterly sums for the space of one year, the Secretary shall publicly read his name with the sum due by him, the next regular meeting after the year is expired, and if the same is not paid to the Treasurer, before the next regular Meeting, he shall be excluded.

But it is provided, that any person who has been so excluded, and shall again incline to become a Member, upon being balloted for, and if admitted, shall, on paying into the hands of the Treasurer, all the ordinary sums which shall remain due at the time of his exclusions, and until his application for re-admission, be then entitled to the same benefit which he otherwise would have enjoyed before his breach of this rule.

XVI. All fines and forfeitures of what kind soever, arising by virtue of the rules and orders of this Society, as also all gifts and legacies by any of the Members, or any other person; and all monies accruing to the society, in any other way whatever, shall be appropriated to the general fund.—Likewise the names of benefactors shall be inserted in a book provided for that purpose; and proper letters of thanks shall be drawn up by the Secretary for any donations received, to be approved by the Society.

XVII. All schoolmasters and teachers are to be appointed by the Society at large, and are not to be discharged on any account, or for any cause, before complaint shall be made, heard, and adjudged to be important and well founded, by the Society, at some Annual or Quarterly Meeting—No person shall be eligible to be a tutor in this Society's school, unless he be of Protestant Religion.

XVIII. The Anniversary and Quarterly Meetings shall be the only time for the admittance of children on the Charity, into the School; which after the Governors have given six weeks' public notice in the Gazettes of this State, informing what number their fund is able or can afford to provide for, shall be performed in the following manner, viz. The children of such indigent Members of this Society, as have been Members for the space of five years have the preference—The poor orphan shall be next noticed; then the child of an indigent widow or widower; and lastly, the children of such poor parents as the Society shall deem worthy of their bounty.

If the parents of the children are able to find cloaths for them, then the Society will find them in board and education; or if the parents of such children live near the school, and are able to board themselves, then the Society will find them in cloaths and education. But if the children be orphans, or their parents in very indigent circumstances, the Society will then find them in cloaths, boarding and education, until they are of a proper age to be put in some trade or profession.—No child whatever shall be admitted who is not above the age of five years.

The names of all children who are candidates for admission, are to be made known to the Society three weeks before the Anniversary; and the Governors shall make strict enquiry whether they are proper objects of charity or not, and report accordingly. Such of the children as the Society, on the consideration of the report, shall adjudge to be proper objects, shall be admitted on the charity. But notwithstanding such admission, if the Society shall afterwards find they were deceived, they shall make such order on the matter as to them shall appear just.

XIX. If any Member should die in such low circumstances, that he cannot out of his estate or effects be decently interred, the President and Wardens shall have power to order all things necessary for his funeral, and the expence shall be paid out of the fund of the Society. In case of the death of any Member in town, the rest of the Members, if regularly invited by the person appointed to invite them shall attend the funeral on the forfeiture of *one shilling* sterling each unless a sufficient excuse is made at the next Meeting; and the Secretary if called upon, shall furnish a list of the Members to the person authorized by the friends of the deceased to invite.

XX. The expence of the Society, at each of their respective Meetings, shall be defrayed by the Town Members, whether present or absent in an equal proportion; which shall not exceed the sum of *one dollar* per Member, at each Annual and Quarterly Meeting, exclusive of *four pence* sterling at each of the Weekly ones throughout the year. The Country Members are to pay the same ratio also, whenever they attend any of the said Meetings.—The President and Wardens shall have power to order, or agree for the entertainment of the Society, at each Anniversary and Quarterly Day, not exceeding the aforesaid sums. Any Member giving one week's notice to the Secretary, of his intention of not attending, shall be excused his fine on the Quarterly Meetings.

XXI. None of the foregoing Rules shall be repealed, nor any new ones made until the same has been proposed and delivered in writing, and undergone three separate readings, at three distinct Meetings, one of which must be a General Meeting, at each of which Meetings, it must have met with the approbation of a majority of the Members then present. All questions in this Society shall be determined by a majority of hands; or by ballot, if any two Members require it, and if the votes are equal, the President shall have the casting vote.

XXII. That no Member be permitted to speak more than twice to one subject, unless with consent of a majority to explain himself. If at any time doubts shall arise concerning the meaning of either of these Rules, the same shall be adjusted and determined by a majority of the Members present at any General Meeting of the Society.

XXIII. Committees (if thought necessary) shall, on application, be permitted to be formed by any five gentlemen, Members of the Society, who reside in the Country. The business of said Committees, which are to be titled from their local situations, shall be, to admit Members into the Society, and receive such donations, gifts, or legacies, as shall from time to time be bestowed or bequeathed to this Society, likewise to collect all annual and quarterly contributions which shall become due from the Members residing in or about their respective neighborhoods, and to do all other business that shall be required of them by the Society. They are also to make proper returns to the Society, at the Annual and Quarterly Meetings, of their proceedings; the names of Members, with the times of their admission, and the sums they have received, so that they may be regularly entered upon the books of the Society. Whoever are appointed officers and refuse to serve, shall pay a fine of *fourteen shillings* sterling, and the Committee shall appoint others, who in like case lie under the same penalty.

XXIV. The Chairman of County Committees shall be appointed annually, and shall have power to make bye-laws for their own government, but no power to alter or amend these Rules, or to dispose of any monies they may receive for the fund, without first obtaining leave from the Society, unless in case of the death of a Member in indigent circumstances; then the Chairman and Members present, shall have full power and authority to act agreeably to Rule the nineteenth: And these Rules shall be binding and in force with all Committees.—C. Meriwether, *History of Higher Education in South Carolina*, pp. 237-41.

5. CHARTER OF THE CATHOLIC SOCIETY, 1778

WHEREAS, several of the inhabitants of this State have associated themselves, under the name of the Catholic Society, for the purpose of founding, endowing and supporting a public school in the district of Camden, eastward of the Wateree river, for the education and instruction of youth, and have made humble application to the General Assembly of this State, to be incorporated as a body politic, and to be invested with such powers and authorities as may be most conducive to answer and further the good intention of the said association.

I. *Be it therefore enacted,* by his Excellency, John Rutledge, Esq., President and Commander-in-Chief in and over the State of South Carolina, by the Honorable the Legislative Council and General Assembly of the said State, and by the authority of the same, That the Rev. Thomas Hill, present president of the said society, and Adam M'Donall and John James, Esq'rs., the present wardens, and the several persons who now are, or shall hereafter be, members of that society in this State commonly called the Catholic Society, and their successors, officers and members of the same, shall be, and they are hereby declared to be, one body corporate and politic, in deed and in name, by the name and style of "The Catholic Society," and by the same name shall have perpetual succession of officers and members, and a common seal, with power to change, alter, break and make new the same, as often as they shall judge expedient; and they, and their successors, shall be able and capable in law to purchase, have, hold, receive, enjoy, possess and retain, to them and their successors, in perpetuity or for any term of years, any estate or estates, real and personal, messuages, lands, tenements or hereditaments, of what kind or nature soever, not exceeding three thousand dollars per annum, and to sell, alien, exchange, demise or lease the same, or any part thereof, as they shall think proper; and by the same name to sue and be sued, implead and be impleaded, answer and be answered unto, in any court of law or equity in this State; and to make such rules and by-laws, (not repugnant and contrary to the laws of the land,) for the benefit and advantage of the said corporation, and for the order, rules and good government and management of the said school, and for the masters, teachers and scholars thereof, as shall be, from time to time, agreed to by the majority of the members of the said society.

II. *And be it further enacted* by the authority aforesaid, That it shall and may be lawful for the corporation hereby erected, to take and hold, in them and their successors, forever, any charitable donations or devises of lands and personal estate, not exceeding, in the whole, the above mentioned sum of three thousand dollars per annum, and to appropriate the same to the endowing and supporting the said school, and to the maintenance and education of such poor and helpless orphans and indigent children as they shall judge proper objects of the charity hereby intended; and to appoint and choose, and at their pleasure to displace, and remove and supply such officers, school-masters, teachers and servants, and other persons to be employed for the above purposes, or other officers of the said society, and to appoint such salaries, perquisites or other rewards for their labor or service therein, as the said society shall, from time to time, approve of and think fit.

III. And *whereas*, there are five hundred acres of vacant pine barren land, adjoining lands given to the said society by Mr. James Bradley, and the said pine barren land would be very advantageous to the said society, for fire-wood and other purposes; *Be it further enacted* by the authority aforesaid, That all that tract of five hundred acres of land, situate, lying and being in Camden district, on the eastward of the Wateree river, butting and bounding to the west, on John Anderson's land; on the northwest, on land given by the said James Bradley to the said society, and to the north, east and south, on vacant land, and having such shape, form and marks as are delineated to the plat hereunto annexed, be given and granted to the said Catholic Society and their successors, forever.

IV. *And be it further enacted* by the authority aforesaid, That this Act shall and may be given in evidence on the trial of any issue or cause in any court of law or equity, without special pleading.— Cooper, *op. cit.*, VIII, 115-16.

6. Charter of Saint David's Society, District of Cheraw, 1778

WHEREAS, sundry inhabitants of the Cheraw district, have formed themselves into a society by the name of the "Saint David's Society," for the express purpose of instituting and endowing a seminary of learning in the district of Cheraw, to instruct and educate youth in the necessary and useful branches of knowledge, and have made humble application to the General Assembly of this State to be incorporated and invested with such powers and privileges as may most effectually advance the views of the said society:

I. *Be it therefore enacted*, by his Excellency Rawlins Lowndes, Esquire, President and Commander-in-chief in and over the State of South Carolina, by the honorable the Legislative Council and General Assembly of the said State, and by the authority of the same, That the Honorable Alexander McIntosh, Esquire, present President of the said society, and George Hext and Abel Kobb, Esquires, the present wardens, and the several persons who now are, or shall hereafter be members of the said society in this State called the "Saint

David's Society," and their successors, officers and members of the same, shall be, and they are hereby declared to be, one body corporate and politic, in deed and in name, by the name and style of the "Saint David's Society," and by the same name shall have perpetual succession of officers and members, and a common seal, with power to change, alter, break, and make new the same, as often as they shall judge expedient, and they and their successors, shall be able and capable in law, to purchase, have, hold, receive, enjoy, possess and retain to them and their successors, in perpetuity, or for any term of years, any estate or estates, real and personal, messuages, lands, tenements or hereditaments, of what kind or nature soever, not exceeding ten thousand dollars per annum, and to sell, alien, exchange, demise or lease the same, or any part thereof, as they shall think proper; and by the same name to sue and be sued, implead and be impleaded, answer and be answered unto in any court of law or equity in this State, and to make such rules and by-laws (not repugnant and contrary to the laws of the land,) for the benefit and advantage of the said corporation, and for the order, rule and good government and management of the said school, and for the masters, teachers and scholars thereof, as shall be from time to time agreed to by the majority of the members of the said society.

II. *And be it further enacted* by (the) authority aforesaid, That it shall and may be lawful for the corporation hereby erected, to take and hold to them and their successors forever, any charitable donations or devisees of lands and personal estate, not exceeding in the whole the above mentioned sum of ten thousand dollars per annum, and to appropriate the same to the endowing and supporting the said seminary of learning, and to the maintenance and education of such poor and helpless orphans and indigent children as they shall judge proper objects of the charity hereby intended; and to appoint and choose, and at their pleasure to displace, remove and supply such officers, school-masters, teachers and servants, and other persons to be employed for the above purposes, or other officers of the said society; and to appoint such salaries, perquisites or other rewards for their labour or service therein, as the said society shall from time to time approve of and think fit.

III. *And be it further enacted* by the authority aforesaid, That this Act shall and may be given in evidence on the trial of any issue or cause in any court of law or equity, without special pleading.—*Ibid.*, pp. 118-19.

7. Charter of John's Island Society, 1779

WHEREAS, several respectable inhabitants of the parish of Saint John's, Colleton county, and others in this State, have associated themselves together for certain benevolent and charitable purposes, and have subsisted for many years past, and been of considerable public utility, by instituting and endowing a seminary of learning, and by supporting poor persons, who, through unavoidable misfortunes, have fallen into indigence, and have made application to the honorable the Senate and House of Representatives to be incorporated, and vested with such powers and privileges as will most effectually promote the good views and intentions of the members thereof:

I. *Be it therefore enacted* by the Honorable the Senate and House of Representatives of the said State, now met and sitting in General Assembly, and by the authority of the same, That the Honorable William Gibbes, Esquire, now President of the said society, and George Abbott Hall, Esquire, Vice-President, the present Stewards and other officers, and the several persons who now are, or shall hereafter be, members of the said society called the "John's Island Society," and their successors, officers and members of the same, shall be, and they are hereby declared to be, a body corporate and politic, in deed and in name, by the style and name of the "John's Island Society," and by the same name shall have perpetual succession of officers and members, and a common seal, with power to change, alter, break and renew the same, as often as may be necessary; and they and their successors, shall be able and capable in law, to purchase, have, hold, receive, enjoy, possess and retain to them and their successors in perpetuity, or for any term of years, any estate or estates, real and personal, messuages, lands, tenements or hereditaments, of what kind or nature soever, not exceeding ten thousand dollars per annum; and to sell, alien, exchange, demise or lease the same, or any part thereof, as they shall think proper, and by the same name to sue and be sued; implead and be impleaded, answer and be answered unto, in any court of law or equity in this State, and to make such rules and by-laws (not repugnant and contrary to the laws of the land) for the benefit and advantage of the said corporation, and for the order, rule and good government and management of the said society, as shall from time to time be agreed to by a majority of them.

II. *And be it further enacted* by the authority aforesaid, That it shall and may be lawful for the corporation hereby established, to take and hold to them and their successors forever, any charitable donations or devises of lands and personal estate, not exceeding in the whole the above mentioned sum of ten thousand dollars per annum, and to appropriate the same to such charitable and benevolent purposes as the said society shall think proper, and to appoint officers for the service of the said society.

III. *And be it further enacted* by the authority aforesaid, That this Act shall be deemed a public Act, and may be given in evidence on the trial of any issue or cause in any court of law or equity, without special pleading.—*Ibid.*, p. 121.

XI

THE RICHARD LUDLAM LEGACY, SOUTH CAROLINA

I. PREVIEW AND COMMENTS

THE REVEREND RICHARD LUDLAM, who served as S.P.G. missionary at St. James, Goose Creek Parish [1] from 1723 to 1728, on October 11 of the latter year left his estate, about 2,000 pounds currency, in part for establishing "a schoole for the instruction of poor children" in that parish. The money seems to have been put at interest until additional practical arrangements could be made to promote Ludlam's benevolent purpose, and the vestry of St. James sought to raise by private subscription additional contributions for the school intended by Ludlam to be established. According to Edward McCrady, Jr., in a paper [2] read before the South Carolina Historical Society August 6, 1883, more than fifty persons in 1744 and subsequently subscribed amounts ranging from five to 100 pounds, a total of more than 2,000 pounds. The preamble to the form under which subscriptions were made stated:

"*Whereas*, Nothing is more likely to promote the practice of Christianity and virtue than the early and pious education of youth, we whose names are underwritten, do hereby agree and oblige ourselves, our executives, and administrators, to pay yearly, for three years successively, viz. on or before June 18, 1745, 1746, and 1747, to the Rev. Mr. Millechamp, [3] or to the Church wardens for the time being, the several and respective sums of money over against our names respectively subscribed, for the setting up of a school in the parish of St. James, Goose Creek, on the land for that purpose purchased, for instructing children in the knowledge and practice of the Christian religion and for teaching them such other things as are suitable to their capacity." The names of the subscribers in 1744 and later were:

S. A. Middleton	£100	James Kinloch	£40	Robert Adams	£5
William Middleton	100	Gideon Faucheraud	10	Mag Eliz Izard	30
John Morton	60	William Allen	25	Maurice Keating	10

1. Pascoe, *op. cit.*, p. 850. Ludlam died in 1728.
2. "Colonial Education in South Carolina," Appendix II in C. Meriwether, *History of Higher Education in South Carolina* (1889), p. 214.
3. Missionary of the S.P.G.

Zach. Villepontoux	£ 50	Martha Izard	£ 20	James Bagby	£ 10
Peter Taylor	25	Mary Izard	20	Joseph Hasfort	15
Thomas Middleton	50	Susanna Lansac	10	James Marion	5
Richard Singleton	20	Jane Morris	20	Peter Porcher	15
Cornelius Dupre	5	Joseph Norman	20	James Singleton	10
Alexander Dingle	5	Richard Tookerman	5	Isaac Porcher	5
Stephen Bull	5	Benjamin Mazyck	15	Benjamin Singleton	10
G. Dupont	7	Paul Mazyck	50	Rachel Porcher	5
Henry Izard	60	Robert Brum	15	Sedgewick Lewis	25
William Wood	8	Thomas Singleton	10	James Lynch	30
Peter Taylor	100	John Tibbin	30	James Coachman	40
John Channing	100	John McKenzie	100	John Dras	100
C. Faucheraud	100	John Moultrie, Jr.	100	Rebecca Singleton	25
Robert Hume	100	W. Blake	100	Peter Tamplet	50
John Parker	70	Benjamin Coachman	100	Joseph Dobbins	25
W. Withers	50	Thomas Smith	50		
Benj. Smith	50	Henry Smith	50		

Exactly what practically resulted from these charitable efforts is not altogether clear, but the following documents throw some light on the undertaking projected by the will of Ludlam in 1728.

II. DOCUMENTS

1. THE WILL OF RICHARD LUDLAM, SOUTH CAROLINA, 1728

Memorandm that on this Eleventh day of Octo. 1728 I the Reverend Richard Ludlam Clerk Rector of St James Goosecreeke in the Province of South Carolina in Sound & disposing mind & memory tho Weak in Body do make & Constitute this my last Will & testament in manner & form following———Imprimis I bequeath my Soul to God who gave it & my body to be decently interred at the discretion of my Exrs hereafter to be named Item—I will that all my just Debts be paid—Item—I give & bequeath unto my brother Thomas Ludlam five Shillings—Item—I give devise & bequeath all my Estate Real & Personal whether in South Carolina or Elsewhere to the honble the Society for propagating the Christian Faith or Gospell in Forreigne parts & to their Successors forever with this trust & Confidence that at their discretion & under their Direction a School for the Instruction of poor Children be erected in the Parish of St. James Goosecreek in Berkly County in the Province of South Carolina out of the money that Shall arise from the Sale of my Said real & personal Estate given & bequeathed as aforesaid And I do hereby Authorise my Exrs hereafter to be named to make Sale of my real Estate for the uses above mentioned & remitt the money arising from Such Sale to the honble The Society or their Order—And Lastly I do nominate & Appoint my Loving friends the right honble Arthur Middleton Esqr Benj: Godin Esqr & Thomas Clifford Exrs of this my last Will & testament revoking all other and former Wills by me made In Witness whereof I do hereunto Sett my hand & seale—The original of this will is in Charleston. Copy is in the South Caroliniana Library of the University of South Carolina and a typescript copy is in the Library of the University of North Carolina.

2. Timothy Millechamp writes to the S.P.G. about Ludlam Legacy, May 22, 1734

We receiv'd Your letter concerning Mr Ludlam's legacy some time Since which Mr Dry was Order'd to answer immediately, tho there was little done; at that time, nor is there any thing Since towards applying the moneys to ye Uses it was Intended.—

The Vestry met and agreed that about 100 Acres of Land belonging to Mr Drye would be the most Convenient place for Erecting a School upon, distant from the Church about a Mile & a half. Since that time Mr Drye has resolved to remove from this province, to Cape Fare, before next Christmas & will therefore sell all his Lands here in one Tract, which is much to large for the Use a part of it was intended but Convenient land may without Doubt be procured, The money now in hand, I think is about 2000 of this Country Currency, besides Lands at Port Royall, & about the Same Vallue, which Cannot be disposed of without a power of Attorney from the Society; if that was Granted I me Inclined to think that the Parishioners would con- tribute towards erecting the School & other Conveniencys So as to Settle at Least a Considerable part of Mr Ludlams benefaction as a fund for a Certain dependance of the master, which besides Some Slaves & Cattle would be tollerable Subsistance for a Man that Should Come well recommended. Had ye money that is in Mr Drys hands been placed out on Security Since Mr Ludlams Death, the Interest by this time would have purchased Land & with the Assistance of the Parishioners built a Convenient house for the Education of them & their Children & Childrens Children; I would by no means be thought to Direct the Society in any of their proceedings, but I am perswaded yt if a power of Attorney, was sent over to any one here to sell the Lands above mentioned & out ye money ariseing from them, as well as that wch is now in hand at Interest ye Charitable work for which it was Intended would Soon be Effected & others by that means might be Inclined to follow yᵉ steps of yᵉ Donor—Foster, *op. cit.*, V, 657-58.

3. THE CHURCHWARDENS OF GOOSE CREEK WRITE ABOUT LUDLAM LEGACY, JULY 6, 1734

We the Minister Church wardens and vestry met on Monday yᵉ 1ˢᵗ instant to Consider what place & building would be most proper for Erecting a School, in our parish according to the Directions of Mʳ Ludlam's will & are of opinion that a Brick house because it is most durable, distant from the Church a Mile or two, that the Master and boys May attend divine Service More Constantly then yᵉ uncertain Seasons of the Year in this Country would otherwise permitt, and being also near the Centre of yᵉ Psh: Most of the Inhabitants May reap yᵉ benefit of it would be very Convenient.—

A Piece of Land belonging to Mʳ Drye was fixed upon soon after we receeded yᵉ Societys letter but his intention of removing to Cape fare, (of which Mʳ Millechamp Informed the Society in May last,) defeats our design. We have at present no opportunity of Makeing any Purchase, but would be much too large, nor Should yᵉ most advantageous one offer, can we Embrace it.—

The Money ariseing from yᵉ Sale of Mʳ Ludlams personall Estate which amounts to about £2000 Currency) is in Mʳ Dry's hands not in his power to dispose of, or Ours to demand of him, without a Letter of Attorney from the Society; without which the real Estate being Lands at Port Royall, cannot be disposed of. If that was Granted to any one here, so yᵗ yᵉ money already in hand, might be Made use of to purchase, or place out a little time on Security, with the Other when receeᵈ the Interest of both Sums at 10 p Cent with the Assistance of the Parishioners would procure all Necessary Conveniencies, establish a Certain Fund for a Master well qualified & recommended and might Encourage others to augment the former Endowment.—

These are yᵉ difficulty's yᵗ Chiefly delay the foundation of a School very much wanting in this Parish. Which we hope the Society will be So good as to remove by a power of Attorney as before Mentioned, and at yᵉ Same time beg leave to give this Caution, from an Uneasiness we See Created in a Neighbouring parish, on the like Occassion (ie:) not to Empower the Vestry (as Such) to receive & dispose of the Moneys above mentioned, but direct the management of it to one or more Persons, (as the Society think most proper) who are always to act with respect to it, as in a private Capacity—*Ibid.*, pp. 660-61.

4. WILLIAM DRYE REMITS TWO HUNDRED POUNDS STERLING ON THE LUDLAM LEGACY, SEPTEMBER 30, 1734

Inclosed I send the Hon: Society a Bill of Exchange for Two hundd pounds Sterling on Account of the late Revd Mr Ludlam's Estate, as Soon as I have Receed the whole that is Outstanding which I hope very Speedily to do, now that there is So good a Crop in all parts of the Country, I will take Care to remitt the ballance with Account Currant—*Ibid.*, p. 664.

5. WILLIAM GUY AND ALEXANDER GARDEN COMMENT ON THE LUDLAM LEGACY, APRIL 16, 1735

The Honourable Society's power of Attorney together with their Free and other papers therewith Enclosed relating to the Legacy of Richd Ludlam late Missionary at St James's Goose Creek this province came Safe to hand last Janry and as we Shall always give ready obedience to their Commands so we shall not be wanting to render them the best Service we Can in that affair with the Utmost Dilligence and fidelity.—

Mr Dry has Delivered Us the Account of his Administration of Mr Ludlams Estate to the 24th of Aprill 1732 together with the proper Vouchers of the Same Copies of the Inventory and Appraismt accounts of Sale, Journall of proceedings, the Severall titles deeds, also of the land and all other Papers in his Custody anywise relating or appertaining to ye sd Estate real or personal. He has also Delivered Us a farther account or Acco Currant—(a Copy of which we have here Enclosed) by which it appears he has remitted to the Honourble Society ye Sum of 200 £ Sterlg pr bills of Exchange at 635 p Ct Advance or £ 1470 of this Currency, So that there remains but a Small Ballance due and which when Recieved (being Still in Some out Standing Debts) he will pay into our hands.—

We have Carefully Examin'd his first Acco Viz: to ye 24th: of Aprill 1732 by the proper Vouchers & found the Same to be Exact & Just in every Article, and are ready to pass a Discharge for it. But as to the farther Account or Account Currant we shall meddle no farther with it then to Transmitt it till Such time as the Hone Society Shall acqut us of their Reciept of the Remittance therein mentioned, We hope the money was Safe in the Hone Society's hands by last Christmas, and as we Concieve their Chief motives for having it remitted them, must have been to Secure and improve it, so we shall only take leave to Intimate that the Legall Interest here is Ten pct pr Annum, and if this appear to them a better Improvement of it, then Can be made in England, they need only give us Ords to Draw for it on their Treasurer and we can Easily put it out at the Interest on Land Security and from the moment we Draw the bills.

Had the power of Attorney we have lately recieved been Sent us Three or four Years agoe it would have been considerably to the advantage of that Legacy—

And as to the State of ye Land or real Estate We have here Enclosed the State of the Case, and the Opinion of a Gentleman learned in the Law upon it. Vizt that the Executors named in the will ought to be made parties with us in the Conveyance of the Said Lands The Said Execrs do readily Consent So to be; but as Mistakes in things of this Nature are not easily rectified, We take leave to pary the Honble Society's Opinion also upon the Case, & to wait their finall Directions —*Ibid.*, pp. 671-72.

6. ACT CONCERNING THE WILL OF RICHARD LUDLAM, MARCH 28, 1778

WHEREAS, the Reverend Richard Ludlam, late of the parish of St. James Goose Creek, in the State of South Carolina, did, in and by his last will and testament, bearing date on or about the eleventh day of October, in the year of our Lord one thousand seven hundred and twenty-eight, give, devise, and bequeath all his estate, both real and personal, whether in South Carolina or elsewhere, to the honorable the Society for propagating the Gospel in Foreign parts, and to their successors forever, upon trust and confidence, that at their discretion and under their directions, a school for the instruction of poor children should be erected in the said parish of St. James Goose Creek aforesaid, out of the monies which should arise from the sale of his real and personal estate; and authorized his executors to make sale of such estate for the uses above mentioned, and remit the money which should arise therefrom to the said Society; And whereas, the said executors, having taken upon themselves the burthen of the execution of the said will, did dispose of part of the real and of all the personal estate of the said Richard Ludlam, for the use of the said Society, upon the trust and confidence abovementioned; And whereas, the said Society having never carried into execution the intentions of the said Richard Ludlam, are now become utterly incompetent to the purposes of his said will; but that the pious designs of the said testator should not be frustrated, it is expedient to vest such part of the real estate of the said Richard Ludlam as is undisposed of, and the monies and securities for monies which have arisen and been taken for the benefit of the said trust, in the vestry of the said parish of St. James Goose Creek, and to incorporate the same;

I. *Be it therefore enacted,* by his Excellency Rawlins Lowndes, Esq., President and Commander-in-chief of the State of South Carolina, by the honorable the Legislative Council and the General Assembly of the said State, and by the authority of the same, That all and every the person and persons who now are vestrymen for the said parish, and their successors hereafter to be chosen and elected to serve as vestrymen for the said parish for the time being, shall be, and they are hereby declared to be, one body corporate and politic, in deed and in name, by the name of the vestry of the parish of St. James Goose Creek; and by the said name the said vestry so to be chosen and elected as aforesaid, shall from time to time, and at all times hereafter, have perpetual succession and a common seal, with full power and authority to change, alter, break and make new the same when and as often as they shall see expedient; and that the said vestry for the time being, and their successors, are hereby declared able and capable in law to have, hold and receive, enjoy, possess and retain to them and their successors the vestry of the said parish for the time being, all such estate, real or personal, goods, chattels and effects, as by the will of the said Richard Ludlam were bequeathed or devised to and from the charitable uses and intents in the aforesaid will mentioned, or which have been or shall be purchased for the use and benefit of the said donation, and all securities for the same; and by the same name shall sue and be sued, implead and be impleaded, answer and be answered, in any court or courts within this State.

II. And whereas, the Reverend James Harrison, late rector of the said parish of St. James Goose Creek, was appointed by the said society for propagating the gospel in foreign parts as their attorney to manage the said trust, whereby he became possessed of and now hath all the monies, bonds and other securities for monies, deeds and other papers relative and belonging to the same; and whereas, the said James Harrison, by his removal from the said parish, is become incapable of transacting the business heretofore committed to his charge, and it is necessary that he should settle the accounts of the said trust; *Be it therefore enacted* by the authority aforesaid, That the said James Harrison, his executors or administrators, shall within three months from the passing of this Act render it upon oath to the said vestry, a true and just account of all sums of money in his possession which belonged to the said trust, and pay the same within one month thereafter to the said vestry for the time being, and deliver to them all bonds and other securities for monies, and also all deeds, evidences and writings touching or concerning any part of the estate of the said Richard Ludlam, deceased, and all other deeds and writings relative to the said trust.

III. *And be it also enacted* by the authority aforesaid, That after an account shall be taken and a copy thereof recorded in the secretary's office by the said vestry of the moneys and effects of and belonging to the said donation, the same shall be deemed and taken as the capital stock of the said vestry, and shall be kept and placed out at interest or otherwise improved as they shall think best; and the future interest and produce thereof shall thereafter be applied towards building and repairing a school or schools, and paying a school master or school masters, and for and towards the support, maintenance, tuition and education of such of the children of the poor of the said parish of St. James Goose Creek as shall be thereafter sent to school, in such manner and according to such rules as shall be established by the vestry for the time being of the said parish.

IV. *And be it further enacted* by the authority aforesaid, That it shall and may be lawful for the vestry of the said parish and their successors for the time being, to sell and dispose at public auction of all such lands as were of the said Richard Ludlam at the time of his decease and have not been heretofore disposed of; and on receipt of the money for which the same shall be sold, to execute conveyance for the same, good and sufficient in law; which said money shall be considered and so as the capital stock of the said vestry, and be kept and placed out at interest, or otherwise improved as aforesaid.

V. *And be it further enacted* by the authority aforesaid, That no person or persons whomsoever shall be elected, deemed or taken as a member or members of the said vestry or have a right to vote as such, until he or they shall have taken and subscribed the following oath, to wit: "I, A.B., do swear that I do not owe or am indebted to the vestry of the parish of St. James Goose Creek on account of the donation of the Reverend Richard Ludlam, deceased, any sum or sums of money whatever; and I do solemnly promise that I will not during the time of my being a vestryman apply for or take up at interest any sum or sums of money of or from the said vestry: So help me God:" which oath shall be administered by some justice of the peace in and for Berkley county, and by him certified to the said vestry.

VI. *And be it further enacted* by the authority aforesaid, That the said vestry shall be, and they are hereby, declared able and capable in law to have, hold, receive, enjoy, possess and retain to them all such other estate, real and personal, money, goods, chattels and effects, as have been already devised or bequeathed, or hereafter shall be devised or bequeathed to charitable uses within the said parish of St. James Goose Creek; subject, nevertheless, to the will, directions or appointments of the donor or donors.

VII. *And be it further enacted* by the authority aforesaid, That this Act shall be deemed and taken as a public Act, and notice shall be taken thereof in all courts of justice and elsewhere in this State, and shall be given in evidence on the trial of any issue or cause without special pleading.—Cooper, *The Statutes at Large of South Carolina,* IV, 438-40 (1778).

7. REPORT OF THE LEGISLATIVE COMMITTEE ON THE LUDLAM LEGACY, DECEMBER 19, 1843

The Committee on Education, to whom was referred the Report of the Attorney General, on the Ludlam School Fund, transmitting the annual Report of the Vestry of St. James, Goose Creek, for the year 1843, beg leave to Report: That they have considered the same, and find that this fund now consists of one hundred and six (106) shares in the Capital Stock of the Bank of the State, seven (7) shares in the Capital Stock of the Bank of South Carolina, and two hundred and fifty dollars ($250) of City six per cent. Stock. The said Vestry of the Protestant Episcopal Church of St. James, Goose Creek, also hold certain claims against Barnard E. Bee, who was several years ago, Chairman of the said Vestry, and had the administration of this charitable fund. It appears by the Report of the Attorney General, to the Legislature, submitted by him on the 30th November, A. D. 1840, that these claims consisted of a Bond dated 1st November, A. D. 1833, conditioned for the payment of the principal sum of three thousand dollars, ($3,000) with interest thereon, from the date thereof, and of the sum of one hundred and sixty-four 31-100 dollars received by him as Chairman aforesaid, on 8th March, A. D., 1829, and of the further sum of two hundred and fifteen dollars, ($215,) received as above, on 2nd January, A. D. 1833. In that Report the Attorney General states, that this bond is not secured by a Mortgage, nor is there any security of any other sort for it, and as he is understood to be insolvent, and has left the State, there seems to be little present prospect of collecting either the amount due on his bond, now amounting with interest to nearly $4,500, or the two other sums of $164 31 and $215. The Committee, so far as they are informed, believe that no legal measures have been adopted by the Vestry, as Trustees of the said charitable Fund, nor by the Attorney General, to recover these claims.

The Committee are aware that the said Barnard E. Bee did recently return to this State for a short time, and are of opinion that whenever he should be within the reach of legal process these claims should be put in suit. The expense would be very inconsiderable, and they should not be allowed to remain in their present situation any longer than is unavoidable.

It appears by the Report and accompanying statement of the Vestry, that there are now established in the Parish of St. James, Goose Creek, and supported by this fund, two Schools, at each of which twenty-two (22) scholars were educated during the last year, at the annual expense of five hundred dollars, ($500) for both schools. The Vestry have not reported "the length of time during which these schools were in operation" as required by this Legislature, at its last Session. The balances reported by your Committee as unaccounted for at that time have been passed to the credit of the fund. The last investment made by the Vestry was by the purchase of two hundred and fifty dollars ($250) six per cent. Stock of the City of Charleston, instead of State six per cent. Stock, as directed by the joint Resolution of this House and the Senate, in December, A. D. 1842; assigning as a reason, which your Committee deem satisfactory, that there was no State six per cent. Stock to be obtained, except at too high a premium.

Your Committee believe, that the present administration of this fund, is prudent and judicious, but the experience of the past has demonstrated the necessity of a strict supervision, and the objects of the benevolent founder of this public charity, will be best secured by a more rigid system of accountability. Your Committee therefore recommend the following resolutions:

Resolved, That the Vestry of the Protestant Episcopal Church of the Parish of St. James, Goose Creek, shall make an annual Report to the Legislature, setting forth therein the number of Schools established by them, the names of the Teachers, the number of the Scholars, and the length of time during which the Schools may be in operation.

Resolved, That the said Vestry shall, on the 1st day of November, in each year, render a statement of the condition of this fund, and an account of the disposition of the income arising therefrom, to the Comptroller General, at Charleston, who shall examine and credit the same: That the said Vestry shall, at the same time, exhibit all bonds, choses in action, and certificates of Stock, of which the said funds consist, and vouchers of the annual amounts: That thereupon, the said statement and account, being first approved by the Comptroller General, shall be appended to the annual Report of the Vestry.

Resolved, That the Vestry be required to put in suit the claims of the said Vestry, as Trustees of the Ludlam School Fund, against the said Barnard E. Bee, and report on the said 1st day of November, in each year, to the Attorney General, the progress of their proceedings; and they are hereby authorized to call on the said Attorney General for any professional assistance that the circumstances of the case may require.

Resolved, That the House do agree to the Report. *Ordered,* That it be sent to the Senate for concurrence.

By order,

T. W. GLOVER, C. H. R.

In the Senate, Dec. 19, 1843.

Resolved, That the Senate do concur in the Report. *Ordered,* That it be returned to the House of Representatives.

By order,

W. E. MARTIN, C. S.

—*Reports and Resolutions of the General Assembly of South Carolina,* 1843, pp. 144-45.

8. OPINION OF THE ATTORNEY-GENERAL IN THE CASE OF BARNARD E. BEE AND THE LUDLAM SCHOOL FUND, DECEMBER 2, 1846

To the Honorable, the President and Members of the Senate of the said State.

The Attorney General, in compliance with the Joint Resolutions of both branches of the Legislature, of December, 1844, directing him to report annually, the state of the proceedings against Barnard E. Bee, for the recovery of the debt due by him, to the Ludlam School Fund, respectfully Reports:

That judgment was obtained, and duly entered, against Mr. Bee, at the last May Term of the Court of Common Pleas for Charleston District, for the whole amount claimed to be due by him, to wit, for the principal sum of $3,000 due on his bond, and the sum of $379 31, received by him on Graves' bond, as stated in the former reports of the Attorney General, together with interest on these sums, from the periods, respectively, from which they bear interest. An execution has been issued on this judgment, but no property of the defendant has been discovered on which it could be levied; nor is there, at the present time, any prospect of payment of any part of the debt, otherwise than by means of the land in Texas, which is mentioned in the Report of last year.

The Attorney General further Reports. That in the exercise of the discretion confided to him by the resolutions of the last session, he accepted the conveyance of Mr. Bee's right to his League of Land in Texas, and thereupon entered an *exonereter* on his bail bond: and immediately afterwards adopted measures to have this right located, in order that the land might be rendered available by means of a sale. It appeared, however, that Mr. Bee had anticipated him in this, and with a view to obviate the objection heretofore made to his conveyance, of being merely the assignment of a right to land, and not a conveyance of any specific lands, had located his right, and obtained a patent for the land, in his own name. This patent was handed to the undersigned during the last summer, but on examining it, he discovered that it had been taken out in January of the present year, and this being subsequent to the date of Mr. Bee's conveyance to the Trustees of the Ludlam fund, a further conveyance, or assignment of the land mentioned in the patent was necessary; and such a conveyance was accordingly demanded, and cheerfully executed by Mr. Bee. Before, however, it was prepared and delivered to the undersigned, the Session of the Legislature was so near at hand, that he did not deem it proper to adopt any decided measures for making the sale of the land until the matter had been submitted to the Legislature for its instructions. He has however, made some inquiries as to the means of effecting a sale of this land, the result of which, together with the conveyance and patent, he is prepared to lay before a Committee of your honorable body whenever requested so to do.

All which is respectfully submitted.

H. BAILEY, *Att'y Gen.*

Columbia, Dec. 2, 1846.

THE STATE OF SOUTH CAROLINA
TO THE HONORABLE THE SENATE
AND HOUSE OF REPRESENTATIVES:

The Report of the Vestry of the Parish of St. James (Goose Creek,) respecting the Ludlam School Fund.

STATEMENT OF THE FUND.

106 State Bank Shares, at $85, ...	$9,010
7 South Carolina Bank Shares, at $38, ...	266
City six per cent. Stock, ...	250

Bond of Barnard E. Bee, dated 1st November 1833, conditioned to pay $3,000, with interest from the date. The sum of $164 31, rec'd by B. E. Bee, 8th March 1829; and $215 rec'd by him 2nd Jan. 1833.

$9,526

The condition of this claim will appear in the Report of the Committee on Education, a. a. 1843. p. 1844.
Since that Report the claim has been put in suit.

STATEMENT OF CASH FOR THE YEAR 1846.

By balance of January dividend on State Bank Stock, left undrawn by Thos. Gadsden former Chairman, ...	$ 55
By July div'd on do.	265
By July div'd on S. C. Bank Stock, ...	7
By January and February div'ds on City Stock, ...	15

$342

To Cash paid Mr. Nichols, teacher of the lower School, ...	150
Nov. 18, 1846.—By balance of Cash, ...	$192

This Report is presented thus imperfectly, in consequence of Mr. Thomas Gadsden, the former Chairman, having left the State,—without having furnished the Chairman with any statement of his receipts and expenditures. There is every reason to believe that the money received by him on account of this fund, has been scrupulously appropriated to its proper objects. The vouchers for the vested fund were delivered to the Chairman of the Vestry, during the past Summer, by the direction of Mr. Gadsden.

It is the intention of the Vestry to apply so much of the balance as may be necessary for the purchase of such books as may form a suitable Library for the use of the Schools, and also for the improvement of the School Houses, so as to make them neat and comfortable.

The salary of the teacher of the Upper School ($100) for the past year has not been paid, and is a charge on the balance reported.

The Comptroller General reports, that in obedience to the Resolutions of 1843, he has audited the Cash account and inspected the evidences of the vested fund, as herein before stated, and certifies the statements to be correct.

W. LAVAL,
For Comp. Gen.

November 21, 1846.

REPORT OF THE SCHOOLS.

The Upper School. Mr. Nichols, teacher. Scholars, ... 26
Period of Instruction—26 Scholars— 3 months.
              24   "   12   "
The Lower School. Mr. McCall, teacher. Scholars, ... 12
Period of Instruction—12 Scholars—12 Months.

    Total number of Scholars, ... $\overline{38}$
    All of which is respectfully submitted.

HENRY R. FROST,
Chairman pro. tem., and
Treasurer to the Vestry.

In a letter recently received from Mr. Thos Gadsden there is the following observations upon the state of the Ludlam Fund. "I enclose," he says, "my account current with the Ludlam Fund, showing a balance in my hands of $176 75. This sum would have been invested, but the Legislature restricted the Vestry in purchasing stocks, to the 5 and 6 per cents of the State; and for so small a sum, such investment could not be made. Having understood that there was no election of a Vestry on Easter Monday, I retained the amount, but am prepared when called upon by that body, to pay it over."

The Vestry then in office still continue, although there was no election held.

HENRY R. FROST,
Chairman pro. tem. and
Treasurer &.c.

—*Reports and Resolutions of the General Assembly of the State of South Carolina*, 1846, pp. 108-11.

9. Report of the House Committee on Education on the Ludlam School Fund, December 18, 1846

COMMITTE ON EDUCATION.

IN THE HOUSE OF REPRESENTATIVES, December 18, 1846.

The Committee on Education, to whom was referred the Report of the Attorney General, on the debt due to the Ludlam School Fund, respectfully Report; That they have considered the same, and recommend that the Attorney General be directed to bring the proceedings of the State in this case, to such a conclusion as he may deem most beneficial, and for this purpose, that he be empowered to have a sale made of all lands heretofore conveyed by Barnard E. Bee, to the Vestry of the Parish; and further, that his proceedings heretofore, be approved by the Legislature.

Resolved, That the House do agree to the Report.

Ordered, That it be sent to the Senate for concurrence.

By order,

T. W. GLOVER, C. H. R.

IN THE SENATE, December 18, 1846.

Resolved, That the Senate do agree to the Report.

Ordered, That it be returned to the House of Representatives.

By order,

W. E. MARTIN, C. S.

—*Ibid.,* p. 121.

XII

THE COLLEGE OF WILLIAM AND MARY

I. PREVIEW AND COMMENTS

ON A TABLET in the arcade of the Sir Christopher Wren Building at the College of William and Mary appears, among other statements, the following: "First College in the United States in its antecedents, which go back to the College proposed at Henrico (1619). Second to Harvard University in actual operation."

Attempts to establish a college in Virginia between 1617 and 1624 (Henrico College and East India School) failed. Documents on those efforts appear in Section I of this volume. Other efforts were made for higher education in that colony, especially in 1660, 1662, and 1691 when the General Assembly petitioned the Crown for "a free schoole & colledge." In 1691 the Reverend James Blair persuaded the Crown to allow funds from quit-rents for the support of a higher educational institution in the colony and two years later the charter for the College of William and Mary was granted.[1] Blair became its first president and served for a half century in that office. The charter of the college, in Latin and in English, follows in this section along with other documents.

The College of William and Mary was the first institution of higher education established in the South before the Revolution. The other eight collegiate institutions established in the American Colonies were Harvard (1636) in Massachusetts, under Puritan auspices; Yale (1701) in Connecticut, under Congregational auspices; Princeton (1746) in New Jersey, under Presbyterian auspices; The Academy and College (1753-55) in Philadelphia, through the efforts of Benjamin Franklin and his co-workers, but under no denominational auspices; King's College (1754) in New York, now known as Columbia University, under Anglican auspices; Brown (1764) in Rhode Island, under Baptist auspices; Rutgers (1766) in New Jersey, under Reformed Dutch auspices; Dartmouth (1769) in New Hamp-

1. Useful secondary accounts of the founding and early development of the College of William and Mary appear in many places, including Herbert B. Adams, *The College of William and Mary*. Circulars of Information of the Bureau of Education. No. 1, 1887. This study contains excellent bibliography and leads to sources. On the reorganization of the College of William and Mary in 1779, see Lyon G. Tyler, "A Few Facts from the Records of William and Mary College," in *Papers of the American Historical Association*, IV (October, 1890), 129-41.

shire, under Congregational auspices. In the establishment of all these institutions, except that which grew into the University of Pennsylvania, the religious or theological purpose was very strong. The very intimate relationship between the College of William and Mary and the Anglican authorities is nowhere shown so clearly perhaps as in Document 17 below, believed to be printed now for the first time. The original of this document, a single sheet of parchment, in the original Latin, is the property of the Library of the College of William and Mary. Photocopy of it is in the Library of the University of North Carolina.

The decline of the College of William and Mary led to energetic efforts in the 1820's to move the institution from Williamsburg to Richmond, documents on which proposal appear in a later volume. Of special interest in the life of the institution before 1800 is the reorganization of curriculum in 1779 when the Board of Visitors changed the college into "a university." [2] In 1819 the General Assembly chartered the University of Virginia which was opened in 1825. A proposal for a college in South Carolina was made in 1723 when "The Secretary Hart brought from the Upper House the Rever'd Mr. Morritts Proposal for a college." [3] The story of later efforts for a college in South Carolina has been excellently told by Professor J. H. Easterby. [4] In 1785 the General Assembly of South Carolina granted charters for colleges at Winnsborough, Charleston and Ninety-Six. [5] In 1801 the College of South Carolina (now the University of South Carolina) was founded at Columbia and opened its doors to students in 1805.

Initial efforts to provide for collegiate education in North Carolina

---

2. Mr. John M. Jennings, librarian of the Virginia Historical Society, says that the "text of the actual statute (probably composed by Thomas Jefferson) is lost—but important extracts were printed in *The Virginia Gazette* (Dixon & Nicolson) on 18 December 1779. This was certainly one of the earliest steps taken by an American college to liberalize its approach to higher education." Letter to Edgar W. Knight, September 10, 1947.

3. *MS House Journal*, Historical Commission of South Carolina, December 7, 1723.

4. "The South Carolina Education Bill of 1770," *The South Carolina Historical and Genealogical Magazine*, XLVIII (April, 1947), 95-111. I am grateful to Professor Easterby for his help with the South Carolina Bill of 1770. He kindly provided me with typescript copy of the document, a photocopy of which is in the Library of the College of Charleston and another is in the Library of the University of North Carolina. The original document is the property of the Historical Commission of South Carolina, Columbia. See Section X below for documents on early higher educational efforts in North and South Carolina.

5. Cooper, *Statutes at Large of South Carolina*, IV, 674-78. (March 19, 1785).

were made under Presbyterian auspices in 1771 when the General Assembly chartered Queen's College at Charlotte, empowered the institution to confer degrees, and provided for its support by a tax on liquors sold in Mecklenburg County for a period of ten years. All except two of the incorporators were Presbyterians, but the charter required that the president of the institution be a member of the Anglican Church. Presumably this requirement was an attempt "to forestall anticipated opposition in England." Governor Tryon urged royal approval of the charter, but the Commissioners for Trade and Plantations, although making a gesture toward religious toleration, seriously raised the question whether the Crown should encourage "toleration by giving Royal Assent to an Establishment, which in all its consequences, promises great and permanent Advantages to a sect of Dissenters from the Established Church who have already extended themselves over the Province in very considerable numbers," and advised that the charter be disallowed. The measure was vetoed [6] April 22, 1772, and Governor Martin, successor to Tryon, proclaimed the royal disallowance in 1773. Meantime, Queen's College had been opened to students and had operated without charter; and in 1777 the General Assembly of the new state granted another charter and changed the name from Queen's College to Liberty Hall Academy. On his Southern tour George Washington wrote in his diary May 28, 1791: "... Charlotte is a trifling place, though the Court of Mecklenburg is held in it. There is a School (called a College) in it at which, at times there has been 50 or 60 boys." [7] In 1789 the General Assembly chartered the University of North Carolina which was opened to students in 1795.

George Whitefield petitioned and made application to the Governor and Council for lands to endow a college in Georgia but it was not until 1785 [8] that provision was made in that State for higher education, through the charter of the University of Georgia (the

6. The question has been raised by some historians whether the veto did not turn in part also on the British mercantile policy.

7. John C. Fitzgerald (ed.), *The Diaries of George Washington, 1748-1799*, IV, 185.

8. The birthday of an educational institution is a bit difficult to establish. Is it the date of its charter, of the laying of the cornerstone of its first building, of the beginnings of instruction, or some other date? Georgia claims to be the oldest state university (chartered first) and North Carolina claims that priority (first to be opened to students). Once, while president of the University of North Carolina, Harry W. Chase undertook graciously to settle the issue, by beginning an address at the University of Georgia: "I bring from the oldest American state university greetings to the oldest American state university."

first American state to provide for a state university), which was opened for instruction in 1801.

Whitefield hoped to call the institution proposed by the name of "Bethesda College in the Province of Georgia." Although the colonial authorities approved the proposal "the English government insisted on conditions which Whitefield refused to meet, and so the charter was never granted. Balked in this far-sighted move, Whitefield turned to developing it into an academy" similar to the insitution Benjamin Franklin and his co-workers had projected in Philadelphia. White-field left the Bethesda property to the Countess Dowager of Hunt-ingdon; but before she could develop the institution into a college, in accordance with his will, the building was destroyed by lightning and the approach of the Revolution made impossible further develop-ment of the institution.[9]

II. DOCUMENTS

1. The need for a college in Virginia, 1660-1662

Bee itt enacted that there bee a petition drawn up by this grand assembly to the king's most excellent majestie for his letters pattents to collect and gather the charity of well disposed people in England for the erecting of colledges and schooles in this countrye and alsoe for his majesties letters to both universities of Oxford and Cambridge to furnish the church here with ministers for the present and this petition to be recommended to the right honourable governor Sir William Berkeley. (March, 1660/61).

Whereas for the advancement of learning, promoteing piety & pro-vision of an able & successive ministry in this country, it hath been thought fitt that a colledge of students of the liberall arts and sciences be erected and maintayned In pursuance whereof the right honour-able his majesties governour, council of state, and burgesses of the present grand assembly have severally subscribed severall consider-able sumes of money and quantityes of tobacco (out of their charity and devotion) to be paid to the honourable Grand Assembly or such treasurer or treasurers as they shall now or their successors hereafter at any time appoint upon demand after a place is provided and built upon for that intent and purpose, *It is ordered* that the commissioners

9. E. Merton Coulter, *Georgia: A Short History* (Chapel Hill: The University of North Carolina Press, 1947), pp. 71, 72. See also the section on Bethesda Orphan House above.

of the severall county courts do att the next followinge court in their severall countys subscribe such sumes of money & tobaccoe towards the furthering and promoteing the said persons and necessary worke to be paid by them or their heires, as they shall think fitt, and that they alsoe take the subscriptions of such other persons at their said courts who shall be willing to contribute towards the same And that after such subscriptions taken they send orders to the vestryes of the severall parishes in their severall countys for the subscriptions of such inhabitants and others who have not already subscribed and that the same be returned to Francis Morrison Esquire. (March, 1660/61).

Whereas the want of able and faithful ministers in this countrey deprives us of those great blessings and mercies that always attend upon the service of God; which want, by reason of our great distance from our native country, cannot in probability be always supplied from thence: Bee it enacted, that for the advance of learning, education of youth, supply of the ministry, and promotion of piety, there be land taken up or purchased for a college and free school: And that there be with as much speed as may be convenient houseing erected thereon, for entertainment of students and scholars. (March, 1661/62).—Hening, *Statutes at Large*, II, 30-31, 37, 56.

2. SOME PIRATES ARE REQUIRED TO SHARE THEIR LOOT WITH THE COLLEGE, ABOUT TO BE CHARTERED, 1689

. . . . Edward Davis,[1] Lional Delewafer and John Hinson were by Cap. Simon Row Commander of his Majesty's Ship Dun seized and Secured at the Mouth of James River, 1688, upon suspicion of being Pirates having a Considerable Quantity of Plate and Money with some other things according to an Inventory thereof taken, and were brought before the Governor (Lord Howard) then in Council and upon their Examination they declared they had been trading and had come from Bermudas to Pensylvania, from Pensylvania to Maryland and from Maryland in a Shallop down the Bay with Intention to go

---

1. These three pirates were probably entitled to the benefits of the royal proclamation, but they had too many valuable possessions for the freebooting naval officers of the time to let them off lightly. They were taken to England, and on March 10, 1691/2, the Privy Council ordered their release and pardon on condition (a condition proposed by the pirates) that £300 of their money then in England, and one-fourth of what was in the hands of one Captain Rowe, should be given to William and Mary College about to be chartered. This "deal" was the handiwork of that shrewd Scotsman, Rev. Dr. James Blair. See the order of the Privy Council, *William and Mary Quarterly Historical Magazine*, VII, 165.

to Lynhaven in this Colony there to set themselves down and Produced Passes under the hand of two Justices of Peace in those Provinces. The Governor suspected the Plate, Money & Goods to be piratical, therefore secured them and Committed the Persons to James City Gaol there to remain till the Matter be represented unto his Majesty and his Majesty's Pleasure: But the 16 of August these Persons Petitioned the Governor and pray'd the Benefit of the King's Proclamation for the more Effectual reducing Pirates and Privateers upon which they affirmed they came in and the Proclamation being Published the 6 of August they apprehended themselves to be within it. The Governor told them the matter lay before the King and that he could not proceed until his Majesty's Pleasure signified. On the 18 of April they again Petitioned the President and Council setting forth their whole case and praying to be enlarged and their Plate &c restored, upon which the Council advised and for answer returned that his Majesty by the Lord Sunderland's Letter was pleased to Signifie that they or any other persons who shall be apprehended for Piracy be prosecuted according to Law at such time & in such Manner as Sir Robert Holmes or his Agent shall desire And Capt. Berry being Sir Robert's Deputy was to be acquainted with the Petition before any Proceeding could be had they Petition'd again the 23 April to which the Council answered that Capt. Berry was expected soon in Town and it was necessary to know what Orders he had received from Sir Robert Holmes and Capt. Berry was afterwards acquainted with this Petition and he answered that according to his direction from Sir Robert he could not Proceed to trial until the Plate &c. were deliver'd to him. Which considered by the Council they were of Opinion it was not consistent with the Present Case that the Money &c. should be removed until the Case was fully heard and determined. The 29 April they petition again to the same Effect as before upon which the Council resolve that as they came in Voluntarily and Capt. Berry refused to proceed to trial of them that the Money should remain where it was lodged by his Excellency and that they giving Security for their good Behaviour should be permitted to take a Voyage to England in Order to receive his Majesty's Pardon or be proceeded Against according to Law and they are allowed 30L apiece out of their Money to defray their Charges and Wm. Edwards, Clerk of Council ordered to take out of the Chest in presence of Ralph Wormeley and Christopher Wormeley Esq'rs and ordered that a further sum be paid out of it to Geo. Marable and another to Nich Spencer.—"The Randolph Manuscript," *The Virginia Magazine of History and Biography*, XX, No. 1 (January, 1912), 5-7.

3. PAPERS RELATING TO THE COLLEGE OF WILLIAM AND MARY, 1690, 1691, 1692 [1]

Severall Propositions to be humbly P'sented to the Consideration of ye next Generall Assembly, for ye better incouragement of Learning By the founding a Colledge in this Country to consist of three Schools, Vizt Grammar, Phylosophy, & Divinity.

It is proposed yt the Genll Assembly would humbly address their sacred Majties to grant their Lysence and Royall Charter to enable & impower certain fitting persons to found & erect a Colledge in some convenient place in this Country, & yt out of their Royall bounty & favour, their Majties would be gratiously pleased, to grant part of their Quittrents of this Country towards the better enabling the sd persons to build the said Colledge, and provide for the yearly maintenance of ye same.

That either by continueing the p'sent dutyes upon all Liquors imported into this country, or an Additionall Duty on ye same, or by any other better wayes or means, as to the Wisdom of the Assembly shall seem most Certaine and effectual, a sufficient yearly maintenance may be settled & provided for ye paying the Stipends and yearly Allowances of ye Mastrs and Professrs and the defraying other charge of the said Colledge.

That Care be taken for ye providing able & fitting Mastrs and Profesrs for the said Schooles, Vizt for the Grammar School, a Master, & an able Usher. For the Phylosophy school, two able Profesrs, one for Logick & natural Phylosophy, & the other for ye Mathematicks; for the Divinitie schoole one able Professor, skill'd in ye Orientall Languages, & one able & grave divine, to be President of the Colledge who may be fitting in case of mortalitie, or Disabilitie of any of the said Profesrs to supply their place while another may be procured.

That for the better Encouragement of able and Learned men, to undertake the said places, there may be allowed to the said President, and to Every of the said Mastrs & Professrs ye yearly allowances following. Vizt:—

To ye President of ye Colledge, ... £150
To ye Professrs of Divinity, ... £150
To Each Professr of Phylosophy, ... £ 80

1. These papers are copied from MSS in the British Record Office.

and liberty to take £1 yearly of each Schollar, excepting tenn poor Schollars who are to be taught gratis.

To the Mastr of ye Grammar schoole £80, with the liberty to take fifteen shillings pr Annum of each scholar, excepting 20 poor schollars, who are to be taught Gratis.

To ye Usher £50 & liberty to take five shillings yearly of each schollar, except the twenty poor schollars aforesd.

That for ye better encouragemt and enabling fitting persons to transport themselves into this Country, to undertake ye said places, there be advance, & allowed to ye President, and each of ye sd Mastrs & Profesrs £50 a piece, & to ye Usher £25.

That a convenient place may be appointed as near as may be to ye Centre of ye Country for ye seating of the said Colledge, and a sufficient Quantity of land purchased for ye same, whereon may with all possible expedicon be builded Convenient & necessary houses.

That due Regard be had for ye making Statutes & Ordinances, for ye well Governmt of ye said Colledge.

Endorsed.

Virginia, 1690.

Proposall of ye Clergy for ye founding a Colledge.

Instrument app'ting Comrs for taking Subscriptions towards a Colledge to be erected:

Whereas I understand that a good Proposicon concerning ye building & endowing of a free school & colledge in this Colony of Virginia, hath been made by several pious, & charitable Gentlemen & by them p'sented to ye honble councel of State; who likewise approved of ye same, as an excellt design, for ye good education of ye youth, & for a continual supply of ye Ministry, of this Colony. And that towards ye effecting of so good a work, the two chief things yt are wanting, are Sufficient subscriptions, for charityes & free gifts, to defray ye charge of ye building, together wth an Act of Assembly, providing a yearly Revenue, for ye Endowing, of ye sd free Schoole & Colledge, according to ye meaning, & intent of ye sd Proposicon: & being most willing & desirous yt so good, & necessary a work may be carried on, wthout farther delay, wee do hereby impower & Authorize you—

Mr James Blair Commissary, Capt Wm Randolph, Coll: Edward Hill, Mr Francis Eppes, & Capt Joseph Foster, Mr Patrick Smith, Minister of Southwark, Mr Benj:Harrisson, Mr Hen: Baker, Coll. Tho: Milner, Coll: Joshua Lawson, & Coll: Lemuel Mason. Mr Samll Ebon,

Minister of Bruton, Edm: Jennings Esqe, Capt Fran: Page, Mr Hen: Hartwel, & Mr Wm Sherwood & Capt: Hen Duke.

Mr Dewel Pead Minister of Middlesex, Mr Christopher Robinson, Mr John Buckner, Majr Lewis Burrell, Coll: Phill: Lightfoot, Majr Hen: Whiteing, Capt: John Smith, Mr Tho: Foster, Coll: Rich: Johnson & Mr Wm Leigh

Mr John Farnefold, Minister of Bowtracey, Capt Geo: Cooper, Mr Christopher Neale, Capt Wm Hardrick, Capt Lawrence Washington, Coll: Wm Fitzhughes, Capt Wm Ball, Capt John Pinkard, Mr Rob: Carter, & Capt Wm Lee

Mr Teagle, Minister of Accomack, Coll Danll Jenefer, Coll Char: Scarborough, Coll Jno West & Capt Jno Custis

—Jointly or Severally, to procure as many Subscriptions gratuities & benevolences as you can wthin this Colony of Virginia, towards ye defraying ye charge of ye sd buildings, hoping if it shall appear by ye largeness & numbers of ye sd subscriptions, yt ye Countrey intends sincerely & seriously to advance so good a work, yt then it will meet wth no Obstruccon, neither from their Majesties, nor from ye generall Assembly but will be duely carried on & receive all Legal approbacon, & encouragemt. Given under my hand & Seal this 25th day of July in ye 2d year of yeir maties reign. Ao Domini 1690.

(Francis Nicholson.)

Wee whose names are Subscribed being desirous to promote ye good design of a free schoole & Colledge in Virginia,—to Show or forwardness therein, for ye good Example of others, Do hereby freely offer towards ye building of ye sd schoole & colledge & other necessary houses, thereunto belonging, the several Sums here affixed to our names wch sums we do hereby bind orselves, or heirs & executrs to pay, or cause to be paid wthin six months after ye Generall Assembly of this Colony shall have passed An act, for endowing of ye sd free schoole & Colledge, & their Majties have confirmed ye same, to such Collector, or Collectors, as by Law shall be appointed, for Receiveing ye sd paymts. In witness whereof we have hereto Set or hands & Seales.

Endorsed:—Virginia, 1690.

To ye Honble Merchts of London, especially such as Traffick in Virginia:

Honble Gentlemen.—The Lieut Governr, Councill, Gentry & Clergy of this Collony being at p'sent about a Charitable design of erecting & founding a Free Schoole & Colledge, for the Education of our youth, a constant supply of our Ministry, & p'haps a foundation for ye Conversion of our neighbouring Heathen to ye Christian Faith, they have not only contributed very liberally themselves, but being well assured of yor Kind Dispositions towards this poor Country, they have commanded us to send you the enclosed Breefe, & withall in their names to entreat, not only yor own charitable subscripcons towards soe good a work; but also yor Intercessions wth such of yor Friends & Acquaintance as you know to be men of Publick Spirits, or to have any p'ticular respect to this place. Your good example herein as it will be rewarded by God, soe shall never be forgotten by us, & we hope our Posterity will have occasion to bless yor memorys, & to Record your names among their first and chief Benefactors: Thus commending this pious & charitable work to Gods blessing & yor Liberality,

Honble Gent: we subscribe ourselves

Your faithfull & ready servst

James Blair, Comiss:

Pat: Smith, Sur:

Sam: Eburn, Sur:

Deuel Pead, Sur:

John Farnefold, Sur:

James Citty in Virginia

July 25th 1690.

Endorsed:—Proposals of the Clergy to the Merchts of London for the founding of a Colledg.

Instructions to Mr James Blair Comissary &c. appointed by ye Genr Assembly of Virga for Soliciting ye business of a free Schoole & Colledge in England.

1. That you goe directly from hence, wth this present Fleet.

2. You shall deliver to my Ld Bishop of London ye Lettr wch you herewith receive, directed to his Lordsp you shall desire his Assistance, & as to ye most Convenient Way, & manner of executing these Instructions, you shall depend on his advice & Directions.

3. You shall Use such means & Applications to deliver our humble Supplication to their Matys as you shall think necessarie.

4. You shall endeavr to procure from their Matys an ample Charter for a Free Schoole & Colledge, wherein shall be taught the Lattin,

Greek, & Hebrew Tongues, together wth Philosophy, Mathematicks & Divinity, & in Ordr to this you shall make itt yor business to peruse ye best Charters in England, whereby Free Schools & Colledges have been founded, haveing Regard alwaies to ye Constitution of this Governmt & particularly to ye Propositions presented to this Generall Assembly for a Free Schoole & Colledge, a Coppy whereof you herewth receive.

5. Pray yt ye Free Schoole & Colledge bee erected & founded on ye South side of Yorke River, upon ye Land late of Coll Townsend deceased, now in ye possession of John Smith, & near to ye Port appointed in Yorke County.

6. Pray yt ye sd Colledge bee incorporated by ye Name of the Colledge of King William & Queen Mary, or if their Matys refuse this Name, by wt other Name they shall thinke fitt.

7. Pray yt ye sd Schoole & Colledge bee founded in ye Names of ye Honble Francis Nicholson Esq., Wm Cole Esq., Ralph Wormeley Esq., Wm Byrd Esq., John Lear Esq., Mr James Blair, Mr John Banister, Mr John Farnifold, Mr Stephen Fouace, Nathl Bacon Esq., John Page Esq., Tho: Milner Gent, Christopher Robinson Gent: Charles Scarbrough Gent, John Smith Gent, Benjamin Harrison Gent, Miles Cary Gent, Hen: Hartwell Gent.

8. Pray yt ye sd Founders may bee alsoe made Governrs of ye Lands, Possessions, Revenues, & Goods, of ye sd Schoole & Colledge.

9. Pray yt ye sd Governrs before their Entry & Admittance to their respective offices, may take ye Oath of Allegiance & Supremacy to King William & Queen Mary, & their Successrs Kings of Engld yt they may alsoe Subscribe ye Test agst Popery, & promise by Oath to bee faithfull in ye sd Office & Trust, & pferr Men according to their Meritts, without Fee, advantage, Favour, or Affection.

10. Pray yt ye sd Governrs & their Successrs may have a Comon Seale for signing all Ordrs & other things touching ye sd Corporation.

11. Pray yt ye sd Governrs & their Successrs may have power from time to tyme to Nominate & appointe to all places & Pfermt wthin ye sd Schoole & Colledge, & to supply ye sd Places in Case of Vacancy by Death, Resignation, Deprivation, or otherwise.

12. And if ye sd Governrs & their Successrs doe not within Eighteen Months after such Vacancy, make such Nomination & appointment, yt then & soe often ye Governr or Commandr in Chief for ye tyme being in this Country, shall & may by writeing under his Hand &

Seale, Nominate & appointe some Learned & meet Person to supply ye sd Place.

13. Pray yt ye Presidt & first Professr of Divinity bee ex officio of ye Number of ye Governrs.

14. Pray yt ye sd Governrs & their Successrs may have Power and Authoritie under their Colledge Seale, to sett down & pscribe such Ordrs, Rules, Statutes, & Ordinances, for ye Ordr, Rule, & Governance of ye sd Colledge, & of all Persons residing therein, as to ye sd Governrs & their Successrs shall seem meet & Convenient. And yt ye sd Ordrs, Rules, Statutes, & Ordinances, soe by them made & Sett downe, shall bee established in full Strength, Force, & Virtue in Law, Provided they be not repugnant to ye Prerogative Royall, to ye Laws & Statutes of England & this Dominion, nor ye Canons & Constitutions of ye Church of England.

15. Pray yt in case of ye Death of any of ye Governrs of ye sd Schoole & Colledge, or ye removing of his Habitation out of this Country, ye remaineing part of them may have power to Nominate their Successr.

16. Pray yt ye sd Governrs & their Successrs may have Power & Authority, to demise & purchase, to sue & bee sued, to take Guifts & Legacies for ye Use of ye sd Colledge. Notwithstanding ye Statute of Mortmaine, or any other Statute whatsoever.

17. Pray yt ye sd Governrs & their Successrs may have Power to Elect a Chancellr, who shall enjoy yt Honr seven Yeares, & noe longer, except hee bee elected de Novo.

18. You shall endeavr yt ye sd Schoole & Colledge, bee under noe other Visitation than by ye sd Governrs & their Successours.

19. To Pvent fraudulent dealings, You shall endeavr to have itt inserted in ye sd Charter, yt noe Leases shall bee granted to any yt are Governrs of ye sd Colledge, nor to any Psons in their Names, or for their behalfe, nor to their Successrs.

20. Haveing obtained ye sd Charter, you shall procure a good Schoolemaster, Usher & Writeing Master to bee sent into this Country; for ye importacon & Sallary of ye Schoolemastr & Usher, you shall in ye Name of ye Assembly, promise according to ye Propositions Psented to this Genll Assembly, to wch we refer you, & to ye Importacon of a fitt Man to teach Writing & Arithmetick you shall offer and for his Yearly Sallary.

21. You shall use yor best endeavrs to obtaine their Marys Lyscence to aske & Collect Benevolences towards ye sd Schoole & Colledge, &

to procure as many Subscriptions, Guifts and Benevolences thereupon as you can.

22. The Moneys, Guifts & Subscriptions soe procured, shall bee safely lodged in such Places & handes, as shall be agreed upon by ye Ld Bsp of London, his Excly ye Ld Howard of Effingham Govr of Virga, Mr Jeffrie Jeoffries, Mr Micajah Perry, & yrself.

23. You shall desire & endeavr yt all accts of ye sd Money bee inspected by ye Ld Bishops of London, Salisbury & St Asaph, ye Ld Howard of Effingham, Mr Jeoffrie Jeoffryes, Mr Micajah Perry, Mr Arthur North, Mr John Cary, Mr Fra: Lee & yorself.

24. And because itt is impossible soe to provide att this distance, yt all matters relateing hereto be duely answer'd & presented, Itt is thought fitt, & you are hereby impower'd in all Cases in wch you are not already directed by these or Instructions, to proceed according to ye Best of yor Judgemt and Discretion, haveing alwaies regard to ye Constitucon of this Country & Governmt.

25. And yt soe good a Worke may not miscarry, nor be unnecessariely delayed for want of Money, to prosecute itt.

Fr: Nicholson

William Cole Secry

Tho Milner Speaker

By Ordr of ye Burgesses

Endorsed. Generall Assembly of Virginia

Instructions to Mr James Blair

(in pencil)   May 1691 Virginia

A Memoriall concerning 200 £ raised out of the Quitt Rents now begg'd for ye Colledge of Virginia.

Observations.

It is very easy to demonstrate that not one farthing of this Revenue has been diverted from the use of the Government of Virginia, ever since it was repurchased by the Crown from my Lord Culpeper, and it is very strange it should be so positively alleadged to

The Quitt-Rents of Virginia since ye first settling of that Colony, have never turned to any Accot neither to the goverement of Virginia nor to the Crown of Engld, but have been unproffitably diverted from any Publick use, first by private Grants to the Lords Arlington & Culpeper, and afterwards promised indeed both have been Employ'd other-wise, when the Contrary may so plainly appear to ye Lords of ye Councill.

by King Charles & King James to ye Countrey of Virginia, but for what reasons I know not, it seems otherwise Employed.

This fund of Money lying ready in the Countrey appropriated to no use, only in Generall promised for the Countries Exigencies, is humbly conceived to be as proper & Convenient a Sum as can well be devised for their Majesties to grant towards the Erecting of this good foundation of a free School and Colledge, Especially since it is acknowledged, that there is no other Exigency of the Countrey as yet foreseen, upon wch the said Money can be so well Employed, but against this an Objection is suggested, that if the Countrey should want Money for fortifications or any other Exigencies of the Governmt (in case this £2000 should be disposed of, to the Colledge) the Govr would have this recourse to their Majts Treasurer here in England.

The Lieut Governr & Councill have represented, that ye Poverty of the Inhabitants, is such, that should any Attempt be made upon the Countrey, the Charge it would bring, would be very near the Ruin of Many of them, and if shipping should fail to come thither to take off their Tobacco, there will not be one penny to defray the charges of the Government, unless the same is paid out of the Quit Rents.

It were a Sufficient Answer to this Objection to Shew that what ever Forts have been built in the Countrey, and whatsoever the Charge has amounted to of Maintaining Garrisons in them, has been still defrayed by a Publick Levy upon the People, who have never been backward when the Governor thought fitt to call a Generll Assembly, but have from time to time raised Sufficient Sums of Money for ye defence of

their Country, when they were far less Numerous, and consequently not so able to bear the charge of a Publick Levy as now they are, but for a More particular Answer to the Objection, I will show that as the Quitt Rents never were laid out for defraying the Contingent Charge of that Governmt so there's no Necessity that they should, ye Countrey having Sufficiently provided for that by other & better Methods.

These Provisions are all precarious, & will not be in ye powr of the Crown as ye Revenue of the Quit Rents is, whch while it is so, The Assembly will not be so easily disposed by unquiet Spirits as often happens in Virginia, to avail themselves of the Necessities of the Govrment.

The Government have represented that ye Inhabitants are so poor & Indigent, that the Officers Cant compell them to find Arms as by Law they are Obliged.

10. By one of the Laws of Virginia, every Master of a family is obliged to keep a well fixed Gun, two pound of powdr and Eight pound of Shott, for every person that is able to carry Arms within his family, to be ready upon all Occasns for the defence of ye Countrey, a Law so dilligently put in practice, that there is no Custome more generally to be observed among ye young Virginians, than that they all learn to keep & use a Gun, wth a Marvellous dexterity as soon as ever they have strength enough to lift it to their heads, ye great Plenty of Game both in their woods & Rivrs paying them well for the trouble & charge they are at in Observing of this Law.

2. All the white men in the Countrey are listed in the Militia of ye Severll Countreys where they reside, Except a very few that are left to look after ye Stocks at home, while the rest are upon Military duty, this Militia is duly Muster'd & well accoutred, ye foot wth guns & Swords, and the Horse with Carbines Swords and pistolls.

3. There is a Certain Numbr of Rangrs kept under constant pay (Except the Govr think fitt to disband them) at ye heads of their great Rivrs from whence they are in danger of Incursions by land, who are at all times to give notice of any vestages they discover of ye Enemy, & are strong enough to fall upon & defeat any Ordinary gang of Indians.

4. In ye same Law which Establishes these Rangers, Entituled an Act for the better defence of the Countrey, there is a Clause giving power to the Lieutent Govr, or Comander in chief for the time being, with ye advice of ye Councill upon all Occasions to raise Levy & Muster such Number of Men, Horses, Arms & Amunition for ye better defence of the Countrey, as they shall think fitt, & obliging themselves to pay to every officer & Soldier, so raised at Certain rates menconed in ye sd Law, out of ye Publick Levy of ye Countrey.

5. And least any time by this means ye Publick Levy should be too great, and so prove burdensome to the Inhabitants, by another Law, Entituled an Act for lessening the Levy by the Poll and laying an

This article shews sufficiently what is before averr'd wch unjustly Suppose an Arbitrary Armed Force, to be made use of by the King, or his Governor to do w^t they please without ye Assembly, but it may be as well apprehend'd that if Their Maj^{ts} part wth this Revenue or this fund, ye Assembly may do what they please or impose upon the Kings Goveru^r when he shall be defeated of this Security.

If their Majesties shall think fitt to dispose of this fund, the only one I believe in their dominions, unanticipated, It may be so, or part of it much better towards repurchasing the other half of the Quit Rents of Virginia, the right of which upon the death of my Lord Culpepper, is Supposed to be vested in my Lord Fairfax and others This would be very acceptable to the People that Complain of Oppression from the Patentees, it would be a lasting benefit to ye Crown & Conduce to further support of the Government.

Imposition on Liqu^{rs}, they raise a fund of about a thousand pounds a Year wch they appropriate to no use, but Expressly reserve to be disposed of by the Govern^r, Counc^{ll} & Burgesses, for lessening ye Levy P Poll & for defraying ye Conting^t *charges of ye Government.*

It is true that these two last are both Temporary Laws, vizt: That wch gives ye Govr & Counc^{ll} Power to make what Military preparations they think fitt, and that which raises such a fund for defraying the Charge of it, The reason whereof is plainly this, that the Govr may be obliged to Call frequent Asemblys, wch are Esteemed as Necessary there as Parliaments are in England, and they reckon that if they gave away ye power of Levying & Maintaining at the Countrys charge, such an Arbitrary armed Force w^{thout} any limitation of time, there would be no more Occasion for Assemblys because the Govern^r might do what he pleased without them, But it is Evident not only from their usuall Practice, but also from the lasting reasons upon wch these Laws are founded, Viz^t: The defence of the Countrey and the defraying the Conting^t Exigencies of the Govern^{mt} that they are resolved from time to time to renew them and Consequently that the Govern^{rs} will not want Sufficient Means wherethall to defend the Countrey, Except there should happen to be so bad an understanding between him & them, that he leavs off Calling of Assemblys, and in that Case it is not this sum of Money now begg'd for the Erecting of the Colledge, nor a much greater One, that will be Sufficient to defend ye Countrey.

Their Lordsp^s may easily be inform'd of ye dayly necessities of the Governm^t for ye supplying of which, it is not always proper or reasonable, to Call an Assembly, nor are they always in Humo^r to grant what is desired of them, at least without much than an Equivalent, by parting with the Rights of the Crown. And it is no less Strange, that in this time of Warr, there neither is nor may be as it is alledged, any Exigency foreseen, to require the use of this fund for the Support of the Governm^t, The Lords of ye Councill will Judge otherwise, and that this Exigency is very near at hand, and more pressing than the Erecting of a Colledge, wch the Assembly of Virginia can easily provide for.

Endorsed:—Memor^{ll} concerning 2000 £ raised out of the Quitt Rents now begg'd for ye Colledge of Virginia—with Observations.

(In pencil.) Virginia, ?—ab^t July, 1692.

Virginia.
At the Court at Whitehall
the 28th July 1692
By the Lords of their Mat^{ys} most Hono^{ble}
Privy Councill.

Upon reading the Petic^{on} of James Blair Clerk touching a Grant for Erecting a free School and Colledge in Virginia and for Settling to the said Colledge & Clergy Severall Branches of the Revenue there not already Appprpriated to any other use in that Colony, And whereas A Report from the R^t Hono^{ble} the Lords Commission^{rs} of Their Mat^{ys} Treasury and other Papers relating thereunto were also read and Considered It is this day Ordered in Councill that A Copy of the s^d Report be sent to Mr Attorney Gener^{ll} who is to Consider the same, And to Report Whether Escheats can be granted before they Actually Accrue.

John Nicholas.

Virginia.
At the Court at Whitehall
the first of September 1692
Present
The Queens Most Excell^t Mat^y
in Councill,

A Report from the Right Hono^{ble} the Lords Com^{rs} of the Treasury having been read at the Board in the words following:
Vide ye Report——

May it please Your Maty

We have considered the two Memorlls hereunto Annexed the one proposing A free School & Colledge in Virginia &c,

Her Maty in Councill is this day graciously pleased to Approve the Same, Except the last Clause thereof Concerning Escheats, And to Order as it is hereby Ordered, That the Sum of £1985: 14: 10 mencon'd in the first Clause of the said Report be Apply'd towards the building of A free School & Colledg and to no other uses whatsoever.

And that the neat Surplusage of ye Quit rents menconed in the Second Clause thereof, After the Lieut Governr is paid £300 P Ann which will Amount to About 500li P Ann be granted and Appointed for three Years next Ensuing for the Maintenance of the Ministers the same to be divided and Apporconed as followeth, £100 P Ann to the Commissary, the remainder to be Equally distributed Amongst the Ministers resident on the place by the Governr and Commissary.

And that the neat produce which shall arise in England by Selling here the Tobacco which shall be Collected in Virginia and Maryland for or in Lieu of the peny P li Imposed by an Act 25 Car. 2d upon Tobacco Exported thence to the other Plantations, with Their Mats Part of the Forfeitures which shall be Sued for and Recovered in Virginia or Maryland upon the said Act or the Acts of Trade and Navigacon. And the Lands on the South side of Blackwater and the Parmunkee Neck And the Office of Surveyor Generll now void, or when it shall become void menconed in the 3d 4th & 5th Clauses of the said Report, be Granted for ever towards the Maintenance of the said Free School and Colledge According to the said Report, Provided they Appoint such under Surveyors from time to time as shall be Approved of by the Governr or Commander in Chief for the time being, and the Councill of that Colony.

And the Lords Commissionrs of the Treasury are to Issue all necessary Orders and directions for the Effectual doing thereof Accordingly.

To the King & Queens most Excellent Majestyes. The humble Addres of yor Majestyes Councill and Burgesses of the Generall Assembly of Virginia:

May it please yor Majestyes. Your Majestyes having been most Graciously pleased upon ye humble Supplication of Your Generall Assembly of Virginia, To grant your Royall Charter for erecting the

Colledge of William and Mary in this Country for the Education of Youth, And a Seminary of a Church of England Ministry amongst us with Severall Royall Donations to the Same We therefore your Majestyes most Loyall Subjects by this our most humble Addres begg leave to returne our most hearty thanks for Such a Signall Testimony of your Majestyes pious and Christian care of your Subjects in this part of the world, and as the best Expression of our gratitude are Resolved to further and promote your Majestyes Pious intentions by giveing such countenance and Encouragement to so Noble an Undertaking as our poor circumstances will aford there being nothing whereof we are more earnestly desirous then that our Children may be Educated in all dutys of Piety towards God and Loyalty to your Sacred Majestyes whose long life and prosperity is the earnest and Constant prayer of

Your Majestyes
most Loyal
Dutifull
and
Obedient Subjects.

May it please yr Excellency

In Obedience to yr Excellys letter of the twenty-fourth of March last wee doe humbly certify to yr Excely that wee have carried on the building of two Sides of the designed Square of the Colledge (wch was all wee judged wee had money to goe through with) and have brought up the Walls of ye Said building to the roof wch hope in a Short time will be finished, Collo Ludwell having promised to Shingle it upon Creditt we transmitt herewith the accounts of the Said building, and other Expences belonging to the Colledge by wch it will appeare that wee have Expended one hundred & Seventy pounds Eight Shillings two pence farthing more than wee have yet received wch has been advanct by Some of or number.

We likewise transmitt to yr Exclly the accounts of the Penny P pound given to the Colledge by his Majt Royall Charter and of the Skinnes & furres granted by an Act of Assembly by wch account it will appear that accrues to the Colledge the Summe of five hundred thirty Seven pounds fifteen shillings three pence three farthings over and above wt has defrayed the Presidt and Masters Sallaries wch Summe wee have applied towards the building the Edifices of the said Colledge

The Rule wee have followed in Settling the penny P pound with the Severall Collections of Virg^a & Maryland is the Same wch was approved by ye Hono^{ble} the Com^{rs} of his Maj^s Customs as by their letters to us of Apr^{ll} 24th 1694 & Jan^{ry} 4th 1695 doth appear Viz^t allowing to ye Said Collect^{rs} twenty P Cent of ye said revenue & reserving the remainder to ye Colledge

And to ye end that the Colle^{rs} accounts of ye penny P pound may bee duly Examind wee have Ordered that ye Rect^r for ye time being the Treasu^r and Presid^t or any one of them wth two more of ye Gov^{rs} of the Colledge (not being Collec^{rs}) shall inspect & Auditt the Said accounts and transmitt ye Same (being sworn to before y^r Exc^{lly}) together with ye Lists of Shipps to the Hono^{ble} the Com^{rs} of his Maj^s Customes wch their Hon^{rs} Expect from us instead of a Compt wch office they have let fall Saveing ye profitts thereof to ye Colledge.

In Maryland his Exc^{lly} Govr Nicholson takes care to have ye Collec^{rs} accounts auditted, & Sworn to before him, & his Maj^s hon^{ble} Councill of ye province, & transmitted to us together wth their lists of Shipps

Wee have likewise Settld ye office of Survey^r Gen^{ll} & did formerly exhibitt to ye Excelly a list of ye particular Surve^{rs} for ye particular Counties of this Country, but these Settlements have not been So long made as to bring in any revenue to ye Colledge, wch wee Expect they will doe about Christmas next.

Wee are beginning to lease out the tenn thousand acres of Land of his Maj^{tes} Royall grant to the Colledge on the black water Swamp, But the other ten thousand acres in Parmunkey neck, haveing a dispute ab^t it with some pretenders, o^r Chaine was Stoppt and the Survey not yet finished, as we hope it will be in a little time.

Wee have founded a grammar School wch is well furnisht wth a good School-master Usher and Writing-master in wch the Scholl^{rs} make great proficiency in their Studies to the Gen^{ll} Sattisfacon of their parents and guardians.

The work of the building and furnishing of the Colledge being now almost at a Stopp for want of money, we have desired Mr President Blair to goe home for England to procure what assistance hee can towards the finishing of it.

This is what occurrs to us at p'sent for y^r Excy's Sattisfacon wch we humbly Submitt, and are

          Yo^r Excys most humble
          Servants

Steph: Fouace Rector, Fr: Nicholson, Wm Byrd,
James Blair, Cha: Scarburgh, Jon Smith,
Benjn Harrison, Miles Cary, Wm Randolph,
Matthew Page.

(In pencil) ? June, 1696.
Virginia. To the Kings Most Excellent Majty
Amidst the Generall Acclamacons of all your Majties Joyfull Subjects for the Signall Deliverance of Your Majties Sacred person and preservacon of our Religion, Lawes and Government from the late horrible Conspiracy of Papists and other wicked and traiterous persons Wee the Subscribers and Trustees and Governors of the Colledge of William and Mary in Virginia Beg Leave to Joyne Our most hearty Congratulacons and withall upon this Occasion to Renew our protestacons of Loyalty, Obedience and Gratutude to Your Majty as Lawfull and Rightfull King of England and the Dominions thereunto belonging together with the Acknowledgmt of Our Lasting Obligations to Your Majty as the Royall Founder and most bountiful benefactor of this Rising Colledge which has the honour to Carry to Posterity the memory of the blessed and Auspicious Names of King William and Queen Mary and will Ever be Devoted to Your Majties Service and Interest against all Your present and future Enemyes.

Jno Smith, Rector; Phill: Ludwell,
Dan Parke, Fra: Nicholson, Matthew
Page. W. Edwards, Lewis Burwell,
Will Fitzhugh, R. Wormeley, William
Byrd, James Blair, Benjn Harrison,
Miles Cary.

Endorsed: Address from Virginia.
—*William and Mary College Quarterly Historical Magazine*,
VII, 158-74.

4. THE GENERAL ASSEMBLY OF VIRGINIA PETITIONS THE CROWN FOR "A FREE SCHOOLE & COLLEDGE," 1691

To *their most Excellt Maties* Wm & Mary *by ye Grace of God of* England, Scotland, France, Ireland, & Virga *King & Queene Defenders of the Faith &c*

The humble Supplication of ye Generall Assembly of Virga

Wee the Lt Governr Councill & Burgesses of this general Assembly which is the first since your Maties most Gracious & happy reigne over us being encouraged by yor Princely Zeall for Promoting Religion & vertue, and incited by ye urgent necessities of this yor Maties Dominion, where our youth is deprived of the benefitt of a liberal & vertuous Education, and many of our Parishes of that instruction & comfort which might be expected from a pious & learned ministry have unanimously Revolved as the best Remedy for those great evills, and as the most Suitable expression wee can make of our hearty concurrence with your Maties in Supporting the Protestant Religion, & the Church of *England*, humbly to Supplicate yor Maties for your Royall grant & Charter to erect & endow a free Schoole & Colledge within this yor Maties Dominion, as to the perticulars relateing to the s^d Desygne wee have given our Instructions to the Reverend Mr *James Blayre* whome wee have appointed to present this our humble Supplication, & to attend & receive your Maties Comands, thereupon, But since wee desygne that our intended free Schoole & Colledge together with learning and vertue may convey to future generations the memory of our Obligacons to your Maties which there is noe fear that wee of the present age can ever forgett, besides what is contained in the s^d Instructions wee humbly pray that the said Schoole & Colledge may transmitt to our Posterity those names which are so deare & auspicious to us, and may accordingly be called the Colledge of King *William* and Queen *Mary*, That God may make yor Maties happy in thankfull & obedient Subjects, as your Subjects are in a King & Queen that answer, their very wishes is the hearty prayers of.—H. R. McIlwaine (ed.), *Journals of the House of Burgesses of Virginia*, 1659/60-1693, p. 368. For the legislative history of this petition, see the same work, *passim*.

5. JAMES BLAIR REPORTS TO GOVERNOR NICHOLSON ON HIS VISIT TO LONDON FOR THE CHARTER OF THE COLLEGE OF WILLIAM AND MARY, 1691

LONDON, Decr 3rd, 1691.

MAY IT PLEASE YOUR HONOR,

In my last from Bristol I gave your Honour an account of our passage, our landing in Ireland, my passage from thence to Bristol, with all the news I had then heard. This letter I left with Mr Henry Daniel, who promised to take care of it, & to send it by a ship that he said was there, almost ready to sail from Bristol to Virginia. Mr Randolph of New England, & Mr Sherwood, who are now both bound for Virginia, will save me the trouble of writing news, so that

I shall need only to give your Honour an account of my proceedings in the affair of the College. When I came first to London, which was the first day of September, there were many things concurred to hinder my sudden presenting of the address about the College, for Mr Jeoffreys was in Wales, & did not come to Town to present the address upon their majesties' accession to the crown; the Bishop of London thought it not so proper to present an address about business; then the King was in Flanders: my friend the Bishop of Salisbury was at Salisbury; the Bishop of St. Asaph at his diocese in Wales, and before Mr Jeoffreys came to Town the Bishop of London was taken very sick, so that for a month's time he was not able to stir abroad; upon all which accounts I found it necessary to delay in the beginning, for which I had one reason which was enough of itself if there had been no more, and that was that I found the court so much altered, especially among the Bishops (who were the most proper persons for me to apply myself to), that really I found myself obliged to take new measures from what I had proposed to myself. The Bishop of London was at this time under a great cloud and mighty unwilling to meddle in any court business, for notwithstanding his great merit from the present government, he had been passed by in all the late promotions, & the two archbishopricks had been bestowed upon two of his own clergy, viz: Dr Tillotson & Dr Sharp, so yet notwithstanding the Bishop of London's great kindness to Virginia, yet I found he was not at this time in so fit circumstances to manage a business at court as we expected. I found that the Archbishop of Canterbury was the man who was wholly entrusted by the King & Court for all Ecclesiastical affairs, & I was told by every body who had skill in Business that it was absolutely necessary to get him to be our friend. Thus the time past on & I did nothing but make friends in private against the King's coming over, which was expected about the beginning of October, but happened not till the 19th of the month. All this while I waited duely on the Bishop of London, as knowing well that whenever this business came to be done he must appear cordially in it, or else no interest that I could make could prevail to get it done without him, it belonging so entirely to his province. I both discoursed him at large, and plyed him with memorials till I got him to be very perfect in the Business of the College, but at the same time I disliked the method in which he was going to put it, which was this. He advised me to put in the address by way of petition to the King in Council, & the council he said would defer it to the committee for plantations where he did not doubt but that it would pass. I told his Lordship that I never doubted the obtaining of the charter, but the great difficulty would be in obtaining a gift of such things from his Majesty as we had a mind to ask for the College, and that in order to this, the best way seemed to me to be to engage the Bishops about Court zealously in the thing & to get the King so prepared that when the address was presented to him he should consult the Bishops in it, it being an Ecclesiastical affair, & that by their advice the whole business should be approved by his majesty & all promises for the encouragement of it that we had a mind to ask, & then at last, if it was necessary, that it might be brought before the Committee of Plantations to see what they had to say against it, but for the council and the Committee of Plantations to be the first meddlers & contrivers of the business I did not like it, because as his Lordship told me himself the church of England party was the weakest in the council, & if there is any of the revenue to be spared the courtiers are more apt to beg it for themselves than to advise the bestowing of it upon any publick use. But all that I could say could not prevail with the Bishop of London to have the business managed in this manner with the King himself. This was the first week in October when the King was daily expected & I was really in a great deal of trouble & knew not how to help myself, when by God's good providence, by means of a minister of my acquaintance, I was introduced to Dr Stillingfleet, Bishop of Worcester, one thought to be as much in favour with the Queen as any Bishop in England. I found the Bishop of Worcester exceeding well prepared to receive me kindly. The first word he said to me was that he was very glad of this opportunity of being acquainted with me, that he had heard a great deal of me from the Bishop of London, of good things I had done and still designed to do for the church in America, & he freely proffered to do me all the service that lay in his power. After some discourse with him I found we had already run into one error & seemed like to run into another. The first was, that all this time we had neglected the Queen, who he assured me would be the best friend that I could find in a business of this nature, as being a person that is a very great encourager of all works of charity. The other was that, as I told him, we intended to bring before the council & committee of Plantations, which he assured me, was the ready way to spoil all. For the first I had this to say, that by my instructions I was to depend upon the Bishop of London, who presently after my coming to London was taken sick & was but just now beginning to stir abroad again. I desired him to be so kind as to acquaint her majesty with it & withall to ask whether her majesty would have the address presented to her, or whether we must wait for his majesty's coming, who was now expected every minute. He promised me that he would do it & for the other wrong step we were like to make I was as much convinced of it as he could be, but I shewed him the difficulty and begged that he would make use of his Interest with the Bishop of London to persuade him to take another course. About the same time I received a letter from the Bishop of Salisbury (whose assistance I had desired) with one enclosed for the Archbishop of Canterbury wherein he recommended me & the business of the college to his Grace. And upon my address to him I was received very kindly, he told me that he remembered me since I was with the master of rolles. He heard me very patiently discourse the business of our college, and enquired concerning the state of our clergy in Virginia, he assured me that he would do me all the kindness that he could in my affair & desired me to draw him up a couple of memorials, one about the college and another about the clergy, and withall told me that if I would follow his advice he did not question but the business would do very well. He told me I must have patience for the King at his first coming would be full of his Parliament business but if I would leave it to him he would tell me when was the proper time to deliver the address & would before hand prepare his majesty. He was utterly against the making of it a council business and promised me to talk with the Bishop of London in it, and to shew him the necessity of manageing it first with the King himself. Both these Bishops were as good as their words for the Bishop of Worcester opened the business of the college to the Queen who seemed to like it extraordinarily, promised to assist in recommending it to the King, but ordered that the address should not be presented till the King came himself. And the Archbishop took an occasion to speak to the Bishop of London about it in the presence of the Bishop of Worcester. They all commended the thing & for the right managing of it, the Archbishop proposed that the King should be prepared and then the address delivered to him, & if he thought fit to make a council business of it he might. The Archbishop desired leave of the Bishop of London to manage it with the King, which the Bp of London willingly assented to & so the thing was put again into a right method. The Archbp told me afterwards that he never saw the King take anything better than he did the very first proposal of our college & that he promised frankly if I could find any thing in that country which was fit for him to give towards it he would give it. After which I made it my whole business to wait upon those Bishops & to give them memorials of my affair. I have already writ out three quires of paper in this sort of work & all things seem to be in a right disposition towards it. After the heat of the parliament business was a little over the Archbishop got the King himself to name a day for presenting the address. It was Novr 12th, in the Council chamber, before the council sat. I was introduced by the Archbishop of Canterbury & my Lord Effingham (the Bishop of London should have been there but was that day taken again with a fit of the stone.) I kneeled down & said these words, "Please your majesty here is an humble supplication from the Government of Virginia for your majesty's charter to erect a free school & college for the education of their youth," & so I delivered it into their hand. He answered, "Sir, I am glad that that colony is upon so good a design & I will promote it to the best of my power." The King gave it to the principal Secretary, my Lord Nottingham, at whose office, within two days, I had it again, with this account from Mr Warre, my Lord's Secretary, that the King had ordered me to give it to the Bishop of London, both a scheme of the college and an account what was expected of him towards the encouragement of it; & if I could concert the matter with the Archbishop and the Bishop of London then it should be brought before the committee for plantations & pass if they had nothing to object against it. The parliament sits so close that it is an hard matter to find anybody at leisure, yet I persuaded the Bishop of London on Wednesday last to come for half an hour to his chamber at Whitehall, where I presented & read to him a memorial I had prepared for his majesty's use, & the Archbishop & he were to wait an opportunity to speak to the King about it. Every one thinks it is in so good a way that it cannot well miscarry. I make it my whole business to wait upon it & if I hear further before the ships go your honour may expect another line about it. I find there will be a great deal of difficulty in finding of able masters & yet I am sensible the life of the business lies in this. In England their masters of their colleges have a much easier life than is designed for the masters & professors of our college in Virginia. I can have several young men that are fit enough to be ushers but can not perswade any of the Eminent experienced masters to go over. I have two in my eye that are very fit for it if I can prevail with them to undertake it. There is one thing which was forgot in my instructions, (and it was my fault for I was not sensible of the necessity of it at this time) that is that I should have been ordered to provide a president of the college at the same time with the schoolmaster & usher. I thought y^t at first a Grammar school being the only thing we could go upon, a good Schoolmaster & Usher were enough to manage that. But the Bishop of London and some other Bishops and a great many other skillfull men whom I have consulted have undeceived me & persuaded me that the president of the College ought to be the first man of all masters we provided for it. Their reasons are these: first that the good success of the whole business depends upon the setting up & executing of a good discipline at first both among masters & Scholars, which, if it be left wholly to the Schoolmaster, he will be sure to make it easy enough for himself & will contrive to lead the scholars in such a method as will keep them a great deal longer at school than they needed to be kept, only for his own advantage. Most of the masters here in England keep their scholars seven years at the Latin which might be as well taught in four if they pleased. 2nd. It may so happen y^t the school master & usher may want as much to be instructed themselves as any of the scholars.—Commissary Blair to Governor Nicholson. William Stevens Perry (ed.), *Historical Collections Relating to the American Colonial Church*, I, 3-8.

6. Action of the Privy Council on the petition of the pirates, 1691

Virginia.
At the Court at Whitehall
the 10 of March 169½
Present
The King's Most Excell^t Ma^ty
in Councill,

Upon reading the Peticon of Edwd Davies, John Hinson and Lionel Delawafer, humbly praying that their Money Plate, Jewells and Cloathing, Seiz'd as Pirats goods in the year 1688 by Capt. Rowe Commander of the Dunbarton Frigatt in Virginia may be restored to them, and it Appearing by the Report of the Right honoble the Lords Comm^rs of the Treasury that ye Pet^rs by writing under their hands had own'd themselves to be Pirats & had Claim'd the Benefitt of a Proclamacon issued by the late King James for the Suppression of Pirats and Privateers in America, by force or Assurance of pardon but

had not strictly comply'd with the Conditions of the said Proclamacon and the Petrs being Willing that the Sum or Value of three hundred pounds of the goods belonging unto them and now lying in their
Maties Warehouse together with the fourth part of wt shall be recovered belonging to the Petrs from the said Capt Rowe or his Executrs shall be employ'd towards the Erecting a Colledg or free
Schoole in Virginia or such other Pious or Charitable uses as their
Maties shall direct. It is this day Ordered in Councill as it is hereby
Order'd that the Money, Plate, Jewells and other goods belonging to
the said Petrs and seiz'd by Capt Rowe now lying in their Mats Warehouse or wherever the Same may be found be forthwith Restored
to the Petrs the Sum or Value of three hundred Pounds only Excepted,
wch together with the fourth part of wt remains in the hands of the
said Capt Row or his Executors or which shall be recovered from
them as belonging to the Petrs is to be dispos'd of towards the Erecting of A Free Schoole or Colledg in Virginia in case the same shall
be founded by grant from their Maties and if the same shall not be
so founded as aforesd to such other pious or Charitable uses as Their
Maties shall direct the petrs giving good Security to answer the said
fourth part of what shall be receiv'd or recovered from the said Capt
Rowe or his Executors to be Applied as Abovemencon'd, and the Rt
Honoble the Lords Commrs of the Treasury are to give all neces-
directions herein.—"Papers Relating to the Founding of the College,"
William and Mary College Quarterly, VII, 165.

THE

CHARTER,

TRANSFER *and* STATUTES,

OF THE

COLLEGE

OF

William and *Mary,*

IN

VIRGINIA:

In *Latin* and *English.*

WILLIAMSBURG:

Printed by WILLIAM HUNTER.

MDCCLVIII.

THE

CHARTER

OF THE

COLLEGE

OF

WILLIAM and *MARY*.

[4]

CHARTA COLLEGII

Gulielmi & *Mariae,*

I N

VIRGINIA.

G*ULIELMUS* & *MARIA*, Dei Gratia, *Angliæ, Scotiæ, Franciæ,* & *Hiberniæ,* Rex & Regina, Fidei Defensores, &c. omnibus ad quos præsentes Literæ nostræ pervenerint, salutem.

Cum perdilecti & fideles subditi nostri constituentes conventum generalem Coloniæ nostræ *Virginiæ,* in animo habuerint, & sibi proposuerint, quo ecclesia *Virginiensis* ministrorum evangelii seminario suppeditetur, juventus in bonis moribus & literis pie educetur, et fides Christiana apud *Indos Occidentales* propagetur, in gloriam Dei Omnipotentis, facere, fundare, & stabilire quoddam studium generale, sive collegium perpetuum s. sanctæ theologiæ, philosophiæ, linguarum aliarumque bonarum artium & scientiarum, de uno præside, sex magistris seu professoribus, & centum scholaribus, pluribus seu paucioribus, secundum dicti collegii facultatem, & statuta ejusdem, per quosdam fiduciarios a conventu generali prædicto, nominatos, & electos, viz. fideles & dilectos *Franciscum Nicholson,* vice-gubernatorem nostrum in coloniis nostris *Virginiæ* & Terræ-Mariæ, *Guliel-*

mum

[5]

THE
CHARTER of the COLLEGE
O F
William *and* Mary,
I N
V I R G I N I A .

WILLIAM *and* MARY, *by the Grace of God, of* England, Scotland, France *and* Ireland, *King and Queen, Defenders of the Faith,* &c. *To all to whom these our present Letters shall come,* Greeting.

Forasmuch as our well-beloved and faithful Subjects, constituting the General-Assembly of our Colony of Virginia, *have had it in their Minds, and have proposed to themselves, to the End that the Church of* Virginia *may be furnished with a Seminary of Ministers of the Gospel, and that the Youth may be piously educated in good Letters and Manners, and that the Christian Faith may be propagated amongst the* Western Indians, *to the Glory of Almighty God; to make, found, and establish a certain Place of universal Study, or perpetual College of Divinity, Philosophy, languages, and other good Arts and Sciences, consisting of one President, six Masters or Professors, and an Hundred Scholars, more or less, according to the Ability of the said College, and the Statutes of the same; to be made, encreased, diminished, or changed there, by certain Trustees, nominated and elected by the General-Assembly aforesaid; to wit, our faithful and well-beloved* Francis Nicholson, *our Lieutenant-Governor in our Colonies of*
Virginia

[6]

mum Cole, Rodolphum Wormley, Gulielmum Byrd, & *Joannem Lear,* Armigeros; *Jacobum Blair, Joannem Farnifold, Stephanum Fouace,* & *Samuelem Gray,* Clericos; *Thomam Milner, Christophorum Robinson, Carolum Scarborough, Joannem Smith, Benjaminum Harrison, Milesium Cary, Henricum Hartwell, Gulielmum Randolph,* & *Mattheum Page,* Generosos, vel majorem partem eorundem, vel eorum diutius viventium, inde faciend' augend' minuend' vel mutand' super *australem* partem fluminis cujusdam communiter vocati *York River,* vel alibi, ubi ipsi conventui generali magis videbitur expedire, intra coloniam nostram *Virginiæ,* perpetuis futuris temporibus sustinend' & alend'.

I. Cumque etiam perdilectus & fidelis conventus generalis coloniæ nostræ *Virginiæ,* prædictæ, per dilectum nobis in Christo, *Jacobum Blair* clericum, agentem suum legitime constitutum, humillime supplicaverit quatenus nos præfatis *Franciso Nicholson, Gulielmo Cole, Rodolpho Wormley, Gulielmo Byrd,* & *Joanni Lear,* Armigeris; *Jacobo Blair, Joanni Farnifold, Stephano Fouace,* & *Samueli Gray,* Clericis; *Thomæ Milner, Christophoro Robinson, Carolo Scarborough, Joanni Smith, Benjamino Harrison, Milesio Cary, Henrico Hartwell, Gulielmo Randolph,* & *Mattheo Page,* Generosis, non tantum ad collegium prædictum faciend' fundand' erigend' & stabiliend' licentiam regiam nostram, sed etiam gratiam & munificentiam nostram regiam, in erectione & fundatione collegii prædicti, graciose concedere & extendere dignaremur, in talibus modo & forma qual' nobis melius videbitur expedire: Nos præmissa prædicta ferio confiderantes, & intime quantum in nobis est veram philosophiam, cæterasque bonas & liberales artes ac scientias promoveri, & fidem Christianam orthodoxam propagari cupientes; & volentes ut de cætero in perpetuum unum tale habeatur collegium, sive Studium generale, & certus ac indubitatus modus in eodem collegio, de, pro, & in regimine & gubernatione ejusdem, & magistrorum seu

professorum,

[7]

Virginia *and* Maryland, William Cole, Ralph Wormley, William Byrd, *and* John Lear, *Esquires;* James Blair, John Farnifold, Stephen Fouace, *and* Samuel Gray, *Clerks;* Thomas Milner, Christopher Robinson, Charles Scarborough, John Smith, Benjamin Harrison, Miles Cary, Henry Hartwell, William Randolph, *and* Matthew Page, *Gentlemen, or the major Part of them, or of the longer Livers of them, on the* South *Side of a certain River, commonly called* York *River, or elsewhere, where the General-Assembly itself shall think more convenient, within our Colony of* Virginia, *to be supported and maintained, in all Time coming.*

I. *And forasmuch as our well-beloved and trusty the General-Assembly of our Colony of* Virginia *aforesaid, has humbly supplicated us, by our well-beloved in Christ,* James Blair, *Clerk, their Agent duly constituted, That we would be pleased, not only to grant our Royal Licence to the said* Francis Nicholson, William Cole, Ralph Wormley, William Byrd, *and* John Lear, *Esqrs;* James Blair, John Farnifold, Stephen Fouace, *and* Samuel Gray, *Clerks;* Thomas Milner, Christopher Robinson, Charles Scarborough, John Smith, Benjamin Harrison, Myles Cary, Henry Hartwell, William Randolph, *and* Matthew Page, *Gentlemen, or the major Part of them, or of the longer Livers of them, to make, found, erect, and establish the said College, but also to extend our Royal Bounty and Munificence, towards the Erection and Foundation of the said College, in such Way and Manner, as to us shall seem most expedient: We taking the Premises seriously into our Consideration, and earnestly desiring, that as far in us lies, true Philosophy, and other good and liberal Arts and Sciences may be promoted, and that the Orthodox Christian Faith may be propagated: And being desirous, that for ever hereafter, there should be one such College, or Place of universal Study, and some certain and un-*
doubted

[8]

professorum, & scholarium, ac omnium aliorum ibidem habitantium & commorantium, & ut collegium illud perpetuis futuris temporibus sit & remaneat, de gratia nostra speciali, ac ex certa scientia & mero motu nostris, concessimus & licentiam dedimus, ac per præsentes concedimus & licentiam damus, pro nobis hæredibus & successoribus nostris, quantum in nobis est præfatis *Francisco Nicholson, Gulielmo Cole, Rodolpho Wormley, Gulielmo Byrd,* & *Joanni Lear,* Armigeris; *Jacobo Blair, Joanni Farnifold, Stephano Fouace,* & *Samueli Gray,* Clericis; *Thomæ Milner, Christophoro Robinson, Carolo Scarborough, Joanni Smith, Benjamino Harrison, Milesio Carey, Henrico Hartwell, Gulielmo Randolph,* & *Mattheo Page,* Generosis, ut ipsi sive major Pars eorum sive eorum diutius vivientium, ad studia veræ philosophiæ, linguarum, cæterarumque aliarum bonarum artium & scientiarum, promovenda, & purum Christi unici mediatoris nostri evangelium propagandum, in laudem & honorem Dei Omnipotentis, quoddam Studium generale, sive Collegium perpetuum sacro sanctæ theologiæ, philosophiæ, linguarum & aliarum bonarum artium & scientiarum, de uno præside, sex magistris sive professoribus, & centum scholaribus, pluribus vel paucioribus, graduatis & non-graduatis, ut prædictum est, juxta ejusdem collegii ordinationes & statuta per ipsos *Franciscum Nicholson, Gulielmum Cole,* &c. sive majorem partem eorum, in ea parte faciend' contend' statuend' & stabiliend' in quodam loco super *australem* partem fluminis *Eboracensis* vulgo vocati *York River,* super terram, nuper terram colonelli *Townsend,* defuncti, nunc in possessione *Joannis Smith,* prope portum in comitatu *Eboracensi,* per conventum generalem prædictum, constitutum vel designatum, intra prædictam coloniam nostram *Virginiæ;* vel si locus iste ob insalubritatem, vel quamcunque aliam ob causam minus arrideat ubicunque alibi visum fuerit conventui generali coloniæ nostræ *Virginiæ,* aut majori parti eorundem, intra

limites

[9]

doubted Way within the said College, for the Rule and Government of the same, and of the Masters or Professors, and Scholars, and all others inhabiting and residing therein, and that the said College should subsist and remain in all Time coming; of our special Grace, certain Knowledge, and mere Motion, HAVE GRANTED and given Leave, and by these Presents do grant and give Leave, for us, our Heirs and Successors, as much as in us lies, to the said Francis Nicholson, William Cole, Ralph Wormley, William Byrd, *and* John Lear, *Esqs;* James Blair, John Farnifold, Stephen Fouace, *and* Samuel Gray, *Clerks;* Thomas Milner, Christopher Robinson, Charles Scarborough, John Smith, Benjamin Harrison, Miles Cary, Henry Hartwell, William Randolph, *and* Matthew Page, *Gentlemen, That they or the major Part of them, or of the longer Livers of them, for promoting the Studies of true Philosophy, Languages, and other good Arts and Sciences, and for Propagating the pure Gospel of Christ, our only Mediator, to the Praise and Honor of Almighty God, may have Power to erect, found, and establish a certain Place of universal Study, or perpetual College, for Divinity, Philosophy, Languages, and other good Arts and Sciences, consisting of One President, Six Masters or Professors, and an Hundred Scholars, more or less, Graduates and Non-Graduates, as abovesaid, according to the Statutes and Orders of the said College, to be made, appointed, and established upon the Place by the said* Francis Nicholson, William Cole, *&c. or the major Part of them, upon the* South *Side of* York River, *on the Land late of Colonel*   Townsend, *deceased, now in the Possession of* John Smith, *near the Port appointed or laid out for* York County, *by the said General Assembly, within our said Colony of* Virginia; *or, if by reason of Unwholsomeness, or any other Cause, the said Place shall not be approved of, wheresoever else the General Assembly of our Colony of* Virginia, *or the major Part of*
them

[10]

limites coloniæ prædictæ, erigere, fundare & stabilire possint
& valeant, perpetuis futuris temporibus duraturum.

II. Et ulterius, de gratia nostra speciali, ac ex certa
scientia, & mero motu nostris concessimus & licentiam dedimus, ac per presentes concedimus, & licentiam damus, pro
nobis hæredibus & successoribus nostris præfatis *Francisco
Nicholson, Gulielmo Cole,* &c. ut ipsi, sive major ipsorum
pars, aut eorum diutius viventium, possint & valeant recipere, retinere, & gaudere, sintque personæ aptæ & capaces in
lege, ad recipiend' retinend' & gaudend' maneria, terras,
tenementa, redditus, servitia, rectorias, portiones, annuitates,
pensiones, & advocationes ecclesiarum, cum omnibus aliis
hæreditamentis, franchesiis & possessionibus quibuscunque
tam spiritualibus, quam temporalibus, ad valorem duarum
mille librarum per annum; ac omnia bona, catalla, pecunias,
& statum personalem qualemcunque, de dono cujuscunque
in hunc usum eadem largiri volentis; aut quæcunque dona,
concessiones, assignamenta, legationes, aut appunctuationes
eorundem, aut cujuscunque eorum, aut aliorum bonorum
qualiumcunque: Sed sub hac expressa intentione, & speciali
fiducia quam in ipsis reponimus, ut ipsi præfati *Franciscus
Nicholson, Gulielmus Cole,* &c. aut major pars ipsorum, aut
eorum diutius viventium, capiant & recipiant præmissa, dis-
ponantque eadem, aut redditus, proventus, aut proficua
eorundem, aut eorum cujuscunque, solummodo ad sustinen-
dos sumptus impendendos, in erigendo, & aptando ædificia
de & pro prædicto designato collegio, eademque libris
aliisque utensilibus convenientibus adornanda aliosque
sumptus ad prædictum futurum collegium pertinentes, prout
ipsis, aut majori ipsorum parti maxime visum fuerit expedite, donec præfatum collegium actu erectum, fundatum
& stabilitum fuerit; & sub hac fiducia ac ea intentione, ut
quam primum prædictum collegium secundum propositum
nostrum regium erectum & fundatum fuerit, præfati *Franciscus Nicholson, Gulielmus Cole,* &c. aut eorum diutius
viventes,

[11]

them shall think fit, within the Bounds of the aforesaid Colony, to continue for all Times coming.

II. *And further, of our special Grace, certain Knowledge, and mere Motion, we HAVE GRANTED, and given Leave, and by these Presents do grant, and give Leave, for us, our Heirs and Successors, to the said* Francis Nicholson, William Cole, *&c. that they, or the major Part of them, or of the longer Livers of them, may be enabled to take, hold, and enjoy, and that they may be Persons apt and capable in Law, for taking, holding and enjoying all Manors, Lands, Tenements, Rents, Services, Rectories, Portions, Annuities, Pensions, and Advowsons of Churches, with all other Inheritances, Franchises, and Possessions whatever, as well Spiritual as Temporal, to the Value of Two Thousand Pounds a Year; and all other Goods, Chattels, Monies, and Personal Estate whatsoever, of the Gift of any Person whatsoever, that is willing to bestow them for this Use; or any other Gifts Grants, Assignments, Legacies, or Appointments, of the same, or of any of them, or of any other Goods whatsoever,: But with this express Intention, and upon the special Trust we put in them, that they the said* Francis Nicholson, William Cole, *&c. or the major Part of them, or of the longer Livers of them, shall take and hold the Premisses, and shall dispose of the same, and of the Rents, Revenues, or Profits thereof, or of any of them only for defraying the Charges that shall be laid out in Erecting and Fitting the Edifices of the said intended College, and furnishing them with Books, and other Utensils, and all other Charges pertaining to the said College, as they, or the major Part of them, shall think most expedient, until the said College shall be actually erected, founded, and established, and upon this Trust and Intention, that so soon as the said College shall, according to our Royal Intent, be erected and founded, the said* Francis Nicholson, William Cole,*
&c.*

[12]

viventes, aut diutius vivens, & illorum, aut illius hæredes, executores, administratores, aut assignati bonis & sufficientibus scriptis & assurantiis in lege, dent, concedant & transferant, prædictis præsidi, & magistris, seu professoribus, aut eorum successoribus, eadem maneria, terras, tenementa, redditus, servitia, rectorias, portiones, annuitates, pensiones, & advocationes ecclesiarum, cum omnibus aliis hæreditamentis, Franchesiis, possessionibus, bonis, catallis, & statibus personalibus prædictis, aut tantum eorundem, quantum in erectione prædicti collegii, aut in alios usus prædictos, non antea expensum & collocatum fuerit.

III. Cumque conventus generalis prædictus coloniæ nostræ *Virginiæ, Jacobum Blair*, clericum prædictum, tanquam personam idoneam in locum præsidis collegii prædicti, nominaverit, elegerit, aut designaverit; nos, de gratia nostra speciali, ac ex certa scientia, & mero motu nostris, prædictam nominationem, & electionem approbamus, confirmamus, & pro rata haberi volumus; eundemque *Jacobum Blair*, primum prædicti collegii præsidem, durante vita sua naturali facimus, creamus, & stabilimus, per presentes.

IV. Et ulterius licentiam nostram specialem concedimus præfatis *Francisco Nicholson, Gulielmo Cole*, &c. eorumque sucessoribus, aut majori ipsorum parti, aut alias personas aptas, idoneas, & habiles, in loca magistrorum, aut professorum collegii prædicti eligere & nominare possint & valeant; utque post mortem, resignationem, aut deprivationem ejusdem, præsidis, aut professorum, aut eorum cujuscunque, prædicti *Franciscus Nicholson, Gulielmus Cole*, &c. eorumque successores, aut major ipsorum pars, in illius, aut illorum locum, aut loca personam idoneam, aut personas idoneas, de tempore in tempus, sufficere & substituere, valeant & possint; secundum ejusdem collegii ordinationes & statuta per ipsos *Francisum Nicholson, Gulielmum Cole*, &c. aut eorum successores, aut majorem partem eorundem,

[13]

&c. or the longer Livers or Liver of them, and their or his Heirs, Executors, Administrators, or Assigns, shall, by good and sufficient Deeds and Assurances in Law, Give, Grant, and Transfer to the said President and Masters, or Professors, or their Successors, the said Lands, Manors, Tenements, Rents, Services, Rectories, Portions, Annuities, Pensions, and Advowsons of Churches, with all other Inheritances, Franchises, Possessions, Goods, Chattels, and personal Estate aforesaid, or as much thereof as has not been laid out and bestowed upon the Building the said College, or to the other Uses above-mentioned.

III. And, seeing the said General Assembly of our Colony of Virginia, *has named, elected, or appointed, the said* James Blair, *Clerk, as a fit Person to be President of the said College; We, of our special Grace, certain Knowledge, and mere Motion, do approve, confirm, and ratify the said Nomination, and Election, and do by these Presents make, create, and establish the said* James Blair *first President of the said College, during his natural Life.*

IV. And further, we grant our special Licence to the said Francis Nicholson, William Cole, *&c. and their Successors, or the major Part of them, That they shall have Power to elect, and nominate other apt, fit, and able Persons, into the Places of the Masters or Professors of the said College; and that, after the Death, Resignation, or Deprivation of the said President, or Professors, or any of them, the said* Francis Nicholson, William Cole, *&c. and their Successors, or the major Part of them, shall have Power to put in, and substitute, a fit Person, or Persons, from Time to Time, into his or their Place or Places, according to the Orders and Statutes of the said College, to be made, enacted, and established, for the good and wholesome Government of the said College, and of all that bear office, or reside therein,*
by

[14]

eorundem, pro bona & salubri gubernatione ejusdem collegii, omniumque in eodem munere aliquo fungentium, aut
ibidem commorantium faciend' condend' & stabiliend'.

V. Et ulterius volumus, & pro nobis, hæredibus & successoribus nostris, per præsentes concedimus, ut cum predic-
tum collegium sic erectum, factum, fundatum, & stabilitum
fuerit, collegium *Gulielmo & Mariæ*, in *Virginia*, in perpetuum appelletur & nuncupetur; & ut præses, & magistri,
seu professores collegii prædicti sint unum corpus cor-
poratum & politicum in re, facto, & nomine, & ut per
nomen præsidis, & magistrorum, seu professorum, collegii
Gulielmi & Mariæ, in *Virginia*, habeant successionem perpetuam; & ut dicti præses, & magistri, seu professores,
præses, magistri, seu professores collegii *Gulielmi & Mariæ*,
in *Virginia*, in perpetuum appellentur & nuncupentur: Et ut
dicti præses, & magistri, seu professores, & eorum successores, per nomen præsidis, & magistrorum, seu professorum
collegii *Gulielmi & Mariæ*, in *Virginia*, sint personæ habiles,
capaces, aptæ, & perpetuæ in lege, ad requirend' & recipiend'
dominia, maneria, terras, tenementa, redditus, reversiones,
rectorias, portiones, pensiones, annuitates, hæreditamenta,
possessiones, & servitia quæcunque, tam spiritualia quam
temporalia, ac omnia bona & catalla quæcunque, tam de
dono nostro, hæredum & successorum nostrorum, quam de
donis ipsorum *Francisci Nicholson, Gulielmi Cole, Rodol-
phi Wormley, Gulielmi Byrd,* & *Joannis Lear,* Armi-
gerorum; *Jacobi Blair, Joannis Farnifold, Stephani Fouace,*
& *Samuelis Gray,* Clericorum, *Thomæ Milner, Christophori
Robinson, Caroli Scarborough, Joannis Smith, Benjamini
Harrison, Milesii Cary, Henrici Hartwell, Gulielmi Randolph,* & *Matthei Page,* Generosorum, seu aliorum quorumcunque ad valorem duarum mille librarum legalis
monetæ *Anglicanæ,* per annum, & non amplius, habend' &
tenend' sibi & successoribus suis in perpetuum.

VI. Ac

[15]

by the said Francis Nicholson, William Cole, *&c. or their Successors, or the major Part of them.*

V. *And further, we Will, and for us, our Heirs, and Successors, by these Presents, do* GRANT, *That when the said College shall be so erected, made, founded, and established, it shall be called and denominated, for ever, the College of* William *and* Mary, *in* Virginia, *and that the President and Masters, or Professors, of the said College, shall be a Body politic and incorporate, in Deed and Name; and that by the Name of the President, and Masters, or Professors, of the College of* William *and* Mary, *in* Virginia, *they shall have perpetual Succession; and that the said President, and Masters, or Professors, shall for ever be called and denominated the President, and Masters, or Professors, of the College of* William *and* Mary, *in* Virginia: *And that the said President, and Masters, or Professors, and their Successors, by the Name of the President, and Masters, or Professors, of the College of* William *and* Mary, *in* Virginia, *shall be Persons able, capable, apt, and perpetual in Law, to take and hold Lordships, Manors, Lands, Tenements, Rents, Reversions, Rectories, Portions, Pensions, Annuities, Inheritances, Possessions, and Services, as well Spiritual as Temporal, whatsoever, and all Manner of Goods and Chattels, both of our Gift, and our Heirs and Successors, and of the Gift of the said,* Francis Nicholson, William Cole, Ralph Wormley, William Byrd, *and* John Lear, *Esqs;* James Blair, John Farnifold, Stephen Fouace, *and* Samuel Gray, *Clerks;* Thomas Milner, Christopher Robinson, Charles Scarborough, John Smith, Benjamin Harrison, Myles Cary, Henry Hartwell, William Randolph, *and* Matthew Page, *Gentlemen, or of the Gift of any other Person whatsoever, to the Value of Two Thousand Pounds of lawful Money of* England, *Yearly, and no more, to be had and held by them and their Successors for ever.*

VI. *And*

[16]

VI. Ac etiam ut iidem præses, & magistri, seu professores, & successores eorum, per nomen præsidis, & magistrorum, seu professorum, collegii, *Gulielmi* & *Mariæ*, in *Virginia*, & sub eodem nomine placitare & implacitari, prosequi, defendere & defendi, respondere & responderi, possint & valeant, in omnibus & singulis causis, quærelis, actionibus realibus, personalibus, & mixtis, cujuscunque generis fuerint sive naturæ, in quibuscunque foris, curiis, & locis nostris, hæredum & successorum nostrorum, ac foris, curiis, & locis, aliorum quorumcunque, coram quibuscunque justitiariis & judicibus ecclesiasticis & secularibus, in quibuscunque regnis, terris, coloniis, dominationibus, aut plantationibus ad nos, aut hæredes nostros pertinentibus, ac ad ea & omnia alia & fingula facienda, agenda, & recipienda, prout, & eodem modo, quo cæteri ligei nostri, personæ habiles & capaces in lege, intra coloniam nostram prædictam; vel alibi intra regnum nostrum *Angliæ*, faciunt & facere poterunt, in foris, curiis, & locis prædictis, & coram justiciariis & judicibus prædictis.

VII. Necnon ut prædictus præses, & magistri, seu professores, & eorum successores habeant unum commune sigillum pro causis & negotiis suis, ac successorum eorum quibuscunque agendis serviturum; & ut bene liceat iisdem præsidi, & magistris, seu professoribus, collegii prædicti, & successoribus eorum, sigillum suum ad libitum, de tempore in tempus frangere, mutare, & de novo facere, prout iis melius expedire videbitur.

VIII. Et ulterius de uberiori gratia nostra speciali, dedimus & concessimus, & pro nobis, hæredibus & successoribus nostris, per præsentes, licentiam damus & concedimus specialem, quantum in nobis est, præfatis *Francisco Nicholson, Gulielmo Cole, Rodolpho Wormley, Gulielmo Byrd,* & *Joanni Lear,* Armigeris; *Jacobo Blair, Joanni Farnifold, Stephano Fouace,* & *Samueli Gray,* Clericis; *Thomæ Milner,*
Christophoro

[17]

VI. *And also, that the said President and Masters or Professors, by and under the Name of the President and Masters or Professors of the College of* William *and* Mary, *in* Virginia, *shall have Power to plead, and be impleaded, to sue, and be sued, to defend, and be defended, to answer, and be answered, in all and every Cause, Complaint, and Action real, personal, and mixed, of what Kind and Nature soever they be, in whatsoever Courts and Places of Judicature belonging to us, our Heirs and Successors or to any other Person whatsoever, before all Sorts of Justices and Judges, Ecclesiastical and Temporal, in whatsoever Kingdoms, Countries, Colonies, Dominions, or Plantations, belonging to us, or our Heirs; and to do, act, and receive, these and all other Things, in the same manner, as our other liege People, Persons able and capable in Law, within our said Colony of* Virginia, *or our Kingdom of* England, *do, or may act, in the said Courts and Places of Judicature, and before the said Justices and Judges.*

VII. *As also, that the said President, and Masters, or Professors, and their Successors, shall have one common Seal, which they may make Use of in any whatsoever Cause and Business belonging to them and their Successors; and that the President, and Masters, or Professors of the said College, and their Successors, shall have Leave to break, change, and renew, their said Seal, from Time to Time, at their Pleasure, as they shall see most expedient.*

VIII. *And further, of our more especial Grace, we have Given and Granted, and for us, our Heirs, and Successors, we Give and Grant our special Licence, as far as in us lies, to the said* Francis Nicholson, William Cole, Ralph Wormley, William Byrd, *and* John Lear, *Esqs;* James Blair, John Farnifold, Stephen Fouace, Samuel Gray, *Clerks;* Thomas Milner, Christopher Robinson, Charles Scarborough, John Smith,

[18]

Christophoro Robinson, Carolo Scarborough, Joanni Smith, Benjamino Harrison, Milesio Cary, Henrico Hartwell, Gulielmo Randolph, & *Mattheo Page,* Generosis, aut ipsi aut aliæ personæ quæcunque, aut alia persona quæcunque, postquam Collegium prædictum, ut prædicitur, fundatum, erectum, factum, creatum, & stabilitum fuerit, maneria, terras, tenementa, redditus, servitia, rectorias, portiones, annuitates, pensiones, & advocationes ecclesiarum, ac omnia & omnimoda alia hæreditamenta, franchesias, & possessiones quascunque, tam spirituales, quam temporales, ad valorem duarum mille librarum, per annum ultra omnia onera & repriz' tam de feodis suis propriis quam alienis, præsidi, & magistris, seu professoribus ejusdem collegii, pro tempore existent' & successoribus suis dare, & concedere, assignare, & legare, possit & possint, valeat & valeant, habend' tenend' & gaudend' iisdem præsidi, & magistris, seu professoribus, & eorum successoribus, in perpetuum: Et ut ipsi præses, & magistri, seu professores, prædicti maneria, terras, tenementa, redditus, reversiones, servitia, rectorias, portiones, pensiones, annuitates, & omnia & omnimoda alia hæreditamenta, & possessiones quascunque, tam spirituales, quam temporales, ad prædictum valorem duarum mille librarum, per annum, ultra omnia onera repriz' & repart' recipere possint, & tenere sibi & successoribus suis prædict' in perpetuum, sicut prædictum est. Nolentes quod præses, & magistri, seu professores præfati collegii, qui pro tempore fuerint, aut successores sui, ratione, seu occasione præmissorum, vel eorum alicujus, per nos, hæredes, & successores nostros, justiciarios, escheatores, vicecomites, seu alios balivos, aut ministros nostros, seu hæredum, aut successorum nostrorum quoscunque impetantur, inquietentur, molestentur, aut in aliquo occasionentur, vexentur, seu graventur.

IX. Et ulterius volumus, & per præsentes, declaramus, nominamus, ordinamus, & constituimus, præfatos *Francis-*
cum

[19]

Smith, Benjamin Harrison, Myles Cary, Henry Hartwell, William Randolph, *and* Matthew Page, *Gentlemen, that they, or any other Person or Persons, whatsoever, after the said College is so founded, erected, made, created, and established, may have Power to Give, and Grant, Assign, and Bequeath, all Manors, Lands, Tenements, Rents, Services, Rectories, Portions, Annuities, Pensions, and Advowsons of Churches, and all Manner of Inheritances, Franchises, and Possessions whatsoever, as well Spiritual as Temporal, to the Value of Two Thousand Pounds a Year, over and above all Burthens, and Reprisals, to the President, and Masters, or Professors, of the said College, for the Time being, and their Successors, to be had, held, and enjoyed, by the said President, and Masters, or Professors, and their Successors, for ever: And that they the said President, and Masters, or Professors aforesaid, may take and hold, to themselves, and their Successors, for ever, as is aforesaid, Manors, Lands, Tenements, Rents, Reversions, Services, Rectories, Portions, Pensions, Annuities, and all, and all Manner of Inheritances, and Possessions whatsoever, as well Spiritual as Temporal, to the aforesaid Value of Two Thousand Pounds a Year, over and above all Burthens, Reprisals, and Reparations: It not being our Will, that the said President, and Masters, or Professors, of the said College, for the Time being, or their Successors, shall be troubled, disquieted, molested, or aggrieved, by Reason, or Occasion, of the Premisses, or any of them, by us, our Heirs, and Successors, or by any of our Justices, Escheators, Sheriffs, or other Bailiffs, or Ministers, whatsoever, belonging to us, our Heirs, and Successors.*

IX. *And further, we Will, and by these Presents, do declare, nominate, ordain, and appoint, the said* Francis Nicholson,

[20]

cum Nicholson, Gulielmum Cole, Rodolphum Wormley,
Gulielmum Byrd, & *Joannem Lear,* Armigeros, *Jacobum*
Blair, Joannem Farnifold, Stephanum Fouace, & *Samuelem*
Gray, Clericos; *Thomam Milner, Christophorum Robinson,*
Carolum Scarborough, Joannem Smith, Benjaminum Har-
rison, Milesium Cary, Henricum Hartwell, Gulielmum
Randolph, & *Mattheum Page,* Generosos, & successores
suos, fore in perpetuum veros, solos & indubitatos visitatores
& gubernatores collegii prædicti; iisque, sive majori eorum
parti, per præsentes literas nostras patentes, damus & concedimus perpetuam successionem, modo & forma inferius
specificat' perpetuand': Ac etiam plenam & absolutam facultatem, potestatem, & authoritatem faciend' ferend' condend'
& stabiliend' tot & tales regulas, injunctiones, leges, statuta,
& ordinationes, pro bono regimine & salubri gubernatione
collegii prædicti qual' iisdem præfatis *Francisco Nicholson,*
Gulielmo Cole, &c. & successoribus suis, de tempore in
tempus, prout res & ratio postulat, melius videbitur expedire,
Quæ omnia & singula regulæ, injunctiones, leges, statuta,
& ordinationes, sicut præfertur faciend' observati volumus,
sub pæna in iisdem content': Ita tamen ut regulæ, injunctiones, leges, statuta, & ordinationes hujusmodi sint nequa-
quam repugnantia sive contraria prærogativæ nostræ regiæ,
legibus & statutis regni nostri *Angliæ,* vel coloniæ nostræ
Virginiæ prædict', vel canonibus & constitutionibus ecclesiæ
Anglicanæ, per easdem leges *Angliæ* stabilit'.

X. Et ulterius volumus, & per præsentes, pro nobis hæredibus & successoribus nostris, concedimus & confirmamus præfatis visitatoribus & gubernatoribus collegii
prædicti, & successoribus suis, quod ipsi & sucessores sui,
sint & erunt in perpetuum octodecem homines, vel aliquis
alius numerus, non excedens numerum viginti in toto, modo
& forma inferius expressa eligend' & constituend'; & ut
habeant unum virum discretum, & idoneum, in forma inferius expressa, ex illorum numero eligend' & nominand',

qui

[21]

Nicholson, William Cole, Ralph Wormley, William Byrd, and John Lear, *Esqs;* James Blair, John Farnifold, Stephen Fouace, *and* Samuel Gray, *Clerks;* Thomas Milner, Christopher Robinson, Charles Scarborough, John Smith, Benjamin Harrison, Myles Cary, Henry Hartwell, William Randolph, *and* Matthew Page, *Gentlemen, and their Successors, to be the true, sole, and undoubted Visitors and Governors of the said College for ever: And we Give, and Grant to them, or the major Part of them, by these our Letters Patents, a continual Succession, to be continued in the Way and Manner hereafter specified; as also full and absolute Liberty, Power, and Authority, of making, enacting, framing, and establishing, such and so many Rules, Laws, Statutes, Orders, and Injunctions, for the good and wholesome Government of the said College, as to them the said* Francis Nicholson, William Cole, *&c. and their Successors, shall, from Time to Time, according to their various Occasions and Circumstances, seem most fit and expedient: All which Rules, Laws, Statutes, and Injunctions, so to be made, as aforesaid, we will have to be observed, under the Penalty therein contained: Provided notwithstanding, that the said Rules, Laws, Statutes, Orders, and Injunctions, be no way contrary to our Prerogative Royal, nor to the Laws and Statutes of our Kingdom of* England, *or our Colony of* Virginia, *aforesaid, or to the Canons and Constitutions of the Church of* England, *by Law established.*

X. *And further, we Will, and by these Presents, for us, our Heirs, and Successors, do Grant, and confirm to the said Visitors, and Governors of the said College, and their Successors, that they, and their Successors, shall, for ever, be Eighteen Men, or any other Number not exceeding the Number of Twenty, in the whole, to be Elected and Constituted in the Way and Manner herein after specify'd; and that they shall have one discreet and fit person, that shall be elected, and nominated, out of their Number, in the*
Manner

[22]

qui erit & nominabitur rector collegii prædicti: Et assignavimus & confirmavimus, ac per præsentes assignamus & confirmamus præfatum *Jacobum Blair*, fore & esse modernum
rectorem collegii prædicti, continuand' in eodem officio pro
uno anno proxime sequent' fundationem collegii prædicti,
& deinde quousque alius quispiam visitatorum & gubernatorum collegii prædicti ad officium illud debito modo
electus, præfectus, & juratus fuerit; utque de tempore in
tempus & ad omnia tempora post expirationem anni illius,
aut post mortem rectoris, intra expirationem anni, visitatores & gubernatores collegii prædicti, sive major pars eorundem, aut successorum suorum, unum alium virum discretum,
& idoneum, de seipsis de tempore in tempus, in rectorem
collegii prædicti eligere & nominare, valeant & possint;
utque qui in locum rectoris collegii prædicti, sicut præfertur,
electus, præfectus, seu nominatus fuerit, officium illud
rectoris collegii prædicti, habere, exercere, & gaudere, possit
& valeat, pro uno ano integro tum proxime sequenti; &
deinde quousque alius Rector collegii prædicti, ad officium
illud debito modo electus, præfectus, & juratus fuerit: Et ad
perpetuandum successionem prædict' rectoris, & prædictorum visitatorum & gubernatorum collegii prædicti, volumus,
ordinamus, & appunctuamus, ut quotiescumque, aliqui, vel
aliquis, e præfatis visitatoribus & gubernatoribus collegii
prædicti, obierit vel obierint, seu se & familiam suam extra
coloniam nostram prædictam amoverit vel amoverint, & inde
in partes peregrinas in perpetuum migraverit vel migra-
verint, quod tunc & toties bene liceat & licebit rectori, qui
pro tempore fuerit, & aliis visitatoribus & gubernatoribus
collegii prædicti tunc superviven' & remanen', sive majori
parti eorundem, unum alium, vel plures alios, de principalibus & melioribus inhabitantibus coloniæ nostræ *Virginiæ*
prædict' in locum, sive loca ipsius visitator' & gubernator',
sive ipsorum visitatorum & gubernatorum, sic mortui vel
amoti, mortuorum vel amotorum, eligere, nominare, &
præficere, ad implendum prædictum numerum de visitatoribus

[23]

*Manner hereafter mentioned, that shall be, and shall be
called Rector of the said College: And we have appointed
and confirmed, and by these Presents, do appoint, and confirm the said* James Blair, *to be the present Rector of the
said College, to be continued in the said Office for one Year
next ensuing the Foundation of the said College, and thereafter, till some other of the Visitors and Governors of the
said College shall be duly elected, preferred, and sworn
into the said Office; and that from Time to Time, and in
all Time coming, after the said Year is expired, or after the
Death of the Rector within the Year, the Visitors and Governors of the said College, or the greater Part of them, or of
their Successors, shall have Power to elect, and nominate
another discreet and fit Person, from amongst themselves,
to be Rector of the said College; and that he who is so
elected, preferred, and nominated, as abovesaid, into the
Place of Rector of the said College, shall have Power to
have, exercise, and enjoy the said Office of Rector of the
said College, for one whole Year, then next ensuing, and
thereafter, until some other Rector of the said College shall
be duly elected, preferred, and sworn into the said Office:
And to perpetuate the Succession of the said Rector, and of
the said Visitors and Governors of the said College, we
Will, ordain, and appoint, that as often as any one or more
of the said Visitors and Governors of the said College, shall
die, or remove himself and Family out of our said Colony,
into any other Country, for good and all, that then, and so
often, the Rector for the Time being, and the other Visitors
and Governors of the said College, then surviving, and
remaining within the Colony, or the major part of them,
shall and may have Leave to elect, nominate, and chuse
one or more of the principal and better Sort of Inhabitants
of our said Colony of* Virginia, *into the Place or Places of
the Visitor and Governor, or Visitors and Governors, so
dead or removed, to fill up the aforesaid Number of Visitors*

[24]

bus & gubernatoribus collegii prædicti; utque ille sive illi sic
elect' & præfect' præstet vel præstent coram rectore & aliis
visitatoribus & gubernatoribus collegii prædicti, vel majore
parte eorundem sacramentum corporale ad officium illud
bene & fideliter exequendum; quod sacramentum prædict'
rector, & duo, vel plures e numero visitatorum, administrare
possint & valeant: Et post sacramentum prædictum sicut
præfertur præstitum, sit & sint de numero prædictorum visitatorum & gubernatorum collegii prædicti.

XI. Et insuper volumus, & per præsentes, pro nobis, hæredibus, & successoribus nostris, concedimus & confirmamus
præfat' præsidi, & magistris, seu professoribus collegii
prædicti, & successoribus suis, ut ipsi, & successores sui,
habeant unum virum præclarum & discretum, in forma inferius expressa eligend' & nominand', qui erit & nominabitur
Cancellarius collegii prædicti, & assignavimus & confirmavimus, & per præsentes, pro nobis, hæredibus, & successoribus
nostris, assignamus & confirmamus prædilectum, & perquam
fidelem reverendum in Christo patrem, *Henricum,* per-
missione divina episcopum, *Londinensem,* fore & esse primum Cancellarium collegii prædicti, continuand' in eodem
officio, proseptem annis proxime sequent', & deinde, quousque alius Cancellarius collegii prædicti, ad officium illud
debito modo electus & præfectus fuerit: Utque de tempore
in tempus, & ad omnia tempora, post expirationem septem
annorum illorum, aut post mortem præfati episcopi, aut
Cancellarii, pro tempore existentis, rector, & visitatores, &
gubernatores collegii prædicti, pro tempore existent', vel
major pars eorundem, unum alium virum præclarum & discretum, de tempore in tempus, in Cancellarium collegii
prædicti, eligere, nominare, & præficere, valeant & possint;
utque qui in Cancellarium collegii prædicti sicut præfertur,
electus, præfectus, & nominatus fuerit, officium illud Cancellarii collegii prædict' habere, exercere, & gaudere, possit
& valeat, pro septem anis integris tunc proxime sequent', &

deinde

[25]

*tors and Governors for the said College; and that he or they
so elected and chosen, shall take his or their corporal Oath
before the Rector, and the other Visitors and Governors
of the said College, or the major Part of them, well and
faithfully to execute the said Office; which Oath the said
Rector, and Two, or more of the Visitors, shall have Power
to administer: And that after the taking of the said Oath,
he, or they, shall be of the Number of the said Visitors and
Governors of the said College.*

XI. *And further, we Will, and by these Presents, for us,
our Heirs, and Successors, do Grant and Confirm, to the
said President, and Masters, or Professors of the said College, and their Successors, that they, and their Successors,
shall have one eminent and discreet Person, to be elected
and nominated, in the Manner hereafter expressed, who
shall be, and shall be called Chancellor of the said College:
And We have appointed and confirmed, and by these Presents, for us, our Heirs, and Successors, do appoint and confirm, our well-beloved and right trusty the Reverend
Father in God,* Henry, *by divine Permission, Bishop of*
London, *to be the first Chancellor of the said College, to be
continued in the said Office, for Seven Years next ensuing,
and thereafter, until some other Chancellor of the said College shall be duly elected and chosen into the said Office:
And that from Time to Time, and in all Time coming,
after these Seven Years are expired, or after the Death of
the said Bishop, or of the Chancellor, for the Time being,
the Rector, and Visitors, and Governors, of the said College, for the Time being, or the major Part of them, shall
and may have Power to elect, chuse, and nominate, some
other eminent and discreet Person, from Time to Time, to
be Chancellor of the said College; and that he who is so
nominated and elected to be Chancellor of the said College,
shall and may have, execute, and enjoy, the said Office of
Chancellor of the said College, for the Space of Seven*
Years

[26]

deinde quousque alius Cancellarius collegii prædicti debito modo electus, præfectus, & constitutus fuerit.

XII. Insuper volumus, per præsentes, & pro nobis, hæredibus, & successoribus nostris, concedimus & confirmamus prefat' præsidi, & magistris, seu professoribus, collegii predicti, & eorum successoribus, retinere & appunctuare, cum collegium prædictum, stabilitum, erectum, & fundatum fuerit, quendam locum convenientem, seu cameram conciliar', intra collegium prædictum; utque idem rector, & alii visitatores, & gubernatores collegii prædicti, vel major pars eorum, pro tempore existent', quoties iis opportunum & necessarium fore videbitur, convocare & tenere, intra eandem cameram quandam curiam, seu convocationem de iisdem rectore, visitatoribus, seu gubernatoribus collegii prædicti, vel eorum majori parte, possint & valeant, perpetuis futuris temporibus, ac in eadem convocatione, tractare, conferre, consultare, consulere, & discernere, de statut', injunct', & ordinationibus collegii prædicti.

XIII. Ac insuper volumus, ac per præsentes, pro nobis, hæredibus, & successoribus nostris, concedimus & confirmamus præfat' præsidi, & magistris, seu professoribus, collegii prædicti, & successoribus suis, seu majori parti eorundem, de tempore in tempus, perpetuis futuris temporibus, ut ipsi rector, & visitatores, seu gubernatores collegii prædicti, & eorum successores seu major pars eorundem, habeant potestatem & authoritatem, annuatim & quolibet anno, primo die *Lunæ*, qui accidet & continget proxime post festum annunciationis beatæ *Mariæ* virginis, eligendi & nominandi, & eligere & nominare, possint & valeant, unum e prædictis visitatoribus seu gubernatoribus collegii prædicti, fore & esse rectorem collegii prædicti, pro uno anno integro ex tunc proxime sequent': Utque ille postquam sicut præfertur elect' præfect' & nominat' fuerit, in officium rectoris collegii prædicti, antequam ad officium prædictum exequend' admittatur,

[27]

Years then next ensuing, and thereafter until some other Chancellor of the said College shall be duly elected and constituted.

XII. *Further, we Will, by these Presents, and for us, our Heirs, and Successors do Grant and Confirm to the said President, and Masters, or Professors, of the said College, and to their Successors, that after the said College is erected, founded, and established, they may retain and appoint some convenient Place, or Council Chamber, within the said College; and that the Rector, and other Visitors, and Governors of the said College, or the major Part of them, for the Time being, as often as they shall think good, and see Cause, may convocate and hold a certain Court or Convocation within the said Chamber, consisting of the said Rector, and Visitors, and Governors, of the said College, or the major Part of them, in all Time coming; and in the said Convocation, may treat, confer, consult, advise, and decree, concerning Statutes, Orders, and Injunctions, for the said College.*

XIII. *And further, we Will, and by these Presents, for us, our Heirs, and Successors, do Grant and Confirm to the said President, and Masters, or Professors, of the said College, and their Successors, or the major Part of them, that from Time to Time, and in all Time coming, the said Rector, and Visitors, or Governors, of the said College, and their Successors, or the major Part of them, shall have Power and Authority, Yearly, and every Year, on the first* Monday *which shall happen next after the Feast of the Annunciation of the blessed Virgin* Mary, *to elect and nominate, and that they shall and may elect and nominate one of the said Visitors or Governors of the said College, to be Rector of the said College, for one whole Year then next ensuing: And that he, after he is so elected and chosen into the said Office of Rector of the said College, before he*

be

[28]

mittatur, sacramentum corporale eodem die, & loco, coram ultimo rectore, & visitatoribus, seu gubernatoribus collegii prædicti (aut quibuscunque tribus eorundem) præstabit ad bene & fideliter officium illud exequend'; & ut post sacramentum prædictum sic præstit', officium illud rectoris collegii prædicti, pro uno anno integro, ex tunc proxime sequent' exequi, valeat & possit: Ac etiam, ut quolibet septennio eodem die *Lunæ* proxime post festum annunciationis beatæ *Mariæ* Virginis prædict' simili modo & forma, habeant authoritatem & potestatem eligendi & nominandi, & eligere & nominare valeant alium Cancellarium collegii prædicti, continuand' pro septennio, ex tunc proxime sequent': Et ut ille qui sic elect' præfect' & nominat' fuerit, in officium Cancellarii collegii prædicti, immediate post talem electionem & nominationem officium illud Cancellarii collegii prædicti pro septennio integro, ex tunc proxime sequent' exequi valeat & possit.

XIV. Et ut onera & expensæ erigendi, ædificandi, fundandi, & adornandi, collegium prædictum in præsens, ac etiam alendi & manutenendi præsidem, & magistros, seu professores prædictos, in futurum sustineri & supportari possint, de uberiori & ampliori gratia nostra speciali, certa scientia, & mero motu nostris, dedimus concessimus, assignavimus, & transtulimus, ac per præsentes, pro nobis, hæredibus, & successoribus nostris, damus, concedimus, assignamus, & transferimus præfatis *Francisco Nicholson, Gulielmo Cole, Rodolpho Wormley, Gulielmo Byrd,* & *Joanni Lear,* Armigeris; *Jacobo Blair, Joanni Farnifold, Stephano Fouace,* & *Samueli Gray,* Clericis; *Thomæ Milner, Christophoro Robinson, Carolo Scarborough, Joanni Smith, Benjamino Harrison, Milesio Cary, Henrico Hartwell, Gulielmo Randolph,* & *Mattheo Page,* Generosis, & executoribus & assignatis eorum in perpetuum, totam illam plenam & integram summam unius mille & noningentarum octogingta quinque librarum quatuordecem solidorum & decem denariorum

bonæ

[29]

be admitted to execute the said Office, shall, on the same Day, and in the same Place, take his corporal Oath before the last Rector, and Visitors, or Governors, of the said College, or any Three of them, well and faithfully to execute the said Office; and that after so taking the said Oath, he shall and may execute the said Office of Rector of the said College, for one whole Year then next ensuing: And also, that every Seventh Year, on the same Monday, *next after the Feast of the Annunciation of the blessed Virgin* Mary, *aforesaid, they shall, in like Manner, have Power and Authority to elect and nominate another Chancellor of the said College, to be continued for Seven Years then next ensuing: And that he who shall be so elected, chosen, and nominated, into the Office of Chancellor of the said College, shall and may, immediately after such Election and Nomination, execute the Office of Chancellor of the said College for Seven Years then next ensuing.*

XIV. *And that the Charge and Expence of erecting, building, founding, and adorning, the said College at present, and also of supporting and maintaining the said President, and Masters, or Professors, for the future, may be sustained and defray'd, of Our more ample and bounteous special Grace, certain Knowledge, and mere Motion, We have Given, Granted, Assigned, and Made over, and by these Presents, for us, our Heirs, and Successors, do Give, Grant, Assign, and Make over to the said* Francis Nicholson, William Cole, Ralph Wormley, William Byrd, *and* John Lear, *Esqs;* James Blair, John Farnifold, Stephen Fouace, *and* Samuel Gray, *Clerks;* Thomas Milner, Christopher Robinson, Charles Scarborough, John Smith, Benjamin Harrison, Myles Cary, Henry Hartwell, William Randolph, *and* Matthew Page, *Gentlemen, and their Executors, and Assigns for ever, the whole and entire Sum of One Thousand Nine Hundred and Eighty Five Pounds Fourteen Shillings and Ten Pence, of good and lawful Money*

[30]

bonæ & legalis monetæ *Angliæ*, de denariis pro redditibus
nostris in colonia prædicta, receptis & levatis in manibus
Gulielmi Byrd, armigeri, auditoris nostri, vel alicuius alius
personæ in colonia prædicta, ad usum nostrum nunc re-
manentibus: Ideoque mandamus & firmiter injungendo præ-
cipimus præfato auditori, vel cuilibet alii apud quem
prædicta pecunia deposita est, aut qui eandem solvere
tenetur immediate super visum literarum harum nostrarum
patentium, solvere, seu solvi facere, præfatam summam unius
mille & noningentarum octoginta quinque librarum quatuordecem solidorum & decem denariorum præfatis *Francisco
Nicholson, Gulielmo Cole*, &c. aut majori parti eorum, aut
eorum diutius viventium, aut eorum attornat', in ea parte
legitime constitut' sine aliquo alio warranto, mandato sive
præcepto nostro, in hac parte inmpetrand' vel expectand',
in, circa, & ad ædificationem, erectionem, & adornationem
collegii prædicti expendend' & applicand', & ad nulla alia
usus, intentiones, & proposita quæcunque.

XV. Cumque etiam, per quendam actum parliamenti
factum anno regni avunculi nostri regii, *Caroli* secundi,
beatæ memoriæ, vicesimo quinto, intitulat', *An Act for the
Encouragement of the* Greenland *and* Eastland *Trades, and
for beter securing the Plantation Trade*, inactitatum fuerit,
ut post primum diem *Septembris*, qui tunc foret anno domini millesimo sexcentesimo septuagesimo tertio, si qua
navis, quæ per legem terræ posset negotiari, in aliquibus
plantationibus, accederet alicui earum ad navem prædict'
nicotiana, aut aliis mercibus, ibidem numeratis onerand', &
si scriptum obligatorium non prius esset datum, cum uno
sufficiente fidejussore, eandam nicotianam transportare in
Angliam, Walliam, sive oppidum *Bervici* super *Twedam*, &
non alio, & ibidem illam exonerare, & in terram exponere
(periculis maris solummodo exceptis;) in tali causa persolve-
retur prædicto avunculo nostro, & hæredibus, ac successoribus ipsius, pro unaquaque nicotianæ libra, sic onerata, unus
denarius

[31]

Money of England, *that has been received and raised out of the Quit-Rents of the said Colony, now remaining in the Hands of* William Byrd, *Esq; our Auditor, or in whose soever other Hands the same now is, for our Use, within the said Colony: And therefore, we command and firmly enjoin the said Auditor, or any other Person with whom the said Money is deposited, or who is obliged to pay the same, immediately upon Sight of these our Letters Patents, to pay, or cause to be paid, the said Sum of One Thousand Nine Hundred and Eighty Five Pounds Fourteen Shillings and Ten Pence, to the Said* Francis Nicholson, William Cole, &c. *or the major Part of them, or of the longer Livers of them, or to their Attorney, in that Part lawfully constituted, without any other Warrant, Mandate, or Precept, to be obtained or expected from us, to be laid out and applied about and towards the building, erecting, and adorning, the said College, and to no other Use, Intent, or Purpose whatsoever.*

XV. *Seeing also, by a certain Act of Parliament, made in the Twenty-fifth Year of the Reign of our Royal Uncle,* Charles *the Second, of blessed Memory, intituled,* An Act for the Encouragement of the *Greenland,* and *Eastland* Trades, and for better securing the Plantation Trade, *it was enacted, That after the First Day of* September, *in the Year of our Lord* M,DC,LXXIII, *if any Ship, which by Law, might trade in any of the Plantations, should come to any of them to load, and take on Board Tobacco, or any other of the Commodities there enumerated, and if Bond were not first given, with one sufficient Surety, to carry the said Tobacco to* England, Wales, *or the Town of* Berwick *upon* Tweed, *and to no other Place, and there to unload and put the same on Shore, (the Dangers of the Sea only excepted;) in such Case there should be paid to our said Uncle, and his Heirs, and Successors, one Penny for every Pound of Tobacco so loaded and put on Board, to be levied,*
                                                        collected

[32]

denarius levand', colligend', & solvend', talibus locis, & collectoribus, sive aliis officiariis, in respectivis plantationi- bus, colligere, levare, & recipere, eosdem instituendis & sub talibus mulctis, tam officiariis, quam mercibus infligendis, quales ob non soluta, aut defraudata regia vectigalia, aut custumas in *Anlia* infligi debent: Et si acciderit aliquas per- sonas sive personam, que debita præmentionata solvere de- bent, non habere pecunias numeratas quibus iisdem satisfacere poterunt, ut officiarii instituti ad colligenda eadem accipiant in loco pecuniarum numeratarum talem proportionem nicotianæ onerandæ qual' ad valorem ejusdem attingeret, secundum usualem ratam mercis prædictæ, in tali plantatione respective: Quæ omnia ordinanda & disponenda sunt, & debita respectiva levari causanda, per Commissiona- rios custumarum nostrarum in *Anglia*, pro tempore existent', sub authoritate & directione domini Thesaurarii *Angliæ*, sive Commissionariorum Thesauri, pro tempore existent', prout per eundem actum parliamenti, intra alia ibidem contenta, relatione inde habita, plenius liquet & apparet; nos de uberi- ori gratia nostra, mero motu, & certa scientia, dedimus & concessimus, ac pro nobis, & successoribus nostris, damus & concedimus præfatis *Francisco Nicholson, Gulielmo Cole*, cæterisque præfatis fiduciariis, & hæredibus suis, in per- petuum, prædictam reventionem unius denarii pro qualibet libra nicotianæ ex *Virginia*, aut terra *Mariæ*, in *America*, aut illarum quacunque, sicut præfertur onerand'; & productum nitidum qui accreverit in *Anglia*, aut alibi, venditione ibidem nicotianæ, in coloniis nostris *Virginiæ*, & terræ *Mariæ* colli- gend', in loco denarii prædicti, pro qualibet libra nicotianæ sic onerandæ persolvend': Proviso tamen semper, ut Com- missionarii custumarum nostrarum in *Anglia*, pro tempore existentes, omnes collectores, & receptores, prædictæ pecu- niæ & nicotianæ, eorumque supervisores, de tempore in tempus, prout antea nominent & constituant: Et ut salaria prædictorum collectorum, receptorum, & supervisorum, ex prædicta reventione deducantur & persolvantur; utque prædicti

[33]

collected, and paid in such Places, and to such Officers, and Collectors, as should be appointed in the respective Plantations, to collect, levy, and receive the same, and under such Penalties, both to the Officers and upon the Goods as for Non-payment of His Majesty's Customs in England: *And if it should happen that any Person or Persons who are to pay the said Duties, shall not have ready Money to satisfy the same, that the Officers who are appointed to collect the said Duties, shall, in Lieu of the said ready Money, take such a Proportion of Tobacco, that was to be ship'd, as may amount to the Value thereof, according to the usual Rate of the said Commodity, in such Plantation, respectively: All which Things are to be ordered, and disposed, and these several Duties are to be caused to be levied, by the Commissioners of our Customs in* England, *for the Time being, under the Authority and Direction of the Lord Treasurer of* England, *or the Commissioners of the Treasury, for the Time being, as by the said Act of Parliament, amongst other Things therein contained, Reference being thereto had, doth more fully appear; We, of our more bounteous Grace, mere Motion, and certain Knowledge, have Given and Granted, and for us, and our Successors, do Give, and Grant, to the said* Francis Nicholson, William Cole, &c. *and the other Trustees above-mentioned, and their Heirs, for ever, the said Revenue of One Penny for every Pound of Tobacco in* Virginia, *or* Maryland, *in* America, *or either of them, that shall be so loaded, and put on Board, as is abovesaid; and the nett Produce which shall accrue in* England, *or elsewhere, by felling there the Tobacco that shall be collected in our Colonies of* Virginia, *and* Maryland, *in Lieu of the Penny that ought to be paid for every Pound of Tobacco so loaded and put on Board, as is abovesaid: Provided always, That the Commissioners of our Customs in* England, *for the Time being, shall name and appoint all the Collectors and Receivers of the said Money and Tobacco, and their*
Inspectors

[34]

dicti *Franciscus Nicholson, Gulielmus Cole, Rodolphus Wormley, Gulielmus Byrd,* & *Joannes Lear,* Armigeri; *Jacobus Blair, Joannes Farnifold, Stephanus Fouace,* & *Samuel Gray,* Clerici; *Thomas Milner, Christophorus Robinson, Carolus Scarborough, Joannes Smith, Benjaminus Harrison, Milesius Cary, Henricus Hartwell, Gulielmus Randolph,* & *Mattheus Page,* Generosi, eorumque successores, ac etiam præses, & magistri, seu professores collegii prædicti, eorumque successores, pro tempore existent', teneantur accipere & observare omnes tales regulas, ordinationes, & instructiones, quales ad melius & exactius colligendos prædictos denarios a prædictis Commissionariis custumarum nostrarum in *Anglia,* pro tempore existentibus, sub inspectione & directione domini Thesaurarii, aut commissionariorum Thesauri nostri in *Anglia,* pro tempore existentium, de tempore in tempus, ad ipsos transmittentur, prout per eundem actum parliamenti, relatione inde habita, magis particulariter, dirigitur, & instituitur: Seb sub hac expressa intentione, & speciali fiducia & confidentia quam reponimus in prædicto *Francisco Nicholson, Gulielmo Cole,* cæterisque præfatis fiduciariis quod ipsi, & eorum diutius viventes, eorumque hæredes, prædictam reventionem unius denarii, pro singulis nicotianæ libris prædictis, tenebunt, capient, & prossidebunt, cum omnibus proficuis, commoditatibus, & emolumentis ejusdem, ut eandem applicent & impendant ad erectionem & adornationem ædificiorum aliorumque, ad prædictum collegium necessariorum, donec collegium prædictum, actu erectum, fundatum, & stabilitum fuerit: Et sub hac expressa intentione, & speciali fiducia & confidentia, quod quamprimum prædictum collegium secundum regium nostrum propositum erectum & fundatum fuerit, præfati fiduciarii, eorumque diutius viventes, aut diutius vivens ejusque, aut eorum hæredes, aut assignati bonis & sufficientibus assurantiis in lege dabunt, concedent, & transferent præsidi, & magistris, seu professoribus collegii prædicti, integram hanc reventionem, prædictam, cum omnibus proficuis, proventibus, & emolu-

mentis

[35]

Inspectors and Comptrolers, from Time to Time, as they have hitherto done: And that the Salaries of the said Collectors, Receivers, and Comptrolers, shall be deducted and paid out of the said Revenue; and that the said Francis Nicholson, William Cole, Ralph Wormley, William Byrd, *and* John Lear, *Esqs;* James Blair, John Farnifold, Stephen Fouace, *and* Samuel Gray, *Clerks;* Thomas Milner, Christopher Robinson, Charles Scarborough, John Smith, Benjamin Harrison, Myles Cary, Henry Hartwell, William Randolph, *and* Matthew Page, *Gentlemen, and their Successors, as also the President, and Masters, or Professors of the said College, and their Successors, for the Time being, shall be obliged to receive, and observe all such Rules, Orders, and Instructions, as shall be transmitted to them, from Time to Time, by the said Commissioners of our Customs in* England, *for the Time being, under the Inspection and Direction of the Lord Treasurer, or the Commissioners of our Treasury in* England, *for the Time being, for the better and more exact collecting of the said Duty, as by the said Act of Parliament, Reference being thereto had, is more particularly directed and appointed; but with this express Intention, and upon the special Trust and Confidence We place in the said* Francis Nicholson, William Cole, *and the rest of the aforesaid Trustees, that they, and the longest Livers of them, and their Heirs, shall take, hold, and possess the said Revenue of a Penny per Pound for every Pound of Tobacco aforesaid, with all its Profits, Advantages, and Emoluments, to apply and lay out the same, for building and adorning the Edifices and other Necessaries for the said College, until the said College shall be actually erected, founded, and established, and with this express Intention, and upon the special Trust and Confidence, that so soon as the said College shall be erected and founded, according to our Royal Purpose, the said Trustees, and the longest Livers or Liver of them, and his or their Heirs, or Assigns, shall, by good and sufficient Deeds*

and

[36]

mentis ejusdem, nuper memoratis, aut tantundem eorum quantum in usus prædictos, nondum expensum & collocatum fuerit, tenend', possidend', & gaudend', prædict' præsidi, & magistris, seu professoribus, eorumque successoribus, in perpetuum.

XVI. Ac etiam, de gratia nostra speciali, mero motu, & certa scientia nostris, dedimus & concessimus, & per præsentes, pro nobis, hæredibus, & successoribus nostris, damus & concedimus *Francisco Nicholson, Gulielmo Cole*, cæterisque præfatis fiduciariis, eorumque diutius viventibus, aut diutius viventi ejusque, aut illorum hæredibus officium Supervisoris generalis coloniæ nostræ *Virginiæ* prædictæ, si modo officium prædictum nunc vacuum sit, vel quandocunque & quotiescunque in posterum vacuum fuerit, habend', tenend', & exercend', cum omnibus vadis, feodis, allocationibus, proficuis, commoditatibus, advantagiis, libertatibus, locis & præeminentiis quibuscunque, ad dictum officium spectant' & pertinent': In tam amplis modo & forma, quam aliquis alius dictum officium, antehac habens, exercens, vel occupans, unquam habuit, percepit, vel gavisus fuit, aut habere, percipere, vel gaudere, debuit per præfatos fiduciarios, eorumque hæredes, aut per tales officiarios & substitutos, quales ipsi, aut major ipsorum pars, aut diutius viventium ipsorum, eorumque hæredum, de tempore in tempus, nominabunt & constituent, donec collegium prædictum actu fundatum & erectum fuerit: Sed sub hac expressa intentione, & speciali fiducia & confidentia, quam reponimus in prædicto *Francisco Nicholson, Gulielmo Cole*, cæterisque præfatis fiduciariis, quod ipsi, & eorum diutius viventes, eorumque hæredes, quicquid restat pecuniarum, ex hoc officio durante sua administratione provenientium, & in erectionem prædicti collegii, cæterosque usus supradictos, nondum impensarum, quam primum collegium prædictum actu erectum & fundatum fuerit, præsidi, & magistris, seu professoribus collegii prædicti, pro tempore existent' reddent, & restituent: Et

postquam

[37]

and Assurances in Law, Give, Grant, and Transfer to the President, and Masters, or Professors, of the said College, this whole Revenue, with all its Profits, Issues, and Emoluments before-mentioned, or so much thereof, as shall not have been expended and laid out for the aforesaid Uses, to be held, possessed, and enjoyed, by the said President, and Masters, or Professors, and their Successors, for ever.

XVI. *And also, of our special Grace, mere Motion, and certain Knowledge, We have Given and Granted, and by these Presents, for us, our Heirs, and Successors, do Give, and Grant, to* Francis Nicholson, William Cole, *and the rest of the said Trustees, and to the longest Livers or Liver of them, and to his or their Heirs, the Office of Surveyor-General of our said Colony of* Virginia, *if the said Office be now void, or whensoever, and how often soever, it shall hereafter fall void, to be had, held and executed, with all its Issues, Fees, Profits, Advantages, Conveniences, Liberties, Places, Privileges, and Preeminences whatsoever, belonging to the said Office, in as ample Form and Manner as any other Person, who has heretofore had, executed, or possessed, the said Office, ever had, received, or enjoy'd, or ought to have, receive, or enjoy, by the said Trustees, and their Heirs; or by such Officers and Substitutes, as they or the major Part of them, or of the longest Livers of them, or of their Heirs, shall from Time to Time nominate and appoint, until the said College shall be actually founded, and erected: But with this express Intention, and upon this special Trust and Confidence, which We place in the said* Francis Nicholson, William Cole, *and the rest of the said Trustees, that they and the longest Livers of them, and their Heirs, shall give back and restore to the President, and Masters, or Professors, of the said College, for the Time being, whatsoever Money remains in their Hands,*
that

[38]

postquam collegium illud actu fundatum & erectum fuerit,
volumus ut officium illud Supervisoris generalis, si modo
tunc vacuum sit & quotiescunque in posterum vacuum fuerit,
habeatur, teneatur & exerceatur, cum omnibus suis proficuis
& pertinentibus supradictis, per præfatos præsidem, & magistros, seu professores supradictos, eorumque successores,
in perpetuum: Proviso tamen, ut præfatus *Franciscus
Nicholson*, cæterique fiduciarii prædicti, aut major ipsorum
pars, aut eorum diutius viventium, & prædicti præses, &
magistri, seu professores, pro tempore existentes, de tempore
in tempus, tot & tales supervisores particulares pro singulis
coloniæ nostræ *Virginiæ* comitatibus nominabunt & substitu-
ent, quales Gubernator noster generalis & Concilium coloniæ nostræ *Virginiæ* supradictæ, pro tempore existent'
necessarios & idoneos fore judicabunt.

XVII. Ac etiam de ampliori gratia nostra speciali, mero
motu, & certa scientia nostris, dedimus, concessimus, & confirmavimus, & per præsentes, pro nobis, & successoribus
nostris, damus, concedimus, & confirmamus, præfatis *Francisco Nicholson, Gulielmo Cole,* cæterisque fiduciariis supradictis, decem mille acrarum terræ, nondum ab aliquibus aliis
subditis nostris, legaliter occupat' sive possessionat', jacent',
& existent', a parte australi plaudis aquæ nigræ vulgo vocat'
Blackwater Swamp, ac etiam, alias decem mille acras terræ
nondum etiam ab aliquibus aliis subditis nostris, legaliter oc-
cupatæ sive possessionatæ, jacent' & existent' in isthmo illo,
vulgo vocato *Pamunkey Neck,* inter furcas, seu ramos fluminis Eboracensis, vulvo vocat' *York River:* Quæ viginti
acrarum mille, volumus limitari & mensurari in locis supradictis, ubicunque libitum fuerit præfatis *Francisco Nicholson, Gulielmo Cole,* cæterisque fiduciariis supradictis, aut
majori parti ipsorum, aut eorum diutius viventium, habend'
& tenend' præfat' *Francisco Nicholson, Gulielmo Cole,* cæterisque præfatis fiduciariis, & hæredibus suis, in perpetuum,
ea tamen intentione, & in speciali fiducia, & confidentia,
quod

[39]

*that has risen from this Office, during their Administration,
not yet laid out upon the building of the said College, and
the other above-mentioned Uses, so soon as the said College shall be actually erected, and founded: And after the
said College shall be actually erected and founded, we Will,
that the said Office of Surveyor-General, if it be then void,
and as often as it shall be void, for the Time to come, shall
be had, held, and executed, with all its Profits and Appurtenances above-mentioned, by the said President, and
Masters, or Professors, and their Successors, for ever,
Provided always, That the said Francis Nicholson, and
the rest of the above mentioned Trustees, or the major
Part of them, or of the longest Livers of them, and the
President, and Masters, or Professors, for the Time being,
shall, from Time to Time, nominate and substitute such,
and so many particular Surveyors for the particular Counties of our Colony of Virginia, as our Governor in Chief,
and the Council of our said Colony of Virginia, for the
Time being, shall think fit and necessary.*

XVII. *And also, of our more bounteous special Grace,
mere Motion, and certain Knowledge, we have Given,
Granted, and Confirmed, and by these Presents, for us, and
our Heirs, and Successors, do Give, Grant, and confirm, to
the said Francis Nicholson, William Cole, and the rest of
the Trustees above-mentioned, Ten Thousand Acres of
Land, not yet legally occupied or possessed by any of our
other Subjects, lying, and being, on the South Side of the
Blackwater Swamp, and also other Ten Thousand Acres of
Land, not yet legally occupied or possessed by any of our
other Subjects, lying and being in that Neck of Land, commonly called Pamunkey Neck, between the Forks or
Branches of York River: Which Twenty Thousand Acres
of Land, we Will have to be laid out and measured in
the Places above-mentioned, at the Choice of the said
Francis Nicholson, William Cole, and the rest of the*
                                                    fore-

[40]

quod præfati *Franciscus Nicholson, Gulielmus Cole,* cæterique fiduciarii prædicti, sive major pars eorundem, sive eorum diutius viventium, cum collegium prædictum, fundatum & stabilitum fuerit, dabunt, concedent, locabunt, & alienabunt, viginti mille acrarum prædict' præfat', præsidi, & magistris, seu professoribus collegii prædicti habend' & tenend', sibi & successoribus suis, in perpetuum, per fidelitatem in libro & commune soccagio, reddendo nobis, & successoribus nostris, duo exemplaria carminum lingua latina conscriptorum, apud domum Gubernatoris, sive Vicegubernatoris coloniæ nostræ *Virginiæ* prædict', pro tempore existent', annuatim ad quemlibet quintum diem *Novembris,* quolibet anno, in perpetuum, in plena exoneratione, acquitantia, & satisfactione, omnium & singulorum redituum quietorum *Anglice Quit-Rents,* servitiorum, consuetudinum, debitorum, & onerum quorumcunque nobis, vel successoribus nostris, pro prædictis viginti mille acris terræ, per leges aut consuetudines *Angliæ,* aut *Virginiæ,* debit' & debend'.

XVIII. Ac etiam, de gratia nostra speciali, certa scientia, & mero motu nostris, dedimus & concessimus præfat' præsidi, & magistris, seu professoribus, collegii prædicti, & per præsentes, pro nobis, & successoribus nostris, damus & concedimus plenam & absolutam facultatem, potestatem, & authoritatem, nominandi, eligendi, & constituendi, unum virum discretum & habilem, ex ipsorum numero, vel e numero visitatorum & gubernatorum prædict', vel deinde, ex aliis principalibus inhabitantibus coloniæ nostræ *Virginiæ* prædictæ, elegendum, ad interessendum in domo Burgensium, Conventus generalis coloniæ nostræ *Virginiæ,* & ibidem, ad faciendum & consentiendum, his, quæ de communi concilio dictæ coloniæ nostræ, favente Deo, contigerint ordinari.

XIX. Et insuper volumus, ut *Francisco Nicholson,* cæterisque fiduciariis prædictis, eorumque secessoribus, vel

præsidi

[41]

fore-mentioned Trustees, or the major Part of them, or of the longest Livers of them, to be had and held by the said Francis Nicholson, William Cole, *and the rest of the above-mentioned Trustees, and their Heirs, for ever; but with this Intention, and upon special Trust and Confidence, that the said* Francis Nicholson, William Cole, *and the rest of the said Trustees, or the major Part of them, or of the longest Livers of them, so soon as the said College shall be actually founded, and established, shall Give, Grant, Lett, and Aleinate the said Twenty Thousand Acres of Land to the said President, and Masters, or Professors of the said College, to be had and held by them, and their Successors, for ever, by fealty, in free and common Soccage, paying to us, and our Successors, Two Copies of* Latin *Verses Yearly, on every Fifth Day of* November, *at the House of our Governor, or Lieutenant-Governor of* Virginia, *for the Time being, for ever, in full Discharge, Acquittance, and Satisfaction of all Quit-Rents, Services, Customs, Dues, and Burdens whatsoever, due, or to be due, to us, or our Successors, for the said Twenty Thousand Acres of Land, by the Laws or Customs of* England, *or* Virginia.

XVIII. *And also, of our special Grace, certain Knowledge, and mere Motion, We have Given, and Granted, and by these Presents, for us, and our Successors, do Give, and Grant, to the said President, and Masters, or Professors, of the said College, full and absolute Power, Liberty, and Authority, to nominate, elect, and constitute one discreet and able Person of their own Number, or of the Number of the said Visitors, or Governors, or lastly, of the better Sort of Inhabitants of our Colony of* Virginia, *to be present in the House of Burgesses, of the General Assembly of our Colony of* Virginia, *and there to act and consent to such Things, as by the common Advice of our said Colony shall (God willing) happen to be Enacted.*

XIX. *And*

[42]

præsidi, ac magistris, seu professoribus, collegii prædicti, aut eorum successoribus, pro tempore existentibus, super humilem eorum petitionem concedantur, de tempore in tempus, per nos, hæredes, & successores nostros, tales ulteriores confirmationes, & ratificationes, præmissorum, sub magno sigillo nostro *Anglia,* aut aliter qual' Attornato nostro generali, aut hæredum, vel successorum nostrorum, pro tempore existen', magis videbitur expedire.

In cujus rei testimonium has literas nostras, fieri fecimus patentes, testibus nobis ipsis, apud *Westmonaster,* octavo die *Februarii,* anno regni nostro quarto.
Per breve de privato sigillo.

PIGOTT.

[43]

XIX. *And further, it is our Pleasure, that such further Confirmations and Ratifications of the Premisses shall be Granted, from Time to Time, by us, our Heirs, and Successors, to the said* Francis Nicholson, *and the rest of the Trustees above mentioned, and to their Successors, or to the President, and Masters, or Professors, of the said College, or to their Successors, for the Time being, upon their humble Petition under the Great Seal of* England, *or otherwise, as the Attorney General of us, our Heirs, or Successors, for the Time being, shall think fit and expedient.*

In Testimony whereof, We have caused these our Letters to be made Patent: Witness our Selves, at Westminster, *the Eighth Day of* February, *in the Fourth Year of our Reign.*

By Writ of the Privy Seal.

P I G O T T .

8. The General Assembly selects the Middle Plantation as the site for the college, 1693

Whereas their majesties have been most graciously pleased upon the humble supplication of the generall assembly of this country by their charter bearing date the 8th day of Ffebruary in the fourth year of theire reign to grant their royall lycence to certaine trustees to make, found, erect and establish a college named the college of William and Mary in Virginia at a certaine place within this government known by the name of *Townsends Land* and heretofore appointed by the generall assembly, or if the same should be found inconvenient at such other place as the generall assembly should think fitt, and whereas the said fformer designed place for divers causes is found to be very unsuitable for such an use and severall other places have been nominated in the room thereof upon consideration of which and a full enquirie into the conveniences of each one of the said places the *Middle Plantation* situate between York and James Rivers appearing to be the most convenient and proper for that designe.

Be it therefore enacted by the governour, councell and burgesses of this present generall assembly and the authority thereof, and it is hereby enacted That *Middle Plantation* be the place for erecting the said college of *William and Mary* in Virginia and that the said college be at that place erected and built as neare the church now standing in *Middle Plantation* old ffields as convenience will permitt.—Hening, *op. cit.*, III, 122.

9. The General Assembly levies duties for the support of the College, 1693

Be it enacted by the governour, councell and burgesses of this present generall assembly and the authority thereof, and it is hereby enacted, That from and after the first day of January next, there shall be sattisfyed and paid to theire majesties theire heires and successors for and towards the better support and maintenance of the colledge of *William and Mary* in Virginia speedily intended by Gods grace to be erected at *Middle Plantation* within this government. The following dutyes, customes and impost for the following goods, wares and merchandises which shall be exported, carryed out of this theire majesties dominion either by land or water (that is to say) for every rawhide three pence for every tan'd hyde six pence, for every dressed buckskin one peney three ffarthings, for every undrest buckskin one peney, for every doe skin dressed one peney halfe peney, for every undrest doeskin three farthings, for every pound of beaver three pence, for every otter skin two pence, for every wild catt skin one peney halfe peney, for every minx skin one peney, for every fox skin one peney halfe peney, for every dozen of racoon skins three pence, and soe proportionably for a greater or lesser quantity, and for every elke skin four pence halfe peney.

And be it enacted by the authority aforesaid, and it is hereby enacted, That the said dutyes, customes and impost shall be paid and satisfyed by the person or persons exporting or carrying out the same either by land or water to the collector or collectors which shall be appointed by the governour or commander in chiefe for the time being to receive the said dutyes, customes and impost before the said goods, wares or merchandises shall be shipped off exported or carryed out of and from this dominion either by land or water and a certificate thereof obtained from the collector or collectors of the district where such goods wares and merchandises shall be soe exported or carryed away signifying the payment and sattisfaction of such dutyes, customes and impost as aforesaid, under the penallty of fforfeiting such of the said goods, wares and merchandizes which shall be shiped off or loaden on board of any boat, sloop, shipp or other vessell, in order to the exportation thereof by water or endeavoured to be carryed out of this countrey by land, the one moyety thereof to their majesties, theire heires and successors to and for the better support of the government and the contingent charges thereof the other moyety to him or them that shall sue or prosecute for the same in any court of record within this colony by action of debt, bill, plaint or information wherein noe essoyn protection or wager of law shall be allowed.

And be it further enacted, That the severall collectors or officers appoynted to collect and receive the said duties, customes and imposts shall from time to time be accountable and pay the same to the governour of the said colledge of William and Mary, or such other person or persons as shall be by them lawfully deputed, and that for the receiveing and paying thereof the said collector or collectors shall be allowed ten per cent—*Ibid.,* pp. 123-24.

10. "A TRUE ACCOUNT OF A CONFERENCE AT LAMBERT," 1697

INTERLOCUTORIES.

C . . .THOMAS, Ld ARCHBISHOP OF CANTERBURY
L . . .HENRY, Ld BISHOP OF LONDON.
P . . .Mr JOHN POVEY.   Bl . . .Mr BLAIR
M . . .Mr MARSHALL.   H . . .Mr HARRISON.
By. . .Mr BYRD.

L. My Lord, it is late (upon which Dr Hutton and Dr Woodward, understanding my L^d of London had business with the Archbishop, rose up and took their leave, then the Archbishop, ordered the Door to be shut and begun thus):

Bl. I suppose we all understand for what business we are met. I am sorry to hear of the differences in Virginia. I hope now ye will freely discourse the matter.

By. My Lord, I understand Mr Blair has accused Sr Edmund Andros to Your Grace and to my Lord of London concerning several things relating to the College of Virginia and therefore I beg that he may now repeat whatsoever he has to say of that nature and that he may do it Article by Article, that so I may make a distinct answer. By this means your Grace will see on which side innocence lies.

C. Nay I must say this for Mr Blair that he has not accused Sir Edmund nor no other person to me. I had heard that he discouraged the Colleg long before Mr Blair came over. If I remember right, the first time I heard it was upon occasion of Mr Boyles' Legacy, for being somewhat concerned in that, I did often talk with one Mr War, one of the executors, who was a very honest man and a great well-wisher to the College of Virginia, and offer my advice that some considerable part of it might be applied to that College; and he told me the chief objection to that was that the Governor of Virginia discouraged the College and he was afraid it would come to nothing. I cannot deny that Mr Blair has talked with me of these matters; but it has been more in answering accusations against himself than in accusing anybody, and therefore I would desire him in the first place to answer those objections that have been made against him, two of which I do at present remember. One is, that he has filled the Church and the College with Scotchmen and endeavored to make a national faction by the name of the Scottish party. The other is that he has misapplied and squandered away the money that should have gone to the building of the College. Say what ye have to say against him upon these or any other subjects, and let me hear his answers.

By. My Lord, for the first, I suppose Mr Blair will not deny that he has brought in several of his countrymen. But indeed my Lord, I cannot blame him much for this, though it makes a great noise in the Country and they are a sort of discontented troublesome Men murmuring at the shortness of their salaries with which the Ministers were very well contented formerly, and they are frequently troubling the Governor and the House of Burgesses with their petition on that subject.

Bl. My Lord, this is quite a new thing to me that Mr Byrd tells me of—the Scotch Ministers troubling the Governor or House of Burgesses with Petitions about their Salaries. I desire him to instance in any one petition of that nature, for I know none. It is true there was a petition presented to the Governor by the Clergy in general at one of their Meetings, but that Petition was signed by all the English as well as the Scotch clergy that were present. And why it should be laid particularly on the Scotch Ministers is only to distinguish them with that mark of Odium. But, my Lord, I desire to know ill things the Scotch Ministers have done there and whether I have supported any of them in any ill thing.

P. My Lord, because Mr Byrd is not so well acquainted with the Minutes of the Council, I beg leave that I may answer Mr Commissary who desires Instances of Scotch Ministers who have done ill things. I find, My Lord, there is one Mr Greig that was guilty of Sodomy and one Mr Doyley that his Parish complained of and one Mr Munroe—

Bl. Sir, That is your mistake. Mr Greg was an English man and Mr Doyley is an English man and what ye have to say to Mr Munroe I cannot Imagine for I take him to be as good a Man as any we have in the Country.

P. Then I am mistaken for I thought Greg and Doyley had been Scotch names.

C. There is nothing as far as I see in all this, for it seems this Greg, the most scandalous of all, was an Englishman. But can ye say anything of any scandalous Scotchman that Mr Blair has brought in and supports.

By. Yes, My Lord, there is one Mr Gordoun, a Scotchman, whom Mr Blair himself has owned to me to be an ill man and one that I myself have seen Drunk, and several others, for he is an habitual Drunkard.

Bl. My Lord, I confess this Mr Gordoun is a Man of very ill fame but sure nobody will say that I brought him into the Country or do in the least support him. He was in the Country before me, for ought I know; I am sure he was in it some time before I was in office there— and I have been so far from supporting that he is the only Man at whose Church I made a visitation on account of the Minister's Scandal. My Lord, there are some Hundreds of Witnesses of persons that were present at that visitation (for it was as publick and solemn as I could make it), and, My Lord, here is one Gentlemen (pointing to Mr Harrison), that happened to be there. They can all bear one witness that I did all that ever I could to have that Man turned out. But drunkenness being hard to prove and the witnesses mincing and ex-tenuating the matter and his vestry appearing in a body—petitioning that their Minister might not be taken from them, I could not for the heart of me, except I would have gone contrary to the *allegata* and *probata* overthrow him. But all the people were sensible I was not backward, if I could have done it. Now, My Lord, I would fain know what any man in my circumstances could have done more, so that, My Lord, there is not the least proof of my supporting any of them in any ill thing. For there being some Scotch Ministers in the Country, what is that to me, My Lord? It is not I that provide Ministers for the Country. If they bring me my Lord Bishop of London's License and behave themselves well in the Country it is not my part to quarrel with them only because they are Scotchmen.

L. My Lord, whatever there is in this, I must take it upon me. Your Grace knows the circumstances of the poor Men in their own Country, and I must confess I thought it both a Charity to the Men and that it was a piece of good service to the plantations, to send them thither. And I think it unkindly done in Sir Edmund Andros to make a noise about this, for I wrote him an account of all that I sent and told him the Characters I had of them, and told him if any of them did not behave himself well, he should be as easily turned out as ever he had been put in. He makes me no returns to this but raises a clamour against these Men only account of their country.

C. We know there are some of the best men of that Country that are not permitted access to the Ministry in their own Country.

Bl. I confess, My Lord, I was very unwilling to take a Scotch Schoolmaster if I could have holpen it. I spoke to all the Bishops with whom I had the Honor to be acquainted, to help me to a good English Schoolmaster and particularly I spoke to your Grace. You was then

Bishop of Lincoln, and I put off providing one till the last month—so that I was like to go without one—and then I took a Scotchman. But, thank God, he is one that is without exception. I hope these Gentlemen wont deny that I made a very good choice.

By. My Lord, the Schoolmaster, Mr. Ingles, is a very good schoolmaster. He has made several good scholars and I believe all people are very pleased with him.

C. That is very well. I confess I have much to do to find Schoolmasters for my own schools and I am very glad ye are so well provided. Well I think we have heard enough on this subject.

By. My Lord, I confess as I said in the beginning that I see no just ground of any accusation against Mr. Blair on this account.

P. I know it is a very hard thing to persuade good men to go over into the Plantations. I confess it is a wonder to me that such a Man as Mr. Commissary Blair went thither and I think My Lord of London does mighty well to send several of the Episcopal Scotch Clergy thither.

By. My Lord, as to the second point, the thing we have to say against Mr. Blair is this, that he has taken Yearly the president's Salary f150 a Year. The first year indeed, he took but f100 which was conscientious, but after that, he has taken the whole f150. Now, my Lord, by the charter the whole Revenue, the penny a pound and everything else, is to go towards the building and furnishing, till the College is finished and then it is to be transferred to the President and Masters. But in the mean time they are to have nothing.

Bl. My Lord, my answer to this shall be very short. Mr. Byrd says the whole revenues are by the Charter to go solely towards Building. This I positively deny. For there is nothing but the ready money, viz: f1985 14s 10d which was appointed to be applied solely towards the building. But all the rest viz: the penny a pound, the Land, and the Surveyor General's place is to go for all other uses of the College till it is actually founded, erected, and established. Particularly, the word founding, which is always the Law Word for a perpetual fund of maintenance, is always put into these Revenues. And indeed, my Lord, by the Order of Council upon which the Charter was to be drawn, it appears that the Revenues were given solely for the maintenance of the President and Masters. But upon my acquainting Mr. Lowndes of the Treasury, who helped to draw the Charter, that at present we were only to have a president and a Grammar Schoolmaster and an Usher and that their salaries came but to f280 a year and that we were to provide and pay the professors of Philosophy and Divinity as we should have occasion for them, he started this objection. "What" says he "if the penny per pound should amount to 1000 pounds per annum? If your President and Masters at present are only to have 280 pounds, what shall become of the rest? For if in the charter it be given only for the maintenance of the President, and Masters and yet these president and Masters are to have but 280 pounds, the overplus being appropriated to no use, ye will be in danger of losing it again if this comes to be observed. And therefore" continued he, "I think you had better give a power to the Governors of your College to bestow this money not only for maintenance of President and Masters but for building, furnishing, buying books, or any other use about the College. I liked this motion and accordingly the Charter was drawn giving them power to put these Revenues to all uses whatsoever about the College till it should be actually erected, founded, and established, but so that still the charges of founding the College consisting of a President and six Masters were actually included. And for this I appeal to the Charter.

By. My Lord, Mr Blair refers himself to the Charter. Here is an English copy of it. Pray give me leave to read this part about the King's gift of the Revenues.

Bl. Pray then read it distinctly—the ready money gift and all—that the different uses between that and the gift of the revenues may appear. For that's to be applied solely to the building, and the other Revenues to all uses whatsoever till it is actually erected and founded.

Upon this Mr Byrd began to read the gift of a penny a pound and Mr Blair prayed him to begin a little before that at the gift of the ready money. Then the Arch Bishop said: C. I perceive it will take a long time to read and examine the Charter and my Lord of London is in haste. But pray let me know one thing, which I have heard something of, that is, I have been told, that the Governor of the College obliged Mr Blair to quit a Living that he had at some considerable distance and to come and attend the business of the College. If so they could not expect but he must have salary. Pray, Sir, (to Mr Blair), tell us in short how that was.

Bl. My Lord, after the general Assembly of Virginia had chosen me president of the College, accordingly I was named first president in the Charter in words of the present tense and as ample words as the law affords for giving any man a good title to any place. But tho' I had the Right and Title to the president's salary which the same general Assembly had settled at 150 a year, yet I thought in good conscience I was bound to take none of it till I came to give attendance and do the duty of a president. In Pursuance of this at the very first Meeting of the Governors of the College in Virginia, I gave some Account of my Negotiation in England and produced the Charter, and after it was read I told them, "Gentlemen, ye see I am here made president of the College, which was not done till after the General Assembly had sent me an acount of their unanimous Election of me. But, gentlemen, tho' I am president yet if you think the business of the President unnecessary at present, I have a good plantation and a good Living where I am—up at Henrico—and I am inducted into it. I will stay there and not put you to one farthing charge till you shall say the attendance of a president is necessary at the College. Whereupon, my Lord, there was a free debate upon the subject and they agreed upon this, that since I had had all the trouble of managing the business of the College both in Virginia and in England, if I was not at the head of it they were afraid it would still come to nothing and therefore voted that I should presently leave my Parish and remove myself to the place where the College should be built and carry it on with all diligence. Accordingly my Lord I gave up my Induction and as soon as I could get an house to live in, I removed to the place appointed for the building of the College and have ever since given all due attendance upon the business of it and indeed my Lord as before I had the right so now I thought I had likewise Equity and good conscience on my side for taking my Salary. The first Year indeed, about 4 or 5 months being lapsed before I could get to this place, I gave down £50 of my salary, but ever since, I think, on account of my Residence and attendance on the business I have right to the whole 150 pound. Thus was the Salary settled by the general Assembly, and how I, or even the Governors of the College who are only Trustees, can alter it or lessen it with a good conscience, I do not understand.

C. If this be the case, it is no more than I or any other person should have done.

By. My Lord, this is the reason men give for not paying their subscriptions. They say they won't give their Money to make a Salary for the President.

Bl. My Lord, this is a very strange reason, for there was always a distinct account kept both of the King's money gift and of all the subscriptions, for all these went solely to the building, there was never one penny taken of them for Salaries. The Salaries were still paid out of the Revenue and what was of the Revenue over and above the Salaries was thrown into the Building too.

H. My Lord, I can give Your Grace an account of the reason they gave for not paying their Subscriptions, for after Col. Hartwell left Virginia, I, being a well wisher to the College and living convenient, was desired to collect the subscriptions of York County. I came to one Man who was a Justice of the peace and asked him for his Subscription. He answered me that he would pay when Secretary Wormley paid. The true reason, my Lord, why others do not pay is because the great men do not pay.

P. My Lord, I think there is all the reason in the world Mr Blair should have his Salary. It is but a mean reward for the extraordinary pains he has taken. But if the College is poor perhaps there might be another way found to make up a Salary for Mr Blair. Here was an hundred pound a year ordered for him as Commissary out of the Quit rents. The Treasury would never settle it but from year to year, and I doubt it has been ill paid, Now, my Lord, it has been as easy a matter to have got £200 a Year for that use as one.

By. My Lord, Mr Blair's taking this Salary has certainly made a great noise in the Country and it is against the Charter which applies all to the Building till all is finished and then it is to be transferred to the president and Masters.

Bl. My Lord, here is their Error. They confound two things that are quite different, viz: the paying of the Master's Salaries, called in the charter the Founding the president and Masters, and the transferring, which is the yielding up of the Trust to them. For the paying their Salaries, there is no doubt they must do that as soon as they set up the men. Otherwise they could not pay Mr Ingles the Schoolmaster no more than me, for this objection strikes against him and all others they may have in time as well as against me. But the transferring is not till the whole erection and founding and establishment is over and it is supposed in the Charter the first president and Masters may be gone and may have successors by that time.

C. Well I think we have heard enough of this. I wish ye would proceed to something else.

By. Then, My Lord, I must desire Mr Blair to say what he has to say against Sir Edmund Andros about his obstructing the business of the College.

Bl. My Lord, it is a pretty hard task for me who am a subject of

Virginia to say anything that may look like an accusation of Sir Edmund Andros, the present Governor. But I think it is my duty to acquaint your Grace with the bad state of the affairs of the College and shall leave it to Your Grace to judge whether Sir Edmund Andros is the root of all or not.

I shall begin with the business of the Subscriptions towards the building. When Governor Nicholson left the Government of Virginia there were subscriptions for near £3000. In that Gentleman's time there has not been a subscription for one penny. Of the 3000 pound Subscription there is come in but about 500 and some odd pounds. The Persons that stand out are the Council and Great Men who have places of profit and preferment under Sir Edmund and it is very observable that the payments which have been made have been made chiefly by such people who lived remote from those Councillors and Great Men particularly the south side of James River where there is no Councillor. There the People have generally paid, but in the rest of the Country except it be here and there a Zealous man for the College, they generally stand out and refuse to pay. Not only so, My Lord, but the Governor of the College presented a Bill to the general assembly for facilitating the payment of the Subscriptions towards the building of the College, and because the King had sometime before written a Gracious letter to the Governor commanding him to carry on the work of the College and to remove the obstructions of it; they thought it was the best way to put it in first to the Upper House, viz: the Council upon whom the Governor has a more immediate influence. But, my Lord, we found no effects of the King's Letter at that time, for these Gentlemen, in presence of the Governor, fell a quarrelling with the Bill and at first found fault with several matters of the form and wording of it; but when all these were mended, that they could object nothing of form, then they very unfairly threw out the Bill without so much as giving it a hazard in the House of Burgesses. The noise of this made people more obstinate in refusing their payments than ever. So that, my Lord, with much ado we have got the roof on but half of the Building, the other half we have not meddled with, and how we shall finish what we have built I cannot tell.

By. Please to go on, Sir, and I will answer all at once.

Bl. My Lord, I come next to the Land the King was pleased to give us. He gave us 20,000 acres of Land in two several Tracts, viz: 10,000 acres in each tract. These two tracts of land had been kept shut up from the first sealing of Virginia till that time which made the

Gift so much more valuable to us. For, there being such a great range for Stocks, abundance of People were desirous to seat there; and so the College might have had Tenants enough had they been so kept. But upon the Grant of this Land to the College, Sir Edmund Andros opened those tracts to all mankind so that we could have no Tenants, since every Man was free to take Land in fee in the same place. Not only so, but he signed Patents for mighty large quantities of Land to several of his creatures in the same places, tho' in the College Charter it was expressly provided that we should have the first choice, and illegal pretenders were so encouraged that they came *vi et armis* when we went to survey the lands and broke our chain and carried away the Surveyor's Instruments so that by main force we are kept out and can't come to the possession of the Land the King gave us to this day.

By. Have you any more to say, sir?

Bl. Yes, Sir, a great deal more.

By. Pray go on then (in the meantime Mr Byrd and Mr Povey took Notes.)

Bl. My Lord, I shall speak next of the Revenue of the penny per pound which is the chief thing we have to subsist upon. And as to this, My Lord, I shall only observe that since that Revenue was bestowed on the College, it is sunk in Virginia at least one-half of what I can prove by the Custom house books it always amounted to formerly. For, my Lord, since that time several collectors have not given us an account of one pound of Tobacco exported out of their precincts, particularly Secretary Wormley and Colonel Park, a thing that was never known before. Not that there is less Tobacco exported now than was formerly, For Maryland which formerly did not export so much as half the proportion of what Virginia exported of the penny per pound Tobacco does now by the good managery of the Governor give us an account of near as much again as Virginia doth. In short, my Lord, I cannot but think the Collectors of Virginia are encouraged to mismanage this Revenue, and that the design is to starve us out that we shall not be able to subsist.

By. Have you done now, Sir?

Bl. No, not yet, Sir.

By. Go on, then.

Bl. My Lord, we are put to strange difficulties in the Government of the College, for by the Constitution the full number of Governors is 40, and by the Charter there must be present a Major part of the whole before we can make a meeting or do business. Now, My Lord, the Governor has several friends and favorites among these men, but not so many as to carry a vote in any full meeting, and therefore they play another sort of game; that is, they generally chuse to absent themselves that so if any one or two of the rest be absent by Sickness or bad weather or necessary Business we can make no Meeting at all. It has often happened, my Lord, that we have been met nine or ten, and have wanted perhaps one or two of the Major part, and of these the Governor of Maryland, has come 150 miles to make one. In this case, by Lord, we have sent expresses to one or two of the nearest of these Gentlemen, and have represented to them how we just wanted one or two to make a number, and therefore begged their Company to a new day to which we adjourned the meeting, but all in vain. They would not budge, and we have been necessitated often to go away without doing any business. My Lord, if this had happened but once or twice it might be some necessary business that occasioned their absence, but when it is always the same sort of men it is very plain that this can be nothing but a Laid designe to obstruct and hinder the business and meetings of the College.

By. Sir, I hope you have done now.

Bl. Sir, I shall say but one thing more of the College. For the Clergy, you know, I have not said a word, and it is this: My Lord, the friends of the College are the men that are marked out to be frowned upon and discountenanced upon all ocasions. If there be any favors to be desired from the Government, they are to expect none of them. If they be lawyers, they shall be discouraged in their practice at the bar; if Ministers, every troublesome Man in the parish shall be encouraged to make them uneasy; if Burgesses are to be chosen for the General Assembly, all the Interest the Government can make shall be made to keep them out; if places of Trust or profit are to be bestowed, they shall have none of them; if they have any Law suit, they shall be generally in the wrong; and, in short, nothing shall recommend a Man to the favor of the Government more than if he be a Zealous Enemy of the College. The Governor of Maryland, who is our more active friend, has been used barbarously and how strangely I have been handled is an unaccountable thing. I have been twice suspended from the Council; all endeavors have been used to deprive me of my salary as president of the College, and to turn me out of a little parish I have there, to that degree that offers have been made to the vestry to find them a Minister gratis if they would make no further agreement with me. And even since I came last from Virginia, he has called two or three Vestries, and endeavored all that ever he could to turn me out. But the Major part of the Vestry have been my friends so that he could not yet compass it. In short, my Lord, I am afraid the friends of the College will be so tired out with ill usage that they will not be able to hold out much longer, and that all will go as fast backward in the matters of the College as ever it went forward in Governor Nicholson's time.

By. Sir, you have done now.

Bl. Sir, I have done what I designed to say at the College, but I have a great deal more to say of the bad circumstances of the Clergy.

By. That is another subject.

C. But it hangs all in a string. You see he's endeavoring to turn Mr Blair out of his parish. This seems to me a very strange way they have there that their Ministers are not inducted, but may be removed like domestic Servants by a Vote of the Vestry. Who would be a Minister in that Country?

By. My Lord, I confess this is very hard upon the Ministers, but this is none of the Governor's fault, for by the law of the Country it is the part of the vestry to present, and then the Governor is to Induct. Now, my Lord, the Vestry does not present and therefore the Governor cannot induct.

Bl. My Lord, it is true what Mr Byrd says that the Vestry in that Country are the Patrons, and they are to present, and the Governor, by the King's instructions, is ordinary as to Inductions. But your Grace knows that if a patron fails of presenting, so many months, then the right of presentation for that times devolves upon the Ordinary, so that it is really in the Governor's power to make presentation *jure devoluto*, which he never does, and that is the reason the Ministers are left in such precarious circumstances.

By. My Lord, there is a great difference between a patron in England and a Vestry in Virginia, and a Vestry cannot lapse their right of presentation as a patron may.

C. Pardon me, it is the very same thing, and we have several Societies of people here in England that have the right of presentation, and if they do not make use of it within six months, the Ordinary presents *jure devoluto*.

M. My Lord, it seems to be a very unreasonable thing that the Ministers should be on such precarious circumstances. But, my Lord, I wish your Grace would enquire whether it was not always so before Sir Edmund Andros's time.

C. Did they before this time remove Ministers by a vote of the Vestry?

Bl. My Lord, Before his time I never heard of a minister involuntarily removed without an accusation of him to the Governor as Guilty of some crime. Sometimes, indeed, the Minister being unwilling to stand a Trial consented to the leaving of them. But I never heard till Sir Edmund Andros's Time, that without an accusation a Minister was turned out against his will, purely by a vote of the Vestry.

By. And who has been turned out in that fashion in Sir Edmund Andros's time? Mr Doyley, you'll say.

Bl. Yes, Mr Doyley is one plain instance.

By. My Lord, Here is an extract out of the Minutes of Council by which it appears that Mr Doyley quit his parish voluntarily. For being interrogated such a Day if he desired to continue Minister of that Parish he answered, No.

L. Both might be true, both that the Vestry turned him out, and that he afterwards considering how unkindly they had used him, did not desire to return to them.

Bl. I am very sure he was turned out by the Vestry, and against his own will, for he presented a petition to the Governor and Council complaining of it.

H. Mr Eburn, too, was turned out of Middle plantation by the Governor's own creatures, and this I have reason to know, for it is the parish where I myself live.

By. By what creatures? By Col. Park?

H. Yes; and by Colonel Jennings.

C. It must be a very pernicious thing. A minister will not know how to preach against any Vice, but some of the Great Men of his parish may fancy the Sermon was made against him, and so make a faction to turn out the Minister, though perhaps the sermon was made seven years before.

M. My Lord, I am confident if your Grace will but write to Sir Edmund Andros about these inductions he will take care to have that matter mended.

By. Indeed, my Lord, I dare say Sir Edmund Andros knows nothing of this right he has *jure devoluto*, or else he would not suffer the clergy to be so precarious.

Bl. I am sure I not only put him in mind of it, but gave it him under my hand and desired him to consult his Lawyers about it.

By. But. Sir, perhaps he thought not your Lawyer enough that he could depend on your opinion.

Bl. He either could not or would not.

By. He shews, himself, upon all occasions, a good friend to the Clergy, and all his Speeches recommend their case to the general Assembly.

H. It is very strange then that in the year 1693, when the King, by an express letter, ordered him to recommend the condition of the Clergy in His Majesty's name to the next general Assembly, and when there was an assembly then called, the Governor said not one word of this to them in his speech, and not only so, but that when the House of Burgesses, who were favourable to the Clergy, did of their own accord take the law about the Clergy's Salaries into consideration, and mended it very considerably for the Clergy's interest, in a Bill which they sent up to the council, and which passed there likewise; yet Sir Edmund Andros dissolved that Assembly without giving his assent to that Bill, which by that means was lost.

By. My Lord, it is true that Assembly was favorable to the Clergy. They were then upon a great work, viz: the revisal of the laws and the amendment of this law about the Clergy was in that revisal. They sat not long enough to go through with it all, so that this law fell among the rest.

L. It seems then this Bill about the Clergy was a tacked Bill, and Sir Edmund could not pass it without passing the whole body of the Laws so revised.

Bl. No, my Lord, it was no tacked Bill, for tho' it came in upon occasion of the revisal of the laws, the whole revisal was not sent up together in one book, but single laws were sent up, 2 or 3 or any other number according as they happened to be dispatched in the House of Burgesses and the Upper house and the Governor could pass any one of these Laws without the rest as they pleased. Now this was the case with the Clergy Bill; it passed both Houses, and if the Governor had but given his assent to it, it had been a law to all intents and purposes. But upon his dissolving the Assembly, without giving his assent to the Law, it fell to the ground.

M. Did he assent to any other laws of that revisal.

Bl. Truly, I cannot tell, for he dissolved the assembly in an Anger.

By. This is a very harsh insinuation, as if Sir Edmund had been so angry with the assembly for bettering the law about the Clergy's Salaries that he dissolved them in anger for that very reason.

Bl. No, Sir, I insinuate no such thing as that he dissolved them for that reason.

L. No, Mr Blair has said nothing to that purpose. I believe, indeed, it was an omission in Sir Edmund, and he has endeavoured to get the same Law renewed again, but could never do it.

By. This Last assembly, there passed a Law which bettered the Clergy's Salaries.

Bl. But that law makes them 13 per cent. worse than this other Law which he refused.

C. It was an unhappy thing, but since the whole revisal fell we must put the best construction upon it.

M. My Lord, Mr Blair has reason to be concerned for the College and Clergy, and indeed these things leave a heavy load upon Sir Edmund, but I hope if your Grace will hear Mr Byrd; he has something to say that will clear him.

C. Well, Mr Byrd, now if you please Let us hear what you have to say to these things.

By. My Lord, Mr Blair has said several things, by which he would make it appear that Sir Edmund has mightily obstructed the business of the College. Now, My Lord, to show the contrary, first of all we produce here an extract out of the Council Books at a Council after the last Fleet came in, and Mr Blair was restored to the Council, which I shall here read. (The Minute of Council he read, was something to this purpose; that the Governor acquainting the Council, that he had been represented in England as one that had trampled upon the Clergy, and ruined the College, &c., and Mr Commissary Blair being particularly interrogated about this, said he knew nothing of it, and that the expressions were very strange. Then immediately the Governor read the Bp of London's Letter to him, and shewed that it contained these expressions.)

Bl. Is this a Minute taken out of the Council Books?

By. Yes, Sir.

Bl. I am sure it was never read in Council while I was there. But I suppose it were true, what is this to the purpose my saying that I knew nothing of these expressions, and thought them very strange; for I took the question to be an accusation of me, as if I had wrote home these expressions for England to which that answer was pertinent enough. But, my Lord, the time is remarkable when it is said that I said the expressions were strange, viz: that it was before I knew that they were anybody's expressions; for it is said that afterwards he read My Lord of London's Letter, wherein these expressions were contained; tho' my Lord of London's Letter was not read, but only the Governor pretended to repeat or recapitulate two or three Lines out of it.

L. Mr Blair might very well say the expressions were strange; for indeed, my Lord, I wrote very frankly and warmly to Sir Edmund Andros, and, instead of giving me any satisfaction it seems he carried my Letter to the Council, and made a noise of it there.

C. I should have been apt to say myself that the expressions were strange, for it seems the question was not about the befriending or not befriending the College, but concerning the softness or harshness of the expressions.

By. But, my Lord, here is another thing of yet greater weight. The Governor at a Meeting of the College, proposed the question whether he had been an obstructer of the College, and the answer is (here he read something to this purpose—that he had been so far from being an obstructor that he had been ready and forward upon all occasions to promote the business of the College).

Bl. Sure, Sir, that is no extract out of the College Records.

By. No, my Lord, this is a Certificate from two of the Governors of the College, my father and Captain Randolph.

Bl. My Lord, if this had signified anything, it should have been taken out of the College Minutes. But I must desire your Grace to observe in the first place how unfair a question this is, which cannot be answered without accusing a Governor to his face; and then that instead of taking the answer out of the proper Record, they only bring a Certificate from two men that have a dependence in the Governor.

By. A dependence, Sir?

Bl. Yes, Sir, I say a dependence.

By. My Lord, the Governor has no other way to Justify himself but by the Testimonies of persons that are concerned.

H. My Lord, I can give your Grace an account of this question that was put to the Governors of the College, for I was then Clerk to the College. A meeting of the Governors of the College was called, to choose a Rector which they are to do yearly by their Charter. They met in the Governor's Great Hall. Before they proceeded to the Election, the Governor said he was never wanting to the College in any thing, and if any of them knew any thing to the contrary, desired them to say. No body saying any thing, they proceeded to the Election of the Rector, and I wrote nothing at all down of this, taking it to be only some by discourse. After the Rector was chosen, I began the Minutes of the day with an account of that Election, and so went on to other business that was done. The Governor and Secretary Wormley in the mean time came and looked upon the minutes at a Sideboard where I was writing, and finding nothing minuted of the Governor, they asked me what I meant that I did not set down the Vote about the Governor. I told them I heard no vote about the Governor, for all questions used to be put by the Rector, and the Votes gathered by him. But, if His Excellency would have any thing entered about that business, but I would ask the Rector and Governors, and know what question was put, and how it was answered. Upon this, the Governor spoke again to the Rector and Governors of the College, and told them that he expected some what should be entered concerning what he had spoke, and get the Rector to put the question whether they knew that the Governor had obstructed the Business of the College. They were strangely confounded and surprized with this Question. Some answered they knew nothing of it; others, they had said nothing of it; others, they had writt nothing of it. I began to take their sense in minute as right as I could, but the Governor and Secretary Wormley and Col. Byrd would give me no rest, alleging that I did not take the Minute full enough for the Governor's honour and Vindication. At last I asked them how they would have it, and writt their sense in a script of Paper, but perceiving that it was a Vote that was Like to cause great division, I entered it not into the Book, till I had consulted those that were present, and so entered it according to the sentiment of the majority, but not so complimenting as the Governor would have had it. But he had no way to help himself, for the Governors of the College were so angry that they suffered themselves to be surprised with such unfair Votes which could not be safely answered but one way, that they seemed to be resolved if the Governor brought it in again to throw it quite out. So it stood upon the Minutes as it was, but far short of this Certificate these two Gentlemen give it.

Bl. My Lord, I would fain know the worst Governor that ever was should ever put such a question to any Meeting of the subjects of his Government as this: "Am I an ill man?" Whether they would think it fit to accuse him to his face or rather to decline the answer.

By. But what other way has a Governor then to vindicate himself?

Bl. Yes, it is a much better way if his Actions will vindicate him:

e.g. Speak to the particulars, and shew us what his conduct has been as to the subscriptions, Lands, revenues, and other things relating to the College and by these it will be seen whether he has been a friend to it or not.

By. Well, Sir, I will come now to answer the particulars.

M. Pray give me leave first to ask one thing upon occasion of What Mr Blair said that the Minute of Council was never read in Council; That seems to be a very strange way. Pray, Sir, is it the custom to read the Minutes of Council in Council?

Bl. No, Sir. Amongst other things, this abuse is so great that we never know what is entered in the Council Books, whether it be the sense of the Council or not.

By. But any Gentleman of the Council may command a sight of the Books when he pleases.

Bl. I know not what others may do, but I could never have that liberty. I have waited on the clerk time after time for a sight only of some order relating to myself, and could not come to the sight of it till it was past time to remedy it.

C. It is a very strange thing. Here where we have better engrossing Clerks than any they have there, we do often see that the Minutes of the Council are rectifyed by advice of the Members that were present. Well, Mr Byrd, if you please to go on with your Answers.

By. The first objection, my Lord, was about the Subscriptions. I find nothing in this but that the Councill and the Great Men do not pay. What is this to the Governor? Then that the Council threw out the Bill for facilitating the payment of the College subscriptions. What is this to the Governor? There might be a thousand reasons for throwing out that Bill.

Bl. My Lord, as little as all this is to the Governor, our Councill of Virginia has such an immediate dependence on him that whatever way the Governor goes they generally follow. What else should be the reason that those very Men who were the forwardest to subscribe in Governor Nicholson's time should be the backwardest to pay in Sir Edmund Andros's time?

C. Has the Governor paid his own subscription?

Bl. My Lord, he never subscribed any thing.

By. The subscriptions, my Lord, were before his time.

C. Nor has he given no thing towards it?

Bl. My Lord, when I left the Country he had given nothing. What he has done since, I know not.

C. I confess it is a very ill sign, that a Governor encourages the thing with others if he gives nothing to it himself. But I think I have been told that he gave Bricks towards building the Chapel.

By. My Lord, Sr Edmund did really give an Order to my Father, if the Governors of the College would carry up the Chapel, to pay for the Bricks. But the Governors of the College slighted it, and told him they had no money to carry up the Chapel. But I am very certain that the Governor gave such an Order to my Father, and here is the Copy of it.

P. It was writ home to us, and we took it for granted that he had given the Bricks.

Bl. No, Sir, he never gave a Brick.

C. But Mr Byrd says he will engage for him that he shall give the Bricks still.

By. My Lord, I will, for here is the Order still.

Bl. I find it has been very confidently reported that the reason why he had not given these bricks was that the College slighted the Gift. Now, my Lord, I know all the parts of that story so well that if Your Grace would please to hear it, it would appear as plain as day-light that the College were so far from slighting that they accepted of that Gift in the thankfullest manner—but yet could not have the Bricks.

C. This is as material to the business as any thing. Let us have it, Sir.

Bl. My Lord, there was a West country fleet a going out of Virginia for England, which occasioned that this Gentleman's father, Collonel Byrd, was down at a place called Kirkotan, where this fleet was made up. While he was there he received this Order concerning bricks that Mr Byrd speaks of, upon which Col Byrd and some others of the Governor's friends wrote home for England that the Governor had given the bricks; but all this while the College knew nothing of the bricks. As Colonel Byrd returned to his own house, my house being in his way, he did me the favor to make me a Visit. I was then sick. Among other News concerning that fleet he told me, as a piece of News that he thought would be very acceptable to me, that the Governor was becoming a friend to the College, and with that he pulled out a Letter out of his pocket, the Original I suppose of this Letter Mr Byrd speaks of, wherein he ordered him, if the College should carry up the Chapel together with the rest of the Building, to pay for making the bricks of the said Chapel. I told him I was very glad of it for the example of it would go a great way towards the bringing in our Subscriptions. I asked him likewise if I might say any thing of it. He told me that I might tell it to any of the Trustees of the College that I should happen to see, but that the Governor would take his own way to propose it to them at their meeting, so I talked of it to any of these Gentlemen I happened to see as a piece of good news, and I told them we should hear more of it at the next meeting of the Committee.

C. What Committee?

Bl. My Lord, this Committee was made up of the Rector and five or six of the Governors of the College that lived nearest the place, who met usually once a Month at the College to inspect the carrying on of the Building. But, my Lord, that Committee came, I was not at it indeed, for I was so sick of a fever and ague that I could not stir abroad. But I had taken care to prepare them all for the kind acceptance of the Governor's Gift which I expected would have been proffered to them at that meeting. But I was strangely surprised to understand that there was no such proposition made to them and so no mention of it. Upon this I spake to Mr Hadley, the Surveyor of our Building, who was pretty well in favor with the Governor and desired him to wait upon His Excellency and let him know that Colonel Byrd had acquainted me with His Excellency's design of giving Bricks for the Chapel, and that I was in hopes that Governors of the College should have heard something of it at their last Meeting, for it was only they that could determine whether they could carry up the Chapel together with the rest of the Building; but since nothing was said of it to them I desired that Mr Hadley would try whether His Excellency would give him leave to propose it to them at their next meeting. The Answer Mr Hadley brought me was, that the Governor still talked of giving the Bricks, but that he found he was not willing that I should meddle with it at all. So, my Lord, the time went on and we heard no more of this gift till at last there being to be another Committee about the latter end of July last year, I urged Mr Hadley to wait upon the Governor again and to represent to him that the Season of the year was so far advanced that if the Bricks were not made very speedily they could not be made that year and therefore begged of him that if he would not give me leave to make the proposition to the Committee, that he would employ him to whom he had talked so much of this gift to do it that we might order the Bricks to be made with all expedition. Upon this Mr Hadley waited again upon the Governor and what passed between them I do not know, but Mr Hadley told me with an abundance of joy that he had now got leave from the Governor to make the proposition about the Bricks to the next Committee. And accordingly at the next Committee where I was present, he acquainted the Governors of the College that he had Orders from His Excellency to propose to them that if they would carry up the Chapel together with the rest of the Building, he would pay for the Bricks that should go to the Building of the Chapel at the rate they had given to Colonel Park for their other Bricks, viz: 14sh a thousand. Upon this proposition the Governors of the College presently ordered more Brickmakers to be set to work and appointed two of their number, viz: one Mr Edwards and myself, to wait upon the Governor next day to return him their hearty thanks for this generous proffer and to acquaint him that they had resolved immediately to comply with it and for that end had set up another Stool of Bricks and would lay the foundation of the Chapel with all expedition. If any of these Gentlemen doubt the truth of this, here I have the very original Order under the Clerk of the College's hand to produce. For we took it out to have it in readiness for Sir Edmund who often, when he would baulk verbal Messages, would ask if we have 'em in writing. Accordingly, my Lord, next day Mr Edwards and I went and waited on the Governor at his House and Mr Fouace who was just come from England and was resolved to see the Governor, desired that he might go along with us. It fell to my turn being the eldest in Commission to make the Governor the compliment. I did it as well as I could, telling him that Mr Hadley having yesterday in his Excellency's name made a generous proposition to the College, viz: that if they would go upon the Chapel His Excellency would pay for the Bricks; The Governors of the College had ordered Mr Edwards and myself to wait upon him to return their most hearty thanks for his generous proffer and to acquaint him that in compliance with it, they had ordered a new Stool of Bricks to be set up and that they would lay the foundation of the Chapel with all expedition and carry it up as high above ground before Winter as the season and weather would permit. My Lord, he heard me with a strange gravity in his countenance and when I had done the first word he said (I shall never forget it) was this, directly or indirectly (says he), I gave no such order to Mr Hadley. Sir, said I, it is very strange that Mr Hadley should do such a thing without orders. I confess I had not the least doubt of his orders for I knew your Excellency was upon such a thing before I heard first of it from Colonel Byrd. Yes, says he, I gave Orders to Colonel Byrd about it and I desired him to speak to you of it and I believe he did speak to you; but you thought it not worth your while to mind it then. Now you may take your own course. I first made an apology for myself confessing indeed that Colonel Byrd told me of the thing as a piece of News, but not as from His Excellency, far less that he desired me to act any thing in it, on the contrary that he told me his Excellency would take his own way to propose it to the Governors of the College. I told him likewise how that after I saw the thing was delayed I had sent Mr Hadley to his Excellency and that I had particularly by him offered my service to propose it and that the answer he brought me was that he found his Excellency did not care that I should meddle in it. But at last, my Lord, I endeavored yet to bring him to the thing telling him that tho' there had been some mistake either in Colonel Byrd or Mr Hadley or myself yet I hoped his Excellency would not on that account retract his designed bounty to the College, that it was a thing that would do a great deal of good and would by the example of it be a great means to bring in our subscriptions that were due. But after all I could not prevail; he grew hot upon it as if we had really slighted him and told us we should not have a Brick. This is the true account of that matter. The Governors of the College were far from refusing his gift. On the contrary they accepted it with all thankfulness but he himself retracted it as I have told.

By. It was your own fault that you had them not for here is the Order.

C. But if that Order never came regularly before them what could they do.

By. As to the Lands my Lord, the Law is open, the Governor cannot hinder people of their rights.

P. My Lord, the Land on the South side of Black water was all along designed to be opened and there was an Order for opening it in my Lord Effingham's time.

Bl. But it is very certain that it was kept shut over till the College's Charter was brought into Virginia.

P. Were there no Inhabitants on the place?

Bl. None that had legal Patents. The Surveyors were all prohibited to Survey there and till that prohibition was taken off we could not get a Surveyor even to survey the College Land.

C. Well I think we heard the most material things.

P. My Lord, there is one thing, Mr Commissary said, in which I suppose he is in error, that is he said Sr Edmund Andros has twice suspended him from the Council. Now, my Lord, this last time he is not suspended but only declared to be within the meaning of the Act of Parliament as to the sitting in the General Court. My Lord, the way I heard this thing represented, it was all Mr Commissary's own doing for the Act being read in order to the swearing the Naval Officers, Mr Blair himself stated the difficulty upon his hearing the Act read and desired the Governor and Council to give their Opinion whether he should sit in the General Court or not. The Governor and Council, as I was told, shifted the question and said to Mr Blair, Sir,—In a few days you are to embark for England what need we trouble ourselves with this question now? But Mr Blair pretended some scruple of conscience, that he could not be satisfied till he had their opinion. The Governor was so averse to it that he adjourned the Council till the afternoon designing the thing should drop and that they should go upon other business. But Mr Blair would come again in the afternoon and would let them enter upon nothing till they had decided that and so soon as they had decided that as to the General Court he was within the meaning of the Act, that Mr Blair got up and went away from the Council tho' they told him he was not suspended. Nay, further, my Lord, I am told that they afterwards sent for him to Council but that he positively refused to act in any Council business. Sir, you know best (to Mr Blair) whether it was thus or not.

Bl. Sir It was quite otherwise. I never heard a story more altered.

C. How was it?

Bl. My Lord, your Grace may remember, how after I was suspended the first time, I was restored to the Council by His Majesty's Warrant. There was a Clause in that warrant, My Lord, which I did not at all deserve, that I should not only be restored to the Council but continue so till it appeared to His Majesty that I had justly forfeited the good opinion he was pleased to say he had of me. This Clause, My Lord, every one construed to be a prohibition of all such suspensions of me for the future. At the same time with this Warrant there was sent into the country a new Act of Parliament of a posterior date to the Warrant. I think the Title of it is "An Act for preventing frauds in the Plantation Trade." If there was any thing in that Act of Parliament disabling me to be of the Council, I ought never to have been received in again upon the Warrant. But, my Lord, they received me in and I stayed there near a year afterwards, till about

the time that the Accounts of the Revenue were going to be laid
before the Council, for I must observe, my Lord, that both times I
was suspended just as these accounts were going to be laid before
the Council and all the time I was of the Council I could never come
by sight of these Accounts and there is a reason for that, my Lord. So
now the accounts being ready to be brought in, it was resolved, it
seems, that I should be removed before they came in. In the Morning
one of the Gentlemen of the Council told me they designed that Day
to remove me from the Council. When the Council was met, the first
thing that I saw was that the Clerk stood with the Act of Parliament
in his hand ready to read and the Governor ordering him to read it
after he had done. It was pretty long. I confess, my Lord, I started the
first difficulty myself in these words: "Sir," said I, to the Governor,
"upon the reading of this Act there occurs a doubt to me whether it
be proper for me to sit in the General Court or not for the words of
the Act are these: provided always that all places of Trust in the
Courts of Law and what relates to the Treasury of the said Islands
shall from the date of this Act be in the Hands of the Native born
subjects of England, Ireland or of the said Islands. Your Excellency
knows when I was first admitted to be of the Council I desired to be
excused from sitting in the General Court. Now I shall be very glad
if these words of the Act of Parliament disable me from it." Upon this
the Governor desired them to consider how far the Act of Parliament
affected me. In Answer to this, as the matter had been said before,
some said I could not be of the Council, because the Accounts of the
Government were laid before the Council and by the Act of Parliament I was disabled from any place of Trust relating to the Treasury.
But seeing the tendency of this I argued against it that the being of
the Council was no place of Trust as to the Treasury for all monies
were Issued out by the Governor's Warrant even out of Council and
tho' he advised with his Council sometimes about Money to be laid
out, yet he might chuse whether he would or not. Upon this it was
confest by the Governor himself that the King had gone sometimes
into the Treasury and signed Warrants without ever bringing the
business before Council. From this they went to another topic, which
gave better satisfaction, viz: that the Governor and Council by the
Constitution of the Country being the sole Judges of the General
Court, if I was consequently disabled likewise from being of the
Council I desired them to consider the King's Warrant for restoring
me and particularly that clause which orders me to continue in the

Council. The Warrant was read and the Governor considering the bold stroke they were going to make attempted first to shift it off on me, by persuading me to remove myself from the Council. "Mr Commissary," says he, "is a going for England in a few days and he might ease us of all this trouble if he pleased." My Lord, though I understood the meaning of this yet I gave no answer to it till one Colonel Jennings, a great Creature of the Governor's, explained it thus. "Yes" says Colonel Jennings "Mr Commissary might ease us of all this trouble if he would absent himself from the Council for these few days what remain." Upon this, my Lord, I made this answer to the Governor which I beseech your Grace to take notice of because it will clear the question whether I removed myself from the Council as it is said or not. "Sir," said I to the Governor, "I must beg your excellency's pardon. The King has now twice commanded me to be here and therefore I shall not take it upon myself to remove myself from this Board though at the same time I shall readily submit to any Sentence your Excellency and the Council shall pronounce about it." Upon this, my Lord, the Governor told the Council that I had given them a very plain answer which was that I would not remove myself and therefore, said he, you must go upon it and give your Opinions. Upon this, My Lord, they discoursed the matter somewhere for making distinctions of the two several capacities of a Judge and Councillour; as to the first they were of Opinion that I was included within the Act. But as to the second they thought I was not included and especially the King's Warrant being so express they thought it was better to let me sit for the three or four days remaining. But others, especially such as were upon the intrigue of business who knew it was resolved I should not see the Accounts and saw no way to avoid my seeing of them if I stayed upon the Council, were very positive that I was included within the Act of Parliament as to the Council too, because they alleged by the constitution of Virginia it was necessary that whosoever was of the Council should sit in the General Court. The Governor perceiving the Division, whether it was that he doubted the Vote would not go clearly of his side or whether he was really afraid to go in the contradiction of the King's Warrant, being disappointed of his aim of making me absent myself, adjourned the Council till the afternoon, and in the mean time which was altogether unusuall sent and adjourned the General Court too where there were several Causes depending and the People were all met about their business for, to make the thing more odious of my side, he was resolved the General

Court should sit no more till this business about my being disabled were decided, that so the odium of the delay of Justice might lie upon me who would not remove myself. In the afternoon, My Lord, it is said I would come again to Council and would not let them go upon other business till they had decided this. I do assure Your Grace I stayed in my chamber in the afternoon till the Messenger of the Council came to call me; he told me the Governor and Council were met and wanted my Company. And if I had not gone then a worse construction would have been put upon it. So soon as I came to the Council it is said I hindered them to go upon other business. My Lord, there is no occasion for that.. The Governor without offering at any thing else told them He hoped they had had their thoughts upon the Question that was proposed to them concerning Mr Commissary, whether as to his being of the Council, he were within the Act of Parliament or not. After the King's Warrant was again read and they had observed that it was of a prior date to the Act of Parliament, they concluded that the Act was to take place before the Warrant and that I was incapacitated by the Act from sitting either in Council or General Court. Only one Gentleman insisted still upon the distinction of the two several Capacities. My Lord, I was so far from removing myself as it is said that I did not offer to remove even after this Vote, but had the impudence to sit still. The Governor casting a strange look at me asked me if I did not hear the vote of the Council. "Yes Sir" said I, "I heard it but your Excellency knows that we cannot suspend one another. I wait for your Excellency's Sentence." "No," said he, "I'll pronounce no Sentence." "Then, Sir," said I, "I cannot remove." Upon this, My Lord, he was strangely surprized for this put him quite out of his Measures for as he had laid the thing first I was to remove myself and if that would not do the Council was to remove me, and in either of these ways the Governor would have pretended to have been an unconcerned person but when he saw that neither of these ways would do and that I brought it home to himself, then he begun to be very uneasy and asked the Council what he should do in this case. Colonel Jennings answered him, "Sir, Your Excellency may signify to Mr Commissary, that you have put the Question to the Council whether he is incapacitated by the Act of Parliament to act as one of the Council and that it is our unanimous Opinion that he is." Upon this the Governor stood up and, in the manner he uses to pronounce sentences, said, "Mr Commissary I have put the Question to this Board how far you are included within the Act of Parliament, and it is our unanimous Opinion that you are incapacitated from acting any further as one of the King's Council." "Sir," said I, "I take this for a sentence," and with that made a bow, and came away.

P. But Sir was you never sent for to the Council after this?

Bl. Sir, I thank you for putting me in mind for I should have forgot that. Truly I cannot tell whether I was sent for to the Council again or not. The matter was thus. It was about Tuesday if I remember right that I was removed from the Council. They went on in their business—received their accounts and wrote their letters for England and by Saturday they had done. On the Saturday the Governor sent Mr Sherlock to me to my house in the country. He brought nothing in Writing; The Message he delivered by word of mouth was this, that His Excellency bid him tell me, They had finished their business and drawn their Letters for England and they desired that I should seem them before they went. My Lord, it was now Saturday afternoon and a very rainy day; I was to preach next day and I confess I was very unwilling to stir abroad but not knowing what use might be made of it if I did not go I ordered my Horse to be got ready and went away to James Town in all the rain with Mr Sherlock. When I came thither I found the Governor and Council together not in the Council Chamber but in the Secretary's Chamber which was at t'other end of the Town nor not set at a Table about any business; so that whether they will call it a Council or not I cannot tell. When I came in I told the Governor I was come in obedience to his Message to see what service his Excellency had for me. He answered me that having prepared their Letters for England they were willing that I should see them if I pleased. To this I replied that if it was any Council business, his Excellency knew I was declared incapable of acting in those affairs. But if they had any thing to say to me, in any other Capacity any thing relating to the Clergy or College for which I was concerned I was ready to hear it. "Yes", says he, "there is in these Letters something relating both to the Clergy and College please to hear 'em read." "If you please Sir," said I, and upon that he called for Chairs and they all sat down not at a table but to and again about the room as we are now sitting. I did not offer to sit down but the Governors had a Chair brought and would oblige me to sit too. Then he ordered the Clerk to read the Letters. If I remember right there were two Letters, one for the Secretary, My Lord Duke of Shrewsbury, another for the Council of Trade. The only thing I spake to in the Letters was one thing relating to the Clergy; for speaking of an Address presented to the Governor by the Clergy they called it an address from part of the Clergy of Virginia. "Sir" I said to the Clerk "I believe that is a mistake. It should be an address from the Clergy of Virginia." It was answered me by some of the Council that the Clergy were not all there. I replied to this that they were all duly summoned and many more than the major part were present & all that were present signed the Address. I asked them if it was their way when any of the Council was absent to call their Orders, Orders of Council or Orders of part of the Council. I told them too, it looked ill to say an Order of part of the Clergy, as if we were all in factions and parties; so my Lord after some dispute I gained the point, and had that word of the letter mended. There was a great deal of Council business in the Letters but I spoke to none of it. Now, my Lord, whether this meeting will be called a Council, or not, or whether it will be said that I acted in it or not I cannot tell. I am apt to think if my suspension is not approved of in England it will be said that I was not suspended & that I was at a Council afterwards and that I spoke and acted in it. But if my suspension is approved of, that then this meeting is no Council and that my acting in it was only as Commissary but not as one of the Council.

P. Nay, certainly, Sir, you are not suspended. Here is a Copy of the Sentence and if it be compared with your first suspension you will find the difference and therefore I should by all means advise that nothing may be said of this suspension but that Mr Commissary take his place at the Council board as if there had been no such thing for the meaning of the Sentence is only that as to the General Court he is within the meaning of the Act of Parliament.

L. Let us hear the sentence. Mr Byrd read it to this purpose that the act for preventing of frauds &c being read in order to the swearing of the Naval Officers, Mr Commissary Blair, of his own accord, acknowledging himself to be a native of Scotland, proposing the doubt whether he was not disabled from sitting as a Judge in the general Court. The Governor and Council were of Opinion that in regard of the Constitution of Virginia the General Court was to be held by the Governor and Council, therefore Mr Commissary is within the meaning of the Act. Then the Bishop of London argued that these very words did bear that sense that Mr Blair was suspended from the Council. The Archbishop said he thought they implied more than a suspension viz: an incapacitating. Mr Povey then blamed Sir Edmund for his short and obscure way of wording things. Then my Lord Archbp said to this purpose to my Lord Bishop of London. "Well, my Lord, I think we have heard all the most material things of both sides; when your Lordship is at leisure we'l appoint another day and get Mr Blaithwait and Mr Blair and consider what we shall do upon all this."

L.. When Your Lordship pleases.

P. My Lord, give me leave to speak to one thing that Mr Commissary mentioned because it seems to reflect on the Office, that is, Mr Blair seems to insinuate that he could never come by a sight of the accounts all the while he was of the Council. Now, my Lord, I think it is for the King's service that every Man should see the accounts and should have leave to make what observations he can against the passing of them. Here are the accounts (holding a paper in his hand) Mr Blair may see them when he pleases.

Bl. "Sir. I humbly thank you; it is a favor I could never have in Virginia," (and with that he step^t to Mr Povey as it were to receive the Accounts from him and taking them in his hand said) "Will you give me leave to peruse them and I will carefully return 'em to you?"

P. "Sir, you may look upon 'em but I cannot part with this; this is the Record but if you will call at the Office you may see them when you will." Upon that Mr Blair restoring them again had returned to his chair. Then Mr Byrd said something to this purpose:

By. "My Lord this is a very uncharitable Insinuation of Mr Blair about his being twice turned out of the Council, just as the Accounts were going to be brought before the Council; for the first time, it was a month after before the Audit and the second time a week, and the accounts are so fairly stated that I believe this will be found to be a very groundless imputation."

P. "My Lord, the accounts of Virginia are the easiest part of my accounts whatsoever. The Revenue is but small and the Salaries are all established."

Bl. My Lord, I am loth to enter into this Subject for it is now late and we have taken up too much of your grace's time already.. But if I were to speak to the accounts I should say something as considerable as all I have yet said to make it appear what Arts have been used to hinder the King's Bounty to the Clergy of Virginia by the mismanagement of the Revenue, for, My Lord, about five years ago My Lord of London knows there was a gift past by the late Queen in Council of the Quit rents of Virginia to the Clergy for three year. But upon a great Clamour that was raised that if the Quit rents were disposed of, that Government would not be able to subsist, the King was prevailed upon to recall that grant and so the Clergy lost it. But my Lord at that same time His Majesty recalled it he was pleased to say that he would make a Tryal for three Years and if he found that the Government could subsist without the Quit rents the Clergy should have 'em still. To prevent this, My Lord, from that time there has been such an unusual lessoning and consumption of the revenue that Quit rents and all had enough to do to defray the charge. I would fain to know why Sir Edmund Andros presently after the news of this, past an Act for enlarging Tobacco Hogsheads by which every Hogshead holds at least a fifth part more than it did and consequently the King's Revenue of Two shillings per hogshead is a fifth part less than it was, that is, six or seven hundred pounds a Year. I would fain know why so much unnecessary charge to New York. Why so much for demolishing old Forts and Building a Powder house and mounting of Guns and maintaining a cruising Sloop upon another footing than was Ordered by the Lords of the Treasury. In short my Lord I would fain know what is become of all the money Governor Nicholson Left in bank and how it comes to pass that the Revenue is now over and above between four and five thousand pound in debt. My Lord, this is a strange thing in a time of peace for it has been profound peace with us. My Lord, the only true reason for all this was to convince the King that that Government could not subsist without the Quit Rents: tho' we know it subsisted very well before upon the Revenue of the two Shillings a Hogshead. But, My Lord, I will forbear till I have seen the accounts only I am very well satisfied that I can discover a great Mystery of iniquity in them.

C. Well, I think all the matters have been sufficiently discoursed. My Lord (to the Bishop of London) we must take a time to consider what is fit to be done upon all this. Then the Bishop of London and all the rest of us got up and after some invitation of the Bishop of London to stay all night which we did not accept of, we parted.—William Stevens Perry (ed.), *Historical Collections Relating to the American Colonial Church*, I, 36-65.

11. THE PRESIDENT AND FACULTY THANK THE HOUSE OF BURGESSES FOR ATTENDANCE UPON "OUR SCHOLASTICK EXERCISES," 1698

To the honourable The Speaker and Gentlemen of the House of Burgesses.

We, the President, Masters, and Scholars of the Royal Colledge of William and Mary in Virginia, being deeply sensible of the great honour lately conferred on this College by the hon'ble House of Burgesses, first in gracing our Scholastick exercises, with your own Countenance and presence on May day last, and then in giveing so favourable a Judgment and Character of the proficiency of our youth in their studies and in recommending the said Colledge to our own good Governour's care and favour in your most hearty address made to his Excellency for that purpose; Desire leave in all humility to offer our most thankfull acknowledgements for the same and withall to assure this honble House that nothing can so effectually encourage us to go on in the cheerful prosecution of our studies as the favourable contenance of so great Patrons as we hope to find both in his Excellency and the present Generall Assembly for which good understanding among yourselves and joint endeavours to carry on this and all other good works we doubt not ye will have the blessings and prayers of all good men to join with those of

> Your most obliged humble servants.
> James Blair, Presidt
> Mungo Inglis, humanity prof.
> John Hodges, Usher.

In name & at the desire of the rest of our Codiciples:
> Orlando Jones,
> Henry Harrison,   Scholars.
> John Allen,
> John Jones,

The Answer sent by Major Custis and Capt. Wilson.

The house have sent us to acquaint you that they have read your address, it is received mighty kindly and they hope you will always merit their esteem.—*William and Mary Quarterly Historical Papers*, II (1893), 36.

12. President James Blair accuses Governor Nicholson of instigating the "barring out" in 1702

There are instances of his [Governor Nicholson's] tampering with my servants & when he had got one of them, to tell a false malicious story he made him put it in writing & sent it home, for Engld, to blacken me without doing me the common Justice to call me to hear what I had to say, for myself, tho' he would send for me upon many much more frivolous occasions, there are instances too of his encouraging my debtors, not to clear accts with me, nor pay one, that I might be put to the Charge & trouble of a Law suit. One of them to whom I had so far condescended, as to refer the business in dispute to an Arbitrator of his own nomination, told me, the Govr even after the Signing of Arbitration bonds & after the day was appointed, to meet with the arbitrators persuaded him not to meet, or submit to any arbitration, but to go to law, advising him if he were cast in the County court, to appeal to the general court, "where", said he, "I am the Chief Judge & will do you right," & accordingly the man was over persuaded & went to Law & the Govr employed a Lawyer for him, as the Lawyer himself told me when I came to retain him. I will not say he has had any design upon my life, though I will give your Lordships an Acct of two Strange passages that have an ill aspect that way. One was this, about a fortnight before Christmas 1702 while I lodged in the College, I heard the School boys about 12 o'clock at night, a driving of great nails, to fasten & barracade the doors of the Grammar School. I was mightily surprized at it for we had banished this custom & it was quite left off for some years. I made haste to get up & with the assistance of 2 servant men, I had in the College, I had almost forced open one of the doors before they sufficiently secured it, but while I was breaking in, they presently fired off 3 or 4 Pistols & hurt one of my servants in the eye with the wadd as I suppose of one of the Pistols, while I press'd forward, some of the Boys, having a great kindness for me, call'd out "for God's sake sir don't offer to come in, for we have shot, & shall certainly fire at any one that first enters." Upon the hearing of this, I began to think there was something more than ordinary in the matter & desired a parley with them, thinking to find out upon what acct it was that they had provided fire arms, Powder & Shot, which they had never used to do formerly, but that night they would not discover it, tho' I confess, I had some suspicion, of the designs of my malicious neighbour; & resolved to let them alone till morning, & then getting all the other masters together & calling for workmen to break open the doors; Before we began, we offered them a pardon, if they would open, of their own accord & tell us the truth, who it was that set them on, tho' by that time we had more than a suspicion of it, for I had seen one of his excellency's servants that morning a handing of them in, some more Powder, upon this, the Boys, sent out a Window by a ladder One of the Chief confederates that knew the whole plot with orders to discover it. The Short of his story was, to the best of my remembrance, that while they had no thoughts of any such thing, the Govr Sent for him, & put him upon it, gave them money to buy victuals & drink & Candles, & Powder, & Shot, & lent them 6 of his own Pistols. Upon hearing that the Governor, was the Author & the contriver of this business, we sent the boys to him, leaving it to his excellency to determine the time when he would have them dismiss'd, for it was then about a week before the usual time. His excellency being out of humor, to the great disappointment of the Boys, ordered that they should continue at their books till the usual time & then be dismiss'd, this decision made them very angry & they said they wondered what he had made all that to do for, when they were not to be dismiss'd one day sooner than ordinary for their pains. When we entered the school we found the Gov^{rs} 3 pair of Pistols, with some swords & other weapons they had provided. It was God's great mercy to me that the boys gave me warning of the Shot & so saved me from the danger, which I have too much reason to suspect, was contrived on purpose upon my acc^t; his excellency being then in too bad a Humor, to do such a thing out of a frolic; besides that the Fire Arms, Powder, & Shot, my lying in the College; & the differences between him & me, which at that time were come to some heighth, made the badness of the design too, too probable. The other Passage was about 6 weeks afterwards. As I was asleep in bed with my wife in my Chamber, in the College, between one & two in the morning, a maid who lay in a Closet just by, heard somebody a opening the door of the outer room & after he had turned the lock of it, come quite thro' to our chamber door, after he had endeavoured to turn that lock likewise, but could not (for it was double locked & the key within) then with all the force he had, he shook that door so violently as if he had designed to break it open, & this making a very great noise (for it was a thin pair of folding doors), awaked my wife & me, & we both call'd out "who's there!" & I call'd to the maid to light a candle; for it was in Winter towards the end of Jany. At last when he observed the door gave no way & that we were all awake (without speaking a word), we heard him march off thro' the outer room again. Upon enquiry I found that the Govr that night had appeared to be in so bad a humor that every body was afraid to speak to him. And a person of good credit told me, he was seen between one & two of the Clock in the morning, to go directly from his own house toward the college without a light, with some other more particular circumstances, which I am afraid to give an acc^t of, lest innocent persons, as yet in his Power, should come to be suspected of this intelligence, but I do solemnly take my oath of it, that I believe he himself was the person, that attempted to break into my chamber, for what reason at such unseasonable hour near 2 o'clock in the morning, in a dark winter night, when he could not be a walking for pleasure, & when he went away without speaking a word. God & his own conscience only know, nor can I imagine what good construction, he could have put upon it, if either the lock or the door had given way, so that he had actually broken in upon us.—Perry, *op. cit.*, I, 136-38.

13. Account of the "barring out" of President James Blair of The College of William and Mary, 1705

About a fortnight before Christmas, 1702, while I lodged in the College, I heard the School boys, about 12 o'clock at night, a-driving of great nails, to fasten & barricade the doors of the Grammar School. I was mightily surprised at it, for we had banished this custom & it was quite left off for some years. I made haste to get up, & with the assistance of 2 servant men, I had in the College, I had almost forced open one of the doors before they sufficiently secured it, but while I was breaking in, they presently fired off 3 or 4 Pistols and hurt one of my servants in the eye with the wadd, as I suppose, of one of the Pistols; while I press'd forward, some of the Boys, having a great kindness for me, called out, "for God's sake, sir, don't offer to come in, for we have shot, & shall certainly fire at any one that first enters." Upon the hearing of this, I began to think there was something more than ordinary in the matter & desired a parley with them, thinking to find out what acct it was that they had provided fire arms, Powder & Shot, which they had never used to do formerly, but that night they would not discover it, tho' I confess, I had some suspicion, of the designs of my malicious neighbour; & resolved to let them alone till morning, & then getting all the other masters together & calling for workmen to break open the doors. Before we began, we offered them a pardon, if they would open, of their own accord, & tell us the truth, who it was that set them on, tho' by that time, we had more than a suspicion of it, for I had seen one of his Excellency's servants that morning a handing of them in some more Powder, upon this, the Boys, sent out at a Window by a ladder One of the Chief confederates that knew the whole plot, with orders to discover it. The Short of this story was, to the best of my remembrance, that while they had no thoughts of any such thing, the Govr Sent for him, & put him upon it, gave them money to buy victuals & Drink & Candles, & Powder, & Shot, & lent them 6 of his own Pistols.. Upon hearing that the Governor was the Author & the contriver of this business, we sent the boys to him, leaving it to his excellency to determine the time when we would have them dismiss'd, for it was then about a week before the usual time. His excellency being out of humor, to the great disappointment of the Boys, ordered that they should continue at their books till the usual time & then be dismiss'd, this decision made them very angry & they said they wondered what he had made all that to do for, when they were not to be dismiss'd one day sooner than ordinary for their pains. When we entered the school, we found the Govr's 3 pair of Pistols, with some swords & other weapons they had provided. It was God's great mercy to me that the boys gave me warning of the Shot & so saved me from the danger, which I have too much reason to suspect, was contrived on purpose upon my acct, his excellency being then in too bad a Humor, to do such a thing out of a frolic; besides that the Fire Arms, Powder, & Shot, my lying in the College; & the differences between him & me, which at that time were come to some height, made the badness of the design too, too probable."

When Governor Nicholson read this statement, he set to work to refute it, and actually prepared in reply the same year (1704) a long pamphlet, which was published in London under the title of "A Modest Answer to a malicious Libel against his Excellency Francis Nicholson, Esq., &c., or an Examination of that Part of Mr. Blair's Affidavit relating to the school boys of the Grammar School in her Majesty's Royal College of William and Mary in Virginia." In this pamphlet Governor Nicholson took issue with Dr. Blair in regard to the facts, and indignantly denied that he had any design upon his life. Barring out the masters, he said, had been the custom every year but one at College since his assuming the government, and the object of the boys was the merely innocent one of getting a little longer holiday at Christmas. The excepted year was 1700, when the General Assembly, banished from Jamestown by the accidental burning of the State house, met in the College hall, December 5, and continued sitting till December 17th. He denied that he had furnished the boys any shot, and explained his loan of his pistols to them and some powder by the fact that it was the custom, and no one thought anything of it. In 1699 the boys had "both Pistols & Powder, and Guns and Swords," at which time Mr. Blair was so far from being under any apprehension that he went in with his Excellency as soon as the boys surrendered, along with Colonel (Philip) Ludwell and Mr. Benjamin Harrison (who also promoted the thing and assisted and encouraged the boys) and other gentlemen of the neighborhood and some of their ladies, and participated of the feast which the boys had provided with the money the Governor gave them. In the opinion of the writer of the pamphlet, Dr. Blair's suspicions were not only an injustice to the Governor, but a reflection "upon the best gentlemen's sons in the country." The fact that "his own Brother's son" (John Blair, born 1687) was a principal actor in the barring out and the master's (Mungo Inglis') son-in-law had no hand in it, was evidence conclusive that the boys were very far from any murderous designs, and that their real purpose was to keep out Mr. Inglis rather than Dr. Blair. "By all of which we may see," concludes the author, "how much this gentleman makes it his study to aggravate things against his Excellency, with all the urging circumstances that come within the invention of Envy."

To this defence Governor Nicholson appended the affidavits of the usher, the clerk of the College, and some of the boys who had attended, in 1702, and before it. They sufficiently protect his intentions, but the wonder remains that a governor should mix up in such a puerile affair and should be unable to see the impropriety, to say no more, of putting pistols, with or without shot, into the hands of thoughtless children. But, after all, neither Blair nor Nicholson should be held to too strict an account, for our ancestors two hundred years ago were not much more than children in some respects. At the least provocation they flew into gusts of anger and uttered language that played the wilds with truth.

The Affidavits.

I, John Allen, Usher of the Grammar School of William and Mary College, do make Oath, that when the School Boys of the College shut out the Masters before Christmas, 1702, I was then in the College and present with Mr Blair almost all the Night, but I don't remember that I heard any of the Boys caution Mr Blair not to offer to come in, saying that they had Shot, and would certainly fire at any one that first enter'd; as he says in his Affidavit of the first of May, 1704.

Neither can I learn that they had any Shot, having made strict Enquiry among the Boys.

As to the custom of shutting out the Masters, which Mr Blair says was banished and quite left off for some years; I do Affirm that it was always practised from the first bringing of it in, to the Year 1702, complained of in the affidavit, except in the Year 1700, when the General Assembly met in the College Hall the 5th of December, and continued setting till the 17th thereof, for which Reason the Scholars were dismissed sooner than ordinary: and I do very well remember that at Christmas, 1699, when I was a Scholar, we shut the Doors against our Masters, at which time his Excellency gave us Money to buy Victuals and Drink, and after we had obtain'd leave to be dismist, and had opened the School Doors. Mr Blair himself, together with several of his Relations, participated of the Entertainment which we had provided with the Money aforesaid; at which time we had Powder, Guns, Pistols, Swords, and other arms, but were taken from us by Surprize.

JOHN ALLEN.

The above affidavit sworn before us this 3d Day of May, 1705.

Hen. Duke, John Smith, John Lewis.

I, William Robertson, make Oath, that at Christmas, 1702. I was Clerk of William and Mary College, and lodged there when the School Boys shut out their Masters. I was called out of Bed to come down to Mr Blair, who I heard talking with them and perswading them to open the Door; but that not succeeding he went to break it open, and called for a Negro Man and a white Servant for that Purpose, and when the Negro went about breaking open the Door, one of the Boys fired at him with Powder; they fired two or three times besides that, whenever any body came nigh to break open the Door, but I did not perceive that they had any manner of Shot, or made use of any, nor did I hear that they had provided Shot to the best of my remembrance. I don't remember that I heard any such caution given by the Boys to Mr Blair, as is mentioned in his Affidavit of the 1st of May, 1704, nor do I know of any Design the Boys had at that time except it was for obtaining leave to break up sooner. As to the Custom of shutting out the Masters I heard it was first practised in 1699, and that the Scholars had provided Fire-Arms, but they were discovered and taken away by one of the Masters, and in 1701,

I heard they shut out the Masters again, but as I was not then concerned about the College, nor present at any of those times, I can say nothing of my own Knowledge.

WILLIAM ROBERTSON.

The above Affidavit sworn before us this 3d. Day of May, 1705.

Hen. Duke, John Smith, John Lewis.

THURSDAY, May the 3d., 1705.

I, The Subscriber, having seen an Affidavit of Mr Commissary Blair, dated the 1st of May, 1704, wherein he says that his Excellency, the Governor, encouraged the Scholars at the Grammar School to shut out their Masters, and gave them money to buy Powder and Shot, &c., and that he had too much Reason to suspect the Shot was contrived on his Account. I do therefore as being at that time at the School, and concerned in shutting out the Masters, declare that I knew of no Design against the life of Mr Blair—or any Person whatsoever, and that I am very sure there was no Shot made use on that occasion, nor heard that any one in the School had Shot—nor did I remember to have heard any such warning given to Mr Blair not to offer to come in, for that we had Shot and would Fire, &c. I believe some of us might say we would Fire (as we actually did) but it was only with Powder, there being no Shot amongst us to the Knowledge of me the Subscriber. As for Powder, we had some belonging to some of the Boys, but I do not know of any bought with the Governor's Money, nor do I remember that any Powder was given us by any of his Excellency's Servants. Some of us having fired some of the Pistols, and I declare there was no Shot in any of them. I declare that we let Charles Doyly and John Grymes and some others out at the School Window by a Rope, and none by a Ladder, except me the Subscriber; Charles Doyly was sent out to bring Powder from Mr Henry Tyler's House, and was taken with the Powder (before he could get back to us) by Mr Allen and Mr Robertson, and we had none of that Powder. John Grymes was sent out because he had accidentally cut his Leg on a Glass Bottle, and I do not remember that any one was sent out to discover as Mr Blair alledges.

I do declare that I was the Person to whom the Governor gave the Money to buy Victuals for our holding out against the Masters, but gave me no Directions to buy Powder or Shot, and I was also the Person sent out to know the Governor's Pleasure when the School should be dismist, but I do not remember that I told Mr Blair, any thing of the Governor's setting us on to shut out the Masters.

But I do declare that the Custom of shutting out the Masters was first begun (by his Excellency's Encouragement) at which time we had Fuzees and other Arms, but made no use of them by Reason they were taken from us by one of the Masters, before we had an opportunity to get them into the School to shut up the Doors. The next Year we shut out the Masters again, and the next Year that we shut them out, was the Year which I find Mr Blair complains of.

JOHN LEAR.

This above Affidavit sworn before us this 3d of May, 1705.

Hen. Duke, John Smith, John Lewis.

THURSDAY, May the 3d., 1705.

I, The Subscriber, having seen an Affidavit of Mr Commissary Blair, dated the 1st of May, 1704, wherein he says that his Excellency, the Governor, encouraged the Scholars at the Grammar School to shut out their Masters, and gave them Money to buy Powder and Shot, &c., and that he had too much Reason to suspect the Shot was contrived on his account, I do therefore as being at that time at the said School, and concerned in shutting out the Masters, declare, that I knew of no Design against the life of Mr Blair or any Person whatsoever, and that I am very sure there was no Shot made use of on that Occasion, nor heard any one in the School had Shot, nor do I remember to have heard any such warning given to Mr Blair not to offer to come in, for that we had Shot and would Fire, &c. I believe some of us might say we would Fire (as we actually did) but it was only with Powder, there being no Shot amongst us to the knowledge of me the Subscriber. As for Powder we had some belonging to some of the Boys, but I do not know of any bought with the Governor's Money, nor do I remember that any Powder was given us by any of his Excellency's servants. Some of us having fired some of the Pistols, and I declare there was no Shot in any of them. I declare that we let Charles Doyly, and John Grymes, and some others out at the School Window by a Rope, and none by a Ladder, except John Lear; Charles Doyly was sent out to bring Powder from Mr Henry Tyler's House, and was taken with the Powder (before he could get back to us) by Mr Allen and Mr Robertson, and we had none of that Powder. John Grymes was sent out because he had accidentally cut his Leg on a

Glass Bottle, and I do not remember that anyone was sent out to discover as Mr Blair alledges.

ROBERT PITT.

The within Affidavit, sworn this 4th Day of May, 1705.

Hen. Duke, John Smith, John Lewis.

THURSDAY, May the 3d., 1705.

I, The Subscriber, having seen an Affidavit of Mr Commissary Blair's, dated May the 1st, 1704, wherein he says that his Excellency encouraged the Scholars of the Grammar School to shut out their Masters, and gave them Money to buy Powder and Shot, and says he had too much Reason to suspect the Shot was contrived on his account; I do therefore as being at that time, and concerned in shutting out the Masters, declare that I knew of no Design against the Life of Mr Blair, or any Person whatever, and am very sure that there was no Shot made use of on that Occasion; nor do I remember that I heard any such warning given Mr Blair, as that we had Shot and would Fire, if he did offer to come in; I do believe that some of the Boys might say, that they would Fire, (as they actually did), being only with Powder, there being no Shot amongst us, to the best of my Knowledge, as to the Powder we had, it did belong to some of the Boys, but know of no Powder or Shot bought with his Excellency's Money, or that any was given us by any of his Excellency's Servants. Charles Doyly and John Grymes and some others were let out by a Rope; Charles Doyly was sent to Mr Henry Tyler's House to fetch Powder, but was taken before he could get back to us (by Mr John Allen and Mr Robertson) and we had none of that Powder. John Grymes was sent out because he had accidentally cut his Leg with a Glass Bottle, but know of none that was sent out by a Ladder, except John Lear, who was sent to know his Excellency's Pleasure when he should be dismist, but doe not know of one that was sent to discover as Mr Blair alledges.

JAMES DAY.

The within Affidavit sworn before us this 4th of May, 1704.

Hen. Duke, John Smith, John Lewis.

MAY the 31st, 1705.

I, The Subscriber, having seen an Affidavit of Mr Commissary Blair, dated the 1st of May, 1704, wherein he says that his Excellency, the

Governor encouraged the Scholars at the Grammar School to shut out their Masters, and gave them Money to buy Powder and Shot, &c., and that he had too much Reason to suspect the Shot was contrived on his Account, I do therefore, as being at that time at the said School, and concerned in shutting out the Masters, declare that I know of no Design against the life of Mr Blair, nor any person whatever, and I am sure there was no Shot made use of on that Occasion, nor did I hear that any one in the School had Shot, nor do I remember to have heard any such Warning given to Mr Blair, not to offer to come in, for that we had Shot and would Fire, &c. I do believe some of us might say we would Fire (as indeed we actually did) but it was only with Powder, there being no Shot amongst us, to the knowledge of me, the Subscriber. As for Powder, we had some belonging to some of the Boys, but I do not know of any that was bought with the Governor's Money. I, the Subscriber, having fired several of the Pistols, do declare that I know nothing of any Shot being in them. I declare that we let Charles Doyly and John Grymes out of the Window by a Rope, and not by a Ladder. Charles Doyly was sent out to bring Powder from Mr Henry Tyler's House, and was taken with the Powder (before he could get back to us), by Mr Allen and Mr Robertson, and we had none of that Powder. John Grymes was sent out, because he had accidentally cut his Leg with a Glass Bottle. I, the Subscriber, do likewise declare that the Masters were thrice shut out of the School (during the time of my Education) but cannot say in what Years.

JOHN TIMSON.

Sworn before us this 31st Day of May, 1705.

John Smith, John Lewis.

MAY the 31st, 1705.

I, The Subscriber, having formerly been Usher of the Grammar School in William and Mary College, do declare, that (to the best of my Remembrance) the Custom of shutting out the Masters commenced first in the Year 1699. And in the Year 1700, the General Assembly meeting and setting in the College, obtain'd Leave of the Masters to dismiss the Scholars somewhat sooner than the usual time. In the Year 1701, the Scholars shut out the Masters again, but the Year 1702, I went to England, and so know nothing of what Mr Blair taxes his Excellency with, as done in the said Year, with a Design of killing or hurting Mr Blair; and farther, that from the beginning of that Custom, while I belonged to the College, there was no Intermission unless in the said Year 1700, nor of any Design of doing Mr Blair any Hurt or Prejudice in the least.

ORLANDO JONES.

Sworn this 31st Day of May, 1705, before us,

John Smith, John Lewis.

JUNE the 1st, 1705.

I, The Subscriber, having seen an Affidavit of Mr Commissary Blair's, dated the first of May, 1704, wherein he says That his Excellency encouraged the Scholars at the Grammar School to shut out their Masters, and gave them Money to buy Powder and Shot, &c., and that he had too much Reason to suspect the Shot was contrived on his Account: I do therefore as being at that time at the said School, and concern'd in shutting out the Masters, declare that I know of no Design against the Life of Mr Blair, nor any Person whatever, and that I am very sure there was no Shot made use of on that Occasion, nor heard that any one in the School had Shot, nor do I remember to have heard any such Warning giving to Mr Blair, nor to offer to come in, for that we had Shot and would Fire, &c., I believe some of us might say we would fire, (as we actually did), but it was only with Powder, there being no Shot amongst us, to the knowledge of me, the Subscriber. As for Powder, we had some belonging to some of the Boys, but I do not know of any bought with the Governor's Money, nor do I remember that any Powder was given us by any of his Excellency's Servants, some of us having fired some of the Pistols, and I declare there was no Shot in any of them; I declare that we let Charles Doyly and John Grymes, and some others, out at the School Window by a Rope, and not by a Ladder. Charles Doyly was sent out to bring Powder from Mr Henry Tyler's House, and was taken with the Powder before he could get back to us by Mr Allen and Mr Robertson, and we had none of the Powder. John Grymes was sent out because he had accidentally cut his Leg on a Glass Bottle. We do not remember that any one was sent out to discover the Plot as he alleges.

GEORGE HUNT.

Sworn this 31st of May, 1705, before us.

John Smith, John Lewis.

I, Thomas Bouth, having been educated for some Years at William and Mary College, do declare, that in the Year 1699, to the best of my remembrance, the School Boys shut out their Masters, and that I was then amongst them in the School, and that was the first beginning of that Custom; next year the Assembly sat in the College, and the School was dismist without shutting out the Masters. I remember that I was also concerned with the other Scholars in shutting out the Masters in 1701. But in the Year 1702, (which is the time mentioned in Mr Blair's Affidavit of the 1st of May, 1704, which I have seen), I was not in the School, nor concerned in the shutting out of the Masters, and can't say any thing of my own Knowledge of what happened then, but only that I saw the Boys shut up in the School.

THOMAS BOUTH.

Sworn this 30th of June, 1705, before us,

John Smith, John Lewis.

I, Ballard Dormer, having for some Years been educated at the Grammar School in William and Mary College, do make Oath, that in the Year 1701, the School Boys shut out their Masters, and I was then in the School, and I remember that the School Boys shut out their Masters in 1702, but I was not then in the School, nor concern'd in it; so know nothing of what happened then, nor heard that the Boys had, or made use of any Shot on that Occasion.

BALLARD DORMER.

Sworn before us this 30th Day of June, 1705,

John Smith, John Lewis.

TUESDAY, July the 17th, 1705.

I, The Subscriber, having seen an Affidavit of Mr Commissary Blair, dated the first of May, 1704, wherein he says that his Excellency, the Governor, encouraged the Scholars at the Grammar School to shut out their Masters, and gave them Money to buy Powder and Shot, &c., and that he had too much Reason to suspect the Shot was contrived upon his Account, I do therefore, as being at that time at the said School, and concerned in shutting out of the Masters, declare that I know of no Design against the life of Mr Blair, or any Person whatsoever, and I am very sure there was no Shot made use of on that Occasion, nor heard that any one had Shot in the School; nor do I remember that there was Powder bought with the Governor's Money, or of any that was given us by his Excellency's Servants; for that Powder as we had was bought with the Boys' Money, which, at last being almost spent, I was let out at one of the School Windows by a Rope to fetch Powder from Mr Tyler's House, and before I could return again into the School (with the Powder) was taken by Mr Allen and Mr Robertson, and they received none of that Powder. What they did after I came out, I can't declare.

CHARLES DOYLY.

Sworn this 17th Day of July, 1705, before us,
John Smith, John Lewis.

July the 17th, 1705.

We, the Subscribers, having seen an Affidavit of Mr Commissary Blair, dated the first of May, 1704, wherein he says that his Excellency, the Governor, encouraged the Scholars at the Grammar School to shut out their Masters, and give them Money to buy Powder and Shot, &c., and that he had too much Reason to suspect the Shot was contriv'd upon his Account, we do therefore, as being at that time at the said School, and concern'd in shutting out of the Masters, declare that we know of no Design against the Life of Mr Blair, or any other Person whatsoever, and we are very sure there was no Shot made use of on that Occasion, nor heard that any one had Shot, in the School, nor do we remember to have heard any such Warning given to Mr Blair not to come in, for that we had Shot and would Fire, &c. We believe some of us might say we would Fire (as we actually did), but it was only with Powder, there being no Shot amongst us, to the knowledge of us, the Subscribers. We declare that Charles Doyly and I, John Grymes, was let out through one of the School Windows by a Rope, and not by a Ladder, and we do not know that any one was sent out to discover as Mr Blair alledges.

JOHN GRYMES, CHARLES GRYMES.

Sworn this 17th day of July, 1705, before us,
John Smith, John Lewis.

TUESDAY, July the 17th, 1705.

I, the Subscriber, being a Scholar at the Grammar School of William and Mary College in Virginia, at the time complained of by

Mr Blair, I do, therefore, as being at that time at the said School, and concerned in the shutting out of the Masters, declare that I know of no Design against the Life of Mr Blair, nor any Person whatsoever; and I am very sure there was no Shot made use of on that Occasion, nor heard of any one in the School that had Shot, nor do I remember to have heard any such Warning given to Mr Blair not to offer to come in, for that we had Shot and would Fire, &c. I believe some of us might say we would Fire (as we actually did), but it was only with Powder, there being no Shot amongst us, to the Knowledge of me, the Subscriber; as for Powder we had, belonging to some of the Boys, but I do not remember any bought with the Governor's Money, nor do I know of any Powder given us by his Excellency's Servants. I declare, likewise, that we let Charles Doyly and John Grymes out by a Rope, and not by a Ladder. Charles Doyly was sent out to fetch Powder from Mr Henry Tyler's House, and was taken with it (before he could get to us), by Mr Robertson and Mr Allen, and we had none of the Powder; John Grymes was sent out because he accidentally cut his Leg on a Glass Bottle, and I do not remember that any one was sent out to discover, as Mr Blair alledges.

EDMUND DUKE.

Sworn this 17th of July, 1705, before us,

John Smith, John Lewis.

WEDNESDAY, June the 27th, Anno, 1705.

I, The Subscriber, having seen an Affidavit of Mr Commissary Blair's, dated May the 1st, 1704, wherein he says, that his Excellency encouraged the Scholars of the Grammar School to shut out their Masters, and gave them Money to buy Powder and Shot, and likewise says that he had too much Reason to suspect the Shot was contrived on his Account, I do, therefore (as being at that Present, and concerned in shutting out the Masters) declare that I knew of no Design against the Life of Mr Blair, or any other Person whatever, and to my knowledge there was no Shot made use of, on that Occasion, nor do I remember that I heard any such Warning given Mr Blair, as that we had Shot and would Fire if he did offer to come in. I do believe that some of the Boys might say they would Fire, (as they actually did) being only with Powder, there being no Shot amongst us, to my knowledge; as to the Powder we had, it did belong to some of the Boys, but I know not of any Shot bought with his Excellency's Money, or that any was given us by any of the Servants. Charles Doyly and John Grymes and some others was let out by a Rope; Charles Doyly was sent to Mr Henry Tyler's House to fetch Powder, but was taken before he could come back to us, by Mr John Allen and Mr William Robertson. John Grymes was sent out because he accidentally cut his Leg with a Glass Bottle, but I know of none was sent out by a Ladder except John Lear, who went to know his Excellency's Pleasure when he should be dismiss'd; I know not of one who was sent to discover as Mr Blair alledges.

Per THOMAS BRAY.

Sworn this 17th Day of July, 1705, before us,

John Smith, John Lewis.

I, John Tyler, having seen an Affidavit of Mr Commissary Blair, dated the first of May, 1704, wherein he says that the Governour gave Money to buy Powder and Shot; I do (therefore as being concerned then in shutting out the Masters) declare that I know of no Shot made use of on that Occasion; as to the Custom of shutting out the Masters, I remember it had been practised twice before that time mentioned in Mr Blair's Affidavit, but do not remember the Years.

JOHN TYLER.

Sworn this 17th Day of July, 1705, before us,

John Smith, John Lewis.

JULY the 17th, 1705.

I, the Subscriber, having seen an Affidavit of Mr Commissary Blair, dated the 1st of May, 1704, wherein he says that his Excellency, the Governour, encouraged the Scholars of the Grammar School to shut out their Masters, and gave them Money to buy Powder and Shot, and that he had too much Reason to suspect that it was contrived upon his Account; I do therefore, as being at that time at the same School and concern'd in shutting out of the Masters, declare that I knew of no Design against the Life of Mr Blair or any other whatsoever, and I am very sure there was no Shot made use of on that Occasion, nor do I remember to have heard any such Warning given to Mr Blair not to come in, for that we had Shot and would Fire. I believe some of us might say that we would Fire (as we actually did) but it was only with Powder, there being no Shot among us to the knowledge of me, the Subscriber.

FRAN. TYLER

Sworn this 17th of July, 1705, before us,

John Smith, John Lewis.

JULY the 17th, 1705.

We, the Subscribers, having seen an Affidavit of Mr Commissary Blair, dated the first of May, 1704, wherein he says that his Excellency, the Governour, encouraged the Scholars at the Grammar School to shut out their Masters, and give them money to buy Powder and Shot, &c., and that he had too much reason to suspect the Shot was contriv'd upon his Account, we do, therefore, as being at that time at the said School and concerned in shutting out the Masters, declare that we know of no Design against the Life of Mr Blair or any other person whatsoever, and we are very sure there was no Shot made use of on that Occasion, nor heard that any one had Shot in the School, nor do we remember to have heard any such Warning given to Mr Blair not to come in, for that we had Shot and would Fire, &c. We believe some of us would say that we would Fire (as we actually did), but it was only with Powder, there being no Shot amongst us to the knowledge of us, the Subscribers. We declare that Charles Doyly and John Grymes was let out through one of the School Windows by a Rope, and not by a Ladder. And we do not know that any one was sent out to discover as Mr Blair alledges.,

WILSON ROSCOW, JAMES ROSCOW.

Sworn this 17th of July, 1705, before us,

John Smith, John Lewis.

Memorandum.

A List of Affidavits of the several Persons here underwritten:

Sworn May 3, 1705—John Allen, Will. Robertson, John Lear; before Hen. Duke, John Smith, John Lewis.

Sworn May 4, 1705—Robert Pitt, James Day; before the aforesaid.

Sworn May 31, 1705—John Timson, Orlando Jones, George Hunt; before John Lewis, John Smith.

Sworn June 30, 1705—Tho. Booth, Ballard Dormer; before John Lewis, John Smith.

Sworn July 17, 1705—Charles Doyly, John Grymes, Charles

Grymes, Edmund Duke, Thomas Bray, John Tyler, Fran. Tyler, Wilson Roscow, James Roscow; before John Smith, John Lewis.

—*William and Mary Quarterly Historical Magazine*, XVI, 181-99.

14. HUGH JONES ON THE COLLEGE OF WILLIAM AND MARY, 1724

Publick Buildings here [Williamsburg] of Note, are the College, the Capitol, the Governor's House, and the Church. The Latitude of the *College* at Williamsburgh, to the best of my Observation, is 37°. 21'. *North.*

The Front which looks due *East* is double, and is 136 Foot long. It is a lofty Pile of Brick Building adorn's with a *Cupola.* At the *North* End runs back a large Wing, which is a handsome *Hall,* answerable to which the *Chapel* is to be built; and there is a spacious *Piazza* on the *West* Side, from one Wing to the other. It is approached by a good Walk, and a grand Entrance by Steps, with good Courts and Gardens about it, with a good House and Apartments for the *Indian Master* and his Scholars, and Out-Houses; and a large Pasture enclosed like a Park with about 150 Acres of Land adjoining, for occasional Uses.

The Building is beautiful and commodious, being first modelled by Sir *Cristopher Wren,* adapted to the Nature of the Country by the *Gentlemen* there; and since it was burnt down, it has been rebuilt, and nicely contrived, altered and adorned by the ingenious Direction of *Governor Spotswood;* and is not altogether unlike Chelsea Hospital.

This *Royal Foundation* was granted and established by *Charter, by King William and Queen Mary,* and endowed by them, with some thousand Acres of Land, with Duties upon Furs and Skins and a Penny a Pound for all Tobacco transported from *Virginia* and *Maryland,* to the other Plantations; to which have been made several additional Benefactions, as that handsome Establishment for Mr. Boyle, for the Education of *Indians,* with the many Contributions of the Country, especially a late one of 1000 l. to buy Negroes for the College Use and Service.

The Society is a Corporation established for a *President, six Masters or Professors,* with a hundred Scholars, more or less.

For some Causes that I can't account for, the Revenue is not improved as much as might be wished; neither is the College brought to that Method of Education and Advantage, as it might be; tho' 'tis hoped, that in a few Years it will, like the Palm Tree, grow to the greater Perfection, under the Weighty Obstacles that load it.

The Salary of the President Mr. *James Blair*, has been lately ordered to be reduced from 150 to 100 l. *per Ann.*

The Salary of the Fellows (one of which I have been several Years, is 80 l. *Per Ann.* each, with 20s. Entrance, and 20s. a Year for Pupilage for each Scholar: The Payments are sometimes made in Current *Spanish Money*, and sometimes in *Sterling* Bills.

The Nature of the Country scarce yet admits of the Possibility of reducing the *Collegians* to the nice Methods of Life and Study observed in *Oxford* and *Cambridge;* tho' by Degrees they may copy from thence many useful Customs and Constitutions.

When the *College* shall be compleatly finished, and Scholarships founded, then is the Trust to be transferred from the *Trustees* to the *President and Masters;* but at present it is managed by a certain Number of Governors or Visitors, (one of which is chosen yearly Rector) appointed first by the Trustees, elected out of the Principal and worthiest Inhabitants.

These appoint a Person, to whom they grant several Privileges and Allowances to board and lodge the Masters and Scholars at an extraordinary cheap Rate.

This Office is at present performed in the neatest and most regular and plentiful Manner, by *Mrs. Mary Stith*, a Gentlewoman of great Worth and Discretion, in good Favour with the Gentry, and great Esteem and Respect with the common People.

Great Pity it is, but the noble Design of this College met with more Friends to encourage, and Benefactors to advance, its flourishing State.

One Happiness is, that it has always a *Chancellor* in *England*, chosen by the *Governors* or *Feoffees;* to whose Patronage and Direction it may have recourse upon emergent Occasions.

The last *Chancellor* was the late *Bishop of London;* and the present is his *Grace the Archbishop of Canterbury.*

The *Chancellor* continues in that office but seven Years; so that it may happen as soon as he has obtained a perfect Knowledge and Acquaintance with the Persons and Affairs belonging to the *College*, his Term is expired: Besides their Business in other momentous Affairs at Home may divert them, and the Distance of the Country may prevent them from obtaining true Notions, and exact Accounts of the Nature of the *Colony* and the *College;* so that for these Reasons, they can't do for it the Good, which they otherwise might: For their better Information, and for Direction of all, in promoting Religion and Learning in this *Plantation*, I have made Publick this Account of *it*, and *its* Inhabitants. . .

The Royal Founders of *William* and *Mary* College, with Prospect of doing the greatest Good for the Colonies of *Virginia* and *Maryland*, conferred this princely Donation upon them; and were seconded with the ample Benefaction of the honourable Mr. *Boyle*, and the Contributions of the Country. But this underwent the common Fate of most other charitable Gifts of this Kind, having met with several Difficulties to struggle with in its Infancy; but the most dangerous was, that it was as it were no sooner finished, but it was unfortunately and unaccountably consumed to Ashes. Yet observe the wonderful *Turns* of Fortune, and Power of *Providence*. This College, *Phoenix-like*, as the City of *London*, revived and improved out of its own Ruins. But though it has found such unexpected Success, and has proved of very great Service already; yet is it far short of such Perfection, as it might easily attain to by the united Power of the Persons concerned about this important Foundation.

For it is now a College without a Chapel, without a Scholarship, and without a Statute.

There is a Library without Books, comparatively speaking, and a President without a fix'd Salary till of late: A Burgess without certainty of Electors; and in fine, there have been disputes and Differences about these and the like Affairs of the College hitherto without End.

These Things greatly impede the Progress of Sciences and learned Arts, and discourage those that may be inclined to contribute their Assistance or Bounty towards the Good of the College.

Nevertheless the Difficulties of this Kind might be removed by some such Regulations as follow, *viz.*

Let none be permitted to teach School in any Parish, but such as shall be nominated by the Minister and Vestry, and licensed by the President of the College.

Let such Lads as have been taught to read and instructed in the Grounds of the *English* Language in those Schools, be admitted into the *Grammar* School at the College, if they pass Examination before the President and Masters; together with such Youth as shall be sent from *Maryland*, who have a Right to be educated at this College.

Provided always that the Number of *Grammar* Scholars shall never exceed one Hundred.

Let them be boarded and lodged in the Dormitory, as they are at present; or upon such Terms as may from Time to Time seem most proper to the President and Masters, or to the Governors, till a Transfer be obtained.

These Lads should be two Years under the Care of the Usher, and two more under the *Grammar* Master; and by them instructed in *Latin* and *Greek*, in such methods as the President and Masters shall direct.

And during these four Years, at certain appointed Times they should be taught to write as they now are in the Writing-School, or in such Methods as the President and Masters may judge better: There also should the Writing Master teach them the Grounds and Practice of Arithmetick, in order to qualify such for Business, as intend to make no farther Progress in Learning.

Out of the *Grammar* School should be yearly elected by the President and Masters (or Professors) five Scholars upon the Foundation, who should be allowed their Board, Education, and Lodging in proper Apartments gratis; and should also be provided with cloaths and Gowns, &c. after the Charter-House Method.

These Scholars should continue three Years upon the Foundation; during which Time, at appointed *Terms* they should be instructed in Languages, in Religion, in Mathematicks, in Philosophy, and in History, by the five Masters or Professors appointed for that Purpose; who with the *Grammar* Master make up the Number appointed by the Charter.

Besides the Scholars, the Professors should for a certain Sum instruct such others as may be enter'd Commoners in the College out of the *Grammar* School, or from elsewhere, by the Approbation of the President and Masters, who should be obliged to wear Gowns, and be subject to the same Statutes and Rules as the Scholars; and as Commoners are in *Oxford*. These should maintain themselves, and have a particular Table, and Chambers for their Accommodation.

For to wait at the four high Tables hereafter mentioned, there should be elected by the President and Masters four Servitors, who should have their Education, and such Allowances, as the Servitors in Oxford.

Such Scholars, Commoners, and Servitors, as have behaved themselves well, and minded their Studies for three Years, and can pass proper Examination, and have performed certain Exercises, should have the Degree of Batchellor of Arts conferred upon them; should eat at a Table together, and be distinguished by a peculiar Habit; maintain themselves, be subject to certain Rules, and pursue proper Studies; being allowed the Use of the Library as well as the Masters, paying proper Fees upon their Admission for the Good of the Library.

Out of these Batchellors should be yearly elected by the Presidents and Masters, one Fellow to be allowed 20 l. for his Passage to *England*, and 20 l. *per Ann.* for three Years after his speedy Entrance and Continuance in some certain College in *Oxford* or *Cambridge*; after which he should commence Master of Arts; which Degree, with all others in our Universities, should be conferred in the same Manner in this College by the President and Masters.

Out of the Graduates above Batchellors should the Masters or Professors be chosen by the Election of the said Masters or Professors, with the President; who also every seven Years should chose a new Chancellor, to whose Determination all Disputes and Differences should be referred.

And when the President's Place is vacant, it should be filled by such of the Masters as has belonged first to the College.

A *Testimonium* from this College should be of the same Use and Force as from others in our Universities.

If the present Fund be insufficient to defray the Expence, proper Improvement should be made of the Revenue, and Application made for additional Benefactions.

A Body of Statutes should be directly formed and established by the Visitors, President, and Masters; and a *Transfer* of the Trust should be then made.

Such an Establishment would encourage the bright Youth of *Virginia* to apply to their Studies, and in some Measure would compel them to improve themselves; whereas now being left to their own Liberty, they proceed but superficially, and generally commence *Man* before they have gone through the *Schools* in the College. Here too would be great Inducements for their Friends to advise and persuade them to go through with their Learning; when they are certain, that they will thus be regularly improved, and have Prospect of a cheap Education, and Hopes of the best Preferment in their Country in Church and State; and have equal (if not superior) Chance with others for Promotion abroad in the World; being bred compleat

Gentlemen and good Christians, and qualified for the Study of the Gospel, Law, or Physick; and prepared for undertaking Trade, or any useful Projects and Inventions.

As for the Accomplishments of Musick, Dancing, and Fencing, they may be taught by such as the President and Masters shall appoint at such certain Times, as they shall fix for those Purposes.

'Till these Regulations (or the like) be made, Matters may be carried on as they are at present; only to me there seems an absolute Necessity now for a Professor of Divinity, in order to instruct the *Indians* and *English* Youth there in the Grounds of Religion, and read Lectures of Morality to the senior Lads, and to read Prayers and preach in the College as Chaplain: This I am certain is very much wanting, and what the present Income of the College with good Management will easily allow of; therefore I hope particular Notice will be taken hereof.

There is as yet no great Occasion for the Hall, so that it might be made a Chapel and Divinity School, for which Purpose it would serve nobly with little or no Alterations.

As there is lately built an Apartment for the *Indian* Boys and their Master, so likewise is there very great Occasion for a Quarter for the Negroes and inferior Servants belonging to the College; for these not only take up a great deal of Room and are noisy and nasty, but also have often made me and others apprehensive of the great Danger of being burnt with the College, thro' their Carelessness and Drowsiness.

Another thing prejudicial to the College, is the Liberty allowed the Scholars, and the negligent Observance of College Hours, and Opportunity they have of rambling Abroad.

To remedy this, there is wanting some Contrivance to secure the Youth within the College at certain Hours; which has hitherto been in vain attempted, because of the many Servants lodged in the College, and the several Doors and Ways to get out of it.

Likewise the Privileges and Apartments of the Presidents and Masters, and House-Keeper, &c. ought to be fix'd and ascertain'd; for these being precarious and doubtful, upon this Account has arose much Difference and Ill-Will, to the great Scandal of the College, and Detriment of Learning.

Little additional Charge would put the Government of the College upon a much better Footing; whereas at present it scarcely merits the name of a College.

As for Election of a Burgess in Pursuance to a Clause in the Charter, he ought to be chosen by the President and as many Masters as there shall actually be at any Time.

The Charter mentions six Masters or Professors, but does not specify the Professions; it directs to the making of Statutes and founding Scholarships, but the particulars are left to the Discretion of the Managers; and some such Establishment as this here mentioned may not be improper, especially if for greater Encouragement the Surveyors of each County were to be appointed by the President and Masters, out of such as have taken a Batchellor of Arts Degree there; and if also the Governor and Council were to elect a certain Number of Batchellors for Clerks into the Secretaries Office; out of which Clerks attending and writing there at certain Times, the County Clerks should be appointed by the Secretary.

The Office of the President would be to govern the College, be Treasurer, and Censor, and have a casting Vote in all Debates.

The six Professors or Masters would be

Divinity, who should be Chaplain and Catechist.

Mathematicks.

Philosophy.

one for

Languages.

History.

Humanity, who should be *Grammar* Master.

The under Masters would be the Usher, the *Indian* Master, and the Writing-Master.

The Town Masters must be such as occasion requires, for Fencing, Dancing, and Musick.

There would be three *English* Fellows.

There would be fifteen Scholars, and a sufficient Number of School-Boys for a constant Supply.

Besides a Number of Batchellors and Masters of Arts, who would wait till they come in Fellows or Professors, or got to be made Surveyors or County Clerks.

For all this there might easily be contrived Room in the College, especially if a Hall was built in the Place intended for the Chapel.

As also would there be Room enough for the House-Keeper, Officers, and Servants; especially if a Quarter was built for the Negroes, &c.

The Tables might then be distinguish'd into four higher or four lower, *viz.*

The upper Table for the President and Masters.

The second for the Masters of Arts, &c.

The third for the Batchellors of Arts.

The fourth for the Scholars and Commoners.

The four lower Tables should be

> The first for the House-Keeper, and the upper School-Boys.
>
> The second for the Usher, Writing-Master, and the lower School-Boys.
>
> The third for the Servitors and College Officers.
>
> And the last for the *Indian* Master and his Scholars.

This Regularity might easily be effected, and would prove not only decent and creditable, but also useful and advantageous to the Country and the College.

The Library is better furnished of late than formerly, by the kind Gifts of several Gentlemen; but yet the Number of Books is but very small, and the sets upon each Branch of Learning are very imperfect, and not the best of the Sort.

To remedy this Defect proper Application should be made to the Societies and to the superior Clergy in *England*, who would give at least what Duplicates they have upon such an useful Occasion; and what necessary Collection of Books cannot be obtain'd by begging, they may buy as soon as they shall be able to stock their Library; as a great Help to which I believe considerable Contributions would be made by the Clergy Burgesses, and Gentry of the Country, if upon easy Terms they were allowed the Use of the Library at certain Hours, at such Times as they shall be at *Williamsburgh*, either for Pleasure or upon Business.

The Office of Librarian is given to Mr. *John Harris* the Usher, in order to make his Place more agreeable to his Merit; and if the Gardener was made to execute the Office of Porter for his present Salary, it would be no great Hardship upon him, and would be an Ease to the College; and for the Benefit and Encouragement of the House-Keeper several small necessary Pensions and Privileges might be contrived more than what are at present allowed; so that it might be made well worth the while of a Person of Integrity, Knowledge, and Prudence, to undertake and carry on so troublesom an Office.

The greater the Number of Collegians, the greater would be the

Gain of the House-Keeper; so that when the College should be full and compleat as here directed and wished, the Collegians may be boarded upon easier Terms; boarded I say; because if any but the President dieted themselves, it would creat Confusion; and if any belonging to the College but such Masters as have Families were permitted to eat elsewhere, it would not be worth any body's while to lay in Provision, when they could not tell what Number they must provide for.

As for the *English* College Customs of *Commons*, &c. it is thought as yet more adviseable to board in the College than to keep to those Methods, till the Country affords better Conveniencies and Opportunities for so doing.

The *Indians* who are upon Mr. *Boyle's* Foundation have now a handsom Apartment for themselves and their Master, built near the College, which useful Contrivance ought to be carried on to the utmost Advantage in the real Education and Conversion of the Infidels; for hitherto but little Good has been done therein, though abundance of Money has been laid out, and a great many Endeavours have been used, and much Pains taken for that Purpose.

The young *Indians*, procured from the tributary or foreign Nations with much Difficulty, were formerly boarded and lodged in the Town; where abundance of them used to die, either thro' Sickness, change of Provision, and way of Life; or as some will have it, often for want of proper Necessaries and due Care taken with them. Those of them that have escaped well, and been taught to read and write, have for the most Part returned to their Home, some with and some without Baptism, where they follow their own savage Customs and heathenish Rites.

A few of them have lived as Servants among the *English*, or loitered and idled away their Time in Laziness and Mischief.

But 'tis great Pity that more Care is not taken about them, after they are dismissed from School.

They have admirable Capacities when their Humours and Tempers are perfectly understood; and if well taught, they might advance themselves and do great Good in the Service of Religion; whereas now they are rather taught to become worse than better by falling into the worst Practices of vile nominal Christians, which they add to their own *Indian* Manners and Notions.

To prevent this therefore, let there be chosen continually four

Indian Servitors out of the *Indian* Schools, as the other four out of the *Grammar* School.

Let these be maintained in the *Indian* House, and wait upon the four lower Tables: Let them be instructed as the other Servitors, or as their Genius most aptly may require, but particularly in Religion; and when they are found qualified let them be sent to *England*, or placed out to Captains of Ships or Trades, as the Mathematical Boys in *Christ-Hospital*, for a few Years; then let them return and be allowed a small Exhibition, and encouraged in their separate Callings and Occupations; and let them settle some among the *English*, and others return to their own Nations.

Undoubtedly many of them would become excellent artists and Proficients in Trade; and thus when Reason and Experience has convinced them of the Preference of our Religion and Manners, certainly they may not only save their own Souls; but also be extreamly instrumental in the Conversion of their barbarous Friends and Relations.

In proceeding thus, any that seem capable or inclinable to study Divinity, should by all Means be encouraged and forwarded in it, and sent over for a small Time to one of our Universities with an Allowance of *Fellows;* after which, if such were admitted into Orders, and then sent out Missionaries among their own Country-Folks, what great Good might we not expect from such, when thoroughly converted and instructed in Christianity, and made truly sensible of the Advantages of Religion, the deadly State of Infidelity, and the miserable Lives and Customs of the *Indians?*

In a Work of this Kind undoubtedly several good Christians would contribute their charitable Assistance; 'till which the present Fund should be applied in this Method, though the Managers should be obliged to reduce the Number of *Indian* Scholars upon this Account; since this was the main Intent of the Benefaction, and no other Method can well answer this Design; which may be evidenced by Experience both from the Colleges of *Virginia* and *New England* too, as I have been credibly informed from good Authors, as well as my own Experience.

By such Methods in Process of Time might the *Indian* Obstinacy be mollified, their seeming Dulness might be cleared from Rust; and the Gates of Heaven be opened for their Admission upon their perfect Conversion to the Faith of Christ. In such glorious Designs as these neighter should Humour, Interest, nor Prejudice divert any from their charitable Assistance therein, especially such as are concerned in Affairs of this Kind, and engaged by Duty to lend their best Aid in *leading* the Infidels into the Pale of Christ's Church, and making them by mild and most gentle Measures to accompany his Flock; since all the Force in the World would rather *drive* them from, than guide them, to the Congregation of the Faithful and Communion of Saints.

By some such prudent and mild Methods along may they be made to live and die as true Christians, and not like the most savage Brutes, as they generally do.

Thus far as to the Education of the young Men in *Virginia*, and the Instruction most proper for the *Indians;* and as for the Negroes each Owner ought to take Care that the Children born his Property, and all his intelligent adult Negroes be taught their Catechism and some short Prayers, be made to frequent the Church and be baptized, and hindered as much as may be from Swearing, Lying, Intemperance, Prophaness, and Stealing and Cheating.

Finally, as to the Education of Girls, it is great Pity but that good Boarding Schools were erected for them at *Williamsburgh* and other Towns.—Hugh Jones, *The Present State of Virginia* (London: Printed for J. Clarke, at the *Bible* under the *Royal-Exchange*, 1724), pp. 26-28, 44, 70, 83-94.

15. The General Assembly makes further provision for the
support of the college, 1726

And, forasmuch as the present revenue of the college of William and Mary, is not sufficient to maintain the full number of masters or professors required by the charter of the said College, and thereby the progress of learning hath been much obstructed, and the will of the roial founders in great measure frustrated,

XX. *Be it further enacted, by the authority aforesaid,* That the sum of two hundred pounds per annum, out of the said duty of one penny upon every gallon of wine, rum, brandy, and other distilled spirits, by this act imposed, as aforesaid, is and shall be appropriated for the relief of the said college; and for and during the said term of twenty-one years, shall be paid by the said treasurer, half-yearly, in equal portions, unto the surviving trustees of the said college, until the same shall be transferred to the president and masters; and from and after such transfer, then to the president and masters, and their successors, for and towards the maintaining and supporting the full number of masters and professors, which are to reside in the said college. —And if, at any time, there shall be no trustee of the said college, residing in this country, before such transfer shall be made, then the said sum of two hundred pounds shall be, in manner aforesaid, paid to the visitors and governors of the said college, or to such person as they shall appoint to receive the same: And after the said sum of two hundred pounds per anum shall be so satisfied, then the overplus of all monies arising from the said duty, shall be applied to such other use or uses, as the general assembly shall think fit to direct, as aforesaid.—Hening, *op. cit.*, IV, 148-49.

[108]

16. The Statutes of William and Mary College in Latin and
English, 1728

STATUTA COLLEGII

Gulielmi & Mariae,

I N

VIRGINIA.

Proœmium.

A D excolendos hominum animos & mores emendandos, quantam vim
habeant bonarum literarum, artiumque liberalium studia vel inde
constat, quod non solum olim apud *Hebræos, Ægyptios, Græcos,* &
Romanos, literarum politiorum studia viguerunt; sed etiam posteriori-
bus hisce seculis, eædem postquam Barbarorum incursionibus profli-
gatæ aliquamdiu a communi hominum consuetudine exulassent,
revocatæ sint, & apud plerasque Nationes in magno honore constitutæ.
Hinc errorum in re religionis reformatio; hinc juventutis ad officia
Virtutum christianarum & humanitatis institutio; hinc ad ecclesiæ &
reipublicæ munia obeunda virorum idoneorum præparatio. Nullibi
tamen apud Christianos ab ignorantia & barbarie magis periclitabatur
quam apud *Anglorum* Colonias in *America;* in quibus quippe primi
possessores duris laboribus in regione sylvis & vepribus obsita, & barbarorum incursionibus infesta, per multos annos vitam ægre admodum
sustinuerunt. Nullæ tum scholæ aperiebantur; nullæ educationis in
regionibus hisce dabatur opportunitas. Pauci admodum opulentiores

filios

THE
STATUTES
OF THE
COLLEGE
OF
WILLIAM *and* MARY,
IN
VIRGINIA.

The Preface

*T*owards *the cultivating the Minds of Men, and rectifying
their Manners, what a mighty Influence the Studies of good
Letters, and the liberal Sciences have, appears from hence, that these
Studies not only flourished of Old amongst those famous Nations the*
Hebrews, Egyptians, Greeks, *and* Romans; *but in the latter Ages
of the World likewise, after a great Interruption and almost Destruc-
tion of them, through the Incursions of the barbarous Nations, they
are at last retrieved, and set up with Honor in all considerable Nations.
Upon this there followed the Reformation of many Errors and
Abuses in the Point of Religion, and the Institution of Youth to the
Duties of Christian Virtues and Civility; and a due Preparation of
fit Persons for all Offices in Church and State. But no where was
there any greater Danger on Account of Ignorance and want of
Instruction, than in the* English *Colonies of* America; *in which the
first Planters had much to do, in a Country over-run with Woods
and Briers, and for many Years infested with the Incursions of the
barbarous* Indians, *to earn a mean Livelyhood with hard Labor. There
were no Schools to be found in those Days, nor any Opportunity
for good Education. Some few, and very few indeed, of the richer*

Sort,

[110]

filios in *Angliam* educationis ergo ablegabant: Illicque post longæ navigationis & varia ab hostibus pericula, cum cæli solique mutatione conjuncta, in varios incidentes morbos, multi morbillus & aliis morbis morte prærepti sunt. Ingens interea ingeniorum omnisque literaturæ defectus surrepserat, & nova hominum succreverat generatio, pejor avis, quæ si prima legendi & scribendi rudimenta didicerat, nullum ulterius cum musis commercium habebat; sed vitam ignobilem inter ligones & rastra, cæteraque instrumenta rustica solum transigebat. Restabat tamen nonullum semen virorum qui saniora concilia in educatione juventutis, aut ipsi experti fuerant, aut ab aliis acceperant; horum privatis primum inter se colloquiis, postea cum pluribus re communicata, specimen quoddam collegii exaratum, ac Præsidi & Concilio exhibitum fuit Anno Dom' 1690; paulo ante adventum Vice-gubernatoris *Nicholsoni*, & ab ipsis proximo Conventui generali cum laude commendatum. Hoc opus sic bene cæptum progressum fecit non mediocrem sub Vice-gubernatore *Nicholsono*. Nam quamvis concilio Gubernatoris supremi, Domini *Howardi Effinghamii*, tunc in *Anglia* absentis, diu retardatus, nullum convocaverat Conventum generalem ante annum milesimum sexcentesimum nonagesimum primum; non tamen interea cessaverat disignatum opus Collegii; ipse enim & Concilium per Brevia, ut vocant, subscriptiones incolarum ad promovendum opus illud pium invitaverant. Brevia isthæc a Præfecto & Concilio commissa curæ *Jacobi Blair*, (qui tunc nuper constitutus fureat Commissarius Episcopi *Londinensis*, quique ab initio operi huic diligenter incubuerat) & paucis aliis verbi Dei ministris, subscriptiones ad valorem duarum mille librarum monetæ *Anglicanæ* procurarunt. Has excipiebat Conventus generalis in *Virginia* celeberrimus Anno 1691. Conventus hic, postquam specimen istud Collegii, tanquam *Virginiæ* aptissimum approbaverant, eundem *Jacobum Blair* Agentem & Oratorem suum constituentes, ipsum cum humili Supplicatione ad Regem *Gulielmum* & Reginam *Mariam* in *Angliam* delegarunt, orantes

ut

[111]

Sort, sent their Children to England *to be educated. And there, after many Dangers from the Seas and Enemies, and unusual Distempers, occasioned by the Change of Country and Climate, they were often taken off by the Small-pox, and other Diseases. It was no Wonder if this occasioned a great Defect of Understanding, and all Sort of Literature, and that it was followed with a new Generation of Men, far short of their Fore-Fathers, which, if they had the good Fortune, tho' at a very indifferent Rate, to read and write, had no further Commerce with the Muses, or learned Sciences; but spent their Life ignobly at the Hoe and Spade, and other Employments of an uncultivated and unpolished Country. There remained still notwithstanding, a small Remnant of Men of better Spirit, who had either had the Benefit of better Education themselves in their Mother-Country, or at least had heard of it from others. These Men's private Conferences among themselves being communicated to greater Numbers in the like Circumstances, produced at last a Scheme of a Free-School and College, which was by them exhibited to the President and Council, in the Year* 1690; *a little before the Arrival of Lieutenant-Governor* Nicholson, *which was afterwards recommended by them with Applause to the next ensuing General Assembly. This Work so luckily begun, made a very considerable Progress under his Government. For, altho' being tied up by Injunctions from my Lord* Effingham, *Chief Governor, who was then in* England, *he was not allowed to call an Assembly so soon as he would, yet that designed good Work did not sleep in the mean Time; for in that Interval of Assemblies he and the Council sent out Briefs, by which, and their own good Example, they invited and encouraged the Subscriptions of the Inhabitants. These Briefs were recommended to the Care and Management of Mr. Commissary* Blair, *a Minister, who had been one of the first Projectors of this good Work, and was a little before this made Commissary to the Bishop of* London; *with the Help of his Surrogats some of the most creditable Ministers of the Country, and brought in Subscriptions to the Value of Two Thousand Pounds Sterling. Upon this followed that famous General Assembly of the Year* 1691. *This Assembly not only approved that Scheme of a College, as well fitted to this Country, but resolved upon an humble Petition to* King William *and* Queen Mary, *for a Charter to impower*
certain

[112]

ut facultas & licentia concederetur quibusdam fiduciariis ab ipsis no-
minatis, ad fundandum ejusmodi collegium; utque ad sumptus in fundatione & edificatione ejusdem requisitos, & alendos Præsidem &
Magistros impendendos, regia munificentia adjutarentur. *Blairus* non
segniter provinciam hanc administravit, & propensos ad tam bonum
opus Regis & Reginæ animos reperiens, fretus etiam præcipue opera
& patrocinio D. *Tillotsoni*, Archi-episcopi *Cantuariensis*, & D. *Comp-
toni*, Episcopi *Londinensis* aliisque ad bona opera promovenda pro-
pensis Episcopis, quibus tum ecclesia *Anglicana* abundabat; post varias
Difficultates & obstacula non pauca, biennio in legatione ista ab-
sumpto, diploma tandem regium quo fundaretur collegium, pecuniam
etiam & varia dona in ædificationem ejusdem, & alendos Præsidem, &
Magistros, seu Professores obtinuit, & ad opus perficiendum, tum
Præses constitutus, fortiter sese accinxit. Sed in *Virginiam* reversus
in multo majores in operis progressu incurrit difficultates, cum quibus
per multos annos sibi colluctandum sensit. Sed omnia ista libenter
prætereuntes (quæ Collegii eversionem minitabantur, presertim postquam incendio ædificiis & bibliotheca subito destructis, nil restabat
pecuniæ, unde reædificationis sumptus exsolverentur, ni patientia &
frugalitate in reservandis Collegii reditibus & Reginæ *Annæ* munificentia, tantum opus tandem cum laude consummatum fuisset) ad id
quod nunc præ manibus est procedamus; Obstructionibus cunctis jam
prope remotis, nihil magis necessarium esse videtur, quam ut secundum Concilium reverendissimi Cancellarii nostri D. *Wake*, Archi-
episcopi *Cantuariensis*, regulæ & statuta ad bene gubernandum
Collegium, omnesque tam Præsidem & Magistros, quam Discipulos
aliosque intra illud inhabitantes, aut res ejusdem foras procurantes,
post maturam cum D. Cancellario deliberationem conficiantur & præ-
scribantur. Quoniam autem multa progressu temporis magis expedi-
entia reperientur, cum Collegium a parvis initiis, ad majorem
pervenerit perfectionem; nonnulla etiam corrigenda & immutanda
pro statu casuum & circumstantiarum quæ tunc existent; omnia ejusmodi Visitatoribus & Gubernatoribus, pro tempore existentibus, ad-
denda, minuenda, seu mutanda pro vario Academiæ statu, & linguarum,

&

[113]

certain Trustees that they named, to found such a College, and that their Majesties would likewise assist in the Funds necessary for building the Edifices, and maintaining the President and Masters. To deliver this Petition, and to negotiate this whole Affair, they made Mr. Blair *their Agent to sollicit it at the Court of* England. *Tho' both the King and Queen were exceeding well inclined, and the good Bishops, especially Dr.* Tillotson, *Archbishop of* Canterbury, *and Dr.* Compton, *Bishop of* London, *gave all Assistance; and Mr.* Blair *followed it with Diligence and Dexterity, it was a long time before all the Difficulties, which were objected, were got over. But at last, after Two Years spent in that Service, an ample Charter was obtained, with several Gifts, both for Building and Endowment, for paying the President's and Masters Salaries; and Mr.* Blair, *by Advice of the General Assembly in* Virginia, *and the Bishops in* England, *being made President of the College, returned to see all put in Execution. In which for many Years afterwards he was involved in a great Number of Difficulties, some of which threatened the total Subversion of the Design. Especially when in the Year* 1705, *the Buildings and Library were destroyed by Fire; and there was no Money to repair the Loss. Yet at Length, by Patience and good Husbandry of the Revenues, and the Bounty of Queen* Anne, *the Work was finished a second Time to every one's Admiration. But to go on to another necessary Branch of this Design, which we are now about, other Obstructions being in good Measure removed, there seems to be nothing more necessary than that, according to the Advice of our most Reverend Chancellor Dr.* Wake, *Archbishop of* Canterbury, *some Rules and Statutes should be made for the good Government of the College, and of the President, and Masters, and Scholars, and all others, that either live in it, or are employed in the Management of its Affairs abroad, after mature Deliberation with the said Lord Archbishop, our Chancellor. But because in Progress of Time many Things will be found to be more expedient, when from small Beginnings the College shall have come to greater Perfection; and some Things too will want to be corrected and altered, as future Cases and Circumstances may require: All these Things we are very willing to leave to the Visitors and Governors, for the Time being, to be added, diminished and changed, according to the different Circumstances*

of

[114]

& artium studia promovendo, secundum potestatem & authoritatem in Charta collegii fundatoria ipsis concessam, haud gravate relinquimus. Tantum ne quid temere sub disputationis adore statuatur aut immutetur, volumus ut nullum novum Statutum inactitatum aut præscriptum sit, nisi postquam in duobus Gubernatorum Academiæ conventibus debite propositum, lectum, & consideratum fuerit.

De Senatu Academico.

DE numero authoritate & potestate Senatus Academici in eligendo Cancellario, præside & magistris, & legibus academicis præscribendis & mutandis satis in Charta fundatoria Academiæ explicatum est. Unde apparet quantum in ipsis momenti sit, & quantum bona ipsorum electio ad probam collegii gubernationem conducat.

In electione igitur omnium Academiæ visitatorum & gubernatorum præferantur, qui moribus probi, doctrina secundum reformatam ecclesiam *Anglicanam* sani, academicæ & politioris literaturæ patroni, & cives ditiores, qui patrocinio suo, collegio, si opus sit, inservire possint.

Caveat Senatus academicus ne ullæ vel inter seipsos, vel inter præsidem & magistros dissensiones, seu partium studia foveantur; curetque ut omnia quiete & moderate & absque ulla erga quemvis gratia aut odio transigantur.

Authoritatem ordinariam præsidis & magistrorum in administrando quotidiano regimine academiæ tueantur & supportent, & querimonias ordinarias domesticas ad ipsos referant; nec nisi in extraordinariis, ubi dignus vindice nodus, aut corruptio aliqua reformanda, aut Statutum novum condendum, aut aliud quidpiam magni momenti transigendum est, molestiam sibi fieri permittant.

In electione Præsidis, & Magistrorum seu Professorum, præcipuam doctrinæ, pietatis, sobrietatis, prudentiæ, morum probitatis, ordinis & disciplinæ observantiæ, & ingenii pacifici considerationem habeant, &

absque

[115]

of the College, for promoting the Study of the learned Languages, and liberal Arts, according to the Powers granted them by the College Charter. Only that nothing may be enacted rashly, in the Heat of Disputation, no old Statute suddenly changed, or new One made; we recommend it for a Rule in these Matters, that no new Statute be enacted or prescribed, until it has been duly proposed, read and considered at Two several Meetings of the Governors of the College.

CONCERNING THE COLLEGE SENATE.

As to the number, *Authority, and Power of the College Senate, in chusing the Chancellor, and the President, and Masters, and in appointing and changing of Statutes, all this is sufficiently set forth in the College Charter. From whence it is evident, how much depends upon them, and how far a good Election of them conduces to the good Government of the College.*

Therefore in the Election of all Visitors and Governors of the College, let such be preferred as are Persons of good Morals, and found in the Doctrine of the reformed Church of England; *and Friends and Patrons of the College and polite Learning; and Gentlemen in good Circumstances, such as by their Interest, if there be Occasion, can patronize and serve the College.*

Let the College Senate beware, that no Differences or Parties be held up and cherished, either amongst themselves, or the President and Masters; and let them take Care that all Things be transacted quietly and moderately, without Favor or Hatred to any Person whatsoever.

Let them maintain and support the ordinary Authority of the President and Masters in the Administration of the daily Government of the College, and let them refer all common domestick Complaints to them: And not suffer themselves to be troubled, except in Matters of great Moment, where there is some Difficulty to be got over, or some Corruption or ill Practice to be reformed, or a new Statute to be made, or some other weighty Business to be transacted.

In the Election of a President or Masters, let them have a principal Regard to their Learning, Piety, Sobriety, Prudence, good Morals, Orderliness and Observance of Discipline, and that they be of a
quiet

[116]

absque personarum respectu tales in loca vacantia eligant.

De Cancellario.

CANCELLARIUS est velut Academiæ *Mecænas*, aut patronus, qui res ipsius apud regem gratia, & apud omnes alios authoritate in *Anglia* administrare possit. Ejus præcipue in omnibus arduis Academiæ negotiis in *Anglia* transigendis Consilium adhibendum est. Si ulli ad Regem aut Reginam libelli supplices ab Academia transmittantur, per Cancellarium præsententur.

Si novo Præside, vel Professore, aut Magistro, ex *Britannia* Academiæ opus erit, ipsius ope & concilio, & recommendatione Senatus Academicus præcipue nitatur.

De Præside, & Magistris, & Scholis.

TRIA sunt quæ fundatores Collegii hujus sibi proposuerunt, ad quæ Statuta ejus omnia respicere & collimare debebant. Primum estut *Virginiæ* juventus in bonis moribus & literis probe educetur. Secundum, ut ecclesia *Americana*, præcipue *Virginiensis* bonis pastoribus, secundum doctrinam & ritus ecclesiæ *Anglicanæ*, tanquam ex seminario debite suppeditetur. Tertium, ut *Indi Americani* in religione Christiana instruantur, & ut ex ipsis quidam maxime probis moribus imbuti, & in schola theologica prius præparati, ad prædicandum Evangelium apud suos, lingua ipsorum propria dimittantur, postquam rite in diaconos & presbyteros ordinati fuerint.

Ad hos tam præclaros fines assequendos, quatuor scholæ intra collegii hujus limites assignentur, de quibus, cum Magistris, seu professoribus, ad easdem pertinentibus, nonnulla decernenda sunt.

[117]

quiet and peaceable Spirit; and let them chuse such Persons into the vacant Places without Respect of Persons.

OF THE CHANCELLOR.

T HE CHANCELLOR IS TO BE *the* Meccœnas *or Patron of the College, such a One as by his Favor with the King, and by his Interest with all other Persons in* England, *may be enabled to help on all the College Affairs. His Advice is to be taken, especially in all such arduous and momentous Affairs, as the College shall have to do in* England. *If the College has any Petitions at any Time to the King or Queen, let them be presented by their Chancellor.*

If the College wants a new President, or Professor, or Master, out of Great-Britain, *let the College Senate rely chiefly on his Assistance, Advice, and Recommendation.*

CONCERNING THE PRESIDENT, AND MASTERS, AND SCHOOLS.

T HERE ARE THREE THINGS *which the Founders of this College proposed to themselves, to which all its Statutes should be directed. The First is, That the Youth of* Virginia *should be well educated to Learning and good Morals. The Second is, That the Churches of* America, *especially* Virginia, *should be supplied with good Ministers after the Doctrine and Government of the Church of* England; *and that the College should be a constant Seminary for this Purpose. The Third is, That the* Indians *of* America *should be instructed in the Christian Religion, and that some of the* Indian *Youth that are well-behaved and well-inclined, being first well prepared in the Divinity School, may be sent out to preach the Gospel to their Countrymen in their own Tongue, after they have duly been put in Orders of Deacons and Priests.*

For carrying on these noble Designs, let there be Four Schools assigned within the College Precincts; of which, together with the Masters, or Professors, belonging to them, some Directions must be given.

[118]

Schola Grammaticalis.

A<small>D</small> hanc scholam pertinent Ludi-magister, & si numerus discipulo-
rum id requirit, hypodidascalus. Ludi-magister est unus e sex
Magistris, e quibus cum Præside & Scholaribus Collegium consistit;
non item hypodidascalus. Pro salario annuo solvantur Ludi-magistro,
centum & quinquaginta libræ monetæ *Anglicanæ;* & ab unoquoque
discipulo viginti solidi ejusdem monetæ, quando nullus est hypodidascalus. Sin vero hypodidascalus sit quoque in ista Schola, quindecem
solidi solvantur Ludi-magistro, & quinque hypodidascalo. Pro salario
annuo solvantur hypodidascalo septuaginta quinque libræ monetæ
Anglicanæ. A pauperioribus tamen, qui Academiæ sumptibus aluntur,
nihil a Ludi-magistro vel hypodidascalo exigatur, sed gratis instruantur.

In hac schola grammaticali linguæ latina & græca accurate doceantur. Pro rudimentis, grammaticis, & authoribus ut vocantur classicis,
utrisque linguæ, iisdem volumus utantur libris, qui lege vel consuetudine in scholis *Angliæ* obtinent. Permittimus tamen Ludi-magistro,
ut si quas habet in grammaticam latinam vel græcam, aut in authores,
quiillic præleguntur, observationes, easdem assentiente, vel saltem non
repugnante Præside, scholaribus dictare liceat. Diligenter caveat Ludi-
magister ne cujusvis, quantumvis probati authoris, partem aliquam
discipulis prælegat, quæ contra pietatem aut bonos mores ipsis quidpiam insinuet.

Morum etiam præcipua erit cura, ut nemo scholarium mentiri,
jurare, obscæne quidpiam loqui vel facere, pugnare, alea vel foliis
lusoriis ludere, compotare, vel aliud quidpiam contra bonos mores
facere audeat; utque omnes ejusmodi culpæ facilius detegantur, fidissi-
mos eliget & constituet observatores Ludi-magister publicos, qui ad
ipsum omnia deferant, & pro culpæ merito disciplina utatur æqua,
absque ullo personarum respectu.

Hypodidascalus, quoad methodum docendi & scholæ regimen, in
omnibus,

[119]

THE GRAMMAR SCHOOL.

To THIS SCHOOL *belongs a School-Master; and if the Number of Scholars requires it, an Usher. The School-Master is One of the Six Masters, of whom, with the President, and Scholars, the College consists. But the Usher is not reckoned a Member of that Body. Let there be paid in yearly Salary to the School-Master, One Hundred and Fifty Pounds* Sterling, *and Twenty Shillings* Sterling *from each Scholar, by the Year, when there is no Usher. But if there be an Usher too in that School, let Fifteen Shillings be paid to the Master, and Five to the Usher; and for a yearly Salary, let there be paid to the Usher, Seventy-five Pounds* Sterling. *But from the poor Scholars, who are upon any charitable College Foundation, neither the Master, nor Usher, are to take any School Wages; but they are to be taught* Gratis.

In this Grammar School let the Latin *and* Greek *Tongues be well taught. As for Rudiments and Grammars, and Classick Authors of each Tongue, let them teach the same Books which by Law or Custom are used in the Schools of* England. *Nevertheless, we allow the School-master the Liberty, if he has any Observations on the* Latin *or* Greek *Grammars, or any of the Authors that are taught in his School, that with the Approbation of the President, he may dictate them to the Scholars. Let the Master take Special Care, that if the Author is never so well approved on other Accounts, he teach no such Part of him to his Scholars, as insinuates any thing against Religion and good Morals.*

Special Care likewise must be taken of their Morals, that none of the Scholars presume to tell a Lie, or curse or swear, or talk or do any Thing obscene, or quarrel and fight, or play at Cards or Dice, or set in to Drinking, or do any Thing else that is contrary to good Manners. And that all such Faults may be so much the more easily detected, the Master shall chuse some of the most trusty Scholars for public Observators, to give him an Account of all such Transgressions, and according to the Degrees of Heinousness of the Crime, let the Discipline be used without Respect of Persons.

As to the Method of teaching, and of the Government of the School,

[120]

omnibus, tanquam superiori, Ludi-magistro morem gerito.

Diebus *Saturni* & profestis, lectio præscribatur sacra ex *Castalionis* dialogis aut *Buchanani* psalmorum paraphrasi, aut quocunque alio libro pio a Præside & Ludi-magistro saltem comprobato, pro captu puerorum, quæ diebus *Lunæ* & post festa mane reddatur.

Curabit etiam Ludi-magister ut catechismum *Anglicanum* lingua vulgari omnes addiscant; provectiores etiam lingua latina.

Priusquam ad scholam philosophicam promoveantur, si qui ad privilegia & reditus scholarium aspirant, examen prius subeant coram Præside, & Magistris, seu Professoribus, aut Pastoribus, & quibusvis aliis linguarum peritis, utrum debitos in lingua latina & græca progressus fecerint. Idem quoque examen habeatur de ipsorum progressu in studio philosophiæ prius quam ad scholam theologicam promoveantur. Et nemo ignavus aut ingenio tardiori in scholarem eligatur.

Sin ampliores sint scholarium proventus quam ut tribus philosophiæ & totidem theologiæ candidatis sussicere possint, quod reliquum est in incipientes in schola grammaticali impendatur.

Schola Philosophica.

QUANDOQUIDEM meliores in philosophia progressus nunc indies videmus quam quos exhibuerunt *Artistotelis* logica & physica, quæ tam diu in scholis, omnibus aliis exclusis, solæ regnarunt, idcirco Præsidi & magistris relinquimus, consulto tamen prius Domino Cancellario, quæ logicæ, physicæ, ethicæ, & mathematicæ, systemata in scholis doceantur. Volumus etiam ut præter disputationes, exerceantur juvenes studiosi in orationibus & thematibus variis, sed non e sacro textu desumptis. Hæc scilicet scholæ theologicæ relinquimus.

In schola philosophica duos magistros seu professores constituimus, qui pro salario annuo octoginta libras monetæ *Anglicanæ* singuli accipiant, & ab unoquoque discipulo viginti solidos per annum; exceptis
pauperioribus,

[121]

School, let the Usher be obedient to the Master in every Thing, as to his Superior.

On Saturdays *and the Eves of Holidays, let a sacred Lesson be prescribed out of* Castalio's *Dialogues, or* Buchanan's *Paraphrase of the Psalms, or any other good Book which the President and Master shall approve of, according to the Capacity of the Boys, of which an Account is to be taken on* Monday, *and the next Day after the Holidays.*

The Master shall likewise take Care that all the Scholars learn the Church of England *Catechism in the vulgar Tongue; and that they who are further advanced learn it likewise in* Latin.

Before they are promoted to the Philosophy School, they who aim at the Privileges and Revenue of a Foundation Scholar, must first undergo an Examination before the President and Masters, and Ministers skilful in the learned Languages; whether they have made due Progress in their Latin *and* Greek. *And let the same Examination be undergone concerning their Progress in the Study of Philosophy, before they are promoted to the Divinity School. And let no Blockhead or lazy Fellow in his Studies be elected*

If the Revenues of the College for the Scholars, are so well beforehand, that they are more than will serve Three Candidates in Philosophy, and as many in Divinity, then what is left let it be bestowed on Beginners in the Grammar School.

The Philosophy School.

F OR AS MUCH AS *we see now daily a further Progress in Philosophy, than could be made by* Aristotle's *Logick and Physicks, which reigned so long alone in the Schools, and shut out all other; therefore we leave it to the President and Masters, by the Advice of the Chancellor, to teach what Systems of Logick, Physicks, Ethicks, and Mathematicks, they think fit in their Schools. Further we judge it requisite, that besides Disputations, the studious Youth be exercised in Declamations and Themes on various Subjects, but not any taken out of the Bible. Those we leave to the Divinity School.*

In the Philosophy School we appoint Two Masters or Professors, who for their yearly Salary shall each of them receive Eighty Pounds Sterling, and Twenty Shillings Sterling a Year from each Scholar, ex-

cept

[122]

pauperioribus, qui Academiæ aluntur expensis; hi enim gratis instituentur.

Magistrorum istorum alter rhetoricam, logicam & ethicam, docebit; alter physicam, metaphysicam, & mathematicam.

Et quo his studiis magis alacriter incumbat juventus Academica, & ad honores aspiret, pro forma & institutione cleberrimarum in *Anglia* Academiarum, quatuor annos assignamus, priusquam gradum Baccalaurii, & septem priusquam lauream magistralem assequantur.

Schola Theologica.

IN hac schola duo sint professores cum salario annuo utrique centum & quinquaginta librarum monetæ *Anglicanæ*; & nihil a studentibus, seu theologiæ candidatis exigatur.

Professorum alter doceat linguam *Hebræam*, & critice exponat sensum literalem S. Scripturæ tam veteris quam novi Testamenti.

Alter explicet locos communes theologiæ, & controversias cum quibusvis hæretecis; & de iisdem lectiones & disputationes habeat.

Inter hos duos studiorum tempora partiantur studiosi theologiæ.

Schola Indica.

IN hac Schola unus Magister *Indorum* pueros doceat legere, scribere, & vulgarem arithmeticam. Præcipue catechismum, & christianæ religionis institutiones diligenter inculcet. Pro salario habeat quadraginta aut quinquaginta libras monetæ *Anglicanæ*, secundum Facultates ejusdem scholæ a prænobili *Roberto Boyle* assignatas, aut ab aliis Benefactoribus postea assignandas. In eadem schola liceat ipsi quoque alios ex urbe docere discipulos, & mercedem pro isto opere solitam viginti solidorum per annum exigere.

[123]

cept such poor Ones as are entertained at the College Charge, upon the Foundations; for they are to be taught Gratis.

One of these Masters shall teach Rhetorick, Logick, and Ethicks. The other Physicks, Metaphysicks, and Mathematicks.

And that the Youth of the College may the more chearfully apply themselves to these Studies, and endeavour to rise to the Academic Degrees, we do, according to the Form and Institution of the Two famous Universities in England, *allot Four Years before they attain to the Degree of Bachelor, and Seven Years before they attain the Degree of Master of Arts.*

THE DIVINITY SCHOOL.

I N THIS SCHOOL *let there be Two Professors, with a Salary of One Hundred and Fifty Pounds* Sterling *to each; they are to have nothing from the Students or Candidates of Theology.*

Let one of these Professors teach the Hebrew *Tongue, and critically expound the literal Sense of the Holy Scripture both of the Old and New Testament.*

Let the other explain the common Places of Divinity, and the Controversies with Hereticks; and let them have Prelections and Disputations on those Subjects.

And let the Students of Divinity divide their Time betwixt those Two Professors.

THE *INDIAN* SCHOOL.

T HERE IS BUT *One Master in this School who is to teach the* Indian *Boys to read, and write, and vulgar Arithmetick. And especially he is to teach them thoroughly the Catechism and the Principles of the Christian Religion. For a yearly Salary, let him have Forty or Fifty Pounds* Sterling, *according to the Ability of that School, appointed by the Honorable* Robert Boyle, *or to be further appointed by other Benefactors. And in the same School the Master may be permitted to teach other Scholars from the Town, for which he is to take the usual Wages of Twenty Shillings a Year.*

[124]

De Præside.

UT muneri quisque suo diligentius incumbat, præter sex Professores seu Magistros, Præsidem cæterorum Supervisorem constituimus. In Præsidem eligatur quidam vir gravis, in sacris ordinibus constitutus, vitæ inculpatæ, & famæ honestæ, & non minus triginta annis natus. Beneficiorum ecclesiasticorum cum cura animarum, non nisi unicum possidebit; idque tam prope a Collegio distans, ut ordinariam Academiæ curam non impediat. Electio ipsius Collegii Gubernatoribus committatur. Præter doctrinam & mores inculpatos curandum est ut sit prudens, peritus, & in negotiis procurandis industrius ac diligens; ac in omnibus honorem & commoda Academiæ suis aut aliorum quorumcunque semper præferat. Cæteris Magistris & professoribus diligenter invigilet, ut muneribus suis non desint. Scholares coram ipso sæpius Professores & Magistri examinent; eosdem ipse etiam seorsim a Præceptoribus sæpius examinabit, ut ad majorem in studiis diligentiam tam Præceptores quam discipuli excitentur. In explicatione quoque S. Scripturæ aut in themate quodam theologico aut controversia aliqua adversus temporis cujusque hæreticos, lectionem theologicam quater in anno habeat. Et curet ut duo reliqui Professores theologici suas lectiones & disputationes diligenter obeant. Collegii reditus & expensas diligenter inspiciat, & curet ut semel saltem quotannis finale computum omnium redituum & expensarum perficiatur, &, si opus est, Visitatoribus & Gubernatoribus in conventu ipsorum generali exhibeatur. Commercio epistolico de Statu & Negotiis Collegii cum omnibus & præcipue cum Cancellario de tempore in tempus incumbat. Conventus ordinarios instituat, & in iisdem præsit, & ut accurate a scriba sensus Conventus in libros transcribatur, omnia ab ipso exscripta prius relegat, & si opus est, errata corrigat, & omissa restituat. Utque ædificia debite reparentur, & sustineantur provide curabit. Utque plenius de omnibus Collegii negotiis informari possint

Visitatores

[125]

CONCERNING THE PRESIDENT.

THAT EVERY ONE *may so much the more diligently wait upon his proper Office, besides the Six Professors or Masters, we have appointed a President to be Supervisor of the rest. Let there be chosen for a President, a Man of Gravity, that is in Holy Orders, of an unblemished Life, and good Reputation, and not under Thirty Years of Age. Of Ecclesiastical Benefices that have a Cure of Souls annexed, he shall not possess above One, and that of so near a Distance from the College, that it may not hinder his ordinary Care and Attendance upon the College. Let the Election of him be entrusted with the Governors of the College. Besides Learning, and an unblemished good Life, Care must be taken that he be a Man of Prudence, and skilful in Business, and industrious and diligent in the Management of all Affairs; always preferring the Honor and Interest of the College, to his own or any other Person's Concerns. Let him have a watchful Eye over the other Masters and Professors, that they be not absent from their Employments. Let the Masters often examine the Scholars in his Presence; and let him likewise often examine them a-part from their Masters, that both Masters and Scholars may be excited to greater Diligence in their Studies. Let him likewise have a Theological Lecture Four Times a Year in the Explication of Scripture, or some Theological Subject, or on some Controversy against Hereticks. And let him take Care that the other Two Professors diligently attend their Lectures and Disputations. Let him diligently inspect into the Revenues and Expences of the College, and see that once a Year at least a full Account be perfected of all Receipts and Issues; and that if there be Occasion for it, it be laid before the Visitors and Governors at their General Meeting. Whatever Business of the College requires Epistolary Commerce with any Persons, he must take Care to write about it, especially to the Chancellor. He is to appoint the Time for the ordinary Meetings of himself and the Masters, at which he is to preside. And to the End, that all Things past at these Meetings may be truly entered in Books by the Scribe of the Meeting, the President shall first read over the Minutes, and if there be Occasion, correct the Errors and Omissions: He must provide in due Time that the Edifices be duly kept up and repaired. And that the Visitors and Governors of the College may be*

[126]

Visitatores & Gubernatores, Præses eorum consessibus & conciliis intersit.

Præsidi in salarium annuum ducenæ libræ monetæ *Anglicanæ* assignentur, cum domo & horto Statui ipsius conveniente quam primum Collegii reditus omnes istiusmodi sumptus suppeditare poterint.

De Gubernatione Collegii ordinaria.

GUBERNATIO Collegii ordinaria sit penes Præsidem & sex Magistros; duos scilicet Professores theologicos, duos philosophicos, duos etiam scholæ grammaticalis, & scholæ *Indicæ* Ludi-magistros. Potestas convocandi, prorogandi, & dimittendi istiusmodi Conventus sit penes Præsidem. Quod ad negotia in ejusmodi Conventibus tractanda, in primis curabunt ut omnia Academiæ Statuta diligenter executioni mandentur. Si quæ incommoda Statuta correctione aut immutatione egeant hæc omnia cum desideratis emendationibus Conventui generali Gubernatorum & Visitatorum modeste proponant, eorumque deliberationi submittant. Querimoniæ omnes, queis præceptores singuli in scholis suis obviam ire nequeunt, huc deferantur, primo sc. ad præsidem; & ab illo ad Conventum Magistrorum. Nominatio & electio omnium officiariorum ad negotia Academiæ necessariorum, Hypodidascali sc. in schola grammaticali, bursarii, bibliothecarii, ostiarii, coqui, mancipis, & hortulani, opificum quoque ad ædificationes aut reparationes requisitorum, eorum etiam qui artem scribendi docent, sit penes ipsos. In negotiis tamen minoribus sufficiat Præsidis mandatum, verbo tenus pronunciatum. Si quæ Statuta debitis pænis aut mulctis non muniantur, istiusmodi pænarum aut mulctarum appunctuatio ad Conventum hunc referatur. Omnia hic, quantum fieri potest, unanimiter, id si nequeat, suffragiorum majore numero transigantur. Si paria sint suffragia, qui a parte Præsidis sunt, pro majore numero habeantur.

In negotiis majoribus, præcipue ubi inter Præsidem & Magistros non bene convenit, consulatur Senatus Academicus, e Gubernatoribus & Visitatoribus constans, eorumque præscripto lites omnes majores determinentur.

[127]

be the better informed of every Thing relating to it, let the President be always allowed to be, and accordingly let him be present at all their Meetings and Councils.

Let the President's yearly Salary be Two Hundred Pounds Sterling, *with an House and Garden suitable to the Place, so soon as the College Revenues will bear all these Expences.*

Of the ordinary Government of the College.

LET THE ORDINARY *Government of the College be in the President and the Six Masters, viz. the Two Professors of Divinity; and the Two Professors of Philosophy, and the Master of the Grammar School, and the Master of the* Indian *School. Let the Power of calling, proroguing, and dismissing this Sort of Meetings be in the President. As to the Business to be treated of in these Meetings, in the first Place it must be their Care that all the Statutes of the College be diligently put in Execution. If any of the Statutes are found to be inconvenient, so as to want to be amended or changed, let them modestly propose all such desired Amendments to the General Meeting of the Visitors and Governors, and submit them to their Deliberation. Let all Complaints and Grievances, which the Masters in their particular Schools cannot redress, be brought first to the President, and by him to the Meeting of the Masters. To this Meeting belongs the Election and Nomination of all Officers that are necessary or requisite for the College Business, such as the Usher in the Grammar School, the Bursar, the Library-keeper, the Janitor, the Cook, the Butler, and Gardener, the Writing-master, the Workmen for building or repairing; Bailiffs and Overseers. But in lesser Matters the President's Order by Word of Mouth may suffice. If any of the Statutes are not backed and fortified with due Penalties and Mulcts, the setting of such Mulcts and Penalties is referred to this Meeting of the President and Masters. Let all things in this Meeting, if possible, be transacted unanimously; if that cannot be, let the Decision be by Plurality of Votes. If the Votes are equal, the Side on which the President is, shall be taken for the major Part.*

In all Business of great Weight and Consequence especially if the President and Masters cannot agree, let the College Senate, consisting of the Visitors and Governors, be consulted; and by their De-
termination

[128]

determinentur.

Præses & Magistri, ad evitandum omne hæresios, scismatis, aut per-
duellionis periculum, priusquam munera ista adeant, assensum dabunt
articulis fidei Christianæ eodem modo, & iisdem verbis quibus verbi
Dei ministri in ecclesia *Anglicana* statuto Parliamenti assentiri tenen-
tur articulis ecclesiæ *Anglicanæ*. Eodem modo quoque fidem præsta-
bunt Regi vel Reginæ pro tempore in *Anglia* regnantibus. Sacramento
etiam de fideli muneris administratione secundum Collegii Statuta
coram Præside & Magistris conscientias suas astringent, tactis S. S.
Evangeliis. Hæc omnia sub pæna privationis muneris & salarii.

De Scholaribus.

SCHOLARES duorum sunt generum; eorum scilicet qui propriis aluntur
expensis, & mercedem solvunt, in scholis, ubi Magistris sc. per-
mittitur mercedem a discipulis accipere; & aliorum qui Academiæ
aluntur expensis.

Quod ad prioris generis scholares, liberum relinquimus ipsorum
parentibus & guardianis utrum ad Collegii mensam, & intra Collegii
septa, an alibi in urbe aut prope Collegium in villa aliqua suburbana
victitent & contubernentur; cum enim consilium & intentio nostra sit,
ut quam minimo sumptu juventus literas humaniores, cæterasque artes
liberales & scientias addiscat. Si qui domos habent tam prope sitas, ut
inde convenienter campanæ Academiæ audiri, & publicæ studiorum
horæ observari possint, nolumus Statutis hisce nostris eos impedire quo
minus filios suos aut amicorum apud se alant, & hospitio accipiant.
Speramus tamen omnia intra Collegium tam bene accommodata fore,
ut non alibi melius, aut pretio minori contubernari possit.

Cubicula Collegii præterquam quæ Præsidi & Magistris, cæterisque
officiariis necessaria sunt mercede moderata pueris ditioribus & natu
majoribus allocentur. Pecunia inde proveniens in reparationem ædi-
ficorum Collegii impendatur.

E scholaribus eligantur quot secundum reditus in illum usum ap-
punctuatos

[129]

termination let all the greater Differences be decided.

For avoiding the Danger of Heresy, Schism, and Disloyalty, let the President and Masters, before they enter upon these Offices, give their Assent to the Articles of the Christian Faith, in the same Manner, and in the same Words, as the Ministers in England, *by Act of Parliament are obliged to sign the Articles of the Church of* England. *And in the same Manner too they shall take the Oaths of Allegiance to the King or Queen of* England. *And further, they shall take an Oath that they will faithfully discharge their Office, according to the College Statutes, before the President and Masters, upon the Holy Evangelists. All this under the Penalty of being deprived of their Office and Salary.*

Of the Scholars.

THERE ARE TWO *Sorts of Scholars; one is of them who are maintained at their own Charge, and pay School Wages in the Schools where the Masters are allowed to take Wages as above; the other Sort is of those who are maintained at the College's Charge.*

As to the First Sort of Scholars, we leave their Parents and Guardians at Liberty whether they shall lodge and eat within the College or elsewhere in the Town, or any Country Village near the Town. For it being our Intention that the Youth, with as little Charge as they can, should learn the learned Languages and the other liberal Arts and Sciences: If any have their Houses so near the College, that from thence the College Bells can be heard, and the public Hours of Study be duly observed, we would not by these our Statutes hinder them from boarding their own Children, or their Friends, or from lodging them at their own Houses. Nevertheless we hope that all Things relating to the Table or Lodging will be so well supplied within the College, that they can be no where cheaper or better accommodated.

Let the spare Chambers of the College, over and above what are necessary for the President and Masters, and other Officers of the College, be let out at moderate Rents to the better Sort of the big Boys; and let the Money they yield be laid out in the Reparation of the Edifices of the College.

Out of the Scholars let there be chosen to be put upon the Foundation,

[130]

punctuatos Collegium alere possit, qui deinceps in schola philosophica & theologica diligenter instituantur & alantur, usque dum ad sacros ordines, & ad munus ac officium aliquod in ecclesia promoti fuerint. In hujusmodi scholaribus eligendis, electio fiat per Senatum Academicum; & præcipua ratio habeatur inopiæ, ingenii, doctrinæ, pietatis, & morum probitatis. Et quo magis quis ex eligendorum numero in his excedit, eo magis, ut æquum est, præferatur.

De Bursario seu Thesaurario.

QUONIAM Collegii hujus status, in hac ipsius infantia, nondum admittit multos officiarios, qui forte auctioribus ipsius reditibus, & crescente Scholarium numero, postea necessarii erunt; idcirco regulas de mancipe, coquo, janitore, bibliothecario, hortulano, & cæteris Collegii officiariis, ad Præsidem & Magistros referentes, qui ipsorum officia & salaria ubi Collegio necessarii fuerint, præscribent, de unico Bursario regulæ quædam in præsens formandæ sunt.

Bursarii est diligenter & mature omnes Collegii reditus & proventus quoscunque colligere, & eosdem in arca bene munita asservare; salaria etiam Præsidi, Magistris, seu Professoribus, & Scholaribus debita omnesque alios Academiæ sumptus juste, & in tempore debito solvere; & pro omnibus apochas recipere. Horum omnium acceptorum sc. & expensorum computa libris computationum inserta exacte describantur, & a Præside & Magistris singulis semestribus examinata, exoneratio eorundem in iisdem libris sub Præsidis & Magistrorum nominibus annotetur.

Præses & Magistri virum ad opus hoc maxime aptum & idoneum, & qui solvendo est, datis quoque fide-jussoribus, de tempore in tempus eligent. Pro salario habebit, quicquid Senatui Academico æquum visum fuerit, habita laboris cujusque bursarii & meriti ratione, ultra omnes expensas, quas in refractariis cogendis, equis, aut nunciis, aut

attornatibus

[131]

tion, as many as the College can maintain out of the Funds allotted for that Purpose. And let them be thereafter diligently instructed and maintained, till they are put in Orders, and preferred to some Place and Office in the Church. The Election of this Sort of Scholars let it be in the Visitors; and in that Election let them chiefly regard besides their Poverty, their Ingeniousness, Learning, Piety, and good Behaviour, as to their Morals. And the more any one of the Candidates excells in these Things, he has so much the better Title to be preferred; and let him be preferred accordingly.

OF THE COLLEGE BURSAR OR TREASURER.

BECAUSE THE CIRCUMSTANCES *of the College in this its Infancy, will not as yet admit of many Officers, who perhaps when it comes to be richer in Revenues, and has a greater Number of Students, will become necessary: Therefore referring the Rules concerning the Butler, Cook, Janitor, Library-keeper, Gardener, and other Officers, to the President and Masters, who are to direct their Offices and Salaries, as the College shall find them useful and necessary; we shall only at present lay down some Rules concerning the Bursar or College Treasurer.*

It belongs to the Bursar timely and diligently to gather in all the College Revenues, or whatever else is due to it; and to keep the Money in a strong Chest. Likewise to pay to the President, Masters, or Professors, and the Foundation Scholars their several Salaries, and to pay all other College Debts and Expences honestly, and in due Time; and to take Discharges and Receipts for every Thing. Let the Accounts of all Incomes and Disbursements be exactly entered in Account Books; and after they are audited and examined once in Half a Year by the President and Masters, that Examination, and their Discharge shall be entered in the same Count-Books, signed by the President's and Masters Names.

Let the President and Masters from Time to Time chuse a Man fit for this Business, such a one as is responsible, and well able to pay, and who shall likewise give good Security. For Salary he shall have whatever the Meeting of the Visitors shall think reasonable, according to the Trouble and Desert of each Bursar, besides his Expences in suing at Law for any Debts due to the College, or any other

[132]

attornatibus conducendis, aut e longinquo, puta terra *Mariæ*, pecunia opportanda, aut recuperanda, solvere necessarium erit.

De Terminis observandis.

TERMINI in quibus aperiuntur scholæ grammaticalis & *Indica* tres sunto; terminus *Hilarii* incipiat die *Lunæ* post *Epiphaniam*; exeat vero die sabbati dominicam *Palmarum* precedente. Terminus *Paschæ* incipiat die *Lunæ* post dominicam in albis; exeat vero in vigilia diei dominicæ ante *Pentecosten*. Terminus Trinitatis incipiat die *Lunæ* post dominicam *Trinitatis*, & finiat *Decembris* decimo sexto. Eosdem terminos observent cæteræ scholæ; excepto solummodo quod scholæ Philosophicæ & Theologicæ ferias concedimus a festo S. *Jacobi* usque ad festum S. *Lucæ*. Quoniam vero frequenti examinatione efficitur ut discentium studia & progressus in bonarum artium disciplinis majorem in modum promoveantur, volumus ut in cujusque termini initio singularum scholarum & classium discipuli publice in aula congregati examinentur, quomodo profecerint in earum linguarum vel artium cognitione quibus studuerint, vel studere debuerint. Examinatores sunto Præses & Magistri; Pastores quoque vel alii quicunque viri docti, qui examinationibus istis interesse dignabuntur.

Quandoquidem proventus annui collegii in præsens tenuiores sunt quam ut omnibus supra constitutis salariis, cæterisque necessariis expendendis pares esse possint, multa discretioni gubernatorum Collegii de tempore in tempus relinquenda sunt, ut pro præsenti Collegii Statu quædam salaria Professoris sc. *Hæbrei* & Hypodidascali grammaticalis prorsus rescindant; aliorum vero Professorum & Magistrorum, secundum operis & residentiæ proportionem pro tempore minuant. Auctioribus vero Collegii proventibus plene & tempestive solvantur.

Nos infra subscripti *Jacobus Blair*, & *Stephanus Fouace*, Clerici, constituentes majorem partem fiduciariorum superviventium pro Academia *Gulielmi* & *Mariæ*, in *Virginia*, considerata necessitate condendi Statuta pro bona regimine ejusdem Collegii, prædicta Statuta duo-
decem

[133]

other Charges he has been out in Horses and Messages, or in recovering the College Dues, or carrying the Money from Maryland, *or any other very remote Place.*

OF THE TERMS TO BE KEPT.

LET THERE BE *Three Terms for opening the Grammar and the* Indian *School. Let* Hilary *Term begin the First* Monday *after* Epiphany, *and end on* Saturday *before Palm-Sunday. Let* Easter *Term begin on* Monday *after the First* Sunday *after* Easter; *and let it end in the Eve of the* Sunday *before* Whit-Sunday. *Let* Trinity *Term begin on* Monday *after* Trinity Sunday; *and end on the Sixteenth Day of* December. *Let the other Schools observe the same Terms; except only, that to the Philosophy and Divinity Schools we grant Vacation from St.* James's *Day to St.* Luke's. *And because by frequent Examination the Studies of Scholars are much promoted, we appoint that in the Begining of every Term the Scholars of all the Schools and the several Classes in them should be examined in Public, in the public Hall, what Progress they have made in the Knowledge of those Languages and Arts in which they have been studying or should have studied. Let the Examiners be the President and Masters; and likewise the Ministers, or any other learned Men that please to afford their Company at these Examinations.*

For as much as the yearly Income of the College at present is so small, that it cannot answer all the above appointed Salaries, and the other Things that there will be Occasion to expend; many Things are from Time to Time to be left to the Discretion of the Governors of the College; that according to the Circumstances of the College, for the Time being, they may entirely cut off some Salaries, particularly those of the Hebrew *Professor, and the* Usher *of the Grammar School; and for a Time may lessen the Salaries of some other Professors and Masters, in Proportion to their Service and Residence. But when the College Revenues increase, and will bear it, they are all to be fully and timely paid.*

We the Subscribers James Blair, *and* Stephen Fouace, *Clerks, being the major Part of the surviving Trustees for the College of* William *and* Mary, *in* Virginia, *having considered the Necessity there was to make Statutes for the good Government of the said College, do approve*

[134]

decem suprascriptis paginis contenta sub manu & Sigillis nostris approbamus & confirmamus, eademque Sigillo Academiæ muniri volumus:
Reservata tamen potestate quæ per chartam fundatoriam concessa est
Visitatoribus & Gubernatoribus ejusdem Collegii ut debite procedentes
nova Statuta addant, aut hæc ipsa immutent, prout res & occasio de
tempore in tempus requirent. In quibus tamen præsertim de rebus
arduis & majoris momenti consilium Cancellarii prius adhibendum esse
arbitramur. Dat. *Londini* 24 die *Junii*, Anno Domini millesimo septingentesimo vigesimo septimo.

Jacobus Blair.

L. S.

Stephanus Fouace.

L. S.

[135]

prove and confirm the aforesaid Statutes contained in the *Twelve above written Pages; and appoint them to be passed under the College Seal. Reserving notwithstanding the Power given by the Charter to the Visitors and Governors of the same College, namely, that proceeding regularly they may add new Statutes, or may even change these, as their Affairs and Circumstances from Time to Time shall require. As to which nevertheless, especially in the arduous Affairs of great Weight and Moment, we are of Opinion that the Chancellor's Advice should be first taken. Dated at London, *the 24th Day of* June, *in the Year of our Lord One Thousand Seven Hundred and Twenty Seven.*

James Blair.

Stephen Fouace.

---

* The Original is in Twelve great Sheets, under the College Seal.

[136]

The following regulations made by the Visitors were ordered to be printed immediately after the Statutes.

I. **T**HAT *all the Masters resident at the College do attend their respective Schools Day by Day (the usual Holidays and Vacation Times excepted.) And that the Divinity Professor do reside in the College.*

II. *That the President and Masters be directed to keep up a strict Discipline among the Scholars.*

III. *That no Repairs be made without the Consent of the President and Masters, and a Warrant to the Bursar for defraying the Charge thereof: Nor any Invoices made out without the like Consent.*

IV. *That each of the Masters, and Ushers, do provide Firing and Candles for their Chambers, at their own Expence. That they respectively pay Fifty Shillings per Annum for their Washing, if they wash in the College. That the Masters and Scholars keeping waiting Boys pay Five Pounds per Annum for their Board.*

V. *That for the future, if the Masters desire hot Suppers, they shall provide them at their own Expence.*

VI. *That the President and Masters take Care to provide proper Quantities of Wheat and Corn, at such Seasons when they may be purchased upon the easiest Terms; and that only one Sort of Bread be used for the Masters and Scholars.*

VII. *That one of the Masters, or the Usher, be always present with the Boys at Breakfast and Supper.*

F I N I S.

17. EDMUND GIBSON, BISHOP OF LONDON, IS APPOINTED CHANCELLOR OF THE COLLEGE OF WILLIAM AND MARY, 1729

OMNIBUS AD QUOS praesentes literae pervenerint Salutem. SCIATIS quod nos Rector, et Visitatores et Gubernatores Collegii GULIELMI et MARIAE in Virginia debite procedentes secundum Mandatum Nobis Officium in Charta fundatoria eiusdem Collegii, quoad Electionem et Nominationem Cancellarii singulis redeuntibus septenniis, prout in eadem Charta fundatoria, relatione inde habita, magis particulariter et expresse continetur; Quodque Reverendissimus in Christo Pater Guilielmus Archiepiscopus Cantuar(en)sis Officium Cancellarii praedicti, pro septem annis proxime elapsis, tenere et exercere dignatus fuerit ELEGIMUS, nominavimus et confirmavimus, Ac per praesentes Eligimus nominamus et confirmamus Reverendum in Christo Patrem Edmundum Episcopum Londinensem in Locum Cancellarii eiusdem Collegii Gulielmi et Mariae in Virginia, continuandum in eodem Officio pro septem annis nunc proxime sequentibus, et deinde quousque alius Cancellarius Collegii praedicti ad Officium illus debito modo electus et praefectus fuerit: Humillime supplicantes quatenus Officium illus Cancellarii Collegii praedicti tenere et exercere, idemque Collegium Favore et Patrocinio suo prosequi dignetur, IN CUIUS REI TESTIMO-NIUM Diploma hoc Sigillo Collegii munitum, Nominee et Jussu Senatus Academici Rector manu propria subscripsit. DAT. in CAMERA CONCIL(I) pridie Calend(as) Aprilis Anno Dom(ini) MDCCXXIX, et Regni GEORGII II. secundo.

Jacobus Blair. Rector.

Translation

To all whom these presents may come, Greetings.

Know that we, the Rector, and the Visitors and Governors of the College of William and Mary in Virginia, duly proceeding according to the duty assigned us in the founding charter of the same College with reference to the naming and electing of a Chancellor for seven year periods, as is more particularly and expressly stated in this same founding charter, after due consultation thereof; and inasmuch as the Most Reverend Father in Christ, William, Archbishop of Canterbury, deigned to hold and exercise the duty of the aforesaid Chancellor for the seven years just elapsed: We have chosen, named and confirmed and through these presents we choose, name and confirm the Reverend Father in Christ, Edmund, Bishop of London, in the position of Chancellor of the same College of William and Mary in Virginia, to be continued in the same office for the seven years next following, and henceforth until another Chancellor of the aforesaid College shall have been elected and installed in the required manner: most humbly beseeching that he deign to hold and exercise this office of Chancellor of the aforesaid College, and to bestow upon this same College his favor and patronage.

In testimony whereof, the Rector has signed with his own hand this diploma, protected by the seal of the College, in the name and at the order of the academic Senate.

Given in the Council chamber on the 31st day of March, in the year of our Lord, 1729, and in the second year of the reign of George II.

James Blair, Rector.

—The original of this document is the property of the Library of the College of William and Mary. Photocopy is in the Library of the University of North Carolina.

18. The General Assembly enacts legislation on the College, 1734

Whereas the college of William and Mary, in Virginia, consisting of a president, six masters, or professors, and one hundred scholars, more or less, graduates, or non-graduates, founded and endowed by William and Mary, of blessed memory, late king and queen of England, etc. by their roial charter, under the great seal of England, bearing date at Westminster, the eighth day of February, in the fourth year of their rein, and since encouraged and supported by several other gifts and donations hath, of late been much injured in its revenues, by divers frauds and abuses, particularly in the exportation of tobacco from hence, to other British plantations in America, without paying the duty of one penny per pound, imposed by a statute of the parliament of England, made in the twenty-fifth year of the reign of king Charles the second, which was granted by the said roial charter, among other things, to certain trustees therein appointed, for erecting building, and founding the said college, and since transferred by the survivors of them, pursuant to the charter, to the said president and masters; and in the exportation of skins and furs, without paying the several duties imposed by an act of the general assembly, of the fourth year of the reign of the late queen Anne, for the better support of the said college: So that, by the deficiency of those revenues, which fall short of the annual expence of the college, about one hundred and fifty pounds per annum, it is fallen much in debt, and that must increase, when the edifices and buildings thereunto belonging shall require repairs, which must necessarily be expected.

II. And, forasmuch as the supporting and encouraging so hopeful a work, is of the greatest importance to the people of this colony, for the advancement of learning, and the good education of their youth, wherein we have already seen some good effects, *Be it enacted, by the Lieutenant-Governor, Council, and Burgesses, of this present General Assembly, and by the authority of the same,* That from henceforth, if any person shall ship on board any ship, or other vessel, bound to any of the British plantations, in America, any goods, merchandize, or commodities whatsoever, such person shall, either before the same shall be shipped, or within five days after, make oath, before some justice of the peace of the county where he lives, to the several parcels or packages of such goods, merchandize, or commodities so shipp'd, and the contents thereof, and that no tobacco is contained therein; or if any tobacco shall be packed in such parcels, he shall make oath to the true quantity, upon pain of forfeiting all goods, merchandize, and commodities, or the value thereof: And the justice of the peace, before whom such oath shall be made, shall certify the same under his hand; and such certificate shall be delivered to the master of the ship or vessel, who shall deliver the same to the naval officer of the district, at the time of his clearing: And no naval officer shall clear any such ship or vessel, until such certificate be produced; and a copy of such certificate shall, by the naval officer, be delivered, or sent, to the collector of the duty of a penny per pound, in the same district, before clearing. And any person making a false oath in the premises, and being thereof lawfully convicted, shall suffer as for perjury in a court of record, by the laws of England.

III. *And be it further enacted,* That every master of any ship or vessel, or other person clearing or concerned in loading any ship, or vessel, going to any British plantation, in America, before his clearing, shall make oath, before the naval officer of the district, to the quantity of tobacco he hath on board, if he hath any, or that he hath no tobacco, and will take none on board without paying the duty; a copy of which oath, such naval officer shall transmit to the collector of the customs, of the port whither such ship or vessel shall be bound: And any person making a false oath therein, and being thereof lawfully convicted, shall suffer as for perjury in a court of record, by the laws of England.

IV. *Provided always*, That nothing herein contained, shall be construed, deemed, or taken, to alter, change, or infringe, the powers, privileges, or allowances, of the several collectors of the said duty of one penny per pound, appointed, or to be appointed by the commissioners of his majesty's customs in Great-Britain, for the time being, pursuant to the act of parliament, made in the twenty fifth year of the reign of king Charles the second, for the collecting, levying, and receiving, the said duty, or penalties therein mentioned.

V. And, to the end no tobacco may be carried into the province of North Carolina, in order to be exported from thence, which is of late much practised, without paying the duty in either colony, *Be it further enacted*, That if any person shall carry any tobacco into the said province, without paying the said duty of one penny per pound, the owner thereof shall forfeit the value of such tobacco.

VI. And, for preventing frauds in the exportation of skins and furs, *Be it further enacted*, That no skins or furs shall hereafter be packed, in order to be shipped off, with any other thing; and every person intending to export any skins or furs, before the same shall be shipped, shall make oath before some justice of the peace of the county where he lives, to the several parcels or packages intended to be shipped, and the number of skins and furs, and the kinds thereof, and pounds of beaver, if any, therein contained; and that no other thing is packed therein: Which oath shall be certified as aforesaid, and the certificate shall be delivered by the master of the ship, or vessel, wherein the same shall be shipped, before his clearing, to the naval officers; who shall receive of the owner of such skins and furs, the several duties by the said act imposed, and, without distinguishing between buck and doe skins, shall account all deer skins, so shipped, to be one third buck, and two thirds doe skins.

VII. And, to the end the said duties upon skins and furs may not be defrauded, by the carrying the same by land or water, into Maryland, Pensilvania, or North Carolina, which is very easie, and much practised by many people, not only to the impoverishing the college, but to the great diminution of the trade of this colony, *Be it further enacted*, That where any person or persons shall be hereafter found travelling upon the frontiers, with any skins or furs, it shall be lawful for any justice of the peace, sheriff, or constable, of the county where such person shall be found, to seize such skins and furs; unless the person or persons carrying the same, shall produce a certificate under the hand of a justice of the peace in this colony, that he is an inhabitant of the colony; and *moreover*, shall make oath, that he will not carry the said skins or furs, or cause the same to be carried, into any other colony or province, without paying the said duties. And in case any skins or furs shall be hereafter seised, by virtue of this act, one moiety thereof shall be forfeited to the person seising the same, and the other moiety to the king, his heirs and successors, for the better support of the college of William and Mary, in Virginia.

VIII. *And be it further enacted*, That where any hides, skins, or furs, shall be exported, either by land, or water, contrary to this or the said former act, the owner shall forfeit the value thereof: And that one moiety of all the penalties herein inflicted, and not otherwise disposed of, shall be to the king, his heirs and successors, for the better support of the college of William and Mary, in Virginia, and the other moiety to the informer; to be recovered, with costs, by action of debt, or information, in any court of record, within this dominion.

IX. And, to the end the said president and masters may not depend altogether upon the provisions herein made, for the improvement of their revenues, which may be perhaps still precarious, but may receive a more certain relief, *Be it further enacted*, That after the twenty fifth day of October, in the year of our Lord one thousand seven hundred and thirty five, the whole duty of one penny, for every gallon of rum, brandy, and other distilled spirits, and of wine, imported, laid by one act of the general assembly, made at a session held in the twelfth year of the reign of the late king George the first, to continue for twenty one years, out of which, two hundred pounds per annum was appropriated for the relief of the said college, be given to the said president, and masters, and their successors, for the residue of the said term; and shall be applied and disposed of, to such good uses, for the better support of the college, as by the visitors and governors of the college, or the greater part of them, shall from time to time be directed, and appointed; so as some part thereof shall be laid out and applied for buying such books, for the use of the scholars and students, in the college, as the said visitors and governors, or the greater part of them, shall think most necessary; and such books, so to be bought, shall be marked thus, *The Gift of the General Assembly of* Virginia, *in the year 1734*, and shall for ever be preserved and kept in the public library of the said college.

X. *And be it further enacted*, That the president, masters, scholars, and students, of the college of William and Mary, in Virginia, and all the domestic servants belonging to the college, be from henceforth exempted from being listed as tithables, in the county of James-City, and from paying any public, county, or parish levies, for ever. —Hening, *op. cit.*, IV, 429-33.

19. SOME MINUTES OF THE FACULTY OF THE COLLEGE OF WILLIAM AND MARY FOR 1743, 1754, 1755, 1756, 1758

At a meeting of the President and Masters of Willm & Mary Coll:
Present:

The Revd Mr William Dawson President.
The Revd Mr Thos Dawson.
The Revd Mr Thos Robinson & John Graeme.

After the Death of the Revnd Mr Jas Blair, late Presidt The Govrs & vistrs having elected the Revend Mr William Dawson President. He qualified himselfe according to the Statutes by subscribing his assent to the 39 articles of the Church of England in the words following:

Ego Guil Dawson Praeses Collegii Gulielmi & Mariae in Virginia, Librum de Religionis articulis, in quos consensum est ab archiepiscopis & Episcopis utrinsq: Provinciae, ac reliquo omno clero, in Synodo, Londinensi, An. 1562 omnine comprobo; et omnes ac singulos articulos in ecdem contentu, (qui triginta novem citra ratificationem numerantur) Verbo Dei consentaneous esse agnosco

WILLIAM DAWSON.

And then the Masters administered the oath de fideli &c to the President in the form following:

Tu fidem dabis te munus Praesidis tibi comissum fideliter administraturum secundum statuta Collegii. Ita Deus te adjuvet tactis sacrosanctis Christi evangeliis.

Jan. ye 14th, 1754.
At a meeting of ye President & Masters of W. & M. College.
Present:

Ye Revd W. Stith, President; Mr Dawson, Mr Robinson, Mr Preston & Mr Graham.

Resolved, yt Will Preston be appointed Clerk to ys Meeting & yt he be allowed ye yearly Salary of ten pounds.

Resolved, yt Mr Dawson be desired to write to Mrs Clayton & enquire, if she will accept of ye Place of House-Keeper to the College, at present vacant by ye Resignation of Mrs Gough.

Resolved, yt a person be appointed to hear such Boys as shall be recommended by their Parents, or Guardians a chapter in the Bible every School-Day at 12 o'clock & yt he have ye yearly salary of one Pistole for each Boy so recommended.

Resolved, yt Mr Jones, ye Usher of ye College, be appointed to hear such Boys.

It was proposed by ye President yt ye Bursar be obliged to give Security according to Statute. But upon a Question: Whether ye present Bursar a sworn Master, shall be obliged to give security & yet not receive 5 per cent, Wch is equally directed by ye same statute? It passed in ye negative.

WILLIAM STITH.

Aug. 29, 1754.

At a Meeting of the President and Masters of William and Mary College:

Present,

The Rev. W. Stith, President,

Mr Dawson, Mr Robinson, Mr Preston, Mr Graham and Mr Camm.

Mr Dawson is desired to acquaint Mr Kemp yt ye President and Masters are very uneasy at his encouraging the boys to Engage in Racing, and other Diversions contrary to the Rules of the College, and that if he do not desist for ye future they are determined to make a proper Representation thereof to the Court.

Mr Dawson is desired to caution Mr Holt agt harbouring any of the College Boys.

Mr Camm is desired to acquaint Mr Secretary Nelson with the disturbances which have been caused in College by ye turbulent and bad Behaviour of Henry Harrison, a clerk in his office, and request Yt he will restrain him from acting in such a manner for the future, by any method he shall think proper.

November 1, 1755.

At a Meeting of the Masters of William and Mary College:

Present,

Ye Revd Mr Dawson, Mr Robinson, Mr Preston and Mr Graham.

After the death of ye Revd W. Stith, A.M., late President of the College, ye visitors having elected the Revd Thomas Dawson President, He qualified himself according to the Statutes by subscribing his Assent to the 39 articles of ye Church of England in ye following words:

Ego, Thom. Dawson, Praeses Collegii Guil: & Mariae in Virginia Librum de Religionis Articulis in quos consensum est ab archi-episcopis and Episcopis utriusque Provinciae, ac reliquo omni Clero, in Synodo Londinensi Anno Dom. 1562 omnio comprobo; et omnes ac singulos Articulos in eodem contentos (qui trigenta novem citra ratificationem numerantur) Verbo Dei consentaneos esse agnosco.

THOMAS DAWSON.

And then ye Masters administered ye following Oath:

In Fidem dabis Te munus Praesidis tibi comissum fideliter administraturum secondum statuta collegii; its Deus te adjuvet tactis sacrosanctis Xti Evangeliis.

Mr Emanuel Jones, being elected Master of ye Indian School by ye Visitors and Govrs, did also subscribe his assent to ye 39 articles and took ye oath de fideli administratione, &c.

They likewise subscribed to ye three articles in ye 36 canon.

Nov. 6, 1755.

At a meeting of the President and Masters:

Present,

Ye Revd Mr Thom: Dawson, President.

Ye Revd Mr Robinson, Mr Preston, Mr Graham, Mr Camm, Mr Jones.

Mr James Hubard is unanimously elected usher of the Grammar School in ye room of Mr Em. Jones.

THOMAS DAWSON, President.

Jan. 1, 1756.

At a meeting of ye President and Masters:

Present,

Ye Revp Mr Thomas Dawson, President.

Ye Mr Robinson, ye Revd Mr Preston and ye Revd Mr Graham.

Mr Richard Collinson was by them examined and is thought capable of teaching the Grammar School at Norfolk.

THO. DAWSON, President.

May ye 3, 1756.

At a Meeting of ye President & Masters &c

Present. Ye Rev: Thomas Dawson A.M. President Ye Rev: Tho: Robinson, A.M., W. Preston A.M. R. Graham A. M. & Em. Jones A.B.

Resol: unanimously Yt Cole Digges & Matthew Hubard be expelled ye College of W. & Mary not only for yir remarkable Idleness and bad Behavior in general, but particularly for whipping ye little Boys in ye Grammar School—for Obstinacy & Disrespect to ye Grammar Master, & refusing to answer before ye President & Masters ye complaints made agt ym.

Resol: unanimously Yt any young Gentleman, who shall keep Company with ye said Cole Digges & Matthew Hubard or shew ym any countenance, shall be looked upon as their abettors & punished accordingly.

Resolved unanimously, Yt yir Parents be acquainted with ye above Resolves, & desired to keep ym fm coming within ye College Bounds, otherwise ye Society will cause them to be punished by ye Civil Magistrate.

James Hubard the Usher of the College having in the Case of Digges & Hubard behaved to the President & Masters in a most scandalous, impudent, & unheard of Manner, by breaking into the Room, where the said President & Masters consult upon Business, & thence, when they were examining upon account of his bad Behavior, forcing away his Brother in opposition to every known Rule of the College, nay even of common Decency & good Manners; was this Day sent for to appear before the said President & Masters to know what he had to alledge in Extenuation of a Crime, which tended entirely to destroy the good Government of the College. Upon his Appearance he pleaded the Heat of Passion, excited by brotherly Affection, that he was very sorry for what had happen'd and asked Pardon sincerely of the Society for so heinous a crime, which he again assur'd them was not the Effect of Deliberation, but of Madness, the Height of Passion.

At a Meeting of the President & Masters of Wm & Mary College, September 27, 1756.

Present The Revd Thomas Dawson A.M. President, The Revd T. Robinson A.M., R. Graham A.M., J. Camm A M, E. Jones A.B.

Resol: that E. Jones be appointed clerk to this meeting.

Whereas all the Masters are fully satisfied that Mr Hubbard continues to behave very ill in his Office, and is the chief occasion of the present Disorders in the College notwithstanding his Promises of better & more respectful Conduct some Time ago upon which he was pardon'd for a very flagrant Affront to the President & Masters assembled in Meeting; we therefore think it necessary for the Quiet and Good of the College that he be remov'd from the ushership, & he is accordingly remov'd.

Resol: that Mr Stringer be appointed usher of the College.

Wednesday February 15th 1758.

Present The Revd Mr Thomas Dawson President & Mr Emanuel Jones Mr of the Indian School.

The President having in pursuance of an Order of the Visitors of the 14th December past, appointed the Revd Mr William Davis to be Master of the Grammar School in the room of Mr Robinson lately deprived by the Visitors until the arrival of the Master expected from England, he qualified himself according to the Statutes, by subscribing his Assent to the 39 Articles of the Church of England in the following words,

Ego infra-scriptus Gulielmus Davis clericus, Magister Ludi-Grammaticalis Collegii Gulielmi et Mariae in Virginia (&c. here follow the words of the oath given on p. (48).—Editor.)

And then Mr President and Mr Jones administered to Mr Davis the following oath:

In Fidem dabis te Munus Ludi Magistri Scholae Gram: maticalis fideliter administraturum secondum Statuta Collegii-ita Deus to adjuret tactis Sacrosanctis Xti Evangelis.

He likewise Subscribed to the three Articles in the 36th Canon.

Friday April 7th 1758.

Present The Revd M Thomas Dawson, President & Emmanual Jones Master of the Indian School.

The Revd Mr Gronow Owen being elected by the Visitors and Governors Master of the Grammar School, and having enter'd on the said Office the 5th Instant, did this Day subscribe his Assent to the Articles of the Church of England as in Page 19th, and did also take the Oath de fideli Administration &c

He likewise subscrib'd to the three Articles in the 36th Canon.

THOMAS DAWSON P.

—*William and Mary Quarterly Historical Papers*, II (1893, 1894), 51, 52; 56, 57; 123, 124; 126, 127; 257-59.

20. The General Assembly enacts further legislation on the College, 1745

And be it further enacted, by the authority aforesaid, That all and every such sum or sums of money, which shall be raised, collected, and levied, by the said duties, the necessary charges of collecting, managing, and accounting for the same, always excepted, shall, from time to time, be accounted for and paid, by the respective collectors thereof, to the treasurer of Virginia, for the time being, upon oath; which oath the said treasurer is hereby impowered to administer; and by the said treasurer accounted for to the General Assembly of this colony, upon oath: And that all and every such sum and sums of money, which shall be raised, collected, and levied, by the said duties of two pence for every gallon of wine, rum, brandy, and other distilled spirits; and one penny upon every gallon of cyder, beer, and ale, over and above the necessary charges aforesaid; are, and shall be appropriated, issued, applied, and disposed to such use or uses, as the General Assembly, from time to time shall think fit to direct, for lessening the levy by the poll, or defraying any public expence, and to and for no other use whatsoever. And that all and every sum and sums of money, to be raised and levied out of the duty of one penny upon every gallon of wine, rum, brandy, and other distilled spirits, by this act imposed as aforesaid is and shall be appropriated to the relief of the college of William and Mary, in this colony, for and during the said term of eleven years; and shall be paid, by the said treasurer, half yearly, in equal portions, unto the president and masters of the college, and their successors; and shall be applied and disposed of for the founding scholarships, and such other good uses, for the better support of the college, or the greater part of them, shall, from time to time, be directed and appointed, and not otherwise; and shall be accounted for the Assembly.—Hening, *op. cit.,* V, 317-18.

21. The General Assembly levies duties for the support of the College, 1748

I. BE *it enacted by the Lieutenant Governor, Council, and Burgesses, of this present General Assembly, and it is hereby enacted, by the authority of the same,* That there shall be paid to his majesty, his heirs and successors, for and towards the better support and maintenance of the college of William and Mary, in Virginia, the following duties, customs, and imposts, for the following goods, wares, and merchandizes, exported out of this dominion, by land or by water: that is to say,

For every raw hide, six pence.

For every tann'd hide, six pence.

For every drest buck skin, one penny three farthings.

For every undrest buck skin, one penny.

For every doe skin drest, one penny half penny.

For every undrest doe skin, three farthings.

For every pound of beaver, three pence.

For every otter skin, two pence.

For every wild cat skin, one penny half penny.

For every mink skin, one penny.

For every fox skin, one penny half penny.

For every dozen of raccons skins, three pence, and so proportionably for a greater or lesser quantity.

For every dozen of musk-rat skins, two pence, and so proportionably for a greater or lesser quantity.

And for every elk skin, four pence half penny.

II. And for preventing frauds in the exportation of skins and furs, *Be it further enacted by the authority aforesaid,* That no skins or furs shall be hereafter packed, in order to be shipped off, with any other thing; and every person intending to export skins, or furs, before the same shall be shipped, shall make oath before some justice of the peace of the county where he lives, to the several parcels, or packages intended to be shipped, and the number of skins and furs, and the kinds thereof, and pounds of beaver, if any therein contained, and that no other thing is packed therein; which oath shall be certified by the justice of peace administering the same, and his certificate delivered by the master of the ship or vessell wherein the same shall be shipped, before his clearing, to the naval officer, who shall receive of the owner of such skins, and furs, the duties by this act imposed, and without distinguishing between buck and doe skins, shall account all deer skins, to be one third buck, and two thirds doe skins.

III. *And be it further enacted, by the authority aforesaid,* That the said duties upon skins and furs shall be paid, and satisfied, by the owner or exporter thereof, either by land or water, to the collector or collectors, appointed to receive the same, by the governor or commander in chief of this colony, for the time being, with advice of the council, and a certificate, that penalty of forfeiture of all hides, skins, and furs, exported or intended to be exported, by land or water, contrary to this act, or value thereof.

IV. And to the end the said duties upon skins and furs may not be defrauded, by clandestine transportation thereof into the neighbouring colonies, *It is hereby further enacted*, That if any person shall be found travelling upon the frontiers of this colony, with hides, skins, or furs, it shall be lawful for any justice of peace, sheriff, or constable, of the county where such person shall be found, to seize such hides, skins, and furs, unless the person carrying the same produce a certificate, under the hand of a justice of peace of this colony, that he is an inhabitant thereof, and shall also make oath, that he will not carry the said hides, skins, or furs, or cause the same to be carried, into any other colony or province, without paying the said duties: And in case any hides, skins or furs, shall be so seized, one moiety thereof shall be to the seizor, and the other moiety to the king, his heirs and successors, for the better support of the said college of William and Mary.

V. And whereas by an act of parliament, passed in the twenty-fifth year of king Charles the second, a duty of one penny per pound was laid upon all tobacco, exported from hence to other British plantations, in America, which, among other donations, was by the late king William, and queen Mary, granted to the said college, for the better support thereof, but by reason of divers frauds and abuses, this branch of their revenue hath of late proved very deficient, *Be it therefore further enacted, by the authority aforesaid*, That every person who shall ship any goods, merchandizes, or commodities whatsoever, on board any ship or vessel bound to any of the British plantations in America, shall, before the same be shipped, or within five days after, make oath before a justice of peace of the county where he lives, to the several parcels, or packages, of goods, merchandize, or commodities so shipped, and the contents thereof, and that no tobacco is contained therein; or if any tobacco, to the true quantity, upon pain of forfeiting all such goods, merchandize, and commodities, or the value thereof: And the justice of peace, before whom such oath shall be made, shall certify the same under his hand; which certificate shall be delivered to the master of the vessel, and by him to the naval officer of the district, at the time of his clearing; and no naval officer shall clear any such ship or vessel, until such certificate be produced, and a copy thereof shall be by the naval officer delivered, or sent, to the collector of the duty of one penny per pound, in the same district, before clearing: And every master of such ship or vessel, or other person clearing, or concerned in loading the same, before his clearing shall make oath, before the naval officer of the district, to the quantity of tobacco on board, if he hath any or that he hath no tobacco, and will take none on board, without paying the duty; a copy of which oath the naval officer shall transmit to the collector of the customs, of the port whither such ship or vessel shall be bound: And every person making a false oath in any of the premises and being thereof lawfully convicted, shall suffer as for wilful perjury.

VI. And to the end no tobacco may be carried into the province of North Carolina, to be exported thence without paying the duty in either colony, *Be it further enacted, by the authority aforesaid,* That if any person shall carry any tobacco into the said province, without paying the said duty of one penny per pound, the owner thereof shall forfeit the value of such tobacco: And that one moiety of all penalties and forfeitures, arising by this act, shall be to the king, his heirs and successors, for the better support of the college of William and Mary, in Virginia, and the other moiety to the informer, recoverable with costs, by action of debt or information, in any court of record within this colony.

VII. *And be it further enacted, by the authority aforesaid,* That the several collectors, appointed to receive the duties aforesaid, shall, from time to time, be accountable and pay the same to the president and masters of the said College of William and Mary, or such other person or persons as shall be by them lawfully deputed; and for receiving and paying thereof, such collectors shall be allowed six per centum: *Provided always,* That nothing herein contained shall be construed to alter or infringe the powers, privileges, or allowances, of collectors of the said duty of one penny per pound, appointed or to be appointed by the commissioners of his majesty's customs of Great Britain, pursuant to the said act of parliament, made in the twenty-fifth year of king Charles the second, for collecting, levying, and receiving the said duty, or penalties therein mentioned.

VIII. *And be it further enacted, by the authority aforesaid,* That all and every other act and acts, clause and clauses heretofore made, for or concerning any matter or thing within the purview of this act, shall be, and are hereby repealed.

IX. *And be it further enacted, by the authority aforesaid,* That this act shall commence and be in force, from and immediately after the tenth day of June, which shall be in the year of our Lord, one thousand seven hundred and fifty-one.—*Ibid.*, VI, 91-94.

22. THE COLLEGE OF WILLIAM AND MARY CONFERS HONORARY DEGREE OF MASTER OF ARTS ON BENJAMIN FRANKLIN, 1756

At a meeting of ye President & Masters of W. & M. College, Present.

Ye Revd T. Dawson, A.M., president; T. Robinson, A.M., W. Preston, A.M., R. Graham, A.M., J. Camm, A.M., and Em. Jones, A.B. Ys Day, Ben. Franklin, Esquire, favored ye Society with his company, and had ye Degree of A.M. conferred upon him by ye Revd T. Dawson, A.M. president to wm he was in publick presented by the Revd W. Preston, A.M. A Copy of ye Diploma:

Praeses et Magistri Collegii Guil: & Mar: in Virginia omnibus, ad quos hoc praesens Scriptum pervenerit, salutem in Domino Septiternam.

Quum in Charta Regia nobis•concessum & confirmatum fuit, ut eos qui se Literis & Studiis praecipue ornarunt, gradibus Academicis decoremus; Quum volumus in hujus modi Honorem imprimis Evehi virum inclytissimum quo nobis & Juventuti Virginiensi Exemplum valde egregium proponamus; Quumque Benjaminum Franklin Armigerum nobis commendarunt Gradus Artium Magistri a diversis Collegiis Americanis in eum collatus, quinetiam Honores a Rege Christianissimo, a regia Scientarum apud Parisios Academia, a regia Societate Londinensi ei accumulati, nec non ejusdem Celebritas & Gloria, ob miras in Philosophia naturali Patefactiones excogitatas, per totam Literarum Rempublicam evulgatae; idcirco in frequenti Senatu Die Secundo mensis Aprilis Anno Domini 1756 habito, conspirantibus omnibus Suffragiis, praefatum Benjaminum Franklin Armigerum, virum omni Laude dignum, Artium magistrum renunciavimus & constituimus. In cujus Rei Testimonium huic Diplomati Sigillum Collegii Gulielmi & Mariae commune apponi fecimus.

Dat Die men: & An: praedict:

Thomas Dawson, President.

—*William and Mary College Quarterly Historical Papers*, II, 208-9.

23. THOMAS JEFFERSON WRITES TO JOHN PAGE ABOUT THE COLLEGE, 1763

Affairs at W. and M. are in the greatest confusion. Walker, M'Clurg and Wat Jones are expelled *pro tempore*, or, as Horrox softens it, rusticated[1] for a month. Lewis Burwell, Warner Lewis, and one Thompson, have fled to escape flagellation. I should have expected Warner Lewis, who came off on his own accord. Jack Walker leaves town on Monday.—Letter to John Page (1763), Ford (ed.), *The Writings of Thomas Jefferson*, I, 353.

24. LATIN VERSES PRESENTED BY THE COLLEGE OF WILLIAM AND MARY, ACCORDING TO THE TERMS OF THE CHARTER, 1771 [2]

[Under the provisions of the charter of William and Mary College, granted by King William and Queen Mary in 1693, two copies of Latin verses were to be presented yearly on the fifth day of November "at the house of our Governor, or Lieutenant Governor of Virginia, for the time being, for ever, in full discharge, acquittance, and satisfaction of all quit-rents, services, customs, dues and burdens whatsoever, due, or to be due, to us, or to our successors, for the said twenty thousand acres of lands, by the laws or customs of England or Virginia." This custom was discontinued in 1774 but was revived in the 1930's. The original of the verses which follow for 1771, as well as those for 1772, 1773, and 1774, is in the New York Public Library. Photographic reproductions of these materials were sent to the editors of *William and Mary College Quarterly Historical Magazine* who used them in that publication in 1930, Vol. X, p. 269.]

To His Excellency, The Right Honourable John Earl of Dunmore, His Majesty's Lieutenant Governor General, Commander in Chief of the Colony and Dominion of VIRGINIA, and Vice Admiral of the same.

Nonis Novembris MDCCLXXI.

Hinc procul O procul este profani. Daedala Tellus
Submittat fruges, pro salvis dona maritis
Grata ferant sponsae, sertisque recentibus halet
Ara Tibi, crebro Britonum celebrata per urbes
Hic et ubique Dies! Memori de pectore grates
Depromant cuncti pariter juvenesque senesque.
Jam nox atra polo piceam detraxerat Umbram
Nec tamen aut roseis digitis Aurora refulget

---

1. Rustication was an old form of collegiate discipline or punishment under which some students delinquent in their academic duties were required to leave the campus and go to the country, sometimes perhaps with a tutor, to catch up with their work.

2. See Section XVII of the charter. Only the verses presented in 1771 are here used. Below are given verses presented when the custom was revived in the 1930's.

Aureus aut Titan ostentat lampada terris;
Cuncta tenent tenebrae: Quin Sol trepidavit et ipse
Mundus ne rueret repetens compage soluta
Antiquum Chaos? En! pavor undique et undique lethum est.
Conscia fama volat; simul et [?] quisque pavendo
Dat Vires illi ignotoque auctore malorum
Quod timuere fovent. Nec solum vulgus acerbo
Perculsum terrore tremit sed Curia et ipse.
Sedibus exiluere patres. Caelestia tangat
Dummodo corda stupor, stupuere. At fallere quicquam
Possit eum mare qui terras qui numine torquet
Caelum, qui motus animi sensusque latentes
Rimatur? Deus ipse Deus qua mole parentur
Insidiae quantumque caput sic fraude petatur
Vidit et ingemuit: Phoebum splendescere clare
Praecipit, "Heus fiat factum": subitoque in apertam
Proripuit lucem quos strinxerat impius Error
Popicolas; ausus sontes patefecit ad auras,
Auctores stravit; nec enim sua dextera aberrat
Cum feriat candente manu. O Jupiter alme,
In quem tota hominum gens inclinata recumbit,
O columen Britonumque stator Britonumque nepotum,
Sis bonus: O felix, tuis [?] sic semper adesto,
Terrarum caelique parens! semperque placeto
Parcere subjectis et debellare superbos.

25. PHILIP VICKERS FITHIAN AND MR. CARTER TALK ABOUT THE COLLEGE OF WILLIAM AND MARY, 1774

After having dismissed the School I went over to Mr Carters Study—We conversed on many things, & at length on the College of William & Mary at *Williamsburg*. He informed me that it is in such confusion at present, & so badly directed, that he cannot send his Children with propriety there for Improvement & useful Education —That he has known the Professors to play all Night at Cards in publick Houses in the City, and has often seen them drunken in the Street!—That the Charter of the College is vastly Extensive, & the yearly income sufficient to support a University being about 4.000L. Sterling—That the Necessary Expence for each Scholar yearly is only 15L Currency.

Two of the officers of the Institution, Mr Bracker, & Mr. Henly

Clergymen are at present engaged in a paper War published weekly in the Williamsburg Gazette's.—*Journal & Letters of Philip Vickers Fithian* (February 12, 1774), 86-87.

26. SOME MINUTES OF THE FACULTY, DECEMBER 4, 1779

At a meeting of the President and Professors of Wm. & Mary College under a statute passed by the Visitors the fourth day of December 1779. Present.

James Madison, President & Professor of Natural Philosophy & Mathematics.

George Wythe, Professor of Law & Police.

James McClurg, Professor of Anatomy & Medicine.

Robert Andrews, Professor of Moral Philosophy, the Laws of Nature & of Nations, & of the Fine Arts.

Charles Bellini, Professor of Modern Languages.

*　　*　　*　　*　　*

For the Encouragement of Science,

Resolved, That a Student on paying annually one thousand pounds of Tobacco shall be entitled to attend any two of the following Professors, viz: of Law & Police, of Natural Philosophy and Mathematics, & of Moral Philosophy, the Laws of Nature and Nations & of the Fine Arts, & that for fifteen hundred pounds he shall be entitled to attend the three said Professors. . . .—*William and Mary College Quarterly*, II, Second Series (January, 1922), 46.

27. JOLIN BROWN WRITES WILLIAM PRESTON THAT WILLIAM AND MARY HAD BEEN MADE INTO A UNIVERSITY, DECEMBER 9, 1779

William & Mary has undergone a very considerable Revolution; the Visitors met on the 4th. Instant & form'd it into a University, annul'd the old Statutes, abolish'd the Grammar School, Continued Mr. Madison President & Professor of Mathematics, Appointed Mr. Wythe Professor of Law, Dr. McClurg of Physick, Mr. Andrews of Moral Philosophy & Monsr. Bellini of modern Languages.—*William and Mary Quarterly*, II, 2d Series (January, 1922), 46.

28. THE BOARD OF VISITORS CHANGES THE COLLEGE OF WILLIAM AND MARY INTO A UNIVERSITY, DECEMBER 4, 1779

At a Convention of the Visitors of the college of William & Mary, on the 4th of December, 1779, a statute was passed, of which the following is an extract.

The funds of the college being no longer competent to support so extensive an institution as that which the charter recommends; and where science at large cannot be cultivated, that scheme of education being most proper, which is more immediately subordinate to the leading objects of society: The scanty stipend lately paid by each scholar for commons having occasioned a considerable expense; It being just, that students inducted into the several scholarships should be equally affected by the depreciation of money, with the college: since the original donations, on which they were founded, cannot be now disposed of, but at a depreciated rate: Experience having proved, that the rarer parts of science have been obstructed in their progress by the maintenance of a Grammar-School within the same; the learning of which may be acquired elsewhere, in a much shorter time: And the necessities of the college rendering it expedient to multiply the sources of revenue by every possible means: Let there be, therefore, six professorships: The 1st of which shall be, Law and Police; the 2nd, Anatomy and Medicine; the 3d, Natural Philosophy and Mathematicks; the 4th, Moral Philosophy, the Laws of Nature and of Nations, and the fine Arts; the 5th, Modern Languages; and the 6th, for Brafferton.

The particular method of instruction, to be pursued in each school, shall be subject to the controul of the President and Professors, with a committee of six of the visitors, conferring and voting together, from time to time, on that subject; their meetings to be called by the President, or by a majority of the said committee, Each Professor, except the master of Brafferton, shall receive for every student who attends him, one thousand pounds of tobacco annually. Commons shall cease at college. The President and Professors shall allow to some sober and discreet male person, the use of the college kitchen and garden. They shall also hire to him the negroes accustomed to labour in the same, taking bond with faculty. He shall furnish the several students with the different meals, at such price as the President and Professors shall establish, from time to time, to be paid by the students themselves. Such students as have been, or shall be, inducted into scholarships, created on private donations actually paid, or established by the General Assembly, shall receive, while they remain at college, the interest of the original sum, at the rate of five per centum per annum, and no more; and scholarships, founded on donations not yet paid, shall be admitted on the same conditions only. The Grammar School shall be discontinued. A sufficient number of slaves shall be reserved for cleaning the college; and if any remain after such reservation, and hiring of the slaves belonging to the garden and kitchen, as aforesaid, they shall be hired out at publick auction.

This statute shall commence in force on the 25th day of *December*, in the year of our LORD 1779.—*Virginia Gazette*, December 18, 1779.

29. THE COLLEGE OF WILLIAM AND MARY CONFERS HONORARY DEGREE OF DOCTOR OF LAWS ON THOMAS JEFFERSON, 1782

At a Meeting of the President & Professors of the University on December 31, 1782.

Present:

> James Madison, Presidt.
> George Wythe,
> Robert Andrews,
> Charles Bellini.

Resolved that a Degree of Doctor of Law be presented to Thomas Jefferson, Esqr, of which the following is a Diploma.

DIPLOMA.

Praeses et Professores universitatis seu Collegii Guilielmi et Mariae in Virginia omnibus ad quos presentes literae pervenerint Salutem: Cum eo gradus Academici instituti fuerint ut viri de Academia, de Republica optime meriti, istis (302) insignibus ornarentur, Sciatis, quod nos ea, sola qua possumus via, gradu doctoris in jure civili libenter studioseque collato, testamur quanti facimus Thomam Jefferson Virginiensem ingremio nostrae matris educatum mira in has Musarum Sedes benevolentia propendentem nec minorem inde reportantem, peritisimum et privati juris et publica; eximio erga patriam Amore, quam aliis in rebus, tam maxime in libertate americana vindicanda insignem; adeo literis qua vulgatis qua interioribus et reconditis imbutum, ut artes omnes bonae in uno homine convenire videantur quas ornat Magnitudo animi, quae nihil ad ostentationem omnia ad conscientiam refert, recteque facti non ex populi sermone (303) Sed es facto petit. Idcirco in solemni convocatione vigesimo die mensis januarii Anno Domini Milessimo Septingentesimo octogesimo tertio habita conspirantibus omnium suffragiis, eundem honorabilem et egregium Thomam Jefferson Doctorem in Jure civili creavimus et constituimus, eumque virtute presentis Diplomatis singulis juribus, privilegiis et honoribus gradui isti quaqua pertinentibus honoris causa frui et gaudere jussimus. In cuius rei testimonium sigillum Universitatis commune quo ac in parte utimur, presentis apponi fecimus. Datum in Domo Nostrae convocationis Anno, die, et mense praedictis.—*William and Mary College Quarterly Review and Historical Magazine*, XVI (1907), 73-74.

30. ELKANAH WATSON FINDS IN NORTH CAROLINA AN INDIAN EDUCATED AT THE COLLEGE OF WILLIAM AND MARY, 1786

I crossed the Yadkin at the ferry, where Green by a hair-breadth, escaped the pursuit of Cornwallis, he having reached one shore with his army, when his pursuer appeared on the opposite bank. Salisbury was a pleasant village, containing fifty dwelling-houses and a large stone prison. The road to Charlotte, in Mecklenburgh county, was equal to any English turnpike, and traversed a beautiful level.

I carried letters to the courteous Gen. Polk, and remained two days at his residence, in the delightful society of his charming family. Having expressed a wish to visit the Catawba Indians, Gen. Polk accompanied me to the Indian foot-path. This I pursued alone on horseback, leaving Mills with my carriage at the tavern. My curiosity had been strongly excited to see an Indian people in their native savage condition, that I might contrast them with the polish and refinement of France. I confess it was somewhat trying to my nerves to penetrate thus solitarily without a guide or protector, into the mazes of a gloomy wilderness, and amid the haunts of a savage race.

When I entered the first village, the young Indians and squaws fled in every direction, the men being absent on a hunting expedition. It was sometime before I could find the residence of their king or chief, New River, alias Gen. Scott. At length an old squaw pointed to a log house, where I was kindly received by the old king, on his crutches. He spoke no English, and to induce him to send for a person to interpret between us, I intimated by signs, that I had an important communication to make. On this, he dispatched a runner across the Catawba river, for an interpreter. In about an hour his cabin was thronged by the savage warriors, and among them one who had been educated at William and Mary College, a sensible and well-informed person; but a perfect Indian in his appearance and habits. I stated to them the probability of a new war with England, on account of that government having retained the western posts on our territory, in violation of the treaty of peace. The king lit up a large pipe, and we each took three or four whiffs. I produced my bottle of rum, my only credential. We circulated the bottle and pipe alternately, drinking from the former, without the intervention of any other vessel. I observed every countenance sedate and attentive, and although they appeared warmly interested in the event, they maintained in the discussion in which they engaged, the utmost decorum, one only speaking at a time. In this council, and strolling through the village with the educated Indian, I spent the residue of the day. We entered their cabins, where I saw several straight-limbed, handsome young girls, daubed with paint, and decorated with feathers, rings, and brooches.— Winslow C. Watson (ed.), *Men and Times of the Revolution; or Memoirs of Elkanah Watson* (New York: Dana and Company, 1856), pp. 256-57.

31. THOMAS JEFFERSON ON THE COLLEGE OF WILLIAM AND MARY, 1787

The college of William and Mary is the only public seminary of learning in this state. It was founded in the time of king William and Queen Mary, who granted to it 20,000 acres of land, and a penny a pound duty on certain tobaccoes exported from Virginia and Maryland, which had been levied by the statute of 25 Car. II. The assembly also gave it, by temporary laws, a duty on liquors imported, and skins and furs exported. From these resources it received upwards of 3000*l* communibus annis. The buildings are of brick, sufficient for an indifferent accommodation of perhaps an hundred students. By its charter it was to be under the government of twenty visitors, who were to be its legislators, and to have a president and six professors, who were incorporated. It was allowed a representative in the general assembly. Under this charter, a professorship of the Greek and Latin languages, a professorship of mathematics, one of moral philosophy, and two of divinity were established. To these were annexed, for a sixth professorship, a considerable donation by Mr Boyle of England, for the instruction of the Indians, and their conversion to Christianity. This was called the professorship of Brafferton, from an estate of that name in England, purchased with the moneys given. The admission of the learners of Latin and Greek filled the college with children. This rendering it disagreeable and degrading to young gentlemen already prepared for entering on the sciences, they were discouraged from resorting to it, and thus the schools for mathematics and moral philosophy, which might have been of some service, became of very little. The revenues too were exhausted in accommodating those who came only to acquire the rudiments of science.—After the present revolution, the visitors, having no power to change those circumstances in the continuation of the college which was fixed by the charter, and being therefore confined in the number of professorships, undertook to change the objects of the professorships. They excluded the two schools for divinity, and that for the Greek and Latin languages, and substituted others; so that a present they stand thus:

A Professorship for Law and Police;
Anatomy and Medicine:
Natural Philosophy and Mathematics:
Moral Philosophy, the Law of Nature and Nations,
the Fine Arts:
Modern Languages:
For the Brafferton.

And it is proposed, so soon as the legislature shall have leisure to take up this subject, to desire authority from them to increase the number of professorships, as well for the purpose of subdividing those already instituted, as of adding others for other branches of science. To the professorships usually established in the universities of Europe, it would seem proper to add one for the ancient languages and literature of the North, on the account of their connexion with our own language, laws, customs, and history. The purposes of Brafferton institution would be better answered by maintaining a perpetual mission among the Indian tribes, the object of which, besides instructing them in the principles of Christianity, as the founder requires, should be to collect their traditions, laws, customs, languages, and other circumstances which might lead to a discovery of their relation with one another, or descent from other nations. When these objects are accomplished with one tribe, missionary might pass on to another.— Jefferson, *Notes on the State of Virginia* (1787), pp. 157-58.

32. LATIN VERSES PRESENTED TO GOVERNOR JOHN G. POLLARD, OF VIRGINIA, BY THE COLLEGE OF WILLIAM AND MARY, 1930

Viro Honestissimo Ioanni Garland Pollard
Praefecto Rei Publicae Virginiae
praeses, professores, discipulique Collegii Regis et Reginae Gulielmi et
Mariae in Virginia, ex praescripto diplomatis antiqui
collegii D.D.D.

Nonis Novembribus, Anno Domini MDCCCCXXX

O felix, talem quae sis dignata saluti,
   Virginia, ipsa tuae praeposuisse virum!
qualem non regalis honos, non saeva cupido
   imperii a patriae dulcis amore vocat.
Civis enim est, civisque iugo te temperat aequo
   civibus et iusto iura dat ore suis.
Tullius alter adest; non inscius hic quoque legum.
   Hunc quoque custodem respicis, alma parens.
At tu, nostra salus, praeclarum imitare prioris
   temporis exemplar, sis patriaeque pater.
Ne tamen haec quaecumque iuvent; maiora sequaris
   et veterum certes exsuperare decus.
Te duce per populum redeant Saturnia regna,
   mox redeat virtus religioque patrum;
Pax iterum laetam lustret cum Virginie terram
   et teneant clausas Martia templa fores.
Tradidit ipse tibi clavum qui rexit in oras
   communem optatas per vada caeca ratem.
His tibi monstret iter, doceat quae flabra minentur,
   qua lateant scopuli, quaeque pericla maris.
Dique deaeque tibi faveant aurisque secundis
   ad Musas revehant Aoniumque nemus.
Namque tui desiderio correpta caterva
   doctorum reditus Pieridumque dolet.
Haec quae praesidibus patres sub rege dederunt
   munera, nunc, eadem dantur, honeste, tibi;
non tamen ut gens serva usum renovamus avorum,
   regis at externi nescia ferre iugum,
Accipe dein nostri quam parva haec pignora amoris
   et studium populi spernere parce tui.

—*William and Mary Quarterly Historical Magazine*, XI, Series 2
(1931), 54.

XIII

THE EDUCATION OF SOUTHERNERS
ABROAD

I. PREVIEW AND COMMENTS

EXACTLY HOW MANY southerners went abroad for their education in the colonial period may never be known, in part because "of the destruction of so many of the records of these early times." [1] But it is known that well-to-do southern families had appreciation of the apparent need for European education and that in the seventeenth and eighteenth centuries the youth of such families were educated at English schools and universities. It seems to have been a somewhat natural practice for young southern colonists to be sent to Europe, especially to England. Educational advantages were greater abroad than in the colonies during the seventeenth century and many of the young colonists would in England be brought "into intimate association with all the members of their family connection who had not gone out to the plantations over-sea." Also, there was a belief in the colonies that in Europe many influences outside the school would "broaden and liberalize" the minds of American students. But this view became less strong as the Revolutionary War approached and the colonial period came to a close. As a matter of fact, as early as 1699 opposition to sending American children abroad for education had been voiced by a student at The College of William and Mary—even if his speech on the subject appears to have been written by a member of the faculty. [2] The young man warned against "Forreigne Education." Hugh Jones, in *The Present State of Virginia* (1724), did not think much of the practice of sending Virginians to Europe for education and believed they could do just as well at Williamsburg. Jedidiah Morse, pioneer American geographer, in the preface to a geography published in 1784, deplored America's cultural dependence on England.

Many wills in seventeenth century Virginia provided for the education of children in Europe. Among the earliest Virginians to be sent to England for education, probably to a school at Yarmouth,

1. Philip A. Bruce, *Institutional History of Virginia in the Seventeenth Century*, I, 317.
2. Edgar W. Knight, "Early Opposition to the Education of American Children Abroad," *Educational Forum*, XI (January, 1947), 193-204.

was Henry Sewell, of Lower Norfolk County. Ralph Wormeley of Middlesex County was matriculated at Oriel College, Oxford, at the age of fifteen; John Catlett of Rappahanock County, left directions for all of his children to be educated in England; Augustine Warner was a pupil in the Merchant Taylor's School in London in the late 1650's; John Lee, oldest son of Colonel Richard Lee, studied at Queen's College and received a Bachelor's degree, and later a diploma in medicine; and his brother, Richard, was also educated in England. Richard Sturman of Westmoreland County, left instructions for his children to be educated in England.[3]

South Carolina youth who were sent to England for education included Arthur Middleton, Thomas Heyward, and Thomas Lynch, Jr., three of the signers of the Declaration of Independence; John Rutledge, Hugh Rutledge, C. C. Pinckney, Thomas Pinckney, W. H. Drayton, Christopher Gadsden, Henry Laurens, John Laurens, Gabriel Manigault, John F. Grimké, William Wragg, and others.[4] More than 350 Americans were admitted to the Inns of Court in London before 1860 and 250 of these "were from the South or intimately connected with that section." There were eighty-nine from South Carolina and seventy-six from Virginia, in contrast to thirty from Massachusetts and forty from New York.[5]

II. DOCUMENTS

1. VIRGINIA STUDENTS AT CHRIST'S COLLEGE, CAMBRIDGE, 1686-1773

Spencer, William—born in Virginia. School: Northill, Beds. Admitted pensioner under Dr. Luke, 16. April 1684. Age not given. Fellow-Commoner 23. July 1686.

Resided till Michs. 1687.

Holt, Arthur—Son of Joseph—Born in Virginia. School: Sedbergh, under Mr. Saunders. Adm. first sizar, and then pensioner 8. Dec. 1716 aet. 20.

LL.B. 1723 Adm. scholar (as of Lancashire) 11. Apr. 1717. At Dec. 1718 he appears as Mr. Holt., having apparently become a

---

3. Bruce, *op. cit.*, pp. 316 ff.

4. In his *Higher Education in South Carolina*, C. Meriwether gives (pp. 25-26) an extract from the *News and Courier* of Charleston, January, 1870, containing a list of Americans admitted to the Inns of Court which shows that South Carolina led all of the colonies and states prior to 1786.

5. J. G. deR. Hamilton, "Southern Members of the Inns of Court," *North Carolina Historical Review*, X (October, 1933), 273-86; Clement Eaton, *Freedom of Thought in the Old South* (Duke University Press, 1940), p. 6.

fellow-commoner. Ordained deacon York, 1718 Sept. priest 1719 Sept. Resided till Mich. 1722.

Corbin, Garvin—E. S. of Richard, armiger; b. at Laneville, Virginia. School: Grinstead, Essex, under Mr. Harris. Admitted pensioner under Mr. Barker 26. Jan. 1756. Aet. 16.

Resided till Ladyday 1759. Admitted at Middle Temple 11. Feb. 1756 as of King's & Queen's County, Virginia.

Lee, Philip Thomas:—S. Richard: b. in Maryland—School Eton, under Dr. Barnard. Admitted pensioner under Mr. Shepherd 4. Jan. 1757, age 19.

Resided till Mich. (or Xmas) 1759. Admitted at the Middle Temple 24. Feb. 1756. Second s. of Ri. Lee of Blenheim on the Potomac and of Grace Ashton. Married a Miss Russell of England and had 5 children. He was of the family from which the Confederate General R. E. Lee sprang. Died at Blenheim 28. Nov. 1778. (Information from Secretary of the Maryland Historical Association, by R. A. Leigh, Esq.,)

Nelson, Thomas—S. Wm: b. at York, Virginia. School: Hackney under Dr. Newcome. Adm. pensioner under Mr. Porteous 15. May 1758, age 19.

Resided till Ladyday 1761: during the last year he pays f1.51.0. a quarter for 'two chambers'

Dana, Edmund—S. of Richard Arm: b. at Boston, 'New England': a master at Cambridge, New England, related to Lord Kinnaird, and ordained by Bishop of Lincoln 1769: adm. sizr under Dr. Shepherd 29. Nov. 1769, age 32.

M. A. of Havard University. Ordained priest Lincoln (*lit. dim.*— at Peterborough, 1769. He pays 3s. od, but I suppose did not reside, till Dec. 1700 (?). Prob. he intended to take the B. D. Degree: but he did not do so.

Lee, George Fairfax—S. George: b. in America: School: Islington under Mr. Davis. Adm. pensioner under Dr. Shepherd and Messrs. Paley and Law. 6. Oct, 1772. age 19. Resided till Mich. 1773. Perhaps akin to Phil. Tho. Lee (1759).—*The Virginia Magazine of History and Biography*, XXI (1913), 433-34.

2. STUDENT AT THE COLLEGE OF WILLIAM AND MARY SPEAKS AGAINST THE EDUCATION OF VIRGINIANS IN FOREIGN COUNTRIES, 1699

Wee have now heard the advantages of Learning towards the Improvmt of any Country. the next Question our Superiours thought proper to be discuss^d before this hono^ble Audience is whether it is better to be furnish^ed with Education & the other means of Learning at home I mean within the Country of Virg^a or to trust to our Childrens procureing of it Abroad in England or other forreigne parts.

Now the Task Assigned to us in this dayes Exercises is to Show the advantages of the first of these a Virg^a Education, & I doe Soe much more willingly Apply mySelf to this Subject because I shall not need to proove it by any Nice and Metaphysicall Arguments, but by Such a plaine and Easy way of Reasoning as I am Confident must bee Obvious to the meanest Capacity

In Short then I think it is noe hard matter to demonstrate that Forreigne Education is not to be purchased but at a farr greater Expence of time health besides the dishonour of wanting it in the Country, And that after all it is much more probable wee shall intirely miss our Learning abroad then at home, And that if wee chance to Acquire it it will bee mixed with soe many other bad Qualities as will render us much more uneasy in this Country & more unserviceable Unto it, than if we had Learned the Same things at home, If I can make out these Assertions I hope it will be noe hard Matter to Resolve the Question where we are to prosecut our Studies in Europe or America in England or Virg^a.

To begin with precious time who Looses most hee that has his School within a dayes Rideing or two at furthest of his Fathers house or he that has it at the distance of 6: 8: 10 or more weeks Sayling, I speak to men acquainted with these things who know how Tedious it is to Rigg out for Remote Voyages to prepare all things Necessary to take a solemn leave of their Friends it being Realy an even Lay whether they shall ever See them againe or not, to Ly in harbours waiting for fair winds or to bee driven back with Contrary ones to bee exposed to all Sorts of Enemies & to their Barbarous Usage of their prisoners, not to Speak of Some of them Soe inexorable, that it is well if all a mans estate can redeem him from a perpetuall Slavery. Let any Impartiall man consider these things and he will be easily Convinced who Loses most time hee that presently with all ease and Security Enters Upon his Studyes at hoe, or hee that in makeing an English Voyage in preparing for it and Settling himselfe after it though hee escapes the danger of Seas & enemies, Spends at Least a greate many moneths before he can enter upon his Businss, and much more afterwards before he can Returne and settle himselfe to any Course of Life in his own Country. Next to pretious time I look upon the Loss of health to be one of the greatest, Not that I can or would Reflect on the wholesomeness of the English air & Clymat, but as it has pleased the wise God to fitt all animals for the severall Elements wherein hee designed they should Live soe he has soe fitted all mens bodies & Constitutions for the severall Aires & Clymats wherein they were Borne & bred, That to carry them out of these into Remote & Forreigne parts is Like the Turning of Creatures out of their owne Element, Particularly it is an Easy thing to observe that every Change of Climat is attended with Certain sorts of dangerous diseases wch the poore Stranger must undergoe before he is seasoned as they call it to that Forreigne Countrey heere is then a double seasoning (we) expose our Children too by Obliging them to Travel into England for their Education One of that Loathsome Vile and dangerous disease of the Small Pox before they are seasoned to the Air of England in wch a greate many of our Countrymen and Women have Lost their Lives the other of Feavors & Agues in wch they must Resolve to Run the Risque of their Lives before they are seasoned againe to their owne Native Air of Virginia both wch Risques are much more Easily prevented by Contriving the means of good Education in our Own Countrys. A third greate Loss wee Sustain by Running into Forreigne Countrys for Education is that of wealth & Riches The Rate of English Education is soe disproportioned to our Virginia Purses & Estates that alass how few are there that were ever able to Come up to it, or to goe therron with it Even when they had not the Advantages they now have of Education at a farr cheaper Rate at home, I doe safely Appeal to those parents who ever sent their Children for England to be Educated Whether the Education of any one Such Child, did not Cost them as dear as what would have been Reckoned A good Portion for him in Virginia, It is true indeed that good Education is Costly everywhere but I believe every one will acknowledge that in this Country it does not Cost neare one halfe of what it does in England. But suposeing it Cost realy as much, I hope all wise Patriots will Consider that though the sumes bestowed by the Parents upon English or Virginia Education were Equal, yet the Loss to the Country would be very unequal & that for this Plain reason because all that goes for English Education is soe much dead Loss to the Country, it is soe much wealth Exported, & not only the expenders but the Country in Genll is soe much the poorer for it, whereas what goes for Virga Education is again spent in the Country, & soe only Circulates from one hand to another, but upon the Ballance of Trade the Country in Generall is nothing the poorer—what doe I say the poorer, I may safely maintain that it is a greate deale the Richer soe much money is saffed that must have gone Yearly out to England & a penny savd is a penny gott and a greate deale of money likewise is Imported from England wch if it had not been for the means of Education here wee should never have seen besides that English Donation wee have had towards the building Viz from his Majtie & others about 2600 pound. there is a perpetuall fund of Settlemt of Guift to our College wch is Equaly for the Honor & profit of the Country I mean the Legacy of the Famous & Honble Robert Boyle by wch a Land Estate in Yorkshire to the Vallue of 140 li a yeare is for ever Granted to our College of Virga for the Education of heathen Children in the Christian Faith by this One Example. it Appeares that in time this may be the meanes of bringing to and Adding to the Countrys Stock of wealth wch I hope all that are Friends to the Common Wealth & more particularly they who have the Honour to be Intrusted with the Managemt of the publick Consultacons for that and will think worthy of their Consideration, and will not bee Led away with a vulgar Error wch has been Industriously spread among the Common people that the College will Ruin the Country. It is plain to any man that without prejudice and partiality will Consider matters that not only all that money will be saved wch went Formerly out for European Education but alsoe that our Neighbouring Provinces on this greate Continent of America wil choose much Rather to send their Children hither for the Benefitt of a good Education than to Europe where the Expence of money & the Loss of time and the danger of sickness is much greater.

But if the profitt were noe greater all men must owne that it is much more for the Credditt and Reputacon of the Country to have the means of Education within ourselves than to be beholding to forreign parts for a thing of soe greate Importance, If it was a greate Signe and Badge of Servitude Among the Israelites when they were not permitted to have any Smiths Among them but were Necessitated to sharpen their Goads & Mattocks to the Philistines it is Certainly a much greater Badge of Servitude that wee cant have a Minister nor a Phisician nor a Lawyer nor a statesman nor a Justice of Peace nor an ingenious gentleman without goeing a greate deal further to sharpen our witts & must be kept with our nose to the grindstone & earn our Living with the hard Labour of the hoe till now the old stock of English Gent being dead for want of Education Among our selves that it is a Common complaint that in many Counteys there are not men enough to be found to fill the Bench & to administer Justice between man and man & wee insensibly decline to a state of Ignorance & Abjectnes of Spirritt wch is the Common consequence of it for after all it is not soe much the fertility of the soil or the Blessings of air earth & water that makes a brave Country as the Improoveing the Spirritts of the inhabitants with useful knowledge and the Inspireing them with Noble & Virtuous Resolutions.

But I will venture to proceed further and assert that our Youth is in a much fairer Election of attaining Learning at home than abroad for supposeing the Circumstances to be Equall in other Respects wch is the only fair way of stating such a Question I say it is noe way probable that a Child should be either soe diligent in his Studies or soe Circumspect in his Manners abroad as at home. For alass what is Youth when remoovd from under the Inspection of their parents and all others that Could have any power with them or Authority over them and what are Masters too when there is noe parent to put them in mind of their duty to the Children or to blame them for their Negligence What is a Bashful stranger when cowed & overaw'd with the insulting reflections of a schoolfull of Boyes that with their Mothers Milk Learn to Contemn all others that are not of their owne Nation? doe wee believe that Learning is to be purchased Like a Cargoe of goods or that a Factor has either the time or the Naturall affection of a Parent, to inspect the Education of Forreigne Children or his Authority to Correct them if they should proove stubborn & headstrong as Youth Generally is when Left to its selfe.

But supposeing wch is not easily to be Granted that A Child should make as good proficiency in his Studies when Left to himselfe as when under the Inspection of his parents Yet there are many other greate inconveniencies wch doe almost Necessarily attend a Forreigne Education. One of the Least of these is that it is Impossible for the Parents to have the Comfort of Frequently seing them or hearing from them or knowing whether they doe well at their studies or not. And ye the Comfort of these things is the greatest reward that parents usually have for all their paynes & Labour Another is that a Child being soe long left to him selfe, has got such a taste of Liberty that it is in Vain to Expect, Especialy if hee bee a Child of any Spirritt that ever hee will kindly submitt himselfe to the Paternall or Maternall Yoke after his Returne to his Owne Country and wch is worse by degrees hee is intirely recovered from his parents & utterly forgott them as if hee were under noe Filiall tye or Relation to them soe that insensibly there growes a strangeness and a want of Naturall affection & a third is that when hee is Called home hee comes fraught more Commonly with the Luxury then with the Learning of England & knowes not how to brook our more simple and Less Costly way of Living in Virginia, Hee has now another Gusto that cannott be Sattisfyed with the plainess of his Country & soe either inclines him to Returne to the & Flesh potts of Egypt the good eating & drinking fine playes & Jovial Company of England or if through the Necessity of his Affaires hee finds himselfe Confined to this Country he becomes soe uneasy to himselfe and all that are About him that Neither Virga victuals nor drink or house nor Furniture nor Wife nor Serts nor Company nor business nor anything else Can suit with his New English humor & soe if hee does not Mortgage or sell his Virginia Estate in England the Chief Fruit hee has reapt by his English Education is that hee spends all his dayes in Misery Cursing his hard Fate that has Condemned him to a Life so unsuitable to his humour and inclination, from all which Considerations I think I may safely Conclude that a Virginia Education is the most proper & suitable to Virga Children & that with noe such Loss of time health Wealth or Reputation & with a greate deale more Comfort to our selves and all our Relations wee may follow our studies at home & Improve our Naturally good Capacityes to the Service of the Church And State in our own Country.—*William and Mary College Quarterly Historical Magazine*, X (October, 1930), Series 2, 325-29. See also E. W. Knight, "Early Opposition to the Education of American Children Abroad," *The Educational Forum*, XI (January, 1947), 193-204.

3. HUGH JONES ON EDUCATION IN EUROPE, 1724

As for Education several are sent to *England* for it; though the *Virginians* being naturally of good Parts, (as I have already hinted) neither require nor admire as much Learning, as we do in *Britain;* yet more would be sent over, were they not afraid of the Small-Pox, which most commonly proves fatal to them.

But indeed when they come to *England* they are generally put to learn to Persons that know little of their Temper, who keep them drudging on in what is of least Use to them, in pedantick Methods, too tedious for their volatile Genius.

For *Grammar* Learning taught after the common round-about Way is not much beneficial nor delightful to them; so that they are noted to be more apt to spoil their School-Fellows than improve themselves; because they are imprisoned and enslaved to what they hate, and think useless, and have not peculiar Management proper for their Humour and Occasion.

A civil treatment with some Liberty, if permitted with Discretion is most proper for them, and they have most Need of, and readily take polite and mathematical Learning; and in *English* may be conveyed to them (without going directly to *Rome* and *Athens*) all the Arts, Sciences, and learned Accomplishments of the Antients and Moderns, without the Fatigue and Expence of another Language, for which few of them have little Use or Necessity, since (without another) they may understand their own Speech; and all other Things requisite to be learn'd by them sooner and better.

Thus the Youth might as well be introduced there (Virginia) as here (England) by proper Methods, without the Expence and Danger of coming hither; especially if they make Use of the great Advantage of the *College* at *Williamsburgh*, where they may (and many do) imbibe the Principles of all human and divine Literature, both in *English* and in the learned Languages.

By the happy Opportunity of this College may they be advanced to religious and learned Education, according to the Discipline and Doctrine of the established *Church of England;* in which Respect this College may prove of singular Service, and be an advantageous and laudable Nursery and strong Bulwark against the contagious dissentions in *Virginia*; which is the most antient and loyal, the most plentiful and flourishing, the most extensive and beneficial Colony belonging to the Crown of *Great Britain*, upon which it is most directly dependant; wherein is established the *Church of England* free from Faction and Sects, being ruled by the Laws, Customs, and Constitutions of *Great Britain*, which it strictly observes, only where the Circumstances and Occasion of the Country by an absolute Necessity require some small Alterations; which nevertheless must not be contrary (though different from and subservient) to the Laws of *England*. —*The Present State of Virginia* (London: Printed for P. Clarke at the Bible under the Royal Exchange, 1724) pp. 45-47. An edition of this book was printed in New York in 1865 "for Joseph Sabin." Jones was a zealous churchman, historian, and mathematician who came to this country in 1716, served as professor of mathematics in The College of William and Mary, as chaplain to the Virginia House of Burgesses and as minister at Jamestown. He was author of *A Short English*

Grammar. An Accidence to the English Tongue, said to be the first grammar written in America.

4. VIRGINIANS AT TRINITY COLLEGE, CAMBRIDGE, 1701-1800

Virginians at Trinity College, Cambridge,
Admissions 1701-1800

Carter, John, son of Robert Carter of Virginia, America. School, Mile End, London (Mr. Maltaire). Age 18 Fellow-Commoner, January 12, 1714. Tutor, Mr. Baker, (Matriculated, 1714). Did not graduate).

Taylor, Daniel, son of Daniel Taylor, Judge of Virginia, America. Educated at the College of William and Mary, Virginia. Age 21. From St. John's College whence he had matriculated, 1724. Sizar, October 14, 1724. Tutor Mr. Parue (B. A. 1727).

Ambler, John, Son of Richard Ambler of York Town, Virginia, America. School Wakefield, Yorkshire (Mr. Clarke) Age 19. Pensioner, October 15, 1753. Tutor, Mr. Whisson. (Matriculated 1753. Did not graduate).

Beverley, Robert, son of William Beverley of Virginia, America. School Wakefield, Yorkshire (Mr. Clarke). Age 17. Pensioner, May 19, 1757, Tutor, Mr. Whisson, (Matriculated, 1757. Did not graduate.)

Smith, Thomas, son of Gregory Smith of Virginia, America. School, Wakefield, Yorkshire (Mr. Atkinson) Age 18. Pensioner, April 21, 1759. Tutor Mr. Whisson (Matriculated 1759; Scholar 1760; B.A. 1763.)

Riddell, George, son of Andrew Riddell of Enfield, Middlesex. School, Hampton, Virginia, America (Dr. Warrington), Age 17. Pensioner, September 29, 1769. Tutor, Mr. Postlethwaite, (Matriculated 1770; Scholar 1771; B. A. 1774.

Beverley, William, son of Robert Beverley of Blandfield, Essex. School, Fredericksburg, Spotsylvania, Virginia, North America (Mr. Denholm). Age 18. Pensioner, April 4, 1781. Tutors Mr. Therond & Mr. Cranke. (Did not Matriculate or graduate).

Skipwith, Gray, Son of Peyton Skipwith of Virginia, America. School, Eton (Dr. Davies'). Age 19. Fellow Commoner, November 25, 1790. Tutor, Mr. Jones. (Did not matriculate or graduate).—*The Virginia Magazine of History and Biography,* XXI (1913), 82.

5. Virginians at Appleby School, 1732-53

Lawrence Washington, eldest son of Augustine Washington, of [River], * * * upon his leaving the School gave ½ a guinea—4th December, 1732.

John Brunskill, eldest son of John Brunskill, Vicar of St. Margaretta, Caroline Co., on the river Virginia, upon going to Pembroke Hall, Cambridge, gave half a guinea—20th February, 1751/2.

John Skinker, 3d son of Major Samuel Skinker, of Rappahannock River, in Virginia, on being called home, gave ½ a guinea—16th April, 1753.—*Ibid.*, XI (October, 1903), 214-15.

6. Peter Manigault writes from London to his father
August 1, 1750; March 13, 1752

Hond Sir

...I shall continue to make the best Use of time, by a vigorous Pursuit of my Studies, in order to enable me to return the sooner home; for though I have been absent but a little while, and I like England tolerably well, I could return with a great deal of Pleasure immediately....—*The South Carolinia Historical and Genealogical Magazine*, XV (July, 1914), 117-18.

Hond Sir

...As you are so kind to offer me the Liberty of returning to Carolina, immediately after I am of Age; or of staying sometime Longer abroad; I am willing to be directed in that Respect, intirely by you; however if my Inclinations, provided they are not unreasonable, are in that case to govern, (upon mature Deliberation of the many advantages that may accrue from a longer stay here,) I would not, without your Desire, leave England, till this time two year, and would imploy all the intermediate time, in a close Application to my Improvement. But as I presume you would like to know particularly, how I would bestow myself during so long a space, so I ought in duty to inform you, that I would chuse to stick close to my Books, all this Summer, in London, & in the fall, go the Northern Circuit & then have an Opportunity of seeing such Relations as I have in that part of England. The next winter, I would also chuse to spend in London, & omit nothing, that can possibly be of any advantage to me. Early in the Spring, I hope you wont be against my going to France, &

seeing some parts of Holland and Flanders; in this Excursion I promise myself that besides other useful Attainments, I shall with the help of what I understand already, make myself a compleat Master of the French Tongue. I should like to return to England, in the beginning of the next winter, which will be chiefly taken up, in preparing myself for my return in the Spring; when I could like to take an Opportunity of going to Boston, & travelling by land to Charlestown, where I would not propose to be, till the Month of October.—*Ibid.*, pp. 120-22.

7. Advertisement of Reverend B. Booth's Academy near Liverpool, 1766

At the Rev. B. BOOTH's ACADEMY, the seat of the late Lady MOLLINEUX's at Woolton, five miles from Liverpool, young GENTLEMEN are educated on the following terms:

	£	s.	d.
FOR Board, and learning English, Latin, Greek, Writing, Arithmetick, Merchants Accounts, Geography, Navigation, Astronomy, Surveying, Mathematicks in general, Drawing and Perspective,	21 *per Ann.*	0	0
Entrance for do	1	1	0
Musick, per quarter,	1	1	0
Entrance for do	0	10	6
Dancing, per quarter,	0	15	0
Entrance for do	0	5	0
Fencing, per quarter,	1	1	0
Entrance for do	0	10	6
Fire, per annum,	0	5	0

Washing, according to their age, from 7 s. 6 d. to 10 s. per quarter.

Particulars relating to those who do not board in the Academy, may be had from the master.

—*The Virginia Gazette* (Williamsburg, Alex. Purdie, and John Dixon), November 27, 1766, p. [2]; also December 4, 1766, p. [3].

8. Advertisement of an academy in County York, England, 1769

At the ACADEMY *in* LEEDS,
Which is pleasantly situated in the county of
York, *in* England,

YOUNG Gentlemen are genteely boarded, and diligently instructed in *English*, the Classicks, Modern Languages, Penmanship, Arithmetick, Merchants Accounts, Mathematicks, Modern Geography, Experimental Philosophy, and Astronomy, for twenty guineas *per annum*, if under twelve years of age, by Mr. AARON GRIMSHAW, and able masters. Drawing, Musick, and Dancing, are extra charges. Due regard is paid to the young Gentlemens health, morals, and behaviour.—*Ibid.*, November 2, 1769, p. [3]; also November 9, 1769, p. [3]; November 16, 1769, p. [3].

9. John Rutledge gives advice to his brother, a student in England, 1769

The very first thing you should be thoroughly acquainted with is the writing of shorthand, which you will find an infinite advantage. Take down notes of everything in Court, even if not worth transcribing, for your time may as well be employed in writing as in hearing. By no means fall into the too common practice of not attending a place of worship. There is generally a good preacher at the Temple Church.... If you stick to French and converse generally in that language you may soon be master of it. Whatever study you attempt, make yourself completely master of it; nothing makes a person so ridiculous as to pretend to things he does not understand. I know nothing more entertaining and more likely to give you a graceful manner of speaking than seeing a good play well acted. Garrick is inimitable, mark him well and you will profit by him. You must not neglect the classics. Get a good private tutor who will point out their beauties to you and at your age you will in six months become better acquainted with them than a boy at school generally in seven or eight years. Read Latin authors, the best frequently ... Read the apothegms of Bacon, English history, and the enclosed list of law books; and when I say read, I don't mean run cursorily through them as you would a newspaper, but read carefully and deliberately and transcribe what you find useful in it. Bacon, you know, is my favourite. You will think I have cut out work enough for you while in England, and indeed though it is a long time to look forward to, if you mind your business you will not have too much time to spare . . . One word in regard to your deportment. Let your dress be plain, always in the city and elsewhere, except when it is necessary that it should be otherwise, and your behaviour rather grave.

Farewell, my dear brother. Let me hear from you by every opportunity.

Believe me,

Yours affectionately

J. RUTLEDGE.

—Mrs. T. P. O'Connor, *My Beloved South*, pp. 140-41.

10. SOME VIRGINIANS EDUCATED IN ENGLAND AND SCOTLAND PRIOR TO 1800

Ambler, John, Yorktown, Wakefield School, Yorkshire. Trinity College, Cambridge, 1753.

Armistead, Henry, Gloucester Co., at school in England, (place unknown) 1702.

Alexander, Philip, Stafford Co., Inner Temple, 1760.

Atchison, Walter, Norfolk, Middle Temple, 1771.

Bland, Theodrick, Jr., Prince George, Wakefield, 1753, Edinburgh, 1761.

Bland, Richard (d. 1776), Prince George, Edinburgh.

Beverley, Robert, Essex, Wakefield, Trinity, Cambridge, 1757.

Beverley, William, Essex, Trinity, Cambridge, 1781.

Beverley, Robert, Essex, Mr. Andrews' School at Highgate, 1784.

Beverley, John, Middlesex, at school in England, (place unknown), about 1694.

Beverley, Robert, Middlesex, at school in England (Place unknown), about 1694.

Beverley, Harry, Middlesex, at school in England (place unknown) about 1694.

Blair, John, Williamsburg, Middle Temple, 1755.

Blair, James, Williamsburg, Edinburgh, 1761.

Baylor, John, (d. 1774), King & Queen, Putney Grammar School, and Caius, Cambridge.

Baylor, John, (Jr.), Caroline, Putney Grammar School and Caius, Cambridge.

Brooke, Lawrence, Spotsylvania, Edinburgh, 1776.

Brooke, Robert, Spotsylvania, Edinburgh, 1777.

Ball, William, Lancaster, Edinburgh, 1773.

Ball, Joseph, Lancaster, Grays Inn, 1720.

Ball, Henry Lee, Lancaster, Middle Temple, 1769.

Bolling, Robert, Chesterfield, Wakefield, 1756.

Boush, William, Norfolk, Edinburgh, 1778.

Byrd, William, Charles City, educated in England and Holland, 1684-1695, Middle Temple, 1690.

Brunskill, John, Caroline, Appleby School, Pembroke, Cambridge, 1752.

Burwell, James, York Co., Eton, 1760.

Burwell, Lewis, Gloucester, Eton, 1725, Caius, Cambridge, 1729.

Burwell, Lewis, Gloucester, Balliol, Oxford, 1765, Inner Temple, 1765.

Carter, George (d. 1742), Lancaster, Middle Temple.

Carter, John, Lancaster, Mile End Schools, Trinity, Cambridge, 1714.

Carter, John, "Cleve," King George, at school in England (place unknown), 1764.

Carter, Landon, "Cleve," King George, at school in England (place unknown), 1764.

Carter, Robert, Lancaster, at school in England (place unknown) about 1678.

Corbin, Francis, King & Queen, Inner Temple, 1777, (stated also to have been at Canterbury School and Cambridge.)

Corbin, Gawin, King & Queen, Middle Temple 1756, Christs, Cambridge, 1756.

Corbin, Richard Henry, King & Queen, St. Johns, Cambridge 1794.

Cary, Wilson, Elizabeth City, Trinity, Cambridge, 1721.

Clayton, Thomas, (b. 1701-1739), Gloucester, Pembroke, Cambridge.

Campbell, Archibald, Westmoreland, Edinburgh, 1770.

Downman, Joseph Ball, Lancaster, Middle Temple, 1773.

Eskridge, Robert, Westmoreland, Wood End Grammar School, (Scotland?) 1719.

Fairfax, William, Fairfax, Wakefield, about 1753.

Fauntleroy, William, Richmond Co., Middle Temple, 1760.

Fitzhugh, Henry, Stafford, Christ Church, Oxford, 1722.

Gilmer, George, Williamsburg, Edinburgh, 1761.

Griffin, Corbin, Richmond Co., Edinburgh, 1765.

Griffin, Cyrus, Richmond Co., Middle Temple, 1771.

Griffin, John, Augusta (?), Edinburgh, 1774.

Goodwin, Joseph, Edinburgh, 1769.

Galt, John M., Williamsburgh, Edinburgh, 1770.

Grymes, Philip Ludwell, Middlesex, Eton, 1760.

Grymes, John Randolph, Middlesex, Eton, 1760.

Jones, Walter, Hanover, Edinburgh, 1769.

Kenner, Rodham, (b. 1707), Northumberland, St Bees Grammar School.

Lee, Arthur, Westmoreland, Eton 1753, Edinburgh, Lincoln's Inn 1770, Middle Temple.

Lee, Henry, Middle Temple, 1773.

Lee, John, Westmoreland, Queens, Oxford, 1658.

Lee, George Fairfax, Westmoreland, Christ, Cambridge, 1772.

Lee, Richard Henry, Westmoreland, Wakefield.

Lee, Philip Ludwell, Westmoreland, Inner Temple.

Lee, Ludwell, Westmoreland, St. Bees, 1776.

Lee, Thomas, Westmoreland, at school in England (place unknown) 1776.

Lee, Lancelot, Westmoreland, at school in England (place unknown) 1771.

Lee, William, Westmoreland, at school in England (place unknown) 1771.

Meade, David, Nansemond, private school at Dalston, and Harrow 1751.

Meade, Richard Kidder, Nansemond, private school at Dalston (and probably Harrow.)

Meade, Everard, Nansemond, private school at Dalston (and probably Harrow.)

Mason, Thompson, Fairfax, Temple.

Munford, Robert, Mecklenburg, Wakefield about 1752.

McClurg, James, Elizabeth City, Edinburgh 1770.

Nelson, Thomas Jr., Yorkton, educated in England 1752-59 under care of Bishop Porteus.

Nicolls, Samuel, Edinburgh 1776.

Parker, George Northampton, at school in Bristol about 1676-79.

Power, James, King William, Wakefield, 1757.

Peyton, Valentine, Stafford, Edinburgh, 1754.

Page, Mann, Gloucester, Eton 1706, St. Johns, Oxford, 1709.

Perrott, Henry, Middlesex, Grays Inn, 1674.

Randolph, Peyton (d. 1776), Williamsburgh, Middle Temple.

Randolph, (Sir) John, Henrico, Grays Inn.

Randolph, Beverley, Williamsburgh, Eton, 1762.

Randolph, William, Williamsburg, Eton 1762.

Robinson, Christopher, Middlesex, Oriel, Oxford, 1721.

Robinson, Christopher, Middlesex, Oriel, Oxford, 1723.

Robinson, Peter, Middlesex, Oxford, 1737.

Robinson, Middlesex, Oriel, Oxford, 1737.

Robinson, John, Middlesex, educated in England 1713 and under care of his uncle Bishop Robinson.

Ravenscroft, John, Prince George, Edinburgh 1770.

Skipwith, Gray, Mechlenburg, Eton 1787, Trinity, Cambridge, 1790.

Spotswood, Alexander, Spotsylvania, Eton 1760.

Scott, Gustavus, Prince Wm., Kings College, Aberdeen 1765, Middle Temple 1767.

Scott, John, Prince Wm., King's College, Aberdeen, 1768.

Smith, Thomas, King & Queen, Trinity, Cambridge, 1759.

Steptoe, George, Westmoreland, Edinburgh, 1767.

Shore, John, Prince George, Edinburgh, 1777.

Stith, William, Charles City, Queens, Oxford, 1724.

Skinker, John, King George, Appleby 1753.

Span, John, Northumberland, Queens, Oxford, 1705.

Tayloe, John, Richmond Co., Eton 1788, St. John's Cambridge 1789.

Thacker, Chichley, Middlesex, Oriel, Oxford, 1724.

Tucker, St. George, Yorktown (born in Bermuda) Inner Temple 1773.

Turberville, George Lee, Westmoreland, Winchester 1771.

Tapscott, James, Edinburgh, 1765.

Turpin, Philip. Chesterfield, Edinburgh, 1774.

Taylor, Daniel, New Kent, Trinity, Cambridge, 1724.

Washington, Augustine Sr., Westmoreland, Appleby.

Washington, Augustine Jr., Westmoreland, Appleby.

Washington, Lawrence, Westmoreland, Appleby, 1722.

Wormeley, Ralph, Middlesex, Oriel, Oxford, 1665.

Wormeley, Ralph, Middlesex, Eton 1757, Trinity, Cambridge.

Wormeley, Ralph, Middlesex, at school in England (place unknown) 1702.

Wormeley, John, Middlesex, at school in England (place unknown) 1702.

Warner, Augustine, Gloucester, Merchant Taylors, London, 1658.
White, Alexander, Frederick, Inner Temple, 1762.
Yates, Bartholomew, Middlesex, Brasenose, Oxford, 1695.
Yates, Bartholomew, Middlesex, Oriel, Oxford, 1732.
Yates, Robert, Middlesex, Oriel, Oxford, 1733.

A number of the persons included in this list also studied at Wm. and Mary. The counties most numerously represented were Westmoreland, 19, and Middlesex, 17.—*The Virginia Magazine of History and Biography*, XXI (1913), 196-99. The Virginia residence is given, and at least one year, preferably the first year, of the student's residence in the school or college.

11. ON SOUTH CAROLINA STUDENTS SENT ABROAD, 1809

The operation of slavery to so great an extent produces, of course, the same effects here as in other places; but the people have considerably improved in education and morals since the revolution. It was customary for a long period, for the more wealthy planters to send their sons to Europe for education; and even now they frequently send them to the northern states; but the practice is gradually declining, and the desire has become general to have respectable seminaries in the state. A college has been founded, and very respectably endowed, at Columbia; and there are several other colleges and academies throughout the state. The towns are pretty well supplied with common schools, but they are defective in the country; and this branch of education, being the basis of the morality of the state, deserves the early attention of the legislature.—John Melish, *Travels Through the United States of America in the Years 1806, 1807, 1809, 1810, and 1811*. I, 283-84.

XIV

TUTORIAL PRACTICES; "OLD FIELD" AND "COMMUNITY" SCHOOLS

I. PREVIEW AND COMMENTS

THE TUTORIAL SYSTEM of education was very popular in the Southern Colonies, particularly in Virginia and South Carolina where educational opportunities for the children of the wealthy planting classes were generally provided by such means. In the early period some of the tutors came from England and in the eighteenth century many came from the northern part of this country. Occasionally an indentured servant served as tutor, as was the case of John Harrower, a part of whose diary is included in this section.

Perhaps the best known account of the tutorial system is given by Philip Vickers Fithian who went to "Nomini Hall" in Westmoreland County, Virginia, in 1773 as tutor of the children of Robert Carter, a member of one of the wealthiest and most influential families in Virginia.

Fithian was born in New Jersey, in 1747, was admitted to the junior class of Princeton November 30, 1770, and was graduated in September two years later, then studied theology in preparation for admission to the Presbyterian ministry. In the fall of 1773 he was offered a position as tutor in the Carter family through a letter which he received from Dr. John Witherspoon who served as president of Princeton intermittently from 1768 until his death in 1794. Dr. Witherspoon advised young Fithian to take the position in Virginia, if only for a short time, although it appears that the staunch Calvinist warned the young man against the moral and physical dangers he would likely face in the conditions many people believed to exist among the wealthy and regal families of the Old Dominion. The young man seems to have been agreeably surprised when he found at Nomini Hall so many evidences of culture, refinement, and elegance of life instead of the alleged revelry and riotous and loose living. The master of Nomini Hall, grandson of "King Carter," was a man of wide culture, of studious habits, and preferred the quietude of his family estate to the "gayeties of the Governor's court at Williamsburg" although he was a member of the King's Council which sat in that town.

Probably no contemporary account now available gives a more interesting and vivid view of life on a plantation in the late eighteenth century than these materials, first published in 1900 by the Princeton Historical Association, edited by John Rogers Williams (Princeton, N. J.: The University Library). Williams also edited and published some of the selections in *The American Historical Review*, January, 1900 (pp. 290-319). At that time the Philip Fithian papers were the property of Mrs. Edward W. Hitchcock, of Philadelphia, who was a descendant of the Fithian family. She died in 1900, while the book, which bore the title *Philip Vickers Fithian, Journal and Letters, 1767-1774*, was in press. In 1943 Colonial Williamsburg, Incorporated, reprinted the work which was edited, with an introduction, by Hunter Dickinson Farish, under the title *Journal & Letters of Philip Vickers Fithian, 1773-1774: A Plantation Tutor of the Old Dominion*, from which the selections that follow are taken, with the permission of the publishers. The Williamsburg edition includes some materials that were omitted from the Princeton edition. The Fithian manuscripts now are in the Princeton University Library.

Among the many unofficial European "inspectors" who visited the United States during the latter part of the eighteenth and the early part of the nineteenth century was John Davis, who was born at Salisbury, Wiltshire, in 1776, came to this country at the age of twenty-two, and in 1805 published in England his *Travels of Four Years and A Half in the United States of America*.[1]

Davis, who was "reared in the lap of opulence," was a man of good education and wide reading, a traveller "who was professedly literary, who cared little for the political aspects of what he saw ... He came here presumably to make a living at least for a time, and numbered among his American friends many men of high political and social station. He was private tutor in New York, South Carolina, and Virginia. His book, from which the excerpts below are taken, was "dedicated by permission to Jefferson from whom Davis bore a letter of recommendation. Davis said: "By imparting what I knew of English, French and Latin to others, I was enabled to gratify my disposition to travel, and to subsist comfortably." The letter to Jefferson bore the date of August 31, 1801, and Jefferson's reply that of September 9, 1801.

Many ministers of the Church of England served also as tutors in

---

1. This book was reprinted in New York in 1909 by Henry Holt and Company, with an introduction by A. J. Morrison.

the Southern Colonies. From 1733 to 1774 more than 400 advertisements relating to schools and schoolmasters were published in *The South Carolina Gazette* at Charleston; and many scores of similar advertisements appeared in Virginia, North Carolina, and Georgia during the late colonial and early national period.[2]

Philip A. Bruce says [3] that perhaps most of the children in Virginia who received education during the seventeenth century obtained it in what came to be known at a later date as the "Old Field School." This type of school has often been referred to and may be described as a "community school" set up at a convenient place by the people of the neighborhood. Sometimes such a school was called "academy," as was the case of the one in charge of John Davis on the plantation of Mr. Ball in Virginia in the latter part of the eighteenth century. The people of the neighborhood assured Davis that if he would continue with them for seven years they would build a "brick seminary" which would be a rival of the College of William and Mary. "It now opened what some called an academy but others an Old Field School." It will be noted also that John Harrower taught children other than those of Colonel Daingerfield at the plantation near Fredericksburg.

II. DOCUMENTS

1. Extracts from the diary and letters of Philip Vickers Fithian, 1773-1774

Nassau-Hall June 26th 1773.

Sir.

I expected notwithstanding your small offence you would have let me know before this time whether you had made any determination different from what you designed when I left you. If you design teaching before you get into business, there are now several considerable offers made to young men who are willing to go to Virginia by some of the first gentlemen in the colony; one particularly who will give as good as 60 £, the best accomodations, a room to study in and the advantage of a library, a horse kept and a servant to wait upon you.

Dr.Witherspoon is very fond of getting a person to send him. I make no kind of doubt but if you were to write to the doctor but

2. Hundreds of these advertisements have been collected and now are in the Library of the University of North Carolina. Only a few are used here.
3. *Institutional History of Virginia in the Seventeenth Century*, I, 331.

he would engage it to you, the terms are exactly as I write you as I have informed myself that I might let you know—...

I am, Sir,

Your very friend,
Andw Hunter.[4]

Philip V. Fithian to Andrew Hunter, Jr.

Deerfield, July 3. 1773.

Sir

...What you write concerning the offer of a Gentleman in Virginia, is, I think of considerable consequence, provided the conditions of teaching are not over burdensome; I should speedily agree to go and apply for the place, were I made satisfied as to this.

I shall however, beg the assistance of your friendship, to enquire in what county the school is; what number and degrees of scholars there are; and if you think the place suitable, and if the Doctor shall think proper to appoint me to it, I am not unwilling to remove and accept it. Please to mention this to the Doctor; and if he has not engaged a teacher, and is pleased to accept me, I hope you will acquaint me as speedily as may be, with what you can learn as to the time of beginning, the custom of the school, &c. You mentioned four in your last, who have applied to Presbytery, and are on tryal, I can tell you another, Mr. Heith; he applied to the Philadelphia Presbytery; but came to town, I understood so late, that before he made application the Presbytery was dissolved, some of the members however, being still in town, at his request, gave him sundry pieces of exercise, which it is expected the Presbytery will acknowledge, so that he is the fifth out of our class who is designing soon to appear in public!

I am Sir yours, &c.

Philip. V. Fithian

Fryday july 30.

...Received several Letters by the Stage to Day; One especially from Mr Hunter, in which I am pressed to accept the proposal by the Gentleman in Virginia. The Offer is very proffitable; Colonel *Carter* has four Sons. To a private Tutor for which he proposes to give sixty-five Pounds pr Year; find him all Accommodations; Allow him a Room for his own Study; And the Use of an eligant Library of

4. Andrew Hunter, Jr., was a resident of Cohansie, New Jersey, the home of Fithian, who studied under the Reverend Andrew Hunter, Sr., in preparation for the Presbyterian ministry.

Books; A Horse to ride; & a Servant to Wait. I am inclined to go, but dont meet with much Encouragement from those who have the Direction of my Studies. ...

Monday August 2.
Concluded, this Day, with the Concurrence of Mr *Hunter*, to set off for Princeton, & know of Dr. Witherspoon something more particular concerning the Proposal for my going to *Virginia*. Busy all the Afternoon in preparing to go.—Evening very hot. Went on foot to the Stage.—Drank a Bowl of Punch with Mr. *Richard* Howel, & to bed by ten.

Monday August 9
Waited on Dr Witherspoon, about nine oClock, to hear his proposal for my going to *Virginia*— He read me a Letter which he receivd from Col: Carter, & proposed the following Terms— To teach his Children, five Daughters, & three Sons, who are from five to seventeen years Old— The young Ladies are to be taught the English Language. And the Boys are to study the English Language carefully; & to be instructed in the Latin, & Greek— And he proposes to give thirty five Pounds Sterling, which is about Sixty Pounds currency; Provide all Accommodations; Allow him the undisturbed Use of a Room; And the Use of his own Library; find Provender for a Horse; & a Servant to Wait—
—By the advice of the Dr & his Recommendation of the Gentleman, & the Place, I accepted the Offer, & agreed to go in the Fall into *Virginia*—...

Monday August 30.
Rose by half after six— Write a Letter to Dr Witherspoon concerning my going to Virginia— I hear that many of my Friends in this Place are unwilling I should go— I am indeed in a Dilimma— But I have agreed— Well, I must away— And I hope in the Kindness of him who was my Fathers God, & has been the Guide of my Youth, that he will save me from being corrupted, or carried away with the Vices which prevail in that Country—...

Philip V. Fithian to Dr. Witherspoon.
Greenwich august 30th 1773.
Revd Sir.
I am sorry that I may inform you of the dissattisfaction which my

friends in general since my return home seem to discover, with my intention of going this fall to *Virginia*. However willing I am myself to accept the proposal and go, it will not be easy to break through the entreaties of those who are my neares[t] relations, and who have all along, with the warmest friendship interested themselves to procure my welfare. I do not intend by any means, abruptly to decline the fulfilling my agreement, but only desire to know, if there are not some to be found among the late Seniors who would willingly discharge me by accepting the offer themselves. If not I have only further to beg, that you would be pleased, Revd Sir, to favour me with the proposal of the gentleman; and so soon as there is a return from him, I shall be glad to know the time when I must leave home;

I am Revd Sir,
with great respect
your humble Servt
Philip V. Fithian

P.S. Letters come safe sent by the princeton stage, and directed to me at Greenwich.

Andrew Hunter to Philip Fithian.
Nassau Hall Septr 6th 1773

Dr Sir.

I am very sorry that I cannot answer your letter so much to your satisfaction as I could desire. Doctor Witherspoon is gone to New-England to the convention and is not expected home 'till the latter end of this week— he received no account from Virginia before he went from home. You may trust that I will let you know when ever I can hear any thing related to your prospect of going to the southward. . .

I am, Sir,
Your friend.
Andw Hunter.

Wednesday Sept: 8
Received a Letter from Mr Hunter—No News from Princeton—Nor Virginia—Evening Mr Paterson came home with Uncle.

Wednesday. Sept: 15.
Rose at seven; slept but little for I was affraid— Breakfasted on Oysters, at the Ferry-Mans, with John Holmes, Esq:—Had an Hours Conversation with him, on Lotteries—Whether they are just & lawful

—He thinks not—At ten we came up to his Brother Benjamin Holmes's Esq:— They mentioned to me an Intention they have to erect, & establish a School, among them, that their Children may be taught, Latin, Greek, & the Practical Branches in Mathematicks— They desired to know if it would be convenient, & agreeable for me to undertake with them, to prosecute their Plan. But I must, with Doubt, away to *Virginia*— It would be a laudable undertaking if such a School could be founded in this Part of our Province; & I think ought to be duely encouraged—...

Monday Octob: 11.
By Six up— Busy in Preparing for my Journey— Agreed with Uncle for his Horse; I am to give him 25 £—The Money to be paid in May next.

Teusday October 12.
Rose early; very busy— Had my Boots altered & mended— Was measured for a Surtout-Coat— Drew up a Form to settle my Affairs before I leave Home—Afternoon Mrs Peck, Mrs Hoshel, Johnny Peck, Stephen Ranney, Miss Abby Peck call to see me & take a final Adieu for the present— The Thought of Leaving Home haunts me at Times!

Wednesday Octob: 13.
Dismissed Study, & begin to take Leave of Relations & Friends!—...

Thursday 28.
Rode after Breakfast to the Honorable Rob: Carters the End of my Journey; 12 Miles, by two o-Clock in the Afternoon. Both Myself, and my Horse seem neither tired nor Dispirited—...

Fryday 29.
Settled myself in the Room appointed me— and adjusted my Affairs after my Ride.

Saturday 30.
Rode with Mr Carters eldest Son to a Store, about seven Miles— Bought half a Box of Wafers for 1/- And a quire of paper for 1/6. Dined at three— And rode into Richmond Parish 15 Miles to Mr Fantleroys— Was introduced to Mr Fantleroy—two of his Sons— Mr. Christian a dancing Master—

Sunday 31.
Rode to Church six Miles—Heard Mr. Gibbern—preach on Felixes trembling at Pauls Sermon.

Monday Novemr 1st.
We began School— The School consists of eight— Two of Mr. Carters Sons— One Nephew— And five Daughters— The eldest Son is reading Salust; Grammatical Exercises, and latin Grammar— The second Son is reading english Grammar Reading English: Writing, and Cyphering in Subtraction— The Nephew is Reading and Writing as above; and Cyphering in Reduction— The eldest daughter is Reading the Spectator; Writing; & beginning to Cypher— The second is reading next out of the Spelling-Book, and begining to write— The next is reading in the Spelling-Book— The fourth is Spelling in the beginning of the Spelling-Book— And the last is beginning her letters—

Letter of Philip V. Fithian to the Reverend Enoch Green.

Westmoreland. Novr. 2d 1773.

Revd Sir.

According as I appointed I take this early oppertunity of acquainting you that I am arrived safe; and I am to assure you that I find the place fully equal to my highest expectations— I am situated in the *Northern-Neck,* in a most delightful Country; in a civil, polite neighbourhood; and in a family remarkable for regularity, and economy, tho' confessedly of the highest quality and greatest worth of any in *Virginia.* I teach only Mr Carters children, and only one of them is to learn Languages, and he is reading Salust and the Greek grammar, is seventeen years old, and seems to be a Boy of Genius— the other two learn writing and Arithmetic— But he has four Daughters, young Misses that are at times to be taught writing and English— I have the terms as I expected, and find the place wholly agreeable— and am strongly solicited to stay many years— But money nor conveniency shall detain me long from my most important connections at home— You may expect me in may at the *Synod.* Please to have my compliments to Mrs Green, to Miss Betsy if at Deerfield, and to my acquaintances that shall enquire and accept to yourself the
Respect of your humble Servt

Philip V. Fithian

Wednesday 3.
Busy in School—

Thursday 4.
Busy in School— To day the two eldest Daughters, and second Son attended the Dancing School.

Fryday 5.
Busy in School—

Saturday 6.
Catechised in School til twelve—the Children. And dismiss'd them. . .

Sunday 7.
Rode to Ucomico Church— 8 Miles— Heard Parson Smith. He shewed to us the uncertainty of Riches, and their Insufficiency to make us happy— Dined at Captain Walkers; With Parson Smith, his Wife; his Sister, a young Lady; &c— Returned in the Evening.

Monday 8.
Busy in School—. . .

Teusday 9.
Busy in School—

Wednesday 10.
Busy in School— The eldest Daughter taken off by her Teacher in Music; Mr Stadley who is learning her to play the *Forte-piano—*

Thursday 11.
Rose by seven— Busy in School—. . .

Fryday 12.
Rose by Seven— Ben begun his Greek Grammar—Three in the Afternoon Mr Carter returned from *Williamsburg.* He seems to be agreeable, discreet, and sensible—He informed me more particularly concerning his desire as to the Instruction of his Children—

Saturday 13.
   Catechised the Children and dismissed them about Eleven —Read in Pictete— and proceeded in writing my Sermon for the Presbytery— Expence for my Horse 1/3.

Sunday 14.

Rode to Nominy Church about six Miles— the day Cold— Parson Smith preached— "What shall a man be profited" &c. Rode home after Sermon— Dined at Mr Carters to day Mrs Turbuville, Miss Jenny Corbin, and Mr Cunningham a young Merchant.

Monday 15.
Busy in School—Wrote in the Evening at my Sermon.

Teusday 16.
In School—Writing at my Sermon.

Wednesday 17.
Busy in School—

Thursday 18.
Busy in School—

Fryday 19.
Busy in School—

Saturday 20.
Rode to Mr Fishers dined with Mr Cunningham at 3 o-Clock— Rode in the evening to Mr Lancelot Lees, a young Gentleman, who has lately come from England; sup'd on Oysters— Rode home about nine o-Clock he along—

Sunday 21.

Rode to Church— Mr Smith preached on the Parable of the rich Man. Dined at home—Mr Lee dined with us—Reading in Pictete— Feel very home-Sick— Saw two Brothers quarrel—Doleful Sight.—

Monday 22.
Busy in School—Mr Lee gave us his Company in the morning in School, and was very chearful— he left us about twelve o-Clock—

Teusday 23.
Busy in School— Miss Carter rode out with her Dady and Mama to the County Court— Writing at my Sermons.

Wednesday 24.
Busy in School.

Thursday 25.
Rode this morning to Richmond Court-house, where two Horses run for a purse of 500 Pounds; besides small Betts almost enumerable...

Fryday 26.
Busy in School— Robin, & Nancy at dancing-School.

Saturday 27.
Robin and Nancy yet at Dancing-School—Mr Harry Fantleroy call'd after dinner to see us. In the Evening Ben & I rode with him to his fathers; I was introduced to one Mr Walker a Scotch Gentleman, lately a School-master but has quit, and is going in the Spring for the Gown to England.

Sunday 28.
Rode to Church— The Parson was absent; it is indeed a little cold! The Clerk read prayers for us—...

Monday 29.
All our Scholars present— Mr Carter has put into my hands; Tyre's Dictionary, & the pronouncing Dictionary, to improve his Sons in Grammar classically, both Latin and English. and he has given me Fenning in Arrithmetic.

Tuesday 30.
Busy in School—I was solicited the other Day at the Race by one Mr *Gorden,* to take and instruct two of his Sons, Saturday also I was again solicited by Mr Fantleroy to take two of his Sons—But I must decline it—

Wednesday Decemr 1st 1773.
Busy in School—...
Afternoon Vacant.

Letter of Philip V. Fithian to the Reverend
Enoch Green.

Decemr 1st 1773.

Revd Sir.
As you desired I may not omit to inform you, so far as I can by a letter, of the business in which I am now engaged, it would indeed be vastly agreeable to me if it was in my power to give you particular intelligence concerning the state and plan of my employment here.

I set out from home the 20th of Octr and arrived at the Hon: Robert Carters, of Nominy, in Westmorland County, the 28th I began to teach his children the first of November. He has two sons, and one Nephew; the oldest Son is turned of seventeen, and is reading Salust and the greek grammer; the others are about fourteen, and in english grammer, and Arithmetic. He has besides five daughters which I am to teach english, the eldest is turned of fifteen, and is reading the spectator; she is employed two days in every week in learning to play the Forte-Piana, and Harpsicord—The others are smaller, and learning to read and spell. Mr Carter is one of the Councellors in the general court at Williamsburg, and possest of as great, perhaps the clearest fortune according to the estimation of people here, of any man in Virginia; He seems to be a good scholar, even in classical learning, and is remarkable one in english grammar; and notwithstanding his rank, which in general seems to countenance indulgence to children, both himself and Mrs Carter have a manner of instructing and dealing with children far superior, I may say it with confidence, to any I have ever seen, in any place, or in any family. They keep them in perfect subjection to themselves, and never pass over an occasion of reproof; and I blush for many of my acquaintances when I say that the children are more kind and complaisant to the servants who constantly attend them than we are to our superiors in age and condition. Mr Carter has an overgrown library of Books of which he allows me the free use. It consists of a general collection of law books, all the Latin and Greek Classicks, vast number of Books on Divinity chiefly by writers who are of the established Religion; he has the works of almost all the late famous writers, as Locke, Addison, Young, Pope, Swift, Dryden, &c. in Short, Sir, to speak moderately, he has more than eight times your number—His eldest Son, who seems to be a Boy of genius and application is to be sent to Cambridge University, but I believe will go through a course either in Philadelphia or Princeton College first. As to what is commonly said concerning Virginia that it is difficult to avoid being corrupted with the manners of the people, I believe it is founded wholly in a mistaken notion that persons must, when here frequent all promiscuous assemblies; but this is so far from truth that any one who does practise it, tho' he is accused of no crime, loses at once his character; so that either the manners have been lately changed, or the report is false, for he seems now to be best esteemed and most applauded who attends to his business, whatever it be, with the greatest diligence. I believe the virginians have of late altered their manner very much, for they begin to find that their estates by even small extravagance, decline, and grow involved with debt, this seems to be the spring which induces the People of fortune who are the pattern of all behaviour here, to be frugal, and moderate...

I am, Sir, yours

Philip V. Fithian

Thursday 2.
Busy in School.

Fryday 3.
Busy in School...
Evening after School walked in the fields with Mrs. *Carter,* Miss Carter, and Miss Nancy.

Tuesday 7.
Mr *Stadley* Miss Priscilla's Music Master arrived this morning—He performed several peices on the Violin. Expence for an Orange half a Bit.

Wednesday 8.
Miss Priscilla with her Music Master, they performed together to day—

Thursday 9.
Mr Stadley left us. Busy in School.

Fryday 10.
Miss Nancy is beginning on the *Guitar.* Ben finished reading Salusts Cataline Conspiracy.

Sunday 12.
Rode to Nominy-Church, parson Smith preached 15 minutes—Advertisement at the Church door dated Sunday Decemr 12th Pork to be sold to-morrow at 20/. per Hundred—dined with us to day Captain Walker. Colonal Richd Lee; & Mr Lanclot Lee. sat after Dinner till Sunset, drank three Bottles of Medaira, two Bowls of Toddy!—

Monday 13.
Mr Carter is preparing for a Voyage in his Schooner, the Hariot, to the Eastern Shore in Maryland, for Oysters: there are of the party, Mr *Carter,* Captain *Walker* Colonel *Richd Lee,* & Mr *Lancelot Lee.* With Sailors to work the vessel—I observe it is a general custom on

Sundays here, with Gentlemen to invite one another home to dine, after Church; and to consult about, determine their common business, either before or after Service—It is not the Custom for Gentlemen to go into Church til Service is beginning, when they enter in a Body, in the same manner as they come out; I have known the Clerk to come out and call them in to prayers.—They stay also after the Service is over, usually as long, sometimes longer, than the parson was preaching—Almost every Lady wears a red Cloak; and when they ride out they tye a white handkerchief over their Head and face, so that when I first came into Virginia, I was distress'd whenever I saw a Lady, for I thought She had the Tooth-Ach!—The People are extremely hospitable, and very polite both of which are most certainly universal Characteristics of the Gentlemen in Virginia—some swear bitterly, but the practise seems to be generally disapproved—I have heard that this Country is notorious for Gaming, however this be, I have not seen a Pack of *Cards*, nor a *Die*, since I left home, nor gaming nor Betting of any kind except at the Richmond-Race. Almost every Gentleman of Condition, keeps a Chariot and *Four*; many drive with six Horses—I observe that all the Merchants & shopkeepers in the Sphere of my acquaintance and I am told it is the Case through the Province, are young Scotch-Men; Several of whom I know, as *Cunningham, Jennings, Hamilton, Blain;*—And it has been the custom heretofore to have all their Tutors, and Schoolmasters from Scotland, tho' they begin to be willing to employ their own Countrymen—Evening Ben Carter and myself had a long dispute on the practice of fighting—He thinks it best for two persons who have any dispute to go out in good-humour & fight manfully, & says they will be sooner and longer friends than to brood and harbour malice—Mr *Carter* is practising this Evening on the *Guittar* He begins with the *Trumpet Minuet*. He has a good Ear for Music; a vastly delicate Taste: and keeps good Instruments, he has here at Home a *Harpsichord, Forte-Piano, Harmonica, Guittar, Violin,* & *German Flutes,* & at Williamsburg, has a good *Organ,* he himself also is indefatigable in the Practice.

Teusday 14.
Busy in School—The Weather vastly fine! . . .

Wednesday 15.
Busy in School—To day Dined with us Mrs Turburville, & her Daughter Miss Letty Miss Jenny Corbin, & Mr Blain. We dined at three. The manner here is different from our way of living in Co-

hansie—In the morning so soon as it is light a Boy knocks at my Door to make a fire; after the Fire is kindled, I rise which now in the winter is commonly by Seven, or a little after, By the time I am drest the Children commonly enter the School-Room, which is under the Room I sleep in; I hear the round one lesson, when the Bell rings for eight o'clock (for Mr Carter has a large good Bell of upwards of 60 Lb. which may be heard some miles, & this is always rung at meal Times;) the Children then go out; and at half after eight the Bell rings for Breakfast, we then repair to the Dining-Room; after Breakfast, which is generally about half after nine, we go into School, and sit til twelve, when the Bell rings, & they go out for noon; the dinner-Bell rings commonly about half after two, often at three, but never before two.—After dinner is over, which is common, when we have no Company, is about half after three we go into School, & sit til the Bell rings at five, when they separate til the next morning; I have to myself in the Evening, a neat Chamber, a large Fire, Books, & Candle & my Liberty, either to continue in the school room, in my own Room or to sit over at the great House with Mr & Mrs Carter—We go into Supper commonly about half after eight or at nine & I usually go to Bed between ten and Eleven. Altho the family in which I live, is certainly under as good political Regulations, and every way as suitable & agreeable as I can expect, or even could desire; & though the Neighbourhood is polite, & the Country pleasant, yet I cannot help reflecting on my situation last winter, which was near the lovely *Laura* for whom I cannot but have the truest, and the warmest Esteem! possibly, If Heaven shall preserve my life, in some future time, I may again enjoy her good society. . .

Fryday 17.

I dismissed the children this morning til' monday on account of Mr Christian's *Dance* which, as it goes through his Scholars in Rotation, happens to be here to Day—and I myself also am unwell, so as not to go out; Mrs Carter sent me over Coffee for Breakfast; & soon after some Spirits of *Hartshorn* for my Head—At twelve she sent the waiting Man to know if I was better, & what I would choose for Dinner. I thank'd her, & desired that She would give herself no trouble; She was careful, however, from her undistinguished kindness, to send me before Dinner some hot *Barley Broth,*—*Ben Carter* before Noon introduced into my Room, Mr *Billy Booth*, a young Gentleman of Fortune, who is one of Mr Christians pupils—The two Master Fantleroys came in also to see me—There came to the dance three *Chariots*, two *Chairs*, & a number of Horses. Towards Evening I grew better, & walked down, with a number of young Fellows to the River; after our return I was strongly solicited by the young Gentlemen to go in and dance I declined it, however, and went to my Room not without Wishes that it had been a part of my Education to learn what I think is an innocent and an ornamental, and most certainly, in this province is a necessary qualification for a person to appear even decent in Compay!—

Mrs *Carter* in the Evening, sent me for Supper, a Bowl of hot Green Tea, & several *Tarts*. I expected that they would have danced till late in the Night, but intirely contrary to my Expectation, the Company were separated to their respective apartments before half after nine *oClock*.

Saturday 18.

Rose by Seven, Sent for Mr Carters Barber and was drest for Breakfast—We went in to Breakfast at ten;—I confess I have been seldom more dash'd than when I entered the dining-Room, for I must of necessity be interrogated by Mr *Carter* before them all, about my indisposition, and if I was better.—I went through the several Ceremonies with as much resolution, and speed as possible, and soon mixed with the Company in promiscuous conversation. There were present of Grown persons Mr & Mrs *Carter*, Mrs *Lee*, and Miss *Jenny Corbin*; young Misses about Eleven: & Seven young Fellows, including myself; —After Breakfast, we all retired into the Dancing-Room, & after the Scholars had their Lesson singly round Mr Christian, very politely, requested me to step a *Minuet*; I excused myself however, but signified my peculiar pleasure in the Accuracy of their performance—There were several Minuets danced with great ease and propriety; after which the whole company Joined in country-dances, and it was indeed beautiful to admiration, to see such a number of young persons, set off by dress to the best Advantage, moving easily, to the sound of well performed Music, and with perfect regularity, tho' apparently in the utmost Disorder—The Dance continued til two, we dined at half after three—soon after Dinner we repaired to the Dancing-Room again; I observe in the course of the lessons, that Mr Christian is punctual, and rigid in his discipline, so strict indeed that he struck two of the young Misses for a fault in the course of their performance, even in the present of the Mother of one of them! And he rebuked one of the young Fellows so highly as to tell him he must alter his manner, which he had observed through the Course of the Dance, to be insolent, and wanton, or absent himself from the School—I thought this a sharp reproof, to a young Gentleman of seventeen, before a large number of Ladies!—When it grew too dark to dance, the young Gentlemen walked over to my Room, we conversed til half after six; Nothing is now to be heard of in conversation, but the *Balls*, the *Fox-hunts* the fine *entertainments*, and the *good fellowship*, which are to be exhibited at the approaching *Christmas*.—I almost think myself happy that my Horses lameness will be a sufficient Excuse for my keeping at home on these Holidays.—Mr Goodlet was barr'd out of his School last Monday by his Scholars, for the Christmas Holidays, which are to continue til twelfth-day; But my Scholars are of a more quiet nature; and have consented to have four or five Days now, and to have their full Holiday in May next, when I propose by the permission of Providence to go Home, where I hope to see the good and benevolent *Laura*.

When the candles were lighted we all repaired, for the last time, into the dancing Room; first each couple danced a Minuet; then all joined as before in the country Dances, these continued till half after Seven when Mr Christian retired; and at the proposal of several, (with Mr Carters approbation) we played *Button*, to get Pauns for Redemption; here I could join with them, and indeed it was carried on with sprightliness, and Decency; in the course of redeeming my Pauns, I had several Kisses of the Ladies!—Early in the Evening cam colonel Philip Lee, in a travelling Chariot from Williamsburg—Half after eight we were rung in to Supper; The room looked luminous and splendid; four very large candles burning on the table where we supp'd, three others in different parts of the Room; a gay, sociable Assembly, & four well instructed waiters!—So soon as we rose from supper, the Company form'd into a semicircle round the fire, & Mr Lee, by the voice of the Company was chosen *Pope*, and Mr Carter, Mr Christian, Mrs *Carter*, Mrs *Lee*, and the rest of the company were appointed Friars, in the Play call'd "break the Popes neck"—Here we had great Diversion in the respective Judgments upon offenders, but we were all dismiss'd by ten, and retired to our several Rooms.

Monday 20.

Rose at half after Seven; the Morning extremely cold—We had in School to Day as visitors Miss Betsy, and Miss Matilda Lee Mr Carter gave me for his Daughter Nancy to Read, the "compleat Letter-writer"—Also he put into my hands for the use of the school, "the British-Grammar."

Saturday 25.

I was waked this morning by Guns fired all round the House. The morning is stormy, the wind at South East rains hard Nelson the Boy who makes my Fire, blacks my shoes, does errands &c. was early in my Room, drest only in his short and Breeches! He made me a vast fire, blacked my Shoes, set my Room in order, and wish'd me a joyful Christmas, for which I gave him a half a Bit.—Soon after he left the Room, and before I was Drest, the Fellow who makes the Fire in our School Room, drest very neatly in green, but almost drunk, entered my chamber with three or four profound Bows, & made me the same salutation; I gave him a *Bit*, and dismissed him as soon as possible.—Soon after my Clothes and Linen were sent in with a message for a Christmas *Box*, as they call it; I sent the poor Slave a Bit, & my thanks.—I was obliged for want of small change, to put off for some days the Barber who shaves & dresses me.—I gave *Tom* the Coachman, who Doctors my Horse, for his care two Bits, & am to give more when the horse is well.—I gave to *Dennis* the Boy who waits at Table half a *Bit*—So that the sum of my Donations to the Servants, for this Christmas appears to be five Bits, a Bit is a pisterene bisected; or an English sixpence, & passes here for seven pence Half-penny. the whole is 3S .. 1½ D.—

At Breakfast, when Mr Carter entered the Room, he gave us the compliments of the Season. He told me, very civily, that as my Horse was Lame, his own riding Horse is at my Service to ride when & where I Choose. . . . We dined at four o-Clock—Mr Carter kept in his Room, because he breakfasted late, and on Oysters—There were at Table Mrs Carter & her five Daughters that are at School with me—Miss *Priscilla, Nancy, Fanny, Betsy,* and *Harriot,* five as beautiful delicate, well-instructed Children as I have ever known!—*Ben* is abroad; *Bob* & *Harry* are out; so there was no Man at Table but myself.—I must carve—Drink the Health—and talk if I can! Our Dinner was no otherwise than common, yet as elegant a *Christmas Dinner* as I ever sat Down to—The table Discourse was Marriage; Mrs *Carter* observ'd that was she a Widow, she should scruple to marry any man alive; She gave a reason, that She did not think it probable a man could love her grown old when the world is thronged with blooming, ripening

Virgins; but in fact Mrs Carter looks & would pass for a younger Woman than some unmarried Ladies of my acquaintance, who would willingly enough make us place them below twenty!—We dined at four; when we rose from table it was growing dark—The wind continues at South East & is stormy and muddy...

Wednesday 29.

This Morning our School begins after the Holidays. Bob seems sorry that he must forsake the Marsh & River when he is daily fowling, & never kills any Game. At Dinner we had the Company of Dr Franks who has been all along Mr Carters Clerk; but is now leaving Him. We had a large Pye cut to Day to signify the Conclusion of the Holidays. I drew, this afternoon more Flowers for Miss Prissy.

Sunday 2.

The weather warm and Damp—The Family rode to Church to-day and are to dine out. Mr Carter at my request, gave me the Keys of his Book-Cases and allowed me to spend the Day alone in his Library...

Wednesday 5.

Rose at Seven. The morning very stormy. *Bob & Nancy* before Breakfast had a quarrel—Bob called Nancy a Lyar; Nancy upbraided Bob, on the other Hand, with being often flog'd by their Pappa; often by the Masters in College; that he had stol'n Rum, & had got drunk; & that he used to run away &c—These Reproaches when they were set off with Miss Nancys truely feminine address, so violently exasperated *Bob* that he struck her in his Rage—I was at the time in my Chamber; when I enter'd the Room each began with loud and heavy complaints, I put them off however with sharp admonitions for better Behaviour...

Thursday 6.

To Day about twelve *Bob* & *Prissy* & *Nancy* went in the Chariot to Stratford, to attend the Dancing-School—Mr Taylor, the Colonels principal Overseer dined with us—After School in the Evening, I sat with *Betsy* & *Fanny* while they sung me many songs, When they had done I waited on them Home, & spent the Evening with Mr & Mrs *Carter*.

Saturday 8.

Catechised the Children, and dismiss'd them about ten...

Monday 10th

The Morning very cold—Dined with us to-day Mr *Sanford* a Captain of a Sloop which trades out of *Potowmack* to *Norfolk*—I wrote out some exercises for *Bob* & *Harry*—In the Evening the Colonel began with a small Still to disstill some Brandy from a Liquor made of Pisimmonds. I set Ben this Evening to writing. I likewise gave *Catalines* Speech in *Salust* to commit to memory in Latin, which he is to pronounce Extempore. In the Evening I borrowed of *Ben Carter* 15s.— I have plenty of Money with me, but it is in Bills of Philadelphia currency & will not pass at all here.

Teusday 11.

... This morning I put Ben to construe some Greek, he has yet no Testament, I gave him therefore Esops Fables in Greek, and Latin. I also took out of the Library, and gave him to read Gordon, upon Geography. Ben seem's scared with his Greek Lesson, he swore, & wished for Homer that he might kick Him, as he had been told Homer invented Greek.

Monday 17.

At Breakfast the Colonel gave orders to the Boys concerning their conduct this Day, & through the course of the Ball—He allows them to go; to stay all this Night; to bring him an Account of all the company at the Ball; & to return tomorrow Evening—All the morning is spent in Dressing.—Mr Carter & Mrs Carter pressed me to go; But, mindful of my Promise when I left Home, I stay and enjoy myself in quiet.—I give the Children a Holiday to Day—I gave Dennis the Waiter half a Bit a Present—Mrs *Carter*, Miss *Prissy*, & *Nancy* dressed splendidly set away from Home at two.

Teusday 18.

Mrs *Carter*, & the young Ladies came Home last Night from the Ball, & brought with them Mrs *Lane*, they tell us there were upwards of Seventy at the Ball; forty one Ladies; that the company was genteel; & that Colonel *Harry Lee*, from *Dumfries*, & his Son *Harrey* who was with me at College, were also there; Mrs. Carter made this an argument, and it was a strong one indeed, that to-day I must dress & go with her to the Ball—She added also that She Desired my Company in the Evening when she should come Home as it would be late— After considering a while I consented to go, & was dressed—we set away from Mr Carters at two; Mrs *Carter* & the young Ladies in the

Chariot, Mrs Lane in a Chair, & myself on Horseback—As soon as I had handed the Ladies out, I was saluted by Parson *Smith;* I was introduced into a small Room where a number of Gentlemen were playing Cards, (the first game I have seen since I left Home) to lay off my Boots Riding-Coat &c—Next I was directed into the Dining-Room to see Young Mr *Lee;* He introduced me to his Father—With them I conversed til Dinner, which came in at half after four. The Ladies dined first, when some Good order was preserved; when they rose, each nimblest Fellow dined first—The Dinner was as elegant as could be well expected when so great an Assembly were to be kept for so long a time.—For Drink, there was several sorts of Wine, good Lemon Punch, Toddy, Cyder, Porter &c.—About Seven the Ladies & Gentlemen begun to dance in the Ball-Room—first Minuets one Round; Second Giggs; third Reels; And last of All Country-Dances; tho' they struck several Marches occasionally—The Music was a French-Horn and two Violins—The Ladies were Dressed Gay, and splendid, & when dancing, their Silks & Brocades rustled and trailed behind them!—But all did not join in the Dance for there were parties in Rooms made up, some at Cards; some drinking for Pleasure; some toasting the Sons of america; some singing "Liberty Songs" as they call'd them, in which six, eight, ten or more would put their Heads near together and roar, & for the most part as unharmonious as an affronted—Among the first of these Vociferators was a young Scotch-Man, Mr. *Jack Cunningham;* he was nimis bibendo appotus; noisy, droll, waggish, yet civil in his way & wholly inoffensive—I was solicited to dance by several, Captain Chelton, Colonel Lee, Harry Lee, and others; But George Lee, with great Rudeness as tho' half drunk, asked me why I would come to the Ball & neither dance nor play Cards? I answered him shortly, (for his Impudence moved my resentment) that my Invitation to the Ball would justify my Presence; & that he was ill qualified to direct my Behaviour who made so indifferent a Figure himself—Parson Smiths, & Parson Gibberns Wives danced, but I saw neither of the Clergymen either dance or game—At Eleven Mrs. Carter call'd upon me to go, I listned with gladness to the summons & with Mrs. Lane in the Chariot we rode Home, the Evening sharp and cold! I handed the Ladies out, waited on them to a warm Fire, then ran over to my own Room, which was warm and had a good Fire; oh how welcome! Better this than to be at the Ball in some corner nodding, and awakened now & then with a midnight Yell!—In my Room by half after twelve; & exceeding happy that I could break away with Reputation.—

Thursday 20.
Ben came Home late in the Night—This morning he looks fatigued out. We began to study to Day but all seem sleepy and dull...

Sunday 30.
Very stormy this morning with Rain and Hail which instantly freezes; the trees hang bending with Ice, & the ways are all glassy & slippery— None think of going to Church this day—Mrs Carter & I after Break- fast had a long conversation on religious affairs—Particularly on differing Denominations of Protestants—She thinks the Religion of the established Church without Exception the best of any invented or practised in the world. & indeed she converses with great propriety on these things, & discovers her very extensive Knowledge; She allows the Difference between the Church, & Presbyterianism to be only exceeding small, & wishes they were both intirely united! ...

Monday 31.
Excessive sloppy—Miss *Nancy* came to School to Day—I finished my verses which are to be presented as a Valantine to Miss *Prissy Carter*.

Teusday February 1st 1774.
Fair & mild but vastly muddy—About twelve Squire *Lee* & young *Harry Lee*, who was a College-Fellow, came to see us. They staid while about five. The Toasts at Dinner were as usual—The Colonel & Mrs Carter seem Much pleased with Harry, & with his manner.

Wednesday 2.
The weather vastly fine. At twelve o-Clock the Colonel & Miss *Prissy* rode out for an airing—*Prissy* This day began Multiplication. We had also a large elegant Writing Table brought to us, so high that the Writers must stand.

Fryday 4.
I put Ben this day into virgil—We had our Room mended & came into it—at twelve I rode out to Mr Taylors about two Miles, in again by Dinner-Time—Dined with us one Mrs Hut—This Evening, in the School-Room, which is below my Chamber, several Negroes & *Ben*, & *Harry* are playing on a *Banjo* & dancing!—

Sunday 6.

I rode to Church; Mrs Carter & Miss Prissy & Nancy were out—Mr Smith gave us a Sermon 14 Minutes long on Charite—But poor Fellow he seem'd Cold as his Subject! Mr Fantleroy; & Mr Goodlett dined with us and set off for Home as soon as we rose from Dinner—This day two Negro Fellows the Gardiner & cooper, wrangled; & at last fought; It happened hard however for the Cooper, who is likely to lose one of his Eyes by that Diabolical Custom of gouging [5] which is in common practise among those who fight here—

Teusday 8.

Before Breakfast *Nancy* & *Fanny* had a Fight about a Shoe Brush which they both wanted—Fanny pull'd off her Shoe & threw at Nancy, which missed her and broke a pane of glass of our School Room. they then enter'd upon close scratching &c. which methods seem instinctive in Women. Harry happen'd to be present & affraid lest he should be brought in, ran and informed me—I made peace, but with many threats— . . .

February, 1774
Teusday 15.

I have a call this morning from *Bob & Harry* for a Holiday, for Shrove Teusday; I shall dismiss them at twelve o-Clock. I gave Miss Carter my Verses for her Valentine, Dined with us Mrs *Ford.* I finished reading the first, & began the Second Volume of *Pictete.*

Wednesday 16.

I happened last monday to offend *Prissy,* She retains her anger & seems peculiarly resentful!—*Ben* agreed for half a Bit a Week to play the Flute every Night, or read, for me, twenty Minutes after I am in Bed.

Thursday 17.

Prissy seems much affronted; The Cause was as follows Monday afternoon, by Chance I tapp'd her on the Head, & wholly in Jest; She seem'd vex'd, but Teusday morning which is her day for practice on the Forte-Piano, after Breakfast, I desir'd her to walk over to the

5. Jedidiah Morse, pioneer American geographer, described this "delicate and entertaining diversion" as follows: "When two boxers are worried with fighting and bruising each other, they come, as it is called, to close quarters, and each endeavours to twist his forefingers in the ear-locks of his antagonist. When these are fast clinched, the thumbs are extended each way to the nose, and the eyes gently turned out of their sockets. The victor, for his expertness, receives shouts of applause from the sportive throng, while his poor eyeless antagonist is laughed at for his misfortune."

School, she refused, & gave for an Excuse that She must begin to play
—Both these things laid together were the cause of her resentment.

Saturday 19.
at Dinner we were conversing on Reading, among many remarks the
Colonel observed that, He would bet a Guinea that Mrs Carter reads
more than the Parson of the parish! No panegyrick on the Gentleman? Mr. Christian the Dancing Master, Came home with the young
Ladies.

    ...Rode to Nomini Church; Parson Smith read Prayers, but it
was too Cold a Day to give us a Sermon; After Service *Mr & Mrs
Carter*, The Parson, his wife & Sister; Mr. *Camel* the Comptroler; *Ben,
Bob*, Miss *Pierce* Miss *Sanford*, and My self were invited to Colonel
Washingtons to Dinner. His House has the most agreeable Situation,
of any I have yet seen in Maryland Or Virginia; the broad Potowmack, which they account between 7 and 8 Miles over, washes his
Garden on the North. the River Nomini is within a stones throw on
the West, a levil open Country on the East; a Lane of a mile & three
quarters accurately measur'd. lies from the House South-East it has
from the House the whole distance a uniform Descent, & at the Gate
at the End of this Lane the Situation is just six feet lower than at the
House—There are no Marshes near, which altogether make the place
exceeding Description. The Roads are now miry & disagreeable.

Sunday 27.
I rode to day to Richmond Church, Parson Gibbern preached about
20 Minutes on the Text "he that walketh uprightly walketh wisely"—
this seems to be a polite part of the parish.—After Sermon Ben & I
rode to Doctor *Jones's;* he was from home. Mrs Jones a young, Handsome, polite Lady, received & entertained us exceeding civilly.—On
our return home, we called to see Mr. Hamilton, who by a accident
was thrown from a Horse, & received a sad cut on his Face! he lies at
Mr Lanes.

March, 1774
Wednesday 2.
I gave my little family a Holiday, with an intention to ride with Mr
Lane after Dinner—We walked to the Mill, & about the works, but
before twelve it began to rain, & prevented our going out—Mrs *Carter*
came out of her chamber & dined with us, & seems to be well over
Illness.

Mr Lane lives in Louden County 20 Miles from Dumfries; & is to return to Princeton towards the close of this month.

Thursday 3.

Late last Evening the Packets came in: In the Pennsylvania Gazette I saw that Doctor *Elmer* of my acquaintance in Jersey; & Doctor Jones at whose House I dined Last Sunday are created members of the American Philosophical Society.—In the virginia Papers there is an Account of an Earthquake felt on monday the 21 ult. at *Williamsburg, Richmond*, & Fredericksburg—After Breakfast Mr. Lane left us, He wast drest in black superfine Broadcloth; Gold-Laced hat; laced Ruffles; black Silk Stockings; & to his Broach on his Bosom he wore a Masons Badge inscrib'd "Virtute and Silentio" cut in a Golden Medal! Certainly he was fine!—Mrs Carter continues better. Evening we performed again in the several parts our Sonata—*Ben* mentioned to his Mama, as Mr. Lane's coming hindred his asking his *Papa* for his Concent to go to Philadelphia.

She seems to be not unwilling.

Expence to Day for Paper a Bitt, or 7½ d.

Saturday 12.

I rose by six—Breakfasted with us Captain *Blackwel*; master of a Ship lying in Ucomico—I heard *Harry*, Miss *Fanny*, & *Besy* repeat their catechism. . .

Monday 14.

Bob this morning begg'd me to learn him lattin; his Reason he tells me is that yesterday Mrs *Taylor* told him he must not have either of her Daughters unless he learn'd Latin he urged me so strong that I put him some Lessons for leasure hours. . . We had with us one Mr. *Neal* a good Sort of self sufficient Gentleman—

Teusday 15.

This morning, as Ben & Bob were agreeing on the price of a Rudiman Grammar, which *Bob* wanted to purchase of *Ben*; after some time when Bob would not give 2/10. Bens great demand for a Book almost worn out, which when new, may, by thousands be had in Philadelphia for 2/. that Currency—He threw his Book into the fire, & destroy'd it at once!—An Instance of two ruling Foibles which I discover in Ben viz. obstinacy, & avarice. And another I mentioned the other day, of his agreeing, for half a Bit, or 3½ d a week, to play the flute for a limited time, every night after I am in Bed; of this however he has grown tired, & given up his wages on account of the Labour, or Confinement of the Task—And I should be deceived, if a very little money would not excite him to submit to almost any menial service—Bob however; for the present is frustrated in his purpose of learning Grammar, & it seems to chagrin him as much, as tho' he actually believed in what Mrs Taylor told him last Sunday, that without he understands Latin, he will never be able to win a young Lady of Family & fashion for his Wife.—At the Noon play-Hours *Bob & Nelson* the Boy waits on the School had a fight, I know not on what account; it was Bobs misfortune in the course of the Battle to receive a blow on his cheek near his Eye, which is visible & brought the intelligence of the Quarrel to me, for all were wholly silent till I made inquiry, when all in a moment seem'd to turn & try to convict him— In the Evening, after School, I took them both to my Room and examined them of the reason, Place, and manner of their fighting; from themselves it seem'd plain that they fought for mere Diversion I therefore dismiss'd Nelson, & kept Bob til near Supper & then gave him a smart correction & dismiss'd him.

Thursday 17.
This morning Mr Carter put Miss *Fanny* to learning the Notes—while we were breakfasting Mr *Stadley* the musician came; Miss *Prissy* is with him; *Nancy* learns the *Guitar*, under the direction of her *Papa*, as Mr Stadley does not understand playing on the *Guitar*—...

Sunday 27.
An odd Jumble of affairs happened this morning—*Bob* drest himself & came into our Room & in his usual way began to be pretty free in telling us *News*. Amongst a vast quantity of other stuff he informed *Ben* & I that he heard Mr *Randolph* has the P.....we both join'd in severely reprimanding for attempting to propogate so unlikely a Tale —Why, Brother Ben, said the mischeivous Wretch I heard in this Neighbourhood, yesterday a Report concerning you not much to your—but I will conceal it—This inraged Ben he at first however persuaded him but soon began to threaten loudly unless he told the whole —why then, Brother said Ben, it is reported that two Sundays ago you took Sukey (a young likely Negro Girl maid to Mrs Carters youngest Son) into your stable, & there for a considerable time lock'd yourselves together!—Before Bob had done, the Bell rung for Breakfast &

we parted—all went to church to-day but Miss *Nancy, Harry, &* *Myself*—I spend the day agreeably in Mr Carters Library—...

Thursday 31.
All our company continue. The morning fair & cool—Yesterday & to-day I am strongly solicited to dance—I decline however & must persevere.—...

Fryday April 1st 1774
Good Fryday—A general Holiday here—Wednesday & thursday I gave up my School on account of the Dance, and they must have this Day for Devotion!—The Colonel, *Ben Harry, & myself* all go to Ucomico Church—Parson *Smith* gave the usual Prayers for the Day and a long Sermon very suitable & well chosen...

Saturday 2.
The morning stormy. I kept the children in til twelve o-Clock then dismissed them—I spent the greater part of this Day in reading Miscellaneous Pieces out of Magazines—The weather cleared before Evening—at five with *Ben*, I rode over to Mr Turburville's, chiefly to see a young Lady lately from London; who has come over at Mr Turburville's Invitation in the character of Governess to Miss Turburville She seems to be young, genteel, & is not without personal excellence— I received together with Mr *Carters* Family an Invitation from Mr Turburville to dine with him to morrow; which I propose to accept.—

Teusday 5.
It is with difficulty I am able to collect the members of our School together for Business. Holidays have become habitual, & they seem unwilling to give them over. As the Negroes have this Day for a Holiday our Schollars thinks it hard that they should be compell'd to attend to Business. I summon them together however, and shall keep them to constant Study until the time of my setting away. Miss Priscilla this morning told me, of Miss Panton, a moving story: Last Sunday Evening after we left there She took a lonely Walk, & being asked why She chose to walk without a companion, she answered that she was thinking of Home & of her Friends, & indulging her fond Grief on account of their absence!—Such a feeling as this I have not been a stranger to, I therefore Sympathize with the poor young Girl. The Day agreeably pleasant—Towards Evening Miss *Corbin* came over to pay us a visit After School I waited on the Ladies in the

Dining-Room the conversation was on Fashions, which instantly introduced the oddity of Miss *Panton*. But Miss Corbin with a *Sneer*, & with ill-nature enough, swore She would not think of imitating such a thing as her!—O!—Tantane Animis caelestibus Irae?—I spent the Evening in cheerful chat with the Ladies. I think I have not had a more sociable & unconstrained feeling since I left Home, & my forgiving Friends.

Wednesday 6.

Ben is making a great Bustle about going to Philadelphia—He almost counts the Hours—We propose to go next Wednesday. But with composure, & Patience, yet with great Satisfaction I anticipate the near approaching Day. *Ben* begs me to acquaint him with the manners of the People in regard to Religion, and he swears he can suit himself to any serious, or formal Visage—

Mrs *Carter*, & Miss *Corbin*, after Breakfast rode to Colonel Frank-Lee's—We dine alone. I informed the Colonel that I do not think it will be convenient for me to continue with him longer than one year—He discovered some dissattisfaction; I told him my reason & he assented—he honours me, by putting in me so much confidence as to commission me to find out and recommend to Him some young Gentleman to succeed me in the instruction of his Children—He flattered my vanity also by reading a Letter to me which I am to bear to Dr. Witherspoon, the contents of it as follows—

"Robert *Carters* compliments to Dr *Witherspoon*: He has the pleasure to acquaint Him that Mr Fithians Method of teaching, & his conduct are highly approved here; He is about to visit his friends in *New-Jersey*, & will bring these from Sir,

Your humble Servt"—

He informed me that he does indeed prefer a Tutor for his Children who has been educated upon the Continent, not on a supposition that such are better Schollars, or that they are of better principles, or of more agreeable Tempers; but only on account of pronunciation in the English Language, (as most of his Children are to be taught chiefly in this) in which he allows young Gentlemen educated in good Schools on the Continent, to excel the Scotch young Gentlemen, & indeed most of the English. ...

Sunday 10.

Mrs *Carter* yesterday, in the Character of a truely fond Mother, altered her mind concerning *Ben* many Times and in several different manners: At first she agreed for him to go with me as far as Anopolis without a waiting Man; then She concluded he was not well and had better decline going entirely; towards Evening She gave him full liberty if he will take a Waiting-Man; & will not set away till Monday morning; This I urged not being pleased from the Begining with going on the Sabbath—I gave yesterday to the Shoemaker a Bit— & a Bit to the Wash woman; half a Bit to her little Girl; & half a Bit to *Nelson* the Boy who waits on our School; the whole is 11½...

Thursday 21.
Spent all this day in preparing for my approaching examination before the Revd Presbytery—I am to review Greek Testament—Moral & Natural Philosophy—Logic—Geography And if I have time I must look over the Lattin Classics.

Wednesday 27.
John Peck agreed to succeed me at Mr Carters in Virginia...
  Paid John Peck for postage of my Letter to him last winter 4/...

Sunday May 8th 1774
To day at Greenwich was administered, & I received the holy Sacrament—Grant, great God, that I may have been a worthy communicant! I dined with Mrs Ward. She speaks with great Respect, Affection, and Sincerity of her late worthy Partner.

Wednesday 18.
I passed my first examination before the Presbytery; after which I read my thesis & Sermon both which were accepted—In this examination I was questioned on my personal Religion, & on the Latin, & Greek Languages...

Saturday 28.
...From Tylers in Virginia where I landed about twelve o-Clock I rode to Mattox Bridge eight miles; thence to Mattox Church six miles—Here I bought some Ears of corn for my Horse—Thence to Westmorland Court House 16 miles—Here is a Tavern I got a Bowl of Punch & fed 2/6—Thence I rode to Nomini Hall about Eeight in the Evening 10 miles—I found Mr & Mrs Carter at home sitting together—They received me with great welcome—*Ben*, *Bob*, Miss *Fanny* & *Betsy* came in to see me—The others in bed—sup'd on *Crabs* & an elegant dish of Strawberries & cream—How natural, how agreeable, how majestic this place seems!

Sunday 29.

I rose by half after six—Ben informed me that Bob has behaved vastly ill since I left him—He has reported several mischievous & false stories of his brother; That has been intimate in some bad families— That he has injured his own fathers Servants &c—The morning pleasant—I did not attend Church, Ben out of kindness kept me company at Home—I had however chosen to stay alone. . .

Monday 30.

Our little beautiful Seminary collected They seem all glad to see me, & willing to enter on business—I am truely fond of the young growing beauties—Soon they will be the admiration of the world, & ornaments in their family. . .

Teusday 31.

Very warm—I feel well reliev'd of the Fatigues of my ride—The lower Class of People here are in a tumult on the account of Reports from Boston, many of them expect to be press'd & compell'd to go and fight the Britains! . . .

Wednesday June 1st 1774

Cool & pleasant—I began my English Exegesis—or Thesis.

Fryday 3.

The dancing School happens in course to day at Mr Washingtons— Mrs *Carter* takes *Bob* & *Nancy* with her—Our School seems silent —Writing at my English Thesis—I put *Harry* & *Bob* this week to read Popes Homer but Homers inimitable fire cannot charm or move them! —Evening *Ben* rode to the Dance. . .

Philip V. Fithian to John Peck

Nomini Hall June 3d 1774.
Virginia.

Sir.

I have the pleasure to inform you I arriv'd safe and had a pleasant ride; I expect to hear from you by every post but have received no letter yet—if you did not receive my letter dated "Delaware-River, on board the Swallow," this is to request you to apply immediately to Dr Witherspoon who promised me in Philadelphia that he would recommend you here; the reason of my demanding dispatch is, that Mr Carter proposes to write to England for a Tutor if he cannot be speedily satisfied of having one from the Northward—If I attempt to write news I must inform you that the Assembly of this province is dissolved on passing a resolve to keep the first day of June through the whole province a solemn fast, the resolve past however, and the day was kept...I expect to hear from you several times this summer, I beg you will not disappoint me.

My compliments to acquaintances—

From, Sir,

yours

Philip V. Fithian

Saturday 4.

The day cool & agreeable—I kept the children in til twelve tho' with great difficulty; they were for asserting their liberty. & pleaded the custom of las[t] winter—I finished a rough incorrect plan of my English Thesis, & laid it by for future examination—

After dinner I begun the Lecture, wrote an introduction—Towards evening I took my hat & a Sermon, & retired to a Shady Green where I rambled about til dusk committing my Sermon to memory—We have omitted Supper, & in its place substituted Coffee which we commonly take about seven in the evening...

Monday 6.

Mr *Carter* rode to richmond court—At Dinner I had a long and useful conversation with Mrs Carter She told me openly & candidly the Several failings of her children, & indeed She knows them perfectly—In particular she knows not what to do with her perverse Son *Bob* —He abuses his Mama, Miss Sally, the children, Family, and is much given to slander. Poor unhappy youth, I fear he will come to an unhappy end! This afternoon I found it necessary to correct Bob severely for impertinence in School—Mr Carter at Court received his Invoice from London for this Spring, in which was a gold Seal for *Ben* with a Coat of Arms price five Guineas!—

Saturday 11.

I was sitting in the Colonels Library I took a Catalogue [6] of the whole of His Books—& he tells me he has left behind him at Williamsburg, with many other things 458 Volumes besides Music & Pamphlets.

It is with considerable Difficulty that I keep the Children in School

---

6. For this catalogue see pp. 285-94 of *The Journal of Philip Vickers Fithian* (Colonial Williamsburg, Incorporated, edition).

til twelve o Clock as they used to go out all the last winter at Break-fast—*Bob* especially is vastly vociferous on the Occasion—Our Bells for School & play-Hours are at present under good Regulations. The Children come in as soon as they rise and are Drest which is usually about seven—The Bell rings at eight for Breakfast—At nine it Rings for two purposes; for the Children to enter School, & for the Gar-diners, Carpenters, & other workmen to come into Breakfast—At ten it rings them to work. At twelve it rings for the School play hours —At two it rings for us to Dine, & the workmen—And the las[t] bell is at three for School & for the workmen to go to Labour—I dismiss them by my watch at half after Five. . .

Wednesday 15.
So cold that I ordered a Fire in the School-Room . . . Close Attention for two weeks past has fatigued me so much, that yesterday, & to Day I have laid aside Study, & read only for Relaxation—I took a whim in my head & would not go to Dinner. my Head was not dress'd, & I was too lazy to change my clothes—Mrs Carter, however, in the evening lash'd me severely. I told her I was engaged in read-ing a pleasant Novel.—That I was not perfectly well—But She would not hear none, & said I was rude, & censurable. . .

Fryday 17.
Bob was missing last night I was at his Room at twelve o Clock he was absent—This morning I examined him, he told me he was at Mr Turburville's, but told me several palpable Lies—I gave him how-ever severe correction. . .

Saturday 18.
Ben not very well—At twelve *Bob* teaz'd me for leave to go to a Cock-Fight & Horse-Race about two Miles off, I gave him Leave with his promising to be home by Sun Set.—Spent the Afternoon in my room writing—Towards evening 'Squire *Lee* call'd in, & brought a late London News-Paper in which we are informed that another Act of Parliament has pass'd taking from the People of Boston all power of trying any Soldier, or Person whether for commiting any Crime; & obliging all such offenders to be sent home for legal Tryal —Heaven only knows where these tumults will End!—He informed us likewise that last Saturday in Richmond (our neighbour County) the people drest & burnt with great marks of Destestation the in-famous Lord *North*—Mrs *Carter*, after the 'Squire left us quite

astonished me in the Course of the evening. with her perfect acquaintance with the American Constitution.

Teusday 21.
Harry is unwel, takes this morning Physick, and keeps his Room— Ben is in the same way—Priscilla & Nancy are practising Musick, so that to Day we have only four in School—At five in the Evening, Ben, *Prissy* & I rode out on Horse back for exercise; before we returned Captain *Dobby*, of the Ship *Susannah* an agreeable, sensible, polite Gentleman came, & 'Squire *Lee*—The conversation, at Coffee was on American affairs, the 'Squire shew'd us one of Mr Dunlaps papers, in which are accounts that the Northern Colonies are zealous & stedfast in resolutions to maintain their Liberties—We sat til eleven—

Saturday 25.
Ben & I slept til eight—we breakfasted at nine, soon after Christien collected his School and gave them a Lesson round. . .

Sunday 26.
Mr *Smith* to Day is out of the Parish so that we have no sermon—I shut up myself therefore in my chamber to reading—Eleven I am sent for to see Mr Lowe who is come—I invite him to my Room, where we sit til Dinner—He informed me of the Manner of Trials in Scotland, which Candidates undergo. It is similar & indeed almost the same as with our Presbytery Evening Mr Carter returned about seven o-Clock from Williamsburg; He has been unwell himself while there, & he informs us that many are indisposed in that City While we were at Coffee I was taken with a Sudden & unusual pain in my Breast, a sickness at my stomach, attended with trembling and dizzy faintness; I retired to my Room immediately, laid myself down in bed but had a Fever most of the Night—

Wednesday 29.
Writing at my Sermon—The day cool & agreeable. I was never so much confined as now, not even when I was at College, for I used to go with my sweet mates, as Virgil calls them, about the Fields, or to the Brooks to wash, & often ride to Trenton for exercise & pleasure— & sometimes to *Newington* & spend an Afternoon with that dear girl *Laura*— Here in Virginia I have no Call out, people seem sociable & kind but I want Spirit to improve & relish Society Soon, however, soon, if I keep my Health, I shall be again at Liberty.

Thursday 30.

The morning pleasant none too hot to be agreeable—My Charge seem rising slowly, & uniformly in their several Parts—Harry begun at Reduction & is now working Fellowship; he improves too in Writing. Bob began at Addition and is working Compound Division: he is the best writer in the School—Ben begun with reading Salust he is now reading Virgil & the Greek-Testament. He writes extremely bad—Priscilla began Addition & is working Division; She improves in writing, & reads tolerably—Nancy mends fast in writing, but reads carelessly thick & inaccurately.

—I mentioned to Day Mr *Peck* to Mr *Carter* He objected at first to his Age as rather too young for the Duty of a Tutor, he assented however & requested me to write him word that he is desired to come by the Time I shall leave Virginia—

Monday 4.

I began to read the first Volume of Tristam-Shandy—He is droll in the account he gives us of his Birth & Family. . .

Fryday 8.

I swear, says Bob, Harry belies me. I never told the Nurse that Harriot should stay in School all Day—It was Mama's order that so long as Mrs *Oakly* the Nurse stays, Harriot is to go into School after Breakfast, & after Dinner, & say a lesson each time—I was passing through the Hall from Breakfast—The Nurse, a short Stump of a (wom)an, who blundered by mere accident, when she was young, out of the road in which Virgins commonly travel, & felt the difficulties of being a Mother, several years before She enjoyed the Pleasures of being a Wife—She call'd to me, & begg'd me to close the Quarrel; You shall have, said I, dear Madam, with the greatest Freedom my consent—Harriot shall be with you—At Breakfast—Where is Ben?—He breakfasts with the House-keeper Madam—At School— What a likeness there is in the manners of Boys; Bob, & Harry had skulk'd behind the writing-Table with their Slates on their Knees, & their Faces close together, just as I have done a thousand Times, in our little School-House in *Greenwich*—But once I was threshed confoundedly for a piece of such hidden play—*Tom Parks* (blotted) asleep, poor Fellow he is now sleeping in the Dust;—Then he was fast asleep on a Bench, with his mouth open—I fill'd his mouth with Snuff!—He sprung up—Nature was in distress, & found all her Avenues too scanty at that time to clear out at once the tickling penetrating Powder—He snuffed—He coughed—He—He told the Master, & then I was tickled—Indeed he made my Feet beat time to his Lash—Says Bob to Harry, behind the Table, I wonder Mr *Fithian* has not fallen in Love yet with some of our Nominy-Girls—Here here he sits from Month to Month—(Not many Months longer said I to myself)—Mr *Marshal* was always out; I suppose Mr *Fithian* never thinks of Girls—Indeed says *Harry*, drawing his chair clos(er) lowering his voice, I never in my Life saw a man who thought so little of these things—Here Tom the Coachman came in with a wood Tarripin which he brought to be a resident in our Room to catch the Bugs & Cockroaches—

Yes, Harry, & Bob, *Fithian* is vulnerable by Cupids Arrows—I assure you, Boys, he is, Not by the Girls of Westmorland—O my dear Laura, I would not injure your friendly Spirit; So long as I breathe Heavens vital air I am unconditionally & wholly Yours...

Saturday 9.

I was waked by *Sam* the Barber thumping at my Door—I was dressed—In Powder too; for I propose to see & dine with Miss *Jenny Washington* to Day. D——n the Bugs & Chinches, says *Ben* rolling over on the Bed, & rubbing his Eyes, I have slept none for them—Mr. Fithian, do you rest any o-Nights? Dont these cursed Bugs keep you awake? —No Sir; for you see I commonly sit & read til half after ten, or eleven—So that by the Time I lay my poor Skin & Bones on the Bed, I am so much fatigued with the tumultuous Business of the Day, & the Study of the Evening that my sleep the rest of the night is sound & unbroken—Priscilla hangs her head a little this morning, She looks feverish, dispirited, sits on a low bench, with her Elbow in her Lap, & Leaning her head upon her hand, swings backwards and forwards, just as I have seen beautiful Quaker Girls when they are weeping at the frightful distortions & Grimaces of some deep-inspired *Father*. But *Priscilla & Tasker* are unwell—Fanny teizes me for a Picture, I must draw her a slip, she says, on Paper like the one I drew for Her the other Day with my finger in the Sand—I love the little careless Girl, & will oblige her—On the writing-Table in the School-Room I found this morning an old Book of Esops Fables done into English Verse; In the Margins of this Book up & Down Bob had in his scribbling Way recorded the Names of several young Ladies of Westmorland & Richmond Counties. I shall set them down, as I turned over the Leaves & found them— I do not insinuate, by writing this Story, the smallest reproach to either of the Ladies; I mention it solely to shew *Bob's* Taste, & the Meditations of his heart when wholly alone. In the Life of Esop, page 23, at the Bottom of the Leaf his own Name is written at full length & in as elegant a hand as he is master of with a Dash below.

Robert Bladen Carter.

He has in the same manner introduced it a few leaves further on, he has done this to be a kind of Preface for what is to follow; he has also very cleverly interspersed it with the Ladies, either that the Ladies Names should be a foil to set his off to advantage, or that his Name be a Foil to adorn the Ladies—In the Life of Woglog the great at the first page

    Miss Lucy Carter of Sabine-Hall.

       Page 3d at the Bottom of the Leaf

    Miss Lettitia Turberville of Hickory Hill.

       Page 8.

    Miss Betsy Carter of Sabine-Hall

       Page 9.

    Miss Priscilla Carter of Nomini-Hall—his Sister:

       Esops Fables Page 1st he writes the Name of the Girl he loves above all others

    Polly Tayloe the Lovely of Mount-Airy.

       Page 39th Miss Betsy Lee.

       Page 41.

    Miss Kitty Tayloe. Mount Airy.

       Page 43.

    Miss Lydia Petit has d—m'd ugly Freckles in her Face, otherways She is handsome & tolerable—

       Page 45.

    Miss Betsy Gaskins.

       Page 47.

    Miss Sally Tayloe.

       Page 50.

    Miss Jenny Washington of Bushfield is very Pretty.

Then he Bolts in

    Robert Carter.

       Page 57.

Miss Polly Tolliver.
   Page 59.
Miss Steerman is a beautiful young Lady.
Miss Jane Corbin.
—Alphia Fantleroy.
— — Edwards.
—Betsy Jones.
—Sally Panton...

Teusday 12.
Indeed I enjoy this fine cool weather, says Ben as he lay on his Back in the Bed rubbing his Eyes, & ears about half after six o-Clock; *Lancelot Lee* had never I am sure, more sensible Pleasure in swallowing a well prepar'd Dinner—To be sure I have slept last Night with the sweetest composure in Spight of the Chinches, & in spight of my Disorder!—Get up, Lump of Indolence, said I to him; Get up & clap to *Virgil* instead of lying there & boasting...

Thursday 14.
To Day is the election of Burgesses in Richmond the neighbouring County—Come, Fithian, will you go? My old objection recurs; I am too busy—I met this morning in Wingates Arithmetic, the following merry Problem—"To discover a Number which any one shall have in his mind, without requiring him to reveal any part of that or any Number whatsoever"—After any one has thought upon any number at Pleasure; bid him double it, & to that double bid him add any such even number as you please to assign: Then from the Sum of that Addition let him reject one half, & reserve the other half; Lastly, from this half bid him subtract the Number which he first thought upon; then you may boldly tell him what Number remains in his mind after that Subtraction is made, for it will be always half the Number which you assigned him to add—A Reason for the Rule is added. "Because, if to the double of any number (which number for Distinction sake I call the first) a second number be added, the half of the Sum must necessarily consist of the said first number, & half the Second: Therefore if from the said half sum the first Number is subtracted, the remainder must of necessity be half the second Number which was added...

Letter of Philip V. Fithian to John Peck

Nomini-Hall. July 15th 1774.

Sir.

I have communicated your intention to Mr *Carter;* he begs you will by no Means disappoint him.

I wrote you a letter by the post early in June possibly it was lost, for either letters are lost, or you and the rest of my friends in *Jersey* use me vastly ill, for I have not received a line since I have been in Virginia—You had better go into the school and acquaint yourself with the method of teaching, and procure some copper plate copies: I am by the goodness of heaven very well; I hope you will remember me to all friends at Princeton to relations and friends at Cohansie; desire *Charles* to carry my *Homer* to cohansie when he goes down in the vacancy; tell him I shall be home if no unforeseen accident prevents by the last of October.

You had better provide yourself with recommendations from several, especially from Doctor Witherspoon, something of the kind will not be a hindrance, but may possibly at some fueture be of eminent Service.

I am, Sir, Yours,

Philip V Fithian

Mr John Peck.
Nassau-Hall

Thursday 21.
Lazy Fellows! *Ben, Bob, Harry, & Myself* all this Morning slept til near seven!—It was a sleepy Morning tho', for the Girls to give us countenance slept too—My Leisure time to Day is spent in forming my Latin Exegesis. . .

Fryday 22.
My Exegesis goes on lustily; I have finished three pages—Indeed Sir, says Harry I cannot reduce 7S . . . 6D into the decimal of a Pound Sterling—you must reduce 7S & 6D to pence; for a numerator; then you must reduce a Pound Sterling to Pence for a Denominator; this Numerator you divide by the denominator & the Quotient will be the Decimal sought—Well *Ben* you & Mr *Fithian* are invited by Mr Turberville, to a Fish feast to-morrow, said Mr Carter when we entered the Hall to Dinner—I am uncertain whether my Latinitas will not be a Shackel too heavy to allow me to favour his kind invitation.

Saturday 23.

Priscilla, & Fanny, each presented me with a fine Jessamine Nose-gay this morning—At eight I dismissed the School: *Ben, Bob, & Harry* go the the *Fish-Feast,* I to making latin . . . the time draws nigh when I must enter on a new, & perhaps less agreable exercise . . . The Colonel shewed me some Powder which was made in *Frederick* in this Province—It seems good—He charged a *Pistol,* it fired quick & strong—

Fryday August) 5(th. 1774)

I have no Stockings; & I swear I wont go to the Dancing School This was the first I heard of *Bob*—Are Bob & Nancy gone to Mr *Turberville's* said the Colonel at Breakfast—*Nancy* is gone Sir, Bob stays at Home he has no shoes! poh! What nonsense! says the Colonel—Call *Bob,* & Call the Clerk—He sent Mr Randolph to the Store for a pair of Shoes, Bob he took to his Study and flogg'd severely for not having given seasonable Notice, & sent him instantly to the Dance—

Monday 8.

All once more in School—Dined with us *George Lee* & Mr *Grubb*— They spent the afternoon at the great House—After Coffee Lee rode Home—Mr *Grubb* staid with us all night—Dennis came into our Room to bring us a Bowl of Punch; Grubb shut the Door, and accused him of having been caught with Bett, the Dairy Girl, in the Stable last Saturday Night—Dennis seem'd in great distress, he denied the Fact tho' with great steadiness—Nelson our Boy came in with a candle— Dennis here, says *Grubb* to *Nelson,* has been accusing you, Sir, of several crimes; he says you gave him half a *Bitt* last Saturday Night, to stand at the Stable-Door while he with Bett—Nelson star'd—Grubb opened a huge *Molls Atlas* that lay in the Room; & read off their Cast & indictment—The Boys seem'd crazy—We dismiss'd them when all the novelty was over, but they darted like Indians so soon as they were at liberty. . .

Wednesday 10.

All in School—Miss *Fanny* very much troubled with the festered Bites of *Seed Ticks*—Mr *Stadley,* whom I always see with Pleasure came towards evening—after School he gave the Girls a lesson each. . .

Letter of Philip V. Fithian to John Peck [7]

Nomini Hall August 12th 1774.

"Si bene moneo, attende."—

Sir.

I never reflect, but with secret, and peculiar pleasure, on the time when I studied in *Deerfield* with you, & several other pleasant Companions, under our common, & much respected instructor, Mr *Green*. And I acknowledge now, with a thankful heart, the many favours, which I received from your family while I was a member of it. This sense of obligation to your Family, And personal friendship for you, have excited me, when it was in my power, to introduce you to the business which I now occupy; into a family, where, if you be prudent and industrious, I am confident you will speedily acquire to yourself both Honour & Profit—But inasmuch as you are wholly a stranger to this Province; & have had little or no Experience in the business which you ar shortly to enter upon; & lest, from common Fame, which is often erroneous, you shall have entertained other notions of the manners of the People here, & of your business as a Tutor, than you will find, when you come, to be actually true; I hope you will not think it *vain* or *untimely*, if I venture to lay before you some Rules for your direction which I have collected from a year's observation. I shall class what I have to say in the following order. First. I shall attempt to give you some direction for the plan of your Conduct among your neighbours, & the People in General here, so long as you sustain the character of a Tutor. Then I shall advise you concerning the rules which I think will be most profitable & convenient in the management of your little lovely charge, the School. Last of all. I shall mention several Rules for your personal conduct. I choose to proceed in the order I have laid down, as well that you may more fully & speedily recieve my mind, as that you may also the more readily select out and apply what you shall find to be most necessary.

First. When you have thought of removinging, for a Time, out of the Colony in which you was born, & in which you have hitherto constantly resided, I make no doubt but you have at the same time expected to find a very considerable alteration of manners, among your new acquaintances, & some peculiarities toto Caelo different, from any you have before been accustomed to. Such a thought is natural; And

7. John Peck and Fithian were classmates at Princeton. Peck succeeded Fithian at Nomini Hall and later married Anne Tasker ("Nancy") Carter and settled in Virginia.

you will if you come into Virginia, in much shorter time than a year be convinced that it is just. In New-Jersey Government throughout, but especially in the Counties where you have any personal acquaintance, Gentlemen in the first rank of Dignity & Quality, of the Council, general Assembly, inferior Magistrates, Clergy-Men, or independent Gentlemen, without the smallest fear of bringing any manner of reproach either on their office, or their high-born, long recorded Families associate freely & commonly with Farmers & Mechanicks tho' they be poor & industrious. Ingenuity & industry are the Strongest, & most approved recommendations to a Man in that Colony. The manners of the People seem to me, (probably I am overborn by the force of prejudice in favour of my native Soil), to bear some considerable resemblance of the manners in the ancient Spartan Common-Wealth— The Valour of its Inhabitants—was the best, & only security of that State against the enemy; & the wise laws of its renowned Legislator were the powerful Cement which kept them firm & invincible—In our Government, the laborious part of Men, who are commonly ranked in the midling or lower Class, are accounted the strenth & Honor of the Colony; & the encouragement they receive from Gentlemen in the highest stations is the spring of Industry, next to their private advantage. The Level which is admired in New-Jersey Government, among People of every rank, arises, no doubt, from the very great division of the lands in that Province, & consequently from the near approach to an equality of Wealth amongst the Inhabitants, since it is not famous for trade. You know very well that the Lands in a small township are divided, & then again subdivided into two & three Hundred Separate, proper, creditable estates; for example *Deerfield & Fairfield* two Townships, or Precincts, in which you & I are tolerably well acquainted, in the former of which, are the Seats of two Judges of the Sessions; & in the latter resides one of the representatives in General Assembly for the County; But if 16000 £ would purchase the whole landed estates of these three Gentlemen, who are supposed to be the most wealthy in the County, if we rate their Land at the Low Consideration of 4L p acre, with all conveniences, each would have 4000 Acres. Now you may suppose how small a quantity many must have when two or three hundred Landholders reside in each of these small Precincts; Hence we see Gentlemen, when they are not actually engaged in the publick Service, on their farms, setting a laborious example to their Domesticks, & on the other hand we see labourers at the Tables & in the Parlours of their Betters enjoying the advantage,

& honor of their society and Conversation—I do not call it an objection to this, that some few, who have no substance but work like Slaves as necessity drives them for a few Months in the year; with the price of this Labour they visit Philadelphia; & having there acquired a fashionable Coat, & a Stock of Impudence, return home to spend the remainder of the year, in idleness & disgrace!—But you will find the tables turned the moment you enter this Colony. The very Slaves, in some families here, could not be bought under 30000 £. Such amazing property, no matter how deep it is involved, blows up the owners to an imagination, which is visible in all, but in various degrees according to their respective virtue, that they are exalted as much above other Men in worth & precedency, as blind stupid fortune has made a difference in their property; excepting always the value they put upon posts of honour, & mental acquirements—For example, if you should travel through this Colony, with a well-confirmed testimonial of your having finished with Credit a Course of studies at Nassau-Hall; you would be rated, without any more questions asked, either about your family, your Estate, your business, or your intention, at 10,000 £; and you might come, & go, & converse, & keep company, according to this value; & you would be dispised & slighted if yo(u) rated yourself a farthing cheaper. But when I am giving directions to you, from an expectation that you will be shortly a resident here, altho you have gone through a College Course, & for any thing I know, have never written a Libel, nor stolen a Turkey, yet I think myself in duty bound to advise you, lest some powdered Coxcomb should reproach your education, to cheapen your price about 5000 £; because any young Gentleman travelling through the Colony, as I said before, is presum'd to be acquainted with Dancing, Boxing, playing the Fiddle, & Small-Sword, & Cards. Several of which you was only entering upon, when I left New-Jersey; towards the Close of last year; and if you stay here any time your Barrenness in these must be detected. I will however allow, that in the Family where you act as tutor you place yourself, according to your most accute Calculation, at a perfect equidistance between the father & the eldest Son. Or let the same distance be observed in every article of behaviour between you & the eldest Son, as there ought to be, by the latest & most approved precepts of Moral-Philosophy, between the eldest Son, & his next youngest Brother. But whenever you go from Home, where you are to act on your own footing, either to a Ball; or to a *Horse-Race*, or to a *Cock-Fight*, or to a *Fish-Feast*, I advise that you rate yourself very low, & if you bett at all, remember that 10,000 £ in Reputation & learning does not amount to a handfull of Shillings in ready Cash!—One considerable advantage which you promise yourself by coming to this Colony is to extend the Limits of your acquaintance; this is laudable, & if you have enough of prudence & firmness, it will be of singular advantage—Yet attempt slowly & with the most Jealous Circumspection—If you fix your familiarity wrong in a single instance, you are in danger of total, if not immediate ruin—You come here, it is true, with an intention to teach, but you ought likewise to have an inclination to learn. At any rate I solemnly injoin it upon you, that you never suffer the spirit of a Pedagogue to attend you without the walls of your little Seminary. In all promiscuous Company be as silent & attentive as Decency will allow you, for you have nothing to communicate, which such company, will hear with pleasure, but you may learn many things which, in after life, will do you singular service.—In regard to Company in general, if you think it worth the while to attend to my example, I can easily instruct you in the manner of my Conduct in this respect. I commonly attend Church; and often, at the request of Gentlemen, after Service according to the custom, dine abroad on Sunday—I seldom fail, when invited by Mr or Mrs *Carter*, of going out with them; but I make it a point, however strongly solicited to the contrary, to return home with them too—Except in one of these cases, I seldom go out, but with a valuable variety of books I live according to Horace's direction, & love "Secretum Iter et fallentis Semita Vitae." Close retirement and a life by Stealth. The last direction I shall venture to mention on this head, is, that you abstain totally from Women. What I would have you understand from this, is, that by a train of faultless conduct in the whole course of your tutorship, you make every Lady within the Sphere of your acquaintance, who is between twelve & forty years of age, so much pleased with your person, & so fully satisfied as to your abilities in the capacity of—a Teacher; & in short, fully convinced, that, from a principle of Duty, you have, both by night & by day endeavoured to acquit yourself honourably, in the Character of a Tutor; & that, on this account, you have their free & hearty consent, without making any manner of demand upon you, either to stay longer in the County with them, which they would choose, or whenever your business calls you away, that they may not have it in their Power either by charms or Justice to detain you, & when you must leave them, have their sincere wishes & constant prayrs for Length of days & much prosperity, I therefore beg that you will attend litterally to this advice, & abstain totally from Women. But this last precaution, which I have been at some pains to dress in the plainest language, I am much inclined to think, will be wholly useless in regard to you, notwithstanding it is founded in that *Honour* and *Equity* which is on all hands allow'd to be due from one Sex to the other, & to many of your *age, & Standing* no doubt would be entirely salutary. Because the necessary connections which you have had with the Fair, from your Puberty upwards have been so unfavourable & ill-fated, that instead of apprehending any danger on the score of over fondness, I am fearful your rancour has grown so inveterate at length, as, not only to preserve you, in thought & practice, pure of every Fleshly foible, but has carried you so far towards the other extream, as that you will need many persuasions, when your circumstances shall seem to require it, to bring you back to a rational & manly habit of thinking & acting with respect to the Sex; which yet, after all (& eternally will continue to be, tho it is much courted & whined after) if considered in the fullest manner, & set forth to the best advantage, never rises above its divine definition Viz "The weaker Vessel." But without detaining you any longer with a matter merely depending on accident or Circumstance I pass on to the second General Head; in which "Ludis atque Jocis amotis" I shall offer to your consideration & recommend for your practice several Rules concerning the management of the School.

2. You will act wisely, if, from the begining, you convince all your Scholars which you may easily do, of your abilities in the several branches, which you shall profess to teach; you are not to tell them, totidem Verbis, "that you understand, perhaps as well as any man on the Continent both the Latin & Greek Classicks"; "& have gone through the usual Course in the noted College of New-Jersey, under Dr Witherspoon, so universally known & admired, where you have studied Criticism, Oratory, History, not to mention Mathematical & philosophical Studies, & dipt a good way into the French-Language, & that you have learn 'd a smattering of Dancing, Cards &c. &c. &c." For Dun-p or Hack--n or the most profound dunce in your College or School would have too much sense to pass such impudence by, & not despise and reproach it; but you may speedily & certainly make them think you a "Clever Fellow" (which is a phrase in use here for a good Scholar) if you never mention any thing before them, only what you seem to be wholly master of—This will teach them never to dispute your determination, & always to rely upon your Judgment;

two things which are most essential for your peace, & their advantage. That you may avoid yourself of this with certainty I shall recommend for your practice the following method, as useful at least, if not intirely necessary. Read over carefully, the lessons in Latin & Greek, in your leisure hours, that the story & Language be fresh in your memory, when you are hearing the respective lessons; for your memory is treacherous, & I am pretty certain it would confound you if you should be accosted by a pert School-Boy, in the midst of a blunder, with "Physician heal thyself"!—You ought likewise to do this with those who are working Figures; probably you may think that because the highest Cypher is only in decimal arithmetic, it is not there fore worth your critical attention to be looking previously into the several Sums. But you are to consider that a sum in the Square-Root, or even in the Single Rule of three direct, is to your Pupils of as great importance, as the most abstruse problem in the Mathematicks to an able artist; & you may lay this down for a Maxim, that they will reckon upon your abilities, according as they find you acquainted & expert in what they themselves are studying. If therefore you have resolution (as I do not question your ability) to carry this plan which I have laid down into execution; you will thereby convince them of the propriety of their Subordination to you, & obedience to your instructions, so that you may lead them, without any resistance, and fix them to the Study of whatever Science you think proper, in which they will rise according to their respective Capacities. I have said that you ought to strive "from the beginning" in fixing this very material article in the minds of your Scholars, Viz a Sense of your authority; for one error of Judgment, or false determination will diminish your Ability with them more than doing forty things with truth would increase your authority—They act in this case as you would do in the company of a number of Strangers—A whole evenings conversation, if it was tolerable good Sense, would perhaps make little or no impression on you; But if through hast in speaking, or inattention, any one should let fall a sentence either remarkably foolish, or grossly wicked, it would be difficult if not impossible to persuade you presently that the author was not either a *thick-Scull*, or a *Villain!*— The education of children requires constant unremitting attention. The meanest qualification you can mention in a useful teacher is *diligence* And without diligence no possible abilities or qualifications can bring children on either with speed or profit. There must be a Combination of qualifications which must all operate strongly & uniformly. In short, give this said Pedagogizing the softest name you will, it is still a "difficult Task." You will meet with numberless difficulties, in your new imployment, which you never dreamt had yet existence. All these you must endeavor to resist & Subdue. This I have seen compared to a Man swimming against a current of Water. But I am mistaken if you will agree, after having six months practice, that the comparison be strong as the truth: You will add to the figure, I am certain, & throw into the Current sharp fragments of *Ice*, & *Blocks*, which would make swimming not only difficult but dangerous! I am not urging these things to discourage you; they are hints for your direction, which, if you will attend to, tho' at first the practice seem rough & unpleasant, shall yet make the remainder of your task pleasing, & the whole of it useful, I will mention several of these Obstacles that you may the more easily guard against them. You will, in the first place, be often solicited, probably oftner than you would wish, to ride abroad; this, however, if you do it moderately, & in seasonable time, & go to proper company, I recommend as conducive to health to one in your sedentary manner of living. But if you go much into company, you will find it extremely difficulty to break away with any manner of credit till very late at night or in most cases for several days, & if you are wanting to your School, you do manifest injury to your Imployer. In this case, I advise you to copy Mr *Carter*. Whenever he invites you, ride. You may *stay*, and talk, & drink, & ride to as great excess as he; & may with safety associate yourself with those whom you find to be his intimates. In all other Cases, except when you ride to Church, at least till you are very intimate in the Colony, you had better ride to a certain Stump, or to some noted plantation, or pretty landscape; you will have in this every advantage of exercise, the additional advantage of undisturbed Meditation, & you will be under no Jealous apprehension in point of behaviour, nor any restraint as to the time of your return.

Another current difficulty will be petitions for holidays. You must have good deal of steadiness if you are able to evade cleverly this practice which has grown so habitual to your little charge from a false method in their early education that they absolutely claim it as a necessary right.

You must also as much as you can, avoid visible partiality. At least you must never suffer your fondness for one Scholar to grow so manifest, as that all your School shall see you look over a fault in him or her which same fault, if commited by another, you severely chastise. This will certainly produce in the others hatred & contempt. A fourth difficulty, and the last I shall mention, consists in knowing when, & in what measure to give the Boys Liberty to go from Home. The two younger Boys are wholly under your inspection; so that not only the progress they make in learning, but their moral Conduct (for both of these are critically observed & examined) either justifies or condemns your management to the World. If you keep them much at home, & close to business, they themselves will call you unfeeling and cruel; & refuse to be industrious; if you suffer them to go much abroad they are certainly out of the way of improvement by study, probably, by discovering their gross Ignorance, they will expose to ridicule both themselves & all their former instructors, & possibly they may commit actual Crimes so as very much to injure themselves; & scandalize their family; but in each of these you will have a large share of blame, perhaps more than the parents, or even the Boys themselves—It will be said that the parents gave them no licence relying wholly on your Judgment & prudence, this will in good measure Justify them to the world. And as to the Boys they are full of youthful impetuosity & vigour, & these compel them, when they are free of restraint, to commit actions which with proper management they had surely avoided. I say, when you lay these things together, & view them on every side you will find so many perplexities arising in your mind, from a sense of ignorance of your duty, that you will proceed with caution & moderation, & will be carefull to examine with some precision into the circumstances of *time, company,* & *Business* when you license them to go out entirely at the risk of your Reputation—But the practice of three or four Weeks will give you a more full notion of these & many other incidents than I am able now either to recollect or express; I shall have gained my End if these hints prevent you from setting off wrong, & doing inadvertantly at first what your Scholars will assert to be precedents for your after conduct. I go on, therefore, in the third place as I proposed,

3. To mention several Rules for your personal conduct. The happy Education which you have had in point of religion, you ought to consider as an important and distinguishing Blessing of Heaven. That train of useful *Instruction, Advice* & *Example* to which you have been accustomed from your infancy is a more perfect, & will be a safer guide in your future walk, than any directions I am able to give you.

You have taken notice of a method for Assistance in Composition, which Longinus recommends.

Place, says he, in imagination, several eminent ancient Authors before your Eyes, & suppose that they inspect your Work, a Sense of Inferiority would make you diligent, & your composition accurate. Perhaps the same advice when transferr'd to Morality, would be equally salutary. Unless it be objected that a Belief of Gods presence at all times in every place is the strongest possible restraint against committing Sin. This I constantly admit; but when I consider how easily our minds are put in motion, & how strongly they are sometimes agitated merely by the senses, & that the senses are affected most by things which fall under their immediate notice, I am fully convinced that if some such plan as I have just mentioned should be fallen upon, & practised, it would make a visible and useful change in our behaviour—In this place I think it needful to caution you against hasty & ill founded prejudices. When you enter among a people, & find that their manner of living, their *Eating*, *Drinking*, Diversions, Exercise &c, are in many respects different from any thing you have been accustomed to, you will be apt to fix your opinion in an instant, & (as some divines deal with poor Sinners) you will condemn all before you without any meaning or distinction what seems in your Judgment disagreeable at first view, when you are smitten with the novelty. You will be making ten thousand Comparisons. The face of the Country, The *Soil*, the *Buildings*, the *Slaves*, the *Tobacco*, the method of spending *Sunday* among Christians; *Ditto* among the Negroes; the three grand divisions of time at the Church on Sundays, Viz. before Service giving & receiving letters of business, reading Advertisements, consulting about the price of Tobacco, Grain &c, & settling either the lineage, Age, or qualities of favourite Horses 2. In the Church at Service, prayrs read over in haste, a Sermon seldom under & never over twenty minutes, but always made up of sound morality, or deep studied Metaphysicks. 3. After Service is over three quarters of an hour spent in strolling round the Church among the Crowd, in which time you will be invited by several different Gentlemen home with them to dinner. The Balls, the Fish-Feasts, the Dancing-Schools, the Christnings, the Cock fights, the Horse-Races, the Chariots, the Ladies Masked, for it is a custom among the Westmorland Ladies whenever they go from home, to muffle up their heads, & Necks, leaving only a narrow passage for the Eyes, in Cotton or silk handkerchiefs; I was in distress for them when I first came into the Colony, for every Woman that I saw abroad, I looked upon as ill either with the *Mumps* or Tooth-Ach!—I say, you will be often observing & comparing these things which I have enumerated, & many more that now escape me, with the manner of spending Money time & credit at Cohansie: You are young, &, (you will allow me the Expression) in the morning of Life. But I hope you have plann'd off, and entered upon the work which is necessary to be performed in the course of your Day; if not, I think it my duty to acquaint you, that a combination of the amusements which I have just now mentioned, being always before your Eyes, & inviting your Compliance will have a strong tendency to keep you doubtful & unsetled, in your notions of Morality & Religion, or else will fix you in a false & dangerous habit of *thinking* & *acting*, which must terminate at length in Sorrow & despair. You are therefore, if you count any thing upon the value of my advice, to fix the plan in which you would spend your life; let this be done with deliberation, Candour, & precission, looking to him for direction, by fervent Prayr, who is the "Wonderful Counsellor"; & when you have done this, let no importunity of whatever kind prevail over you, & cause you to transgress your own Limitations. I have already exceeded the usual bounds of an Epistle. But you will easily pardon a little prolixity, when I assure you it flows from a heart deeply impressed with a sense of the many difficulties which you must encounter, & the dangers which will surround you when you come first out from the peaceful recess of Contemplation, & enter, young and unexperienced, into the tumultuous undiscerning World. I submit these hints to your consideration, & have nothing more than sincere & ardent wishes for your present & perpetual Felicity.

> I am, Sir,
> yours.
> Philip V. Fithian

To Mr John Peck.
on going to Virginia in
Character of a Tutor.

Teusday 16.
The Colonel is summoned to a Meeting of Vestry-Men, at the Glebe —Nothing very extraordinary occurs, unless I mention that *Bob* in the former part of this Day kept pretty quiet in his Seat, and worked out three Sums in Reduction compound, without much direction! ...

Saturday 27.
The morning spent in setting coppies, Sums &c, for the School—After Breakfast, I spent a couple of Hours in the Dancing-Room...

Monday 29.
Miss *Fanny* in School to Day, but not entirely well of her Sores made by the *Ticks*—*Ben* complaines of a pain in his breast; he seems to have many symptoms of Weakness in his breast—I attempted to take a rough Draught of the Great House for myself...

Fryday [September] 2[nd, 1774]
Extreme hot today—Yesterday a Negro Child about six years old sickened as to appearance with the Ague & Fever, & to Day about eleven in the morning it expired! It is remarkable that the Mother has now lost seven successively, none of which have arrived to be ten years old!—The Negroes all seem much alarm'd & our School make it a Subject for continual Speculation; They seem all to be free of any terror at the Prescence of Death; *Harry* in special signified a Wish that his turn may be next. I should be glad if his desire were wise; & he was as fit for the business of the other world, as he seems willing to leave the business of this—In the evening this unexpected Death was the Subject of Conversation in the House—Mr *Carter* observed, that he thought it the most desirable to die of a Short Illness. If he could have his wish he would not lie longer than two days; be taken with a Fever, which should have such an unusual effect on his Body as to convince him that it would be fatal, and gradually increase till it effected a Dissolution—He told us that his affairs are in Such a state that he should be able to dictate a Will which might be written in five minutes, & contain the disposal of his estate agreeable to his mind—He mentioned to us the Substance—"That he would leave Mrs. Carter 6000 £ Sterling; & leave the remainder of his Estate to be disposed among his children as the Law directs."—

He told us likewise, with great firmness, that if he lives to see his children grown, he will pay no regard to age, but give his wealth to Him who bids fairest to be useful to mankind—That he allows all an equal oppertunity of improvement, but the One who is found then improved shall with the Learning inherit also the Substance—*Dennis* the Lad who waits at Table, I took into the School to day at his Fathers request, He can spell words of one syllable pretty readily. He is to come as he finds oppertunity.

Monday 5.

There is wonderful *To do*, this morning among the Housekeeper & children, at the great house. They assert that a Man or a Spirit came into the Nursery about one o-Clock this morning—That if it was indeed a Spirit the Cause of his appearance is wholly unknown; but if it was Flesh & blood they are pretty confident that the design was either to rob the House, or commit fornication with *Sukey*, (a plump, sleek, likely Negro Girl about sixteen)—That the doors & windows were well secured, but that by some secret manner, unknown to all, the *Thing* opened the Cellar door, went through the Cellar, & up the narrow dark Stairs (which are used only on necessary occasions, as when the great Stair way is washing or on some such account)— That it left the said Cellar door standing open, & besides unbar'd, & threw open the East Window in the little Room, in order, as they wisely supposed, to have, if it should be hurried, a ready passage out —That it had previously put a small wedge in the Lock of the Nursery Door, where several of the young Ladies, & the said *Sukey* sleep, so that when they were going to Bed they could not Lock nor bolt the door, but this they all believed was done in mischief by the children, & went thereupon to bed, without suspicion of harm, with the door open—That Sukey some time in the Night discovered Something lying by her Side which she knew to be a Man by his having Breeches —That She was greatly surprised, & cry'd out suddenly to the others that a Man was among them, & that the Man *tickled* her, & said *whish, whish*—That on this She left the Bed & run & Squeased herself in by the side of Miss Sally the House-keeper, but that by this time the Whole Room was awake & alarmed—That when the thing knew there was a discovery it stamped several times on the floor, shook the Bedstead by the side of which it lay, rattled the Door several Times & went down Stairs walking very heavy for one barefoot— That on its leaving the Room the Housekeeper went to Ben Carters Chamber, & that he rose & they all went down & found the Doors & window as I have mentioned—All this with many other material accidents is circulating through the family to Day; some conclude it was a Ghost because it would not speak—But, more probably it was one of the warm-blooded, well fed young Negroes, trying for the company of buxom *Sukey*—The Colonel however, at Breakfast gave out that if any one be caught in the House, after the family are at Rest, on any Pretence what ever, that Person he will cause to be hanged! ...

Thursday [October] 6[th 1774]
I paid Natt who drives the Team half a Bit as a Forfeit for taking hold of his plough—And to Harry 18d for a stirrup-leather & sundry other Articles—The School presented me with a petition formally drawn up for a holiday to day on account of the race at Mr Turberville's, which I granted—*Priscilla, Nancy, Ben, & Bob* go Harry & I, making in my opinion the wisest choice both stay.

Philip V. Fithian to Harry Willis and Robert Bladen Carter

Nomini Hall Octr 6th 1774.

For Masters Harry & Bob.

I approve highly of the method you have taken in asking for liberty to attend the race this afternoon, and think myself bound to give you an answer in the same manner.

This Race happening so soon after the other, which was at the same place, and so much like it seems to promise nothing that can require your attendance, it is therefore my *desire* and *advice* that you stay contented at home. But if your inclination be stronger than either of these, and you still choose to go, you have my consent provided you return by Sun set in the Evening.

Yours

Philip V. Fithian

Wednesday 12.
I was told often before I left Home that coming into Virginia would bring me into the midst of many dangerous Temptations: Gay Company, frequent entertainments, little practical devotion, no remote pretention to Heart religion, daily examples in Men of the highest quality, of Luxury, intemperance, & impiety; these were urged, by my kind acquaintances, as very strong dissuasions against my leaving home; the admonitions I accepted with great Thankfulness, tho' I could not allow them to turn me off from my purpose & I resolved with as much sincerity & Firmness as I could to carry them with me in every part of my behaviour. The close of the time of my Stay here is I expect now near at hand: And if I may judge myself of the carrying my resolutions into practice, I should pronounce that I have not been wanting in my duty in this respect. Some few who frequently ask me to go from home, say I am dull, unsociable, & splenetic: But the Gentlemen generally here have a good & reasonable manner of judging in this case they are well pleased with strict & rigid virtue in those who have the management of their children,

if it does not grow to factious enthusiasm; so that Levity, tho perhaps they would wink at it lessens, & in a while would take away the Reputation & business of a Family Tutor—Of this I was fully convinced in a short time after my coming into the Colony, & saw too the very great advantage of the Precaution which I received from my friends, for they assisted me in setting out on a safe, and prudent Plan, which has, I hope directed me to propriety of conduct with regard to my private character, & likewise to my little lovely Charge.

Saturday 15

...Soon after my return, when I was in the Chamber adjusting my articles Ben came bawling at my window Mr Peck's come, Mr Peck's come! I step'd to the window, & saw presently that what he said was fact, my Heart bounc'd & I with it bolted down to meet him...

Sunday 16

A fine morning—We rose by Seven but we were informed that there is no Sermon so that out of compliment to Mr Peck's weariness we kept close at home rather than ride to Richmond. We spent the Day in our chamber til towards evening when with the young Ladies we took a turn down the River Many we saw fishing—Mrs Carter with *Priss* rode to Captain Turberville's—We all return'd and assembled by evening at the great House—

Monday 17.

Before Breakfast I heard all the School a lesson round Mr Peck Present—After Breakfast I heard their Tables, Grammar &c &c then in Spite of my resolution with great reluctance, I resigned up to Mr Peck my little much-loved Charge!—The pain in my Face is quite gone—To day I saw a Phenomenon, Mrs Carter without Stays!—She complains of a pain in her breast, that prevents her wearing them, she says that She is always supposing the worst, & fears it is a Cancer breeding there—I hope it may be only fear—I am more & more every day pleased with the manner, Temper, oconomy, & whole management of this good Lady—Now I am to take my final Leave!

2. JOHN DAVIS TO THOMAS JEFFERSON

SIR,

IN frequent journeyings through your country, I have made remarks on the character, the customs and manners of the people; these remarks I purpose to systematize into a Volume, and to you I should be happy to be allowed the honour of dedicating them. The object of my speculations has been Human Nature; speculations that will lead the reader to the contemplation of his own manners, and enable him to compare his condition with that of other men.

In my uncertain peregrinations, I have entered with equal interest the mud-hut of the negro, and the log-house of the planter; I have alike communed with the slave who wields the hoe, and the task-master who imposes his labour. My motto has been invariably *Homo sum! humani nihil a me alienum puto*, and after saying this, whatever I were to say more, would be idle declamation.

I am, SIR,
Your most obedient, most humble Servant,
John Davis

THOMAS JEFFERSON, Esq.
President of the United States
of America, Monticello, Virginia.

3. THOMAS JEFFERSON TO JOHN DAVIS.

Sir,

I received your letter of August 31, in which you do me the honour to propose to dedicate to me the work you are about to publish. Such a testimony of respect from an enlightened Foreigner cannot but be flattering to me, and I have only to regret that the choice of the patron will be little likely to give circulation to the work; its own merit however will supply that defect.

Should you in your journeyings have been led to remark on the same objects on which I gave crude notes [1] some years ago, I shall be happy to see them confirmed or corrected by a more accurate observer.

I pray you to accept the assurances of
my respect and consideration.

TH: JEFFERSON

Mr. Davis,
Occoquan, Virginia.

3. MR. CARITAT DOES NOT THINK WELL OF PRIVATE TUTORING

Upon my landing at *New-York*, my first care was to deliver a letter of recommendation which I had been favoured with by a

---

1. *Notes on the State of Virginia.*

friend to a merchant in the city; together with a volume of Travels from *Boston* to *Philadelphia*, which he had recently published. But I cannot say that I was received with the urbanity I had anticipated. Neither my friends letter, nor his book, could soften the features of the stern American; and were the world to read the volume with as little interest as he, it would soon be consigned to the peaceful shelf. . . .

But I was not long depressed by melancholy reflection over my condition, for I found a friend in a man,[1] who, having himself been unfortunate, could feel for another in adversity. . . .

He inquired into my projects. I told him that my scheme was to get into some family as a private tutor. A private Tutor! said he. Alas! The labour of Sisyphus in hell is not equal to that of a private Tutor in America! . . .

Do you write a good hand, and understand all the intricacies of calculation? No. Then you will not do for a private Tutor. It is not your Latin and Greek, but your handwriting and cyphering, that will decide your character. Penmanship, and the figures of arithmetic, will recommend you more than logic and the figures of rhetoric. Can you passively submit to be called Schoolmaster by the children, and *Cool Mossa* by the negroes? No. Then you will not do for a private Tutor. Can you comply with the humility of giving only one rap at the door that the family may distinguish it is the Private Tutor; and can you wait half an hour with good humour on the steps, till the footman or housemaid condescends to open the door? No. Then you will not do for a private Tutor. Can you maintain a profound silence in company to denote your inferiority; and can you endure to be helped always the last at table, aye even after the clerk of the counting-house? No. Then you will not do for a private Tutor. Can you hold your eyes with your hands, and cry Amen! when grace is said; and can you carry the childrens' bibles and prayer-books to church twice every Sunday? No. Then you will not do for a private Tutor. Can you rise with the sun, and teach till breakfast; swallow your breakfast, and teach till dinner; devour your dinner, and teach till tea-time; and from tea-time to bed-time sink into insignificance in the parlour? No. Then you will not do for a private Tutor. Do you expect good wages? Yes. Then you will never do for a private Tutor. No, sir, the place of private Tutor is the last I would recommend you; for as Pompey, when he entered a tyrant's

1. Mr. Caritat, a bookseller.

dominions, quoted a verse from Euripides that signified his liberty was gone, so a man of letters, when he undertakes the tuition of a family in *America,* may exclaim he has lost his independence. Though not a countryman of your's, continued Mr. *Caritat,* I am from the same division of the globe, for I was born and educated in *France.* I should be happy to serve you, but I have not the hypocrisy to pretend that my offers of service are disinterested: interest blends itself with all human actions, and you, sir, have it in your power to be useful to me; I know you are skilled in French, because I have conversed with you in that language; of your own idiom you also discover an intimate acquaintance. *Vous etes donc mon homme.* I have just imported Buonaparte's campaign in *Italy,* from *Bourdeaux,* and the people are eager for a translation. Will you undertake the task? Will you translate the work for two hundred dollars? This is not the land of literature; booksellers in this country are not the patrons of authors, and therefore the remunerations for literary labour are not munificent. But the notoriety of Bounaparte will sell the work; and the translation make your name known beyond the mountains of the Blue Ridge. In a word, if you will translate the volume, I will pay you two hundred dollars.

Less declamation would have made me undertake the translation. I could hardly conceal my transports; and hugging the volume to my breast I danced home to my lodgings.—John Davis, *Travels of Four Years and A Half in the United States of America* (Morrison Edition), pp. 17-21.

4. JOHN DAVIS HAS A LIVELY INTERVIEW WITH A SOUTH CAROLINA PLANTER AND HIS WIFE

I landed at *Charleston* with Doctor *De Bow,* who had clad himself in his black suit, and though a young man, wore a monstrous pair of spectacles on his nose. Adieu jollity! adieu laughter! the Doctor was without an acquaintance on a strange shore, and he had no other friend but his Solemnity to recommend him. It was to no purpose that I endeavoured to provoke him to laughter by my remarks; the Physician would not even relax his risible muscles into a smile.

The Doctor was right. In a few days he contrived to hire part of a house in Union-street; obtained credit for a considerable quantity of drugs; and only wanted a chariot to equal the best Physician in *Charleston.*

The Doctor was in possession of a voluble tongue; and I furnished him with a few *Latin* phrases, which he dealt out to his hearers with an air of profound learning. He generally concluded his speeches with *Nullius addictus jurare in verba magistri!*

Wishing for some daily pursuit, I advertised in one of the papers for the place of Tutor in a respectable family; not omitting to observe that the advertiser was the translator of *Buonaparte's* Campaign in *Italy.* The editor of the Gazette assured me of an hundred applications; and that early the next morning I should not be without some. His predictions were verified; for the following day, on calling at the office, I found a note left from a Planter who lived a mile from the town, desiring me to visit him that afternoon at his house. I went thither accordingly. Every thing indicated opulence and ease. Mr. H————— received me with the insolence of prosperity. You are, said he, the person who advertised for the place of Tutor in a respectable family? I answered with a bow.

Planter. What, Sir, are your qualifications?

Tutor. I am competently skilled, Sir, in the *Latin* and *French* languages, not unacquainted with *Greek*, conversant with Geography, and accustomed to composition in my vernacular idiom.

Planter. But if you possess all *that there* learning, how comes it you could not get into some College, or School.

Tutor. Why, Sir, it is found even in Colleges that dunces triumph, and men of letters are disregarded by a general combination in favour of dulness.

Planter. Can you *drive* well, Sir?*

Tutor. Drive, Sir, did you say? I really do not comprehend you.

Planter. I mean, Sir, can you keep your scholars in order?

Tutor. Yes, Sir, if they are left entirely to my direction.

Planter. Ah! that would not be. Mrs. H—————, who is a woman of extensive learning, (she lost a fine opportunity once of learning *French*, and only a few years ago could write the best hand of any lady in *Charleston*,) Mrs. H————— would superintend your management of the school.

Tutor. Mrs. H—————, Sir, would do me honour.

Planter. Mrs. H—————, Sir, is in the real sense of the word, a woman of literature; and her eldest daughter is a prodigy for her

* The term *drive*, requires some little note explanatory to the *English* reader. No man forgets his original trade. An Overseer on a Plantation, who preserves subordination among the negroes, is said to *drive well;* and Mr. H——*having once been an Overseer himself,* the phrase very naturally predominated in his mind.

age. She could tell at nine years old whether a pudding was boiled enough; and, now, though only eleven, can repeat *Pope's* Ode on Solitude by heart. Ah! *Pope* was a *pretty* poet; my wife is very fond of *Pope.* You have read him, I make make no doubt, Sir. What is your opinion of his works?

Tutor. In his Rape of the Lock, Sir, he exhibits most of the *vis imaginandi* that constitutes the poet; his Essay on Criticism is scarcely inferior to *Horace's* Epistle to the Pisoes; his Satires——

Planter. But I am surprised, Sir, you bestow no praise on his Ode on Solitude. Mrs. H————, who is quite a critic in those matters, allows the Ode on Solitude to be his best, his noblest, his sublimest production.

Tutor. Persuaded, Sir, of the critical acuteness of Mrs. H————, it is not safe to depart from her in opinion;—and if Mrs. H———— affirms the Ode on Solitude to be the sublimest of Mr. *Pope's* productions, it would be rather painful than pleasant to undeceive her in opinion.

Planter. That is right, Sir, I like to see young men modest. What spelling-book do you use?

Tutor. What spelling-book, Sir? Indeed—really—upon my word Sir,—any—oh! *Noah Webster's,* Sir.

Planter. Ah! I perceive you are a New England man, by giving the preference to *Noah Webster.*

Tutor. Sir, I beg your pardon; I am from Old England.

Planter. Well, no matter for that,—but Mrs. H————, who is an excellent speller, never makes use of any other but *Matthew Carey's* spelling-book. It is a valuable work, the copyright is secured. But here comes Mrs. H———— herself.

Mrs. *H————* now entered, followed by a negro girl, who held a peacock's feather in her hand. Mrs. H———— received my bow with a mutilated curtesey, and throwing herself on a sopha, called peremptorily to *Prudence* to brush the flies from her face. There was a striking contrast between the dress of the lady and her maid; the one was tricked out in all the finery of fashion; while the black skin of the other peeped through her garments.

Well, my dear, said Mr. H————, this young man is the person who advertised for the place of tutor in a respectable family. A little conversation with him will enable you to judge, whether he is qualified to instruct our children in the branches of a liberal education.

Mrs. H.—— Why independent of his literary attainments, it will be necessary for him to produce certificates of his conduct. I am not easily satisfied in my choice of a tutor; *a body* should be very cautious in admitting a stranger to her family. This gentleman is young, and young men are very frequently addicted to bad habits. Some are prone to late hours; some to hard drinking; and some to Negur girls: the last propensity I could never forgive.

Mr. H. Yes, my dear, you discharged Mr. *Spondee,* our last tutor, for his intimacy with the Negur girls:—*Prudence* had a little one by him. *Prudence* looked reproachfully at her master; the child was in reality the offspring of Mr. H———, who fearing the inquiries of the world on the subject, fathered it upon the last tutor. But they must have been blind who could not discover that the child was sprung from Mr. H———; for it had the same vulgar forehead, the same vacant eye, and the same idiot laugh.

Mr. H. Do, my dear, examine the young man a little on literary matters. He seems to have read *Pope.*

Mrs. H. What, Sir, is your opinion of Mr. *Pope's* Ode on Solitude?

Tutor. It is a tolerable production, madam, for a child.

Mrs. H. A tolerable production for a child! Mercy on us! It is the *most sublimest* of his productions. But tastes differ. Have you read the works of *Dr. Johnson?* Which do you approve the most.

Tutor. Why, Madam, if you allude to his poems, I should, in conformity with your judgment, give a decided preference to his Epitaph on a Duck, written, if I mistake not, when he was four years old. It need scarcely fear competition with *Pope's* Ode on Solitude. At this moment the eldest daughter of this learned lady, of this unsexed female, tripped into the room on light, fantastic toe. Come, my daughter, said the lady, let this gentleman hear you repeat the Ode on Solitude.

Excuse me, Madam, cried I, taking up my hat and bowing.

Do you hear the child, Bawled Mr. *H*———. I pray you, sir, to excuse me, rejoined I.

Mrs. H. It will not take the child ten minutes.

Tutor. Ten minutes, Madam, are the sixth part of an hour that will never return!

Mr. H. Politeness dictates it.

Tutor. Excuse me, I entreat you, Sir.

Mr. H. I cannot excuse you, I shall hire you as tutor, and I have a right to expect from you submission. I may perhaps give you the sum of fifty pounds a year.

Don't mention it, Sir, said I. There again you will have the goodness to excuse me. Madam, your most obedient. Miss, your very obsequious. Sir, your humble servant.*

My walk back to *Charleston* was along the shore of the *Atlantic,* whose waves naturally associated the idea of a home I despaired ever again to behold. . .—*Ibid.,* 51-58.

5. John Davis takes a post in the College of Charleston

It was not long before my advertisement brought me other applications. The principal of Charleston College honoured me with a letter, whom, pursuant to his desire, I waited on at his house.

I found Mr. *Drone* in his study, consulting with great solemnity the ponderous lexicon of *Schrevelius.*[1] I could not but feel a secret veneration from the scene before me. I was admitted to the presence of a man who was not less voluminous than learned; for no book under a folio ever stood on his shelf.

How stupendous, thought I, must be the erudition of this professor, who holds in sovereign contempt a volume of ordinary dimensions! Every animal has an aliment peculiarly suited to its constitution. The ox finds nourishment only from the earth; and a professor cannot derive knowledge from any volume but a folio.

Mr. *Drone* received me with all the little decorums of dulness. He, however, talked learnedly. He lamented the degeneracy of literature in England and America; discovered that taste was on the decline; and despaired of ever beholding the spirit of that age revived when writers sought not for new combinations of imagery, but were content to compile lexicons, and restore the true punctuation to an ancient poet.

Mr. *Drone* asked me whether I was conversant with Latin; and on my replying in the affirmative, he produced a Horace in folio, and desired I would construe the Ode of *Quem tu Melpomene.*

Horace had never before assumed so formidable an aspect. In the

* It has been my object in this scene to soften the condition of private tutors in America, by putting up Mr. H——— *in signum terroris et Memoriae* to other purse-proud planters. I write not from personal pique, but a desire to benefit society. Happy shall I think myself should this page hold the mirror up to the inflation of pride, and the insolence of prosperity.

1. Seventeenth century Dutch philologist.

ordinary editions he had always looked at me *placido lumine*; but he now appeared crabbed and sour, and I found his text completely buried amidst the rubbish of annotations.

By making *isthmius labor* the agent to *clarabit* the difficulty of the inversion vanished; but when I came to analyze the construction of the ode, not having some rule for verbs construed at memory, I think it was the important one of *mo fit ui*, as *vomo vomui*; the Professor, with a shake of his head, which doubtless put all his sagacity into motion, told me very gravely I had yet something to learn.

I ought to apologize to my reader for detaining him so long in the company of Professor *Drone*; but it is a link in the chain of my history, however rusty. To be brief, he engaged me as an Assistant to his sublime College for three months; and had the vanity to assert, that in consequence of it I should become *fama super aethera notus*.

I was about to take leave of Mr. *Drone*, when his principal Tutor entered the room, to whom he introduced me. Mr. *George* taught the *Greek* and *Latin* classics at the *College*, and was not less distinguished by his genius than his erudition.

On surveying my new acquaintance, I could not but think that he deserved a better office than that of a Gerund-grinder. Nature seemed to have set her seal on him to give the world assurance of a man...

Two young men, of similar pursuits, soon become acquainted. The day of my introduction to Mr. *George*, we exchanged thoughts without restraint; and during three months that I continued at *Charleston*, we were inseparable companions.

I know not whether I was qualified to fill the vacant chair of instruction at the College; but I remember, that zealous to acquit myself with dignity in my new office, I assumed the aspect of a pedagogue, and when an idle boy stared at me, I checked him with a frown. I, however, was not ambitious of this honour more than six weeks; a space of time, which, however it cannot be long, may surely be tedious. The Professor complained that I was always last in the College; and I replied by desiring my discharge.

I was now dismissed from the College; but I was under no solicitude for my future life. A planter of the name of *Brisbane*, had politely invited me to his plantation, to partake with him and his neighbours, the diversion of hunting, during the winter; and another of the name of Drayton, the owner of immense forests, had applied to me to live in his family, and undertake the tuition of his children. Of these proposals, the first flattered my love of ease, and the other insured me an augmentation of wealth. I was not long held in suspense which of the two to chuse; but I preferred the summons of industry to the blandishments of pleasure.—*Ibid.*, pp. 58-62.

6. JOHN DAVIS TAKES A POST ON MR. BALL'S PLANTATION IN VIRGINIA

In my way through the garden I passed two young ladies gathering roses, who, however immured in the woods, were clad with not less elegance than the most fashionable females of *Europe*. They were beautiful in face and form; I asked them with a bowing mien, whether Mr. *Ball* was at home. They replied, that their papa was in the parlour, and with much sweetness of manner directed me by the shortest path to the house.

Mr. *Ball* received me with undissembled accents of joy; he said he had long expected my coming and was gratified at last. A nod to a mulatto boy placed refreshments on the side-board, and in a few minutes the family assembled to take a peep at the Schoolmaster.

The first impression made by Mr. *Ball* decided that he was a Gentleman; and I was not a little delighted with the suavity of his manners, and the elegance of his conversation.

When the children withdrew, I entered on the terms of my proposed engagement, and presented to him a letter which I had been honoured with from Mr. *Jefferson.* I knew my host to be a *Virginian* who favoured the Administration, and thought a letter from the President would operate on him like witchcraft. But I was unacquainted with my man. Mr. *Ball* was not to be biassed by the whistling of a name; he read my letter more from complaisance than any motive of curiosity; observed, that a man's conduct could alone decide his character; congratulated himself upon the acquisition of a man of letters in his family; and offered to engage me for twelvemonth, at a salary of a hundred guineas. I acknowledged the honour he did me, and engaged with him for a quarter of a year.

The following day every farmer came from the neighbourhood to the house, who had any children to send to my Academy, for such they did me the honour to term the log-hut in which I was to teach. Each man brought his son, or his daughter, and rejoiced that the day was arrived when their little ones could light their tapers at the torch of knowledge! I was confounded at the encomiums they heaped upon a man whom they had never seen before, and was at a loss what construction to put upon their speech. No price was too great for the services I was to render their children; and they all expressed an eagerness to exchange perishable coin for lasting knowledge. If I would continue with them seven years! only seven years! they would erect for me a brick seminary on a hill not far off; but for the present I was to occupy a log-house, which, however homely, would soon vie with the sublime College of *William and Mary*, and consign to oblivion the renowned Academy in the vicinity of *Fauquier Court-House*. I thought *Englishmen* sanguine; but these *Virginians* were infatuated.

I now opened what some called an *Academy,** and others an Old Field School; and, however it may be thought that content was never felt within the walls of a seminary, I, for my part, experienced an exception from care, and was not such a fool as to measure the happiness of my condition by what others thought of it.

It was pleasurable to behold my pupils enter the school over which I presided; for they were not composed only of truant boys, but some of the fairest damsels in the country. Two sisters generally rode on one horse to the school-door, and I was not so great a pedagogue as to refuse them my assistance to dismount from their steeds. A running footman of the negro tribe, who followed with their food in a basket, took care of the beast; and after being saluted by the young ladies with the curtesies of the morning, I proceeded to instruct them, with gentle exhortations to diligence of study.

Common books were only designed for common minds. The unconnected lessons of *Scot*, the tasteless Selections of *Bingham*, the florid Harangues of *Noah Webster*, and the somniferous Compilations of *Alexander*, were either thrown aside, or suffered to gather dust on the shelf; while the charming Essays of *Goldsmith*, and his not less delectable Novel, together with the impressive work of *De Foe*, and the mild productions of *Addison*, conspired to enchant the fancy, and

---

* It is worth while to describe the *Academy* I occupied on Mr. *Ball's* plantation. It had one room and a half. It stood on blocks about two feet and a half above the ground, where there was free access to the hogs, the dogs, and the poultry. It had no ceiling, nor was the roof lathed or plastered; but covered with shingles. Hence, when it rained, like the nephew of old *Elwes*, I moved my bed (for I slept in my Academy) to the most comfortable corner. It had one window, but no glass, nor shutter. In the night to remedy this, the mulatto wench who waited on me, contrived very ingeniously to place a square board against the window with one hand, and fix the rail of a broken down fence against it with the other. In the morning when I returned from breakfasting in the "great big-house," (my scholars being collected,) I gave the rail a forcible kick with my foot, and down tumbled the board with an awful roar. "Is not my window," said I to *Virginia*, "of a very curious construction?" "Indeed, indeed, Sir," replied my fair disciple, "I think it is a mighty noisy one."

kindle a love of reading. The thoughts of these writers became engrafted on the minds, and the combinations of their diction, on the language of the pupils.

Of the boys I cannot speak in very encomiastic terms; but they were perhaps like all other school boys, that is, more disposed to play truant than enlighten their minds. The most important knowledge to an American, after that of himself, is the Geography of his country. I, therefore, put into the hands of my boys a proper book, and initiated them by an attentive reading of the Discoveries of the *Genoese;* I was even so minute as to impress on their minds the man who first described land on board the ship of *Columbus.* That man was *Roderic Triana,* and on my exercising the memory of a boy by asking the name, he very gravely made answer *Roderic Random.*

Among my male students was a *New Jersey* gentleman of thirty, whose object was to be initiated in the language of *Cicero* and *Virgil.* He had before studied the *Latin* grammar at an *Academy School* (I use his own words) in his native State, but the *Academy School* being burnt down, his grammar, alas! was lost in the conflagration, and he had neglected the pursuit of literature since the destruction of his book. When I asked him if he did not think it was some Goth who had set fire to his *Academy School,* he made answer, "So, it is like enough."

Mr. *Dye* did not study *Latin* to refine his taste, direct his judgment, or enlarge his imagination: but merely that he might be enabled to teach it when he opened school, which was his serious design. He had been bred a carpenter, but he panted for the honours of literature. . . .

Several families from *New Jersey* were settled in the neighborhood. The characters of men are best illustrated by comparison, and it may not be useless to compare the *Jersey* man with the native *Virginian.*

The *New Jersey Man* puts his hand to the plough; the *Virginian* only inspects the work of his farm. The *New Jersey Man* lives with the strictest economy, and very seldom visits or receives visits. The *Virginian* exceeds his income, loves to go abroad, and welcomes his guest with the smiles of hospitality. The *New Jersey Man* turns every horse out to labour, and walks whither he has to go on business; the *Virginian* thinking it degrading to be seen on foot, has always his riding nag saddled and fastened to the fence. The *New Jersey Man* is distinguished by his provincial dialect, and seldom enlarges his mind, or transfers his attention to others; the *Virginian* is remarkable for his colloquial happiness, loses no opportunity of knowledge, and delights to shew his wit at the expence of his neighbour. Neither a dancing-master, a pedlar, or a maker of air balloons, was ever encouraged by a *New Jersey Man;* but on a *Virginian* they never fail to levy contributions. The treasury of the pedlar is in vain laid open to the eyes of the *New Jersey Man;* neither the brilliant water of the diamond, the crimson flame of the ruby, nor the lustre of the topaz has charms to allure him; but the *Virginian* enamoured of ornament cannot gaze on them with impunity; he empties his coffers of every dollar to adorn the apparel of his wife and daughters.

Of my female students there was none equal in capacity to *Virginia.* The mind of this fair creature was susceptible of every culture; but it had been neglected, and I opened to her worlds of sentiment and knowledge.

Geography was one of our favourite studies. The greatest trifler can scarce inspect a map without learning something; but my lovely pupil always rose from it with a considerable accession of knowledge. Imparting such new ideas was no undelightful employment, and I often addressed my rose of May in an appropriate Ode. . . . .

Succession is only perceived by variation, and in the delightful employment of *teaching my lovely pupil all I knew,* the hours of the morning were contracted to a moment by the earnest application of my mind to its object; time took a new pair of wings, and the school-door, which faced the south, had the sun staring full upon it, before I recollected that my attention ought to be divided, and not consecrated to one scholar.

Hence I frequently protracted the studies of the children till one, or half past one o'clock; a practice that did not fail to call forth the exclamations both of the white and the black people. Upon my word, Mr. *Ball* would say, this gentleman is diligent; and Aunt *Patty* the negro cook would remark, "*He good cool-mossa that; he not like old Hodgkinson and old Harris, who let the boys out before twelve. He deserve good wages!*"

Having sent the young ladies to the family mansion, I told the boys to break up; and in a few minutes they who had even breathed with circumspection, now gave loose to the most riotous merriment, and betook themselves to the woods, followed by all the dogs on the plantation.

Let the reader throw aside my volume, whose mind feels disgust from the images afforded by a school in the woods of *America.* I deprecate not his severity; I write not for such feelings. But, reader, if thou art a father, or if thy mind uncorrupted by the business and vanities of life, can delight in the images of domestic privacy, thou wilt derive more real satisfaction from the picture of a groupe of school-boys at play, than from the conflict of the *Austrians* with the *French* on the plains of *Maringo*.....

Finding the hours hang heavy, I bethought myself of some invitation that had been given me to a neighboring plantation, and one visit leading to another, in my round of calling on one or another, I came to the house whither *Virginia* had gone before me. *Virginians* are ever hospitable; ever open-hearted to the stranger who enters their doors. The house of a *Virginian* is not less sacred to hospitality than the tent of an *Arab*. I was received always with transport. "Here, *Will*, take this gentleman's horse. *Edward*, run up stairs, "my dear, and tell your mother and the girls to come down."

My recreation after school in the evening was to sit and meditate before my door, in the open air, while the vapours of a friendly pipe administered to my philosophy. In silent gravity I listened to the negro calling to his steers returning from labour, or contemplated the family groupe on the grass-plot before the dwelling-house, of whom the father was tuning his violin, the mother and daughters at their needles, and the boys running and tumbling in harmless mirth upon the green. Before me was an immense forest of stately trees; the cat was sitting on the barn door; the fire-fly was on the wing, and the whip-poor-will in lengthened cries was hailing the return of night.....

But the period is hasting when I must leave Mr. *Ball* and the worthy families in his neighbourhood, and another page or two will conduct me out of the woods of *Pohoke*. I had been three months invested in the first executive office of Pedagogue, when a cunning old fox of a *New Jersey* planter (a Mr. *Lee*) discovered that his eldest boy wrote a better hand than I. Fame is swift-footed; *vires acquirit eundo*; the discovery spread far and wide; and whithersoever I went, I was an object for the hand of scorn to point his slow unmoving finger at, as a schoolmaster that could not write. *Virginia* gave me for the persecutions I underwent a world of sighs, her swelling heavens rose and with indignation at old *Lee* and his abettors. The boys caught spirit from the discovery. I could perceive a mutiny breaking out among them; and had I not in time broke down a few branches from an apple tree before my door, it is probable they would have displayed their gratitude for my instructions by throwing me out of my school-window. But by arguing with one over the shoulders, and another over the back, I maintained with dignity the first executive office of Pedagogue.... —*Ibid.*, 394-99, 401-02, 406-07.

7. EXTRACTS FROM THE DIARY AND LETTERS OF JOHN HARROWER, INDENTURED SERVANT, 1773-1776 [1]

Wednesday, 26th. (January, 1774) This day I being reduced to the last shilling I hade was obliged to engage to go to Virginia for four years as a schoolmaster for Bedd, Board, washing and five pound during the whole time. I have also wrote my wife this day a particular Accot of everything that has happned to me since I left her untill this date; At 3 pm this day I went on board the Snow Planter Capt Bowers Comr for Virginia now lying at Ratliff Cross, and imediatly as I came Onbd I recd my Hammock and Bedding. at 4 pm came Alexr Steuart onbd the same Ship. he was Simbisters Servt and had only left Zetland about three weeks before....

Freiday, 13th. (May) This forenoon put ashore here what bale goods we hade remaining onboard. in the afternoon Mr. Burnet, Stewart and myself went ashore on liberty to take a walk and see the Toun, who's principal street is about half an English Mile long, the houses generally at a little distance one from another, some of them being built of wood and some of them of brick, and all covered with wood in the form of sclates about four Inches broad, which when painted blue you wou'd not know it from a house sclated with Isedell sclate. In this Toun the Church, the Counsell house, the Tolbooth the Gallows and the Pillory are all within 130 yds of each other. The Market house is a large brick Building a litle way from the Church. here we drank some Bottles of beer of their own brewing and some bottles of Cyder for which we paid 3½ per bottle of each. returned on board in the evening. Turner still in handcuffs.

Munday, 16th. This day severalls came onbd to purchase servts Indentures and among them there was two Soul drivers. they are men who make it their business to go onbd all ships who have in either Servants or Convicts and buy sometimes the whole and sometimes a parcell of them as they can agree, and then they drive them through

1. The diary is published in full in *The American Historical Review*, VI (October, 1900), No. I, 65-107. The extracts used here are with the permission of that publication. The diary begins with an entry of December 6, 1773, when Harrower left his house in Lerwick in Shetland. After describing his journey to London and his difficulties in getting work there, he sails with Captain Bowers for Virginia.

the Country like a percell of Sheep untill they can sell them to advantage, but all went away without buying any.

Tuesday, 17th. This day Mr Anderson the Mercht sent for me into the (cabin) and verry genteely told me that on my recomendations he would do his outmost to get me settled as a Clerk or bookeeper if not as a schoolmaster which last he told me he thought wou'd turn out more to my advantage upon being settled in a good famely...

Munday, 23d. This morning a great number of Gentlemen and Ladies driving into Town it being an annuall Fair day and tomorrow the day of the Horse races. at 11 AM Mr Anderson begged to settle as a schoolmaster with a friend of his one Colonel Dangerfield and told me he was to be in Town tomorrow, or perhaps tonight, and how soon he came he shou'd acquant me. at same time all the rest of the servants were ordred ashore to a tent at Fredericksbg and severall of their Indentures were then sold. about 4 pm I was brought to Colonel Daingerfield, when we immediately agreed and my Indenture for four years was then delivered him and he was to send for me the next day. at same time ordred to get all my dirty Cloaths of every kind washed at his expense in Toun; at night he sent me five shillings onbd by Capt Bowers to keep my pocket.

Tuesday, 24th. This morning I left the Ship at 6 AM having been sixteen weeks and six days on board her. I hade for Breackfast after I came ashore one Chappin sweet milk for which I paid 3½ Cury at 11 AM went to see a horse race about a mille from Toun, where there was a number of Genteel Company as well as others. here I met with the Colonel again and after some talk with him he gave me cash to pay for washing all my Cloaths and something over. The reace was gain'd by a Bay Mare, a white boy ridder. There was a gray Mare started with the Bay a black boy ridder but was far distant the last heat.

Wednesday, 25th. I Lodged in a Tavern last night and paid 7½ for my Bedd and 7½ for my breackfast. this morning a verry heavy rain untill 11 AM. Then I recd my Linens &c. all clean washed and packing every thing up I went onboard the ship and Bought this Book for which I paid 18d. Str. I also bought a small Divinity book called the Christian Monitor and a spelling book, both at 7½ and an Arithmetick at 1/6d. all for my Accot

Thursday, 26th. This day at noon the Colonel sent a Black with a cuple of Horses for me and soon after I set out on Horseback and aravied at his seat of Belvidera about 3 pm and after I hade dined the Colonel took me to a neat little house at the upper end of an Avenue of planting at 500 y^d from the Main house, where I was to keep the school, and Lodge myself in it.

This place is verry pleasantly situated on the Banks of the River Rappahannock about seven miles below the Toun of Fredericksburgh and the school's right above the Warff so that I can stand in the door and pitch a stone onboard of any ship or Boat going up or coming doun the river.

Freiday, 27th. This morning about 8 AM the Colonel delivered his three sons to my Charge to teach them to read write and figure. his oldest son Edwin 10 years of age, intred into two syllables in the spelling book, Bathourest (Bathurst) his second son six years of age in the Alphabete and William his third son 4 years of age does not know the letters. he has likeways a Daughter whose name is Hanna Basset   Years of age. Soon after we were all sent for to breackfast to which we hade tea, Bread, Butter and cold meat and there was at table the Colonel, his Lady, his Children, the housekeeper and myself. At 11 AM the Colonel and his Lady went some where to pay a visite, he upon horseback and she in her Charriot. At 2 pm I dined with the Housekeeper the Children and a stranger Lady. at 6 pm I left school, and then I eat plenty of fine strawberries, but they neither drink Tea in the afternoon nor eat any supper here for the most part. My school Houres is from 6 to 8 in the morning, in the forenoon from 9 to 12 and from 3 to 6 in the afternoon. . .

Wednesday, June 1st. This day there was prayers in all the Churches in Virginia on Accot of the disagreement at present betwixt great Brittain and her Colonies in North America, On Accot of their not agreeing to pay a duty on Tea laid on them by the british parliament and the Bostonians destroying a Quantity of Tea belonging to the British East India Compy in 1773. . .

Saturday, 11th. At 9 AM left the school and went a fishing on the River with the Colonel his eldest (Son) and another Gentleman in two Canoes, Mrs. Dangerfield another Lady and the other two boys mett us at Snow Creek in the Chair at 2 pm when we all dined on fish under a tree.

Sunday, 12th. This day at Church at Fredericksburgh and at same time settled a Correspondance at Glasgow for getting letters from home, by their being put under cover to Messrs. Anderson and Horsburgh Merch^{ts} in D^o and the expence charged to Mr. Glassel Merch^t in Fredericksbg Virginia.

Tuesday, 14th. This morning entred to school William Pattie son to John Pattie wright, and Salley Evens daughter to Thomas Evens Planter. This day I wrote my wife a particular Accot of all my transactions since I wrote her from London 26th Jany last, the Coppy of which I have by me...

Munday, 20th. This morning entred to school Philip and Dorothea Edge's Children of Mr Benjaman Edge Planter...

Tuesday, 21st. This day Mr Samuel Edge Planter came to me and begged me to take a son of his to school who was both deaf and dum, and I consented to try what I cou'd do with him...

Thursday, 23d. This day entred to school John Edge son to the above named Mr Sam: Edge, he is a lad about 14 years of age and is both deaf and dum.

Saturday, 25th. This afternoon I went and took a walk in the wheat field and under a tree I filled all my pockets of as fine walnuts as ever I eat, But so hard shell that I was obledged to have a hammer to breack them.

Sunday, 26th. After Breackfast I took a walk 3 Miles to Mr. Edge's, the dum lad's fathers where I dined and drank some grogg and returned home in the afternoon. at night I had a small Congregation of Negroes, learng their Catechisim and hearing me read to them.

Sunday, July 3d. At home all the forenoon, in the afternoon went to see One Mr. Richards an Overseer and his wife where I eat plenty of honney out of the Comb, it being taken out of a Beehive in a tree in the woods last night.

Freiday, 8th. After school houres I went two Miles to see the Taylor who made my Cloaths he being a Brittoner but married to a Buckskine, and I found his wife and Daughters drinking tea, at which I joyned them, The Taylor not being at home.

Tuesday, 12th. Sold the spelling book that I bought Onbd the Planter 25th May last, and got the same money for it that I paid for the Christian Monitor and it.

Saturday, 16th. This afternoon the Colonel finished the cutting down of His wheat which cost of wages to hired people £ 23: 10 Curry besides their victualls and drink.

Munday, 18th. This morning entred to School Lewis Richards. Same day I put on a pair of new shoes made in Fredericksburgh of English calf leather the price of them 12/6 Curry. Same day gave one pair of old worsted stockins for 22 foot of Gum plank 10 Inch broad and one thick to make me a Chest.

Tuesday, 19th. On Freiday 15th, Inst John Edge the Dum lad left the school at 6 pm and has not returned since.

Wednesday, 20th. On Munday 4th, Inst at 6 pm William Pattie left the school and has not returned since.

Munday, 25th. Nothing remarkable. Jno Edge returnd to school...

Belvidera 14th June 1774.

My Dearest Life

I wrote you from London on Wednesday 26th Jany last which Im hopefull came safe to hand, and found you and my dear Infants in perfect health, and am hopefull this will find both you and them in the same state, As I am at present and have been I bless God since I left you. You will remember when I wrote you last, I informed you that I was to go for Baltimore in Maryland. But I altred my design in that and came here it being a more healthy pleace. I sailed from London on Freiday the 4th Feby last, and arrived in Hampton roads in Virginia on the 27 April, having been a Month of the time at Spithead in England. As to particulars of our Voyage &ca it would take up too much room here to insert it. But I have a Journal of every days transactions and remarcable Occurrances since the morning I left you which will be amusing to you when please God we are spared to meet, for I design to see and prepare a way for you all in this Country how soon I am able.— I shall now aquant you wt my situation in this Country. I am now settled with on Colonel Wm Dangerfield Esqr of Belvidera, on the Banks of the River Rappahannock about 160 miles from the Capes or sea mouth, and seven Miles below the Toun of Fredericksburgh. My business is to teach his Children to read write and figure, Edwin his oldest son about 8 years of (age) Bathurest his second 6 years of age and William his youngest son 4 years of age. He has also a Daughter whose name is Hanna Basset. I came to this place on Thursday 26th May and next morning I received his three sons into my charge to teach, the two youngest boys I got in A:B:C. and the oldest Just begun to syllab and I have now the two youngest spelling and the oldest reading. I am obliged to teach in the English method which was a little aquard to me at first but now quite easy. I am also obliged to talk english the best I can, for Lady Dangerfield speacks nothing but high english, and the Colonel hade his Education in England and is a verry smart Man. As to my agreement it is as follows Vizt I am obliged to continue with Col. Dangerfield for four years if he insists on it, and for teaching his own children I have Bed, Board, washing and all kind of Cloaths during the above time, and for what schoolars I can get more than his Children I have five shillings currency per Quarter for each of them, which is equall to four shillings sterling, and I expect ten or twelve to school next week, for after I hade been here eight days and my abilities and my behavior sufficiently tried, the Colonel rode through the neighbouring Gentlemen and Planters in order to procure scollars for me, so that I hope in a short time to make something of it. And as I have no Occasion to spend a farthing on myself every shillg I make shall be carefully remitted you, for your support and my Dear Infants. But I must be some time here before any thing can be done, for you know every thing must have a beginning.

As to my living I eat at their own table, and our witualls are all Dressed in the English taste. we have for Breackfast either Coffie or Jaculate,[1] and warm Loaf bread of the best floor, and we have also at table warm loaf bread of Indian corn, which is extreamely good but we use the floor bread always at breackfast. for Dinner smoack'd bacon or what we cal pork ham is a standing dish either warm or cold. when warm we have greens with it, and when cold we have sparrow grass. we have also either warm roast pigg, Lamb, Ducks, or chickens, green pease or any thing else they fancy. As for Tea there is none drunk by any in this Government since 1st June last, nor will they buy a 2ds worth of any kind of east India goods, which is owing to the difference at present betwixt the Parliment of great Britton and the North Americans about laying a tax on the tea; and I'm afraid if the Parliment do not give it over it will cause a total revolt as all the North Americans are determined to stand by one another, and resolute on it that they will not submit. I have the news paper sent me to school regularly every week by the Coll.—Our family consists of the Coll his Lady and four Children a housekeeper an Overseer and myself all white. But how many blacks young and old the Lord only knows for I belive there is about thirty that works every day in the field besides the servants about the house; such as Gardner, livery men and pages, Cooks, washer and dresser, sewster and waiting girle. They wash here the whitest that ever I seed for they first Boyle all the Cloaths with soap, and then wash them, and I may put on clean linen every day if I please. My schoole is a neate little House 20 foot long and 12 foot wide and it stands by itself at the end of an Avenue of planting about as far from the main house as Robt Forbes's is from the burn, and there comes a bonny black bairn every morning to

1. Chocolate.

clean it out and make my bed, for I sleep in it by myself. I have a verry fine feather bed under me, and a pair of sheets, a thin fold of a Blanket and a Cotton bed spread is all by bed cloaths, and I find them just enough. as for myself I supose you wou'd scarce know me now, there being nothing either brown, blew, or black about me but the head and feet, I being Dressed in short cloath Coat, vest Coat, and britches all made of white cotton without any lyning and thread stockins and wearing my own hair curled round like a wigg. at present a suite of Cloaths costs five and twenty shillings here of making which I really think verry high.

I was Sunday last at Fredericksburgh at church and I then settled a safe Correspondance for your letters to come to me, and shall give you the proper directions below. As for myself I thank God I want for nothing that is necessary, But it brings tears from my eyes to think of you and my infants when at the same time it is not in my power at present to help you. But how soon I am able you may depend upon it. I have litle else to say at present; only may the great God who governs all things wisely suport you and my Infants, and guide and direct you in all your ways.

I shall write you again soon and when you write me direct my letters as follows Viz^t to John Harrower at the seat of Colonel Wm Dangerfield Esqr of Belvidera near Fredericksburgh on Rappahannock River Virginia; Then you must take half a sheet of paper and write another letter the contents of which may be as follows Viz^t Gentlemen, being desired by my husband to send his letters under cover to you, You will please forward the inclosed by the first ship bound for any part in Virginia and charge Mr Glassel Merch^t in Fredericksburgh with the expence you are at; I am yours &^{c} Signed A. H. After you have closed my letter and directed it as above, You will inclose it in the above, and direct it as follows To Messrs Anderson and Horsburgh Merch^{ts} in Glasgow. You must get some person to fold up your letter properly and on who writes a clear Distinct hand to direct them. Pray write me verry particularly how it is with you and my Dr Infants, likeways any thing that is remarcable in the Country. I shall conclude this with offering my Comp^{ts} to all enquiring freinds if I have any and my sinceer prayers both evening and morng for you and my Children. My Blessing to you all, is all at prsent from my Dearest Jewell your ever aff^{te} Husband untill Death. Signed, John Harrower.

Addressed, To Mrs. John Harrower in Lerwick, Zetland. . .

Wednesday, 17th. (August) This evening entred to school Thomas

Brooks Mr Spotswoods carpenter in order to learn Writing and Arithmetick at nights and on Sundays...

Sunday, 28th. At home all day teaching Brooks.

Sunday, September 11th. Do teaching Brooks. at 1 pm came Mr Kennedy from Fredericksburgh here to see me and after we had dined we ended the Quart of Rum I bought 16th Last Mo.

Tuesday, October 4th. Went to Fredericksbg and seed a Horse Race for a Hundred Guineas, Gained by Mr Fitchews Horse...

Belvidera 6th Decr 1774.

My Dearest Life...

I have as yet only ten scollars One of which is both Deaff and Dumb and his Father pays me ten shilling per Quarter for him he has been now five Mos with (me) and I have brought him tolerably well and understands it so far, that he can write mostly for anything he wants and understands the value of every figure and can work single addition a little. he is about fourteen years of age. Another of them is a young man a house Carpenter who attends me every night with candle light and every Sunday that I don't go to Church for which he pays me fourty shillings a year. He is Carpenter for a gentleman who lives two miles from me and has Thirty pound a year, free bedd and board.

The Colls Children comes on pretty well. the Eldest is now reading verry distinctly in the Psalter according to the Church of England and the other two boys ready to enter into it; the Coll and his Lady being extreamly well satisfied wt my Conduct in every respect; On 31st Jully last Mrs Daingerfield was delivd of a fourth son who is now my nameson...

I yet hope please God, if I am spared, some time to make you a Virginian Lady among the woods of America which is by far more pleasant than the roaring of the raging seas round abo't Zetland. And yet to make you eat more wheat Bread in your old age than what you have done in your Youth. But this I must do by carefullness, industry and a Close Application to Business, which ye may take notice of in this letter I am doing Sunday as well as Saturday nor will I slip an honest method nor an hour whereby I can gain a penny for yours and my own advantage...

Sunday, 25th. Christmas day, stayed at home all day along wt the Overseer and Children because I hade no saddle to go to the Church with. In the morning the Coll Ordred up to school two Bottles of the best Rum and some suggar for me.

Munday, 26th. This forenoon the Coll wou'd have me to take his saddle and ride to Toun and Amuse myself, and when I was going gave me Six Shillings for pocket money. I went to Toun and Dined in a private house and after buying 1½ Dozn Mother of Pearle buttons for my white morsyld Vest I return'd home in the evening.

Tuesday, 27th. St. John's day. This day a Grand Lodge in Toun, And the whole went to Church in their Clothing and heard sermon.

Thursday, 29th. I began to keep school.

Freiday, 30th. This day there was severall Gentlemen from Fredericksburgh here at Dinner with whom I dined.

Tuesday, January 10th, 1775. This day Thos Brooks who has atten(d) ed ever night and on Sundays left school being obliged to go 40 miles up the country to work. at same time he gave me an order on Coll Daingerfield for £1. 10. 8. Curry of which £1. 5. 2 was for teaching him. . .

Tuesday, 31st. 1 pm yesterday Jas and Wm Porters, sons of Mr William Porter Mercht in Fredericksbg came here to School. . .

Munday, 27th. This day Mr Fraser came here and entred to take his charge as Overseer, and he is to have his bed in the school along with me. he appears to be a verry quiet young man and has hade a tolerable education. his Grandfather came from Scotland. . .

Saturday, 25th. At noon went to Newport to see Mr Martin Heely schoolmaster to Mr Spotswood's Children, and after Dinner I spent the afternoon with him in conversation and hearing him play the Fiddle. He also made a Niger come and play on an Instrument call'd a Barrafou. . .

Saturday, April 1st. At 6 pm Mr Martin Heely schoolmaster at Newport for Mr Spotswoods Children came here to pay me a Visite and staid with me all night.

Sunday, 9th. This day a good number of Company dined here among which was Mr and Mrs Porter from Town, who heard their eldest son read and seemed verry well pleased with his performance since he came to me; Myself at home all day.

Freiday, 14th. This being good Frieday, I broke up school for Easter Holly day, and the Colls three sons went to Town with Mr Porter's two sons this forenoon I went a money hunting but catc'd none. . .

Thursday, 20th. This morning all the boys came to school again at their Usual hour. . .

Sunday, 7th. (May) At 2 houses this day seeking money that was owing me but got none. . .

Saturday, 20th. This day I wrote the following letter to Saml Edge for twenty shillings that has been due me since the 25th Novr 1774. Mr Samuel Edge

*Sir—*I wrote you 18th March last requesting you then to send me per the Bearer then sent, the twenty shillings you are indebted to me, which money you promised to have paid a Month before that time. Notwithstanding of which I have neither seen nor heard from you since, which to me appear some what Strange.

On Saturday last I was informed you intended to send me a wild Goose hunting by giving me a Draught on another. But if any one is owing you I do not chuse to demand the debt; Therefore I hereby aquant you that I will not accept a draught upon none; Therefore I am hopefull you will now send the money by the bearer hereof as I really have pressing occasion for it and cannot be longer without it, having neither stock nor store here to receive money with to purchase what I really cannot be without. your complyance to the above will greatly oblige and wherein I can serve you may freely command Sir yours &c

Signed J H

Addressed to Mr. Samuel Edge, Overseer. . .

Saturday, June 3d. At 9 AM Mr Porter's two son's was sent for and they went to Toun to keep Whitsuntide holliday. . .

Wednesday, 19th. (July) This day I was Informed that Mrs Daingerfield hade made a Complaint upon me to the Colo for not not waiting after Breackfast and dinner (sometimes) in order to take the Children along with me to scholl; I imagine she has a grudge against me since the middle of Feby last the reason was, that one night in the Nursery I wheep'd Billie for crying for nothing and she came in and carried him out from me. Some nights after he got into the same humour and his Papa The Colo hearing him call'd me and Asked why I cou'd hear him do so and not correct him for it; Upon that I told him how Mrs Daingerfield had behaved when I did correct him. At that he was angry wt her. . .

Sunday, 23d. Mrs Porter having been here all night from Town; I this day after breackfast brought all the boys with their books into the passage to the Colo who heard each of them read and was highly pleased with their performance. Mrs Porter likeways told that her sons did me great honour; as well as the rest. . .

Wednesday, August 2d. This day came to School Wm John and Lucy Patties, and are to pay conform to the time they attend. . .

Munday, 28th. (August) Coppy of my 4th Letter wrote this day to my wife.

My Dearest Life...

About 7 months ago a Gentleman in Fredericksbg hade his two sons taken from the high school there and put under my care for which he pays me £5 a year. He is an English man himself and his Lady from Edinburgh, and I have the pleasure to have given the parents such satisfaction that I hade sent me in a present two silk vestcoats and two pairs of britches ready to put on for changes in summer. I observe my Dear Dogg George writes me his name at the foot of your letter, But I am surprized that you take no notice of Jack and Bettie. But I hope you will not faill to be more particular about them in your next, and give my blessing to them all and tell them from me that I hope they will be obedient to you in every respect and mind their books...

Wednesday, 6th. (September, 1775). This day I was informed by Mr Frazer that Mrs Daingerfield talking to them of me that morning about some Glue disresptfully calld me Old Harrower by which and her behaveiour to myself I find her grudge continous tho she has not courage to say any thing to myself well knowing she has (no) foundation to go upon.

Sunday, 10th. This day came Dick a Servt belonging to Mr Anderson from Toun and a Comerade of his to see me and Brought me a pair new shoes and a pair for Mr Frazer also a Bottle Vest India Rum which we drank in school in Company with Mr Frazer.

Thursday, 28th. This morning I recd from Benjamin Edge by the hand of his daughter two Dollars, one half and one Quarter Dollar being in all sixteen shillings and Sixpence in part payment for teaching his son and daughter.

Thursday, October 12th. Company here last night Vizt Old Mrs Waller, her son and his wife and at school there Mr Heely Schoolmaster and Mr Brooks Carpenter and they wt Mr Frazer and myself played whist and danced untill 12 OClock, Mr Heely the Fidle and dancing. We drank one bottle of rum in time. Mr Frazer verry sick after they went home.

Saturday, 28th. Last night came here to school Mr Heely and Thos Brooks in order to spend the evening, but by reason of Mr Frazer's not coming from the House, and some stories told them by Mrs Richards in order to sow disention, She being really a Wolf cloathed with a lambs skin and the greatest Mischief maker I have seen in all my Travels, The first time I seed her, I cou'd observe in her countenance Slyness and deceit, and I have always avoided going to the House as much as possible, But now I really think she ought to be avoided by every christian who regairds peace and their own character, They both went home at 10 pm.

Wednesday, January 10th, 1776. This day we hade the Confirmation of Norfolk being reduced to ashes by the Men of War and British Troops under Command of Lord Dunmore. It was the Largest Toun in the Collony and a place of great Trade, it being situated a little within the Capes. Severall Women and Childn are killed.

Tuesday, 23. This day I entred Edwin into the Latin Gramer.

Tuesday, March 5th. This morning Bathurest Daingerfield got don reading through the Bible and the Newtestament, and began to learn to write 15 Ulto I gave them Holyday this Afternoon.

Saturday, April 20th. At noon I asked the Colo for a bottle of rum as I expected two Countrymen to see me tomorrow, which he verry cheerfully gave and desired me to ask him for one any time I wanted it and told me to take them to the Howse to dinner with me. in the afternoon he, his Lady, and Daughter went over the river to Mr Jones's in King George County.

Sunday, 28th. This day came here to pay me a visit Mr Reid from Mansfield and Mr Scott from Toun and dined with me in the great house by the Colos order, and after we hade spent the afternoon verry agreeably together they returned home in the evening.

Sunday, May 5th. Early this morning I went to Mr McCalley's and entred his oldest son (about 8 years of age) to writting, stayed there all day and rode his horse home in the evening. The Colo went to Newport and dinned there.

Tuesday, 7th. Billie ended reading through his Bible.

Thursday, 9th. After dinner I took the boys with me to Massaponacks Briges to see 56 prisoners that was taken at the late battle in North Carolina, among them was a great many Emigrants from Scotland who were all officers. I talked with several of them from Ross Shr and the Isle of Sky.

Thursday, June 6th. In the afternoon I went to Mr Becks, when he told me that Mrs Battle wanted to see me and to talk to me about teaching her two daughters to write, upon which I imediately waited upon her and engaged to return upon Saturd next by 1 pm and begin them to write but made no bargain as yet.

Saturday, 8th. At noon I went to Mrs Bataile's and entred two of her Daughters to writing, Viz. Miss Sallie and Miss Betty and continoued teaching them until night, when I agreed to attend them every Saturday afternoon and every other Sunday from this date until 8th June 1777 (If it please God to spare me) for four pound Virginia currancy.

Sunday, 9th. After breackfast I rode to Mr McAlleys and teach'd his son to write untill 4 pm and then came home in the evening.

Wednesday, 19th. At noon went to snow creek and the boys and dined at the spring on Barbaque and fish. At 5 pm I went to Mrs Bataile, and teac'd until ½ an hour past 7.

Wednesday, 10th. At 6 pm went to Mrs Battaile's and teach'd untill sunset and then return'd home and soon after hea(r)d a great many guns fired towards Toun. about 12 pm the Colo Despatched Anthy Frazer there to see what was the cause of (it) who returned, and informed him that there was great rejoicings in Toun on Accot of the Congress having declared the 13 United Colonys of North America Independent of the Crown of great Britain.

8. WILLIAM C. PRESTON'S ACCOUNT OF HIS EDUCATION, 1800-1812

Our letters were taught to us by an Irishman named Peter Byrnes, a weaver by trade who had come into my grandfather's family as far back as 1780, and had continued to teach letters to successive children of the family and lived to teach her letters to my daughter Sally, in 1824. He had always been a member of the Preston family, died in it at the age of 82 and is buried in the family grave yard at Aspenvale, Washington County, amidst numbers of his pupils, he being the only one (except another) a stranger to the blood whose remains are buried there. He taught us to read in the Testament and to cipher as far as the rule of three, which was the extent of his curriculum. I learned with facility and was I suppose of good behaviour—at least the *Master*, as all called him, never complained of us, and in after life confirmed the favourable opinion he had conceived of William and Eliza. We never failed to love and cherish him.

The next step in my education was to be placed under the tuition of a Mr. Hercules Whaley, a private tutor brought into the family, a man of rare and curious accomplishments. My father picked him up in remote valleys of Lee County, where he accidentally met him apparently shrinking from exposure and seeking obscurity. My father struck with his conversation prevailed upon him to enter our family as a tutor. He continued with us for many years but there was always a mystery hanging about him. In the course of time we gradually learned that he was a native of New York, that he had been bred for the ministry, that he had become an actor and at length had joined Gen. Wayne's army as a dragoon. These circumstances gradually dropped or rather leaked out in the course of our intimate relations with him for several years. He never entered upon any distinct account of himself and having dropped a hint, would lead off in some other direction. He was found to be a capital Latin scholar, familiar with the Classics contained in that language, not ignorant of Greek, and speaking French pretty well. Besides he had eminent skill in music, sang and played upon the violin with wonderful execution, and read and recited poetry with exquisite power. In reading to me fine passages of poetry he would be seized with such enthusiasm as to rise from his seat, assume a theatrical attitude in the floor and acclaim it with dramatic intonations swept away with excitement. So too playing on the violin (which he did from any music at sight) he would become entirely rapt and elicit the most exquisite tones. I can hardly restrain myself from drawing a full portrait of this strange and mysterious man. He took charge of my entire training (and slept in the same room); we cut our own wood and made our own fires. Each of us had two horses, groomed by ourselves, we rose and walked and sat together and slept in the same room, so that my process of education was continually going on. The only thing which we had not in common was my taste for hunting. With this he had no sympathy. I had a passion for dogs and guns. On the wild mountains and in the lonely valleys about the Saltworks,[1] with a gun in my hand I passed many hours day and night, solitary and alone. In the shade of deep hollows or on the sunny summit of some lofty mountain I staid frequently all day.

Whaley and I read together most of the Latin classics and many of the English, for my father had a very good library. But my parents thought (mistakenly as I have since believed) that their boy ought to be sent to a public school, and so at 14 I was sent to what was called the Washington College at Lexington,[2] a college superintended by lazy and ignorant Presbyterian preachers, and filled with dirty boys of low manners and morals. In six months at this place I unlearned as

1. The salt works in Smythe County, Virginia, owned by the Preston family.
2. Originally Liberty Hall Academy, then Washington Academy in honor of George Washington, now Washington and Lee University.

much as it was possible for a boy of sprightly parts to unlearn in six months, when being affected with some slight hemorrhage of the lungs my anxious parents thought it necessary for me to be sent into a Southern latitude and Florida was fixed on.

Mounted on horseback with a negro servant to wait on and to take charge of me, I proceeded on my lonely journey. Columbia lay in my way. There I put up at a tavern situated on the spot now occupied by the high sounding Congaree house— then bearing the most characteristic appelation of Goat-hall. There I met with several young men, Charleston boys who had come up to join the South Carolina College. These youngsters whose address and manners were very attractive very easily persuaded me that I was far enough South for my health and that the new and flourishing college which they were about to enter was a fit place to obtain an education. So after a night of anxious thought I acquiesced. I knew that my father's plan of education for me was that I should go thro' some Southern College, then to Yale or Princeton and complete my course in Europe. His notion, impressed upon me from my earliest days, was that I was to be a well educated man and then to study law as my life time profession. This was always his purpose and my own never deviated from it. I entered the Sophomore class, December 1809, being a few days under 15 years old, but looking several years older, so that no questions were asked as to my age. In College I took and maintained a good stand. The state of discipline nor the course of instruction at that time were much calculated to confer a high education. I graduated with distinction in 1812, having gone thro pretty much such acquaintances as I had made under Whaley. I had a considerable reputation for speaking and that was the principal source of reputation at that time. Legare [3] and McDuffie [4] were the most distinguished students of my day, and they maintained it thro' life. Indeed I think that in most instances the relative position of students in College has been continued afterwards. When I was graduated I was not quite 18 years old.—Minnie Clare Yarborough (ed.), *The Reminiscences of William C. Preston* (Chapel Hill, N.C.: The University of North Carolina Press, 1933), pp. 2-6.

3. Hugh Swinton Legaré (1789-1843), eminent orator and statesman, who served as Attorney-General of the United States and also for a time as Secretary of State.
4. George McDuffie (1788-1849), who served as Governor of South Carolina from 1834 to 1836, and later as United States Senator.

9. ADVERTISEMENTS OF TUTORS AND TEACHERS

At the house of Mrs. Delaweare on Broad Street is taught these sciences.

Arithmetic	Surveying	Astronomy
Algebra	Dialling	Gauging
Geometry	Navigation	Fortification
Trigonometry		

The STEREOGRAPHIC or ORTHOGRAPHIC Projection of the Sphere. The use of the Globe and the Italian method of Bookkeeping by

John Miller.
—*The South Carolina Gazette*, May 12, 1733.

Reading, writing and arithmetick to be taught by *Edward Clark* at the House of one Mrs. *Lydia Viart's* near the new intended Market. —*The South-Carolina Gazette*, December 13 to December 20, 1735.

Reading, Writing, Arithmetick vulgar and decimal, Geometry, Trigonometry plain and spherical, Mensuration of solid and superficial Bodies, Navigation, Surveying, Gaging, and many other useful Branches of the Mathematicks, Euclid's Elements, Italian, bookkeeping, and Grammar, &c: explain'd and taught in the clearest manner by *Archibald Hamilton*, who may be heard of at Mr. *Coon's* Taylor in *Church-street*. N.B. He attends at any time and Place requir'd to teach, or to keep Books; and is willing upon a reasonable and speedy Encouragement yo undertake a School in Town or Country for teaching all or any Part of what is above specified, otherwise to go off the country.—*The South-Carolina Gazette*, February 12 to February 19, 1737. Also February 19 to 26 and February 26 to March 5, 1737.

This is to give Notice, That the Subscriber having resigned teaching the Free School in the Parish of St. Thomas, intends (in the middle of March next) to remove to his plantation at Cainhoy situate bluff on Wando River, Twelve Miles from Charles-Town, being a very pleasant healthful Situation, where I intend to continue to keep a boarding School, having built a convenient Mansion house, school-house &c. for that Purpose. And whereas it may be objected that I keep a Store and Ferry at the said Plantation, and therefore I give this further Notice, that I have other Persons employed to do those Businesses, and that I intend to do not Manner of Business in School hours; but constantly and diligently to attend the school and doubt not but that I shall (as I have for these 18 years past) give a general satisfaction.

Robert How.

—*The South-Carolina Gazette*, Feb. 6, 1744; Reprinted in *The South Carolina Historical and Genealogical Magazine*, XXXVIII (April, 1937) p. 64.

On Monday, being the 25th Instant June, the Subscriber intends (God willing) to open School in the Parish of St. Thomas, at the Place where Mr. Robert How formerly taught, being about Half a Mile from the Brick Church and Twelve from Charles-Town. The House erected for that Purpose is a fine spacious Building, wherein an Hundred Children may be genteely accommodated: Those inclinable for boarding their Children with me, may depend on the utmost Care and Diligence, by teaching them exactly and expeditiously Reading; Writing in all the usual Hands; Arithmetick, in all its Parts; Merchant's Accompts, or, the Italian Method of Book-keeping, &c.

Stephen Hartley.

—*The South-Carolina Gazette*, June 4, 1744; Reprinted, *ibid.*

WHITE POINT

Reading, Writing in all the Hands us'd in Great Briatain, Arithmetick in whole Numbers, and Fractions vulgar and decimal, Merchants Accompts, in the true Italian Method of double Entry, by Debtor and Creditor, and Dancing are taught at the House of Mrs. Fisher on White Point, by

George Brownell and John Pratt

—*The South-Carolina Gazette*, Sept. 3, 10, 17, 1744. Reprinted, *ibid.*, p. 65.

Nathaniel and Mary Gittens have open'd a School in King street, where will be taught reading, writing, arithmetic, and several sorts of Needle work. They likewise intend to commence an Evening School the 10th of September for writing, arithmetick, and young Ladies to draw. Great care will be taken in teaching, and good Attendance by Nath & Mary Gittens.

—*The South-Carolina Gazette*, Sept. 17, 1744. Reprinted, *ibid.*

This is to give Notice, to all young Gentlemen and Ladies inclinable to be taught the Art of DRAWING, That an Evening School for that Purpose will be open'd on the first of November next, at my House in Friend street, where every Branch of that Art will be taught with the greatest Exactness by

Jeremiah Theus

—*The South-Carolina Gazette*, Nov. 5, 1744. Reprinted, *ibid.*

ANY sober diligent Person that is duly qualified to keep a Country School, is desired to apply to Mr. Thomas Brewer, *of* Nansemond *County; where he will meet with Encouragement; he promising to assure such Master Twenty Four Scholars.*—*The Virginia Gazette* (Williamsburg, W. Parks), February 9, 1738, p. [4]; February 16, 1738, p. [4], February 23, 1738, p. [4].

A SOBER, diligent Person, of a good Character, that is qualified to teach Children to write and cypher, and read good *English*, and is willing to agree for 3, 5 or 7 Years, by applying to the Subscriber, living in *Prince-George* County, may meet with an Employer, who will give as an Encouragement to such Person 20 *l. per Annum*.

Theophilus Field

—*The Virginia Gazette* (Williamsburg, W. Parks), December 12, 1745, p. [4]; December 19, 1745, p. [4].

A SOBER Person, of good Morals, capable of teaching Children to Read *English* well, and to Write and Cypher, by applying to the Subscriber, living in the lower Part of *Prince George* County, and the Neighbours adjacent, may depend on meeting with good Encouragement, as a School-Master.

Thomas Hall

—*The Virginia Gazette* (Williamsburg, William Hunter), March 21, 1750/1, p. [4]; March 28, 1751, p. [4]; April 4, 1751, p. [4]; July 11, 1751, p. [4]; July 18, 1751, p. [4]; July 25, 1751, p. [4]

Williamsburg, June 13, 1751.

A SOBER Person, of good Morals, capable of teaching Children to Read *English* well, and to Write and Cypher, by applying to the

Subscriber, at the *Capitol* Landing of this City, may depend on meeting with good Encouragement, as a School-Master.

Matthew Moody

—*The Virginia Gazette* (Williamsburg, William Hunter), June 13, 1751, p. [4]; June 20, 1751, p. [4]; June 27, 1751, p. [4].

ANY single Man, capable of teaching *Greek, Latin,* and the Mathematicks, who can be well recommended, may meet with good Encouragement, by applying to the Subscriber, in *Prince-George* County.

Theophilus Field

—*The Virginia Gazette* (Williamsburg, William Hunter), March 27, 1752, p. [3]; April 3, 1752, p. [3]; April 10, 1752, p. [4].

Williamsburg, June 12, 1752.

MR. SINGLETON takes this Opportunity of informing Gentlemen and Others, That he proposes to Teach the VIOLIN in this City, and Places adjacent, at a Pistole each *per* Month, and a Pistole Entrance, provided a sufficient Number of Scholars can be engaged, (not less than Six in any one Place:) He will give Attendance at *York, Hampton,* and *Norfolk,* on the aforesaid Terms.—*The Virginia Gazette* (Williamsburg, William Hunter), June 12, 1752, p. [2]

JOHN WALKER,

LATELY arriv'd in *Williamsburg* from *London,* and who for ten Years past has been engag'd in the Education of Youth, undertakes to instruct young Gentlemen in Reading, Writing, Arithmetick, the most material Branches of Classical Learning, and ancient and modern Geography and History; but, as the noblest End of Erudition and Human Attainments, he will exert his principal Endeavours to improve their Morals, in Proportion to their Progress in Learning, that no Parent may repent his Choice in trusting him with the Education of his Children.

Mrs. *Walker,* likewise, teaches young Ladies all Kinds of Needle Work; makes Capuchins, Shades, Hats, and Bonnets; and will endeavour to give Satisfaction to those who shall honour her with their Custom.

The above-mentioned *John Walker,* and his Wife, live at Mr.

Cobb's new House, next to Mr. *Coke*'s, near the Road going down to the Capitol Landing; where there is also to be sold, Mens Shoes and Pumps, *Turkey* Coffee, Edging and Lace for Ladies Caps, and some Gold Rings.—*The Virginia Gazette* (Williamsburg, William Hunter), November 17, 1752, p. [2]; also November 24, 1752, p [3]; December 1, 1752, p. [3].

A PERSON who understands teaching of Reading, Writing and Arithmetic, and comes well recommended, may meet with good Encouragement, by applying to the Subscriber in *Prince-George* County.

Theodorick Bland.
—*The Virginia Gazette* (Williamsburg, William Hunter),
August 27, 1756, p. [4]

COROTOMAN, *May* 20, 1766.

A Person well recommended for his sobriety and good behaviour, and is capable of teaching children to read and write, will meet with employment by applying to

CHARLES CARTER.

—*The Virginia Gazette* (Williamsburg, Alex. Purdie, and
Company), May 23, 1766, p. [3]; May 30, 1766, p. [3];
June 6, 1766, p. [4]

WILLIAMSBURG, SEPTEMBER 4, 1766.

THE Trustees for Mrs. WHALEY'S charity to MATTEY'S School (the Minister and Church-Wardens of *Bruton* parish) give this notice that in the forenoon of *Monday* the 22d instant they will meet in the Church of *Williamsburg*, to choose a master for that school. They hope they have it in their power to make such proposals as shall encourage a diligent and useful person to accept of the office.—*The Virginia Gazette* (Williamsburg, Alex. Purdie, and John Dixon), September 5, 1766. *Supplement*, p. [3]; also September 12, 1766, p. [3]; September 19, 1766, p. [3]

Norfolk county, *March* 23, 1767.

IF WILLIAM JONES, teacher of *Latin, &c.* and was tutor to my children last summer, is now unengaged, and will return to me, he shall meet with encouragement from

JOHN BRICKELL.

—*The Virginia Gazette* (Williamsburg, Alex. Purdie and
John Dixon), April 2, 1767, p. [3]; also April 9, 1767,
p. [3].

WANTED SOON,

A TUTOR for a private family, who, among other things, thoroughly understands the mathematicks. Also a FARMER, who will undertake the management of about 80 slaves, all settled within six miles of each other, to be employed in making of grain. Any such, well recommended, will meet with encouragement by applying to Mr. *John Mercer* in *Stafford*, or to the subscriber in *Williamsburg*, during the sitting of the present General Court.

October 10.   JAMES MERCER.

—*The Virginia Gazette* (Williamsburg, Alex. Purdie and John Dixon), October 15, 1767, p. [2]; also October 22, 1767, p. [2]; November 5, 1767, p. [4].

ANY Gentleman that wants to employ a man in his family to teach the *Latin* and *Greek* languages, will meet with a young man qualified, and well recommended, on applying to the Printer.—*The Virginia Gazette* (Williamsburg, William Rind), May 4, 1769, p. [3].

THE Rev. W. DUNLAP, of *Stratton Major* parish, *King* and *Queen* county, *Virginia*, having engaged a tutor for his own sons, properly qualified to teach the learned languages, as well as writing and accounts, would have no objection to take in two or three boys to board and educate with them. Mr. *Dunlap* is possessed of a library of several thousand volumes in most arts and sciences, which shall be free to the inspection of such youth as may be under his care.—*The Virginia Gazette* (Williamsburg, Alex. Purdie, and John Dixon), June 8, 1769, p. [3]; also June 15, 1769, p [3].

WANTED,

AN ELDERLY WOMAN capable of educating and bringing up children. Such a one, well recommended, will hear of good encouragement by applying to the Printer hereof.—*The Virginia Gazette*, March 8, 1770.

I WILL give THIRTY POUNDS a year for a good SCHOOLMASTER capable of teaching ENGLISH and ARITHMETICK.

SAMUEL DU VAL.

—*The Virginia Gazette* (Williamsburg, William Rind), November 15, 1770, p. [2]; also November 29, 1770, p. [4].

To the PUBLIC.

A CLERGYMAN of character, of the church of *England;* addresses himself to the churches of all his Majesty's plantations, that if they want a sober young man for their Minister, on trial, on reasonable terms: Or, he proposes to teach young Gentlemen and Ladies *French*, *Latin*, *Greek*, and *English*, book keeping by double entry, algebra, geometry, measuring, surveying, mechanics, fortification, gunnery, navigation, and the use of the globes and maps, after a natural, easy, and concise method, without burthen to the memory. Any person or persons who chuse to engage him for any of the above purposes are desired to send their letters post paid, and directed to the Rev. W. S. to be left to the care of Mr. *Thomas Smith*, Rector of *Cople* parish, in *Westmoreland*, *Potomack*, *Virginia*, will receive proper answer as soon as possible.—*The Virginia Gazette* (Williamsburg, William Rind), May 2, 1771, p. [3]; also May 9, 1771, p. [4].

WILLIAM ATTWOOD

Begs leave to inform the Gentlemen of *Williamsburg* that he teaches the *French* HORN, HAUTBOY, and *German* FLUTE; and has, for that Purpose, rented a Room near the College. Gentlemen who are desirous to learn any of those Instruments (should they think it inconvenient to attend) will be waited upon at such Times as they shall please to appoint.—*The Virginia Gazette*, May 23, 1771.

ESSEX, *April* 21, 1771.

WANTED as a tutor, in a private family, a single man, who is master of the languages, and will teach the *English* tongue, and arithmetic. Such a person, properly recommended, as well for his abilities, as his moral character, may find employment, and suitable encouragement, by applying to

JOHN LEE.

—*The Virginia Gazette* (Williamsburg, William Rind), May 30, 1771, p. [3].

Amelia, July 12, 1771.

WANTED as a Tutor in a private Family, a single Man who is master of the Languages, and will teach *English* and Arithmetick. Such a Person, properly recommended, as well for his Abilities as his moral Character, may find Employment, and suitable Encouragement, by applying to

David Grenhill.

N.B. The School is worth FIFTY Pounds a Year, clear of Board.—*The Virginia Gazette*, July 18, 1771. (Also in issues of July 25; August 1, 8).

Wanted in Norborne *Parish*, Frederick *County*, A Schoolmaster well qualified to teach Writing and Arithmetick; if *Latin* also, the more agreeable, and the Salary enlarged. It will not be expected that he should teach more than fifteen or twenty Scholars. For farther Particulars inquire of the Printer of this Paper; or of J. *Nourse* at *Piedmont*, in the said County. None need apply but such as can have an undoubted Character for Diligence and Sobriety.

N.B. It is thought a Dancing Master likewise would meet with encouragement in the above county.—*The Virginia Gazette*, April 11, 1771. Same advertisement appeared in issues of April 18, 25; May 2, 9, 16, 23, 30; June 6, 13, 20, 27.

WANTED IMMEDIATELY,

A SOBER diligent Schoolmaster capable of teaching READING, WRITING, ARITHMETICK, and the *Latin* TONGUE. The School is quite new, has a convenient Lodging Room over it, is situated in a cheap Neighbourhood, and its Income estimated at between sixty and eighty Pounds a Year. Any Person qualified as above, and well recommended, will be put into immediate Possession of the School, on applying to the Minister of *Charles* Parish, *York* County. —*The Virginia Gazette*, ([Williamsburg], Alex Purdie and John Dixon), August 20, 1772, p. [2]; also August 27, 1772, Supplement, p. [1]; September 3, 1772, p. [3].

A WELL bred Woman of Character, capable of teaching young Ladies the Degrees of NEEDLEWORK, together with READING and WRITING, &c. &c. will meet with great Encouragement by applying to the Ladies in the Borough of NORFOLK.—*The Virginia Gazette* ([Williamsburg], Alex. Purdie and John Dixon), November 26, 1772, p. [2].

WANTED,

A PERSON about forty Years old, and past the Vanities of Life, who is judicious, accurate, and acquainted with the most intricate Accounts. If he could be of Service in teaching a Child or two, he would be the more acceptable; good Wages will be given. Inquire at the Post Office in *Williamsburg*.—*The Virginia Gazette* ([Williamsburg], Alex. Purdie and John Dixon), December 10, 1772, p. [2]; also December 17, 1772, p. [3]; December 24, 1772, p. [4].

JOHN BRUCE, M. A.

WILL give very good Encouragement to a Person of irreproachable Morals, capable of assisting him to teach the GREEK, LATIN, and ENGLISH LANGUAGES. Such a Person's being acquainted with the different Branches of the MATHEMATICKS, and excelling in WRITING, will be an additional Recommendation. Application may be made to himself, at his own Room, over against the Church, Head of *Cumberland* Street, *Norfolk.—The Virginia Gazette* ([Williamsburg], Alex. Purdie and John Dixon), December 31, 1772, p. [3].

The Subscriber begs leave to inform his friends That he intends opening a school, on Monday the 20th of this instant April, at the house of Mr. Christian Camphire, adjoining the Collector William Spencer, Esq., where he. . . . designs teaching Latin, Reading, Writing, and Arithmetic.

James Whitefield

N.B. A few Masters and Misses will be also lodged and boarded.—*The Georgia Gazette*, (Savannah), April 8; April 15, 1766.

A single man of good character who Teacheth the Principles of the Latin, the French as accented in Paris, the right Spanish Castellans, and children to Read and Write English, would be glad of employment in a Latin School as an assistant, or in a private family in town or country. Any gentlemen or ladies desirous to employ him in such capacity may hear of him by applying to the printer.—*Georgia Gazette* (Savannah), Sept. 23; Oct. 7, 1767.

A Single man, qualified for a Schoolmaster, will meet with encouragement by applying at Midway to John Baker. St. John's Parish, May 2, 1774.—*The Georgia Gazette* (Savannah), May 11, 1774.

A School

The Publick are hereby informed, that a School is now opened, at the Parsonage House in this place, by the subscriber, who will instruct in the Latin and Greek Languages, and also the Reading and Writing of the English. . . .

Samuel Bird.

—*The Georgie Gazette*, (Savannah), Nov. 27, 1783.

The Rev. Edw. Lucas has opened in the Parsonage House, A Grammar School, where a number of young Gentlemen, not exceeding twelve, will be taught the Greek and Latin Classics, on the most approved plan. Terms: A Guinea and a Half Entrance, and Two Guineas a Quarter.—*The Georgia Gazette*, (Savannah), Feb. 2, 1786.

The Rev. Benj. Lindsay and Robert Walker, lately from the U. of Edinburgh, whose testimonials will bear the minutest inspection, intend to open an Academy, on the 1st of September next in the house formerly occupied by the Rev. Mr. Bowen .... The terms are as follows, viz. On admission, One Guinea. For Greek, Latin, French, and Mathematics, Two Pounds Sterling per Quarter. For English, Writing and Arithmetic, Thirty Shillings Sterling per Quarter.... N.B. The patronage of the inhabitants of Savannah and its vicinity is solicited, as long as the proficiency of the pupils comitted to their charge shall merit it. The strictest attention to morals, as well as other improvements, may be depended on.—*The Georgia Gazette*, (Savannah), Aug, 28, 1788. (Repeated Sept. 11, 18, 25)

Wants employment as Tutor in a genteel family.... a person who is capable of teaching the French and Latin Languages, Reading, Writing, and Arithmetic, Book-keeping and Geography.—*Georgia Gazette* (Savannah), Oct. 15, 1789.

Wanted as a Schoolmaster, A Single man, who understands and can teach the different Branches of Arithmetic, and can be recommended. Inquire to the Printers.—*The Georgia Gazette* (Savannah), May 27, 1790.

By Permission and Encouragement of the Trustees the Public School House of this Town is again opened, where Youth may be taught the *English, Latin,* or *French* Tongue; as also Writing, Arithmetic, Algebra, Trigonometry plain and spherical, Astronomy, Navigation, Surveying, Geography, the Use of Globes, or any other Part of the Mathematics, the *Italian* method of Bookkeeping, at the established Price of the said School, which may be known by enquiring of Mr. Davis, Printer of this Paper, and one of the Trustees. Newbern, June 30, 1775.—*North Carolina Gazette*, June 30, 1775. (This advertisement appeared in later issues of the paper)

As Mr. Beaufort has attended to the house mentioned in his former advertisement, and has not met with such encouragement as he deserves in teaching the French, he intends to continue by one month if no better encouragement; he hopes that such gentlemen and ladies that intend to be taught that useful and genteel language, will not neglect this opportunity, as he is wanted where he may have encouragement suitable to his merit.—*North Carolina Gazette* (James Davis), March 13, 1778.

TUITION.

THE Rev. W. MEREDITH, wishing to employ his leisure hours while in Wilmington, intends opening a seminary for useful literature where the Latin and English languages will be taught grammatically.—The MORALS of the youths committed to his care will be particularly attended to, as being part of his duty,—The terms may be known by applying to him.

—*The Wilmington Chronicle: and North-Carolina Weekly Advertiser*,
April 14, 1796, p. 1.

✵✵✵✵✵✵✵✵✵✵✵✵✵✵✵✵✵✵✵✵✵✵✵✵✵✵✵✵✵✵✵✵✵

DANCING SCHOOL

HARRY CLAY MILBURN, respectfully informs the Ladies and Gentlemen of Nixonton, Hertford, Edenton, and its vicinities, that he will attend at the Court-House in Nixonton, on Monday, the 11th of July, in order to open a *Dancing-School*, at 10 o'clock in the forenoon, and at Hertford, on Thursday, the 14th of July, at 10 o'clock in the forenoon, and at Edenton, the 21st of the same month, at 10 o'clock in the forenoon; to be continued three days in each month, for six months, at each of the aforesaid places: Those who will please to honour him with the instruction of their children in this polite accomplishment, may depend on having the strictest attention paid to their morals, and the utmost care and assiduity to accomplish them with all the graces, not only in ball-room, but in their general deportment. His terms are 4 dollars per quarter, and one third at entrance.

June 13, 1796.   2 W
—*The State Gazette of North-Carolina*,
June 16, 1796, p. 3.

♕♕♕♕♕♕♕♕♕♕♕♕♕♕♕♕♕♕♕♕♕♕♕♕♕♕♕♕♕♕♕♕♕

DANCING SCHOOL.

RICHARD COLEMAN,

RESPECTFULLY informs the Ladies and Gentlemen of Fayetteville and its vicinity, that he will open a DANCING SCHOOL in the State-House on Friday and Saturday next—Those who please to honour him with instructing their children in that polite accomplishment, may depend on having them taught on the most approved principles.

Mr. Coleman's stay will be very short, he will therefore open an Evening school from candle light until 9 o'clock, for the benefit of those young gentlemen whose business will not admit of their attendance in the day.

.*. His terms will be made known on application.

Fayetteville, Oct. 8.

—*The North-Carolina Minerva, and Fayetteville Advertiser,*
October 15, 1796, p. 3, col. 1.

F. RABINEAU,

L I M N E R ,

LAST FROM WILMINGTON,

RESPECTFULLY informs the Ladies and Gentlemen of the town of Fayetteville and its vicinity, that he has arrived, and wishes to please those who desire to employ him.—He paints in Miniature, Crayon, &c &c. Hair work with natural or dissolved hair; Mourning pieces for Bracelets; Breast Pins, or Rings, emblematical to the wish and desire of those Ladies and Gentlemen who will please to employ him. They will be waited upon punctually on application.

Mr. Rabineau will take a Young Gentleman for the purpose of teaching him in the above art, during his stay, provided he is of a natural genius.

—*The North-Carolina Minerva, and Fayetteville Advertiser,*
May 19, 1798, p. 4, col. 1.

THE public are hereby informed, that the subscriber proposes opening a SCHOOL at his house, where Geography, Natural Philosophy and Astronomy will be taught; the Orfery will be of infinite advantage in these studies, especially the latter.—Teaching will commence as soon as 150 dollars shall be subscribed—The rates of teaching will be 12 dollars per year, eight dollars the half month, and two dollars per month.—He will board as many as eight or ten; others may be boarded very conveniently in the neighbourhood, at the rate of three dollars per month, the boarders finding their own bedding—washing will be considered as part of boarding—one half of the money both for teaching and boarding, is to be paid at the opening of the school, the other half at the expiration of their time— The Students finding their own books & paper—He would recommend Guthrie's Georgraphy, Martin's Natural Philosophy, and Ferguson's Astronomy—The knowledge of the languages, that is, Latin, &c. is by no means essential to this study.   Wm. THOMAS.

Richmond County, May 12.   14 4

—*The North-Carolina Minerva, and Fayetteville Advertiser,*
June 16, 1798, p. 4, col. 3.

TUITION.

The subscriber respectfully informs his friends and the public, that he intends continuing his School during the Summer months. Those parents and guardians who will honor him with their patronage, may rely upon the greatest attention being paid those pupils, they may please to put under his care.

Those indebted to him for tuition, are requested to make payment previous to the first day of August, to enable him to settle his creditors.

W. Macvurrich.

Wilmington, July 26.

—*Hall's Wilmington Gazette,*
August 30, 1798, p. 3.

MISCELLANEOUS INTERESTS AND ACTIVITIES

I. PREVIEW AND COMMENTS

THE DOCUMENTS IN THIS section do not lend themselves to easy classification in any of the preceding sections but are important in reflecting significant if miscellaneous educational interests and activities. The documents that follow include the requirement that ministers in Virginia teach children to read (1631); that priests in charge of Indian missions in Florida teach Christian doctrines to the Indians (1634); Sir William Berkeley's report on Virginia (1671); description of Indians and Indian missions in Florida (1674, 1675, 1676); petition to the General Assembly of Virginia for change in the licensing of schoolmasters (1686); acts for establishing free schools in South Carolina (1710-1712); some educational matters in Louisiana (1726, 1728); other materials on education in the 18th century, including some educational activities of the Moravians in North Carolina; the desire of Scotch-Irish Presbyterians for "a teacher of their own opinion and choice" in North Carolina (1775); petition of a schoolmaster at Pensacola, Florida; certificate of a schoolmaster in North Carolina; rules of a school in St. Augustine; the work of the Capuchin missions and of the Ursulines in Louisiana; and other documents.

II. DOCUMENTS

1. MINISTERS IN VIRGINIA ARE REQUIRED TO TEACH CHILDREN TO READ, 1631

IT is also thought fit, That upon every Sunday the mynister shall halfe an hower or more before evenenge prayer examine, catechise, and instruct the youth and ignorant persons of his parrish, in the ten commandments the articles of the beliefe and in the Lord's prayer; and shall diligentlie heere, instruct and teach them the catechisme, sett forth in the booke of common prayer   And all fathers, mothers, maysters and mistrisses shall cause theire children, servants or apprentizes which have not learned the catechisme to come to the church at the tyme appoynted, obedientlie to heare, and to be ordered by the mynister untill they have learned the same: And yf any of the sayd ffathers, mothers, maysters and mistrisses, children, servants or apprentises, shall neglect theire duties as the one sorte in not causinge them to come and the other in refusinge to learne as aforesayd, they shall be censured by the corts in those places holden. And this act to take beginninge at Easter next.—Hening, *Statutes at Large*, I, 157.

2. Priests in charge of Indian missions in Florida must teach Christian doctrines to the Indians, 1634

One of the obligations of evangelical ministers is to teach the Christian doctrine to their parishioners, and preach the word of the holy Gospel to them; and the priests having charge of Indians are especially under this obligation, because their capacity is less: Wherefore we command priests having charge of Indians to teach them the Christian doctrine on Sundays and holidays of obligation throughout the year, and on Sundays in Advent and Lent to explain the holy Gospel to them, as becomes zealous ministers desirous of serving God; for we are greatly consoled and thankful for the apostolical zeal with which they administer them. And let them teach it to the boys every day, as they now do; and we beseech and charge them that they teach it in Spanish where they can, as his Majesty has commanded in a special edict, on account of the many benefits resulting from so doing.— Cedula of March 2, 1634. Given in *Statutes Relating to Florida in the Docesan Synod Held by His Majesty's Command*, by the Right Rev. Dr. John Gareiade Palacios, Bishop of Cuba, June 1684, (Translated by John Dawson Gilmary Shea.) Published between 1860-1875.

3. Sir William Berkeley's report on Virginia, 1671

The questions from the Commissioners of Trade and Plantations in 1670 and the replies the following year from Sir William Berkeley, governor of Virginia, throw interesting light on conditions in that colony at that time. Hening says of this material: "A more correct statistical account of Virginia, at that period, cannot, perhaps, anywhere be found. The answers appear to have been given with great candor, and were from a man well versed in every thing relating to the country, having been for many years governor. As it respects the *inhabitants* of Virginia, *Sir William Berkeley* seems to have been well qualified to rear them up as food for despots, since, in his answer to the last enquiry, he thanks God that there are no '*free-schools* or *printing*,' and 'hopes' that we shall have none these hundred yeares." [1]

1. Hening, *op. cit.*, II, 511.

Berkeley's historic exclamation in his answer to the last question has often been misquoted or misunderstood. There had been in Virginia for a long time foundations for English "free" schools and the governor himself had approved an act of 1642 which incorporated the school established in Elizabeth City County on the will of Benjamin Syms who provided the first educational endowment in English North America. Only the question on education and Berkeley's answer are given here:

What course is taken about the instructing the people, within your government in the christian religion; and what provision is there made for the paying of your ministry?

Answer: The same course that is taken in England out of towns; every man according to his ability instructing his children. We have fforty eight parishes, and our ministers are well paid, and by my consent should be better *if they would pray oftener and preach less.* But of all other commodities, so of this, *the worst are sent us,* and we had few that we could boast of, since the persicution in *Cromwell's* tiranny drove divers worthy men hither. But I thank God, *there are no free schools* nor *printing,* and I hope we shall not have these hundred years, for *learning* has brought disobedience, and heresy, and sects into the world, and *printing* has divulged them, and libels against the best government. God keep us from both!—Hening, *op. cit.,* II, 511-17. Here may be found all the questions and Berkeley's answers to the inquiry from the Commissioners of Trade and Plantations.

4. THE BISHOP OF CUBA DESCRIBES THE INDIANS AND INDIAN MISSIONS
IN FLORIDA, 1674, 1675, 1676

Señora:

Your Majesty is pleased to command me, in the two royal cédulas of the 4th of March of the year 73, to visit at this time the provinces of Florida and apply the proper remedy in the matter presented to Your Majesty by the Bishop of the city, Rodrigo, my predecessor here. No bishop has gone there (to Florida) in more than 60 years, and the presence of one is needed, not only to celebrate confirmations and correct the faults and abuses that have come in during so long a time in the case of (a) people so recently converted, and to investigate the state in which the priests of San Francisco have the work of converting the Indians and the instruction of the converts under their care, but also to lend encouragement to the converting of the Indians of the province of Apalachocoli who have for years been asking that missionaries be sent to teach and baptize them; a request never yet granted for lack (of missionaries). In this field the Bishop believes the Dominican priests of this city would accomplish much.

Señora, this my predecessor said to me in the city of San Lucar where I was by order, awaiting the first opportunity of passage to this incumbency. I replied to him that I wished first to come to the city of Cuba, seat of this bishopric, visiting it, and to go then to the mission. Accordingly, as soon as I entered this city, obeying your Majesty I began to plan for the carrying out of that purpose. Having now completed the visitation of this entire island, I have it in such good condition that within 8 days under the favor of God I shall set forth.

And because (although I recognize the great zeal of the Dominican priests, who have offered themselves to me willingly), to take them now would be to introduce great discord with the Franciscans and jeopardize the conversion of those miserable heathen, it has seemed to me wiser to make use of the latter, both because they are well versed in that language and because they are in control of the entire province of Apalache which borders upon that of Apalachocoli. (I go) to investigate first the condition of that land, and then to enter upon the work of conversion for which I am taking chalices and all the necessary vestments of the Divine Cult. May it please Our Lord that the holy zeal of Your Majesty attain its end for the greater glory of the Divine One and the salvation of those souls.

May Our Lord keep the Catholic Royal Person of Your Majesty in His holy grace with health and complete felicity to the greatest good of Your vassals.

Your Majesty's humble servant and chaplain,

Havana, Gabriel, Bishop of Cuba.

August 14, 1674

Señora:

Your Majesty is pleased to command me, by the royal cédula of June 24, of this year, to apply some financial aid to the repairing of the convent of San Lorenzo el Real del Escurial.

The financial obligations Señora, which I have, with the expenditures I made during the visit to the provinces of Florida, where I maintained eight months, at my own expense, a company of Spanish infantry of the Post (of St. Augustine), and two of Indians, arquebusiers and archers, because I had to traverse the frontier of the country of the Chiscas and Chichimecos, barbarous and warlike heathen, and with the construction of the main bastion of the wall of this city which I have done at my expense and that of the ecclesiastics, have made it impossible for me to do at this time what I shall do when my debts are paid.

May Our Lord keep the Catholic Royal Person of Your Majesty to the greatest blessing and comfort of your vassals.

Your Majesty's humble servant and chaplain,

Havana,
November 20, 1675. Gabriel, Bishop of Cuba.

My Lord:

In the despatch-ship which went out from here last month, I gave you felicitations on your elevation to the Secretaryship, then hoping to give them to you (also) as Secretary of State.

With this goes a packet to Her Majesty with my brief summary account of all that I have discovered in the territory of the provinces of Florida, conversions that I have made and characteristics of the Indians, (I) being by the Divine Mercy the first to tread those lands. And to the hands of the President went my map of the country. It is duplicated by this; and in the one (go) the original *autos* that have resulted from the visitation, and in the other an authenticated copy of them.

I remain at your service for all that you may be pleased to command me, to which I shall respond with good will. May God keep you many years.

Your humble servant kisses your hands,

Gabriel, Bishop of Cuba

Havana,
January 4, 1676,
To Senor Don Antonio de Rojas.

—Smithsonian Miscellaneous Collections, XCV, No. 16, 2-4.

5. GENERAL ASSEMBLY OF VIRGINIA PETITIONS FOR CHANGE IN THE LICENSING OF SCHOOLMASTERS AND THE REPLY OF THE GOVERNOR, 1686

To *his Excellencie* ffrancis *Lord* Howard *Baron* of Effingham *his Majesties Lt & Governor Genl of Virginia.*
The house of Burgesses now assembled, humbly present.

That whereas your Excellencie has been pleased by your late precept to command that all Schoolmasters should make their personall appearance at *James City*, there to receive your Excellencies License & approbation to teach & that none Shall be admitted to that Office before they haue there taken out such a qualification and whereas this house doe too Sencibly vnderstand from their Respective Counties, that severall knowing skilfull Schoolmasters leave of their imploy because they are vnable out of such small allowance as they yearly have to endure the charge they are now necessarily exposed to, for the procuring of their Licenses to teach. This house doe therefore in the Name of themselves and all the inhabitants of this Countrey, humbly pray that for the greater ease of such as are willing to employ themselves in so necessary an vndertakeing, your Excellencie would please to appoint in every Countie, some One of such person or persons as to your Excellencie shall seem most fit, for the due examination of them, & that such persons vpon their well approueing their Capacities, may likewise haue power from your Excellency to grant them a license for so moderate & reasonable a fee, as in the like cases is vsuall & Customary to be paid in *England*.

Mr Speaker *and Gentlemen.*

I haue rec^d from you an Address relateing to Schoolmasters in that as in all other matters, I shall give you all reasonable satisfaction and therefore am to tell you, that what Comands to me I have giuen therein are pursueant to his Majesties Speciall Comands to me, as by the Instruction herewith sent vnto you, you may observe, in which not being so forward, as it was expected I should haue been, my memory was therein refreshed by the Lord Bishop of *London*, and as I am Comanded to haue it performed, so I am desireous to have it done with as much ease & encouragement to the inhabitants, as possible may be and as testimonies thereof I will direct, that Examination shall be taken of the fitness & abilities of persons presented for Schoolmasters by the next of his Majesties Councell of this Colonie, & vpon his approueing of the persons they shall be accordingly lycenced for Schoolmasters, with whom I shall cause to be left blanke lycenses vnder my hand & seale to be filled up with the name & names of such person & persons approued of, for which shall be required no more than a Small fee to my Clerke for the writing the same. Signed

By his Excellencies Comand.

E Chilton C Genl Assmbly

—H. R. McIlwaine (ed.), *Journals of the House of Burgesses of Virginia*, 1659/60-1693, pp. 270, 274.

6. An act for the Founding and Erecting of a Free School, for the use of the Inhabitants of South Carolina, 1710

WHEREAS, it is necessary that a Free School be erected, for the instruction of the youth of this Province in grammar and other arts and sciences and useful learning, and also in the principles of the christian religion; and whereas several charitable and well disposed christians, by their last wills and testaments, have given several sums of money for the founding of a free school, but no person as yet is authorized to take the charge and care of erecting a free school, according to the intent of the donors, and to receive the said legacies, if tendered, nor to demand the same, in case of refusal to pay the same; so that, for want of some person or persons, or body politick and corporate, proper for the lodging the said legacies therein, the same are not applied according to the pious and charitable intention of the testators or donors;

I. *Be it therefore enacted,* by His Excellency William Lord Craven, Palatine, and the rest of the true and absolute Lords and Proprietors of this Province, by and with the advice and consent of the rest of the members of the General Assembly, now met at Charlestown for the south-west part of this Province, and by the authority of the same, That the Honourable Colonel Edward Tynte, Esq., Governour, Colonel Thomas Broughton, Esq., Landgrave Joseph Morton, Mr. William Gibbon, Colonel George Logan, Richard Beresford, Esq., Arthur Middleton, Esq., Captain John Abraham Motte, Colonel Hugh Grange, Ralph Izard, Esq., Lieutenant Colonel Alexander Parris, Esq., Captain Lewis Pasquereau, Doctor Gideon Johnston, Doctor Francis Lejau, Mr. Alexander Wood, and Nicholas Trott, Esquire, or any nine of them, and their successors, to be elected in manner as hereafter is directed, be, and shall forever hereafter be one body politick and corporate, in deed and in name, by the name of the Commissioners for founding, erecting, governing, ordering and visiting a School for the use of the Inhabitants of South Carolina; and that they and their successors, by the same name, by the authority aforesaid, be fully made, ordained, constituted and declared one body politick and corporate, in deed and in name, and that by the same name they and their successors shall and may have perpetual succession; and that they and their successors by that name shall and may forever hereafter be persons able and capable in law to purchase, have, take, receive and enjoy to them and their successors, lands, messuages, tenements, rents, liberties, privileges, jurisdictions, franchises, and other hereditaments whatsoever, of whatsoever nature, kind, quality or value they be, in fee, and in perpetuity; and also estates for lives and for years, and all other manner goods, chattels and things whatsoever, of what name, nature, quality and value soever they be, for the better support and maintenance of masters or teachers for the said school, and also for the erecting of school houses and convenient dwelling houses for the accommodation of the said several masters and teachers. And that, by the name aforesaid, they shall and may be able to plead and be impleaded, answer and be answered unto, defend and be defended, in all courts and places whatsoever, and before whatsoever judge or judges, justice or justices, or other officer or officers belonging to this Province, in all and singular actions, plaints, pleas, matters and demands of what kind, nature and quality soever they be. And to act and do all other matters and things in an ample manner and form as any other the inhabitants of this Province, being persons able and capable in law, or any other body corporate or politick, by the laws of England can or may have, purchase, receive, possess, take, enjoy, grant, set, let, demise, plead and be impleaded, answer and be answered unto, defend and be defended, do, permit and execute. And that the said commissioners and their successors for ever hereafter, shall and may have a common seal to serve for the causes and business of them and their successors, to change, break, alter and make new the said seal, from time to time, and at their pleasure, as they shall think best.

II. And for the better execution of the purposes aforesaid, *Be it further enacted* by the authority aforesaid, That the said commissioners and their successors for ever, shall and may on the second Tuesday in July, yearly, meet at some convenient place, to be appointed by the President of the said commissioners, between the hours of eight in the morning and five in the afternoon, and that they, or the major part of such of them that shall then be present, shall choose one president and vice president, and such other officers, ministers and servants as shall be thought convenient, to serve in the said offices for the year ensuing; and that the said president and all officers then elected shall, before they act in their respective offices, take an oath, to be to them administered by the president, or, in his absence, by one of the vice presidents of the year preceeding, who are hereby authorized to administer the same, for the faithful and due execution of their respective offices and places, during the said year.

III. *And be it further enacted* by the authority aforesaid, That the first president of the said commissioners shall be the Honourable Colonel Edward Tynte, Esq., Governour, and that the said president shall, within three days after the ratification of this Act, cause summons to be issued to the several commissioners herein particularly mentioned, to meet on the second Tuesday of June next ensuing, at such place as he shall appoint, and that they, or the major part of such of them as shall then be present, shall proceed to the election of such other officers, ministers and servants, as to them shall seem meet; which said officers, from the time of their election into their respective offices, shall continue therein until the second Tuesday in July, which will be in the year of our Lord one thousand seven hundred and eleven, and from thenceforward until others shall be chosen in their places, in manner aforesaid.

IV. *And be it further enacted* by the authority aforesaid, That if it shall happen that any of the persons at any time chosen into any of the said offices, shall die, or, on any account, be removed from such office, at any time between the said yearly days of election, that, in such case, it shall be lawful for the surviving and continuing president, or any one of the vice-presidents, to issue summons to the several members of the body corporate, to meet at the usual place of the annual meeting of the said commissioners, at such time as shall be specified in the said summons, and such members as shall meet upon such summons, or the major part of them, shall and may choose an officer or officers in the room or place of such person or persons, so dead or removed, as to them shall seems meet.

V. *And be it further enacted,* by the authority aforesaid, That in case of the death or removal from this Province of any of the said commissioners, that then it shall be lawful for the president, or any one of the vice-presidents, to issue summons to the several surviving commissioners to meet at the usual place of the annual meeting of the said commissioners, at such time as shall be specified in the said summons, and that such members as shall meet upon such summons, or the major part of them, shall or may choose a commissioner or commissioners in the room or place of such person or persons, so dead or removed, as to them shall seem meet.

VI. *And be it further enacted* by the authority aforesaid, That it shall and may be lawful for the said commissioners and their successors to meet at some convenient place to be appointed for that purpose, on the second Tuesday in February and July, and oftener if occasion requires, upon publick summons given five days before, then and there to transact the business of the said commissioners, and to put in force and execute the several powers given them by this Act; and no act done in any assembly of the said commissioners shall be effectual and valid, unless the president or some one of the vice-presidents and eight members of the said commissioners, at least, be present, and the major part consenting thereunto.

VII. *And be it further enacted,* by the authority aforesaid, That all gifts or legacies formerly given, for the use of a free school for this Province, by any person or persons whatsoever, are hereby appropriated for the use of the school intended to be founded and erected, pursuant to the several powers granted to the said commissioners by this Act; and the said commissioners and their lawful successors are hereby authorized and impowered to demand and sue for the same, either by action of debt, suit, bill, plaint or information, in any court of record in this Province, wherein no essoign, protection, privilege, injunction, or wager of law, or stay of prosecution by *non vult ulterius prosequi,* or otherwise, shall be admitted or allowed.

VIII. *And be it further enacted* by the authority aforesaid, That if any action, claim, suit or information shall be commenced or prosecuted against any person or persons, for what he or they shall do in pursuance or execution of this Act, such person or persons so sued may plead the general issue not guilty, and upon issue joined, give this Act and the special matter in evidence; and if the plaintiff or prosecutor shall become non-suit, or suffer discontinuance, or if a verdict pass against him, the defendant or defendants shall recover his or their treble costs, for which he or they shall have the like remedy as in any case by law is given to the defendants. And a receipt signed by such person or persons as shall be lawfully chosen and appointed treasurer to the said commissioners, shall be a sufficient discharge to such executor or executors as shall pay such legacies. And the moneys so received by such treasurer, shall be disposed of, by order of the said commissioners and their successors, towards the purchasing of lands, and the erecting of a school house and dwelling houses, for the use of the several masters and professors.

IX. *And be it further enacted* by the authority aforesaid, That the said commissioners and their successors shall have power, and they are hereby authorized and impowered, to take up by grant from the Lords Proprietors, or purchase, have, take and receive, from any other person or persons whatsoever, so much land as they shall think necessary for the use and conveniency of the several masters and teachers;

and shall also direct the building a school house upon the same, and such dwelling houses and convenient out-houses and buildings for the accommodation of the several masters or teachers; and shall also nominate and appoint one or more persons to be supervisor or supervisors for the said buildings. The said several buildings to be on such places on the said land, so taken up or purchased or received as aforesaid, and of such dimensions and of such materials, as the said commissioners shall order and direct.

X. *And be it further enacted* by the authority aforesaid, That the said commissioners and their successors shall have full power and lawful authority to nominate and appoint a fit person to be master of the said school, by the name and stile of Praeceptor and Teacher of Grammar and other the arts and sciences to be taught in the School for the Province of South Carolina; and so, from time to time, when and as often as the said place of master of the said school, by death, resignation, deprivation, or other wise, shall become void, shall nominate and appoint a fit person to succeed to be master of the said school.

XI. *And be it further enacted* by the authority aforesaid, That the person to be master of the said school, shall be of the religion of the Church of England, and conform to the same, and shall be capable to teach the learned languages, that is to say, the Latine and Greek tongues, and also the useful parts of the mathematicks.

XII. *And be it further enacted* by the authority aforesaid, That these commissioners and their successors shall have power and authority, under their common seal, to set down and prescribe such orders, rules, statutes, and ordinances, for the order, rule and good government of the said school, and of the masters, teachers, ushers and scholars thereof, as to them and their successors shall seem meet and convenient; and that the same orders, rules, statutes and ordinances, so by them made and set down, shall be and stand in full force and strength in law, so always that the same be reasonable, and not repugnant nor contrary to the established laws of this Province. And the said commissioners for the time being shall have full power and authority to visit the said school, and to order, reform, and redress all disorders and abuses in and touching the government of the same; and further, to censure, suspend and deprive any of the masters, teachers or professors of the said school, or the usher or ushers thereof, for the time being, as to them shall seem just, fit and convenient.

XIII. *And be it further enacted* by the authority aforesaid, That the said master or teacher of the said school shall have, hold, occupy, possess and enjoy, to him and his lawful successors, all such land as shall, pursuant to this Act, be taken up, purchased, had or received for the use of the master of the said school, and the school house, and dwelling house, and the out houses, and other buildings upon the same.

XIV. *And be it further enacted* by the authority aforesaid, That in case the commissioners shall think it necessary that there be an usher appointed for the said school, that then the usher of the said school shall be chosen by the master, but approved of by the said commissioners and their successors.

XV. And because it is necessary that a fit person to teach the youth of this Province to write, and also the principles of vulgar arithmetick and merchant's accompts, *Be it further enacted* by the authority aforesaid, That a fitting person shall be nominated and appointed by the said commissioners, to teach writing, arithmetick, and merchant's accounts. [This act was repealed by an act of December 12, 1712, which follows].—Cooper, *Statutes at Large of South Carolina*, II, 342-46.

7. An act for Founding and Erecting of a Free School in Charleston, for the use of the Inhabitants of this Province of South Carolina, 1712

WHEREAS, it is necessary that a free school be erected for the instruction of the youth of this Province in Grammar, and other arts and sciences and useful learning, and also in the principles of Christian religion; and whereas several charitable and well disposed christians, by their last will and testaments, have given several sums of money for the founding of a free school, but no person yet is authorized to take the charge and care of erecting a free school, according to the intent of the donors, and to receive the said legacies if tendered, nor to demand the same in case of refusal to pay the same; so that for want of some person or persons, or body politick and corporate, proper for the lodging the said legacies therein, the same are not applied according to the pious and charitable intent of the donors;

I. *Be it therefore enacted* by the most noble Prince, Henry Duke of Beaufort, Palatine, and the rest of the true and absolute Lords and Proprietors of this Province, by and with the advice and consent of the rest of the members of the General Assembly, now met at Charlestown for the south-west part of this Province, and by the authority of the same, That the Honourable Charles Craven, Esq., Governour, Charles Hart, Esq., Thomas Broughton, Nicholas Trott, Arthur Middleton, and Richard Beresford, Esqs., William Rhett, Esq., the Reverend Mr. Gideon Johnston, the Reverend Dr. Francis Lejau, Mr. Robert Maul, Mr. Ralph Izard, Landgrave Joseph Morton, Colonel George Logan, Colonel Alexander Parris, Colonel Hugh Grange, and Mr. William Gibbon, or any seven of them, or their successors to be elected in manner as is hereafter directed, be, and shall forever hereafter be one body politick and corporate in deed and in name, by the name of the Commissioners for founding, erecting, governing, ordering and visiting a School for the use of the inhabitants of South Carolina; and that they and their successors by the same name, by the authority aforesaid, be fully made, ordained, constituted and declared one body politick and corporate, in deed and in name, and that by the same name they and their successors shall and may have perpetual succession, and that they and their successors by that name shall and may forever hereafter be persons able and capable in law to purchase, have, take, receive and enjoy, to them and their successors, lands, messuages, tenements, rents, liberties, privileges, jurisdictions, franchises, and other hereditaments, of whatsoever nature, kind, quality or value they be, in fee, and in perpetuity, and also estates for lives and for years, and all other manner of goods, chattels and things whatsoever, of what name, nature, quality or value soever they be, for the better support and maintenance of masters or teachers for the said school, and also for the erecting of school houses, and convenient dwelling houses for the accommodation of the said several school masters and teachers; and that by the name aforesaid they shall and may be able to plead and be impleaded, answer and be answered unto, and to defend and be defended, in all courts and places whatsoever, and before whatsoever judge and judges, justice or justices, or other officer or officers belonging to this Province, in all and singular actions, plaints, pleas, matters and demands, of what kind, nature or quality soever they form as any other the inhabitants of this province being persons able and capable in law, or any other body corporate or politick by the laws of England can or may have, purchase, receive, possess, take, enjoy, grant, sell, lett, demise, plead and be impleaded, answer and be answered unto, and to defend and be defended, do, permit and execute; and that the said commissioners and their successors forever hereafter, shall and may have a common seal to serve for the common businesses of them and their successors, to change, break, alter and make new the said seal, from time to time and at their pleasure, as they shall think best.

II. And for the better execution of the purposes aforesaid, *Be it further enacted* by the authority aforesaid, That the said commissioners and their successors forever, shall and may on the third Wednesday in March, meet at some convenient place to be appointed by the president of the said commissioners, between the hours of five and eight of the evening of the said day, and that they, or the major part of such of them that shall then be present, shall choose one president and vice president, and such other officers, ministers and servants, as shall be thought convenient to serve in the said offices, for the year ensuing; and that the said president, and all officers then elected, shall before they act in their respective offices, take an oath, to be to them administered by the president, or in his absence by one of the vice presidents of the year preceeding, who are hereby authorized to administer the same, for the faithful and due execution of their respective offices and places during the said year, and until discharged of the same.

III. *And be it further enacted* by the authority aforesaid, That the first president of said commissioners shall be the Honourable Charles Craven, Esq., Governour, and that the said president shall within forty days after the ratification of this Act, cause summons to be issued to the several commissioners herein before particularly mentioned, to meet on such a day, and at such a place as he shall appoint, and that they, or the major part of such of them as shall then be present, provided the number present with the said Governour are not less than seven, shall proceed to the election of one or more vice president or vice presidents, one treasurer, two or more auditors, one secretary, and such other officers, ministers, and servants as to them shall seem meet, which said officers, from the time of their election into their respective offices, shall continue therein until the third Wednesday in March, which will be in the year of our Lord one thousand seven hundred and thirteen, according to the supputation of the Church of England, and from thence forward until others shall be chosen in their places, in manner aforesaid; and upon such first day of the meeting of the said president and the members, in order to elect a vice president or vice presidents, and other officers as before directed, that the president shall take an oath for the faithful and due discharge of his trust, to be administered unto him by the Chief Justice of this Province, if present, or in case of his absence by any two of the said commissioners, who are hereby impowered to administer the same accordingly, and that each of the other officers then elected, shall take an oath, to be to them administered by the president, for the faithful and due execution of their respective offices and places, until discharged of the same.

IV. *And be it further enacted* by the authority aforesaid, That if it shall happen that any of the persons at any time chosen into any of the said offices shall dye, resign, or on any account be removed from such office, at any time between the said yearly days of election, that in such case it shall be lawful for the surviving and continuing president, or any one of the vice presidents, to issue summons to the several members of the body corporate to meet at the usual place of the annual meeting of the said commissioners, at such time as shall be specified in the said summons; and such members as shall meet upon such summons, provided not less than seven in the whole or the major part of them, shall and may choose an officer or officers in the room or place of such person or persons so dead or removed, as to them shall seem meet.

V. *And be it further enacted* by the authority aforesaid, That in case of the death, resignation, or removal from this Province, of any of the said commissioners, that then it shall be lawful for the President, or any of the vice presidents, to issue summons to the several surviving commissioners, to meet at the usual place of the annual meeting of the said commissioners, at such time as shall be specified in the said summons, and that such members as shall meet upon any summons, provided not less than seven in the whole or the major part of them, shall or may choose a commissioner or commissioners in the room or place of such person or persons so dead or removed, as to them shall seem meet.

VI. *And be it further enacted* by the authority aforesaid, That it shall and may be lawful for the said commissioners and their successors to meet at some convenient place to be appointed for that purpose, on the third Wednesday in March and October, and oftener if occasion requires, upon publick summons given five days before, then and there to transact the business of the said commissioners, and to put in force and to execute the several powers given to them by this Act; and no act done in any assembly of the said commissioners shall be effectual and valid, unless the president, or some one of the vice presidents, and six members of the said commissioners, at least, be present, and the major part consenting thereunto.

VII. *And be it further enacted*, That if any of the said commissioners shall neglect to attend, being duly summoned as in the said Act is directed, such commissioner or commissioners shall forfeit ten shillings for every day that the commissioners shall meet, to transact the business of this Act, unless he or they so neglecting to attend, shall give the commissioners, or the major part of the, such reasons as to them shall be satisfactory; and the forfeitures arising by the neglect of the said commissioners to attend, shall be disposed of as the majority of the commissioners then met shall order and appoint.

VIII. *And be it further enacted* by the authority aforesaid, That all gifts or legacies formerly given for the use of the free school of this Province, by any person or persons whatsoever, are hereby appropriated for the school intended to be founded and erected, pursuant to the several powers granted to the said commissioners by this Act; and the said commissioners and their lawful successors are hereby authorized and impowered to demand and sue for the same, in the courts of this Province, by all such lawful ways and means for the recovery and obtaining of the same, as they might or could do if the said gifts or legacies had been given to them expressly by name; and a receipt signed by such person or persons as shall be lawfully chosen and appointed treasurer to the said commissioners, shall be a sufficient discharge of such executor or executors as shall pay such legacies; and the monies so received by such treasurer, shall be disposed of by order of the said commissioners and their successors, towards the purchasing of lands, and the erecting of a school house and dwelling houses for the use of the several masters and professors.

IX. *And be it further enacted* by the authority aforesaid, That the said commissioners and their successors shall have power, and they are hereby authorized and impowered, to take up by grant from the Lords Proprietors, or purchase, have, take and receive from any other person or persons whatsoever, so much land as they shall think necessary and convenient for the several masters, teachers or professors, and shall also direct the building a school house upon the same, and such dwelling houses, and convenient out houses and buildings, for the accommodation of the several masters or teachers, and shall also nominate and appoint one or more persons to be supervisor or supervisors of the said buildings; the said several buildings to be in such places on the said land so taken up, or purchased, or received as aforesaid, and of such dimensions, and of such materials, as the said commissioners shall order and direct.

X. *And be it further enacted* by the authority aforesaid, That Mr. John Douglas shall be and is hereby declared to be master of the said school, by the name and stile of Preceptor or Teacher of Grammar, and other the Arts and Sciences to be taught in the Free School at Charlestown, for the Province of South Carolina.

XI. *And be it further enacted*, by the authority aforesaid, That upon the death, departure out of this Province, resignation or removal, of the said John Douglas, that the said commissioners and their successors shall have full power and lawful authority to nominate and appoint another fit person to be master of the said school, by the same name and stile; and so from time to time, when and as often as the said place of master of the said school, by death, resignation, deprivation, or otherwise, shall become void, shall nominate and appoint a fit person to succeed, to be the master of the said school.

XII. *And be it further enacted* by the authority aforesaid, That the person to be master of the said school shall be of the religion of the Church of England, and conform to the same, and shall be capable to teach the learned languages, that is to say, Latin and Greek tongues, and to catechise and instruct the youth in the principles of the Christian religion, as professed in the Church of England.

XIII. *And be it further enacted* by the authority aforesaid, That the said commissioners and their successors shall have power and authority, under their common seal, to set down and prescribe such orders, rules, statutes and ordinances for the order, rule and good government of the said school, and for the masters, teachers, ushers and scholars thereof, as to them and their successors shall seem meet and convenient, and that the same orders, rules, statutes and ordinances so by them made and set down, shall be and stand in full force and virtue in law, so always that the same be reasonable, and not repugnant nor contrary to the established laws of this Province. And the said commissioners for the time being, shall have full power and authority to visit the said school, and to order, reform and redress all disorders and abuses in and touching the government of the same, and further to censure, suspend and deprive any of the masters, teachers or professors of the said school, or the usher or ushers thereof, for the time being, as to them shall seem just, fit and convenient.

XIV. And for an encouragement to all charitable and well-disposed persons to contribute liberally towards the erecting and founding of the said school or academy, *Be it further enacted* by the authority aforesaid, That any person or persons that within seven years after the ratification of this Act, will contribute twenty pounds, current money of this Province, towards the erecting and founding of the said school, and will pay the same to the treasurer appointed by the said commissioners, that he or they shall have power to nominate any one person to be taught free in the said school for the space of five years after such gift, provided the person nominated by him or them shall so long live, but in case of the death of the person so nominated to be taught free, then that privilege to cease, and not another person to be nominated in his room or place; and so proportionably for so many twenty pounds as any person will give, so many persons to be taught free for five years, as aforesaid: *Provided* the number of scholars so in the whole to be taught free, do not exceed the number of twenty.

XV. *And be it further enacted* by the authority aforesaid, That the school-master shall have, hold, occupy, possess and enjoy to him and his lawful successors, all such land as shall, pursuant to this Act, be taken up, purchased, had or received for the use of a school-master of the said school, and the school house, and dwelling houses, and the out-houses and other buildings upon the same; and also, as a further encouragement unto him, shall have and receive out of the publick treasury of this Province, the full sum of one hundred pounds per annum, to be paid him half-yearly, and the publick Receiver for the time being is hereby authorized, required and commanded punctually to pay the same out of the publick treasury.

XVI. *And be it further enacted* by the authority aforesaid, That in consideration of the said school-master being allowed the use of the lands, dwelling house and other buildings upon the same land, and also the yearly salary of one hundred pounds per annum, he shall teach freely, and without any manner of fee or reward whatsoever, over and above the number of free scholars to be appointed by each person contributing twenty pounds as aforesaid, any number of scholars not exceeding twelve, the same scholars to be taught free, to be nominated and appointed by the above named commissioners and their lawful successors.

XVII. *And be it further enacted* by the authority aforesaid, That for every scholar the said master shall teach, besides those who by this Act are appointed to be taught free, he shall be allowed at the rate of four pounds per annum, current money of this Province, to be paid him by the parent or guardian of such scholar.

XVIII. *And be it further enacted* by the authority aforesaid, That in case the said school master shall have more scholars in his said school than one man can well manage, then and in such case the said commissioners, or the major part of them that shall meet, shall order and appoint a fit person to be usher of the said school, and for his encouragement shall be allowed by order of the said commissioners and their successors, not exceeding fifty pounds per annum, to be paid him half-yearly out of the publick treasury of this Province, and the publick Receiver for the time being is hereby authorized, required and commanded punctually to pay the same out of the publick treasury of this Province, as is hereafter directed by this Act; And over and above that, shall be allowed for every scholar that is under his charge (excepting those that by this Act are appointed to be taught free) at the rate of thirty shillings per annum, which sum of thirty shillings shall be allowed out of the four pounds per annum before directed to be paid for each scholar that is not taught free; and in case any dispute or difference shall arise between the master and the usher, what scholars shall belong to the more immediate charge of the master and which to the usher, that the same shall be decided by the commissioners and their sucessors.

XIX. And because it is necessary to give encouragement to a fit person that will undertake to teach the youth of this Province to write, and also the principles of vulgar arithmetick, and merchants' accompts; *Be it further enacted* by the authority aforesaid, That a fit person shall be nominated and appointed by the said commissioners, to teach writing, arithmetick, and merchants' accompts, and also the art of navigation and surveying, and other useful and practical parts of the mathematicks, and for his encouragement shall be allowed by order of the said commissioners and their successors, not exceeding fifty pounds per annum, to be paid him half-yearly, out of the publick treasury of this Province, and the publick Receiver for the time being is hereby authorized, required and commanded, punctually to pay the same out of the publick treasury of this province, as is hereafter directed by this Act; and in consideration of the said yearly salary to be paid him, he shall be obliged to teach free all such persons as by this Act are appointed to have their learning free and for other scholars that are not to be taught free, he shall be allowed for teaching them writing, at the rate of thirty shillings per annum, if writing and arithmetick, forty shillings, if merchants accounts, fifty shillings per annum, and if the mathematicks, at such rate as he shall agree with the several parents and guardians of the said children, not exceeding six pounds per annum.

XX. *And be it further enacted* by the authority aforesaid, That as to the publick salaries appointed by this Act to be paid out of the publick treasury of this Province, the publick Receiver for the time being is hereby authorized, required and commanded to pay the same out of the remaining part of the monies received for the duties upon skins and furs, after payment of the ministers' salaries appointed by the Act of Assembly of this Province commonly called the Church Act, and also of the parochial charges, and all other charges and sums of money that are appointed to be paid by one Act of Assembly of this Province, entituled a further Additional Act to an Act entituled an Act for the Establishment of Religious Worship in this Province, according to the Church of England, and for erecting of Churches for the Publick Worship of God, and also for the maintenance of Ministers, and the building convenient houses for them, ratified in open Assembly the eighth day of April, one thousand seven hundred and ten; and also all the monies appointed to be paid by one other Act of Assembly of this Province, entituled an Additional Act to the several Acts relating to the Establishment of Religious Worship in this Province, and now in force in the same, and also to the Act for securing the Provincial Library at Charlestown, in Carolina, ratified in open Assembly the seventh day of June, one thousand seven hundred and twelve; and the remaining part of the monies received upon the duties upon skins and furs, after the payment above mentioned being deducted, is hereby appropriated, to the payment of the several salaries appointed by this Act to be paid, and the publick Receiver for the time being is hereby strictly charged and required to reserve and pay the same accordingly, under the same penalties and forfeitures which are to be incurred by the Act entituled an Act to continue and Act for laying an imposition on Furs, &c. and for Appropriating the same, for misapplying of monies thereby raised, any thing in the same Act to the contrary hereof in any wise notwithstanding. And in the case the remaining part of the monies received out of the said duties upon skins and furs, after the deduction aforesaid, shall not be sufficient to discharge the several salaries appointed to be paid by this Act, that in such case, what is wanting to discharge the same, the said publick Receiver for the time being is hereby strictly charged and required to pay what is wanting to discharge the same, out of the publick treasury.

XXI. And as a further and more general encouragement for the instructing of the youth of this Province in useful and necessary learning; *Be it enacted* by the authority aforesaid, That as soon as a school master is settled in any other, or all the rest of the parishes of this Province, and approved by the vestry of such parish or parishes, such school master so approved, from time to time, shall receive the sum of ten pounds per annum, out of the publick treasury, by quarterly payments, and the publick Receiver is hereby required to pay the same.

XXII. *And be it further enacted* That the vestry of each parish in this Province shall have power, and they are hereby impowered, to appoint a place where the parish school shall be built, and shall draw upon the publick Receiver towards building the same, the sum of twelve pounds current money, and the publick Receiver is hereby required to pay the same accordingly.

XXIII. *And be it further enacted* by the authority aforesaid, That if any action, claim, suit or information shall be commenced or prosecuted against any person or persons, for what he or they shall do in pursuance or execution of this Act, such person or persons so sued may plead the general issue, not guilty, and upon issue joyned, give this Act and the special matter in evidence, and if the plaintiff or prosecutor shall become non-suit, or suffer discontinuance, or if a verdict pass against him, the defendant or defendants shall recover his or their treble costs, for which he or they shall have the like remedy as in any case when costs by law are given to the defendant.

XXIV. *And be it further enacted* by the authority aforesaid, That one Act of Assembly of this Province, entituled an Act for founding and erecting of a Free School, for the use of the inhabitants of South Carolina, ratified in open Assembly the eighth day of April, Anno Domini one thousand seven hundred and ten, and one other Act entituled an Act for the Encouragement of Learning, ratified in open Assembly the seventh day of June, Anno Domini one thousand seven hundred and twelve, be repealed; and it is hereby enacted and declared, that the said Acts, and every clause, article, sentence, word, matter or thing contained in the same, from henceforth shall be repealed, annulled, revoked and for ever made void, any thing in the said Acts to the contrary whatsoever in any wise notwithstanding. —*Ibid.*, pp. 389-96.

8. Instructions for building schoolhouse in South Carolina, 1715

4th That in Case there Shall be any Sum remaining after the finishing of these buildings y^t ye Same Shal be disposed of towards ye Building & endowing of A Publick School for ye use of this province —A. S. Salley, Jr. (Ed.), *Commissions and Instructions from the Lords Proprietors of Carolina to Public Officials of South Carolina, 1685-1715* (Columbia, S. C., 1916), p. 270. (1715)

9. Father Raphael, in charge of the Capuchin missions in Louisiana, writes to Father Raguet about some educational matters, September 15, 1725, and May 18, 1726

I have just made an establishment for a little school at New Orleans. To direct it I have found a man who knows Latin, mathematics, drawing singing and whose handwriting is fairly good. The copies enclosed herewith are from his hand. He is of our order and left it through a thoughtlessness of youth. For more than five years he has been serving in the quality of an officer on the concession of count D' Asfeld. Since our arrival in the country he has several times petitioned us to have him sent back to France in order to re-enter his convent, but as his practical ability made him useful to the concession the directors of this concession have employed every means to retain him until the present time. During this time I have examined his conduct and having found it exempt from certain vices that ordinarily cause (monks) to leave the cloister I have proposed to him that he should devote himself to the education of youth in our mission, convinced that the superiors of the order will approve the views that I have in that, the more so because the thing is not without precedent. He accepted this offer joyfully, and in the two or three months that he has been with us I have been able to do nothing but congratulate myself on his application to his duties.

As the engineers have not indicated the site for the schools of New Orleans I have been obliged to have one bought with a house adjacent to the one that was built for the parsonage. Several private persons have advanced me the sum of three thousand livres for this purchase. I have no other resource than Providence for paying this sum which is loaned with a mortgage on the house, but I hope, Sir, that you will kindly exert yourself with the gentlemen interested to have them share at least to some extent such a necessary expense, since there is nothing upon which the establishment of a colony more essentially depends than upon the education of the young. The house that has been bought is too small for the plan that I have of forming a little seminary of twelve or fifteen pupils who are now in the colony of age and in a position to be admitted to it. I am yet assured of only nine, but I do not doubt that the others who are at the distant posts will soon present themselves. This obliges me to enlarge the house to lodge them, and that is what I am working at now with the assistance of several inhabitants who are furnishing me materials. The way to induce the parents to send us their children is not to ask them anything for education, but as thereby I shall find myself burdened with the support of the two teachers—one who will teach Latin and the liberal arts to the more advanced, the other who will teach the beginners to read—I am convinced that the Company without entering into a new expense will approve that what it already grants for the support of a lay-brother and of a schoolmaster at New Orleans be applied to the support of these two teachers. I am sending the lay-brother back on this vessel and I shall get along without him. He had the same support from the State as a missionary and so the Company by granting the same thing to the master of the school will only change into an undertaking (that is) useful to the public what it was spending for our private use. While waiting, Sir, for a ruling in this matter I shall continue the execution of my plan, relying on Providence which has never failed me in time of need.

I should like to add to this establishment another that would not be less necessary, for the education of several young Indians. That is the only means we have in the present circumstances for working for the salvation of these poor people. We have neither the sufficient number of missionaries nor the necessary means to establish ourselves in their villages, and we could at small cost obtain several pupils who later would serve the missionaries usefully for the education of their nations. There are already some of the nation of the Natchez who have presented themselves of their own accord attracted by a young Indian of this same nation whom we have had with us for about twenty months. It is true that the curiosity to learn to speak and to live like the French is perhaps for the the present the only motive that influences them, but education supported by the habit of observing the practices of religion will be able later to make good Christians of them. We have had one with us for some time and I have had the satisfaction of seeing the fervor with which he applied himself to learning the prayers that our young Indian taught him and which he made him say on his knees...

I had asked the gentlemen of the Company for primers in order to teach the children to read. Instead of that a box of catechisms was sent to us which we do not need since we had brought a rather large quantity of them with us from France. I pray you then, Sir, to please to give your orders that there be sent to us a sufficient number of copies both of little primers for the beginning pupils and of elementary books, grammars and other necessary books for those who are learning Latin. I see that the majority of the inhabitants are disposed to profit by the establishment of the school in order to have their children study. I think that several will be successful especially among the Creoles. They have good memories and sprightliness. I have already had definite proofs of it in the short time that our school has been open...

I have done myself the honor, Sir, to inform you by my preceding letter that I had established a small school at New Orleans. I have the honor to assure you that the studies are progressing very well there. The pupils are yet a small number but there are few young people in the colony. The majority of the inhabitants who are in a position to send their children to school are satisfied to have them taught to read and write and regard all the rest as useless. However, there are five or six of them who are pursuing other subjects and are succeeding wonderfully in them. I am only embarrassed with the payment for the house in which the school is conducted. Those who had promised me to make advances for that purpose seem to withdraw from it in the fear of not being reimbursed because they do not wish to put themselves to an expense for the public. I beg you, Sir, to honor me with your protection in this crisis for if I am obliged to abandon the house this establishment, so necessary and so useful, will inevitably collapse.—Dunbar Rowland and Albert G. Sanders (editors), *Mississippi Provincial Archives*, 1701-1729, II, 507-08, 514, 519-20.

10. TREATY OF THE COMPANY OF THE INDIES WITH THE URSULINES,
1726

Article I. The Company will maintain at the hospital six religious, including the Superior, and will grant to each one a gratuity of five hundred francs to facilitate the means to make their voyage; they shall have gratis their passage and that of four servants on the vessels of the Company.

Article II. When they arrive in Louisiana, they shall be put in possession of the hospital such as it is, namely: The house and its appurtenances, all appearing to consist of a ward which can accommodate sixty or eighty patients; a suite of rooms where live the manager, the infirmarians and the cooks, and a ward which was to be constructed for the convalescent and which ought to be finished at present.

Article III. These six religious will make themselves comfortable in those apartments the best they can, while awaiting the proper buildings which the Company will have constructed for their establishment, which will be executed little by little, according as the funds of the hospital and those destined for the fortifications and the construction of the buildings of the Colony will permit.

Article IV. Sufficient ground, adjoining the house, shall be granted to the said hospital, both to erect there the new buildings of which there may be need and to make a poultry-yard and a garden for the religious.

Article V. The negroes and negresses, cattle, furniture, beds, linen and utensils destined for the use of the hospital, and all that it will be necessary to provide in addition for the service of the patients, shall be given by inventory to the religious, who will be obliged to render an account thereof to the Company.

Article VI. The Superior will appoint a religious as housekeeper, who in this quality will be charged with the effects of the hospital, and with all that will there be furnished for the sustenance of the sick: she will appoint two other Religious to be continually occupied in the service of the patients, another to keep the school of the young girls, and the sixth will serve as aid to those who will find themselves overburdened in their functions, and she shall always be ready to fill the place of those of her sisters who, through illness, may be unable to act.

Article VII. The religious shall not have a right to dispose of any fund or anything belonging to the hospital, without the consent of the administrators, ordered by deliberation taken in their council which shall be held for this purpose every time it will be judged appropriate and which shall be composed of the Commandant General of the Colony; of the First Councillor of the Superior Council, who may substitute another Councillor; of the Procurator General; of the Parish Priest of New Orleans; of the Superior of the Jesuits; of two notable inhabitants who will be elected by the Superior Council, by summoning the administrators to the election, and who will be changed every two years so that one of the two remain; and of the physician maintained by the King.

The Superior of the hospital shall have admission to this Council when she will have something to propose, without having, however, any right of suffrage.

Article VIII. There shall be kept by the Administrators an exact account of the property of the hospital, and the use of it shall be made by their orders; also of that of all which it may get through legacies, donations, and fines, which should never be applied to the religious.

Article IX. The Company will grant to the said hospital a lot of eight acres in front, and of the ordinary depth, along the river as near as possible to New Orleans, in order to there form a plantation which may in the course of time provide a maintenance for the Ursulines on account of the said hospital.

Article X. There shall be conceded by the Company three hundred francs a year to him who will take care of said plantation, during the first five years only.

Article XI. As long as the said plantation will not be in a state to provide for the maintenance and subsistence of the said religious, the Company will grant to each, six hundred francs a year for all things, which will be calculated from the day of their arrival at the port of embarkation, but as soon as the said plantation will produce enough to pay their expenses, this pension will cease to be paid to them, and the said religious will dispose of the income of the said plantation as a thing destined solely for their maintenance and subsistence.

Article XII. There shall be furnished to them by the Company, during each of the five years of the establishment of the said plantation, eight negroes (pieces d'Inde) that shall be paid for by the said Ursulines in the same terms on the same conditions regulated for the planters, by means of which the Company will cease to pay them the annual pension of six hundred francs to each from the time of the expiration of the first five years which will commence on the day of delivery of the first eight negroes.

Article XIII. If for any cause the Ursulines should cease to take charge of the hospital, they shall be obliged to remit to those who take their place, the hospital, the plantation, and all that they will have received by inventory. As to their clothes, furniture, cattle, negroes, etc., that they will have acquired, they will dispose of them as of things belonging to themselves and shall be reimbursed for the buildings which they will have caused to be erected at their own expense either on the grounds of the hospital or on the plantation, provided these constructions had been made with the consent of the Superior Council: they shall also be reimbursed for the expense of clearings made on the land of the plantation: all according to the estimate which will be made thereof, the said religious being obliged to remit to their successors only what they will have received from the Company or the hospital.

Article XIV. The company shall cause to be furnished to said religious all that will be necessary for the sick of the hospital, and the housekeeper shall be answerable for the receipt of it in registers signed by the administrators by opening an account for each kind of provision; in which register she (the housekeeper) will write down the provisions consumed (*consommations*) day by day, so that the said accounts may be balanced by the Administrators at the end of each month.

Article XV. But as it is proper that the religious have the liberty to live according to their own way, they will have for themselves in particular a treasurer (*depositaire*) in addition to her who will be the treasurer of the hospital, and who will be accountable to her Superioress to provide for the needs of the sisters, from funds such as pensions and income from the plantation, and they will govern themselves as to the interior of the house according to their rule and the spirit of their Institute, without the service of the hospital suffering from it in the least.

Article XVI. The Superior will cause an exact record to be kept of the patients that enter the said hospital and of those who will leave it by death or otherwise.

Article XVII. All persons sick of ordinary maladies or not incurable will be admitted to the hospital through a ticket from the physician and in his absence from the head surgeon (*chirugien major*); if they are poor, they will be treated gratis by bringing a certificate from their Parish Priest, signed by the Procurator General, that they have not the means to pay.

Article XVIII. The inhabitants who do not find themselves in the same case, and who will cause themselves to be taken to the hospital, shall be obliged to pay the sum which will be regulated by the administrators of the hospital, and the money will be remitted to the treasurer to be carried on account.

Article XIX. All persons in the service of the Company who will be sick, will be received in preference at the hospital; and the rations of which they have the enjoyment will belong to the hospital for which they shall be charged by the Company for the time the patients shall have remained in the hospital.

Article XX. An account shall also be kept at the hospital of the loans to the sick soldiers during the stay which they will there make.

Article XXI. The Administrators shall pay attention to establish a separate and select place at the hospital to which the officers and employees of the Company who will be sick, can have themselves taken to be treated; and the Administrators shall regulate what will be kept for each day from the salary of the said officers and employees for the benefit of the hospital.

Article XXII. The religious who will have care of the sick, shall not permit any of them, even the convalescent, to receive any food but that furnished by the house.

Article XXIII. In order to give to the hospital the means of providing a part of its expenses, the Company shall grant it, as near as possible, a tract of land of eight acres (*arpents*) in front, and of the ordinary proportions, to there form a plantation on which will be raised provisions, and cattle for the use (*consommation*) of the household; and the income of this plantation, of whatever it may consist, will belong to the said hospital, but there shall be opened for the said plantation a particular account in which it will be charged for all the things furnished by the Company and credited with its products, so that when the said hospital will be in a condition to do without the charities of the Company, it will be bound to refund to the Company the sum in which it will be indebted to the plantation.

Article XXIV. When the religious can do so conveniently, they will take, if they judge proper, girl-boarders at the rate which the Superioress will have regulated, and the payment of the pensions will be remitted into the hands of the treasurer of the religious, but some of those who will be charged with the sick shall be taken away from them, or applied to the education of the boarders.

Article XXV. As soon as the income from the plantation will be sufficient for the maintenance of the six said religious, they will be permitted to increase their number, if they judge proper, in proportion to the income, and passage only will be granted gratis to those whom they will cause to come from France; but they will not receive as religious any girl born in the country without the permission of the Council.

Article XXVI. If any religious, being unable to accommodate her self to the country, or for some other particular reason, be obliged to return to France, she shall have passage gratis for her and one servant, and her pension will cease from the day of embarkation.

Article XXVII. If any religious become through infirmity unable to work, she will not be counted as one of the six who ought to be maintained; and, however, she shall be equally treated during her life at the expense of the hospital, in case the religious are not yet able to do without this help.

Article XXVIII. The present Treaty shall be addressed to the Council of Louisiana to be there registered, and in case of any contests about the articles which it contains, they shall be decided by the Council, to whose judgment the parties have engaged themselves to submit.

Done at Paris, in the Hotel of the Company of the Indies,
> *September* 13, 1726. *Signed* L'Abbe Raguet.—J.
> Morin. — D'Artaguette — Diron. — Castanier.
> — Deshayer. — P. Saintard
> Soeur Catherine de Bruscoly, de St. Amand, *premiere Superieure des Ursulines de France*
> Soeur Marie Tranchepain, de St. Augustin, *Superieure*
> Soeur Marie-Anne Le Boullenger de Ste. Angelique, *Depositaire*

—Henry Churchill Semple, S. J., *The Ursulines in New Orleans*, pp. 167-73.

11. Petition to the King to approve the treaty of the Ursulines, 1726

The Directors of the Company of the Indies very respectfully petition His Majesty to approve, by commission, the Treaty which the Sisters Marie Tranchepain de St. Augustin and Marie-Anne Le Boullenger de Ste. Angélique, Ursulines of Rouen with the assistance of Sister Catherine de Bruscoly de St. Amand, first Superior of the Ursulines of France, have entered into, on the 13th of the present month with the said Company of the Indies for the establishment of six religious of their order, at New Orleans, where they will take care of the hospital of that city and employ themselves in the education of young girls, according to their Institute.

Done in Paris, *September* 17, 1726.—*Ibid.*, p. 174.

12. Brevet or commission of Louis XV, King of France, in favor of the Ursulines of Louisiana, 1726

Today, the eighteenth of September, one thousand seven hundred twenty-six, the King being at Fontainebleau, it has been represented to His Majesty on the part of the Sisters Marie Tranchepain de St. Augustin and Marie-Anne Le Boullenger de Ste. Angélique, Ursuline Religious of Rouen, that they had with the assistance of Sister Catharine of Bruscoly, First Superior of the Ursulines of France, entered into a treaty with the Directors of the Company of the Indies, on the thirteenth of the present month, by which the said Sisters of St. Augustine and Ste. Angélique, on the one side, engage themselves to go to Louisiana with four other religious of their order, to take charge of the Hospital of New Orleans and to employ themselves in the education of young girls, comformably to their Institute; and the Company of the Indies, on the other side, obliges itself to provide not only for the needs of the said hospital, but also for the sustenance of the said religious according as is explained in the said Treaty; that, in fine, they hope with God's blessing for a happy success in their enterprise, whose charitable and pious principles promise them the King's protection, very humbly begging His Majesty to be pleased, as a proof that their undertaking is agreeable to him, to approve of their establishment in the province of Louisiana; in consideration of which His Majesty, wishing to favor all that can contribute to the relief of the poor and the sick and to the education of youth, has approved the conditions of the treaty made between the Company of the Indies and the Ursuline Religious, on the thirteenth of the present month, the intention of His Majesty being that they enjoy without molestation all that will be granted them by the said Company comformably to the agreements that may have been made, or will be made between the said Company of Indies and the said religious, for the purpose of which His Majesty places them under his protection and safeguard, and for assurance of his will his Majesty has commanded me to dispatch the present Brevet which he has been pleased to sign with his own hand, and to be countersigned by me, his Councillor, Secretary of State and of his commandments and finances.

Louis—

Phélypeaux

—Ibid., pp. 175-76.

13. EXTRACTS OF LETTERS BY SISTER MARY MAGDELEINE HACHARD OF ST. STANISLAUS TO HER FATHER, JANUARY 1, 1728, APRIL 24, 1728

New Orleans
January 1, 1728

My dear Father:

... They are working hard on our house. Mr. Perier, our Commandant, always interested in everything that can afford us pleasure, promises to lodge us there within this year. The engineer came to show us the plan. We desire nothing so much as to see ourselves in this house, in order to be also occupied at the hospital to attend the sick, for we learn every day that it is the greatest pity in the world to see the bad arrangement there, and that the greater part of the patients die for want of help. The intention of M. the Commandant and of the inhabitants of this city is that we should also take care of the girls and women of evil life; this is not yet determined on our side; but we have been given to understand that it would do a great good to the colony; and for that they propose to build for us a special apartment at the end of our enclosure to shut up all these people.

We keep also a school to instruct the negro and Indian girls and women; they come every day from one o'clock in the afternoon to half-past two. You see, my dear father, that we are not useless in this country, I assure you that all our moments are counted and that we have not a single one to ourselves. We have lately taken charge of a little orphan girl who was serving in a house where she did not have a very good example. It is further the intention of Rev. Father de Beaubois that we should take charge, through charity, of some little orphan girls; and he tells us, in order to engage us to do it, that he and Mr. Perier charge themselves with all the orphan boys...

My dear father,
Your very humble and very obedient daughter and servant,
MARIE MAGDELEINE HACHARD DE ST. STANISLAS

New Orleans, *April* 24, 1728

My very dear Father:

... The women, while ignorant about things concerning their salvation, are not so about vanity. The luxury which prevails in this city is the reason that nobody can here be distinguished. All is of equal magnificence. The generality are obliged to live with their families on *sagamité*, which is a sort of pap, and are dressed in stuffs of damask full of ribbons, notwithstanding the dearness, for these stuffs usually cost in this country three times more than in France. Women here, as elsewhere, paint white and red, (*portent du blanc et du rouge*) to hide the wrinkles of their faces, on which they also wear beauty spots. In fine, the demon possesses here a great empire, but that does not take away our hope of destroying it, God desiring, as often before, to display His strength in our weakness. The more the enemy is powerful, the more are we encouraged to fight him. What causes us great pleasure, is the docility of the children, whom we can direct as we wish. The negresses are also easy to be instructed when they know how to speak French. But it is not the same with the savages, who are baptized only with fear and trembling, because of the inclination which they seem to have to sin; above all, the women who under a modest air hide beastly passions. . .

The house which they are building for us is at the other extremity of the city. Father de Beaubois and the engineers of the Company who supervise the work, following the idea we have given them, often show us the plan. It will be all in brick and of sufficient size to lodge a large community. There will be in it all the apartments which we could wish. It would be very regularly built, and wainscotted, and with large glass windows. But the construction advances slowly. Mr. Perier, our Governor and Commandant, caused us to hope that it would be ready at the end of this year; but workmen are scarce; we will be happy to take possession of it and of our hospital at Easter, 1729; then we shall need new help, and I pray the Lord that He may send us some good subjects. . .

Our little community is increasing from day to day. We have twenty boarders, of whom eight have to-day made their First Communion; three lady boarders, and three orphans whom we take through charity. We have also seven slave boarders to teach and prepare for Baptism and First Communion. Besides we have a large number of day-scholars and negresses and savages who come two hours a day to be instructed. . .

Your very humble and very obedient daughter and servant,

MARIE MAGDELEINE HACHARD DE ST. STANISLAS

—*Ibid.*, 198-200, 224-38.

14. Salaries of masters in free school at Charleston, South Carolina, 1734

AN ACT for settling the Salarys of the Masters of the Free School in Charlestown, for the use of the Inhabitants of the Province of South Carolina.

WHEREAS, in and by an Act entituled an Act for founding and erecting a free school in Charlestown, for the use of the inhabitants of this Province of South Carolina, among other things it is enacted, that the master of the said school thereby erected, for a further encouragement to him, should have and receive out of the publick treasury of this Province the full sum of one hundred pounds per annum, to be paid him half yearly, and the Publick Receiver for the time being is thereby authorized, required and commanded, punctually to pay the same out of the said publick treasury: And whereas, also in and by the said Act, the commissioners therein named and their successors, are authorized and impowered to appoint an usher and a writing master, who shall also teach arithmetic and merchants accounts, and also the art of navigation and surveying, and other practical parts of the mathematicks, who for their encouragement should be allowed, by order of the said commissioners, not exceeding fifty pounds per annum each, to be paid in the same manner by the Publick Treasurer, as the master's salary is appointed to be paid: And whereas, since the passing of the said Act, being now upwards of twenty-one years, the alteration that hath happened in the currency of this Province, hath reduced the said salarys to one-fifth part of their original values, for remedy whereof we humbly pray your most sacred Majesty, that it may be enacted,

I. *And be it enacted*, by his Excellency Robert Johnson, Esq. Governour, Captain General and Commander-in-chief, in and over his Majesty's Province of South Carolina, by and with the advice and consent of his Majesty's honourable Council and the Commons House of Assembly of this Province, and by the authority of the same, That from and after the ratification of this Act, and the settlement of the said masters and ushers in the said school, or any of them, the said salaries of such masters and ushers so settled, or so much thereof as from time to time shall grow due, shall be paid by the Publick Treasurer of this Province, to the said masters and ushers respectively, as shall be so settled, in manner as is directed by the said herein before in part recited Act, in the current money of this Province, at four hun-

dred per centum advance; any thing to the contrary notwithstanding.
—Cooper, *op. cit.*, III, 377-78.

15. AN ACT FOR THE ESTABLISHMENT OF A FREE SCHOOL IN THE TOWN
OF DORCHESTER, APRIL 9, 1734

Whereas, by the blessing of almighty God, the youth of this Province are become very numerous, and their parents so well inclined to have them instructed in grammar, and other liberal arts and sciences, and other useful learning, and also in the principles of the christian religion, that the free school erected, authorized and established in Charlestown for this purpose, is not sufficient fully to answer the good intent of such an undertaking: And whereas, several of the inhabitants of this Province who have a numerous issue, and live at such a distance from the said free school now established in Charlestown, that their circumstances may not be sufficient to permit them to send their children thither to be educated, whereby they may be deprived of so great a benefit; and it therefore appearing necessary that one or more schools be founded and erected in other part or parts of this Province as shall be most convenient for the carrying on so laudable a design, we therefore most humbly pray your most sacred Majesty that it may be enacted.

I. *And be it enacted,* by his Excellency Robert Johnson, Esq., Governor of this his Majesty's Province of South Carolina, by and with the advice and consent of his Majesty's honourable Council and the Assembly of this Province, and by the authority of the same, That the honourable Alexander Skene, Thomas Waring, Joseph Blake, Arthur Middleton, Ralph Izard, Robert Wright, Paul Jenys, Walter Izard, Benjamin Waring, Esqrs. the Reverend Francis Vernod, and William Cattell and John Williams, Esqrs. and their successors to be elected as hereinafter directed, be and shall forever hereafter be one body politick and corporate in deed and in name, by the name of the commissioners for founding, erecting, governing, ordering and visiting a free school at the town of Dorchester, in the parish of St. George, in Berkley county, for the use of the inhabitants of South Carolina; and that they and their successors by the same name, by the authority aforesaid, be fully made, ordained, constituted and declared one body politick and corporate in deed and in name; and that by the same name, they and their successors shall and may have perpetual succession; and that they and their successors by that name, shall and may forever hereafter be persons able and capable in law to purchase, have, take, receive and enjoy to them and their successors, lands, messuages, tenements, rents, libertys, privileges, jurisdictions, franchises and other hereditaments, of whatsoever nature, kind, quality or value they be, in fee, and in perpetuity, and also estates for lives, and for years; and all other manner of goods, chattels and things whatsoever, of what name, nature, value or quality soever they be, for the better maintenance and support of masters or teachers for the said school; and also for the erecting of school-houses and convenient dwelling houses for the accomodation of the said school masters and teachers; and that by the name aforesaid, they shall and may be able to plead and be impleaded, answer and be answered unto, and to defend and be defended in all courts and places whatsoever, and before whatsoever judge or judges, justice or justices, or other officer or officers belonging to this Province, in all and singular actions, plaints, pleas, matters and demands, of what nature, kind, or quality soever may be, and to act and do all other matters and things in an ample manner and form as any other the inhabitants of this Province being persons able and capable in law, or any other body politick or corporate, by the laws of England can or may have, purchase, receive, possess, take, enjoy, grant, set, let, demise, plead and be impleaded, answer and be answered unto, defend and be defended, do, permit and execute; and that the said commissioners and their successors for ever hereafter, shall and may have a common seal to serve for the causes and business of them and their successors, and to change, break, alter and make new the said seal from time to time, and at their pleasure, as they shall think best; and the said commissioners shall take the State oaths, and an oath for the faithful execution of their offices.

II. And for the better execution of the purposes aforesaid, *Be it further enacted* by the authority aforesaid, That the said commissioners and their successors forever, shall and may yearly on St. George's day, being the three-and-twentieth day of April (unless it shall be on Sunday, and then on the Monday following) meet at some convenient place to be appointed by the President of the said commissioners, for the time being, between the hours of nine and twelve in the morning of the same day, and that they, or any three of them that shall then be present, shall choose a President for the year ensuing, and that such President shall (before he acts in his said office) take the State oaths, to be administered to him by any one justice of the peace, who is hereby authorized and impowered to administer the same, as also an oath for the faithful and due execution

of his office and place during the said year, and until discharged of
the same.

III. *And be it further enacted* by the authority aforesaid, That the
president of the said commissioners shall be the honourable Alexander
Skene, Esq. and that the said president shall, within forty days after
the ratification of this Act, cause summons to be issued to the several
commissioners hereinbefore particularly mentioned, to meet on such
a day, and at such a place as he shall appoint; and the said president
is hereby impowered then and there to administer to the said com-
misssioners the State oaths, as also the oath for the due execution of
their offices; and that they, or the major part of them as shall be then
present, shall proceed to the election of such officers, ministers and
servants as shall be thought convenient, to serve for the year ensuing;
and that each of such officers, ministers and servants as shall be then
elected, shall take the State oaths, and an oath to be to them administered by the president of the said commissioners, for the faithful and due execution of their respective offices and places, until duly
discharged of the same.

IV. *And be it further enacted* by the authority aforesaid, That if
any of the persons at any time chosen into any of the said offices shall
dye, resign, or on any account be removed from such office, at any
time between such yearly days of election, that in such case it may
and shall be lawful for the president for the time being, to issue summons to the other commissioners to meet at the usual place of annual
meeting, at such time as shall be specified in the said summons; and
such commissioners as shall meet upon such summons, (provided not
less than five in the whole,) or the major part of them, shall and may
choose an officer or officers, in the room or place of such person or
persons so dead or removed, as to them shall seem meet.

V. *And be it further enacted* by the authority aforesaid, That in
case of the death, resignation or removal from this Province of any
of the said commissioners, that then it shall be lawful for the president, for the time being, to issue out his summons to the several surviving and remaining commissioners, to meet at the usual place of the
annual meeting of the said commissioners, at such time as shall be
specified in the said summons; and that such members as shall meet
upon any summons, (provided not less than five in the whole,) or
the major part of them, shall or may choose a new commissioner or
commissioners, in the room or place of such person or persons so dead
or removed, as to them shall seem meet.

VI. *And be it further enacted* by the authority aforesaid, That in case of the death, resignation or removal from this Province, of the president any five or more of the commissioners shall meet and choose another president for the remaining part of the year, who shall have and enjoy all the powers and authoritys given and granted to the president by this Act appointed.

VIII. *And be it further enacted* by the authority aforesaid, That it shall and may be lawful for the said commissioners and their successors, to meet at some convenient place in the said parish, to be appointed for that purpose, on the twenty-third day of April, being St. George's day, or oftener of occasion require, upon publick summons given ten days before, then and there to transact the business of the said commissioners, and to put in force and execute the several powers given them by this Act; and no act done in any assembly of the said commissioners, shall be effectual and valid, unless the president and four members of the said commissioners at least be present, and the major part consenting thereunto.

VIII. *And be it further enacted* by the authority aforesaid, That if any of the said commissioners shall neglect to attend, being duly summoned, as in this Act is directed, such commissioners or commissioner, shall forfeit ten shillings for every day that the commissioners shall meet to transact the business of this Act, unless he or they so neglecting to attend, shall give the commissioners, or the major part of them, such reasons as to them shall be satisfactory; and the forfeitures arising by the neglect of the said commissioners to attend, shall be disposed of as the majority of the commissioners then met shall order and appoint.

IX. *And be it further enacted* by the authority aforesaid, That all gifts, legacys and voluntary subscriptions that shall or may hereafter be given or subscribed to or for the use of the free school by this present Act established, by any person or persons, are hereby appropriated to and for the sole use and benefit of the said school; and the several commissioners appointed by this Act, and their lawful successors, are hereby authorized and impowered to demand and sue for the same in the courts of this Province or elsewhere, by all such lawful ways and means for the recovery and obtaining of the same, as they might or could do if the said gifts, legacys and subscriptions had been given to them expressly by name, and a receipt signed by such person or persons as shall be appointed treasurer to the said commissioners, shall be a sufficient discharge to such executor or executors as shall pay such legacys and subscriptions; and the money so received by such treasurer, shall be disposed of by order of the said commissioners or their successors, for the use and benefit of the school by this Act intended to be established, in such manner as the majority of them shall think most proper and convenient.

X. *And be it further enacted* by the authority aforesaid, That the said commissioners and their successors, shall have power, and they are hereby authorized and impowered, to take up by grant from his Majesty, or purchase, have, take, and receive from any other person or persons whatsoever, so much land as they shall think necessary and convenient for the masters and teachers of the school hereby intended to be established, and shall direct the building of such houses as may be necessary to be erected thereon for their accomodation; the said buildings to be in such places on the said lands so taken up or purchased as aforesaid, and of such dimensions and materials as the said commissioners shall order and appoint.

XI. *And be it further enacted* by the authority aforesaid, That the master of the said school shall be capable to teach the learned languages, Latine and Greek tongues, and to catechise and instruct the youth in the principles fo the christian religion.

XII. *And be it further enacted* by the authority aforesaid, That the said commissioners and their successors, shall have power and authority under their common seal, so [to] set down and prescribe such orders, rules, statutes and ordinances for the order, rule, good government and management of the said school, and for the master or teacher and scholars thereof, as to them and their successors, from time to time shall seem meet and convenient; and that the same orders, rules, statutes and ordinances so by them made and set down, shall be and stand in full force and virtue in law: Provided always, that the same be reasonable and fit, and not repugnant or contrary to the established laws of this Province; and the said commissioners for the time being, shall have full power and authority to visit the said school, and to order, reform and redress all disorders and abuses in and touching the government of the same; and further to censure, suspend and deprive any of the masters, ushers or teachers of the said school, as to them shall seem just, fitting and convenient.

XIII. *And be it further enacted* by the authority aforesaid, That if any action, claim, suit or information, shall be commenced or prosecuted against any person or persons, for what he or they shall do in pursuance or execution of this Act, such person or persons so sued,

may plead the general issue, not guilty, and upon issue joined, give this Act and the special matter in evidence; and if the plaintiff or prosecutor shall become nonsuit or suffer discontinuance, or if a verdict pass against him, the defendant or defendants shall recover his or their treble costs, for which he or they shall have the like remedy as in any case where costs by law are given to the defendant.
—*Ibid.*, pp. 378-81.

16. Governor Gabriel Johnston to the General Assembly of North Carolina on schools, September 22, 1736

At a General Assembly begun and held at Edenton on Tuesday the 21st day of September 1736...

Wednesday Septr 22d The House met according to adjournment Present as before.

His Excellency came to the Upper House and by a Messenger required the attendance of the House of Burgesses, who came in a full body, and presented William Downing Esqre their Speaker, whom his Excellency was pleased to approve of; and then delivered his speech to both Houses in the following words, vizt

GENTLEMEN OF THE UPPER HOUSE, Mr SPEAKER AND GENTLEMEN OF THE HOUSE OF BURGESSES...

I shall begin with observing the deplorable & almost totall want of divine worship throughout the Province, I believe it is impossible to instance in any Country, I am sure it is in any Collony belonging to a Christian nation, where some effectuall provision has not been made for paying in Publick, and at stated times that adoration, and Homage to Almighty God, so highly becoming all rational creatures; and for instructing the People in their duty to the supream Author of their being to one another and to themselves: After observing this, nobody will be surprized at the many disorders, which have always prevailed among us; especially when it is considered how little care is taken of the education of youth.

In all civilized Societys of men, it has always been looked upon as a matter of the greatest consequence to their Peace and happiness, to polish the minds of young Persons with some degree of learning, and early to instill into them the Principles of virtue and religion, and that the Legislature has never yet taken the least care to erect one school, which deserves the name in this wide extended country, must in the judgement of all thinking men, be reckoned one of our greatest misfortunes. To what purpose Gentlemen is all your toil and labour, all your pains and endeavours for the advantage and enriching your families and Posterity, if within ourselves you cannot afford them such an education as may qualify them to be usefull to their Country and to enjoy what you leave them with decency.—William L. Saunders (compiler), *The Colonial Records of North Carolina*, IV, 225-27.

17. THE GENERAL ASSEMBLY REPLIES TO GOVERNOR GABRIEL JOHNSTON'S SPEECH, SEPTEMBER 25, 1736

To His Excellency Gabriel Johnston Esqre Captain General Governor & Commander in Chief in and over His Majesty's Province of North Carolina and Vice Admiral of the same.

The Humble Address of his Majestie's Council of the said Province now met in General Assembly.

MAY IT PLEASE YOUR EXCELLENCY,

 ...We lament very much the want of Divine Publick worship (a crying scandal in any, but more especially in a Christian Community;) as well as the general neglect in point of education, the main sources of all disorders and Corruptions, which we should rejoice to see removed and remedeyed, and are ready to do our parts, towards the reformation of such flagrant and prolifick Evils...—*Ibid.*, pp. 230-31.

18. GOVERNOR GABRIEL JOHNSTON REPLIES TO THE GENERAL ASSEMBLY, OCTOBER 7, 1736

GENTLEMEN,

To every Article of this your Representation of grievances I shall give you a particular answer...

This is Gentlemen what I have to say to those grievances your Committee have been pleased to make a report of to you; I am sorry they have been so remiss in their duty as to present so few grievances and those so little material, In any other Country besides this I am satisfied they would have taken notice of the want of divine worship, the neglect of the education of youth, the bad state of your Laws and the impossibility to execute them, such as they are Grievances which will deserve redress, but these it seems are not reckoned grievances in this part of the world. The more unhappy for the People whom you represent; for all the world must now see who is to be blamed for neglecting matters so essential to the peace quiet and good government of the Province.—*Ibid.*, pp. 237-39.

19. GOVERNOR GABRIEL JOHNSTON TO THE GENERAL ASSEMBLY AGAIN
ON THE NEED FOR EDUCATION, MARCH 4, 1737

GENTLEMEN OF THE COUNCIL MR SPEAKER AND
GENTLEMEN OF THE HOUSE OF BURGESSES

It is so short a time since I laid the miserable state of your public
Affairs before you that I flatter myself I have no occasion to remind
you of them at present I shall only therefore once more assure you
that if you are disposed to take any measure for maintaining and establishing the public Worship of Almighty God making any provision
for the Education of Youth or the Reformation and better execution
of your Laws I am come with a most sincere intention of concurring
with you in promoting such valuable Ends or in any other Law which
may be proposed for the real advantage of the province.... —*Ibid.*,
pp. 271-72.

20. PROHIBITION AGAINST TEACHING SLAVES IN SOUTH CAROLINA TO
WRITE, 1740

And *whereas,* the having of slaves taught to write, or suffering them
to be employed in writing, may be attended with great inconveniences;
Be it therefore enacted by the authority aforesaid, That all and every
person or persons whatsoever, who shall hereafter teach, or cause any
slave or slaves to be taught, to write, or shall use or employ any slave
as a scribe in any manner of writing whatsoever, hereafter taught to
write, every such person and persons, shall, for every such offence,
forfeit the sum of one hundred pounds current money.
—David J. McCord, *The Statutes at Large of South Carolina.* VII, 413.

21. GOVERNOR DOBBS OF NORTH CAROLINA TO THE BOARD OF TRADE
CONCERNING SCHOOL MASTERS, JANUARY 4, 1755

MY LORDS [OF THE BOARD OF TRADE]

By my 128th Instruction I am commanded to lay before your Lordships the Wants & Defects of the Province, the chief Products, what
new Improvements are made or may be made by the Industry of the

Planters or what Advantages may be made by trade, and which way his Majesty may contribute thereto.

What I have chiefly observed since I came here as to the wants & Defects of this Province is first the want of a sufficient Number of Clergymen to instil good principals and Morality into the Inhabitants, & proper Schoolmasters to instruct their Youth, the want of which occasions an Indolence & want of Attention to their own good, which with the warmth of the climate & plenty they have of Cattle & fruit without Labour, prevents their Industry, by which Means the Price of Labour is very high, and the Artificers and Labourers being scarce in comparison to the number of Planters, when they are employed they wont work half, scarce the third part of work in a Day of what they do in Europe, and their wages being from 2 Shilling to 3, 4, & 5 Shillings per diem this Currency, the Planters are not able to go on with Improvements in building or clearing their Lands, and unless they are very industrious to lay up as much as can purchase 2 or 3 Negros, they are no ways able to cultivate their Lands as Your Lordships expect and consequently the Clause of Cultivation must be lessened or relaxed, and only be kept as a Rod over them to prompt them to be industrious, and therefore young or new Planters could not venture to take up Lands, and those who are rich can't get hands to assist them to cultivate, until they can buy Slaves and teach them some handicraft Trades But as all the chief Planters now are sensible of their wants and Difficulties, the Assembly is determined to give a proper Encouragement to learned and pious Clergymen and to encourage Schools. . . . —Saunders, *op. cit.*, V, 314-15.

22. MESSAGE CONCERNING AID TO HIS MAJESTY FOR DEFENSE OF THE FRONTIER, JANUARY 4, 1755

MR. SPEAKER AND GENt OF THE ASSEMBLY

On reading the third time the bill for granting an aid to his Majesty we find we cannot agree to pass the Bill in the manner you have sent it to us therefore we propose the following Amendments Vizt that the eight thousand pounds be made up out of the six thousand pounds for the founding and endowing of Publick School and two thousand pounds out of the moneys appropriated for building a Fort at or near Occacock called fort Granville not hitherto applyed that the Governor may have the disposal of the said eight thousand pounds as may be most effectual for his Majestys service Agreable to the Intent of the said Bill if you agree to those Amendments send up two of your members to see the Bill altered accordingly

Mr. Heron and Mr. Harvey brought up a Message from the other House wh was read and is as follows

GENt OF HIS MAJESTYS HONble COUNCIL,

By your message of the fourth Inst we observe that you propose amendmts to the Bill for granting an aid to his Majesty &c vizt That the £8000 be made up out of the £6000 for the founding and endowing a Publick school & £2000 out of the moneys appropriated for building a Fort at or near Ocacock called Fort Granville not yet applied and [give] the Govr the Disposal of the said eight thousand pounds in the most effectual manner for his Majestys service According to the Direction of the said Bill upon consideration of which this House have resolved that They do Consent to the first Amendments by you proposed & Disagree to the Second That they cannot receede from their Amendments to the said Bill Whereof a Discretionary power is given to the Governor either to raise recruits with the five thousand pounds in the Bill mentioned for that purpose to be sent to Ohio, or remit the same in Provision for accomodating his Majestys Troops Already ordered to serve there as shall seem most Convenient for his Majestys service.—*Ibid.*, pp. 267, 268.

23. Report of legislative committee on propositions and grievances, January 9, 1755

11th That under a Sence of the many Advantages that will arise to the province from giving our Youth a Liberal Education (whether considered in a Moral Religious or political Light) a publick School or Seminary of Learning be erected and properly Endowed—And that for effecting the same the Sum of six thousand pounds already appropriated for that purpose be properly applied.—*Ibid.*, pp. 298-99.

24. Governor Dobbs writes the Board of Trade that Scotch Irish Presbyterians desire a "teacher of their own opinion and choice," August 24, 1755

There are at present 75 families on my Lands I viewed betwixt 30 and 40 of them, and except two there was not less than from 5 or 6 to 10 children in each family, each going barefooted in their shifts in the warm weather, no woman wearing more than a shift and one thin petticoat; They are a Colony from Ireland removed from Pennsylvania, of what we call Scotch Irish Presbyterians who with others in the neighbouring Tracts had settled together in order to have a teacher of their own opinion and choice; . . . —*Ibid.*, pp. 355-56.

25. GOVERNOR DOBBS RECOMMENDS SCHOOLS TO GENERAL ASSEMBLY, SEPTEMBER 25, 1755

GENTm OF THE COUNCIL MR. SPEAKER AND GENT: OF THE ASSEMBLY.

There was so much business before your last Sessions which you could not finish that I must earnestly desire your application in finishing it. The revisal of your Laws is absolutely necessary to be brought soon to a conclusion a General Inspection Law upon your exports, The giving encouragement for erecting County or Parish schools for the education of your youth in the knowledge of religion and moral duties is become absolutely necessary to promote industry and to preserve the appearance of religion amongst Us...

I must also recommend to you the consideration of a proper Law to encourage the Indians within this Province by making it equally Penal to kill, maim or wound an Indian or negro servant, as any other of his Majesty's subjects, and to encourage the education of the Indian youth in the knowledge of the English language & Customs by giving them schoolmasters in their Towns, who may assist in civilizing them and inducing them to live industriously by the Produce of their own Lands which Law should also extend to our neighbouring Indian Allies.—*Ibid.*, pp. 496-97.

26. SOME EDUCATIONAL ACTIVITIES OF THE MORAVIANS IN NORTH CAROLINA, 1756-1779

November 30, 1756

After supper an English class was begun for the Single Brethren.— Adelaide L. Fries, translator and editor, *Records of the Moravians in North Carolina*, I, 173.

Br. Petersen has begun a day school for our boys and his wife assists Sr. Kalberlahn with the girls. Br. and Sr. Bachhoff have taken charge of the children in Bethania.—*Ibid.*, p. 241.

January 28, 1765

A school was begun for our older boys. It will be held in the evening between seven and nine o'clock, and they will be taught reading, writing, and arithmetic.—*Ibid.*, p. 331.

February 4, 1768

Br. Reuter has begun a class in arithmetic for the younger boys early in the morning, and one for older boys in the evening. Br. Utley will have evening classes for the older boys and certain Brethren in English reading and writing.—*Ibid.*, p. 377.

The school for children in Bethania was continued by Br. Bachhoff. —*Ibid.*, p. 267 (1763).

Adam Spach, from the South Fork, brought his son to Bethania. He will attend Br. Bachhoff's school, and will lodge with Michael Ranke.—*Ibid.*, p. 285.

April 17, 1765

Adam Spach and the wife of Peter Frey took their daughters, nine and six years old, to the school at Bethania.—*Ibid.*, p. 301.

In February (1770) Br. and Sr. Bachhoff were succeeded by Br. and Sr. Ernst, Br. Bachhoff having served here for eleven years as schoolteacher and Reader.—*Ibid.*, p. 400.

Bro. and Sr. Ernst have moved into the new house, and he conducts a school for the little boys and girls.—*Ibid.*, p. 435.

December 1, 1772

I sent a letter to Br. Marshall, protesting against the requested change in the school, according to which boys and girls would attend at the same time.—*Ibid.*, II, 745.

December 6, 1772

Br. Marshall met with the Society to discuss the school matter, and, in spite of all representations, we had to agree that the custom of the Pennsylvania country congregations should be adopted, and that boys and girls should attend together.—*Ibid.*, p. 745.

December 7, 1772

A beginning was made with the new school arrangement, eight little boys and nine little girls attending. I seated the reading boys and girls on one bench, and the writing and A. B. C. children on the other. At dinner I seated the children of each family together at the table, sang a grace for them before and after the meal, remained with them while they ate, and appointed one little girl to bring water and pour it for them, and to clear the table afterwards. Then they all wanted to pick cotton until time for school to begin again; and so today all went smoothly and in good order. A class for the older boys was begun in the evening.—*Ibid.*, p. 745.

December 9, 1772

Two older girls joined the reading and writing school.—*Ibid.*, p. 745.

January 25, 1773

Adam Spach, Jr. joined the evening school for older boys.—*Ibid.*, p. 781.

February 15, 1773

Three years ago today Br. and Sr. Bachhoff moved to this school-house.—*Ibid.*, p. 781.

January 2, 1775

Br. Stach has been ill, but today was able to again begin the school for boys.—*Ibid.*, p. 900.

November 2, 1773

In the Brothers House a class in writing and arithmetic shall again be begun for the boys. We must also see that the younger Sisters and girls in the Sisters House have practice in writing.—*Ibid.*, p. 774.

September 30, 1772

Today Br. Matthew Stach began a school for the local children, taking several boys in the morning, and three girls in the afternoon; may the Lord lay a rich blessing upon them. This evening we began the winter arrangement of services; Br. Marshall held the twilight service, and communicated the news from Br. Mattheus Hehl's last letter, among other things that August Schubert, who left here a few years ago, has died peacefully, fifteen miles from Philadelphia.—*Ibid.*, p. 740.

April 9, 1770

Little Gottlob Krause, who has been in the care of Br. and Sr. Bachhoff in Bethania, returned to Bethabara. To date we have had a day school for our boys, but no institution in which they could live; this can be no longer postponed, and the transfer to Salem has released space which can be used. The institution now cares for three orphans, Gottlob Krause and the two sons of the widow Dixon. They are in the charge of the single Brother, Würtele, who also conducts the day school, and the young Single Brother Nilson is his Assistant, going there after work hours, to sleep, and also alternating with Br. Würtele in taking them to the services. In the morning the Brn. Graff, Lorenz and Reuter have classes for them and the other boys; in the afternoon

Br. Würtele takes them out to cut wood, or for other work. The eldest of them is ten years old.—*Ibid.*, pp. 612-13.

March 30, 1775

In the presence of Br. Bonn, as Justice, the boys John Jacob Wohlfahrt and Martin Lück were apprenticed to Br. Friedrich Beck, master joiner; the boy John Dixon to Br. Herbst that he may learn to be a tanner; and Gottlieb Strehle to Br. Lund.—*Ibid.*, p. 896.

June 2, 1776

The Committee discussed the school, and thought that the children who can already read well should give more time to writing and ciphering.—*Ibid.*, III, 1097.

November 18, 1776

Br. Fisher has finished the school-table, and brought it to the Gemein Haus, so I began an evening school for the older boys, thirteen in number.—*Ibid.*, p. 1109.

October 7, 1777

Old Br. Stack, in Bethabara, has given up the school for little boys, finding them too troublesome for him.—*Ibid.*, p. 1178.

December 28, 1777

The House-fathers had a meeting about the paying of their rents. As they were leaving several spoke to me, asking that the boys who could no longer attend the day school might have an evening school. I answered that it could be begun after New Year, on condition that no boys under twelve years of age should attend.—*Ibid.*, p. 1199.

April 29, 1778

It was reported that a school for little boys will be begun, and the old Skin-House was suggested for the schoolroom. Br. Jens Schmid will teach the school.—*Ibid.*, p. 1260.

May 20, 1778

Under the changed scale of prices in the Sisters House Sr. Oesterlein, who is now receiving 2/6 for teaching the three little girls, is not able to pay the doubled board rate. It was decided that Br. Bragge shall pay 10 sh. each four weeks for his child and Miksch's and Br. Meyer shall pay 5 sh. each four weeks for his daughter, and Brn. Steiner and Baumgarten pay at the same rate it will give her an annual income of £6: to £8.

To Br. Jens Schmid the three fathers will pay as follows:

Bagge for 12 months @ 30 sh. and the 13th month 40 sh.   20:—:—,
Meyer for 12 months @ 12 sh. and the 13th month 16 sh.   8:—:—,
Stockburger will pay for the year   3:—:—,
   and will furnish wood for the school fire for the winter

£ 31:—:—.
—*Ibid.*, p. 1261.

January 25, 1778

I spoke with the fathers and mothers about the school, to which few children are coming, although the weather is good. Last year there were from 25 to 27, now only 7 to 10. I told them their children would never learn anything if they did not see to it that they attended better. They could say nothing, for the children have stayed away on trivial excuses.—*Ibid.*, p. 1274.

December 15, 1779

As. Br. Fritz has been called to the Maryland Settlement he will not be able to continue with the school for the larger little boys, and it is proposed that Br. Heckewälder shall take his place. We think that the time of instruction, or at least the time that they spend in his care, shall be from 8 to 11 in the morning, and from 1 to 4 or 5 in the afternoon, without leaving Wednesday and Saturday afternoon free as is customary in other schools. Reading, writing and arithmetic are the foundation studies, geography, music, geometry, and speaking are of the next importance. The school for the littlest boys, which Br. Jens Schmid has held, shall continue; both schools shall meet in the house opposite the Two-story House, but in separate rooms.

Arrangements should be made to give our little girls lessons in arithmetic. Sr. Oesterlein has taught them reading and writing, sewing and knitting, with good success, and that arithmetic has been lacking is only because the Sister knows none.—*Ibid.*, p. 1329.

27. ACT CONCERNING FREE SCHOOL AT DORCHESTER, SOUTH CAROLINA, 1756

WHEREAS, the persons appointed commissioners, in and by an Act of the General Assembly of this Province, passed the ninth day of April, one thousand seven hundred and thirty-four, entitled "an Act for founding and erecting, governing, ordering and visiting, a free school at the town of Dorchester, in the parish of St. George, in Berkley county, for the use of the inhabitants of the Province of South

Carolina," are all dead, without having any successors appointed, as by the said Act is directed, whereby the good intent of the said Act hath been in a great measure frustrated; we therefore humbly pray his most sacred Majesty that it may be enacted.

I. *And be it enacted*, by his Excellency James Glen, Esquire, Governor-in-chief and Captain General in and over the Province of South Carolina, by and with the advice and consent of his Majesty's Council, and the Commons House of Assembly of the said Province, and by the authority of the same, That the rector of the said Parish for the time being, Henry Middleton, Walter Izard, Ralph Izard, Daniel Blake, John Ainslie, Esqrs. Mr. Benjamin Waring, Mr. Richard Waring and Mr. Joseph Waring, shall be, and they are hereby appointed, commissioners for the purposes in the said Act mentioned, and invested with the same powers and authorities, to all intents, constructions and purposes whatsoever, for carrying the several matters comprized in the said recited Act into execution, as the commissioners therein nominated and appointed were invested with.

II. *And be it further enacted* by the authority aforesaid, That the commissioners herein named, or any five of them, shall meet in the vestry room of the parish church of St. George's Dorchester, on the twenty-third day of April next, between the hours of nine and twelve of the clock in the morning, and then and there make choice of a president, for the ensuing; and the commissioners hereby appointed, or such as shall at any time hereafter be appointed, in pursuance of the powers of this or the said recited Act, or any five of them, shall every year in like manner, upon the twenty-third day of April, (unless the same shall happen on a Sunday, and in such case upon the day following) proceed to the choice of a president; and the said commissioners, before they begin to act as such, and the president when chosen, shall take such oaths as are in the said Act appointed to be taken, which shall be administered by any two of the commissioners to the others of them respectively, and to the president; and they, or any two of them, are hereby authorized and impowered to administer the same accordingly.

III. *And be it further enacted* by the authority aforesaid, That if at any time hereafter the said commissioners shall be reduced by death, resignation, refusal to act, or departure from this Province for more than twelve months, and the said commissioners shall neglect or refuse to choose a new commissioner or commissioners, in the manner prescribed and directed by the said Act, for the space of six months after any such vacancy as aforesaid, it shall and may be lawful for the vestry and church-wardens of the said parish to choose a new commissioner or commissioners, to make up the number nine; any thing in the said recited Act contained, to the contrary notwithstanding.

IV. *And be it further enacted* by the authority aforesaid, That the said commissioners shall have power, and they are hereby fully authorized and impowered, to nominate and appoint a school-master, ushers or teachers, and to censure, suspend or deprive any of the said masters, ushers or teachers, as they, or any five of them, in their discretion shall see fit: Provided nevertheless, that such nomination and appointment, or censure, suspension or deprivation, shall not take effect unless the same respectively shall be agreed to and resolved upon at a meeting for that purpose to be appointed, and particularly specified in the summons to be issued by the president and served upon each respective commissioner personally, at least ten days before such meeting, or left at his most usual place of abode with one of his known domestic servants.

V. *And be it further enacted* by the authority aforesaid, That the schoolmaster nominated and appointed in the manner above mentioned, shall have, hold, occupy, possess and enjoy, to him and his lawful successors, all such lands as shall, pursuant to the above recited Act, be taken up, purchased, had or received for the use of a schoolmaster for the said school, and the school house, dwelling house, out-houses and other buildings thereon; and also, as a further encouragement, shall have and receive out of the public treasury of this Province the sum of fifty pounds proclamation money, or the value thereof in the current money of this Province, to be paid him half-yearly by the public treasurer, who is hereby authorized, required and commanded, punctually to pay the same out of the fund appropriated for payment of the salarys of the clergy, by draughts to be made for the purpose by the president and any four of the said commissioners, or their successors.

VI. *And be it further enacted* by the authority aforesaid, That the school-master, ushers and teachers to be appointed as aforesaid, shall freely and without any manner of fee or reward whatsoever, teach and instruct ten poor scholars, and as many more as the president and any four of the said commissioners shall from time to time, according as the public or school salarys may or shall be hereafter increased, approve of and judge fit to nominate and appoint.—Cooper, *op. cit.*, IV, 23-24.

28. Board of Trade to Governor Dobbs concerning use of funds for churches and schools, March 10, 1757, December 27, 1757

It is in this light and upon this Opinion that we greatly approve the Measures of sending three Companies to New York to join the Army under the command of the Earl of Loudoun and we sincerely wish that the circumstances and state of the Province would have admitted of these Companies continuing in the Service but as you seem to be of opinion that they would not and that the defence of your own Frontiers called for every support which the Province is capable of affording, we do not see what more could be done than dismissing them in the manner you did, and the Assembly did well in enabling you by a vote of Credit to discharge the debt incurred on this account nor do we see any objection to your Applying the Bills appropriated to the erecting Churches and Schools, to this Service in case you think it advisable so to do.—William L. Saunders (ed.), *The Colonial Records of North Carolina.* V, 749.

I leave it therefore to your Lordships Judgment whether you will advise his Majesty to repeal that Aid Act passed in 1754 and to send me an Instruction for the future not to pass any Law for appointing provincial Treasurers without excluding them from being Members of either House the Inconveniency in Virginia is evident where the Speaker as Treasurer rules the Assembly and they pass his Accounts without ever examining them, the only thing material in the Bill besides the Treasurer's Clause in the aid of 9ᵈ per Taxable for 7 years from the 1ˢᵗ of July 1755 of which three years of the 7 years Tax will be received by July 1758 so that 4 years Tax would be lost. The Tax raises about £900 so that the whole Sum not raised would be £3600 the 4 years Tax. But when it is considered it is only to repay the Bills that were issued for erecting publick Schools £6000 which were not to be issued until his Majesty gave leave, it will be only continuing £3600 of these Bills in Circulation which when others are paying off will be no inconvenience to the Province and may be remedied by a future Bill.—*Ibid.*, pp. 948-49.

29. The General Assembly of North Carolina addresses His Majesty, December 22, 1758

We observe with unfeigned Concern, great Immorality and Profaneness in the Lives and Manners of many of your Subjects in this Province, as well as gross ignorance; the Cause of which we must ascribe to the Want of an orthodox and pious Clergy and regular and proper Schools and Seminaries of Learning.

In this present Session of Assembly we have passed a Bill whereby better provision is made for the Clergy than has been at any Time heretofore in this Government and more we should have gladly done; but alas, S^r, the Country is so impoverished in its circumstances through granting repeated Aids to your Majesty for making the same defensible, and in carrying on Expeditions in Conjunction with your other Colonies against the French and their Indian Allies, that we cannot give sufficient Encouragement to the Clergy, nor Erect proper Schools for the Education of our Youth.

Permit us therefore, most earnestly to intreat your Majesty, to order and direct, that the proportion of the said sum which shall be allotted to this Country, be laid out and applied under such Rules and Regulations as to you, in your great Wisdom, may seem expedient, in purchasing a Glebe for each parish in this province and making suitable improvements thereon, and erecting and establishing a free School in every County. This application we humbly apprehend, will tend to promote the Honour and Glory of God, true Religion, Piety, and Useful Learning, as well as root out Profaneness and Immorality; and cause the rising Generation to add their grateful Prayers and Wishes to those of your loyal Assembly, that your Majesty may long possess and enjoy the Crown of Great Britain and the Dominions thereto belonging; together with the Acquisitions lately made by your Majesty's Arms; and that the same may thereafter be transmitted, through a succession of illustrious Princes, descended from you, until the latest Period of Time.—*Ibid.*, p. 1095.

30. GOVERNOR DOBBS TO THE BOARD OF TRADE, JANUARY 22, 1759

The Assembly then cooled and it ended in an application to me that I would concur with them in recommending so much of the money they were in arrear to their former Agent to be paid out of that sum, this I thought just and concurred with them in it; they then appointed an Agent of their own, without the approbation of the Governor & Council, & resolved to pay him £150 p. ann: for 2 years out of their proportion of the dividend of the £50,000 and then addressed His Majesty congratulating him upon the success of His Arms, at the same time praying that part of the sum should be laid out in purchasing Glebes and establishing Free Schools in each County —This address they never communicated to me, but are to send it to their Agent to deliver it, otherwise the Council would have concurred in a proper Address, upon which the Governor in Council have sent separately a congratulatory address to His Majesty, and then I closed the session. . .

. . . . . but I must remind your Lordships that there was £7200. granted in Bills for building Churches & purchasing Glebes and £6000 for publick schools, which notes were not to be issued without His Majesty's approbation, which Bills were borrowed and issued to answer the expenses of this war to be sunk by proper taxes, as these Bills are restored by the taxes His Majesty may either allow these to be applied for Glebes or schools, or order them to be burnt as they are paid in to lessen the Paper Currency. But I should think one Public Provincial school for the languages &c would be enough to be endowed, and the County schools be only for English scholars to learn to read write and account with some other branches of the Mathematicks.—*Ibid.*, VI, 3, 5.

31. THE GENERAL ASSEMBLY TO GOVERNOR DOBBS, NOVEMBER 28, 1759

. . . . . And as it is Absolutely Necessary to Enact other Laws to Answer the Purposes Intended by those repealed, In the Bill we shall prepare for that End shall endeavor to avoid Incerting Clauses which may be lyable to any Just Exception. We observe what your Excellency mentions relating to the Schools so much Wanted and desired, A former Assembly Granted £6,000 for the founding of a School which is still under a suspending Clause, and until his Majesty shall be pleased to declare his pleasure therein we are at a Loss to proceed. —*Ibid.*, p. 139.

32. MONEY PROVIDED FOR PUBLIC SCHOOL TO BE USED FOR MILITARY PURPOSES, 1759

An Act for Granting an Aid to His Majesty for paying and Subsisting the Forces and Militia now in the pay of this Province, and for other Purposes.

V. And whereas, there is no Money in the Publick Treasury to Answer the said Sum to the End that His Majesty's Service may not be Delayed for want thereof, nor the Credit of the Province affected.

VI. Be it further enacted by the Authority aforesaid, That John Starkey and Thomas Barker, Esquires, Public Treasurers of this Province, out of the Public Notes of Credit already replaced and hereafter to be replaced in their Hands as a Fund for endowing a Public School, building Churches and purchasing Glebes so soon as may be after the passing of this Act when thereunto Required shall make payment out of the said Notes of Credit so as aforesaid Replaced, and to be Replaced with them, for the Purposes aforesaid to the several Creditors of the Public Claims Chargeable on the Contingent Fund to the Amount of Two Thousand Pounds, which said Sum is hereby appropriated to and for Payment of the Debts of the Public, and shall not be applied to any other Intent or Purpose whatsoever. And the sum of Three Thousand Five Hundred Pounds, the remainder of the said sum of Five Thousand Five Hundred Pounds, shall by the said Treasurer be paid to such Person or Persons as the Governor or Commander in Chief for the Time being, shall by his Warrant, Order and appoint.—Walter Clark (ed.), *The State Records of North Carolina*, XXV, 394-95.

33. THE GENERAL ASSEMBLY REPLIES TO GOVERNOR DOBBS, NOVEMBER 14, 1760

The Public Schools (so much wanted and earnestly desired) had, by a former Assembly, £6,000 appropriated for their Establishment but that Law lies under a suspending Clause for his Majesty's Royal approbation, and the Money has since been borrowed for the Service of the War.—Saunders, *op. cit.*, VI, 477.

34. LEGISLATIVE RESOLUTION TO PROVIDE CLOTHING FOR MILITARY FORCES OUT OF SCHOOL FUNDS, APRIL 28, 1762

. . . . . and also, such sums of money as shall be necessary for Cloathing the said forces, not exceeding Forty shillings for each man, out of the money appropriated for founding Schools, and that the same be Replaced by a poll Tax to be laid for that purpose; which said men shall be kept in pay six Months from the first day of May next, and no longer.—*Ibid.*, pp. 830-31.

35. ASSEMBLY THANKS REVEREND JAMES REID FOR HIS SERMON ON EDUCATION, DECEMBER 9, 1762

Ordered that the thanks of this House, be given to the Reverend James Reid for his sermon [1] preached at the beginning of this Session of Assembly, Recommending the Establishing Public Schools for the

1. We have not been able to find copy of the sermon.

Education of Youth, and that he be desired to furnish the Printer with a copy thereof, in order that the same may be printed and dispersed in the several Counties within this Province.—*Ibid.*, p. 955.

36. MEMORIAL OF THE INHABITANTS OF NEWBERN TO WILLIAM TRYON, CONCERNING SCHOOL IN THAT TOWN, MAY 16, 1765

To the Honorable William Tryon Esqr Commander in Chief in and over the Province of North Carolina
The memorial of the Inhabitants of the Town of Newbern and County of Craven in the said Province
Humbly Sheweth.

That there never has been in this Province any regular settled Schoolmaster.

That Thomas Thomlinson arrived from England about 15 Months ago well recommended with regard to his abilities Sobriety and good Conduct and at our Request opened a school at the said Town of Newbern.

That to encourage said Thomas Thomlinson as much as in our power a Number of the Inhabitants of the said town and County as well as several of the adjacent counties who are very desirous to have their children under the Tuition of the said T. Thomlinson have subscribed considerable Sums of money Part of which is already expended in purchasing Materials for the Building of a large and commodious School house that the said T. Thomlinson may be enabled to take a greater Number of Scholars under his Care and provide himself with proper assistant.

That being fully sensible of the great advantage it must be to the rising Generation to have a good Schoolmaster settled in the Town of Newbern they are very desirous that the said T. Thomlinson should continue amongst them as a Schoolmaster whom to their general satisfaction they have experienced to be well qaulified by Precept and Example to instruct their children in such Branches of useful learning as are necessary in several of the Offices and Stations in Life and imprint on their tender Minds the Principles of the Christian Religion agreeable to the Establishment of the Church of England. And your Memorialists having been informed that Salaries have been and continue to be granted for the Encouragement of Schoolmasters in Infant Colonies by the Honorable and Reverend Society for Propagating the Gospel in foreign Parts and being sensible that your Honour has much at Heart the prosperity of this colony by having strongly recommended the Cause of Religion and Virtue to the General Assembly of this Province.

Your Memorialists therefore humbly hope for your Honour's Application in favor of the said T. Thomlinson to the Society for the propagating the Gospel in foreign Parts that for his encouragement he may be allowed from Home such a yearly Salary as to the said Society may seem meet.

And as in Duty bound your Memorialists shall ever pray.

That the Honorable and Reverend Society may be well satisfied with Regard to his Abilities and Character the said T. Thomlinson has begged leave to refer to the Revd John Brown D. D. Chaplain to the late Lord Bishop of London.

Newbern 16. May 1765.

James Reed Missionary

Copy of the Original and of the Gentlemen's Names who attested it.

Thos Cliffd Howe	John Franck
Samuel Cornell	Tho Pollock
John Williams	Bernard Parkinson
Richd Cogdell	Wm. Wilton
Richd Caswell	Christ. Neale
James Davis	Thos Sitgreaves
Peter Conway	Corn Grosnendeyk
John Clitherall	Jno Green
Jacob Blount	John Fonville
Richd Ellis	Longfield Cox
Francis Macilwean	Jno Smith
Alexdr Gaston	Cullen Pollock
Phil Ambrose	Richd Fenner
Jacob Sheppard	Amb. Cox Bagley
Jos. Jones	Andr Scott
John Daly	Andr Stewart
Will Euen	Eliu Cotting
Timo. Clear	Jno. Moore
Jno Pindar	Alex. Eagles
Pat Gordon	

—Ibid., VII, 35-36.

37. General Assembly sends message to William Tryon, May 31, 1765

The order of the day being read the House took under Consideration His Honour's the Governor's Letter, & the Extract of the Minutes of the Proceedings of the Lords Commissioners for Trade and Plantations dated the 13th of December 1763 and after maturely considering the same Resolved the following Message be sent to His Honour the Governor. Vizt

TO THE HONble WILLIAM TRYON ESQre LIEUTENt GOVERNOR ETC

SIR

In Answer to your Message of the 10th inst. you will be pleased to understand that, that Act of Assembly referred to by the Extract of the Minutes of the Proceedings of the Lords Commissioners for Trade and Plantations sent with your Message is an Act entituled "An Act for granting to His Majesty the sum of Forty Thousand Pounds" etc by which among other things the sum of £18000 Procl: is appropriated for erecting Public Schools and purchasing Glebes in the several Parishes in this Province subject to a suspending Clause in the said Act until His Majesty's Royal approbation thereof should be had soon after the passing the said Act the Assembly instructed their Agent to apply for such his Majesties Approbation on which occasion it seems their Lordships were of opinion that it was improper to report the said Act as fit to receive the Royal sanction on Account of several objections which were pointed out and the late Governor instructed to lay before the Assembly in order that it might be amended and the particulars objected to, but for what reason we know not, the said objections have never yet been laid before the Assembly. We therefore request your Honor to represent the state of this case truely to His Majesty that the Assembly may thereby be acquitted from the imputation of having neglected to pay a dutiful obedience to His Majestys Commands, and the impropriety of making a second application to the Board of Trade without taking proper notice of the answer given by their Lordships to their first request and this House further requests that your Honor will obtain a Copy of the said objections and lay them before the Assembly that they may have an opportunity of manifesting their readiness to comply with His Majestys Instructions in amending the said Act, as far as may be compatable with the Interest of the Country and that Duty which the Members owe to their Constituents.

JOHN ASHE Speaker.

May 13th 1765

—*Ibid.*, pp. 73-74.

38. ACT TO ESTABLISH A SCHOOLHOUSE IN NEWBERN, DECEMBER 1, 1766

I. Whereas a Number of well-disposed Persons, taking into consideration the great necessity of having a proper School or Public Seminary of Learning established, whereby the rising Generation may be brought up and instructed in the Principles of the Christian Religion, and fitted for the several Offices and Purposes of Life, have, at a great Expence, erected and Built the Town of New Bern, a convenient House for the Purpose aforesaid; and being desirous that the same may be established by Law on a Permanent Footing, so as to answer the good Purposes by the said Persons intended:

II. Be it Enacted by the Governor, Council, and Assembly, and by the Authority of the same, That the said Persons or other Contributors to said School House, or the Majority of Them, are hereby Authorized, required, and directed, to meet at the Court House in New Bern on the First Tuesday in April next, and then and there to elect and choose, out of their Number, Eleven of the most able and discreet Persons, to be Trustees or Directors of the said School; and that after the said Election, which is to be made before the Sheriff, and a due Return thereof made to the said Directors, they shall be, and are hereby incorporated into a Body Politic and Corporate, by the Name of the Incorporated Society for promoting and establishing the Public School in New Bern; and by that Name to have perpetual Succession, and a Common Seal; and that they and their Successors, by the Name aforesaid, shall be able and Capable in Law to have, purchase, receive, enjoy, possess, and retain, to them and their Successors, forever, in Trust and Confidence for the said School, any Lands, Rents, Tenements, and Hereditaments of what kind, nature or Quality soever; and also to sell, grant, demise, alien, or dispose of the same; and also to receive and take any Charity, Gift, or Donation whatsoever, to the said School; and by the same Name to sue and implead, be sued and impleaded, answer and be answered, in all Courts of Record whatsoever; and from Time to Time under their Common Seal, to make such Rules, Regulations, and Ordinances, for the Admission, or Dismission of the several Masters of the said School, and the better regulating and well ordering the same, as to them shall seem requisite and necessary, and best answer the Purposes intended: Provided the said Rules correspond, and be as near as may be, agreeable to the Laws of Great Britain and this Province.

III. Provided always, That no Person shall be admitted to be Master of the said School, but who is of the Established Church of England; and who, at the Recommendation of the Trustees or Directors, or the Majority of them, shall be duly Licensed by the Governor, or Commander in Chief for the Time Being.

IV. And be it further Enacted, by the Authority aforesaid, That one Lot of Land in the Town of New Bern, lately purchased from William Bastin Whitford, by the Proprietors of the aforesaid School House, and whereon they have erected the same, be from henceforth vested in the Trustees by this Act incorporated, and their Successors, forever, in Trust and Confidence, to and for the Uses and Purposes by the said Society intended.

V. And be it further Enacted, by the Authority aforesaid, That the said Trustees, before they be deemed qualified to enter on the Execution of the Trust reposed in them by this Act, do, before some Magistrate, take the several Oaths of Government, subscribe the Test, and also take the following Oath, to-wit:

I, A.B., do swear that I will duly and faithfully, to the best of my skill and Ability, execute and discharge the several Powers and Authorities given me by an Act of Assembly, for establishing a School House in the Town of New Bern; and that in all Things for the well ordering and good government thereof, I will do equal and Impartial Justice, to the extent of my understanding. So help me God.

VI. And be it further Enacted by the Authority aforesaid, That the said Trustees, or the Majority of them, after their Qualification, shall meet at the said School House, and elect, out of their Number, a fit and Proper Person to be Treasurer to the said Society: which Treasurer shall be annually elected on the first Tuesday in April; into whose Hands shall be paid all Monies of or belonging to the said School, he first giving Bond and Security, in the Sum of Two Thousand Pounds, Proclamation Money, to the Trustees, for the faithful Discharge of his Office, and the Trust reposed in him; and that the said Treasurer shall annually, on the said First Tuesday in April, settle his Accounts with the Trustees, of all Disbursements, Donations, Gifts, Bequests, or other Charities, that may belong or accrue to the

724 DOCUMENTARY HISTORY OF EDUCATION IN THE SOUTH

said School the preceding Year: And upon the said Treasurer's Neglect or Refusal to settle and pay over to the succeeding Treasurer what Money may be in his Hands belonging to the said Society, the same Method of Recovery may be had against Him, as is provided for the Recovery of Monies from Sheriffs, or other Persons chargeable with Public Monies.

VII. And whereas it will be necessary that a Regular Succession of the said Trustees should be kept up, Be it Enacted by the Authority aforesaid, That on the Death, Refusal to Qualify, or Removal out of the Province, of any of the said Trustees, the remaining Trustees, or the Majority of them then in Office, shall elect and Choose, out of the Number of Contributors, other Trustees, in the Room and stead of Those Dead, removed, or refusing to qualify as aforesaid; who shall be invested with the same Powers and Authorities as the other Trustees, first taking the several Oaths appointed by this Act for their Qualification.

VIII. And be it further Enacted by the Authority aforesaid, That an Act of Assembly passed at Wilmington, in One Thousand Seven Hundred and Sixty Four, intituled, An Act for building a House for a School, and the Residence of a School Master, in the Town of New Bern, be, and is hereby repealed; and the Piece or Parcel of ground mentioned in the said Act, being Half of Two Lots known in the Plan of the said Town by the Numbers Fifty Nine and Sixty, beginning at the Corner of Craven and Pollock Streets, and running along Pollock Street Six and a Half Poles; then across said two Lots Fifty Nine and Sixty, in a Parallel Line with Craven Street, Thirteen Poles to the North Side of Lot Number Sixty; then along the said Lot, Six and a Half Poles, to Craven Street; then along Craven Street, Thirteen Poles, to the beginning: Also Two Lots of Land in the said Town of New Bern, adjoining the said School House, known in the Plan of the said Town by the Numbers Three Hundred and Thirteen and Three Hundred and Twenty Seven, which are hereby vested in the Trustees by this Act to be appointed, and to their Successors forever, in Trust and Confidence, to and for the Use of the said School.

IX. And whereas the aforesaid Contributors being desirous that the Benefits arising from the said School may be as extensive as possible, and that the Poor, who may be unable to educate their Children there, may enjoy the Benefits thereof: Be it Enacted by the Authority aforesaid, That a Duty of One Penny per Gallon on all Rum, or other

Spirituous Liquors imported into the River Neuse, be paid, for and during the Space of Seven Years, from and after the passing of this Act, by the Importers thereof, for and towards raising a Fund for the Education of Ten Poor Children in the said School (to be chosen by the Trustees) whose Parents may be unable to pay for the same; and that the said Duty be Part of the common Stock of the said School, and be appropriated as aforesaid, and towards giving a Salary of Twenty Pounds per Year to the Master of the said School, toward enabling him to keep an Assistant; which said Duty shall be collected, accounted for, and paid to the Treasurer of the said School, in the same Manner, and under the same Penalties and Restrictions, as the Duty of Four Pence per Gallon on Spirituous Liquors is now paid and collected.—Clark, *op. cit.*, XXIII, 678-80.

39. GOVERNOR TRYON TO THE BOARD OF TRADE CONCERNING BILL FOR SCHOOL IN NEWBERN, DECEMBER 3, 1766

Newbern 3d December 1766

A Bill is passed for erecting an edifice in Newbern for the use of the Governor for the time being to be built solely under my orders and directions. Another Bill is also passed for erecting a public school at Newbern, (the first in this province) and appropriating a fund for the support thereof, together with many other usefull public Acts. —Saunders, *op. cit.*, VII, 266.

40. TRUSTEES FOR PROMOTING THE PUBLIC SCHOOL IN NEWBERN TO COLLECT THE SUBSCRIPTIONS DUE THE SCHOOL, 1768

An Act for declaring certain Lots in the Town of New Bern taken up by the Trustees for Promoting the Public School in the said Town, saved and improved acording to Law; and to impower the said Trustees to collect the subscriptions due to the said School.

I. Whereas, the Incorporated Society for Promoting the Public School in New Bern have taken up two Lots of Land lying and being in the said Town and known in the plan thereof by the Numbers or Figures 328 and 329, and are contiguous to and in the same Square in which the said Society have erected a large and convenient Building for the Use and Accommodation of the Master and Scholars of the said School. And it being inconvenient that any other Building should be Erected on the said Lots.

II. Be it Enacted by the Governor, Council and Assembly, and by the Authority of the same, That the said Building already Erected shall be held, deemed and taken to be a Sufficient saving and improvement of the said Lots Number 328 and 329 within the extent and meaning of the Act of Assembly in that case made and provided, And the said two Lots are hereby declared to be saved and improved Lots accordingly; anything in the said Act of Assembly to the Contrary notwithstanding.

III. And whereas, Sundry Donations have been made by Subscription for the benefit of the said school, which the said Society have neglected to collect and receive; And Whereas, it is apprehended that the Statute of Limitations will be a Barr to any action that may be brought by the said Society for recovering of the said Subscriptions.

IV. Be it therefore Enacted by the Authority aforesaid, That it shall and may be Lawful for the said Society to commence an Action or Actions on the said Subscriptions against all and every person or persons for any Sum or Sums by him or them subscribed for, and that upon such Action or Actions the said Statute of Limitations shall be no barr; Provided, That such Action or Actions shall be brought by the said Society within the space of Twelve Months from and after the passing of this Act and not after.—Clark, *op. cit.*, XXV, 516.

41. JOHN FIRBY, SCHOOLMASTER AT PENSACOLA, PETITIONS THE PROVINCIAL COUNCIL FOR HOUSE AND LANDS FOR SCHOOL, MARCH 3, 1772

Read the Petition of John Firby Setting Forth

That he was appointed schoolmaster by the Right Rev Father in God the Lord Bishop of London with the approbation of the archbishops and was then Informed That your Petitioner should have a Dwelling House and School found at the Province Expence, at same time ordered your Petitioner to demand 200 acres of Land free of Expence to be granted the School forever, on your Petitioners arrival at this Place in September 1765 his Excellency Govr Johnstone informed your Petitioner "That the School Land should be laid out the Town do not appear to be able to build a School House you must have an allowance for a House," Your Petitioner applyd to Lieutenant Governor Browne and received for answer "a full Governor will soon arrive I advise you to wait a Little; Your Petitioner applyd to the Vestry and requested them for to Erect a House and Fix on a proper Place for the School Land and received for answer "It ought to be done but we cannot raise money for to do it," Your Petitioner has been in this Province near Six years and a half during which time he has had no allowance for House Rent notwithstanding the First year he paid Six Dollars a month Rent—Your Petitioner—Therefore most Humbly prays That your Excellency and the Honorable Council will order the said Land to be laid out and allow your Petitioner what shall be thought Convenient for House Rent by which means he may be able to take all the children belonging the poor and use his best endeavours for to teach them Religion and Virtue That the Goode Intentions of his Majesty may be answered and your Petitioner as in Duty Bound shall ever pray &c

It was the opinion of the Board That the 200 acres of Land mentioned in the Petition Should be run out for the use of the school on the Surveyor Generals Return to Town and the Board are Further of opinion That his Excellency Should recommend to his majestys Secretary of State for north america to Direct a reasonable annual sum to be allowed the Schoolmaster for House Rent.—Manuscript Minutes of the Provincial Council; in Manuscripts Division, Library of Congress.

42. Certificate of John Gottfried Arends as teacher to North Carolina, October 16, 1772

Of his most serene Highness, most mighty Prince and Lord, Lord George the Third, King of Great Britain, France, and Ireland, Defender of the Faith, Duke of Brunswick and Lüneburg, Arch Treasurer of the Holy Roman Empire, and Elector, etc., real Privy Counselor and authorized President of the Royal and Electoral Consistory of this place, also of the Counselors of the Church Consistory, certifies herewith that the bearer of this, John Gottfried Arends, of Göttingen, in compliance with the desire of the Evangelical Lutheran congregation in North Carolina, namely, in Rowan County, to have a capable school teacher; and to this end, according to the attestation of the Governor, has sent deputies, and his royal Majesty and Electoral and serene Highness, our most gracious Lord, has commanded us to be serviceable to them; after due examination for such an office, found him to be experienced, he also having promised, according to the custom of this country and the published appointment for a future school teacher, to conduct his office with all fidelity and diligence, and manifest obedience towards his pastor, modesty toward the congregation, and love for the children.

On the other hand, we do not doubt that the congregation will amply remunerate his serviceable labor, and make his stay, as well as that of the pastor, agreeable.

However, should he desire to return, and be able to do so, then we promise him a proportional school service in this country according to the measure of his deportment and the time of his service, provided he has labored six years, at least.

In testimony whereof we have affixed the royal and electoral seal and signature of the Consistory.

Given in Hannover, the sixteenth day of October, 1772.

Respectfully,

Kauff.

—G. D. Bernheim and George H. Cox, *The History of the Evangelical Lutheran Synod and Ministerium of North Carolina* (Philadelphia: Lutheran Publication Society, 1902), p. 15.

43. RULES OF A SCHOOL IN ST. AUGUSTINE, 1786

1. In accordance with the devout intentions of his majesty, no one shall be qualified to teach except upon examination and approval of the ecclesiastical and civil superiors of the province and every teacher shall be bound to observe these rules and such other orders and resolutions or any part of them, as the said superiors may see fit to communicate from time to time in the interest of the fullest advancement of the pupils.

2. The schools shall be designated as first and second. Children who are beginners and others who are more advanced, but not yet ready to begin writing, shall alone be admitted to the first school. When they are ready to begin writing they shall pass from the first to the second school where they shall be taught writing and arithmetic, while being perfected in reading, etc. Only children of this higher grade shall be admitted to the second school unless the superior authority determines otherwise.

3. His majesty having assigned to the teachers an income sufficient for their decent maintenance, no one of them shall demand of the parents any recompense whatever for the instruction of their children.

4. Every year at Easter the teachers shall prepare a list of the children based on the parish register and, informed of the place of residence, ages, etc., shall request the parents to send their children to school. If this request does not have the desired effect, whether by reason of the culpable neglect of the parents or the indolence and

indifference of the children themselves, the teachers shall report to the parish priest, who will determine the just and proper procedure in the matter. The teacher shall make like reports in the case of pupils kept away from school as a result of idle complaints made to their parents.

5. Throughout the year the schools shall be opened at seven o'clock in the morning and at two in the afternoon. At no time shall the pupils be dismissed in the morning before twelve o'clock, nor in the afternoon in the afternoon in winter before sunset. In the rest of the year the dismissal in the afternoon may be a half hour before sunset.

6. As each pupil enters school in the morning and in the afternoon he shall greet with proper courtesy first his teacher and then his fellow pupils. He shall then hang up his hat in the [proper] place and then seat himself in all modesty. After blessing himself in the name of the Blessed Trinity, he shall take up the book or paper with which his study is to begin.

7. Each teacher shall keep in the school a list of the pupils under his instruction from which, every day at eight o'clock in the morning and a quarter past two in the afternoon, he shall call the roll, designating each pupil by both his christian and his family name. In case anyone fails to answer, the teacher shall immediately send one or two of the boys to the home of the parents to learn the cause of his absence and if necessary bring him to school. If the information obtained warrants it, the teacher shall apply appropriate punishment to the delinquent.

8. In reproving and punishing the pupils, the teacher shall endeavor to be moderate; and as for the same, moral suasion is better than corporal punishment, the teacher shall take special care to learn the character and disposition of each child. In the case of such children the teacher shall not break out into imprecations or epithets, much less throw in their faces the faults of their parents or relatives, nor permit them under any circumstances to talk to one another in this manner in the school or out of it. Each and all should be treated impartially as faithful christians worthy of love and charity.

9. The children shall present themselves in their respective schools mornings and afternoons with all possible cleanliness, with their hair combed and with their faces, hands and feet (if they come barefoot) clean. The teacher shall not permit children in the school with contagious diseases, such as the itch and other diseases of like nature, the parents being first informed in order that they may not be of-

fended at having their children kept out of school while they are being cured.

10. The schoolrooms shall be swept at least once a week by the pupils themselves, and the teacher shall appoint a sufficient number of pupils for this purpose, treating all alike and beginning with the highest class and continuing to the lowest so that each class in turn shall fulfill this obligation.

11. No pupil shall leave the classroom except when necessity demands without the express permission of the teacher; and in order that not more than one shall go out at a time, the teacher shall deliver a ruler which he shall have on his desk for the purpose, to the one being excused, and a second permission shall not be given until the said ruler is returned. The length of the pupils absence shall be measured by the movement of a pendulum hung from the ceiling of the classroom, which pendulum the pupil himself will put in motion at the time of his going out, the teacher taking note whether the pendulum is still in motion when the ruler is returned.

12. The schools shall be divided according to the capacity and advancement of the pupils, by numbers and separate seats into distinct classes, and to the first or most capable of each class shall be given some title, reserving for the first of the highest class the title of Emperor of the whole school, and these titles shall prevail until others more striking can be found.

13. At the beginning of every month there shall be a general examination before the parish priest and the teachers to determine the advancement the pupils may have made during the previous month in writing, reading, arithmetic, christian doctrine, etc., and, as a reward of merit for the advancement shown in the examination, each pupil shall be assigned to a seat or place of preference corresponding to his progress. He shall occupy his place until the next examination when he shall be awarded it again, provided no one excels him in merit. In this latter case he shall descend to occupy the place corresponding to his merit.

14. From pupils studying the alphabet, the syllabary, and reading, the teacher shall hear four lettons a day, two in the morning and two in the afternoon. The teacher shall instruct these pupils at the same time, morning and afternoon, in christian doctrine and in prayers and litanies. He shall endeavor (by his own efforts and not those of some other person) with consummate care and attention to inculcate a clear and distinct pronunciation and understanding in their reading,

requiring the commas, semicolons, etc., to be observed. The teacher of the second school shall proceed by this same method in the teaching of writing with the sole difference that the pupils in this school shall write only two exercises a day. The teacher shall instruct the pupils in the correct position of the hand and how to hold the pen; and after the exercises are finished, he shall point out the faults and reprove the pupils for making them.

15. Pupils in arithmetic or counting shall solve two problems a day, write one or two exercises, read two lessons and receive instructions in christian doctrine once in the afternoon; and the teacher shall never allow his pupils to pass on to new matter until the old is thoroughly learned. It shall be the duty of the teacher to correct and reprove as provided in the rule immediately preceding.

16. The teacher of the second school shall require his pupils, as they advance, to memorize the tables of arithmetic; in order that this may not interfere with other tasks in the school, the pupils may take the tables home and learn them at night, reciting them to the teacher the next morning; and provided the pupils of reading are not occupied with matters of this sort the teachers may assign in the afternoon to each one according to his capacity, a portion of the historical cate-chism of Father Flaure, or of some other author, to be memorized at night, thus preventing the pupils from being idle at home.

17. The teachers shall instruct their pupils how to assist at Mass, and every Saturday night and on the eve of the other feasts of the year when there is to be a congregation in the church, they shall name by turns two of their pupils to assist the sacristan in the conduct of divine services.

18. On nights when the Procession of the Rosary leaves the parish church and passes through the streets, the teachers shall attend with their pupils, no exception being allowed and no excuse being valid. The teachers shall take care that the pupils comport themselves with proper modesty and devotion.

19. The teachers shall attend with their pupils the Salve on Satur-days, the Vespers of Sundays, and other principal days, and at all the services of the church when there is preaching of the Gospel.

20. Whenever God may be pleased to call to judgment any of the children the teachers shall go with their pupils in procession to the funeral, and if necessary the remains shall be borne by four of the pu-pils to the burial place.

21. During each of the Four Ember Seasons of the year, all pupils

of seven years of age and above, shall go to make confession in the presence of their teachers, to which end the teachers shall notify their pupils a day or two beforehand, in order that they may examine their consciences. The teacher shall instruct the pupils in a manner appropriate to their age, how they should prepare themselves, the method they should observe to avoid, by negligence or other culpable reasons, omitting sins that ought to be confessed, and the teachers should inform the pupils also of the necessity of repentence to make the sacrament valid, etc. The teachers shall give these same instructions to the pupils who are of an age to receive the Holy Sacrament of the Eucharist; and in order that everything may be done with system, the pupils shall be divided into three equal divisions and each teacher shall assign one division of his school for each of the Ember days, in order that by this means the pupils may be attended to with dispatch in the church and sent back promptly to school.

22. The teachers shall endeavor to obtain the most instructive books to be read by their pupils. They shall not permit any other language than Spanish to be spoken in the school.

23. The pupils shall ask with most profound humility that the blessings of their parents accompany them on their way to and from school, and whenever they meet any of their elders in the street, they should salute them with proper courtesy.

24. On leaving school the pupils shall go directly home without loitering, or shouting or committing mischievous pranks in the streets.

25. If any negroes or mulattoes should attend the schools, they shall be placed near the door in seats apart; but in matters of instruction, spiritual and temporal, the teachers shall do to them the same justice as to all the rest.

26. The teachers shall have in their respective schools a copy of these regulations in order that everyone may be promptly informed of their provisions and in order that they may be invariably and duly observed as his majesty desires.—East Florida Papers, 41 B 4, in The Library of Congress; translated from the Spanish in Michael J. Curley, C.SS.R., *Church and State in the Spanish Floridas* (*1783-1822*), pp. 78-82. (Studies in American Church History, The Catholic University of America, Vol. XXX.)

INDEX